Harcourt

FLORIDA

GO MATH

Advanced Mathematics 1

© Houghton Mifflin Harcourt Publishing Company
Image Credits: (beach umbrellas) ©Ocean/Corbis.

Edward B. Burger

Juli K. Dixon

Timothy D. Kanold

Matthew R. Larson

Steven J. Leinwand

Martha E. Sandoval-Martinez

Special thanks to the students, teachers, staff, and principal Cheri Godek at Gotha Middle School, Windermere, FL.

Cover Image Credits: (beach umbrellas) ©Ocean/Corbis.

Printed in the U.S.A.

ISBN 978-0-544-20090-6

9 10 11 12 0868 25 24 23 22 21 20 19 18 17

4500652333   E F G

Authors

Edward B. Burger, Ph.D., is the president of Southwestern University, a former Francis Christopher Oakley Third Century Professor of Mathematics at Williams College, and a former vice provost at Baylor University. He has authored or coauthored more than sixty-five articles, books, and video series; delivered over five hundred addresses and workshops throughout the world; and made more than fifty radio and television appearances. He is a Fellow of the American Mathematical Society as well as having earned many national honors, including the Robert Foster Cherry Award for Great Teaching in 2010. In 2012, Microsoft Education named him a "Global Hero in Education."

Juli K. Dixon, Ph.D., is a Professor of Mathematics Education at the University of Central Florida. She has taught mathematics in urban schools at the elementary, middle, secondary, and post-secondary levels. She is an active researcher and speaker with numerous publications and conference presentations. Key areas of focus are deepening teachers' content knowledge and communicating and justifying mathematical ideas. She is a past chair of the NCTM Student Explorations in Mathematics Editorial Panel and member of the Board of Directors for the Association of Mathematics Teacher Educators.

Timothy D. Kanold, Ph.D., is an award-winning international educator, author, and consultant. He is a former superintendent and director of mathematics and science at Adlai E. Stevenson High School District 125 in Lincolnshire, Illinois. He is a past president of the National Council of Supervisors of Mathematics (NCSM) and the Council for the Presidential Awardees of Mathematics (CPAM). He has served on several writing and leadership commissions for NCTM during the past decade. He presents motivational professional development seminars with a focus on developing professional learning communities (PLC's) to improve the teaching, assessing, and learning of students. He has recently authored nationally recognized articles, books, and textbooks for mathematics education and school leadership, including *What Every Principal Needs to Know about the Teaching and Learning of Mathematics*.

Matthew R. Larson, Ph.D., is the K-12 mathematics curriculum specialist for the Lincoln Public Schools and served on the Board of Directors for the National Council of Teachers of Mathematics from 2010-2013. He is a past chair of NCTM's Research Committee and was a member of NCTM's Task Force on Linking Research and Practice. He is the author of several books on implementing the Common Core Standards for Mathematics. He has taught mathematics at the secondary and college levels and held an appointment as an honorary visiting associate professor at Teachers College, Columbia University.

Steven J. Leinwand is a Principal Research Analyst at the American Institutes for Research (AIR) in Washington, D.C., and has over 30 years in leadership positions in mathematics education. He is past president of the National Council of Supervisors of Mathematics and served on the NCTM Board of Directors. He is the author of numerous articles, books, and textbooks and has made countless presentations with topics including student achievement, reasoning, effective assessment, and successful implementation of standards.

Martha E. Sandoval-Martinez is a mathematics instructor at El Camino College in Torrance, California. She was previously a Math Specialist at the University of California at Davis and former instructor at Santa Ana College, Marymount College, and California State University, Long Beach. In her current and former positions, she has worked extensively to improve fundamental pre-algebra and algebra skills in students who have historically struggled with mathematics.

© Houghton Mifflin Harcourt Publishing Company (Timothy D. Kanold) Photo courtesy of Tim Kanold; (Juli K. Dixon) Photo courtesy of Juli Dixon; (Martha E. Sandoval) Carlos Delgado/AP Images for HMH

Florida Reviewers

Richard Austin
University of South Florida, Retired
Tampa, Florida

Lori Bartholomew
Girls Preparatory Academy
School District of
Hillsborough County
Tampa, Florida

Sharon Brown
Instructional Staff Developer
Pinellas County Schools
St. Petersburg, Florida

Jackie Cruse
Math Coach
Ferrell GPA
Tampa, Florida

Princess Hemingway
Mathematics Instructor
Clearwater High School
Clearwater, Florida

Donald Hoessler
Math Teacher
Discovery Middle School
Orlando, Florida

Becky (Rebecca) Jones, M.Ed.
NBCT EA-Math
Orange County Public Schools
Orlando, Florida

Danon Noga
Adams Middle School
Tampa, Florida

Debbi Petrone-Cosme
Buchanan Middle School
School District of Hillsborough County
Tampa, Florida

Bennie Royal Smith
Bay Point Middle School
Pinellas County Schools
St. Petersburg, Florida

Jean Sterner
Thurgood Marshall Fundamental
Middle School
Pinellas County Schools
St. Petersburg, Florida

UNIT 1 Numbers

Careers in Math 1
Vocabulary Preview 2

MODULE 1 Integers

Real-World Video. 3
Are You Ready?. 4
Reading Start-Up 5
Unpacking the Standards. . . . 6

FL
6.NS.3.5   **1.1** Identifying Integers and Their Opposites 7
6.NS.3.7b   **1.2** Comparing and Ordering Integers 13
6.NS.3.7c   **1.3** Absolute Value 19
    Ready to Go On? 25
    Module 1 Assessment Readiness 26

MODULE 2 Factors and Multiples

Real-World Video. 27
Are You Ready?. 28
Reading Start-Up 29
Unpacking the Standards. . . 30

FL
6.NS.2.4   **2.1** Greatest Common Factor 31
6.NS.2.4   **2.2** Least Common Multiple 37
    Ready to Go On? 41
    Module 2 Assessment Readiness 42

MODULE 3 Rational Numbers

Real-World Video. 43
Are You Ready?. 44
Reading Start-Up 45
Unpacking the Standards. . . 46

FL

6.NS.3.6   3.1 Classifying Rational Numbers. 47
6.NS.3.6c   3.2 Identifying Opposites and Absolute Value of
                Rational Numbers 53
6.NS.3.7a   3.3 Comparing and Ordering Rational Numbers 59
                Ready to Go On? 65
                Module 3 Assessment Readiness 66

                Study Guide Review. 67
                Unit 1 Assessment Readiness 71

UNIT 2 Number Operations

Careers in Math 73
Vocabulary Preview 74

MODULE 4 Operations with Fractions

Real-World Video. 75
Are You Ready?. 76
Reading Start-Up 77
Unpacking the Standards. . . 78

FL

6.NS.2.4   **4.1 Applying GCF and LCM to Fraction Operations** **79**
6.NS.1.1   **4.2 Dividing Fractions** **85**
6.NS.1.1   **4.3 Dividing Mixed Numbers** **91**
6.NS.1.1   **4.4 Solving Multistep Problems with Fractions and Mixed Numbers** **97**
      Ready to Go On? **101**
      Module 4 Assessment Readiness **102**

MODULE 5 Operations with Decimals

Real-World Video. 103
Are You Ready?. 104
Reading Start-Up 105
Unpacking the Standards. . 106

FL

6.NS.2.2   **5.1 Dividing Whole Numbers** **107**
6.NS.2.3   **5.2 Adding and Subtracting Decimals** **113**
6.NS.2.2   **5.3 Multiplying Decimals** **119**
6.NS.2.3   **5.4 Dividing Decimals**. **125**
6.NS.2.3   **5.5 Applying Operations with Rational Numbers** **131**
      Ready to Go On? **135**
      Module 5 Assessment Readiness **136**

Study Guide Review. 137
Unit 2 Assessment Readiness 141

© Houghton Mifflin Harcourt Publishing Company • Image Credits: (t) Tetra Images/Alamy; (b) ©PhotoDisc/Getty Images

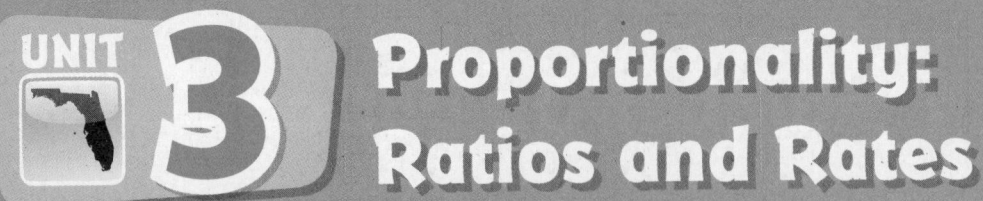

UNIT 3 Proportionality: Ratios and Rates

Careers in Math 143
Vocabulary Preview 144

MODULE 6 Representing Ratios and Rates

Real-World Video. 145
Are You Ready?. 146
Reading Start-Up 147
Unpacking the Standards. . 148

FL
6.RP.1.1   6.1 Ratios 149
6.RP.1.2   6.2 Rates 155
6.RP.1.3   6.3 Using Ratios and Rates to Solve Problems 161
                 Ready to Go On? 167
                 Module 6 Assessment Readiness 168

MODULE 7 Applying Ratios and Rates

Real-World Video. 169
Are You Ready?. 170
Reading Start-Up 171
Unpacking the Standards. . 172

FL
6.RP.1.3a   7.1 Ratios, Rates, Tables, and Graphs. 173
6.RP.1.3   7.2 Solving Problems with Proportions 179
6.RP.1.3d   7.3 Converting Within Measurement Systems 185
6.RP.1.3d   7.4 Converting Between Measurement Systems 191
                 Ready to Go On? 197
                 Module 7 Assessment Readiness 198

MODULE 8 Percents

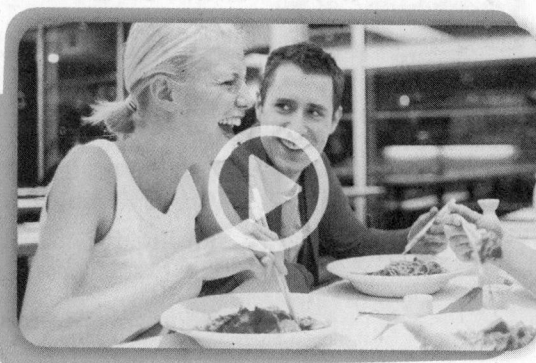

Real-World Video. 199
Are You Ready?. 200
Reading Start-Up 201
Unpacking the Standards. . 202

FL

6.RP.1.3c **8.1 Understanding Percent** **203**

6.RP.1.3 **8.2 Percents, Fractions, and Decimals** **209**

6.RP.1.3c **8.3 Solving Percent Problems** **215**

Ready to Go On? **223**

Module 8 Assessment Readiness **224**

Study Guide Review. **225**

Unit 3 Assessment Readiness. **229**

UNIT 4 Equivalent Expressions

Careers in Math 231
Vocabulary Preview 232

MODULE 9 Generating Equivalent Numerical Expressions

Real-World Video. 233
Are You Ready?. 234
Reading Start-Up 235
Unpacking the Standards. . 236

FL

6.EE.1.1   9.1   Exponents. 237
6.EE.1.1   9.2   Prime Factorization 243
6.EE.1.1   9.3   Order of Operations. 249
            Ready to Go On? 255
            Module 9 Assessment Readiness 256

MODULE 10 Generating Equivalent Algebraic Expressions

Real-World Video. 257
Are You Ready?. 258
Reading Start-Up 259
Unpacking the Standards. . 260

FL

6.EE.1.2a   10.1   Modeling and Writing Expressions. 261
6.EE.1.2c   10.2   Evaluating Expressions 269
6.EE.1.3   10.3   Generating Equivalent Expressions 275
            Ready to Go On? 283
            Module 10 Assessment Readiness 284

            Study Guide Review. 285
            Unit 4 Assessment Readiness 289

© Houghton Mifflin Harcourt Publishing Company • Image Credits: (t) Vladimir Ivanovich Danilov/Shutterstock.com; (b) ©Lloyd Sutton/Alamy

UNIT 5 Equations and Inequalities

Careers In Math 291
Vocabulary Preview 292

MODULE 11 Equations and Relationships

Real-World Video 293
Are You Ready? 294
Reading Start-Up 295
Unpacking the Standards . . 296

FL
6.EE.2.7   **11.1 Writing Equations to Represent Situations** 297
6.EE.2.7   **11.2 Addition and Subtraction Equations** 303
6.EE.2.5   **11.3 Multiplication and Division Equations** 311
6.EE.2.8   **11.4 Writing Inequalities** 319
            Ready to Go On? 325
            Module 11 Assessment Readiness 326

MODULE 12 Relationships in Two Variables

Real-World Video 327
Are You Ready? 328
Reading Start-Up 329
Unpacking the Standards . . 330

FL
6.NS.3.6c   **12.1 Graphing on the Coordinate Plane** 331
6.EE.3.9   **12.2 Independent and Dependent Variables in Tables
                 and Graphs** 337
6.EE.3.9   **12.3 Writing Equations from Tables** 345
6.EE.3.9   **12.4 Representing Algebraic Relationships in Tables
                 and Graphs** 351
            Ready to Go On? 357
            Module 12 Assessment Readiness 358

            Study Guide Review 359
            Unit 5 Assessment Readiness 363

UNIT 6 Relationships in Geometry

Careers In Math 365
Vocabulary Preview 366

MODULE 13 Area and Polygons

Real-World Video 367
Are You Ready? 368
Reading Start-Up 369
Unpacking the Standards . . 370

FL
6.G.1.1 **13.1 Area of Quadrilaterals** 371
6.G.1.1 **13.2 Area of Triangles** 377
6.G.1.1 **13.3 Solving Area Equations** 383
6.G.1.1 **13.4 Area of Polygons** 389
         Ready to Go On? 395
         Module 13 Assessment Readiness 396

MODULE 14 Distance and Area in the Coordinate Plane

Real-World Video 397
Are You Ready? 398
Reading Start-Up 399
Unpacking the Standards . . 400

FL
6.NS.3.8 **14.1 Distance in the Coordinate Plane** 401
6.G.1.3   **14.2 Polygons in the Coordinate Plane** 407
          Ready to Go On? 413
          Module 14 Assessment Readiness 414

Surface Area and Volume of Solids

Real-World Video. 415
Are You Ready?. 416
Reading Start-Up 417
Unpacking the Standards. . 418

6.G.1.4 15.1 Nets and Surface Area. 419
6.G.1.2 15.2 Volume of Rectangular Prisms .425
6.G.1.2 15.3 Solving Volume Equations 431
        Ready to Go On?. 435
        Module 15 Assessment Readiness 436

        Study Guide Review. 437
        Unit 6 Assessment Readiness 441

UNIT 7 Measurement and Data

Careers In Math 443
Vocabulary Preview 444

MODULE 16 Displaying, Analyzing, and Summarizing Data

Real World Video 445
Are You Ready? 446
Reading Start-Up 447
Unpacking the Standards . . 448

FL

6.SP.2.5   **16.1 Measures of Center** 449
6.SP.2.5c   **16.2 Mean Absolute Deviation** 455
6.SP.2.4   **16.3 Box Plots** 463
6.SP.2.4   **16.4 Dot Plots and Data Distribution** 469
6.SP.2.4   **16.5 Histograms** 477
            Ready to Go On? 483
            Module 16 Assessment Readiness 484

            Study Guide Review 485
            Unit 7 Assessment Readiness 487

UNIT 8 — The Number System

Careers in Math. 489
Vocabulary Preview. 490

MODULE 17 — Adding and Subtracting Integers

Real-World Video. 491
Are You Ready?. 492
Reading Start-Up 493
Unpacking the Standards. . 494

FL

7.NS.1.1   **17.1 Adding Integers with the Same Sign** 495
7.NS.1.1   **17.2 Adding Integers with Different Signs.** 501
7.NS.1.1c   **17.3 Subtracting Integers.** 507
7.NS.1.3   **17.4 Applying Addition and Subtraction of Integers** 513
      Ready to Go On? 519
      Module 17 Assessment Readiness 520

MODULE 18 — Multiplying and Dividing Integers

Real-World Video. 521
Are You Ready?. 522
Reading Start-Up 523
Unpacking the Standards. . 524

FL

7.NS.1.2   **18.1 Multiplying Integers** 525
7.NS.1.2   **18.2 Dividing Integers** 531
7.NS.1.3   **18.3 Applying Integer Operations** .537
      Ready to Go On? 543
      Module 18 Assessment Readiness 544

© Houghton Mifflin Harcourt Publishing Company • Image Credits: (t) ©Peter Haigh/Digital Vision/ Getty Images; (b) ©wusuowei/Fotolia

MODULE 19 Rational Numbers

Real-World Video. 545
Are You Ready?. 546
Reading Start-Up 547
Unpacking the Standards. . 548

FL

7.NS.1.2c   19.1   **Rational Numbers and Decimals**. **549**

7.NS.1.1d   19.2   **Adding Rational Numbers**. **555**

7.NS.1.1c   19.3   **Subtracting Rational Numbers** **563**

7.NS.1.2   19.4   **Multiplying Rational Numbers** **571**

7.NS.1.2   19.5   **Dividing Rational Numbers**. **577**

7.EE.2.3   19.6   **Applying Rational Number Operations** **583**

7.EE.1.1   19.7   **Algebraic Expressions** **589**

  Ready to Go On? **595**

  Module 19 Assessment Readiness **596**

  Study Guide Review. **597**

  Unit 8 Assessment Readiness **603**

UNIT 9 Ratios and Proportional Relationships

Careers in Math 605
Vocabulary Preview 606

MODULE 20 Rates and Proportionality

Real-World Video 607
Are You Ready? 608
Reading Start-Up 609
Unpacking the Standards . . 610

FL
7.RP.1.1 20.1 Unit Rates 611
7.RP.1.2 20.2 Constant Rates of Change 617
7.RP.1.3 20.3 Proportional Relationships and Graphs 623
                 Ready to Go On? 629
                 Module 20 Assessment Readiness 630

MODULE 21 Proportions and Percent

Real-World Video 631
Are You Ready? 632
Reading Start-Up 633
Unpacking the Standards . . 634

FL
7.RP.1.3 21.1 Percent Increase and Decrease 635
7.EE.1.2 21.2 Rewriting Percent Expressions 641
7.RP.1.3 21.3 Applications of Percent 647
                 Ready to Go On? 653
                 Module 21 Assessment Readiness 654

                 Study Guide Review 655
                 Unit 9 Assessment Readiness 659

APPENDIX

FL
6.RP.1.3e **A1 Ratios and Pi** 661

© Houghton Mifflin Harcourt Publishing Company • Image Credits: (t) ©OSO Media/Alamy Images

Florida Standards for Mathematics

Correlations for *HMH Florida Go Math* Advanced Mathematics 1

Standard	Descriptor	Citations
MAFS.6.EE.1 Apply and extend previous understandings of arithmetic to algebraic expressions.		
MAFS.6.EE.1.1	Write and evaluate numerical expressions involving whole-number exponents.	Develop Conceptual Understanding: SE: 237, 238, 239, 243, 244, 245, 249, 250 Fluency: SE: 240, 241, 242, 243, 246, 247, 248, 250, 251, 252, 253, 254 Application: SE: 241, 242, 246, 248, 253, 254
MAFS.6.EE.1.2	Write, read, and evaluate expressions in which letters stand for numbers.	Develop Conceptual Understanding: SE: 261, 265, 269, 271, 279 Fluency: SE: 262, 265, 266, 267, 268, 270, 271, 272, 273, 274, 280, 281, 282 Application: SE: 266, 267, 268, 271, 272, 273, 274, 281, 282
MAFS.6.EE.1.2a	Write expressions that record operations with numbers and with letters standing for numbers.	Develop Conceptual Understanding: SE: 260, 261, 265, 283 Fluency: SE: 262, 263, 264, 265, 266, 267, 268 Application: SE: 263, 264, 266, 267, 268
MAFS.6.EE.1.2b	Identify parts of an expression using mathematical terms (sum, term, product, factor, quotient, coefficient); view one or more parts of an expression as a single entity.	Develop Conceptual Understanding: SE: 261, 265, 279 Fluency: SE: 265, 266, 268, 280, 281, 282 Application: SE: 265, 266, 268, 282
MAFS.6.EE.1.2c	Evaluate expressions at specific values of their variables. Include expressions that arise from formulas used in real-world problems. Perform arithmetic operations, including those involving whole-number exponents, in the conventional order when there are no parentheses to specify a particular order (Order of Operations).	Develop Conceptual Understanding: SE: 258, 259, 260, 269, 271, 275, 276, 283 Fluency: SE: 265, 270, 271, 272, 273, 274, 280 Application: SE: 265, 271, 272, 273, 274
MAFS.6.EE.1.3	Apply the properties of operations to generate equivalent expressions.	Develop Conceptual Understanding: SE: 277, 278, 279, 283 Fluency: SE: 277, 278, 280, 281, 282 Application: SE: 278, 282
MAFS.6.EE.1.4	Identify when two expressions are equivalent (i.e., when the two expressions name the same number regardless of which value is substituted into them).	Develop Conceptual Understanding: SE: 263, 265, 275, 276, 277, 278, 279 Fluency: SE: 264, 265, 266, 267, 268, 277, 278, 280, 281, 282 Application: SE: 263, 265, 266, 267, 268, 281, 282

© Houghton Mifflin Harcourt Publishing Company

Standard	Descriptor	Citations
MAFS.6.EE.2 Reason about and solve one-variable equations and inequalities.		
MAFS.6.EE.2.5	Understand solving an equation or inequality as a process of answering a question: which values from a specified set, if any, make the equation or inequality true? Use substitution to determine whether a given number in a specified set makes an equation or inequality true.	Develop Conceptual Understanding: SE: 297, 303, 312, 313, 314, 319, 320 Fluency: SE: 300, 301, 302, 308, 309, 310, 316, 317, 318, 322, 323, 324, 343, 344 Application: SE: 300, 301, 302, 305, 308, 309, 310, 317, 318, 343, 344
MAFS.6.EE.2.6	Use variables to represent numbers and write expressions when solving a real-world or mathematical problem; understand that a variable can represent an unknown number, or, depending on the purpose at hand, any number in a specified set.	Develop Conceptual Understanding: SE: 263, 297, 298, 299, 303, 306, 311, 321 Fluency: SE: 264, 265, 267, 268, 298, 300, 301, 302, 306, 308, 309, 310, 316, 317, 318, 322, 323, 324, 343, 344 Application: SE: 264, 267, 268, 298, 300, 301, 302, 308, 309, 310, 317, 318, 322, 344
MAFS.6.EE.2.7	Solve real-world and mathematical problems by writing and solving equations of the form $x + p = q$ and $px = q$ for cases in which p, q and x are all non-negative rational numbers.	Develop Conceptual Understanding: SE: 299, 303, 306, 314, 315, 383, 384, 431, 432 Fluency: SE: 300, 301, 302, 306, 308, 309, 310, 315, 316, 317, 318, 343, 344, 386, 387, 388, 431, 432, 433, 434 Application: SE: 300, 301, 302, 308, 309, 310, 316, 317, 318, 344, 386, 387, 388, 433, 434
MAFS.6.EE.2.8	Write an inequality of the form $x > c$ or $x < c$ to represent a constraint or condition in a real-world or mathematical problem. Recognize that inequalities of the form $x > c$ or $x < c$ have infinitely many solutions; represent solutions of such inequalities on number line diagrams.	Develop Conceptual Understanding: SE: 296, 319, 320, 321 Fluency: SE: 322, 323, 324, 325 Application: SE: 322
MAFS.6.EE.3 Represent and analyze quantitative relationships between dependent and independent variables.		
MAFS.6.EE.3.9	Use variables to represent two quantities in a real-world problem that change in relationship to one another; write an equation to express one quantity, thought of as the dependent variable, in terms of the other quantity, thought of as the independent variable. Analyze the relationship between the dependent and independent variables using graphs and tables, and relate these to the equation.	Develop Conceptual Understanding: SE: 337, 338, 339, 340, 345, 346, 347, 351, 352, 353 Fluency: SE: 341, 342, 343, 344, 346, 348, 349, 350, 354, 355, 356, 357 Application: SE: 337, 338, 339, 340, 341, 342, 343, 344, 345, 349, 350, 354, 355, 356

Standard	Descriptor	Citations
MAFS.6.G.1 Solve real-world and mathematical problems involving area, surface area, and volume.		
MAFS.6.G.1.1	Find the area of right triangles, other triangles, special quadrilaterals, and polygons by composing into rectangles or decomposing into triangles and other shapes; apply these techniques in the context of solving real-world and mathematical problems.	Develop Conceptual Understanding: SE: 371, 372, 373, 377, 378, 379, 383, 384, 385, 389, 390, 391 Fluency: SE: 373, 374, 375, 376, 379, 380, 381, 382, 383, 384, 386, 387, 388, 392, 393, 394, 395 Application: SE: 375, 376, 381, 382, 383, 384, 386, 387, 388, 392, 393, 394, 395
MAFS.6.G.1.2	Find the volume of a right rectangular prism with fractional edge lengths by packing it with unit cubes of the appropriate unit fraction edge lengths, and show that the volume is the same as would be found by multiplying the edge lengths of the prism. Apply the formulas $V = l\,w\,h$ and $V = b\,h$ to find volumes of right rectangular prisms with fractional edge lengths in the context of solving real-world and mathematical problems.	Develop Conceptual Understanding: SE: 425, 426, 427, 431, 432 Fluency: SE: 427, 428, 429, 430, 431, 432, 433, 434, 435 Application: SE: 429, 430, 431, 432, 433, 434
MAFS.6.G.1.3	Draw polygons in the coordinate plane given coordinates for the vertices; use coordinates to find the length of a side joining points with the same first coordinate or the same second coordinate. Apply these techniques in the context of solving real-world and mathematical problems.	Develop Conceptual Understanding: SE: 400, 407, 408, 409 Fluency: SE: 398, 409, 410, 411, 412, 413 Application: SE: 410, 411, 412, 413
MAFS.6.G.1.4	Represent three-dimensional figures using nets made up of rectangles and triangles, and use the nets to find the surface area of these figures. Apply these techniques in the context of solving real-world and mathematical problems.	Develop Conceptual Understanding: SE: 417, 418, 419, 420, 421 Fluency: SE: 420, 422, 423, 424, 435 Application: SE: 423, 424
MAFS.6.NS.1 Apply and extend previous understandings of multiplication and division to divide fractions by fractions.		
MAFS.6.NS.1.1	Interpret and compute quotients of fractions, and solve word problems involving division of fractions by fractions, e.g., by using visual fraction models and equations to represent the problem.	Develop Conceptual Understanding: SE: 85, 86, 87, 88, 91, 92, 93, 97, 98 Fluency: SE: 88, 89, 90, 93, 94, 95, 96, 97, 98, 99, 100, 101 Application: SE: 89, 90, 93, 94, 95, 96, 98, 99, 100
MAFS.6.NS.2 Compute fluently with multi-digit numbers and find common factors and multiples.		
MAFS.6.NS.2.2	Fluently divide multi-digit numbers using the standard algorithm.	Develop Conceptual Understanding: SE: 106, 107, 108, 109 Fluency: SE: 108, 109, 110, 111, 112, 135 Application: SE: 109, 110, 111, 112

| MAFS.6.NS.2.3 | Fluently add, subtract, multiply, and divide multi-digit decimals using the standard algorithm for each operation. | **Develop Conceptual Understanding:** SE: 113, 114, 115, 119, 120, 121, 125, 126, 127, 131, 132
Fluency: SE: 114, 116, 117, 118, 120, 121, 122, 123, 124, 126, 127, 128, 129, 130, 132, 133, 134, 135
Application: SE: 116, 117, 118, 123, 124, 128, 129, 130, 133, 134 |
| MAFS.6.NS.2.4 | Find the greatest common factor of two whole numbers less than or equal to 100 and the least common multiple of two whole numbers less than or equal to 12. Use the distributive property to express a sum of two whole numbers 1–100 with a common factor as a multiple of a sum of two whole numbers with no common factor. | **Develop Conceptual Understanding:** SE: 31, 32, 33, 37, 38, 79, 80
Fluency: SE: 32, 34, 35, 36, 38, 39, 40, 41, 81, 82, 83, 84
Application: SE: 35, 36, 38, 39, 40, 83, 84 |

MAFS.6.NS.3 Apply and extend previous understandings of numbers to the system of rational numbers.

Standard	Descriptor	Citations
MAFS.6.NS.3.5	Understand that positive and negative numbers are used together to describe quantities having opposite directions or values (e.g., temperature above/below zero, elevation above/below sea level, credits/debits, positive/negative electric charge); use positive and negative numbers to represent quantities in real-world contexts, explaining the meaning of 0 in each situation.	**Develop Conceptual Understanding:** SE: 4, 5, 6, 7, 8, 9, 13, 14, 15, 19, 20, 21, 22, 55 **Fluency:** SE: 10, 11, 12, 14, 15, 16, 17, 18, 21, 22, 23, 24, 25, 55, 56, 57, 58, 65 **Application:** SE: 11, 12, 14, 16, 17, 18, 21, 22, 23, 24, 57, 58
MAFS.6.NS.3.6	Understand a rational number as a point on the number line. Extend number line diagrams and coordinate axes familiar from previous grades to represent points on the line and in the plane with negative number coordinates.	**Develop Conceptual Understanding:** SE: 7, 9, 25, 47, 48, 49, 53, 54, 332 **Fluency:** SE: 10, 11, 12, 17, 50, 51, 52, 56, 58, 65, 332, 334, 335, 336, 357 **Application:** SE: 11, 12, 17, 51, 52, 335, 336
MAFS.6.NS.3.6a	Recognize opposite signs of numbers as indicating locations on opposite sides of 0 on the number line; recognize that the opposite of the opposite of a number is the number itself, e.g., $-(-3) = 3$, and that 0 is its own opposite.	**Develop Conceptual Understanding:** SE: 8, 9, 53, 54 **Fluency:** SE: 10, 11, 12, 25, 54, 55, 56, 57, 58, 65 **Application:** SE: 11, 12, 57, 58
MAFS.6.NS.3.6b	Understand signs of numbers in ordered pairs as indicating locations in quadrants of the coordinate plane; recognize that when two ordered pairs differ only by signs, the locations of the points are related by reflections across one or both axes.	**Develop Conceptual Understanding:** SE: 331, 332, 333, 401, 402, 403 **Fluency:** SE: 332, 333, 334, 335, 336, 357, 402, 404, 405, 406, 413 **Application:** SE: 333, 335, 336, 404, 405, 406
MAFS.6.NS.3.6c	Find and position integers and other rational numbers on a horizontal or vertical number line diagram; find and position pairs of integers and other rational numbers on a coordinate plane.	**Develop Conceptual Understanding:** SE: 9, 53, 54, 55, 331, 332 **Fluency:** SE: 10, 17, 25, 56, 58, 65, 332, 334, 335, 336, 357 **Application:** SE: 17, 58, 335, 336

Standard	Descriptor	Citations
MAFS.6.NS.3.7	Understand ordering and absolute value of rational numbers.	Develop Conceptual Understanding: SE: 13, 14, 19, 20, 21, 55, 60 Fluency: SE: 14, 16, 17, 18, 21, 22, 23, 24, 25, 55, 56, 57, 58, 60, 62, 63, 64, 65 Application: SE: 17, 18, 21, 22, 23, 24, 57, 58, 63, 64
MAFS.6.NS.3.7a	Interpret statements of inequality as statements about the relative position of two numbers on a number line diagram.	Develop Conceptual Understanding: SE: 13, 15, 59, 60, 61 Fluency: SE: 15, 16, 17, 18, 61, 62, 63, 64 Application: SE: 16, 17, 18, 63, 64
MAFS.6.NS.3.7b	Write, interpret, and explain statements of order for rational numbers in real-world contexts.	Develop Conceptual Understanding: SE: 15, 61 Fluency: SE: 15, 16, 17, 18, 61, 62, 63, 64, 65 Application: SE: 17, 18, 61, 62, 63, 64
MAFS.6.NS.3.7c	Understand the absolute value of a rational number as its distance from 0 on the number line; interpret absolute value as magnitude for a positive or negative quantity in a real-world situation.	Develop Conceptual Understanding: SE: 19, 20, 21, 55 Fluency: SE: 21, 22, 23, 24, 25, 55, 56, 57, 58 Application: SE: 20, 22, 23, 24, 57, 58
MAFS.6.NS.3.7d	Distinguish comparisons of absolute value from statements about order.	Develop Conceptual Understanding: SE: 19, 20, 21, 53, 54, 55 Fluency: SE: 21, 22, 23, 24, 25, 57, 58 Application: SE: 21, 22, 55, 57, 58
MAFS.6.NS.3.8	Solve real-world and mathematical problems by graphing points in all four quadrants of the coordinate plane. Include use of coordinates and absolute value to find distances between points with the same first coordinate or the same second coordinate.	Develop Conceptual Understanding: SE: 333, 403 Fluency: SE: 333, 334, 335–336, 403, 404, 405–406, 413–414 Application: SE: 333, 336
MAFS.6.RP.1 Understand ratio concepts and use ratio reasoning to solve problems.		
MAFS.6.RP.1.1	Understand the concept of a ratio and use ratio language to describe a ratio relationship between two quantities.	Develop Conceptual Understanding: SE: 149, 150, 151 Fluency: SE: 150, 152, 153, 154, 167, 197 Application: SE: 150, 152, 153, 154, 197
MAFS.6.RP.1.2	Understand the concept of a unit rate $\frac{a}{b}$ associated with a ratio $a{:}b$ with $b \neq 0$, and use rate language in the context of a ratio relationship.	Develop Conceptual Understanding: SE: 147, 148, 155, 156, 157, 163 Fluency: SE: 158, 159, 160, 164, 167 Application: SE: 158, 159, 160, 164, 167

Standard	Descriptor	Citations
MAFS.6.RP.1.3	Use ratio and rate reasoning to solve real-world and mathematical problems, e.g., by reasoning about tables of equivalent ratios, tape diagrams, double number line diagrams, or equations.	**Develop Conceptual Understanding:** SE: 151, 157, 161, 162, 163, 173, 174, 175, 179, 180, 186, 193, 215, 216, 217, 218, 219 **Fluency:** SE: 152, 153, 154, 157, 158, 159, 160, 164, 165, 166, 167, 176, 177, 178, 179, 180, 182, 183, 184, 194, 197, 217, 218, 220, 221, 222, 223 **Application:** SE: 152, 153, 154, 157, 158, 159, 160, 164, 165, 166, 167, 176, 177, 178, 179, 180, 182, 183, 184, 197, 217, 218, 220, 221, 222
MAFS.6.RP.1.3a	Make tables of equivalent ratios relating quantities with whole-number measurements, find missing values in the tables, and plot the pairs of values on the coordinate plane. Use tables to compare ratios.	**Develop Conceptual Understanding:** SE: 151, 161, 162, 163, 173, 174, 175 **Fluency:** SE: 152, 153, 154, 164, 165, 166, 176, 177, 178 **Application:** SE: 152, 153, 154, 164, 165, 166, 176, 177, 178
MAFS.6.RP.1.3b	Solve unit rate problems including those involving unit pricing and constant speed.	**Develop Conceptual Understanding:** SE: 155, 156, 157, 175, 179, 180, 181, 193 **Fluency:** SE: 158, 159, 160, 167, 175, 177, 178, 179, 180, 181, 182, 183, 184, 194, 195, 196 **Application:** SE: 158, 159, 160, 167, 175, 177, 178, 179, 180, 181, 182, 183, 184, 195, 196
MAFS.6.RP.1.3c	Find a percent of a quantity as a rate per 100 (e.g., 30% of a quantity means $\frac{30}{100}$ times the quantity); solve problems involving finding the whole, given a part and the percent.	**Develop Conceptual Understanding:** SE: 203, 204, 205, 216, 217, 219 **Fluency:** SE: 206, 207, 208, 217, 218, 219, 220, 221, 222, 223 **Application:** SE: 207, 208, 218, 220, 221, 222
MAFS.6.RP.1.3d	Use ratio reasoning to convert measurement units; manipulate and transform units appropriately when multiplying or dividing quantities.	**Develop Conceptual Understanding:** SE: 185, 186, 187, 191, 192, 193 **Fluency:** SE: 188, 189, 190, 192, 194, 195, 196, 197 **Application:** SE: 188, 189, 190, 194, 195, 196
MAFS.6.RP.1.3e	Understand the concept of Pi as the ratio of the circumference of a circle to its diameter.	**Develop Conceptual Understanding:** SE: 661–664 **Fluency:** SE: 664–666 **Application:** SE: 665–666
MAFS.6.SP.1 Develop understanding of statistical variability.		
MAFS.6.SP.1.1	Recognize a statistical question as one that anticipates variability in the data related to the question and accounts for it in the answers.	**Develop Conceptual Understanding:** SE: 447, 469, 470 **Fluency:** SE: 473, 474, 475 **Application:** SE: 473, 474

© Houghton Mifflin Harcourt Publishing Company

Standard	Descriptor	Citations
MAFS.6.SP.1.2	Understand that a set of data collected to answer a statistical question has a distribution which can be described by its center, spread, and overall shape.	**Develop Conceptual Understanding:** SE: 449, 450, 451, 471 **Fluency:** SE: 452, 453, 454, 471, 473, 474, 475, 476 **Application:** SE: 452, 453, 454, 471, 473, 474, 475, 476
MAFS.6.SP.1.3	Recognize that a measure of center for a numerical data set summarizes all of its values with a single number, while a measure of variation describes how its values vary with a single number.	**Develop Conceptual Understanding:** SE: 447, 449, 450, 451 **Fluency:** SE: 452, 453, 454 **Application:** SE: 452, 453, 454
MAFS.6.SP.2 Summarize and describe distributions.		
MAFS.6.SP.2.4	Display numerical data in plots on a number line, including dot plots, histograms, and box plots.	**Develop Conceptual Understanding:** SE: 463, 470, 477, 478 **Fluency:** SE: 466, 467, 468, 470, 473, 474, 475, 476, 480, 481, 482, 483 **Application:** SE: 467, 468, 470, 473, 474, 475, 476, 480, 481, 482, 483
MAFS.6.SP.2.5a	Summarize numerical data sets in relation to their context, such as by: Reporting the number of observations.	**Develop Conceptual Understanding:** SE: 449, 450, 451, 455, 456, 457, 458, 463, 464, 465, 471, 472, 477, 478 **Fluency:** SE: 452, 453, 454, 457, 459, 460, 461, 462, 464, 465, 466, 467, 468, 471, 473, 474, 475, 476, 479, 480, 481, 482, 483 **Application:** SE: 452, 453, 454, 457, 459, 460, 461, 462, 464, 466, 467, 468, 473, 474, 475, 476, 479, 480, 481, 482 **Develop Conceptual Understanding:** SE: 449, 477, 478 **Fluency:** SE: 452, 453, 454, 479, 480, 481, 482 **Application:** SE: 452, 453, 454, 479, 480, 481, 482
MAFS.6.SP.2.5b	Summarize numerical data sets in relation to their context, such as by: Describing the nature of the attribute under investigation, including how it was measured and its units of measurement.	**Develop Conceptual Understanding:** SE: 477, 478 **Fluency:** SE: 452, 453, 454, 479, 480, 481, 482 **Application:** SE: 452, 453, 454, 479, 480, 481, 482
MAFS.6.SP.2.5c	Summarize numerical data sets in relation to their context, such as by: Giving quantitative measures of center (median and/or mean) and variability (interquartile range and/or mean absolute deviation), as well as describing any overall pattern and any striking deviations from the overall pattern with reference to the context in which the data were gathered.	**Develop Conceptual Understanding:** SE: 449, 450, 451, 455, 456, 457, 458, 463, 464, 465, 471, 472, 477, 478 **Fluency:** SE: 452, 453, 454, 457, 459, 460, 461, 462, 464, 465, 466, 467, 468, 471, 473, 474, 475, 476, 479, 480, 481, 482, 483 **Application:** SE: 452, 453, 454, 457, 459, 460, 461, 462, 464, 466, 467, 468, 473, 474, 475, 476, 479, 480, 481, 482

© Houghton Mifflin Harcourt Publishing Company

Standard	Descriptor	Citations
MAFS.6.SP.2.5d	Summarize numerical data sets in relation to their context, such as by: Relating the choice of measures of center and variability to the shape of the data distribution and the context in which the data were gathered.	Develop Conceptual Understanding: SE: 451, 471, 472, 477, 478 Fluency: SE: 452, 453, 454, 471, 473, 474, 475, 476, 479, 480, 481, 482, 483 Application: SE: 452, 453, 454, 473, 474, 475, 476, 479, 480, 481, 482
MAFS.7.EE.1 Use properties of operations to generate equivalent expressions		
MAFS.7.EE.1.1	Apply properties of operations as strategies to add, subtract, factor, and expand linear expressions with rational coefficients.	Develop Conceptual Understanding: SE: 583, 584, 589, 590, 591 Fluency: SE: 588, 589, 590, 592, 593, 594, 595 Application: SE: 592, 593, 594
MAFS.7.EE.1.2	Understand the rewriting an expression in different forms in a problem context can shed light on the problem and how the quantities in it are related.	Develop Conceptual Understanding: SE: 589, 590, 591, 641, 642, 643 Fluency: SE: 589, 590, 592, 593, 594, 642, 643, 644, 645, 646, 653 Application: SE: 593, 642, 643, 644, 645, 646, 653
MAFS.7.NS.1 Apply and extend previous understandings of operations with fractions to add, subtract, and multiply, and divide rational numbers.		
MAFS.7.S.NS.1.1	Apply and extend previous understandings of addition and subtraction to add and subtract rational numbers; represent addition and subtraction to add and subtract rational numbers on a horizontal or vertical number line diagram.	Develop Conceptual Understanding: SE: 496, 497, 501, 502, 503, 507, 508, 509, 510, 513, 563, 564, 565, 566 Fluency: SE: 497, 498, 499, 500, 503, 504, 505, 506, 510, 511, 512, 518, 563, 564, 567, 568, 569, 570 Application: SE: 499, 500, 505, 506, 511, 512, 518, 567, 568, 569, 570
MAFS.7.NS.1.1a	Describe situations in which opposite quantities combine to make 0.	Develop Conceptual Understanding: SE: 501, 503, 558 Fluency: SE: 503, 504, 505, 506, 560, 561, 562 Application: SE: 505, 506, 560, 561, 562
MAFS.7.NS.1.1b	Understand $p + q$ as the number located a distance $|q|$ from p, in the positive or negative direction depending on whether q is positive or negative. Show that a number and its opposite have a sum of 0 (are additive inverses). Interpret sums of rational numbers by describing real-world contexts.	Develop Conceptual Understanding: SE: 496, 497, 501, 502, 503, 555, 556, 557, 558, 565, 566 Fluency: SE: 497, 498, 499, 500, 503, 504, 556, 557, 558, 560, 567 Application: SE: 499, 500, 560, 567
MAFS.7.NS.1.1c	Understand subtraction of rational numbers as adding the additive inverse, $p - q - p + (-q)$. Show that the distance between two rational numbers on the number line is the absolute value of their difference, and apply this principle in real-world contexts.	Develop Conceptual Understanding: SE: 507, 508, 509, 510, 565, 566 Fluency: SE: 510, 511, 512, 519, 567, 568, 569, 570, 595 Application: SE: 511, 512, 567, 568, 569, 570

Standard	Descriptor	Citations
MAFS.7.NS.1.1.d	Apply properties of operations as strategies to add and subtract rational numbers.	**Develop Conceptual Understanding:** SE: 497, 513 **Fluency:** SE: 497, 498, 500, 518, 561, 562, 567, 568, 569, 570 **Application:** SE: 499, 500, 518, 561, 562, 567, 568, 569, 570
MAFS.7.NS.1.2	Apply and extend previous understandings of multiplication and division and of fractions to multiply and divide rational numbers.	**Develop Conceptual Understanding:** SE: 525, 526, 527, 531, 532, 533, 571, 572, 573, 577 **Fluency:** SE: 527, 528, 529, 530, 532, 533, 534, 535, 536, 543, 571, 572, 573, 574, 575, 576, 580, 581, 582, 595 **Application:** SE: 528, 529, 530, 533, 534, 535, 536, 575, 576, 581, 582
MAFS.7.NS.1.2.a	Understand that multiplication is extended from fractions to rational numbers by requiring that operations continue to satisfy the properties of operations, particularly the distributive property, leading to products such as $(-1)(-1) = 1$ and the rules for multiplying signed numbers. Interpret products of rational numbers by describing real-world contexts.	**Develop Conceptual Understanding:** SE: 525, 526, 537, 571, 572, 573, 577 **Fluency:** SE: 529, 530, 540, 541, 542, 543, 571, 572, 573, 574, 575, 576, 595 **Application:** SE: 529, 530, 541, 542, 575, 576
MAFS.7.NS.1.2.b	Understand that integers can be divided, provided that the divisor is not zero, and every quotient of integers (with non-zero divisor) is a rational number. If p and q are integers, then $-\left(\frac{p}{q}\right) = \frac{(-p)}{q} = \frac{p}{(-q)}$. Interpret quotients of rational numbers by describing real-world contexts.	**Develop Conceptual Understanding:** SE: 531, 532, 533, 549, 577, 578, 579 **Fluency:** SE: 532, 534, 535, 536, 552, 554, 580, 581, 582, 595 **Application:** SE: 534, 535, 536, 552, 554, 580, 581, 582
MAFS.7.NS.1.2c	Apply properties of operations as strategies to multiply and divide rational numbers	**Develop Conceptual Understanding:** SE: 537, 573, 577, 578, 579 **Fluency:** SE: 540, 541, 542, 543, 544, 573, 574, 575, 576, 580, 581, 582, 595 **Application:** SE: 541, 542, 575, 576, 580, 581, 582
MAFS.7.NS.1.2d	Convert a rational number to a decimal using long division; know that the decimal form of a rational number terminates in 0s or eventually repeats.	**Develop Conceptual Understanding:** SE: 549, 550, 551, 579 **Fluency:** SE: 551–554, 580, 582, 595 **Application:** SE: 551–554, 582
MAFS.7.NS.1.3	Solve real-world and mathematical problems involving the four operations with rational numbers.	**Develop Conceptual Understanding:** SE: 513, 514, 515, 531, 532, 533, 537, 538, 559, 583, 584, 589, 590 **Fluency:** SE: 513, 514, 515, 516, 517, 518, 519, 533, 534, 535, 536, 538, 539, 540, 541, 542, 543, 560, 561, 562, 583, 586, 587, 588, 593, 594 **Application:** SE: 513, 514, 515, 516, 517, 518, 519, 533, 534, 535, 536, 538, 539, 540, 541, 542, 543, 560, 561, 562, 586, 587, 588, 593, 594

Standard	Descriptor	Citations
MAFS.7.RP.1	**Analyze proportional relationships and use them to solve real-world and mathematical problems.**	
MAFS.7.RP.1.1	Compute unit rates associated with rations of fractions, including ratios of lengths, areas, and other quantities measured in like or different units.	Develop Conceptual Understanding: SE: 609, 610, 611, 612, 613 Fluency: SE: 613, 614, 615, 616, 621, 622, 629 Application: SE: 613, 614, 615, 616, 621, 622
MAFS.7.RP.1.2	Recognize and represent proportional relationships between quantities.	Develop Conceptual Understanding: SE: 617, 618, 619, 623, 624, 625 Fluency: SE: 619, 620, 621, 622, 624, 625, 626, 627, 628, 629 Application: SE: 619, 620, 621, 622, 624, 625, 626, 627, 628, 629
MAFS.7.RP.1.2a	Decide whether two quantities are in proportional relationship, e.g., by testing for equivalent ratios in a table or graphing on a coordinate plane and observing whether the graph is a straight line through the origins.	Develop Conceptual Understanding: SE: 617, 618, 619, 623, 624, 625 Fluency: SE: 619, 620, 621, 622, 624, 625, 626, 627, 628, 629 Application: SE: 619, 620, 621, 622, 624, 625, 626, 627, 628, 629
MAFS.7.RP.1.2b	Identify the constant of proportionality (unit rate) in tables, graphs, equations, diagrams, and verbal descriptions of proportional relationships.	Develop Conceptual Understanding: SE: 617, 618, 619, 625 Fluency: SE: 619, 620, 621, 622, 625, 626, 627, 628, 629 Application: SE: 619, 620, 621, 622, 625, 626, 627, 628, 629
MAFS.7.RP.1.2c	Represent proportional relationships by equations.	Develop Conceptual Understanding: SE: 619, 625 Fluency: SE: 619, 620, 621, 622, 625, 626, 627, 628, 629 Application: SE: 619, 620, 621, 622, 625, 626, 627, 628, 629
MAFS.7.RP.1.2d	Explain what a point (x, y) on the graph of a proportional relationship means in terms of the situation with special attention to the points $(0, 0)$ and $(1, r)$ where r is the unit rate.	Develop Conceptual Understanding: SE: 609, 610, 623, 624, 625 Fluency: SE: 608, 624, 625, 626, 627, 628, 629 Application: SE: 624, 625, 626, 627, 628, 629
MAFS.7.RP.1.3	Use proportional relationships to solve multistep ratio and percent problems.	Develop Conceptual Understanding: SE: 635, 636, 637, 641, 642, 643, 647, 648, 649 Fluency: SE: 635, 636, 637, 638, 639, 640, 642, 643, 644, 645, 646, 648, 649, 650, 651, 652, 653 Application: SE: 635, 636, 637, 638, 639, 640, 642, 643, 644, 645, 646, 648, 649, 650, 651, 652, 653

Standard	Descriptor	Citations
MP Mathematical Practices Standards		*The mathematical practices standards are integrated throughout the book. See, for example, the citations below.*
MAFS.K12.MP.1.1	**Make sense of problems and persevere in solving them.** Mathematically proficient students start by explaining to themselves the meaning of a problem and looking for entry points to its solution. They analyze givens, constraints, relationships, and goals. They make conjectures about the form and meaning of the solution and plan a solution pathway rather than simply jumping into a solution attempt. They consider analogous problems, and try special cases and simpler forms of the original problem in order to gain insight into its solution. They monitor and evaluate their progress and change course if necessary. Older students might, depending on the context of the problem, transform algebraic expressions or change the viewing window on their graphing calculator to get the information they need. Mathematically proficient students can explain correspondences between equations, verbal descriptions, tables, and graphs or draw diagrams of important features and relationships, graph data, and search for regularity or trends. Younger students might rely on using concrete objects or pictures to help conceptualize and solve a problem. Mathematically proficient students check their answers to problems using a different method, and they continually ask themselves, "Does this make sense?" They can understand the approaches of others to solving complex problems and identify correspondences between different approaches.	SE: 8, 10, 11–12, 18, 22, 24, 32, 34, 36, 38, 40, 47–52, 58, 63, 81–84, 88, 89, 93–100, 110–112, 117, 122–124, 128–131, 133–134, 150, 152–154, 158, 158–160, 164–166, 176–178, 182–184, 188, 190, 194–196, 207–208, 212–214, 220–222, 241, 242, 247–248, 252–254, 264–268, 272–274, 278, 280–282, 300–302, 308, 310, 314, 316–318, 322, 324, 336, 341–344, 347, 349–350, 355–356, 374, 376, 380–382, 385–388, 393–394, 403, 405–406, 410, 412, 423–424, 428, 430, 433–434, 453–454, 461–462, 467–468, 474, 476, 481–482, 498–500, 506, 511–512, 514–515, 517–518, 528–530, 534, 536, 537, 540, 542, 553, 554, 561– 562, 567–570, 575–576, 581–582, 584, 587–588, 594, 614–616, 621–622, 627–628, 639, 640, 646, 649, 650–652
MAFS.K12.MP.2.1	**Reason abstractly and quantitatively.** Mathematically proficient students make sense of quantities and their relationships in problem situations. They bring two complementary abilities to bear on problems involving quantitative relationships: the ability to decontextualize—to abstract a given situation and represent it symbolically and manipulate the representing symbols as if they have a life of their own, without necessarily attending to their referents—and the ability to contextualize, to pause as needed during the manipulation process in order to probe into the referents for the symbols involved. Quantitative reasoning entails habits of creating a coherent representation of the problem at hand; considering the units involved; attending to the meaning of quantities, not just how to compute them; and knowing and flexibly using different properties of operations and objects.	SE: 9, 12, 17, 18, 24, 35–36, 38, 40, 51, 57, 64, 90, 95, 100, 111–112, 117–118, 134, 178, 183–184, 193, 207, 213, 215–216, 241–242, 249, 252, 254, 265, 268, 277, 280, 282, 297–298, 300, 306, 319, 320, 322, 323, 324, 335, 336, 348, 351, 355, 382, 385, 374, 389, 394, 401, 406, 411–412, 423, 429–430, 434, 450, 462, 468, 497, 499, 500, 505, 530, 534, 540, 554, 561, 569, 575–576, 582, 593–594, 616, 627, 639, 643, 645

Standard	Descriptor	Citations
MAFS.K12.MP.3.1	**Construct viable arguments and critique the reasoning of others.** Mathematically proficient students understand and use stated assumptions, definitions, and previously established results in constructing arguments. They make conjectures and build a logical progression of statements to explore the truth of their conjectures. They are able to analyze situations by breaking them into cases, and can recognize and use counterexamples. They justify their conclusions, communicate them to others, and respond to the arguments of others. They reason inductively about data, making plausible arguments that take into account the context from which the data arose. Mathematically proficient students are also able to compare the effectiveness of two plausible arguments, distinguish correct logic or reasoning from that which is flawed, and—if there is a flaw in an argument—explain what it is. Elementary students can construct arguments using concrete referents such as objects, drawings, diagrams, and actions. Such arguments can make sense and be correct, even though they are not generalized or made formal until later grades. Later, students learn to determine domains to which an argument applies. Students at all grades can listen or read the arguments of others, decide whether they make sense, and ask useful questions to clarify or improve the arguments.	SE: 10, 12, 16, 19, 22, 24, 25, 38, 40, 48, 51, 58, 82, 83–84, 89, 90, 94, 96, 98, 109–110, 112, 116, 118, 123, 125, 128, 129, 134, 149, 153–154, 158, 159, 160, 166, 176, 177–178, 182, 183, 189–190, 195, 204, 206, 207, 212, 214, 222, 242, 247–248, 250, 251, 253, 268, 272, 273, 274, 276, 280, 281–282, 299–300, 301–302, 307, 308, 309–310, 316, 318, 320, 332, 338–339, 341, 344, 350, 355–356, 376, 382, 386, 388, 404, 406, 407, 410, 422, 424, 434, 451–452, 453, 459, 460, 462, 468, 476, 479, 480, 482, 496, 500, 502, 506, 509, 512, 526, 529, 536, 538, 552, 557, 562, 565, 566, 570, 575, 578, 582, 586, 587–588, 589, 593, 594, 615–616, 622, 623, 624, 627–628, 636–637, 640, 641, 652
MAFS.K12.MP.4.1	**Model with mathematics.** Mathematically proficient students can apply the mathematics they know to solve problems arising in everyday life, society, and the workplace. In early grades, this might be as simple as writing an addition equation to describe a situation. In middle grades, a student might apply proportional reasoning to plan a school event or analyze a problem in the community. By high school, a student might use geometry to solve a design problem or use a function to describe how one quantity of interest depends on another. Mathematically proficient students who can apply what they know are comfortable making assumptions and approximations to simplify a complicated situation, realizing that these may need revision later. They are able to identify important quantities in a practical situation and map their relationships using such tools as diagrams, two-way tables, graphs, flowcharts and formulas. They can analyze those relationships mathematically to draw conclusions. They routinely interpret their mathematical results in the context of the situation and reflect on whether the results make sense, possibly improving the model if it has not served its purpose.	SE: 7, 9, 11, 14, 15, 17, 18, 20, 21, 23, 24, 31, 32, 37, 38, 51–52, 53–54, 57, 61, 63, 64, 83–84, 85, 89–90, 91, 95–96, 97, 100, 107, 111–112, 117, 123–124, 128, 129–130, 132–134, 150, 153, 157–159, 161, 162, 165–166, 177, 181, 184, 189–190, 195–196, 207–208, 213–214, 215, 216, 221–222, 241, 247, 249, 254, 264, 267–268, 272, 273–274, 281–282, 301, 309–310, 315, 317, 324, 333, 335, 343, 349, 354, 373, 375, 381, 384, 385, 387, 393, 404, 407, 409, 423, 429–430, 433, 434, 449, 453, 457–461, 464, 467–468, 477–478, 496, 499, 500, 505, 511, 518, 528, 529–530, 535, 536, 561, 567, 568–569, 575, 577, 581, 593, 616, 620–622, 627–628, 639, 644, 645–646, 650–652

Standard	Descriptor	Citations
MAFS.K12.MP.5.1	**Use appropriate tools strategically.** Mathematically proficient students consider the available tools when solving a mathematical problem. These tools might include pencil and paper, concrete models, a ruler, a protractor, a calculator, a spreadsheet, a computer algebra system, a statistical package, or dynamic geometry software. Proficient students are sufficiently familiar with tools appropriate for their grade or course to make sound decisions about when each of these tools might be helpful, recognizing both the insight to be gained and their limitations. For example, mathematically proficient high school students analyze graphs of functions and solutions generated using a graphing calculator. They detect possible errors by strategically using estimation and other mathematical knowledge. When making mathematical models, they know that technology can enable them to visualize the results of varying assumptions, explore consequences, and compare predictions with data. Mathematically proficient students at various grade levels are able to identify relevant external mathematical resources, such as digital content located on a website, and use them to pose or solve problems. They are able to use technological tools to explore and deepen their understanding of concepts.	SE: 8, 11, 12, 21, 33, 37, 59, 91, 113, 119, 122, 123–124, 125, 129–130, 151, 153, 155, 157–158, 159–160, 161, 163–164, 166, 175–176, 177, 183, 185, 188, 191, 194, 203, 207, 210, 213, 215, 220, 245–246, 247, 249, 263–264, 266, 276, 278, 280, 281, 303–304, 305, 308, 311, 319, 321–322, 351–352, 371, 377, 405, 419–420, 449, 458, 463–464, 477, 481, 501–502, 507–508, 525–526, 531, 549, 571, 585, 588, 623–624, 626, 641, 644
MAFS.K12.MP.6.1	**Attend to precision.** Mathematically proficient students try to communicate precisely to others. They try to use clear definitions in discussion with others and in their own reasoning. They state the meaning of the symbols they choose, including using the equal sign consistently and appropriately. They are careful about specifying units of measure, and labeling axes to clarify the correspondence with quantities in a problem. They calculate accurately and efficiently, express numerical answers with a degree of precision appropriate for the problem context. In the elementary grades, students give carefully formulated explanations to each other. By the time they reach high school they have learned to examine claims and make explicit use of definitions.	SE: 13, 20, 23, 35, 39, 48, 52, 53, 55–56, 59, 69, 86, 90, 93, 96, 111, 114, 115, 120, 124, 126, 127, 155–156, 162, 164, 173–174, 179–180, 185, 192, 193, 209, 214, 216–217, 219–220, 237–238, 242, 247–248, 261–262, 270, 303–304, 305, 313, 320, 332, 334, 336, 349–350, 352, 371–372, 382, 384, 412, 424, 430, 431, 452, 456, 468, 471, 495–496, 498, 504, 508–509, 510, 582, 530, 536, 540, 541, 549–550, 553–554, 556, 562, 564, 567, 574, 582, 616, 622, 625, 628, 635, 638, 643–644, 646, 650

Standard	Descriptor	Citations
MAFS.K12.MP.7.1	**Look for and make use of structure.** Mathematically proficient students look closely to discern a pattern or structure. Young students, for example, might notice that three and seven more is the same amount as seven and three more, or they may sort a collection of shapes according to how many sides the shapes have. Later, students will see 7×8 equals the well remembered $7 \times 5 + 7 \times 3$, in preparation for learning about the distributive property. In the expression $x^2 + 9x + 14$, older students can see the 14 as 2×7 and the 9 as $2 + 7$. They recognize the significance of an existing line in a geometric figure and can use the strategy of drawing an auxiliary line for solving problems. They also can step back for an overview and shift perspective. They can see complicated things, such as some algebraic expressions, as single objects or as being composed of several objects. For example, they can see $5 - 3(x - y)^2$ as 5 minus a positive number times a square and use that to realize that its value cannot be more than 5 for any real numbers x and y.	SE: 12, 18, 23, 24, 40, 52, 57, 58, 63, 70, 84, 90, 96, 118, 124, 130, 153–154, 160, 165–166, 177–178, 184, 189–190, 196, 204, 207, 214, 222, 238, 239–240, 242, 244, 245, 248, 249, 253–254, 263–264, 266, 274, 282, 302, 309, 311, 318, 323–324, 336, 342, 344, 349–350, 355–356, 371–372, 376, 380, 382, 387–388, 406, 430, 434, 453–454, 461–462, 467–468, 471, 474, 480, 481, 500, 505–506, 512, 518, 531, 535, 542, 554, 576, 577, 585, 588, 590, 591–592, 617, 621–622, 623, 626, 628, 640, 645–646, 651–652
MAFS.K12.MP.8.1	**Look for and express regularity in repeated reasoning.** Mathematically proficient students notice if calculations are repeated, and look both for general methods and for shortcuts. Upper elementary students might notice when dividing 25 by 11 that they are repeating the same calculations over and over again, and conclude they have a repeating decimal. By paying attention to the calculation of slope as they repeatedly check whether points are on the line through (1, 2) with slope 3, middle school students might abstract the equation $\frac{(y-2)}{(x-1)} = 3$. Noticing the regularity in the way terms cancel when expanding $(x-1)(x+1)$, $(x-1)(x^2+x+1)$, and $(x-1)$ (x^3+x^2+x+1) might lead them to the general formula for the sum of a geometric series. As they work to solve a problem, mathematically proficient students maintain oversight of the process, while attending to the details. They continually evaluate the reasonableness of their intermediate results.	SE: 18, 19, 23, 24, 39, 52, 58, 64, 87, 90, 93, 124, 125, 130, 149, 156, 173–174, 175–176, 196, 208, 216–218, 237, 242, 310, 311, 335, 337–338, 344, 349, 352, 378, 425–426, 428, 462, 511–512, 530, 535–536, 541, 549, 553–554, 570, 573, 582, 611, 614, 615, 621–622, 628, 646, 652

Florida English Language Arts Standards

HMH Florida Go Math supports English language learners at all proficiency levels. The *HMH Florida Go Math Student Edition* provides integrated resources to assist all levels of learners, as shown in the correlation tables provided below.

In addition, students at various levels may benefit from additional program support:

Beginning - Students at a Beginning level are supported by *Spanish Student Edition, Spanish Assessment Resources*, Success for Every Learner and Leveled Practice A worksheets in *Differentiated Instruction, Math On the Spot* videos with Spanish closed captioning, and the *Multilingual Glossary*.

Intermediate - Students at the Intermediate level may use any of the resources above, and may also use Reading Strategies in *Differentiated Instruction*.

Advanced and Advanced High - Students at these levels will be successful as the *Student Edition* promotes vocabulary development through visual and context clues. The *Multilingual Glossary* may also be helpful.

English Language Arts Standard	Student Edition Citations
LAFS.6.SL.1.1 Engage effectively in a range of collaborative discussions (one-on-one, in groups, and teacher-led) with diverse partners on grade 6 topics, texts, and issues, building on others' ideas and expressing their own clearly. a. Come to discussions prepared, having read or studied required material; explicitly draw on that preparation by referring to evidence on the topic, text, or issue to probe and reflect on ideas under discussion. b. Follow rules for collegial discussions, set specific goals and deadlines, and define individual roles as needed. c. Pose and respond to specific questions with elaboration and detail by making comments that contribute to the topic, text, or issue under discussion. d. Review the key ideas expressed and demonstrate understanding of multiple perspectives through reflection and paraphrasing.	Develop Conceptual Understanding: SE: 10, 13, 20, 79, 81, 91, 150, 162, 237, 238, 244, 250, 270, 303, 313, 332, 337, 338, 371, 389, 401, 451, 452, 456, 479 Fluency: SE: 10, 13, 20, 79, 81, 91, 150, 162, 237, 238, 244, 250, 270, 303, 313, 332, 337, 338, 371, 389, 401, 451, 452, 479 Application: SE: 9, 13, 20, 91, 149, 150, 161, 162, 163, 237, 249, 303, 314, 337, 338, 451, 452, 479
LAFS.6.SL.1.2 Interpret information presented in diverse media and formats (e.g., visually, quantitatively, orally) and explain how it contributes to a topic, text, or issue under study.	Develop Conceptual Understanding: SE: 5, 9, 28, 77, 88, 99, 100, 147, 171, 181, 210, 239, 259, 282, 295, 368, 447, 301, 302, 332, 408, 433, 434, 467, 468, 471, 472 Fluency: SE: 9, 77, 88, 99, 100, 181, 239, 301, 302, 332, 408, 433, 434, 467, 468, 471, 481 Application: SE: 99, 100, 181, 282, 301, 302, 408, 433, 434, 467, 468, 481
LAFS.6.SL.1.3 Delineate a speaker's argument and specific claims, distinguishing claims that are supported by reasons and evidence from claims that are not.	Develop Conceptual Understanding: SE: 25 Fluency: SE: 12, 112, 208, 248, 309, 376, 468 Application: SE: 12, 25, 112, 208, 376, 468
LAFS.6.SL.2.4 Present claims and findings, sequencing ideas logically and using pertinent descriptions, facts, and details to accentuate main ideas or themes; use appropriate eye contact, adequate volume, and clear pronunciation.	Develop Conceptual Understanding: SE: 7, 13, 81, 92, 115, 125, 173, 217, 218, 249, 250, 270, 319, 333, 340, 372, 384, 407, 450, 457, 469 Fluency: SE: 7, 13, 81, 92, 174, 217, 218, 249, 250, 251, 319, 340, 469 Application: SE: 7, 13, 92, 217, 218, 249, 250, 319, 469

English Language Arts Standard	Student Edition Citations
LAFS.68.RST.1.3 Follow precisely a multistep procedure when carrying out experiments, taking measurements, or performing technical tasks.	Develop Conceptual Understanding: SE: 47, 48, 85, 97, 98, 149, 244, 347, 389, 451 Fluency: SE: 47, 48, 51, 95, 97, 98, 153, 183, 267, 318, 376, 379, 462 Application: SE: 47, 48, 51, 85, 95, 97, 98, 153, 183, 267, 318, 376, 462
LAFS.68.RST.2.4 Determine the meaning of symbols, key terms, and other domain-specific words and phrases as they are used in a specific scientific or technical context relevant to grades 6–8 texts and topics.	Develop Conceptual Understanding: SE: 5, 6, 77, 78, 147, 148, 171, 236, 259, 295, 296, 369, 370, 447, 448 Fluency: SE: 22, 112, 152, 301, 411, 474 Application: SE: 31, 411, 474
LAFS.68.RST.3.7 Integrate quantitative or technical information expressed in words in a text with a version of that information expressed visually (e.g., in a flowchart, diagram, model, graph, or table).	Develop Conceptual Understanding: SE: 6, 78, 148, 236, 296, 370, 448 Fluency: SE: 17, 154, 184, 282, 468 Application: SE: 17, 154, 156, 184, 282, 468

LAFS.68.WHST.1.1 Write arguments focused on *discipline-specific content*.
  a. Introduce claim(s) about a topic or issue, acknowledge and distinguish the claim(s) from alternate or opposing claims, and organize the reasons and evidence logically.
  b. Support claim(s) with logical reasoning and relevant, accurate data and evidence that demonstrate an understanding of the topic or text, using credible sources.
  c. Use words, phrases, and clauses to create cohesion and clarify the relationships among claim(s), counterclaims, reasons, and evidence.
  d. Establish and maintain a formal style.
  e. Provide a concluding statement or section that follows from and supports the argument presented.
	Develop Conceptual Understanding: SE: 19, 389, 401
	Fluency: SE: 40, 91, 112, 208, 248, 324, 424, 482
	Application: SE: 91, 112, 162, 204, 208, 248, 324, 482

LAFS.68.WHST.2.4 Produce clear and coherent writing in which the development, organization, and style are appropriate to task, purpose, and audience.	Develop Conceptual Understanding: SE: 120 Fluency: SE: 64, 214, 242, 344, 382, 468 Application: SE: 344, 468

Succeeding with HMH Florida Go Math

Actively participate in your learning with your write-in Student Edition. Explore concepts, take notes, answer questions, and complete your homework right in your textbook!

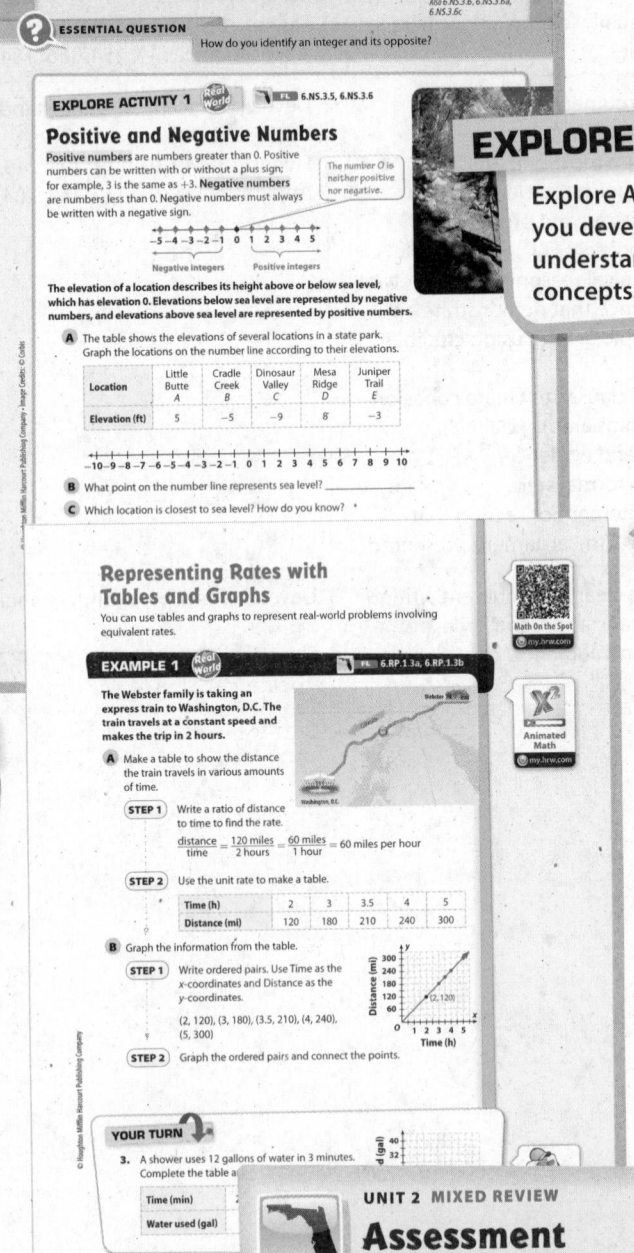

EXPLORE ACTIVITY

Explore Activities help you develop a deeper understanding of math concepts.

YOUR TURN

Your Turn exercises check your understanding of new concepts.

Math On the Spot
⏻ my.hrw.com

Scan QR codes with your smart phone to watch Math On the Spot tutorial videos for every example in the book!

Assessment Readiness

Check your mastery of concepts through review and practice for high-stakes tests.

Enhance Your Learning!

GO DIGITAL
my.hrw.com

my.hrw.com

The Interactive Student Edition provides additional videos, activities, tools, and learning aids to support you as you study!

Practice skills and complete your homework online with the Personal Math Trainer. Your Personal Math Trainer provides a variety of learning aids that develop and improve your understanding of math concepts including videos, guided examples, and step-by-step solutions.

Personal Math Trainer

Online Assessment and Intervention

my.hrw.com

Math On the Spot

my.hrw.com

Math On the Spot video tutorials provide step-by-step instruction of the math concepts covered in each example.

Animated Math activities let you interactively explore and practice key math concepts and skills.

Animated Math

my.hrw.com

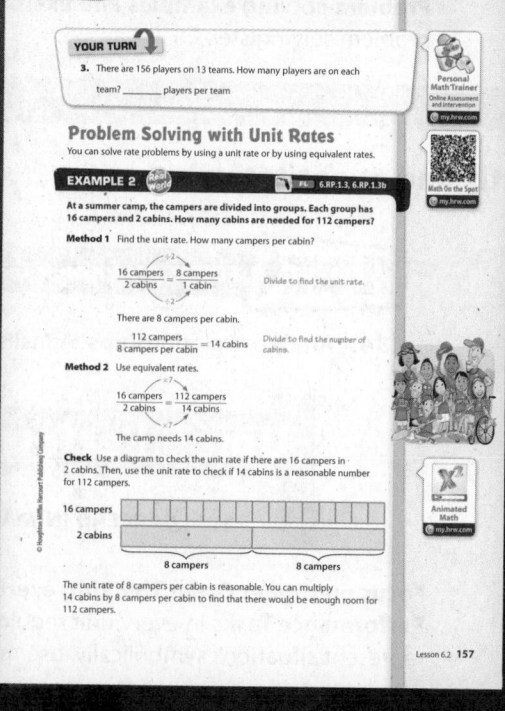

Standards for Mathematical Practice

The topics described in the Standards for Mathematical Content will vary from year to year. However, the *way* in which you learn, study, and think about mathematics will not. The Standards for Mathematical Practice describe skills that you will use in all of your math courses. These pages show some features of your book that will help you gain these skills and use them to master this year's topics.

MP.1.1 Make sense of problems and persevere in solving them.

Mathematically proficient students start by explaining to themselves the meaning of a problem… They analyze givens, constraints, relationships, and goals. They make conjectures about the form… of the solution and plan a solution pathway…

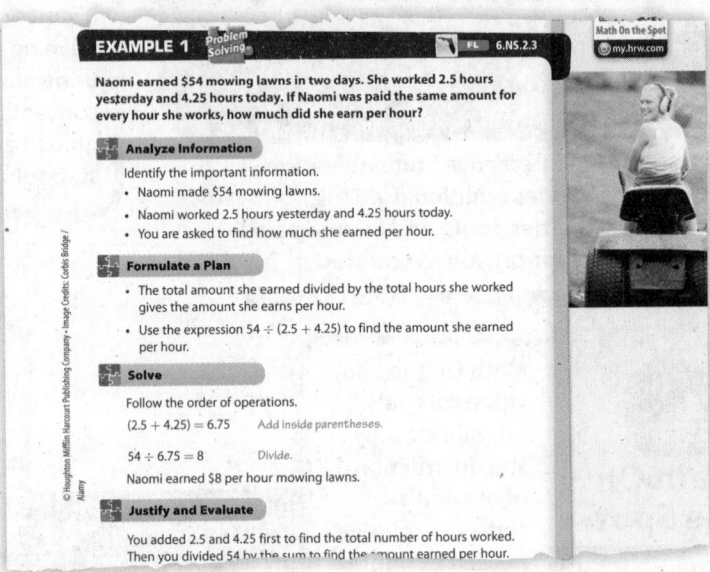

Problem-solving examples and exercises lead students through problem solving steps.

MP.2.1 Reason abstractly and quantitatively.

Mathematically proficient students… bring two complementary abilities to bear on problems…: the ability to decontextualize— to abstract a given situation and represent it symbolically… and the ability to contextualize, to pause… in order to probe into the referents for the symbols involved.

Focus on Higher Order Thinking exercises in every lesson and **Performance Tasks** in every unit require you to use logical reasoning, represent situations symbolically, use mathematical models to solve problems, and state your answers in terms of a problem context.

MP.3.1 Construct viable arguments and critique the reasoning of others.

Mathematically proficient students... justify their conclusions, [and]... distinguish correct... reasoning from that which is flawed.

Reflect

1. **Critique Reasoning** Jo says she can find the percent equivalen[t] multiplying the percent equivalent of $\frac{1}{4}$ by 3. How can you use bar model to support this claim?

? ESSENTIAL QUESTION CHECK-IN

Essential Question Check-in and **Reflect** in every lesson ask you to evaluate statements, explain relationships, apply mathematical principles, make conjectures, construct arguments, and justify your reasoning.

MP.4.1 Model with mathematics.

Mathematically proficient students can apply... mathematics... to... problems... in everyday life, society, and the workplace.

EXAMPLE 2 | FL 6.RP.1.3, 6.RP.1.3a

You make 5 cups of punch by mixing 3 cups of cranberry juice with 2 cups of apple juice. How much cranberry juice and how much apple juice do you need to make four times the original recipe?

Method 1 Use a table.

STEP 1 Make a table comparing the number of cups of cranberry juice and apple juice needed to make two times, three times, and four times the original recipe.

> Multiply both terms of the original ratio by the same number to find an equivalent ratio.

		3×2	3×3	3×4
Cranberry Juice	3	6	9	12
Apple Juice	2	4	6	8

My Notes

Real-world examples and **mathematical modeling** apply mathematics to other disciplines and real-world contexts such as science and business.

MP.5.1 Use appropriate tools strategically.

Mathematically proficient students consider the available tools when solving a... problem... [and] are... able to use technological tools to explore and deepen their understanding...

EXPLORE ACTIVITY | FL 6.NS.1.1

Modeling Mixed Number Division

Antoine is making sushi rolls. He has $2\frac{1}{2}$ cups of rice and will use $\frac{1}{4}$ cup of rice for each sushi roll. How many sushi rolls can he make?

A To find the number of sushi rolls that can be made, you need to determine how many fourths are in $2\frac{1}{2}$. Use fraction pieces to represent $2\frac{1}{2}$ on the model below.

B How many fourths are in $2\frac{1}{2}$? _____

Antoine has enough rice to make _____ sushi rolls.

Reflect

1. Communicate Mathematical Ideas. Whi[ch] mathematical operation

Exploration Activities in lessons use concrete and technological tools, such as manipulatives or graphing calculators, to explore mathematical concepts.

MP.6.1 Attend to precision.

Mathematically proficient students… communicate precisely… with others and in their own reasoning… [They] give carefully formulated explanations…

31. **Communicate Mathematical Ideas** Write an example of an that cannot be simplified, and explain how you know that it simplified.

Key Vocabulary

rate *(tasa)*
> A ratio that compares two quantities measured in different units.

Precision refers not only to the correctness of calculations but also to the proper use of mathematical language and symbols. **Communicate Mathematical Ideas** exercises and **Key Vocabulary** highlighted for each module and unit help you learn and use the language of math to communicate mathematics precisely.

MP.7.1 Look for and make use of structure.

Mathematically proficient students… look closely to discern a pattern or structure… They can also step back for an overview and shift perspectives.

A scientist observed the hourly growth of bacteria and recorded his observations in a table.

Time (h)	Total bacteria
0	1
1	2
2	$2 \times 2 =$ ☐
3	$2 \times 2 \times 2 =$ ☐
4	$2 \times 2 \times 2 \times 2 =$ ☐

After 2 hours, there are $2 \cdot 2 = ?$ bacteria.

A Complete the table. What pattern(s) do you see in the Total bacteria column?

Throughout the lessons, you will observe regularity in mathematical structures in order to make generalizations and make connections between related problems. For example, you can use what you known about multiplication to understand how to use exponents.

MP.8.1 Look for and express regularity in repeated reasoning.

Mathematically proficient students… look both for general methods and for shortcuts… [and] maintain oversight of the process, while attending to the details.

46. **Look for a Pattern** Find the values of the powers in the follo pattern: $10^1, 10^2, 10^3, 10^4$…. Describe the pattern, and use it 10^6 without using multiplication.

25. **Justify Reasoning** Determine whether $3x + 12 + x$ is e $4(3 + x)$. Use properties of operations to justify your ans

Reflect

8. **Make a Conjecture** Use the pattern in the table to make a c about how you can use multiplication to divide one fraction

You will look for repeated calculations and mathematical patterns in examples and exercises. Recognizing patterns can help you make generalizations and obtain a better understanding of the underlying mathematics.

MATHEMATICS GRADE 5 PART 1
Review Test

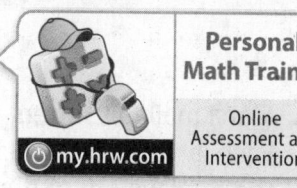

Personal Math Trainer
Online Assessment and Intervention
my.hrw.com

Selected Response

1. Al used the expression $8 + 25 \times 2 - 45$ to find how many CDs he has. How many CDs does he have?

   Ⓐ 3   Ⓒ 21
   Ⓑ 13   Ⓓ 103

2. Jamie baked 24 biscuits. Her sister Mia ate 3 biscuits, and her brother David ate 2 biscuits. Which expression can Jamie use to find how many biscuits are left?

   Ⓐ $24 + (3 + 2)$ Ⓒ $(24 - 3) + 2$
   Ⓑ $24 - (3 + 2)$ Ⓓ $24 - (3 - 2)$

3. What is the unknown number in sequence 2 in the chart?

Sequence Number	1	2	3	5	7
Sequence 1	3	6	9	15	21
Sequence 2	15	30	45	75	?

   Ⓐ 63   Ⓒ 105
   Ⓑ 90   Ⓓ 150

4. Patel hopes to be one of the first fans to get into the stadium for the baseball game because the first 30,000 fans will receive a baseball cap. Which shows 30,000 as a whole number multiplied by a power of ten?

   Ⓐ 3×10^1 Ⓒ 3×10^3
   Ⓑ 3×10^2 Ⓓ 3×10^4

5. The Davis family pays $200,000 for a new house. They make a down payment that is $\frac{1}{10}$ of the price of the house. How much is the down payment?

   Ⓐ $20   Ⓒ $2,000
   Ⓑ $200   Ⓓ $20,000

6. Jackie found a rock that has a mass of 78.852 grams. What is the mass of the rock rounded to the nearest tenth?

   Ⓐ 78.85 grams   Ⓒ 79 grams
   Ⓑ 78.9 grams   Ⓓ 80 grams

7. A company manufactures 295 toy cars each day. How many toy cars does the company manufacture in 34 days?

   Ⓐ 3,065   Ⓒ 10,065
   Ⓑ 7,610   Ⓓ 10,030

8. There are 6 buses transporting students to a baseball game, with 32 students on each bus. Each row at the baseball stadium seats 8 students. If the students fill up all of the rows, how many rows of seats will the students need altogether?

   Ⓐ 22   Ⓒ 24
   Ⓑ 23   Ⓓ 1,536

9. The portions of a house that need to be heated can be modeled by one rectangular prism with a length of 45 feet, a width of 20 feet, and a height of 18 feet, and a second rectangular prism with a base area of 350 square feet and a height of 9 feet. What is the total volume?

   Ⓐ 12500 cubic feet

   Ⓑ 16,200 cubic feet

   Ⓒ 16,550 cubic feet

   Ⓓ 19,350 cubic feet

10. Marci mailed 9 letters at the post office. Each letter weighed 3.5 ounces. What was the total weight of the letters?

(A) 33.5 ounces   (C) 31.5 ounces

(B) 32.5 ounces   (D) 27.5 ounces

11. Denise, Keith, and Tim live in the same neighborhood. Denise lives 0.3 mile from Keith. The distance that Tim and Keith live from each other is 0.2 times as great as the distance between Denise and Keith. How far from each other do Tim and Keith live?

(A) 0.6 mile   (C) 0.1 mile

(B) 0.5 mile   (D) 0.06 mile

12. Madison needs to buy enough meat to make 1,000 hamburgers for the company picnic. Each hamburger will weigh 0.25 pound. How many pounds of hamburger meat should Madison buy?

(A) 2.5 pounds   (C) 250 pounds

(B) 25 pounds   (D) 2,500 pounds

Mini-Tasks

13. Rayna wrote 260,980 as $(2 \times 100,000) + (6 \times 10,000) + (9 \times 1,000) + (8 \times 100)$. What error did Rayna make? Write the correct expanded form.

_____

_____

_____

_____

14. The highest scores at a gymnastics meet were 9.675, 9.25, 9.325, and 9.5. Write the scores in order from least to greatest.

_____

15. Ann and Joe's father donated $3 for every lap they swam in a swim-a-thon. Ann swam 21 laps, and Joe swam 15 laps. Use the Distributive Property to find the amount of money their father donated.

_____

_____

_____

_____

16. A grain of sand has a diameter of 0.049 millimeter. Write 0.049 in words.

_____

Performance Task

17. Jennifer has $12 to spend on lunch and the roller rink. Admission to the roller rink is $5.75. Jennifer estimates that she can buy a large drink and a turkey sandwich and still have enough money to get into the rink. Do you agree? Support your answer.

Sandwiches	Drinks
Tuna $3.95	Small $1.29
Turkey $4.85	Medium $1.59
Grilled Cheese $3.25	Large $1.79

_____

_____

_____

_____

_____

MATHEMATICS GRADE 5 PART 2

Review Test

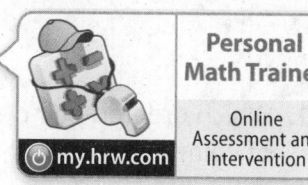

Personal Math Trainer

Online Assessment and Intervention

my.hrw.com

Selected Response

1. Charles bought $\frac{7}{8}$ foot of electrical wire and $\frac{5}{6}$ foot of copper wire for his science project. What is the least common denominator of the fractions?

   Ⓐ 14   Ⓒ 24

   Ⓑ 18   Ⓓ 48

2. Tom jogged $\frac{3}{5}$ mile on Monday and $\frac{2}{6}$ mile on Tuesday. How much farther did Tom jog on Monday than on Tuesday?

   Ⓐ $\frac{1}{30}$ mile   Ⓒ $\frac{8}{30}$ mile

   Ⓑ $\frac{3}{15}$ mile   Ⓓ $\frac{14}{15}$ mile

3. Three fences on a ranch measure $\frac{15}{16}$ mile, $\frac{7}{8}$ mile, and $\frac{7}{16}$ mile. Which is the best estimate of the total length of all three fences?

   Ⓐ $1\frac{1}{2}$ miles   Ⓒ $2\frac{1}{2}$ miles

   Ⓑ 2 miles   Ⓓ 3 miles

4. Lawrence bought $\frac{2}{3}$ pound of roast beef. He used $\frac{3}{4}$ of it to make a sandwich. How much roast beef did Lawrence use for his sandwich? You may use a model to help you solve the problem.

   Ⓐ $\frac{5}{12}$ pound   Ⓒ $\frac{5}{7}$ pound

   Ⓑ $\frac{1}{2}$ pound   Ⓓ $\frac{6}{7}$ pound

5. Sarah built a table using 6 pieces of wood that were each $3\frac{3}{4}$ inches wide. How wide was the table?

   Ⓐ $18\frac{1}{8}$ inches   Ⓒ $21\frac{1}{4}$ inches

   Ⓑ $18\frac{3}{4}$ inches   Ⓓ $22\frac{1}{2}$ inches

6. Vanessa made 6 sandwiches for a party and cut them all into fourths. How many $\frac{1}{4}$-sandwich pieces did she have?

   Ⓐ $1\frac{1}{2}$ Ⓒ 4

   Ⓑ $2\frac{1}{4}$ Ⓓ 24

7. Dr. Watson combines 400 mL of detergent, 800 mL of alcohol, and 1,500 mL of water. How many liters of solution does he have?

   Ⓐ 2.7 liters   Ⓒ 270 liters

   Ⓑ 27 liters   Ⓓ 2,700 liters

8. Give the most descriptive name for the figure.

   Ⓐ square   Ⓒ parallelogram

   Ⓑ rectangle   Ⓓ rhombus

9. Find the volume of the rectangular prism.

   5 cm

   5 cm

   13 cm

   Ⓐ 310 cm³   Ⓒ 325 cm³

   Ⓑ 184 cm³   Ⓓ 23 cm³

10. Which ordered pair describes the location of Point A?

Ⓐ (0, 2)   Ⓒ (4, 0)

Ⓑ (2, 4)   Ⓓ (4, 2)

11. Which ordered pair describes the location of Point A?

Ⓐ (0, 5)   Ⓒ (5, 5)

Ⓑ (5, 0)   Ⓓ (1, 5)

Mini-Tasks

12. When Bruce started bowling, he won $\frac{1}{4}$ of the games he played. Within six months, he was winning $\frac{7}{16}$ of his games. If he improves at the same rate, what fraction of his games should he expect to win after another six months?

_____

13. Gina wants to ship three books that weigh $2\frac{7}{16}$ pounds, $1\frac{7}{8}$ pounds and $\frac{1}{2}$ pound. The maximum weight she can ship is 6 pounds. Estimate to see if Gina can ship all 3 books. Explain your answer.

_____

_____

_____

14. How much trail mix will each person get if 5 people share $\frac{1}{2}$ pound of trail mix?

_____

15. Write a story to represent the division problem $6 \div \frac{1}{3}$.

_____

_____

_____

_____

16. What is the volume in cubic centimeters of the solid?

_____

Performance Task

17. Shia measured the thickness of some buttons. She graphed the results in a line plot.

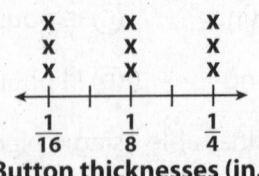
Button thicknesses (in.)

Part A: Suppose Shia makes a stack of all the buttons. How tall will the stack be?

_____

Part B: Suppose Shia wants the stack to be 2 inches high. How many buttons that are $\frac{1}{16}$ inch thick must be added to the stack of buttons?

_____

ADVANCED MATHEMATICS 1 PART 1

Benchmark Test

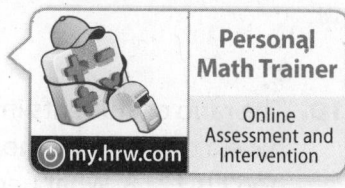

Personal
Math Trainer

Online
Assessment and
Intervention

my.hrw.com

Selected Response

1. Suppose you have developed a scale that indicates the brightness of sunlight. Each category in the table is 9 times brighter than the category above it. For example, a day that is dazzling is 9 times brighter than a day that is radiant. How many times brighter is a dazzling day than an illuminated day?

Sunlight Intensity	
Category	**Brightness**
Dim	2
Illuminated	3
Radiant	4
Dazzling	5

- Ⓐ 2 times brighter
- Ⓑ 729 times brighter
- Ⓒ 81 times brighter
- Ⓓ 9 times brighter

2. Which group of numbers is in order from least to greatest?

- Ⓐ $2.58, 2\frac{5}{8}, 2.6, 2\frac{2}{3}$
- Ⓑ $2\frac{2}{3}, 2\frac{5}{8}, 2.6, 2.58$
- Ⓒ $2\frac{5}{8}, 2\frac{2}{3}, 2.6, 2.58$
- Ⓓ $2.58, 2.6, 2\frac{5}{8}, 2\frac{2}{3}$

3. Which temperature is coldest?

- Ⓐ $-13\,°F$
- Ⓒ $-20\,°F$
- Ⓑ $20\,°F$
- Ⓓ $13\,°F$

4. Patricia paid $385 for 5 nights at a hotel. Find the unit rate.

- Ⓐ $\frac{\$77}{1\ \text{night}}$
- Ⓒ $\frac{\$385}{1\ \text{night}}$
- Ⓑ $\frac{\$154}{1\ \text{night}}$
- Ⓓ $\frac{\$39}{1\ \text{night}}$

5. The fuel for a chain saw is a mix of oil and gasoline. The label says to mix 6 ounces of oil with 16 gallons of gasoline. How much oil would you use if you had 32 gallons of gasoline?

- Ⓐ 3 ounces
- Ⓒ 18 ounces
- Ⓑ 12 ounces
- Ⓓ 85.3 ounces

6. Lee is putting together fruit baskets for gifts. He has 18 apples, 24 pears, and 30 oranges What is the greatest number of fruit baskets he can make if he uses all the fruit and each basket is the same?

- Ⓐ 2 baskets
- Ⓒ 4 baskets
- Ⓑ 3 baskets
- Ⓓ 6 baskets

7. It takes light about 134 milliseconds to travel the distance around Earth's Equator. How many seconds is this?

- Ⓐ 0.000134 sec
- Ⓒ 0.134 sec
- Ⓑ 0.0134 sec
- Ⓓ 1.34 sec

8. From the beginning of cross country season to the end, Tisha reduced her time by 17%, Anchara reduced hers by $\frac{1}{6}$, Juanita reduced hers by $\frac{4}{25}$, and Julia reduced hers from 16:00 to 13:30. Who reduced her time by the greatest percent?

- Ⓐ Tisha
- Ⓒ Juanita
- Ⓑ Anchara
- Ⓓ Julia

9. A stack of blocks is 15.2 inches tall. If there are 10 blocks stacked one on top of the other, how tall is each block?

- Ⓐ 1.62 inches
- Ⓒ 1.72 inches
- Ⓑ 1.52 inches
- Ⓓ 5.2 inches

10. The ratio of students in Jaíme's class who have a dog or cat at home to those who don't is 12 : 8. What percent of the class do NOT have a dog or cat at home?

(A) $33\frac{1}{3}\%$ (C) 60%

(B) 40%   (D) $66\frac{2}{3}\%$

11. Ninety percent of a school's students, or 540 students, attended a school assembly. How many students are there at the school?

(A) 486 students   (C) 600 students

(B) 594 students   (D) 621 students

12. Find the quotient $9\frac{3}{5} \div \frac{8}{15}$.

(A) 2   (C) $16\frac{7}{8}$

(B) 18   (D) $18\frac{3}{4}$

13. Find the product 4.51×3.4.

(A) 153.34   (C) 7.91

(B) 1.5334   (D) 15.334

14. Jorge is building a table out of boards that are 3.75 inches wide. He wants the table to be at least 36 inches wide. What is the least number of boards he can use?

(A) 9   (C) 10

(B) 9.6   (D) 135

Mini-Tasks

15. Nikita is making spaghetti sauce and pizzas for a large party. Her spaghetti sauce recipe calls for $1\frac{3}{4}$ cups of tomato paste, and her pizza recipe uses $\frac{2}{3}$ cup of tomato paste per pizza. She will triple her spaghetti sauce recipe and make 6 pizzas. Write and evaluate an expression for how many $\frac{3}{4}$ cup cans of tomato paste she will need in all.

_____

_____

16. Explain how you can use multiplication to find the quotient $\frac{3}{4} \div \frac{3}{16}$. Then evaluate the expression.

_____

_____

17. A chef has 6 cups of berries and will use $\frac{2}{3}$ cup of berries for each serving of fruit salad. How many servings can be made?

_____

Performance Task

18. School A has 480 students and 16 classrooms. School B has 192 students and 12 classrooms.

Part A: What is the ratio of students to classrooms at School A?

Part B: What is the ratio of students to classrooms at School B?

Part C: How many students would have to transfer from School A to School B for the ratios of students to classrooms at both schools to be the same? Explain your reasoning.

_____

_____

_____

_____

_____

_____

_____

_____

_____

ADVANCED MATHEMATICS 1 PART 2

Benchmark Test

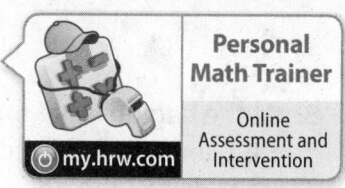

Personal
Math Trainer

Online
Assessment and
Intervention

my.hrw.com

Selected Response

1. Kahlil is recording a beat for a song that he is working on. He wants the length of the beat to be more than 10 seconds long. His friend tells him the beat needs to be 5 seconds longer than that to match the lyrics he has written.

Write an inequality to represent the beat's length. Give three possible beat lengths that satisfy the inequality.

(A) $t > 5$; 16, 21, 22

(B) $t > 15$; 16, 21, 22

(C) $t < 15$; 4, 3, 2

(D) $t < 10$; 4, 3, 2

2. Write an expression for the missing value in the table.

Tom's Age	Kim's Age
10	13
11	14
12	15
a	?

(A) $a + 1$

(C) $a + 3$

(B) $a + 15$

(D) $a + 10$

3. What is the area of the polygon?

(A) 3.15 cm²

(C) 13.95 cm²

(B) 10.8 cm²

(D) 1395 cm²

4. A plant's height is 1.4 times its age. Write an equation for this situation.

(A) $h =$ plant's height; $y =$ plant's age; $h = 1.4y$

(B) $h =$ plant's age; $y =$ plant's height; $h = 1.4y$

(C) $h =$ plant's height; $y =$ plant's age; $y = 1.4h$

(D) $h =$ plant's height; $y =$ plant's age; $1.4 = hy$

5. A rectangular box is $8\frac{1}{2}$ inches long, $5\frac{1}{4}$ inches wide, and 4 inches high. What is its volume?

(A) 160 cubic inches

(B) 168 cubic inches

(C) $178\frac{1}{2}$ cubic inches

(D) 180 cubic inches

6. Write the phrase as an algebraic expression.

4 times the sum of a number and 20

(A) $20 \div y$　　(C) $4(y + 20)$

(B) $20 + y$　　(D) $4y - 20y$

7. Wilson bought gift cards for some lawyers and their assistants. Each lawyer got a gift card worth ℓ dollars. Each assistant got a gift card worth a dollars. There are 14 lawyers. Each lawyer has 3 assistants. The expression for the total cost of the gift cards is $14\ell + 42a$. Write an expression that is equivalent to the given expression.

(A) $14(\ell + 2a)$　　(C) $14(\ell + 42a)$

(B) $14(\ell + 3a)$　　(D) $42(\ell + 3a)$

8. At the beginning of the year, Jason had $120 in his savings account. Each month, he added $15 to his account. Write an expression for the amount of money in Jason's savings account each month. Then use the expression to find the amount of money in his account at the end of the year.

Month	January	February	March	m
Amount	$135	$150	$165	$?

Ⓐ $120 + 12m$; $264

Ⓑ $135 + 15m$; $315

Ⓒ $135 + m$; $147

Ⓓ $15m + 120$; $300

9. Which question is a statistical question?

Ⓐ What are the ages of schools in the school district?

Ⓑ How old is the middle school building?

Ⓒ How many classrooms are there in the elementary school building?

Ⓓ How many daily class periods are there in the high school?

10. Find the interquartile range for the data set: 10, 3, 8, 6, 9, 12, 13.

Ⓐ 12   Ⓒ 6

Ⓑ 8   Ⓓ 7

11. Which problem will have a negative integer as the solution?

Ⓐ -4.6×-7 Ⓒ $\frac{5}{9} - \frac{1}{3}$

Ⓑ $-7 + 9$ Ⓓ $-45 \div 5$

Mini-Tasks

12. Mike was in charge of collecting contributions for the Food Bank. He received contributions of $80, $70, $60, $40, and $80. Find the mean, and the median of the contributions.

_____

13. One side of trapezoid is 10 inches. The side parallel to this is twice as long as this side. The height is half as long as the given side length. Find the area of the trapezoid.

_____

14. Find the perimeter of the rectangle with vertices at $R(-2, 3)$, $S(4, 3)$, $T(4, -1)$ and $U(-2, -1)$.

_____

15. Brian is ordering tickets online for a concert. The price of each ticket for the concert is t dollars. For online orders, there is an additional charge of $11 per ticket, and a service charge of $14 for the entire order. The cost for 7 tickets can be represented by the expression $7(t + 11) + 14$.

Write two expressions equivalent to the cost expression. Then, find the total cost of Brian's online order if the price of each ticket for this concert is $33.

_____

Performance Task

16. Jillian wants to find the surface area of a pyramid. The base is a square with with sides that are 4 inches long. The other faces are isosceles triangles. The ratio of the height of each triangle to its base is 3 : 2.

Part A: Give the base length and the height of each triangular face.

Part B: Find the combined area of the triangular faces.

Part C: Find the surface area of the pyramid.

_____

_____

_____

_____

right© Houghton Mifflin Harcourt Publishing Company

UNIT 1

Numbers

MODULE **1**

Integers

FL 6.NS.3.5, 6.NS.3.7b, 6.NS.3.7c

MODULE **2**

Factors and Multiples

FL 6.NS.2.4

MODULE **3**

Rational Numbers

FL 6.NS.3.6, 6.NS.3.6c, 6.NS.3.7a

CAREERS IN MATH

Climatologist A climatologist is a scientist who studies long-term trends in climate conditions. These scientists collect, evaluate, and interpret data and use mathematical models to study the dynamics of weather patterns and to understand and predict Earth's climate.

If you are interested in a career in climatology, you should study these mathematical subjects:
- Algebra
- Trigonometry
- Probability and Statistics
- Calculus

Research other careers that require the analysis of data and use of mathematical models.

Unit 1 Performance Task

At the end of the unit, check out how **climatologists** use math.

Vocabulary Preview

Use the puzzle to preview key vocabulary from this unit. Unscramble the circled letters within found words to answer the riddle at the bottom of the page.

```
E R I N E Q U A L I T Y I L N
U S E R O J U J P Z Y M B E M
L U E B P P H K F J A L G R Z
A M G Z M Y P G C R Y A R A D
V K B E D U G O C T K W G X
E D M F S L N A S I J J H Z C
T B K H V M I L V I Q E L D R
U R I M R D I E A Y T Z G K P
L V N T N H N D Y N L E F T H
O X T N K U K Q F X O A S T E
S R E B M U N E V I T I S O P
B V G B D Z A F E A X Y T Y A
A D E P X N V I U B V S T A A
O R R V R R X I R G L V B U R
S X S M I Q V Y N L N P S S I
```

- Any number that can be written as a ratio of two integers. (Lesson 3.1)
- The greatest factor shared by two or more numbers. (Lesson 2.1)
- A diagram used to show the relationship between two sets or groups. (Lesson 3.1)
- A mathematical statement that shows two quantities are not equal. (Lesson 1.2)
- The set of all whole numbers and their opposites. (Lesson 1.1)
- The distance of a number from zero on the number line. (Lesson 1.3)
- Numbers less than zero. (Lesson 1.1)

Q: Why did the integer get a bad evaluation at work?

A: He had a ___ ___ ___ ___ ___ ___ ___
___ ___ ___ ___ ___ ___ ___!

Integers

? ESSENTIAL QUESTION

How can you use integers to solve real-world problems?

LESSON 1.1
Identifying Integers and Their Opposites
FL 6.NS.3.5, 6.NS.3.6, 6.NS.3.6a, 6.NS.3.6c

LESSON 1.2
Comparing and Ordering Integers
FL 6.NS.3.7, 6.NS.3.7a, 6.NS.3.7b

LESSON 1.3
Absolute Value
FL 6.NS.3.7, 6.NS.3.7c, 6.NS.3.7d

Real-World Video

Integers can be used to describe the value of many things in the real world. The height of a mountain in feet may be a very great integer while the temperature in degrees Celsius at the top of that mountain may be a negative integer.

my.hrw.com

GO DIGITAL
my.hrw.com

my.hrw.com

Go digital with your write-in student edition, accessible on any device.

Math On the Spot

Scan with your smart phone to jump directly to the online edition, video tutor, and more.

Animated Math

Interactively explore key concepts to see how math works.

Personal Math Trainer

Get immediate feedback and help as you work through practice sets.

Are YOU Ready?

Complete these exercises to review skills you will need for this module.

Personal Math Trainer

Online Assessment and Intervention

my.hrw.com

Compare Whole Numbers

EXAMPLE

3,564 ⬤ 3,528   Compare digits in the thousands place: $3 = 3$

3,564 ⬤ 3,528   Compare digits in the hundreds place: $5 = 5$

$3,564 > 3,528$ Compare digits in the tens place: $6 > 2$

Compare. Write <, >, or =.

1. 471 ◯ 468   2. 5,005 ◯ 5,050   3. 398 ◯ 389

4. 10,973 ◯ 10,999   5. 8,471 ◯ 9,001   6. 108 ◯ 95

Order Whole Numbers

EXAMPLE

356, 348, 59, 416   Compare digits. Find the greatest number.

356, 348, 59, 416   Find the next greatest number.

356, 348, 59, 416   Find the next greatest number.

356, 348, 59, 416   Find the least number.

$416 > 356 > 348 > 59$ Order the numbers.

Order the numbers from greatest to least.

7. 156; 87; 177; 99   8. 591; 589; 603; 600

_____   _____

9. 2,650; 2,605; 3,056; 2,088   10. 1,037; 995; 10,415; 1,029

_____   _____

Locate Numbers on a Number Line

EXAMPLE

Graph $+4$ by starting at 0 and counting 4 units to the right.
Graph -3 by starting at 0 and counting 3 units to the left.

Graph each number on the number line.

11. 12   12. 20   13. 2   14. 9

Reading Start-Up

Visualize Vocabulary

Use the ✔ words to complete the chart. Write the correct vocabulary word next to the symbol.

Symbol
<
>
=
+
−

Vocabulary

Review Words
- ✔ equal *(igual)*
- ✔ greater than *(más que)*
- ✔ less than *(menos que)*
- ✔ negative sign *(signo negativo)*
- number line *(recta numérica)*
- ✔ plus sign *(signo más)*
- symbol *(símbolo)*
- whole number *(número entero)*

Preview Words
- absolute value *(valor absoluto)*
- inequality *(desigualdad)*
- integers *(enteros)*
- negative numbers *(números negativos)*
- opposites *(opuestos)*
- positive numbers *(números positivos)*

Understand Vocabulary

Complete the sentences using the preview words.

1. An _____ is a statement that two quantities are not equal.

2. The set of all whole numbers and their opposites are _____.

3. Numbers greater than 0 are _____. Numbers less than 0 are _____.

Active Reading

Key-Term Fold Before beginning the module, create a key-term fold to help you learn the vocabulary in this module. Write the highlighted vocabulary words on one side of the flap. Write the definition for each word on the other side of the flap. Use the key-term fold to quiz yourself on the definitions in this module.

Unpacking the Standards

Understanding the standards and the vocabulary terms in the standards will help you know exactly what you are expected to learn in this module.

 FL 6.NS.3.6a

Recognize opposite signs of numbers as indicating locations on opposite sides of 0 on the number line; recognize that the opposite of the opposite of a number is the number itself, e.g., $-(-3) = 3$, and that 0 is its own opposite.

Key Vocabulary

integers *(enteros)*
The set of all whole numbers and their opposites.

opposites *(opuestos)*
Two numbers that are equal distance from zero on a number line.

What It Means to You

You will learn that opposites are the same distance from 0 on a number line but in different directions.

UNPACKING EXAMPLE 6.NS.3.6A

Use the number line to determine the opposites.

$-(5) = -5$	The opposite of 5 is -5.
$-(-5) = 5$	The opposite of -5 is 5.
$-(0) = 0$	The opposite of 0 is 0.

 FL 6.NS.3.7

Understand ordering and absolute value of rational numbers.

Key Vocabulary

absolute value *(valor absoluto)*
A number's distance from 0 on the number line.

rational number
(número racional)
Any number that can be expressed as a ratio of two integers.

What It Means to You

You can use a number line to order rational numbers.

UNPACKING EXAMPLE 6.NS.3.7

At a golf tournament, David scored $+6$, Celia scored -16, and Xavier scored -4. One of these three players was the winner of the tournament. Who won the tournament?

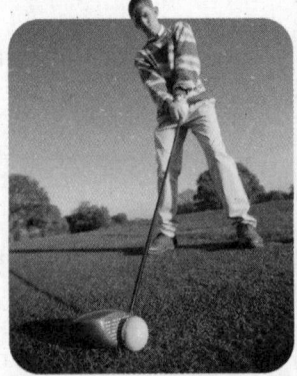

The winner will be the player with the lowest score. Draw a number line and graph each player's score.

Celia's score, -16, is the farthest to the left, so it is the lowest score. Celia won the tournament.

Visit **my.hrw.com** to see all **Florida Math Standards** unpacked.

my.hrw.com

LESSON 1.1 Identifying Integers and Their Opposites

FL 6.NS.3.5

Understand that positive and negative numbers are used together to describe quantities having opposite directions or values.... *Also 6.NS.3.6, 6.NS.3.6a, 6.NS.3.6c*

ESSENTIAL QUESTION

How do you identify an integer and its opposite?

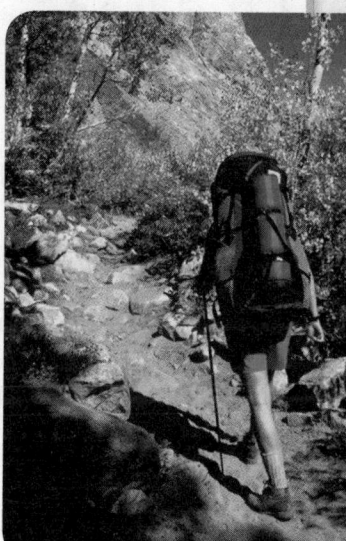

EXPLORE ACTIVITY 1 *Real World* **FL** 6.NS.3.5, 6.NS.3.6

Positive and Negative Numbers

Positive numbers are numbers greater than 0. Positive numbers can be written with or without a plus sign; for example, 3 is the same as +3. **Negative numbers** are numbers less than 0. Negative numbers must always be written with a negative sign.

> The number 0 is neither positive nor negative.

−5 −4 −3 −2 −1 0 1 2 3 4 5

Negative integers   **Positive integers**

The elevation of a location describes its height above or below sea level, which has elevation 0. Elevations below sea level are represented by negative numbers, and elevations above sea level are represented by positive numbers.

A The table shows the elevations of several locations in a state park. Graph the locations on the number line according to their elevations.

Location	Little Butte *A*	Cradle Creek *B*	Dinosaur Valley *C*	Mesa Ridge *D*	Juniper Trail *E*
Elevation (ft)	5	−5	−9	8	−3

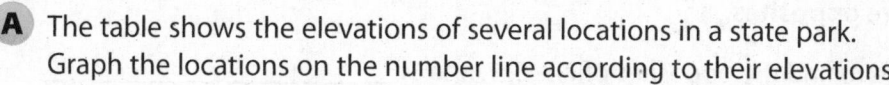

−10 −9 −8 −7 −6 −5 −4 −3 −2 −1 0 1 2 3 4 5 6 7 8 9 10

B What point on the number line represents sea level? _____

C Which location is closest to sea level? How do you know?

_____

D Which two locations are the same distance from sea level? Are these locations above or below sea level?

_____

E Which location has the least elevation? How do you know?

_____

© Houghton Mifflin Harcourt Publishing Company • Image Credits: © Corbis

Reflect

1. **Analyze Relationships** Morning Glory Stream is 7 feet below sea level. What number represents the elevation of Morning Glory Stream?

   _____

2. **Multiple Representations** Explain how to graph the elevation of Morning Glory Stream on a number line.

   _____

EXPLORE ACTIVITY 2 **FL** 6.NS.3.6a

Opposites

Two numbers are **opposites** if, on a number line, they are the same distance from 0 but on different sides of 0. For example, 5 and −5 are opposites. 0 is its own opposite.

Integers are the set of all whole numbers and their opposites.

> Remember, the set of whole numbers is 0, 1, 2, 3, 4, 5, 6, …

On graph paper, use a ruler or straightedge to draw a number line. Label the number line with each integer from −10 to 10. Fold your number line in half so that the crease goes through 0. Numbers that line up after folding the number line are opposites.

A Use your number line to find the opposites of 7, −6, 1, and 9. _____

B How does your number line show that 0 is its own opposite?

   _____

C What is the opposite of the opposite of 3? _____

Reflect

3. **Justify Reasoning** Explain how your number line shows that 8 and −8 are opposites.

   _____

4. **Multiple Representations** Explain how to use your number line to find the opposite of the opposite of −6.

   _____

   _____

Integers and Opposites on a Number Line

Positive and negative numbers can be used to represent real-world quantities. For example, 3 can represent a temperature that is 3 °F above 0. −3 can represent a temperature that is 3 °F below 0. Both 3 and −3 are 3 units from 0.

EXAMPLE 1 Real World   FL 6.NS.3.6a, 6.NS.3.6c

My Notes

Sandy kept track of the weekly low temperature in her town for several weeks. The table shows the low temperature in °F for each week.

Week	Week 1	Week 2	Week 3	Week 4
Temperature (°F)	−1	3	−4	2

A Graph the temperature from Week 3 and its opposite on a number line. What do the numbers represent?

STEP 1 Graph the value from Week 3 on the number line.
The value from Week 3 is −4.
Graph a point 4 units below 0.

STEP 2 Graph the opposite of −4.
Graph a point 4 units above 0.

The opposite of −4 is 4.

−4 represents a temperature that is 4 °F below 0 and 4 represents a temperature that is 4 °F above 0.

B The value for Week 5 is the opposite of the opposite of the value from Week 1. What was the low temperature in Week 5?

STEP 1 Graph the value from Week 1 on the number line.
The value from Week 1 is −1.

STEP 2 Graph the opposite of −1.
The opposite of −1 is 1.

STEP 3 Graph the opposite of 1.
The opposite of 1 is −1.

−6 −5 −4 −3 −2 −1 0 1 2 3 4 5 6

The opposite of the opposite of −1 is −1.
The low temperature in Week 5 was −1 °F.

Reflect

5. **Analyze Relationships** Explain how you can find the opposite of the opposite of any number without using a number line.

_____

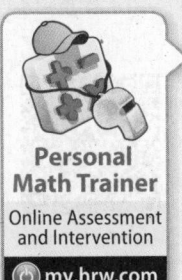
YOUR TURN

Graph the opposite of the number shown on each number line.

6.

7.

Write the opposite of each number.

8. 10 _____

9. −5 _____

10. 0 _____

11. What is the opposite of the opposite of 6? _____

Guided Practice

1. Graph and label the following points on the number line.
    (Explore Activity 1)

    a. −2   b. 9   c. −8   d. −9   e. 5   f. 8

Graph the opposite of the number shown on each number line.
(Explore Activity 2 and Example 1)

2.

3.

4.

Write the opposite of each number. (Explore Activity 2 and Example 1)

5. 4 _____

6. −11 _____

7. 3 _____

8. −3 _____

9. 0 _____

10. 22 _____

❓ ESSENTIAL QUESTION CHECK-IN

11. Given an integer, how do you find its opposite?

_____

_____

1.1 Independent Practice

 FL 6.NS.3.5, 6.NS.3.6, 6.NS.3.6a, 6.NS.3.6c

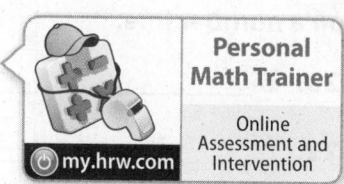
Personal
Math Trainer

Online
Assessment and
Intervention

my.hrw.com

12. Chemistry Atoms normally have an electric charge of 0. Certain conditions, such as static, can cause atoms to have a positive or a negative charge. Atoms with a positive or negative charge are called *ions*.

Ion	A	B	C	D	E
Charge	−3	+1	−2	+3	−1

a. Which ions have a negative charge?

_____

b. Which ions have charges that are opposites?

_____

c. Which ion's charge is not the opposite of another ion's charge?

_____

Name the integer that meets the given description.

13. the opposite of −17 _____

14. 4 units left of 0 _____

15. the opposite of the opposite of 2 _____

16. 15 units right of 0 _____

17. 12 units right of 0 _____

18. the opposite of −19 _____

19. Analyze Relationships Several wrestlers are trying to lose weight for a competition. Their change in weight since last week is shown in the chart.

Wrestler	Tino	Victor	Ramsey	Baxter	Luis
Weight Change (in pounds)	−2	6	2	5	−5

a. Did Victor lose or gain weight since last week? _____

b. Which wrestler's weight change is the opposite of Ramsey's? _____

c. Which wrestlers have lost weight since last week? _____

d. Frankie's weight change since last week was the opposite of Victor's.

What was Frankie's weight change? _____

e. Frankie's goal last week was to gain weight. Did he meet his goal? Explain.

_____

Find the distance between the given number and its opposite on a number line.

20. 6 _____

21. −2 _____

22. 0 _____

23. −7 _____

24. What If? Three contestants are competing on a trivia game show. The table shows their scores before the final question.

Contestant	Score Before Final Question
Timothy	−25
Shawna	18
Kaylynn	−14

    a. How many points must Shawna earn for her score to be the opposite of Timothy's score before the final question?_____

    b. Which person's score is closest to 0? _____

    c. Who do you think is winning the game before the final question? Explain.

    _____

H.O.T. FOCUS ON HIGHER ORDER THINKING

Work Area

25. Communicate Mathematical Ideas Which number is farther from 0 on a number line: −9 or 6? Explain your reasoning.

_____

_____

26. Analyze Relationships A number is k units to the left of 0 on the number line. Describe the location of its opposite.

_____

_____

27. Critique Reasoning Roberto says that the opposite of a certain integer is −5. Cindy concludes that the opposite of an integer is always negative. Explain Cindy's error.

_____

_____

28. Multiple Representations Explain how to use a number line to find the opposites of the integers 3 units away from −7.

_____

_____

_____

LESSON
1.2 Comparing and Ordering Integers

 FL 6.NS.3.7b
Write, interpret, and explain statements of order for rational numbers in real-world contexts. *Also 6.NS.3.7, 6.NS.3.7a*

? ESSENTIAL QUESTION

How do you compare and order integers?

EXPLORE ACTIVITY FL 6.NS.3.7, 6.NS.3.7a

Comparing Positive and Negative Integers

The Westfield soccer league ranks its teams using a number called the "win/loss combined record." A team with more wins than losses will have a positive combined record, and a team with fewer wins than losses will have a negative combined record. The table shows the total win/loss combined record for each team at the end of the season.

Team	Sharks A	Jaguars B	Badgers C	Tigers D	Cougars E	Hawks F	Wolves G
Win/Loss Combined Record	0	4	−4	−6	2	−2	6

A Graph the win/loss combined record for each team on the number line.

−10 −9 −8 −7 −6 −5 −4 −3 −2 −1 0 1 2 3 4 5 6 7 8 9 10

B Which team had the best record in the league? How do you know?

_____

C Which team had the worst record? How do you know?

_____

Reflect

1. Analyze Relationships. Explain what the data tell you about the win/ loss records of the teams in the league.

_____

_____

_____

_____

Ordering Positive and Negative Integers

When you read a number line from left to right, the numbers are in order from least to greatest.

EXAMPLE 1   **FL** 6.NS.3.7

Fred recorded the following golf scores during his first week at the golf academy. In golf, the player with the lowest score wins the game.

Day	Mon	Tues	Wed	Thurs	Fri	Sat	Sun
Score	4	–2	3	–5	–1	0	–3

Graph Fred's scores on the number line, and then list the numbers in order from least to greatest.

STEP 1   Graph the scores on the number line.

STEP 2   Read from left to right to list the scores in order from least to greatest.

The scores listed from least to greatest are –5, –3, –2, –1, 0, 3, 4.

YOUR TURN

Graph the values in each table on a number line. Then list the numbers in order from greatest to least.

2.

Change in Stock Price ($)					
–5	4	0	–3	–6	2

_____

3.

Elevation (meters)							
9	–1	–6	2	–10	0	5	8

_____

Writing Inequalities

An **inequality** is a statement that two quantities are not equal. The symbols $<$ and $>$ are used to write inequalities.

- The symbol $>$ means "is greater than."
- The symbol $<$ means "is less than."

You can use a number line to help write an inequality.

EXAMPLE 2   FL   6.NS.3.7a, 6.NS.3.7b

A In 2005, Austin, Texas, received 51 inches in annual precipitation. In 2009, the city received 36 inches in annual precipitation. In which year was there more precipitation?

Graph 51 and 36 on the number line.

```
 20  24  28  32  36  40  44  48  52  56  60
```

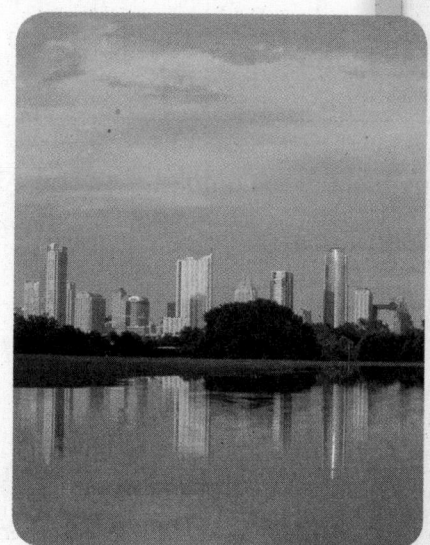

- 51 is to the *right* of 36 on the number line.

  This means that 51 is **greater than** 36.

  Write the inequality as $51 > 36$.

- 36 is to the *left* of 51 on the number line.

  This means that 36 is **less than** 51.

  Write the inequality as $36 < 51$.

  There was more precipitation in 2005.

B Write two inequalities to compare -6 and 7.
$-6 < 7; 7 > -6$

C Write two inequalities to compare -9 and -4.
$-4 > -9; -9 < -4$

> **Math Talk**
> Mathematical Practices
>
> Is there a greatest integer? Is there a greatest negative integer? Explain.

YOUR TURN

Compare. Write $>$ or $<$. Use the number line to help you.

4. $-10 \bigcirc -2$ **5.** $-6 \bigcirc 6$ **6.** $-7 \bigcirc -8$

```
 -10 -9 -8 -7 -6 -5 -4 -3 -2 -1  0  1  2  3  4  5  6  7  8  9  10
```

7. Write two inequalities to compare -2 and -18. _____

8. Write two inequalities to compare 39 and -39. _____

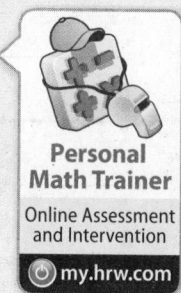

1a. Graph the temperature for each city on the number line. (Explore Activity)

City	A	B	C	D	E
Temperature (°F)	−9	10	−2	0	4

b. Which city was coldest? _____

c. Which city was warmest? _____

List the numbers in order from least to greatest. (Example 1)

2. 4, −6, 0, 8, −9, 1, −3

_____

3. −65, 34, 7, −13, 55, 62, −7

_____

4. Write two inequalities to compare −17 and −22. _____

Compare. Write < or >. (Example 2)

5. −9 ◯ 2   **6.** 0 ◯ 6   **7.** 3 ◯ −7   **8.** 5 ◯ −10

9. −1 ◯ −3   **10.** −8 ◯ −4   **11.** −4 ◯ 1   **12.** −2 ◯ −6

13. Compare the temperatures for the following cities. Write < or >. (Example 2)

City	Alexandria	Redwood Falls	Grand Marais	Winona	International Falls
Average Temperature in March (°C)	−3	0	−2	2	−4

a. Alexandria and Winona _____

b. Redwood Falls and International Falls _____

? ESSENTIAL QUESTION CHECK-IN

14. How can you use a number line to compare and order numbers?

_____

_____

_____

1.2 Independent Practice

FL 6.NS.3.7, 6.NS.3.7a, 6.NS.3.7b

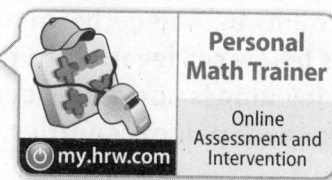

Personal Math Trainer

Online Assessment and Intervention

my.hrw.com

15. Multiple Representations A hockey league tracks the plus-minus records for each player. A plus-minus record is the difference in even strength goals for and against the team when a player is on the ice. The following table lists the plus-minus values for several hockey players.

Player	A. Jones	B. Sutter	E. Simpson	L. Mays	R. Tomas	S. Klatt
Plus-minus	−8	4	9	−3	−4	3

a. Graph the values on the number line.

b. Which player has the best plus-minus record? _____

Astronomy The table lists the average surface temperature of some planets. Write an inequality to compare the temperatures of each pair of planets.

Planet	Average Surface Temperature (°C)
Mercury	167.
Uranus	−197
Neptune	−200
Earth	15
Mars	−65
Jupiter	−110

16. Uranus and Jupiter _____

17. Mercury and Mars _____

18. Arrange the planets in order of average surface temperature

from greatest to least. _____

_____

19. Represent Real-World Problems For a stock market project, five students each invested pretend money in one stock. They tracked gains and losses in the value of that stock for one week. In the following table, a gain is represented by a positive number and a loss is represented by a negative number.

Students	Andre	Bria	Carla	Daniel	Ethan
Gains and Losses ($)	7	−2	−5	2	4

Graph the students' results on the number line. Then list them in order from least to greatest.

a. Graph the values on the number line.

b. The results listed from least to greatest are _____

Geography The table lists the lowest elevation for several countries. A negative number means the elevation is below sea level, and a positive number means the elevation is above sea level. Compare the lowest elevation for each pair of countries. Write < or >.

Country	Lowest Elevation (feet)
Argentina	−344
Australia	−49
Czech Republic	377
Hungary	249
United States	−281

20. Argentina and the United States _____

21. Czech Republic and Hungary _____

22. Hungary and Argentina _____

23. Which country in the table has the lowest elevation? _____

24. Analyze Relationships There are three numbers a, b, and c, where a > b and b > c. Describe the positions of the numbers on a number line.

_____

_____

_____

_____

 FOCUS ON HIGHER ORDER THINKING

25. Critique Reasoning At 9 A.M. the outside temperature was −3°F. By noon, the temperature was −12°F. Jorge said that it was getting warmer outside. Is he correct? Explain.

_____

26. Problem Solving Golf scores represent the number of strokes above or below par. A negative score means that you hit a number below par while a positive score means that you hit a number above par. The winner in golf has the lowest score. During a round of golf, Angela's score was −5 and Lisa's score was −8. Who won the game? Explain.

_____

27. Look for a Pattern Order −3, 5, 16, and −10 from least to greatest. Then order the same numbers from closest to zero to farthest from zero. Describe how your lists are similar. Would this be true if the numbers were −3, 5, −16 and −10?

_____

_____

_____

_____

Work Area

1.3 Absolute Value

FL 6.NS.3.7c
Understand the absolute value of a rational number... interpret absolute value as magnitude... in a real-world situation. *Also 6.NS.3.7, 6.NS.3.7d*

? ESSENTIAL QUESTION

How do you find and use absolute value?

EXPLORE ACTIVITY 1 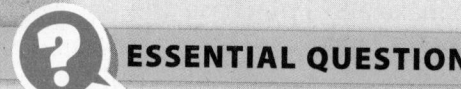 FL 6.NS.3.7, 6.NS.3.7c

Finding Absolute Value

The **absolute value** of a number is the number's distance from 0 on a number line. For example, the absolute value of −3 is 3 because −3 is 3 units from 0. The absolute value of −3 is written |−3|.

$|-3| = 3$

Because absolute value represents a distance, it is always nonnegative.

Graph the following numbers on the number line. Then use your number line to find each absolute value.

−7   5   7   −2   4   −4

−10 −9 −8 −7 −6 −5 −4 −3 −2 −1 0 1 2 3 4 5 6 7 8 9 10

A $|-7| =$ _____   **B** $|5| =$ _____   **C** $|7| =$ _____

D $|-2| =$ _____   **E** $|4| =$ _____   **F** $|-4| =$ _____

Reflect

1. Analyze Relationships Which pairs of numbers have the same absolute value? How are these numbers related?

_____

_____

2. Justify Reasoning Negative numbers are less than positive numbers. Does this mean that the absolute value of a negative number must be less than the absolute value of a positive number? Explain.

_____

_____

_____

_____

Absolute Value In A Real-World Situation

In real-world situations, absolute values are often used instead of negative numbers. For example, if you use a $50 gift card to make a $25 purchase, the change in your gift card balance can be represented by −$25.

EXAMPLE 1 Real World   FL 6.NS.3.7c

Jake uses his online music store gift card to buy an album of songs by his favorite band.

Find the negative number that represents the change in the balance on Jake's card after his purchase. Explain how absolute value would be used to express that number in this situation.

Music Online

Account Balance		$25.00
Cart	1 album	$10.00

STEP 1 Find the negative integer that represents the change in the balance.

−$10   *The balance decreased by $10, so use a negative number.*

_____

_____

Math Talk

Mathematical Practices

Explain why the price Jake paid for the album is represented by a negative number.

STEP 2 Use the number line to find the absolute value of −$10.

−10 is 10 units from 0 on the number line.

10 units

−10 −9 −8 −7 −6 −5 −4 −3 −2 −1 0 1 2 3 4 5 6 7 8 9 10

The absolute value of −$10 is $10, or |−10| = 10.

The balance on Jake's card decreased by $10.

Reflect

3. **Communicate Mathematical Ideas** Explain why the absolute value of a number will never be negative.

_____

_____

_____

YOUR TURN

4. The temperature at night reached −13 °F. Write an equivalent statement about the temperature using the absolute value of the number.

_____

Find each absolute value.

5. |−12| _____ **6.** |91| _____ **7.** |−55| _____

8. |0| _____ **9.** |88| _____ **10.** |1| _____

EXPLORE ACTIVITY 2 Real World FL 6.NS.3.7c, 6.NS.3.7d

Comparing Absolute Values

You can use absolute values to compare negative numbers in real-world situations.

Maria, Susan, George, and Antonio checked their credit card balances on their smartphones. The amounts owed are shown.

You owe: $20   You owe: $25   You owe: $30   You owe: $45

_____ _____ _____ _____

Answer the following questions. When you have finished, you will have enough clues to match each smartphone with the correct person.

Remember: When someone owes a positive amount of money, this means that he or she has a *negative* balance.

A Maria's credit card balance is less than −$30. Does Maria owe more than $30 or less than $30? _____

B Susan's credit card balance is greater than −$25. Does Susan owe more than $25 or less than $25? _____

C George's credit card balance is $5 less than Susan's balance. Does George owe more than Susan or less than Susan? _____

D Antonio owes $15 less than Maria owes. This means that Antonio's balance is _____ than Maria's balance.

E Write each person's name underneath his or her smartphone.

Reflect

11. **Analyze Relationships** Use absolute value to describe the relationship between a negative credit card balance and the amount owed.

_____

Guided Practice

1. **Vocabulary** If a number is _____, then the number is less than its absolute value. (Explore Activity 1)

2. If Ryan pays his car insurance for the year in full, he will get a credit of $28. If he chooses to pay a monthly premium, he will pay a $10 late fee for any month that the payment is late. (Explore Activity 1, Example 1)

   a. Which of these values could be represented with a negative number? Explain.

   _____

   _____

   b. Use the number line to find the absolute value of your answer from

   part a. _____

    −10 −9 −8 −7 −6 −5 −4 −3 −2 −1 0 1 2 3 4 5 6 7 8 9 10

3. Leo, Gabrielle, Sinea, and Tomas are playing a video game. Their scores are described in the table below. (Explore Activity 2)

Name	Leo	Gabrielle	Sinea
Score	less than −100 points	20 more points than Leo	50 points less than Leo

   a. Leo wants to earn enough points to have a positive score. Does he need to earn more than 100 points or less than 100 points? _____

   b. Gabrielle wants to earn enough points to not have a negative score. Does she need to earn more points than Leo or less points than Leo? _____

   c. Sinea wants to earn enough points to have a higher score than Leo. Does she need to earn more than 50 points or less than 50 points? _____

? ESSENTIAL QUESTION CHECK-IN

4. When is the absolute value of a number equal to the number?

_____

Name_____ Class_____ Date_____

1.3 Independent Practice

FL 6.NS.3.7, 6.NS.3.7c, 6.NS.3.7d

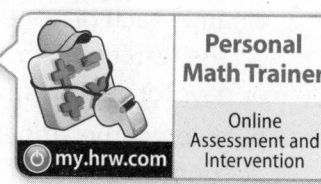

Personal
Math Trainer

Online
Assessment and
Intervention

my.hrw.com

5. Financial Literacy Jacob earned $80 babysitting and deposited the money into his savings account. The next week he spent $85 on video games. Use integers to describe the weekly changes in Jacob's savings account balance.

_____

_____

6. Financial Literacy Sara's savings account balance changed by $34 one week and by −$67 the next week. Which amount represents the greatest

change? _____

7. Analyze Relationships Bertrand collects movie posters. The number of movie posters in his collection changes each month as he buys and sells posters. The table shows how many posters he bought or sold in the given months.

Month	January	February	March	April
Posters	Sold 20	Bought 12	Bought 22	Sold 28

a. Which months have changes that can be represented by positive numbers? Which months have changes that can be represented by negative numbers? Explain.

_____

_____

_____

_____

b. According to the table, in which month did the size of Bertrand's poster collection change the most? Use absolute value to explain your answer.

_____

_____

_____

8. Earth Science Death Valley has an elevation of −282 feet relative to sea level. Explain how to use absolute value to describe the elevation of Death Valley as a positive integer.

_____

_____

9. **Communicate Mathematical Ideas** Lisa and Alice are playing a game. Each player either receives or has to pay play money based on the result of their spin. The table lists how much a player receives or pays for various spins.

Red	Pay $5
Blue	Receive $4
Yellow	Pay $1
Green	Receive $3
Orange	Pay $2

   a. Express the amounts in the table as positive and negative numbers.

   _____

   b. Describe the change to Lisa's amount of money when the spinner lands on red.

   _____

   _____

10. **Financial Literacy** Sam's credit card balance is less than −$36. Does Sam owe more or less than $36? _____

11. **Financial Literacy** Emily spent $55 from her savings on a new dress. Explain how to describe the change in Emily's savings balance in two different ways.

   _____

   _____

   _____

 FOCUS ON HIGHER ORDER THINKING

12. **Make a Conjecture** Can two different numbers have the same absolute value? If yes, give an example. If no, explain why not.

   _____

13. **Communicate Mathematical Ideas** Does $-|-4| = |-(-4)|$? Justify your answer.

   _____

14. **Critique Reasoning** Angelique says that finding the absolute value of a number is the same as finding the opposite of the number. For example, $|-5| = 5$. Explain her error.

   _____

   _____

   _____

Work Area

Ready to Go On?

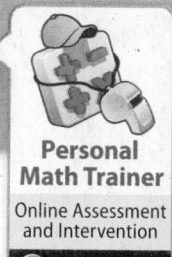

Personal Math Trainer

Online Assessment and Intervention

my.hrw.com

1.1 Identifying Integers and Their Opposites

1. The table shows the elevations in feet of several locations around a coastal town. Graph and label the locations on the number line according to their elevations.

Location	Post Office A	Library B	Town Hall C	Laundromat D	Pet Store E
Elevation (feet)	8	−3	−9	3	1

Write the opposite of each number.

2. −22 _____

3. 0 _____

1.2 Comparing and Ordering Integers

List the numbers in order from least to greatest.

4. −2, 8, −15, −5, 3, 1 _____

Compare. Write < or >.

5. −3 ◯ −15

6. 9 ◯ −10

1.3 Absolute Value

Graph each number on the number line. Then use your number line to find the absolute value of each number.

7. 2 _____

8. −8 _____

9. −5 _____

? ESSENTIAL QUESTION

10. How can you use absolute value to represent a negative number in a real-world situation?

_____

_____

MODULE 1 MIXED REVIEW

Assessment Readiness

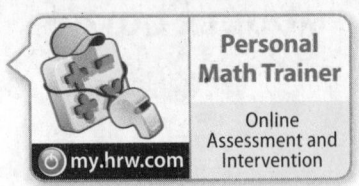

Personal Math Trainer

Online Assessment and Intervention

my.hrw.com

Selected Response

1. Which number line shows 2, 3, and −3?

Ⓐ

Ⓑ

Ⓒ

Ⓓ

2. What is the opposite of −3?

Ⓐ 3   Ⓒ $-\frac{1}{3}$

Ⓑ 0   Ⓓ $\frac{1}{3}$

3. Darrel is currently 20 feet below sea level. Which correctly describes the opposite of Darrel's elevation?

Ⓐ 20 feet below sea level

Ⓑ 20 feet above sea level

Ⓒ 2 feet below sea level

Ⓓ At sea level

4. Which has the same absolute value as −55?

Ⓐ 0   Ⓒ 1

Ⓑ −1   Ⓓ 55

5. In Bangor it is −3°F, in Fairbanks it is −12°F, in Fargo it is −8°F, and in Calgary it is −15°F. In which city is it the coldest?

Ⓐ Bangor   Ⓒ Fargo

Ⓑ Fairbanks   Ⓓ Calgary

6. Which shows the integers in order from least to greatest?

Ⓐ 20, 6, −2, −13   Ⓒ −13, −2, 6, 20

Ⓑ −2, 6, −13, 20   Ⓓ 20, −13, 6, −2

7. How would you use a number line to put integers in order from greatest to least?

Ⓐ Graph the integers, then read them from left to right.

Ⓑ Graph the integers, then read them from right to left.

Ⓒ Graph the absolute values of the integers, then read them from left to right.

Ⓓ Graph the absolute values of the integers, then read them from right to left.

Mini-Task

8. The table shows the change in the amounts of money in several savings accounts over the past month.

Account	Change
A	$125
B	−$45
C	−$302
D	$108

a. List the dollar amounts in the order in which they would appear on a number line from left to right.

_____

b. In which savings account was the absolute value of the change the greatest? Describe the change in that account.

_____

c. In which account was the absolute value of the change the least?

_____

Factors and Multiples

MODULE **2**

ESSENTIAL QUESTION

How can you use greatest common factors and least common multiples to solve real-world problems?

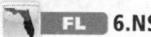

LESSON 2.1
Greatest Common Factor

FL 6.NS.2.4

LESSON 2.2
Least Common Multiple

FL 6.NS.2.4

Real-World Video

Organizers of banquets and other special events plan many things, including menus, seating arrangements, table decorations, and party favors. Factors and multiples can be helpful in this work.

my.hrw.com

© Houghton Mifflin Harcourt Publishing Company • Image Credits: STOCK4B-RF/ Getty Images

GO DIGITAL
my.hrw.com

my.hrw.com

Go digital with your write-in student edition, accessible on any device.

Math On the Spot

Scan with your smart phone to jump directly to the online edition, video tutor, and more.

Animated Math

Interactively explore key concepts to see how math works.

Personal Math Trainer

Get immediate feedback and help as you work through practice sets.

27

Are YOU Ready?

Complete these exercises to review skills you will need for this module.

Personal Math Trainer

Online Assessment and Intervention

⊙ my.hrw.com

Multiples

EXAMPLE	5×1 $= 5$	5×2 $= 10$	5×3 $= 15$	5×4 $= 20$	5×5 $= 25$	To find the first five multiples of 5, multiply 5 by 1, 2, 3, 4, and 5.

List the first five multiples of the number.

1. 7 _____

2. 11 _____

3. 15 _____

Factors

EXAMPLE	$1 \times 12 = 12$ $2 \times 6 = 12$ $3 \times 4 = 12$ The factors of 12 are 1, 2, 3, 4, 6, 12.	To find the factors of 12, use multiplication facts of 12. Continue until pairs of factors repeat.

Write all the factors of the number.

4. 24 _____

5. 36 _____

6. 45 _____

7. 32 _____

Multiplication Properties (Distributive)

EXAMPLE	$7 \times 14 = 7 \times (10 + 4)$ $= (7 \times 10) + (7 \times 4)$ $= 70 + 28$ $= 98$	To multiply a number by a sum, multiply the number by each addend and add the products.

Use the Distributive Property to find the product.

8. $8 \times 15 = 8 \times \left(\boxed{} + \boxed{} \right)$

$= \left(\boxed{} \times \boxed{} \right) + \left(\boxed{} \times \boxed{} \right)$

$= \boxed{} + \boxed{}$

$= \boxed{}$

9. $6 \times 17 = 6 \times \left(\boxed{} + \boxed{} \right)$

$= \left(\boxed{} \times \boxed{} \right) + \left(\boxed{} \times \boxed{} \right)$

$= \boxed{} + \boxed{}$

$= \boxed{}$

Reading Start-Up

Visualize Vocabulary

Use the ✔ words to complete the graphic.

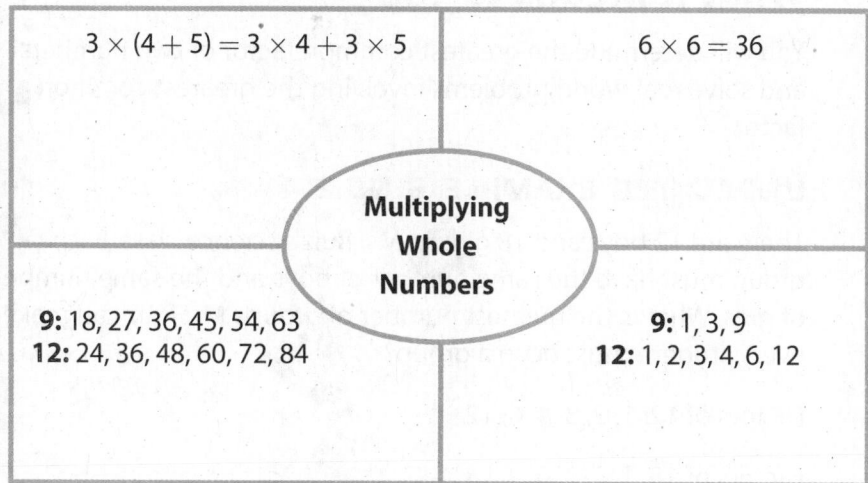

$3 \times (4 + 5) = 3 \times 4 + 3 \times 5$	$6 \times 6 = 36$
Multiplying Whole Numbers	
9: 18, 27, 36, 45, 54, 63 **12:** 24, 36, 48, 60, 72, 84	**9:** 1, 3, 9 **12:** 1, 2, 3, 4, 6, 12

Vocabulary

Review Words
- ✔ area *(área)*
- ✔ Distributive Property *(Propiedad distributiva)*
- ✔ factor *(factor)*
- ✔ multiple *(múltiplo)*
- ✔ product *(producto)*

Preview Words
- greatest common factor (GCF) *(máximo común divisor (MCD))*
- least common multiple (LCM) *(mínimo común múltiplo (m.c.m.))*

Understand Vocabulary

Complete the sentences below using the preview words.

1. Of all the whole numbers that divide evenly into two or more numbers, the one with the highest value is called the _____.

2. Of all the common products of two numbers, the one with the lowest value is called the _____.

Active Reading

Two-Panel Flip Chart Create a two-panel flip chart to help you understand the concepts in this module. Label one flap "Greatest Common Factor." Label the other flap "Least Common Multiple." As you study each lesson, write important ideas under the appropriate flap.

Unpacking the Standards

Understanding the standards and the vocabulary terms in the standards will help you know exactly what you are expected to learn in this module.

 FL 6.NS.2.4

Find the **greatest common factor** of two whole numbers less than or equal to 100 and the least common multiple of two whole numbers less than or equal to 12. Use the Distributive Property to express a sum of two whole numbers 1–100 with a common factor as a multiple of a sum of two whole numbers with no common factor.

Key Vocabulary

greatest common factor (GCF)
(máximo común divisor (MCD))
The largest common factor of two or more given numbers.

What It Means to You

You will determine the greatest common factor of two numbers and solve real-world problems involving the greatest common factor.

UNPACKING EXAMPLE 6.NS.2.4

There are 12 boys and 18 girls in Ms. Ruiz's science class. Each lab group must have the same number of boys and the same number of girls. What is the greatest number of groups Ms. Ruiz can make if every student must be in a group?

Factors of 12: 1, 2, 3, 4, 6, 12

Factors of 18: 1, 2, 3, 6, 9, 18

The GCF of 12 and 18 is 6. The greatest number of groups Ms. Ruiz can make is 6.

 FL 6.NS.2.4

Find the greatest common factor of two whole numbers less than or equal to 100 and the **least common multiple** of two whole numbers less than or equal to 12. …

Key Vocabulary

least common multiple (LCM)
(mínimo común múltiplo (m.c.m.))
The smallest number, other than zero, that is a multiple of two or more given numbers.

What It Means to You

You will determine the least common multiple of two numbers and solve real-world problems involving the least common multiple.

UNPACKING EXAMPLE 6.NS.2.4

Lydia's family will provide juice boxes and granola bars for 24 players. Juice comes in packs of 6, and granola bars in packs of 8. What is the least number of packs of each needed so that every player has a drink and a granola bar and there are none left over?

Multiples of 6: 6, 12, 18, 24, 30, …

Multiples of 8: 8, 16, 24, 32, …

The LCM of 6 and 8 is 24. Lydia's family should buy $24 \div 6 = 4$ packs of juice and $24 \div 8 = 3$ packs of granola bars.

Visit **my.hrw.com** to see all **Florida Math Standards** unpacked.

my.hrw.com

LESSON 2.1 Greatest Common Factor

FL 6.NS.2.4

Find the greatest common factor of two whole numbers....

ESSENTIAL QUESTION

How can you find and use the greatest common factor of two whole numbers?

EXPLORE ACTIVITY 1   **FL** 6.NS.2.4

Understanding Common Factors

The **greatest common factor (GCF)** of two numbers is the greatest factor shared by those numbers.

A florist makes bouquets from 18 roses and 30 tulips. All the bouquets will include both roses and tulips. If all the bouquets are identical, what are the possible bouquets that can be made?

A Complete the tables to show the possible ways to divide each type of flower among the bouquets.

Roses

Number of Bouquets	1	2	3	6	9	18
Number of Roses in Each Bouquet	18	9				

Tulips

Number of Bouquets	1	2	3	5	6	10	15	30
Number of Tulips in Each Bouquet	30							

B Can the florist make five bouquets using all the flowers? Explain.

_____

C What are the common factors of 18 and 30? What do they represent?

_____

D What is the GCF of 18 and 30? _____

Reflect

1. **What If?** Suppose the florist has 18 roses and 36 tulips. What is the GCF of the numbers of roses and tulips? Explain.

_____

© Houghton Mifflin Harcourt Publishing Company

Finding the Greatest Common Factor

One way to find the GCF of two numbers is to list all of their factors. Then you can identify common factors and the GCF.

EXAMPLE 1   **FL 6.NS.2.4**

My Notes

A baker has 24 sesame bagels and 36 plain bagels to put into boxes. Each box must have the same number of each type of bagel. What is the greatest number of boxes that the baker can make using all of the bagels? How many sesame bagels and how many plain bagels will be in each box?

STEP 1 List the factors of 24 and 36. Then circle the common factors.

> The baker can divide 24 sesame bagels into groups of 1, 2, 3, 4, 6, 8, 12, or 24.

Factors of 24: ① ② ③ ④ ⑥ 8 ⑫ 24

Factors of 36: ① ② ③ ④ ⑥ 9 ⑫ 18 36

STEP 2 Find the GCF of 24 and 36.

The GCF is 12. So, the greatest number of boxes that the baker can make is 12. There will be 2 sesame bagels in each box, because $24 \div 12 = 2$. There will be 3 plain bagels, because $36 \div 12 = 3$.

Reflect

2. **Critical Thinking** What is the GCF of two prime numbers? Give an example.

_____

YOUR TURN

Find the GCF of each pair of numbers.

3. 14 and 35 _____   4. 20 and 28 _____

5. The sixth-grade class is competing in the school field day. There are 32 girls and 40 boys who want to participate. Each team must have the same number of girls and the same number of boys. What is the greatest number of teams that can be formed? How many boys and how many girls will be on each team?

_____

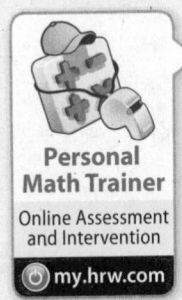

Using the Distributive Property

Animated Math

my.hrw.com

You can use the Distributive Property to rewrite a sum of two or more numbers as a product of their GCF and a sum of numbers with no common factor. To understand how, you can use grid paper to draw area models of 45 and 60. Here are all the possible area models of 45.

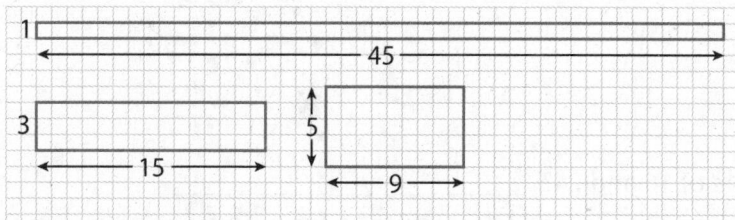

A What do the side lengths of the area models (1, 3, 5, 9, 15, and 45)

represent? _____

B On your own grid paper, show all of the possible area models of 60.

_____

C What side lengths do the area models of 45 and 60 have in common? What do the side lengths represent?

_____

D What is the greatest common side length? What does it represent?

_____

E Write 45 as a product of the GCF and another number. _____

Write 60 as a product of the GCF and another number. _____

F Use your answers above to rewrite 45 + 60.

$45 + 60 = 15 \times$ ____ $+ 15 \times$ ____

Math Talk
Mathematical Practices
How can you check to see if your product is correct?

Use the Distributive Property and your answer above to write 45 + 60 as a product of the GCF and a sum of two numbers.

$15 \times$ ____ $+ 15 \times$ ____ $= 15 \times ($ ____ $+$ ____ $) = 15 \times 7$

Reflect

Write the sum of the numbers as the product of their GCF and another sum.

6. 27 + 18 _____   **7.** 120 + 36 _____

8. 9 + 35 _____

1. Lee is sewing vests using 16 green buttons and 24 blue buttons. All the vests are identical, and all have both green and blue buttons. What are the possible numbers of vests Lee can make? What is the greatest number of vests Lee can make? (Explore Activity 1, Example 1)

   List the factors of 16 and 24. Then circle the common factors.

Factors of 16:						
Factors of 24:						

   What are the common factors of 16 and 24? _____

   What are the possible numbers of vests Lee can make? _____

   What is the GCF of 16 and 24? _____

   What is the greatest number of vests Lee can make? _____

Write the sum of numbers as a product of their GCF and another sum.
(Explore Activity 2)

2. $36 + 45$

   What is the GCF of 36 and 45? _____

   Write each number as a product of the GCF and another number.
   Then use the Distributive Property to rewrite the sum.

$$\left(\boxed{} \times \boxed{}\right) + \left(\boxed{} \times \boxed{}\right) = \left(\boxed{}\right) \times \left(\boxed{} + \boxed{}\right)$$

3. $75 + 90$

   What is the GCF of 75 and 90? _____

   Write each number as a product of the GCF and another number.
   Then use the Distributive Property to rewrite the sum.

$$\left(\boxed{} \times \boxed{}\right) + \left(\boxed{} \times \boxed{}\right) = \left(\boxed{}\right) \times \left(\boxed{} + \boxed{}\right)$$

? ESSENTIAL QUESTION CHECK-IN

4. Describe how to find the GCF of two numbers.

   _____

   _____

2.1 Independent Practice

 FL 6.NS.2.4

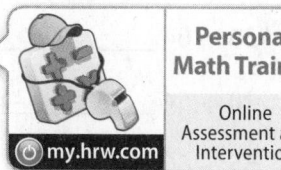

Personal Math Trainer

my.hrw.com

Online Assessment and Intervention

List the factors of each number.

5. 12 _____

6. 50 _____

7. 39 _____

8. 64 _____

Find the GCF of each pair of numbers.

9. 40 and 48 _____

10. 30 and 45 _____

11. 10 and 45 _____

12. 25 and 90 _____

13. 21 and 40 _____

14. 28 and 70 _____

15. 60 and 72 _____

16. 45 and 81 _____

17. 28 and 32 _____

18. 55 and 77 _____

19. Carlos is arranging books on shelves. He has 24 novels and 16 autobiographies. Each shelf will have the same numbers of novels and autobiographies. If Carlos must place all of the books on shelves, what are the possible numbers of shelves Carlos will use?

_____

20. The middle school band has 56 members. The high school band has 96 members. The bands are going to march one after the other in a parade. The director wants to arrange the bands into the same number of columns. What is the greatest number of columns in which the two bands can be arranged if each column has the same number of marchers? How many band members will be in each column?

_____

21. For football tryouts at a local school, 12 coaches and 42 players will split into groups. Each group will have the same numbers of coaches and players. What is the greatest number of groups that can be formed? How many coaches and players will be in each of these groups?

_____

22. Lola is placing appetizers on plates. She has 63 spring rolls and 84 cheese cubes. She wants to include both appetizers on each plate. Each plate must have the same numbers of spring rolls and cheese cubes. What is the greatest number of plates she can make using all of the appetizers? How many of each type of appetizer will be on each of these plates?

_____

Write the sum of the numbers as the product of their GCF and another sum.

23. $56 + 64$ _____

24. $48 + 14$ _____

25. $30 + 54$ _____

26. $24 + 40$ _____

27. $55 + 66$ _____

28. $49 + 63$ _____

29. $40 + 25$ _____

30. $63 + 15$ _____

31. Vocabulary Explain why the greatest common factor of two numbers is sometimes 1.

_____

_____

_____

 FOCUS ON HIGHER ORDER THINKING

32. Communicate Mathematical Ideas Tasha believes that she can rewrite the difference $120 - 36$ as a product of the GCF of the two numbers and another difference. Is she correct? Explain your answer.

_____

_____

_____

33. Persevere in Problem Solving Explain how to find the greatest common factor of three numbers.

_____

_____

_____

_____

34. Critique Reasoning Xiao's teacher asked him to rewrite the sum $60 + 90$ as the product of the GCF of the two numbers and a sum. Xiao wrote $3(20 + 30)$. What mistake did Xiao make? How should he have written the sum?

_____

_____

_____

Work Area

Least Common Multiple

FL 6.NS.2.4
Find . . . the least common multiple of two whole numbers. . . .

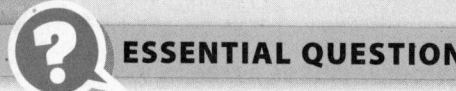 **ESSENTIAL QUESTION**

How do you find and use the least common multiple of two numbers?

EXPLORE ACTIVITY   FL 6.NS.2.4

Finding the Least Common Multiple

A multiple of a number is the product of the number and another number. For example, 9 is a multiple of the number 3. The **least common multiple (LCM)** of two or more numbers is the least number, other than zero, that is a multiple of all the numbers.

Ned is training for a biathlon. He will swim every sixth day and bicycle every eighth day. On what days will he both swim and bicycle?

A In the chart below, shade each day that Ned will swim. Circle each day Ned will bicycle.

1	2	3	4	5	6	7	8	9	10
11	12	13	14	15	16	17	18	19	20
21	22	23	24	25	26	27	28	29	30
31	32	33	34	35	36	37	38	39	40
41	42	43	44	45	46	47	48	49	50
51	52	53	54	55	56	57	58	59	60
61	62	63	64	65	66	67	68	69	70
71	72	73	74	75	76	77	78	79	80
81	82	83	84	85	86	87	88	89	90
91	92	93	94	95	96	97	98	99	100

B On what days will Ned both swim and bicycle? _____

The numbers of the days that Ned will swim and bicycle are common multiples of 6 and 8.

Reflect

1. Interpret the Answer What does the LCM represent in this situation?

_____

Math On the Spot
⊙ my.hrw.com

Applying the LCM

You can use the LCM of two whole numbers to solve problems.

EXAMPLE 1   **FL** 6.NS.2.4

A store is holding a promotion. Every third customer receives a free key chain, and every fourth customer receives a free magnet. Which customer will be the first to receive both a key chain and a magnet?

STEP 1 List the multiples of 3 and 4. Then circle the common multiples.

Multiples of 3: 3   6   9   (12)   15   18   21   (24)   27

Multiples of 4: 4   8   (12)   16   20   (24)   28   32   36

STEP 2 Find the LCM of 3 and 4.

The LCM is 12.

The first customer to get both a key chain and a magnet is the 12th customer.

Math Talk
Mathematical Practices

What steps do you take to list the multiples of a number?

Personal Math Trainer

Online Assessment and Intervention

⊙ my.hrw.com

YOUR TURN

2. Find the LCM of 4 and 9 by listing the multiples. _____

   Multiples of 4: _____

   Multiples of 9: _____

Guided Practice

1. After every ninth visit to a restaurant you receive a free beverage. After every twelfth visit you receive a free appetizer. If you visit the restaurant 100 times, on which visits will you receive a free beverage and a free appetizer? At which visit will you first receive a free beverage and a free appetizer? (Explore Activity 1, Example 1)

   _____

? **ESSENTIAL QUESTION CHECK-IN**

2. What steps can you take to find the LCM of two numbers?

   _____

   _____

© Houghton Mifflin Harcourt Publishing Company

2.2 Independent Practice

FL 6.NS.2.4

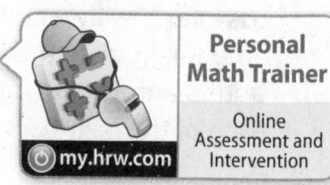

Personal Math Trainer

Online Assessment and Intervention

my.hrw.com

Find the LCM of each pair of numbers.

3. 8 and 56 _____

4. 25 and 50 _____

5. 12 and 30 _____

6. 6 and 10 _____

7. 16 and 24 _____

8. 14 and 21 _____

9. 9 and 15 _____

10. 5 and 11 _____

11. During February, Kevin will water his ivy every third day, and water his cactus every fifth day.

a. On which date will Kevin first water both plants together?

_____

_____

b. Will Kevin water both plants together again in February? Explain.

_____

_____

12. Vocabulary Given any two numbers, which is greater, the LCM of the numbers or the GCF of the numbers? Why?

_____

_____

_____

Use the subway train schedule.

13. The red line and the blue line trains just arrived at the station. When will they next arrive at the station at the same time?

In _____ minutes

14. The blue line and the yellow line trains just arrived at the station. When will they next arrive at the station at the same time?

In _____ minutes

15. All three trains just arrived at the station. When will they next all arrive at the station at the same time?

In _____ minutes

Train Schedule	
Train	**Arrives Every...**
Red line	8 minutes
Blue line	10 minutes
Yellow line	12 minutes

16. You buy a lily and an African violet on the same day. You are instructed to water the lily every fourth day and water the violet every seventh day after taking them home. What is the first day on which you will water both plants on the same day? How can you use this answer to determine each of the next days you will water both plants on the same day?

_____

_____

_____

H.O.T. FOCUS ON HIGHER ORDER THINKING

17. What is the LCM of two numbers if one number is a multiple of the other? Give an example.

_____

_____

18. What is the LCM of two numbers that have no common factors greater than 1? Give an example.

_____

_____

19. **Draw Conclusions** The least common multiple of two numbers is 60, and one of the numbers is 7 less than the other number. What are the numbers? Justify your answer.

_____

_____

_____

20. **Communicate Mathematical Ideas** Describe how to find the least common multiple of three numbers. Give an example.

_____

_____

_____

_____

Ready to Go On?

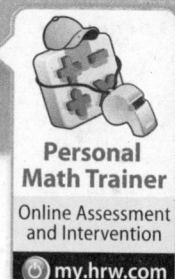

Personal Math Trainer

Online Assessment and Intervention

⏻ my.hrw.com

2.1 Greatest Common Factor

Find the GCF of each pair of numbers.

1. 20 and 32 _____

2. 24 and 56 _____

3. 36 and 90 _____

4. 45 and 75 _____

5. 28 girls and 32 boys volunteer to plant trees at a school. The principal divides the girls and boys into identical groups that have girls and boys in each group. What is the greatest number of groups the principal can make? _____

Write the sum of the numbers as the product of their GCF and another sum.

6. 32 + 20 _____

7. 18 + 27 _____

2.2 Least Common Multiple

Find the LCM of each pair of numbers.

8. 6 and 12 _____

9. 6 and 10 _____

10. 8 and 9 _____

11. 9 and 12 _____

12. Juanita runs every third day and swims every fifth day. If Juanita runs and swims today, in how many days will she run and swim again on the same day? _____

? ESSENTIAL QUESTION

13. What types of problems can be solved using the greatest common factor? What types of problems can be solved using the least common multiple?

_____

_____

_____

_____

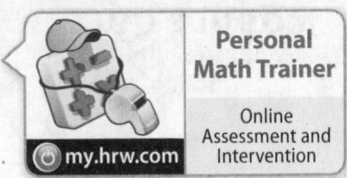

Selected Response

1. What is the least common multiple of 5 and 150?

Ⓐ 5 Ⓒ 15

Ⓑ 50 Ⓓ 150

2. Cy has 42 baseball cards and 70 football cards that he wants to group into packages. Each package will have the same number of cards, and each package will have the same numbers of baseball cards and football cards. How many packages will Cy make if he uses all of the cards?

Ⓐ 7 Ⓒ 14

Ⓑ 10 Ⓓ 21

3. During a promotional event, a sporting goods store gave a free T-shirt to every 8th customer and a free water bottle to every 10th customer. Which customer was the first to get a free T-shirt and a free water bottle?

Ⓐ the 10th customer

Ⓑ the 20th customer

Ⓒ the 40th customer

Ⓓ the 80th customer

4. The table below shows the positions relative to sea level of four divers.

Kareem	Li	Maria	Tara
−8 ft	−10 ft	−9 ft	−7 ft

Which diver is farthest from the surface?

Ⓐ Kareem Ⓒ Maria

Ⓑ Li Ⓓ Tara

5. What is the greatest common factor of 12 and 16?

Ⓐ 2 Ⓒ 12

Ⓑ 4 Ⓓ 48

6. Which expression is equivalent to $27 + 15$?

Ⓐ $9 \times (3 + 5)$

Ⓑ $3 \times (9 + 15)$

Ⓒ $9 \times (3 + 15)$

Ⓓ $3 \times (9 + 5)$

7. During a science experiment, the temperature of a solution in Beaker 1 was 5 degrees below zero. The temperature of a solution in Beaker 2 was the opposite of the temperature in Beaker 1. What was the temperature in Beaker 2?

Ⓐ −5 degrees Ⓒ 5 degrees

Ⓑ 0 degrees Ⓓ 10 degrees

Mini-Task

8. Tia is buying paper cups and plates. Cups come in packages of 12, and plates come in packages of 10. She wants to buy the same number of cups and plates, but plans to buy the least number of packages possible. How much should Tia expect to pay if each package of cups is $3 and each package of plates is $5? Explain.

_____

_____

_____

_____

_____

_____

Rational Numbers

ESSENTIAL QUESTION

How can you use rational numbers to solve real-world problems?

LESSON 3.1

Classifying Rational Numbers

FL 6.NS.3.6

LESSON 3.2

Identifying Opposites and Absolute Value of Rational Numbers

FL 6.NS.3.6, 6.NS.3.6a, 6.NS.3.6c, 6.NS.3.7, 6.NS.3.7c

LESSON 3.3

Comparing and Ordering Rational Numbers

FL 6.NS.3.7, 6.NS.3.7a, 6.NS.3.7b

Real-World Video

In sports like baseball, coaches, analysts, and fans keep track of players' statistics such as batting averages, earned run averages, and runs batted in. These values are reported using rational numbers.

my.hrw.com

GO DIGITAL

my.hrw.com

my.hrw.com

Go digital with your write-in student edition, accessible on any device.

Math On the Spot

Scan with your smart phone to jump directly to the online edition, video tutor, and more.

Animated Math

Interactively explore key concepts to see how math works.

Personal Math Trainer

Get immediate feedback and help as you work through practice sets.

Are YOU Ready?

Complete these exercises to review skills you will need for this module.

Personal Math Trainer

my.hrw.com

Online Assessment and Intervention

Write an Improper Fraction as a Mixed Number

EXAMPLE

$$\frac{11}{3} = \frac{3}{3} + \frac{3}{3} + \frac{3}{3} + \frac{2}{3}$$

Write as a sum using names for one plus a proper fraction.
Write each name for one as one.

$$= 1 + 1 + 1 + \frac{2}{3}$$

$$= 3 + \frac{2}{3}$$

Add the ones.

$$= 3\frac{2}{3}$$

Write the mixed number.

Write each improper fraction as a mixed number.

1. $\frac{7}{2}$ _____   2. $\frac{12}{5}$ _____   3. $\frac{11}{7}$ _____   4. $\frac{15}{4}$ _____

Write a Mixed Number as an Improper Fraction

EXAMPLE

$$3\frac{3}{4} = 1 + 1 + 1 + \frac{3}{4}$$

Write the whole number as a sum of ones.

$$= \frac{4}{4} + \frac{4}{4} + \frac{4}{4} + \frac{3}{4}$$

Use the denominator of the fraction to write equivalent fractions for the ones.

$$= \frac{15}{4}$$

Add the numerators.

Write each mixed number as an improper fraction.

5. $2\frac{1}{2}$ _____   6. $4\frac{3}{5}$ _____   7. $3\frac{4}{9}$ _____   8. $2\frac{5}{7}$ _____

Compare and Order Decimals

EXAMPLE   Order from least to greatest: 7.32, 5.14, 5.16.

7.32 is greatest.

$5.14 < 5.16$

The order is 5.14, 5.16, 7.32.

Use place value to compare numbers, starting with ones, then tenths, then hundredths.

Compare the decimals.

9. 8.86 _____ 8.65   10. 0.732 _____ 0.75   11. 0.22 _____ 0.022

12. Order 0.98, 0.27, and 0.34 from greatest to least. _____

Reading Start-Up

Visualize Vocabulary

Use the ✔ words to complete the web. You may put more than one word in each box.

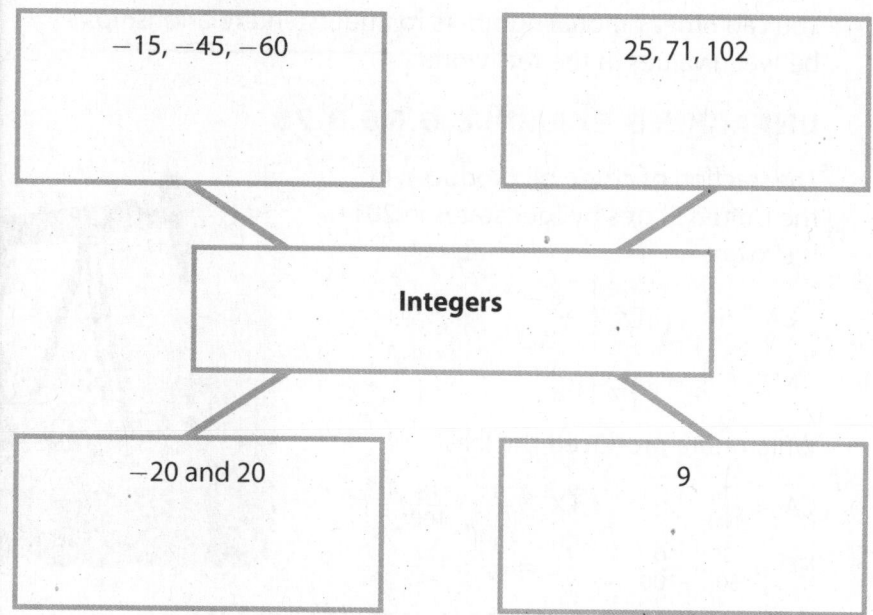

−15, −45, −60		25, 71, 102
	Integers	
−20 and 20		9

Understand Vocabulary

Fill in each blank with the correct term from the preview words.

1. A _____ is any number that can be written as a ratio of two integers.

2. A _____ is used to show the relationships between groups.

Active Reading

Tri-Fold Before beginning the module, create a tri-fold to help you learn the concepts and vocabulary in this module. Fold the paper into three sections. Label the columns "What I Know," "What I Need to Know," and "What I Learned." Complete the first two columns before you read. After studying the module, complete the third column.

Unpacking the Standards

Understanding the standards and the vocabulary terms in the standards will help you know exactly what you are expected to learn in this module.

FL 6.NS.3.7b

Write, interpret, and explain statements of order for rational numbers in real-world contexts.

Key Vocabulary

rational number *(número racional)*
Any number that can be expressed as a ratio of two integers.

What It Means to You

You can order rational numbers to understand relationships between values in the real world.

UNPACKING EXAMPLE 6.NS.3.7B

The fraction of crude oil produced in the United States by four states in 2011 is shown.

CA	$\frac{1}{100}$	TX	$\frac{9}{50}$
ND	$\frac{3}{50}$	AL	$\frac{3}{25}$

Which state produced the least oil?

$CA = \frac{1}{100}$ $\qquad$ $TX = \frac{9}{50} = \frac{18}{100}$

$ND = \frac{3}{50} = \frac{6}{100}$ $\qquad$ $AL = \frac{3}{25} = \frac{12}{100}$

California (CA) produced the least crude oil in 2011.

FL 6.NS.3.7c

Understand the absolute value of a rational number as its distance from 0 on the number line; interpret absolute value as magnitude for a positive or negative quantity in a real-world situation.

Key Vocabulary

absolute value *(valor absoluto)*
A number's distance from 0 on the number line.

What It Means to You

You can use absolute value to describe a number's distance from 0 on a number line and compare quantities in real-world situations.

UNPACKING EXAMPLE 6.NS.3.7C

Use the number line to determine the absolute values of −4.5°F and −7.5°F and to compare the temperatures.

$|-4.5| = 4.5$ $\qquad$ The absolute value of −4.5 is 4.5.

$|-7.5| = 7.5$ $\qquad$ The absolute value of −7.5 is 7.5.

−7.5 is farther to the left of 0 than −4.5, so −7.5 < −4.5 and −7.5°F is colder than −4.5°F.

Visit **my.hrw.com** to see all **Florida Math Standards** unpacked.

my.hrw.com

LESSON 3.1 Classifying Rational Numbers

 FL 6.NS.3.6
Understand a rational number as a point on the number line…

 ESSENTIAL QUESTION

How can you classify rational numbers?

EXPLORE ACTIVITY   Prep for 6.NS.3.6

Representing Division as a Fraction

Alicia and her friends Brittany, Kenji, and Ellis are taking a pottery class. The four friends have to share 3 blocks of clay. How much clay will each of them receive if they divide the 3 blocks evenly?

A The top faces of the 3 blocks of clay can be represented by squares. Use the model to show the part of each block that each friend will receive. Explain.

_____

_____

B Each piece of one square is equal to what fraction of a block of clay?

_____

C Explain how to arrange the pieces to model the amount of clay each person gets. Sketch the model.

Alicia   Brittany   Kenji   Ellis

_____

D What fraction of a square does each person's pieces cover? Explain.

_____

_____

E How much clay will each person receive?

_____

F **Multiple Representations** How does this situation represent division?

_____

_____

Reflect

1. **Communicate Mathematical Ideas** $3 \div 4$ can be written $\frac{3}{4}$. How are the dividend and divisor of a division expression related to the parts of a fraction?

_____

_____

2. **Analyze Relationships** How could you represent the division as a fraction if 5 people shared 2 blocks? if 6 people shared 5 blocks?

_____

Rational Numbers

A **rational number** is any number that can be written as $\frac{a}{b}$, where a and b are integers and $b \neq 0$.

EXAMPLE 1   FL   6.NS.3.6

Math Talk
Mathematical Practices

What division is represented by the fraction $\frac{34}{1}$?

Write each rational number as $\frac{a}{b}$.

A $3\frac{2}{5}$ Convert the mixed number to a fraction greater than 1. $3\frac{2}{5} = \frac{17}{5}$

B 0.6 The decimal is six tenths. Write as a fraction. $0.6 = \frac{6}{10}$

C 34 Write the whole number as a fraction with a denominator of 1. $34 = \frac{34}{1}$

D -7 Write the integer as a fraction with a denominator of 1. $-7 = \frac{-7}{1}$

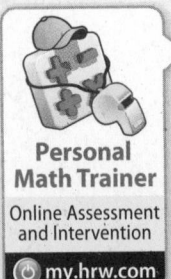

YOUR TURN

Write each rational number as $\frac{a}{b}$.

3. -15 _____

4. 0.31 _____

5. $4\frac{5}{9}$ _____

6. 62 _____

Classifying Rational Numbers

A **Venn diagram** is a visual representation used to show the relationships between groups. The Venn diagram below shows how rational numbers, integers, and whole numbers are related.

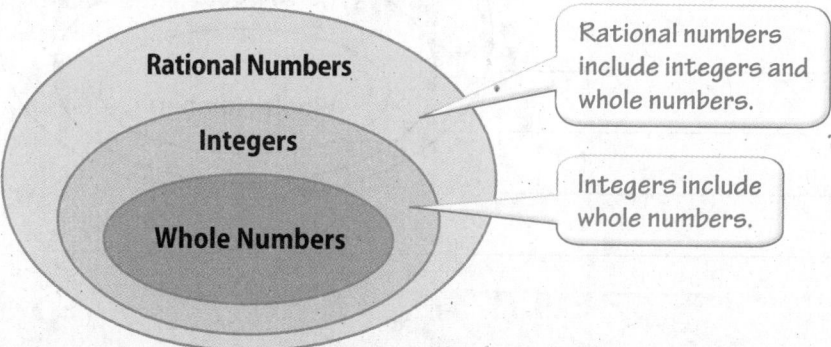

Rational numbers include integers and whole numbers.

Integers include whole numbers.

Math On the Spot

⏻ my.hrw.com

EXAMPLE 2

FL 6.NS.3.6

My Notes.

Place each number in the Venn diagram. Then classify each number by indicating in which set or sets each number belongs.

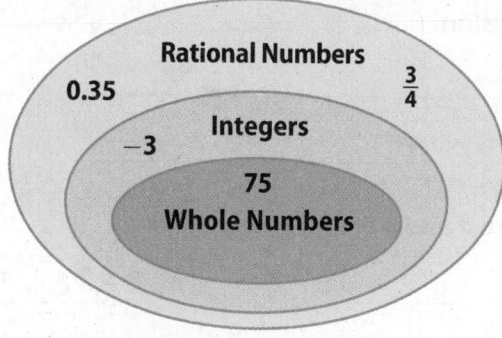

A 75 — The number 75 belongs in the sets of whole numbers, integers, and rational numbers.

B −3 — The number −3 belongs in the sets of integers and rational numbers.

C $\frac{3}{4}$ — The number $\frac{3}{4}$ belongs in the set of rational numbers.

D 0.35 — The number 0.35 belongs in the set of rational numbers.

Reflect

7. **Analyze Relationships** Name two integers that are not also whole numbers.

_____

_____

8. **Analyze Relationships** Describe how the Venn diagram models the relationship between rational numbers, integers, and whole numbers.

_____

_____

© Houghton Mifflin Harcourt Publishing Company

YOUR TURN

Place each number in the Venn diagram. Then classify each number by indicating in which set or sets it belongs.

9. 14.1 _____

10. $7\frac{1}{5}$ _____

11. −8 _____

12. 101 _____

Rational Numbers

Integers

Whole Numbers

Guided Practice

1. Sarah and four friends are decorating picture frames with ribbon. They have 4 rolls of ribbon to share evenly. (Explore Activity 1)

   a. How does this situation represent division?

   _____

   b. How much ribbon does each person receive? _____

Write each rational number in the form $\frac{a}{b}$, where a and b are integers. (Example 1)

2. 0.7 _____

3. −29 _____

4. $8\frac{1}{3}$ _____

Place each number in the Venn diagram. Then classify each number by indicating in which set or sets each number belongs. (Example 2)

5. −15 _____

6. $5\frac{10}{11}$ _____

Rational Numbers

Integers

Whole Numbers

ESSENTIAL QUESTION CHECK-IN

7. How is a rational number that is not an integer different from a rational number that is an integer?

_____

_____

_____

Name_____ Class_____ Date_____

3.1 Independent Practice

 FL 6.NS.3.6

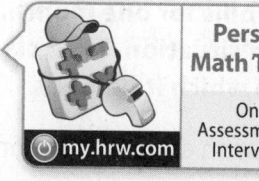

Personal Math Trainer

Online Assessment and Intervention

my.hrw.com

List two numbers that fit each description. Then write the numbers in the appropriate location on the Venn diagram.

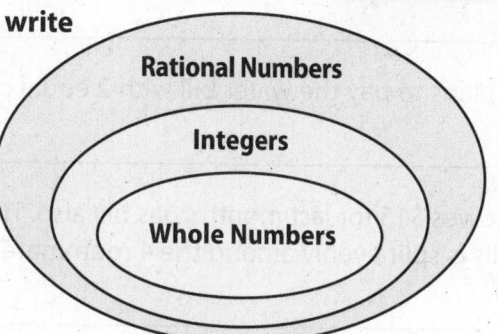

Rational Numbers

Integers

Whole Numbers

8. Integers that are not whole numbers

_____

9. Rational numbers that are not integers

_____

10. Multistep A nature club is having its weekly hike. The table shows how many pieces of fruit and bottles of water each member of the club brought to share.

Member	Pieces of Fruit	Bottles of Water
Baxter	3	5
Hendrick	2	2
Mary	4	3
Kendra	5	7

a. If the hikers want to share the fruit evenly, how many pieces should each person receive?

_____

b. Which hikers received more fruit than they brought on the hike?

_____

c. The hikers want to share their water evenly so that each member has the same amount. How much water does each hiker receive?

_____

11. Sherman has 3 cats and 2 dogs. He wants to buy a toy for each of his pets. Sherman has $22 to spend on pet toys. How much can he spend on each pet? Write your answer as a fraction and as an amount in dollars and cents.

_____

12. A group of 5 friends are sharing 2 pounds of trail mix. Write a division problem and a fraction to represent this situation.

_____

13. Vocabulary A _____ diagram can represent set relationships visually.

© Houghton Mifflin Harcourt Publishing Company

Financial Literacy For 14–16, use the table. The table shows Jason's utility bills for one month. Write a fraction to represent the division in each situation. Then classify each result by indicating the set or sets to which it belongs.

March Bills	
Water	$35
Gas	$14
Electric	$108

14. Jason and his 3 roommates share the cost of the electric bill evenly.

_____

15. Jason plans to pay the water bill with 2 equal payments.

_____

16. Jason owes $15 for last month's gas bill also. The total amount of the two gas bills is split evenly among the 4 roommates.

_____

17. Lynn has a watering can that holds 16 cups of water, and she fills it half full. Then she waters her 15 plants so that each plant gets the same amount of water. How many cups of water will each plant get?

_____

 FOCUS ON HIGHER ORDER THINKING

18. **Critique Reasoning** DaMarcus says the number $\frac{24}{6}$ belongs only to the set of rational numbers. Explain his error.

_____

_____

_____

_____

19. **Analyze Relationships** Explain how the Venn diagrams in this lesson show that all integers and all whole numbers are rational numbers.

_____

_____

_____

_____

20. **Critical Thinking** Is it possible for a number to be a rational number that is not an integer but is a whole number? Explain.

_____

_____

Work Area

LESSON 3.2 Identifying Opposites and Absolute Value of Rational Numbers

FL 6.NS.3.6c

Find and position integers and other rational numbers on a horizontal or vertical number line diagram... *Also 6.NS.3.6, 6.NS.3.6a, 6.NS.3.7, 6.NS.3.7c*

? ESSENTIAL QUESTION

How do you identify opposites and absolute value of rational numbers?

EXPLORE ACTIVITY   **FL** 6.NS.3.6, 6.NS.3.6c

Positive and Negative Rational Numbers

Recall that positive numbers are greater than 0. They are located to the right of 0 on a number line. Negative numbers are less than 0. They are located to the left of 0 on a number line.

Water levels with respect to sea level, which has elevation 0, may be measured at beach tidal basins. Water levels below sea level are represented by negative numbers.

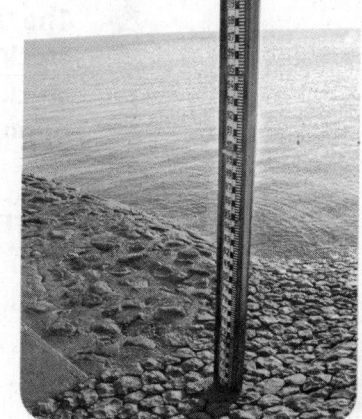

A The table shows the water level at a tidal basin at different times during a day. Graph the level for each time on the number line.

Time	4 A.M. A	8 A.M. B	Noon C	4 P.M. D	8 P.M. E
Level (ft)	3.5	2.5	−0.5	−2.5	0.5

B How did you know where to graph −0.5? _____

C At what time or times is the level closest to sea level? How do you know?

_____

D Which point is located halfway between −3 and −2? _____

E Which point is the same distance from 0 as *D*? _____

Reflect

1. **Communicate Mathematical Ideas** How would you graph −2.25? Would it be left or right of point *D*?

_____

© Houghton Mifflin Harcourt Publishing Company • Image Credits: ©Anna Blume/ Alamy

Lesson 3.2 **53**

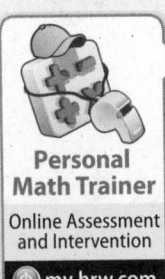
Rational Numbers and Opposites on a Number Line

You can find the opposites of rational numbers the same way you found the opposites of integers. Two rational numbers are opposites if they are the same distance from 0 but on different sides of 0.

$2\frac{3}{4}$ and $-2\frac{3}{4}$ are opposites.

EXAMPLE 1   **FL** 6.NS.3.6a, 6.NS.3.6c

Until June 24, 1997, the New York Stock Exchange priced the value of a share of stock in eighths, such as $27\frac{1}{8}$ or at $41\frac{3}{4}$. The change in value of a share of stock from day to day was also represented in eighths as a positive or negative number.

The table shows the change in value of a stock over two days. Graph the change in stock value for Wednesday and its opposite on a number line.

Day	Tuesday	Wednesday
Change in value ($)	$1\frac{5}{8}$	$-4\frac{1}{4}$

STEP 1 Graph the change in stock value for Wednesday on the number line.

The change in value for Wednesday is $-4\frac{1}{4}$.

Graph a point $4\frac{1}{4}$ units below 0.

STEP 2 Graph the opposite of $-4\frac{1}{4}$.

The opposite of $-4\frac{1}{4}$ is the same distance from 0 but on the other side of 0.

The opposite of $-4\frac{1}{4}$ is $4\frac{1}{4}$.

The opposite of the change in stock value for Wednesday is $4\frac{1}{4}$.

> $-4\frac{1}{4}$ is between -4 and -5. It is closer to -4.

YOUR TURN

2. What are the opposites of 7, -3.5, 2.25, and $9\frac{1}{3}$?

Absolute Values of Rational Numbers

You can also find the absolute value of a rational number the same way you found the absolute value of an integer. The absolute value of a rational number is the number's distance from 0 on the number line.

EXAMPLE 2   FL   6.NS.3.7, 6.NS.3.7c

The table shows the average low temperatures in January in one location during a five-year span. Find the absolute value of the average January low temperature in 2009.

My Notes

Year	2008	2009	2010	2011	2012
Temperature (°C)	−3.2	−5.4	−0.8	3.8	−2

STEP 1   Graph the 2009 average January low temperature.

The 2009 average January low is −5.4 °C.
Graph a point 5.4 units below 0.

STEP 2   Find the absolute value of −5.4.

−5.4 is 5.4 units from 0.

$|-5.4| = 5.4$

Reflect

3. **Communicate Mathematical Ideas** What is the absolute value of the average January low temperature in 2011? How do you know?

_____

_____

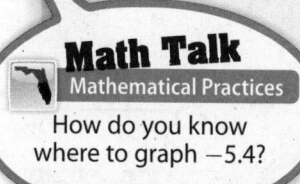

Math Talk
Mathematical Practices

How do you know where to graph −5.4?

YOUR TURN

Graph each number on the number line. Then use your number line to find each absolute value.

-5 0 5

4. $-4.5; |-4.5| = $ _____

5. $1\frac{1}{2}; \left|1\frac{1}{2}\right| = $ _____

6. $4; |4| = $ _____

7. $-3\frac{1}{4}; \left|-3\frac{1}{4}\right| = $ _____

Graph each number and its opposite on a number line. (Explore Activity and Example 1)

1. −2.8

2. 4.3

3. $-3\frac{4}{5}$

4. $1\frac{1}{3}$

Find the opposite of each number. (Example 1)

5. 3.78 _____

6. $-7\frac{5}{12}$ _____

7. 0 _____

8. 4.2 _____

9. 12.1 _____

10. 2.6 _____

11. Vocabulary Explain why 2.15 and −2.15 are opposites. (Example 1)

_____

_____

Find the absolute value of each number. (Example 2)

12. 5.23 _____

13. $-4\frac{2}{11}$ _____

14. 0 _____

15. $-6\frac{3}{5}$ _____

16. −2.12 _____

17. 8.2 _____

 ESSENTIAL QUESTION CHECK-IN

18. How do you identify the opposite and the absolute value of a rational number?

_____

_____

_____

_____

3.2 Independent Practice

FL 6.NS.3.6, 6.NS.3.6a, 6.NS.3.6c, 6.NS.3.7, 6.NS.3.7c

Personal
Math Trainer

Online
Assessment and
Intervention

my.hrw.com

19. **Financial Literacy** A store's balance sheet represents the amounts customers owe as negative numbers and credits to customers as positive numbers.

Customer	Girardi	Lewis	Stein	Yuan	Wenner
Balance ($)	−85.23	20.44	−116.33	13.50	−9.85

a. Write the opposite of each customer's balance.

_____

_____

b. Mr. Yuan wants to use his credit to pay off the full amount that another customer owes. Which customer's balance does Mr. Yuan

have enough money to pay off? _____

c. Which customer's balance would be farthest from 0 on a number line? Explain.

_____

_____

20. **Multistep** Trina and Jessie went on a vacation to Hawaii. Trina went scuba diving and reached an elevation of −85.6 meters, which is below sea level. Jessie went hang-gliding and reached an altitude of 87.9 meters, which is above sea level.

a. Who is closer to the surface of the ocean? Explain.

_____

b. Trina wants to hang-glide at the same number of meters above sea level as she scuba-dived below sea level. Will she fly higher than Jessie did? Explain.

_____

_____

21. **Critical Thinking** Carlos finds the absolute value of −5.3, and then finds the opposite of his answer. Jason finds the opposite of −5.3, and then finds the absolute value of his answer. Whose final value is greater? Explain.

_____

_____

22. Explain the Error Two students are playing a math game. The object of the game is to make the least possible number by arranging the given digits inside absolute value bars on a card. In the first round, each player will use the digits 3, 5, and 7 to fill in the card.

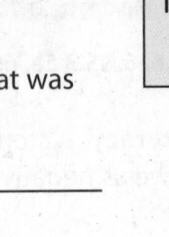

$|-75.3|$

a. One student arranges the numbers on the card as shown. What was this student's mistake?

_____

_____

_____

b. What is the least possible number the card can show? _____

Work Area

23. Analyze Relationships If you plot the point −8.85 on a number line, would you place it to the left or right of −8.8? Explain.

_____

_____

24. Make a Conjecture If the absolute value of a negative number is 2.78, what is the distance on the number line between the number and its absolute value? Explain your answer.

_____

_____

25. Multiple Representations The deepest point in the Indian Ocean is the Java Trench, which is 25,344 feet below sea level. Elevations below sea level are represented by negative numbers.

a. Write the elevation of the Java Trench. _____

b. A mile is 5,280 feet. Between which two integers is the elevation

in miles? _____

c. Graph the elevation of the Java Trench in miles.

−5   0   5

26. Draw Conclusions A number and its absolute value are equal. If you subtract 2 from the number, the new number and its absolute value are <u>not</u> equal. What do you know about the number? What is a possible number that satisfies these conditions?

_____

_____

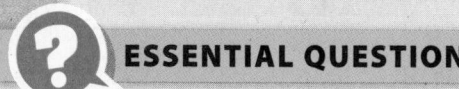

FL 6.NS.3.7a
Interpret statements of inequality as statements about the relative position of two numbers on a number line diagram. *Also 6.NS.3.7, 6.NS.3.7b*

? **ESSENTIAL QUESTION**

How do you compare and order rational numbers?

EXPLORE ACTIVITY   FL Prep for 6.NS.3.7a

Equivalent Fractions and Decimals

Fractions and decimals that represent the same value are *equivalent*. The number line shows equivalent fractions and decimals from 0 to 1.

A Complete the number line by writing the missing decimals or fractions.

B Use the number line to find a fraction that is equivalent to 0.25. Explain.

_____

_____

C Explain how to use a number line to find a decimal equivalent to $1\frac{7}{10}$.

_____

_____

D Use the number line to complete each statement.

0.2 = _____   _____ = $\frac{3}{10}$ 0.75 = _____   1.25 = _____

Reflect

1. Communicate Mathematical Ideas How does a number line represent equivalent fractions and decimals?

_____

_____

2. Name a decimal between 0.4 and 0.5.

_____

Ordering Fractions and Decimals

You can order fractions and decimals by rewriting the fractions as equivalent decimals or by rewriting the decimals as equivalent fractions.

EXAMPLE 1

 FL 6.NS.3.7, 6.NS.3.7a

A Order 0.2, $\frac{3}{4}$, 0.8, $\frac{1}{2}$, $\frac{1}{4}$, and 0.4 from least to greatest.

STEP 1 Write the fractions as equivalent decimals.

$$\frac{1}{4} = 0.25 \qquad \frac{1}{2} = 0.5 \qquad \frac{3}{4} = 0.75$$

STEP 2 Use the number line to write the decimals in order.

0   0.1   0.2   0.3   0.4   0.5   0.6   0.7   0.8   0.9   1

$$0.2 < 0.25 < 0.4 < 0.5 < 0.75 < 0.8$$

The numbers from least to greatest are 0.2, $\frac{1}{4}$, 0.4, $\frac{1}{2}$, $\frac{3}{4}$, 0.8.

B Order $\frac{1}{12}$, $\frac{2}{3}$, and 0.35 from least to greatest.

STEP 1 Write the decimal as an equivalent fraction.

> 60 is a multiple of the denominators of all three fractions.

$$0.35 = \frac{35}{100} = \frac{7}{20}$$

STEP 2 Find equivalent fractions with 60 as the common denominator.

$$\frac{1}{12} \overset{\times 5}{=} \frac{5}{60} \qquad \frac{2}{3} \overset{\times 20}{=} \frac{40}{60} \qquad \frac{7}{20} \overset{\times 3}{=} \frac{21}{60}$$

STEP 3 Order fractions with common denominators by comparing the numerators.

$$5 < 21 < 40$$

The fractions in order from least to greatest are $\frac{5}{60}$, $\frac{21}{60}$, $\frac{40}{60}$.

The numbers in order from least to greatest are $\frac{1}{12}$, 0.35, and $\frac{2}{3}$.

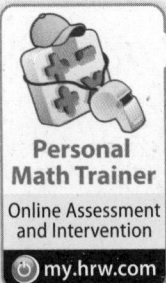
YOUR TURN

Order the fractions and decimals from least to greatest.

3. 0.85, $\frac{3}{5}$, 0.15, $\frac{7}{10}$ _____

© Houghton Mifflin Harcourt Publishing Company

Ordering Rational Numbers

You can use a number line to order positive and negative rational numbers.

EXAMPLE 2   FL 6.NS.3.7a, 6.NS.3.7b

Five friends completed a triathlon that included a 3-mile run, a 12-mile bike ride, and a $\frac{1}{2}$-mile swim. To compare their running times they created a table that shows the difference between each person's time and the average time, with negative numbers representing times less than the average.

Runner	John	Sue	Anna	Mike	Tom
Time above or below average (minutes)	$\frac{1}{2}$	1.4	$-1\frac{1}{4}$	-2.0	1.95

Order the numbers from greatest to least.

STEP 1 Write the fractions as equivalent decimals.

$\frac{1}{2} = 0.5$ $-1\frac{1}{4} = -1.25$

STEP 2 Use the number line to write the decimals in order.

$$-2.0 \quad -1.5 \quad -1.0 \quad -0.5 \quad 0.0 \quad 0.5 \quad 1.0 \quad 1.5 \quad 2.0$$

★ Average Time

$$1.95 > 1.4 > 0.5 > -1.25 > -2.0$$

The numbers in order from greatest to least are 1.95, 1.4, $\frac{1}{2}$, $-1\frac{1}{4}$, -2.0.

Math Talk
Mathematical Practices

Who was the fastest runner? Explain.

Reflect

4. **Communicate Mathematical Ideas** Describe a different way to order the numbers.

_____

_____

_____

5. To compare their bike times, the friends created a table that shows the difference between each person's time and the average bike time. Order the bike times from least to greatest.

Biker	John	Sue	Anna	Mike	Tom
Time above or below average (minutes)	-1.8	1	$1\frac{2}{5}$	$1\frac{9}{10}$	-1.25

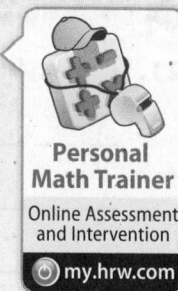

Personal Math Trainer

Online Assessment and Intervention

my.hrw.com

Find the equivalent fraction or decimal for each number.
(Explore Activity 1)

1. $0.6 =$ _____

2. $\frac{1}{4} =$ _____

3. $0.9 =$ _____

4. $0.1 =$ _____

5. $\frac{3}{10} =$ _____

6. $1.4 =$ _____

7. $\frac{4}{5} =$ _____

8. $0.4 =$ _____

9. $\frac{6}{8} =$ _____

Use the number line to order the fractions and decimals from least to greatest. (Example 1)

10. $0.75, \frac{1}{2}, 0.4,$ and $\frac{1}{5}$

```
   0   0.1  0.2  0.3  0.4  0.5  0.6  0.7  0.8  0.9   1
 <─┼────┼────┼────┼────┼────┼────┼────┼────┼────┼────┼──>
```

_____

11. The table shows the lengths of fish caught by three friends at the lake last weekend. Write the lengths in order from greatest to least. (Example 1)

Lengths of Fish (cm)		
Emma	**Anne**	**Emily**
12.7	$12\frac{3}{5}$	$12\frac{3}{4}$

_____

List the fractions and decimals in order from least to greatest.
(Example 1, Example 2)

12. $2.3, 2\frac{4}{5}, 2.6$

13. $0.5, \frac{3}{16}, 0.75, \frac{5}{48}$

14. $0.5, \frac{1}{5}, 0.35, \frac{12}{25}, \frac{4}{5}$

_____

_____

_____

15. $\frac{3}{4}, -\frac{7}{10}, -\frac{3}{4}, \frac{8}{10}$

16. $-\frac{3}{8}, \frac{5}{16}, -0.65, \frac{2}{4}$

17. $-2.3, -2\frac{4}{5}, -2.6$

_____

_____

_____

18. $-0.6, -\frac{5}{8}, -\frac{7}{12}, -0.72$

19. $1.45, 1\frac{1}{2}, 1\frac{1}{3}, 1.2$

20. $-0.3, 0.5, 0.55, -0.35$

_____

_____

_____

? ESSENTIAL QUESTION CHECK-IN

21. Explain how to compare 0.7 and $\frac{5}{8}$.

_____

_____

_____

3.3 Independent Practice

FL 6.NS.3.7, 6.NS.3.7a, 6.NS.3.7b

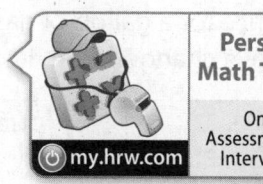

Personal Math Trainer

Online Assessment and Intervention

my.hrw.com

22. Rosa and Albert receive the same amount of allowance each week. The table shows what part of their allowance they each spent on video games and pizza.

	Video games	Pizza
Rosa	0.4	$\frac{2}{5}$
Albert	$\frac{1}{2}$	0.25

a. Who spent more of their allowance on video games? Write an inequality to compare the portion spent on video games.

_____

b. Who spent more of their allowance on pizza? Write an inequality to compare the portion spent on pizza.

_____

c. Draw Conclusions Who spent the greater part of their total allowance? How do you know?

_____

_____

23. A group of friends is collecting aluminum for a recycling drive. Each person who donates at least 4.25 pounds of aluminum receives a free movie coupon. The weight of each person's donation is shown in the table.

	Brenda	Claire	Jim	Micah	Peter
Weight (lb)	4.3	5.5	$6\frac{1}{6}$	$\frac{15}{4}$	$4\frac{3}{8}$

a. Order the weights of the donations from greatest to least.

_____

b. Which of the friends will receive a free movie coupon? Which will not?

_____

c. What If? Would the person with the smallest donation win a movie coupon if he or she had collected $\frac{1}{2}$ pound more of aluminum? Explain.

_____

_____

24. Last week, several gas stations in a neighborhood all charged the same price for a gallon of gas. The table below shows how much gas prices have changed from last week to this week.

Gas Station	Gas and Go	Samson Gas	Star Gas	Corner Store	Tip Top Shop
Change from last week (in cents)	-6.6	5.8	$-6\frac{3}{4}$	$\frac{27}{5}$	$-5\frac{5}{8}$

a. Order the numbers in the table from least to greatest.

_____

b. Which gas station has the cheapest gas this week? _____

c. **Critical Thinking** Which gas station changed their price the least this week?

_____

 FOCUS ON HIGHER ORDER THINKING

25. **Analyze Relationships** Explain how you would order from least to greatest three numbers that include a positive number, a negative number, and zero.

_____

_____

_____

26. **Critique Reasoning** Luke is making pancakes. The recipe calls for 0.5 quart of milk and 2.5 cups of flour. He has $\frac{3}{8}$ quart of milk and $\frac{18}{8}$ cups of flour. Luke makes the recipe with the milk and flour that he has. Explain his error.

_____

_____

_____

27. **Communicate Mathematical Ideas** If you know the order from least to greatest of 5 negative rational numbers, how can you use that information to order the absolute values of those numbers from least to greatest? Explain.

_____

_____

_____

_____

Work Area

Ready to Go On?

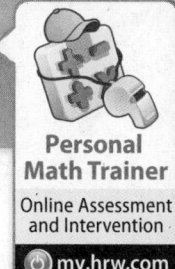

Personal Math Trainer

Online Assessment and Intervention

my.hrw.com

3.1 Classifying Rational Numbers

1. Five friends divide three bags of apples equally between them. Write the division represented in this situation as a fraction. _____

Write each rational number in the form $\frac{a}{b}$, where a and b are integers.

2. $5\frac{1}{6}$ _____

3. -12 _____

Determine if each number is a whole number, integer, or rational number. Include all sets to which each number belongs.

4. -12 _____

5. $\frac{7}{8}$ _____

3.2 Identifying Opposites and Absolute Value of Rational Numbers

6. Graph -3, $1\frac{3}{4}$, -0.5, and 3 on the number line.

7. Find the opposite of $\frac{1}{3}$ and of $-\frac{7}{12}$. _____

8. Find the absolute value of 9.8 and of $-\frac{10}{3}$. _____

3.3 Comparing and Ordering Rational Numbers

9. Over the last week, the daily low temperatures in degrees Fahrenheit have been -4, 6.2, $18\frac{1}{2}$, -5.9, 21, $-\frac{1}{4}$, and 1.75. List these numbers in order from greatest to least.

_____

 ESSENTIAL QUESTION

10. How can you order rational numbers from least to greatest?

_____

_____

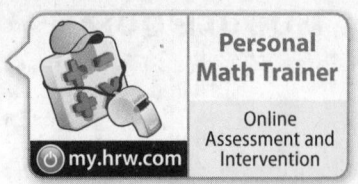
Selected Response

1. Suki split five dog treats equally among her six dogs. Which fraction represents this division?

   Ⓐ $\frac{6}{5}$ of a treat   Ⓒ $\frac{1}{5}$ of a treat

   Ⓑ $\frac{5}{6}$ of a treat   Ⓓ $\frac{1}{6}$ of a treat

2. Which set or sets does the number 15 belong to?

   Ⓐ whole numbers only

   Ⓑ rational numbers only

   Ⓒ integers and rational numbers only

   Ⓓ whole numbers, integers, and rational numbers

3. Which of the following statements about rational numbers is correct?

   Ⓐ All rational numbers are also whole numbers.

   Ⓑ All rational numbers are also integers.

   Ⓒ All rational numbers can be written in the form $\frac{a}{b}$, where a and b are integers and $b \neq 0$.

   Ⓓ Rational numbers cannot be negative.

4. Which of the following shows the numbers in order from least to greatest?

   Ⓐ $-\frac{1}{5}, -\frac{2}{3}, 2, 0.4$

   Ⓑ $2, -\frac{2}{3}, 0.4, -\frac{1}{5}$

   Ⓒ $-\frac{2}{3}, 0.4, -\frac{1}{5}, 2$

   Ⓓ $-\frac{2}{3}, -\frac{1}{5}, 0.4, 2$

5. What is the absolute value of -12.5?

   Ⓐ 12.5   Ⓒ -1

   Ⓑ 1   Ⓓ -12.5

6. Which number line shows $-\frac{1}{4}$ and its opposite?

   Ⓐ

   Ⓑ

   Ⓒ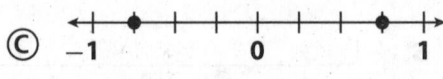

   Ⓓ

7. Horatio climbed to the top of a ladder that is 10 feet high. Which number is the opposite of the number that represents Horatio's height?

   Ⓐ -10 Ⓒ 0

   Ⓑ 10   Ⓓ $\frac{1}{10}$

Mini-Task

8. The table shows the heights in feet of several students in Mrs. Patel's class.

Name	Height (ft)
Olivia	$5\frac{1}{4}$
James	5.5
Carmela	4.9
Feng	5

   a. Write each height in the form $\frac{a}{b}$.

   _____

   b. List the heights in order from greatest to least.

   _____

Integers

> **Key Vocabulary**
> absolute value *(valor absoluto)*
> inequality *(desigualdad)*
> integers *(enteros)*
> negative numbers *(números negativos)*
> opposites *(opuestos)*
> positive numbers *(números positivos)*

? ESSENTIAL QUESTION

How can you use integers to solve real-world problems?

EXAMPLE 1

James recorded the temperature at noon in Fairbanks, Alaska, over a week in January.

Day	Mon	Tues	Wed	Thurs	Fri
Temperature	3	2	7	−3	−1

Graph the temperatures on the number line, and then list the numbers in order from least to greatest.

Graph the temperatures on the number line.

Read from left to right to list the temperatures in order from least to greatest.

The temperatures listed from least to greatest are −3, −1, 2, 3, 7.

EXAMPLE 2

Graph −4, 0, 2, and −1 on the number line. Then use the number line to find each absolute value.

A number and its opposite are the same distance from 0 on the number line. The absolute value of a negative number is its opposite.

$$|-4| = 4 \qquad |0| = 0 \qquad |2| = 2 \qquad |-1| = 1$$

EXERCISES

1. Graph 7, −2, 5, 1, and −1 on the number line. (Lesson 1.1)

List the numbers from least to greatest. (Lesson 1.2)

2. 4, 0, −2, 3 _____

3. −3, −5, 2, −2 _____

Compare using < or >. (Lesson 1.2)

4. 4 ◯ 1   5. −2 ◯ 2   6. −3 ◯ −5   7. −7 ◯ 2

Find the opposite and absolute value of each number. (Lessons 1.1, 1.3)

8. 6 _____

9. −2 _____

MODULE 2 — Factors and Multiples

Key Vocabulary
greatest common factor
  (GCF) (*máximo común
  divisor (MCD)*)
least common multiple
  (LCM) (*mínimo común
  múltiplo (mcm)*)

? ESSENTIAL QUESTION

How do you find and use the greatest common factor of two whole numbers? How do you find and use the least common multiple of two numbers?

EXAMPLE 1

Use the Distributive Property to rewrite 32 + 24 as a product of their greatest common factor and another number.

A. List the factors of 24 and 32. Circle the common factors.

  24: ① ② 3 ④ 6 ⑧ 12 24
  32: ① ② ④ ⑧ 16 32

B. Rewrite each number as a product of the GCF and another number.

  24: 8×3 **32:** 8×4

C. Use the Distributive Property and your answer above to rewrite 32 + 24 using the GCF and another number.

  $32 + 24 = 8 \times 3 + 8 \times 4$

  $32 + 24 = 8 \times (3 + 4)$

  $32 + 24 = 8 \times 7$

EXAMPLE 2

On Saturday, every 8th customer at Adam's Bagels will get a free coffee. Every 12th customer will get a free bagel. Which customer will be the first to get a free coffee and a free bagel?

A. List the multiples of 8 and 12. Circle the common multiples.

  8: 8 16 ㉔ 32 40 ㊽
  12: 12 ㉔ 36 ㊽

B. Find the LCM of 8 and 12.

  The LCM is 24. The 24th customer will be the first to get a free coffee and a free bagel.

EXERCISES

1. Find the GCF of 49 and 63 (Lesson 2-1) _____

Rewrite each sum as a product of the GCF of the addends and another number. (Lesson 2-1)

2. $15 + 45 =$ _____   **3.** $9 + 27 =$ _____

4. Find the LCM of 9 and 6 (Lesson 2-2) _____

MODULE 3 Rational Numbers

Key Vocabulary
rational number (*número racional*)
Venn diagram (*diagrama de Venn*)

ESSENTIAL QUESTION

How can you use rational numbers to solve real-world problems?

EXAMPLE 1

Use the Venn diagram to determine in which set or sets each number belongs.

A. $\frac{1}{2}$ belongs in the set of rational numbers.

B. −5 belongs in the sets of integers and rational numbers.

C. 4 belongs in the sets of whole numbers, integers, and rational numbers.

D. 0.2 belongs in the set of rational numbers.

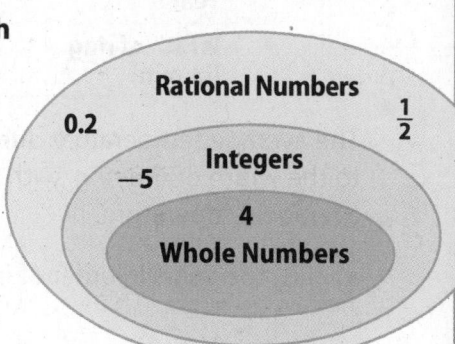

EXAMPLE 2

Order $\frac{2}{5}$, 0.2, and $\frac{4}{15}$ from greatest to least.

Write the decimal as an equivalent fraction. $0.2 = \frac{2}{10} = \frac{1}{5}$

Find equivalent fractions with 15 as the common denominator.

$\frac{2 \times 3}{5 \times 3} = \frac{6}{15}$ $\frac{1 \times 3}{5 \times 3} = \frac{3}{15}$ $\frac{4}{15} = \frac{4}{15}$

Order fractions with common denominators by comparing the numerators.

$6 > 4 > 3$ $\frac{6}{15} > \frac{4}{15} > \frac{3}{15}$

The numbers in order from greatest to least are, $\frac{2}{5}$, $\frac{4}{15}$, and 0.2.

EXERCISES

Classify each number by indicating in which set or sets it belongs.
(Lesson 2.1)

1. 8 _____

2. 0.25 _____

Find the absolute value of each rational number. (Lesson 2.2)

3. |3.7| _____   **4.** $\left|-\frac{2}{3}\right|$ _____

Graph each set of numbers on the number line and order the numbers from greatest to least. (Lesson 2.1, 2.3)

5. $-0.5, -1, -\frac{1}{4}, 0$

_____

© Houghton Mifflin Harcourt Publishing Company

1. **CAREERS IN MATH** Climatologist Each year a tree is alive, it adds a layer of growth, called a tree ring, between its core and its bark. A climatologist measures the width of tree rings of a particular tree for different years:

Year	1900	1910	1920	1930	1940
Width of ring (in mm)	$\frac{14}{25}$	$\frac{29}{50}$	$\frac{53}{100}$	$\frac{13}{20}$	$\frac{3}{5}$

The average temperature during the growing season is directly related to the width of the ring, with a greater width corresponding to a higher average temperature.

a. List the years in order of increasing ring width.

_____

b. Which year was hottest? How do you know?

_____

c. Which year was coldest? How do you know?

_____

2. A parking garage has floors above and below ground level. For a scavenger hunt, Gaia's friends are given a list of objects they need to find on the third and fourth level below ground, the first and fourth level above ground, and ground level.

a. If ground level is 0 and the first level above ground is 1, which integers can you use to represent the other levels where objects are hidden? Explain your reasoning.

_____

_____

b. Graph the set of numbers on the number line.

c. Gaia wants to start at the lowest level and work her way up. List the levels in the order that Gaia will search them.

_____

d. If she takes the stairs, how many flights of stairs will she have to climb? How do you know?

_____

_____

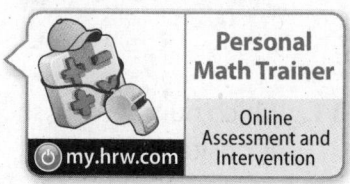

Personal
Math Trainer
Online
Assessment and
Intervention
my.hrw.com

Selected Response

1. What is the opposite of −9?

Ⓐ 9

Ⓑ −$\frac{1}{9}$

Ⓒ 0

Ⓓ $\frac{1}{9}$

2. Kyle is currently 60 feet above sea level. Which correctly describes the opposite of Kyle's elevation?

Ⓐ 60 feet below sea level

Ⓑ 60 feet above sea level

Ⓒ 6 feet below sea level

Ⓓ At sea level

3. What is the absolute value of 27?

Ⓐ −27

Ⓑ 0

Ⓒ 3

Ⓓ 27

4. In Albany it is −4°F, in Chicago it is −14°F, in Minneapolis it is −11°F, and in Toronto it is −13°F. In which city is it the coldest?

Ⓐ Albany

Ⓑ Chicago

Ⓒ Minneapolis

Ⓓ Toronto

5. Which shows the integers in order from greatest to least?

Ⓐ 18, 4, 3, −2, −15

Ⓑ −2, 3, 4, −15, 18

Ⓒ −15, −2, 3, 4, 18

Ⓓ 18, −15, 4, 3, −2

6. Joanna split three pitchers of water equally among her eight plants. What fraction of a pitcher did each plant get?

Ⓐ $\frac{1}{8}$ of a pitcher

Ⓑ $\frac{1}{3}$ of a pitcher

Ⓒ $\frac{3}{8}$ of a pitcher

Ⓓ $\frac{8}{3}$ of a pitcher

7. Which set or sets does the number −22 belong to?

Ⓐ Whole numbers only

Ⓑ Rational numbers only

Ⓒ Integers and rational numbers only

Ⓓ Whole numbers, integers, and rational numbers

8. Carlos swam to the bottom of a pool that is 12 feet deep. What is the opposite of Carlos's elevation relative to the surface?

Ⓐ −12 feet   Ⓒ 12 feet

Ⓑ 0 feet   Ⓓ $\frac{1}{12}$ foot

9. Which number line shows $\frac{1}{3}$ and its opposite?

10. Which of the following shows the numbers in order from least to greatest?

Ⓐ −$\frac{2}{3}$, −$\frac{3}{4}$, 0.7, 0

Ⓑ 0.7, 0, −$\frac{2}{3}$, −$\frac{3}{4}$

Ⓒ −$\frac{2}{3}$, −$\frac{3}{4}$, 0, 0.7

Ⓓ −$\frac{3}{4}$, −$\frac{2}{3}$, 0, 0.7

11. Which number line shows an integer and its opposite?

Ⓐ −5   0   5
Ⓑ −5   0   5
Ⓒ −5   0   5
Ⓓ −5   0   5

12. Which is another way to write 42 + 63?

Ⓐ 7 × (6 + 7)   Ⓒ 7 × 6 × 9
Ⓑ 7 × 15   Ⓓ 7 + 6 + 9

13. What is the LCM of 9 and 15?

Ⓐ 30   Ⓒ 90
Ⓑ 45   Ⓓ 135

14. What is the GCF of 40 and 72?

Ⓐ 2   Ⓒ 8
Ⓑ 4   Ⓓ 12

Mini-Task

15. Stella is recording temperatures every day for 5 days. On the first day, Stella recorded a temperature of 0 °F.

a. On the second day, the temperature was 3 °F above the temperature on the first day. What was the temperature on the

second day? _____

b. On the third day, it was 4 °F below the temperature of the first day. What was

the temperature? _____

c. The temperature on the fourth day was the opposite of the temperature on the second day. What was the temperature?

_____

d. The temperature on the fifth day was the absolute value of the temperature on the fourth day. What was the

temperature? _____

e. Write the temperatures in order from

least to greatest. _____

f. What is the difference in temperature between the coldest day and the

warmest day? _____

16. Marco is making mosaic garden stones using red, yellow, and blue tiles. He has 45 red tiles, 90 blue tiles, and 75 yellow tiles. Each stone must have the same number of each color tile. What is the greatest number

of stones Marco can make? _____

a. How many of each color tile will Marco use in each stone?

_____

b. How can Marco use the GCF to find out how many tiles he has in all?

_____

_____

_____

_____

_____

UNIT 2

Number Operations

MODULE **4**

Operations with Fractions

FL   6.NS.1.1, 6.NS.2.4

MODULE **5**

Operations with Decimals

FL   6.NS.2.2, 6.NS.2.3

CAREERS IN MATH

Chef The role of a chef is diverse and can include planning menus, overseeing food preparation, training staff, and ordering and purchasing food items. Chefs use mathematics when scaling recipes as well as in budgeting and financial planning.

If you are interested in a career as a chef, you should study these mathematical subjects:
- Basic Math
- Business Math

Research other careers that require the use of scaling quantities, and financial planning.

Unit 2 Performance Task

At the end of the unit, check out how **chefs** use math.

© Houghton Mifflin Harcourt Publishing Company •Image Credits: ©Corbis

Use the puzzle to preview key vocabulary from this unit. Unscramble the circled letters to answer the riddle at the bottom of the page.

1. ISROPCALCER

2. INERADRME

3. RENNOOAIDTM

4. DXMIE RUBMEN

5. NEIDIDDV

6. DRVIOSI

1. Two numbers whose product is one. (Lesson 4.2)
2. The whole number left over when you divide and the divisor doesn't divide the dividend evenly. (Lesson 5.1)
3. The part of a fraction that represents how many parts the whole is divided into. (Lesson 4.1)
4. A number that is a combination of a whole number and a fraction. (Lesson 4.3)
5. The amount that you want to divide in a division problem. (Lesson 5.4)
6. The number you divide by in a division problem. (Lesson 5.4)

Q: Decimals always win in arguments with fractions. What do decimals have that fractions don't?

A: __ __ __ __ __ __!

Operations with Fractions

 ESSENTIAL QUESTION

How can you use operations with fractions to solve real-world problems?

LESSON 4.1

Applying GCF and LCM to Fraction Operations

FL 6.NS.2.4

LESSON 4.2

Dividing Fractions

FL 6.NS.1.1

LESSON 4.3

Dividing Mixed Numbers

FL 6.NS.1.1

LESSON 4.4

Solving Multistep Problems with Fractions and Mixed Numbers

FL 6.NS.1.1

my.hrw.com

Real-World Video

To find your average rate of speed, divide the distance you traveled by the time you traveled. If you ride in a taxi and drive $\frac{1}{2}$ mile in $\frac{1}{4}$ hour, your rate was 2 mi/h which may mean you were in heavy traffic.

GO DIGITAL
my.hrw.com

my.hrw.com

Go digital with your write-in student edition, accessible on any device.

Math On the Spot

Scan with your smart phone to jump directly to the online edition, video tutor, and more.

Animated Math

Interactively explore key concepts to see how math works.

Personal Math Trainer

Get immediate feedback and help as you work through practice sets.

Are YOU Ready?

Complete these exercises to review skills you will need for this module.

Personal Math Trainer

Online Assessment and Intervention

my.hrw.com

Write an Improper Fraction as a Mixed Number

EXAMPLE $\frac{13}{5} = \frac{5}{5} + \frac{5}{5} + \frac{3}{5}$ Write as a sum using names for one plus a proper fraction.

$= 1 + 1 + \frac{3}{5}$ Write each name for one as one.

$= 2 + \frac{3}{5}$ Add the ones.

$= 2\frac{3}{5}$ Write the mixed number.

Write each improper fraction as a mixed number.

1. $\frac{9}{4}$ _____   2. $\frac{8}{3}$ _____   3. $\frac{23}{6}$ _____   4. $\frac{11}{2}$ _____

5. $\frac{17}{5}$ _____   6. $\frac{15}{8}$ _____   7. $\frac{33}{10}$ _____   8. $\frac{29}{12}$ _____

Multiplication Facts

EXAMPLE $7 \times 6 = $ ▩   Use a related fact you know.
$6 \times 6 = 36$
Think: $7 \times 6 = (6 \times 6) + 6$
$= 36 + 6$
$= 42$

$7 \times 6 = 42$

Multiply.

9. 6×5 _____   10. 8×9 _____   11. 10×11 _____   12. 7×8 _____

13. 9×7 _____   14. 8×6 _____   15. 9×11 _____   16. 11×12 _____

Division Facts

EXAMPLE $63 \div 7 = $ ▩   Think: 7 times what number equals 63?
$7 \times 9 = 63$

$63 \div 7 = 9$ So, $63 \div 7 = 9$.

Divide.

17. $35 \div 7$ _____   18. $56 \div 8$ _____   19. $28 \div 7$ _____   20. $48 \div 8$ _____

21. $36 \div 4$ _____   22. $45 \div 9$ _____   23. $72 \div 8$ _____   24. $40 \div 5$ _____

Reading Start-Up

Visualize Vocabulary

Use the ✔ words to complete the triangle. Write the review word that fits the description in each section of the triangle.

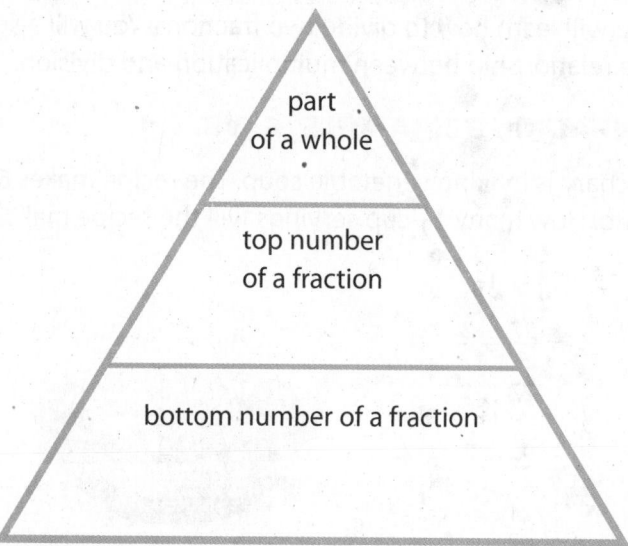

part of a whole

top number of a fraction

bottom number of a fraction

Vocabulary

Review Words
- area (*área*)
- ✔ denominator (*denominador*)
- ✔ fraction (*fracción*)
- greatest common factor (GCF) (*máximo común divisor (MCD)*)
- least common multiple (LCM) (*mínimo común múltiplo (m.c.m.)*)
- length (*longitud*)
- ✔ numerator (*numerador*)
- product (*producto*)
- width (*ancho*)

Preview Words
- mixed number (*número mixto*)
- order of operations (*orden de las operaciones*)
- reciprocals (*recíprocos*)

Understand Vocabulary

In each grouping, select the choice that is described by the given vocabulary word.

1. reciprocals   (A) 1:15   (B) $\frac{3}{4} \div \frac{1}{6}$ (C) $\frac{3}{5}$ and $\frac{5}{3}$

2. mixed number   (A) $\frac{1}{3} - \frac{1}{5}$ (B) $3\frac{1}{2}$ (C) -5

3. order of operations   (A) $5 - 3 + 2 = 0$ (B) $5 - 3 + 2 = 4$ (C) $5 - 3 + 2 = 6$

Active Reading

Layered Book Before beginning the module, create a layered book to help you learn the concepts in this module. Label each flap with lesson titles. As you study each lesson, write important ideas, such as vocabulary and processes, under the appropriate flap. Refer to your finished layered book as you work on exercises from this module.

Unpacking the Standards

Understanding the standards and the vocabulary terms in the standards will help you know exactly what you are expected to learn in this module.

 FL 6.NS.1.1

Interpret and compute quotients of fractions, and solve word problems involving division of fractions by fractions, e.g., by using visual fraction models and equations to represent the problem.

Key Vocabulary

quotient *(cociente)*
The result when one number is divided by another.

fraction *(fracción)*
A number in the form $\frac{a}{b}$, where $b \neq 0$.

What It Means to You

You will learn how to divide two fractions. You will also understand the relationship between multiplication and division.

UNPACKING EXAMPLE 6.NS.1.1

Zachary is making vegetable soup. The recipe makes $6\frac{3}{4}$ cups of soup. How many $1\frac{1}{2}$-cup servings will the recipe make?

$$6\frac{3}{4} \div 1\frac{1}{2}$$
$$= \frac{27}{4} \div \frac{3}{2}$$
$$= \frac{27}{4} \times \frac{2}{3}$$
$$= \frac{9}{2}$$
$$= 4\frac{1}{2}$$

The recipe will make $4\frac{1}{2}$ servings.

 FL 6.NS.2.4

Find the greatest common factor of two whole numbers less than or equal to 100 and the least common multiple of two whole numbers less than or equal to 12. Use the Distributive Property to express a sum of two whole numbers 1–100 with a common factor as a multiple of a sum of two whole numbers with no common factor.

What It Means to You

You can use greatest common factors and least common multiples to simplify answers when you calculate with fractions.

UNPACKING EXAMPLE 6.NS.2.4

Add. Write the answer in simplest form.

$\frac{1}{3} + \frac{1}{6} = \frac{2}{6} + \frac{1}{6}$	Use the LCM of 3 and 6 as a common denominator.
$= \frac{2+1}{6}$	Add the numerators.
$= \frac{3}{6}$	
$= \frac{3 \div 3}{6 \div 3}$	Simplify by dividing by the GCF. The GCF of 3 and 6 is 3.
$= \frac{1}{2}$	Write the answer in simplest form.

Visit **my.hrw.com** to see all **Florida Math Standards** unpacked.

my.hrw.com

Applying GCF and LCM to Fraction Operations

FL 6.NS.2.4
Find the greatest common factor...and the least common multiple of two whole numbers...

? ESSENTIAL QUESTION

How do you use the GCF and LCM when adding, subtracting, and multiplying fractions?

Multiplying Fractions

To multiply two fractions you first multiply the numerators and then multiply the denominators.

$$\frac{\text{numerator} \times \text{numerator}}{\text{denominator} \times \text{denominator}} = \frac{\text{numerator}}{\text{denominator}}$$

The resulting product may need to be written in simplest form. To write a fraction in simplest form, you can divide both the numerator and the denominator by their greatest common factor.

Example 1 shows two methods for making sure that the product of two fractions is in simplest form.

Math On the Spot
my.hrw.com

EXAMPLE 1   FL 6.NS.2.4

Multiply. Write the product in simplest form.

A $\frac{1}{3} \times \frac{3}{5}$

$\frac{1}{3} \times \frac{3}{5} = \frac{1 \times 3}{3 \times 5}$ Write the problem as a single fraction.

$= \frac{3}{15}$ Multiply numerators. Multiply denominators.

$= \frac{3 \div 3}{15 \div 3}$ Simplify by dividing by the GCF.
The GCF of 3 and 15 is 3.

$= \frac{1}{5}$ Write the answer in simplest form.

> 6 in the numerator and 3 in the denominator have a common factor other than one. Divide by the GCF 3.

B $\frac{6}{7} \times \frac{2}{3}$

$\frac{6}{7} \times \frac{2}{3} = \frac{6 \times 2}{7 \times 3}$ Write the problem as a single fraction.

$= \frac{\overset{2}{6} \times 2}{7 \times \underset{1}{3}}$ Simplify before multiplying using the GCF.

$= \frac{2 \times 2}{7 \times 1}$ Multiply numerators. Multiply denominators.

$= \frac{4}{7}$

Math Talk
Mathematical Practices

Compare the methods in the Example. How do you know if you can use the method in **B** ?

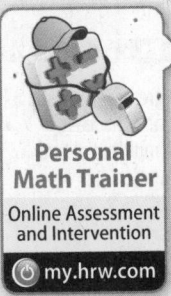
YOUR TURN

Multiply. Write each product in simplest form.

1. $\frac{1}{6} \times \frac{3}{5}$ _____

2. $\frac{3}{4} \times \frac{7}{9}$ _____

3. $\frac{3}{7} \times \frac{2}{3}$ _____

4. $\frac{4}{5} \times \frac{2}{7}$ _____

5. $\frac{7}{10} \times \frac{8}{21}$ _____

6. $\frac{6}{7} \times \frac{1}{6}$ _____

Math On the Spot

⏻ my.hrw.com

Multiplying Fractions and Whole Numbers

To multiply a fraction by a whole number, you rewrite the whole number as a fraction and multiply the two fractions. Remember to use the GCF to write the product in simplest form.

EXAMPLE 2   **FL 6.NS.2.4**

A class has 18 students. The teacher asks how many students in the class have pets and finds $\frac{5}{9}$ of the students have pets. How many students have pets?

STEP 1 Estimate the product. Multiply the whole number by the nearest benchmark fraction.

$\frac{5}{9}$ is close to $\frac{1}{2}$, so multiply $\frac{1}{2}$ times 18.

$\frac{1}{2} \times 18 = 9$

STEP 2 Multiply. Write the product in simplest form.

> You can write $\frac{5}{9}$ times 18 three ways.
>
> $\frac{5}{9} \times 18 \qquad \frac{5}{9} \cdot 18 \qquad \frac{5}{9}(18)$

$\frac{5}{9} \times 18$

$\frac{5}{9} \times 18 = \frac{5}{9} \times \frac{18}{1}$ Rewrite 18 as a fraction.

$= \frac{5 \times \overset{2}{\cancel{18}}}{\cancel{9} \times 1}$ Simplify before multiplying using the GCF.

$= \frac{5 \times 2}{1 \times 1}$ Multiply numerators. Multiply denominators.

$= \frac{10}{1} = 10$ Simplify by writing as a whole number.

10 students have pets.

Math Talk

Mathematical Practices

How can you check to see if the answer is correct?

Reflect

7. Analyze Relationships Is the product of a fraction less than 1 and a whole number greater than or less than the whole number? Explain.

_____

_____

Multiply. Write each product in simplest form.

8. $\frac{5}{8} \times 24$ _____

9. $\frac{3}{5} \times 20$ _____

10. $\frac{1}{3} \times 8$ _____

11. $\frac{1}{4} \times 14$ _____

12. $3\frac{7}{10} \times 7$ _____

13. $2\frac{3}{10} \times 10$ _____

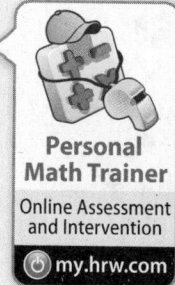

Adding and Subtracting Fractions

You have learned that to add or subtract two fractions, you can rewrite the fractions so they have the same denominator. You can use the least common multiple of the denominators of the fractions to rewrite the fractions.

EXAMPLE 3 FL 6.NS.2.4

Add $\frac{8}{15} + \frac{1}{6}$. Write the sum in simplest form.

STEP 1 Rewrite the fractions as equivalent fractions. Use the LCM of the denominators as the new denominator.

$\frac{8}{15} \rightarrow \frac{8 \times 2}{15 \times 2} \rightarrow \frac{16}{30}$ The LCM of 15 and 6 is 30.

$\frac{1}{6} \rightarrow \frac{1 \times 5}{6 \times 5} \rightarrow \frac{5}{30}$

STEP 2 Add the numerators of the equivalent fractions. Then simplify.

$\frac{16}{30} + \frac{5}{30} = \frac{21}{30}$

$= \frac{21 \div 3}{30 \div 3}$ Simplify by dividing by the GCF.
The GCF of 21 and 30 is 3.

$= \frac{7}{10}$

Reflect

14. Can you also use the LCM of the denominators of the fractions to rewrite the difference $\frac{8}{15} - \frac{1}{6}$? What is the difference?

_____

My Notes

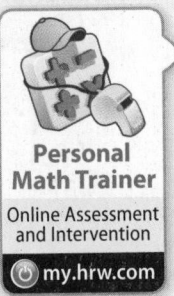
YOUR TURN

Add or subtract. Write each sum or difference in simplest form.

15. $\frac{5}{14} + \frac{1}{6}$ _____

16. $\frac{5}{12} - \frac{3}{20}$ _____

17. $\frac{5}{12} - \frac{3}{8}$ _____

18. $1\frac{3}{10} + \frac{1}{4}$ _____

19. $\frac{2}{3} + 6\frac{1}{5}$ _____

20. $3\frac{1}{6} - \frac{1}{7}$ _____

Guided Practice

Multiply. Write each product in simplest form. (Example 1)

1. $\frac{1}{2} \times \frac{5}{8}$ _____

2. $\frac{3}{5} \times \frac{5}{9}$ _____

3. $\frac{3}{8} \times \frac{2}{5}$ _____

4. $2\frac{3}{8} \times 16$ _____

5. $1\frac{4}{5} \times \frac{5}{12}$ _____

6. $1\frac{2}{10} \times 5$ _____

Find each amount. (Example 2)

7. $\frac{1}{4}$ of 12 bottles of water = _____ bottles

8. $\frac{2}{3}$ of 24 bananas = _____ bananas

9. $\frac{3}{5}$ of $40 restaurant bill = $ _____

10. $\frac{5}{6}$ of 18 pencils = _____ pencils

Add or subtract. Write each sum or difference in simplest form.

11. $\frac{3}{8} + \frac{5}{24}$ _____

12. $\frac{1}{20} + \frac{5}{12}$ _____

13. $\frac{9}{20} - \frac{1}{4}$ _____

14. $\frac{9}{10} - \frac{3}{14}$ _____

15. $3\frac{3}{8} + \frac{5}{12}$ _____

16. $5\frac{7}{10} - \frac{5}{18}$ _____

? ESSENTIAL QUESTION CHECK-IN

17. How can knowing the GCF and LCM help you when you add, subtract, and multiply fractions?

_____

_____

_____

_____

4.1 Independent Practice

 FL 6.NS.2.4

Personal Math Trainer

Online Assessment and Intervention

my.hrw.com

Solve. Write each answer in simplest form.

18. Erin buys a bag of peanuts that weighs $\frac{3}{4}$ of a pound. Later that week, the bag is $\frac{2}{3}$ full. How much does the bag of peanuts weigh now? Show your work.

_____

_____

19. Multistep Marianne buys 16 bags of potting soil that comes in $\frac{5}{8}$-pound bags.

a. How many pounds of potting soil does Marianne buy?

_____

b. If Marianne's father calls and says he needs 13 pounds of potting soil, how many additional bags should she buy?

_____

_____

20. Music Two fifths of the instruments in the marching band are brass, one third are percussion, and the rest are woodwinds.

a. What fraction of the band is woodwinds?

_____

b. One half of the woodwinds are clarinets. What fraction of the band is clarinets?

_____

c. One eighth of the brass instruments are tubas. If there are 240 instruments in the band, how many are tubas?

_____

21. Marcial found a recipe for fruit salad that he wanted to try to make for his birthday party. He decided to triple the recipe.

Fruit Salad
$3\frac{1}{2}$ cups thinly sliced rhubarb
15 seedless grapes, halved
$\frac{1}{2}$ orange, sectioned
10 fresh strawberries, halved
$\frac{3}{5}$ apple, cored and diced
$\frac{2}{3}$ peach, sliced
1 plum, pitted and sliced
$\frac{1}{4}$ cup fresh blueberries

a. What are the new amounts for the oranges, apples, blueberries, and peaches?

_____

_____

_____

_____

b. Communicate Mathematical Ideas The amount of rhubarb in the original recipe is $3\frac{1}{2}$ cups. Using what you know of whole numbers and what you know of fractions, explain how you could triple that mixed number.

_____

_____

_____

_____

© Houghton Mifflin Harcourt Publishing Company

22. One container holds $1\frac{7}{8}$ quarts of water and a second container holds $5\frac{3}{4}$ quarts of water. How many more quarts of water does the second container hold than the first container?

_____

23. Each of 15 students will give a $1\frac{1}{2}$-minute speech in English class.

  a. How long will it take to give the speeches? _____

  b. If the teacher begins recording on a digital camera with an hour available, is there enough time to record everyone if she gives a 15-minute introduction at the beginning of class and every student takes a minute to get ready? Explain.

  _____

  _____

  _____

  c. How much time is left on the digital camera? _____

24. **Represent Real-World Problems** Kate wants to buy a new bicycle from a sporting goods store. The bicycle she wants normally sells for $360. The store has a sale where all bicycles cost $\frac{5}{6}$ of the regular price. What is the sale price of the bicycle?

_____

25. **Error Analysis** To find the product $\frac{3}{7} \times \frac{4}{9}$, Cameron simplified $\frac{3}{7}$ to $\frac{1}{7}$ and then multiplied the fractions $\frac{1}{7}$ and $\frac{4}{9}$ to find the product $\frac{4}{63}$. What is Cameron's error?

_____

_____

_____

Work Area

26. **Justify Reasoning** To multiply a whole number by a fraction, you can first write the whole number as a fraction by placing the whole number in the numerator and 1 in the denominator. Does following this step change the product? Explain.

_____

_____

_____

LESSON
4.2 Dividing Fractions

FL 6.NS.1.1

Interpret and compute quotients of fractions, . . . , e.g., by using visual fraction models. . . .

? ESSENTIAL QUESTION

How do you divide fractions?

EXPLORE ACTIVITY 1 Real World   **FL** 6.NS.1.1

Modeling Fraction Division

In some division problems, you may know a number of groups and need to find how many or how much are in each group. In other division problems, you may know how many there are in each group, and need to find the number of groups.

A You have $\frac{3}{4}$ cup of salsa for making burritos. Each burrito requires $\frac{1}{8}$ cup of salsa. How many burritos can you make?

To find the number of burritos that can be made, you need to determine how many $\frac{1}{8}$-cup servings are in $\frac{3}{4}$ cup. Use the diagram. How many eighths

are there in $\frac{3}{4}$? _____

You have enough salsa to make _____ burritos.

B Five people share $\frac{1}{2}$ pound of cheese equally. How much cheese does each person receive?

To find how much cheese each person receives, you need to determine how

much is in each of _____ parts.

How much is in each part? _____

Each person will receive _____ pound.

Reflect

1. Write the division shown by each model.

_____

© Houghton Mifflin Harcourt Publishing Company

Lesson 4.2 **85**

Reciprocals

Another way to divide fractions is to use *reciprocals*. Two numbers whose product is 1 are **reciprocals**.

$$\frac{3}{4} \times \frac{4}{3} = \frac{12}{12} = 1 \qquad \frac{3}{4} \text{ and } \frac{4}{3} \text{ are reciprocals.}$$

To find the reciprocal of a fraction, switch the numerator and denominator.

$$\frac{numerator}{denominator} \cdot \frac{denominator}{numerator} = 1$$

EXAMPLE 1 **FL** **Prep for 6.NS.1.1**

Find the reciprocal of each number.

A $\frac{2}{9}$ ⤬ $\frac{9}{2}$ *Switch the numerator and denominator.*

The reciprocal of $\frac{2}{9}$ is $\frac{9}{2}$.

Math Talk

Mathematical Practices

How can you check that the reciprocal in **A** is correct?

B $\frac{1}{8}$ ⤬ $\frac{8}{1}$ *Switch the numerator and denominator.*

The reciprocal of $\frac{1}{8}$ is $\frac{8}{1}$, or 8.

C 5

$5 = \frac{5}{1}$ *Rewrite as a fraction.*

$\frac{5}{1}$ ⤬ $\frac{1}{5}$ *Switch the numerator and the denominator.*

The reciprocal of 5 is $\frac{1}{5}$.

Reflect

2. Is any number its own reciprocal? If so, what number(s)? Justify your answer.

_____

3. Communicate Mathematical Ideas Does every number have a reciprocal? Explain.

_____

_____

4. The reciprocal of a whole number is a fraction with _____ in the numerator.

 YOUR TURN

Find the reciprocal of each number.

5. $\frac{7}{8}$ _____   **6.** 9 _____   **7.** $\frac{1}{11}$ _____

Using Reciprocals to Find Equivalent Values

A Complete the table below.

Division	Multiplication
$\frac{6}{7} \div \frac{2}{7} = 3$	$\frac{6}{7} \times \frac{7}{2} =$
$\frac{5}{8} \div \frac{3}{8} = \frac{5}{3}$	$\frac{5}{8} \times \frac{8}{3} =$
$\frac{1}{6} \div \frac{5}{6} = \frac{1}{5}$	$\frac{1}{6} \times \frac{6}{5} =$
$\frac{1}{4} \div \frac{1}{3} = \frac{3}{4}$	$\frac{1}{4} \times \frac{3}{1} =$

B How does each multiplication problem compare to its corresponding division problem?

_____

_____

_____

C How does the answer to each multiplication problem compare to the answer to its corresponding division problem?

_____

_____

Reflect

8. Make a Conjecture Use the pattern in the table to make a conjecture about how you can use multiplication to divide one fraction by another.

_____

_____

_____

9. Write a division problem and a corresponding multiplication problem like those in the table. Assuming your conjecture in **8** is correct, what is the answer to your division problem?

_____

_____

Using Reciprocals to Divide Fractions

Dividing by a fraction is equivalent to multiplying by its reciprocal.

$$\frac{1}{5} \div \frac{1}{4} = \frac{4}{5} \qquad \frac{1}{5} \times \frac{4}{1} = \frac{4}{5}$$

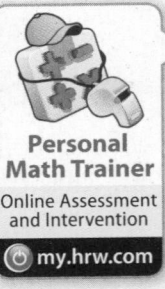

Animated Math
my.hrw.com

EXAMPLE 2

FL 6.NS.1.1

Divide $\frac{5}{9} \div \frac{2}{3}$. Write the quotient in simplest form.

STEP 1 Rewrite as multiplication, using the reciprocal of the divisor.

$$\frac{5}{9} \div \frac{2}{3} = \frac{5}{9} \times \frac{3}{2}$$

The reciprocal of $\frac{2}{3}$ is $\frac{3}{2}$.

STEP 2 Multiply and simplify.

$$\frac{5}{9} \times \frac{3}{2} = \frac{15}{18}$$

Multiply the numerators. Multiply the denominators

$$= \frac{5}{6}$$

Write the answer in simplest form.

$$\frac{5}{9} \div \frac{2}{3} = \frac{5}{6}$$

$$\frac{15 \div 3}{18 \div 3} = \frac{5}{6}$$

Personal Math Trainer

Online Assessment and Intervention

my.hrw.com

YOUR TURN

Divide.

10. $\frac{9}{10} \div \frac{2}{5} = $ _____

11. $\frac{9}{10} \div \frac{3}{5} = $ _____

Guided Practice

Find the reciprocal of each fraction. (Example 1)

1. $\frac{2}{5}$ _____

2. $\frac{1}{9}$ _____

3. $\frac{10}{3}$ _____

Divide. (Explore 1, Explore 2, and Example 2)

4. $\frac{4}{3} \div \frac{5}{3} = $ _____

5. $\frac{3}{10} \div \frac{4}{5} = $ _____

6. $\frac{1}{2} \div \frac{2}{5} = $ _____

? ESSENTIAL QUESTION CHECK-IN

7. How do you divide fractions?

_____

4.2 Independent Practice

FL 6.NS.1.1

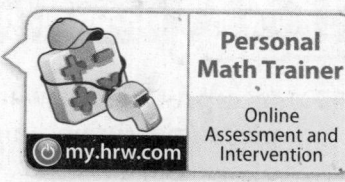

Personal Math Trainer

Online Assessment and Intervention

my.hrw.com

8. Alison has $\frac{1}{2}$ cup of yogurt for making fruit parfaits. Each parfait requires $\frac{1}{8}$ cup of yogurt. How many parfaits can she make?

_____

9. A team of runners is needed to run a $\frac{1}{4}$-mile relay race. If each runner must run $\frac{1}{16}$ mile, how many runners will be needed?

_____

10. Trevor paints $\frac{1}{6}$ of the fence surrounding his farm each day. How many days will it take him to paint $\frac{3}{4}$ of the fence?

_____

11. Six people share $\frac{3}{5}$ pound of peanuts equally. What fraction of a pound of peanuts does each person receive?

_____

12. Biology If one honeybee makes $\frac{1}{12}$ teaspoon of honey during its lifetime, how many honeybees are needed to make $\frac{1}{2}$ teaspoon of honey?

_____

13. Jackson wants to divide a $\frac{3}{4}$-pound box of trail mix into small bags. Each of the bags will hold $\frac{1}{12}$ pound of trail mix. How many bags of trail mix can Jackson fill?

_____

14. A pitcher contains $\frac{2}{3}$ quart of lemonade. If an equal amount of lemonade is poured into each of 6 glasses, how much lemonade will each glass contain?

_____

15. How many tenths are there in $\frac{4}{5}$?

_____

16. You make a large bowl of salad to share with your friends. Your brother eats $\frac{1}{3}$ of it before they come over.

a. You want to divide the leftover salad evenly among six friends. What expression describes the situation? Explain.

_____

_____

_____

b. What fractional portion of the original bowl of salad does each friend receive?

_____

_____

_____

FOCUS ON HIGHER ORDER THINKING

© Houghton Mifflin Harcourt Publishing Company

Work Area

17. **Interpret the Answer** The length of a ribbon is $\frac{3}{4}$ meter. Sun Yi needs pieces measuring $\frac{1}{3}$ meter for an art project. What is the greatest number of pieces measuring $\frac{1}{3}$ meter that can be cut from the ribbon? How much ribbon will be left after Sun Yi cuts the ribbon? Explain your reasoning.

_____

_____

_____

_____

18. **Represent Real-World Problems** Liam has $\frac{9}{10}$ gallon of paint for painting the birdhouses he sells at the craft fair. Each birdhouse requires $\frac{1}{20}$ gallon of paint. How many birdhouses can Liam paint? Show your work.

_____

_____

19. **Justify Reasoning** When Kaitlin divided a fraction by $\frac{1}{2}$, the result was a mixed number. Was the original fraction less than or greater than $\frac{1}{2}$? Explain your reasoning.

_____

_____

_____

20. **Communicate Mathematical Ideas** The reciprocal of a fraction less than 1 is always a fraction greater than 1. Why is this?

_____

_____

_____

_____

21. **Make a Prediction** Susan divides the fraction $\frac{5}{8}$ by $\frac{1}{16}$. Her friend Robyn divides $\frac{5}{8}$ by $\frac{1}{32}$. Predict which person will get the greater quotient. Explain and check your prediction.

_____

_____

_____

LESSON 4.3 Dividing Mixed Numbers

FL 6.NS.1.1
Interpret and compute
quotients of fractions,
and solve word problems
involving division of fractions
by fractions. . . .

? **ESSENTIAL QUESTION**

How do you divide mixed numbers?

EXPLORE ACTIVITY Real World   FL 6.NS.1.1

Modeling Mixed Number Division

Antoine is making sushi rolls. He has $2\frac{1}{2}$ cups of rice and will use $\frac{1}{4}$ cup of rice for each sushi roll. How many sushi rolls can he make?

A To find the number of sushi rolls that can be made, you need to determine how many fourths are in $2\frac{1}{2}$. Use fraction pieces to represent $2\frac{1}{2}$ on the model below.

1				1				$\frac{1}{2}$	
$\frac{1}{4}$	$\frac{1}{4}$	$\frac{1}{4}$	$\frac{1}{4}$	$\frac{1}{4}$	$\frac{1}{4}$	$\frac{1}{4}$	$\frac{1}{4}$	$\frac{1}{4}$	$\frac{1}{4}$

B How many fourths are in $2\frac{1}{2}$? _____

Antoine has enough rice to make _____ sushi rolls.

Reflect

1. **Communicate Mathematical Ideas** Which mathematical operation could you use to find the number of sushi rolls that Antoine can make? Explain.

   _____

   _____

2. **Multiple Representations** Write the division shown by the model.

   _____

3. **What If?** Suppose Antoine instead uses $\frac{1}{8}$ cup of rice for each sushi roll. How would his model change? How many rolls can he make? Explain.

   _____

   _____

   _____

Using Reciprocals to Divide Mixed Numbers

Dividing by a fraction is equivalent to multiplying by its reciprocal. You can use this fact to divide mixed numbers. First rewrite the mixed numbers as fractions greater than 1. Then multiply the dividend by the reciprocal of the divisor.

My Notes

EXAMPLE 1   FL 6.NS.1.1

One serving of Harold's favorite cereal contains $1\frac{2}{5}$ ounces. How many servings are in a $17\frac{1}{2}$-ounce box?

STEP 1 Write a division statement to represent the situation.

$$17\frac{1}{2} \div 1\frac{2}{5}$$

> You need to find how many groups of $1\frac{2}{5}$ are in $17\frac{1}{2}$.

STEP 2 Rewrite the mixed numbers as fractions greater than 1.

$$17\frac{1}{2} \div 1\frac{2}{5} = \frac{35}{2} \div \frac{7}{5}$$

STEP 3 Rewrite the problem as multiplication using the reciprocal of the divisor.

$$\frac{35}{2} \div \frac{7}{5} = \frac{35}{2} \times \frac{5}{7} \qquad \text{The reciprocal of } \frac{7}{5} \text{ is } \frac{5}{7}.$$

STEP 4 Multiply.

$$\frac{35}{2} \times \frac{5}{7} = \frac{\cancel{35}^{5}}{2} \times \frac{5}{\cancel{7}_{1}} \qquad \text{Simplify first using the GCF.}$$

$$= \frac{5 \times 5}{2 \times 1} \qquad \text{Multiply numerators. Multiply denominators.}$$

$$= \frac{25}{2}, \text{ or } 12\frac{1}{2} \qquad \text{Write the result as a mixed number.}$$

There are $12\frac{1}{2}$ servings of cereal in the box.

Reflect

4. **Analyze Relationships** Explain how can you check the answer.

_____

_____

5. **What If?** Harold serves himself $1\frac{1}{2}$-ounces servings of cereal each morning. How many servings does he get from a box of his favorite cereal? Show your work.

_____

6. Sheila has $10\frac{1}{2}$ pounds of potato salad. She wants to divide the potato salad into containers, each of which holds $1\frac{1}{4}$ pounds. How many containers does she need? Explain.

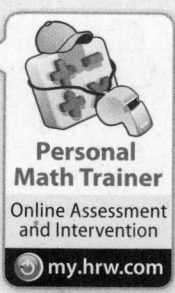

Personal Math Trainer

Online Assessment and Intervention

⟳ my.hrw.com

_____

Solving Problems Involving Area

Recall that to find the area of a rectangle, you multiply length × width. If you know the area and only one dimension, you can divide the area by the known dimension to find the other dimension.

Math On the Spot

⟳ my.hrw.com

EXAMPLE 2   FL 6.NS.1.1

The area of a rectangular sandbox is $56\frac{2}{3}$ square feet. The length of the sandbox is $8\frac{1}{2}$ feet. What is the width?

STEP 1 Write the situation as a division problem.

$$56\frac{2}{3} \div 8\frac{1}{2}$$

STEP 2 Rewrite the mixed numbers as fractions greater than 1.

$$56\frac{2}{3} \div 8\frac{1}{2} = \frac{170}{3} \div \frac{17}{2}$$

STEP 3 Rewrite the problem as multiplication using the reciprocal of the divisor.

$$\frac{170}{3} \div \frac{17}{2} = \frac{170}{3} \times \frac{2}{17}$$

$$= \frac{\overset{10}{\cancel{170}} \times 2}{3 \times \cancel{17}_{1}}$$ Multiply numerators. Multiply denominators.

$$= \frac{20}{3}, \text{ or } 6\frac{2}{3}$$ Simplify and write as a mixed number.

The width of the sandbox is $6\frac{2}{3}$ feet.

Math Talk
Mathematical Practices

Explain how to find the length of a rectangle when you know the area and the width.

Reflect

7. **Check for Reasonableness** How can you determine if your answer is reasonable?

_____

_____

_____

_____

© Houghton Mifflin Harcourt Publishing Company

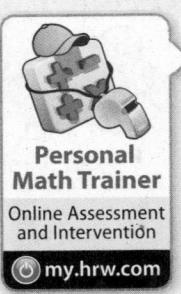

Personal Math Trainer

Online Assessment and Intervention

⏻ my.hrw.com

YOUR TURN

8. The area of a rectangular patio is $12\frac{3}{8}$ square meters. The width of the patio is $2\frac{3}{4}$ meters. What is the length? _____

9. The area of a rectangular rug is $14\frac{1}{12}$ square yards. The length of the rug is $4\frac{1}{3}$ yards. What is the width? _____

Guided Practice

Divide. Write each answer in simplest form. (Explore Activity and Example 1)

1. $4\frac{1}{4} \div \frac{3}{4}$

$$\frac{\boxed{}}{4} \div \frac{3}{4} =$$

$$\frac{\boxed{}}{4} \times \frac{\boxed{}}{\boxed{}} =$$

_____

2. $1\frac{1}{2} \div 2\frac{1}{4}$

$$\frac{\boxed{}}{2} \div \frac{\boxed{}}{4} =$$

$$\frac{\boxed{}}{2} \times \frac{\boxed{}}{\boxed{}} =$$

_____

3. $4 \div 1\frac{1}{8} =$ _____

4. $3\frac{1}{5} \div 1\frac{1}{7} =$ _____

5. $8\frac{1}{3} \div 2\frac{1}{2} =$ _____

6. $15\frac{1}{3} \div 3\frac{5}{6} =$ _____

Write each situation as a division problem. Then solve. (Example 2)

7. A sandbox has an area of 26 square feet, and the length is $5\frac{1}{2}$ feet. What is the width of the sandbox?

_____

8. Mr. Webster is buying carpet for an exercise room in his basement. The room will have an area of 230 square feet. The width of the room is $12\frac{1}{2}$ feet. What is the length?

_____

❓ ESSENTIAL QUESTION CHECK-IN

9. How does dividing mixed numbers compare with dividing fractions?

_____

_____

4.3 Independent Practice

Personal Math Trainer

Online Assessment and Intervention

my.hrw.com

FL 6.NS.1.1

10. Jeremy has $4\frac{1}{2}$ cups of iced tea. He wants to divide the tea into $\frac{3}{4}$-cup servings. Use the model to find the number of servings he can make.

_____

11. A ribbon is $3\frac{2}{3}$ yards long. Mae needs to cut the ribbon into pieces that are $\frac{2}{3}$ yard long. Use the model to find the number of pieces she can cut.

_____

12. Dao has $2\frac{3}{8}$ pounds of hamburger meat. He is making $\frac{1}{4}$-pound hamburgers. Does Dao have enough meat to make 10 hamburgers? Explain.

_____

_____

13. Multistep Zoey made $5\frac{1}{2}$ cups of trail mix for a camping trip. She wants to divide the trail mix into $\frac{3}{4}$-cup servings.

a. Ten people are going on the camping trip. Can Zoey make enough $\frac{3}{4}$-cup servings so that each person on the trip has one serving?

_____

b. What size would the servings need to be for everyone to have a serving? Explain.

_____

c. If Zoey decides to use the $\frac{3}{4}$-cup servings, how much more trail mix will she need? Explain.

_____

_____

14. The area of a rectangular picture frame is $30\frac{1}{3}$ square inches. The length of the frame is $6\frac{1}{2}$ inches. Find the width of the frame.

_____

15. The area of a rectangular mirror is $11\frac{11}{16}$ square feet. The width of the mirror is $2\frac{3}{4}$ feet. If there is a 5 foot tall space on the wall to hang the mirror, will it fit? Explain.

_____

16. Ramon has a rope that is $25\frac{1}{2}$ feet long. He wants to cut it into 6 pieces that are equal in length. How long will each piece be?

_____

17. Eleanor and Max used two rectangular wooden boards to make a set for the school play. One board was 6 feet long, and the other was $5\frac{1}{2}$ feet long. The two boards had equal widths. The total area of the set was $60\frac{3}{8}$ square feet. What was the width?

_____

 FOCUS ON HIGHER ORDER THINKING

Work Area

18. Draw Conclusions Micah divided $11\frac{2}{3}$ by $2\frac{5}{6}$ and got $4\frac{2}{17}$ for an answer. Does his answer seem reasonable? Explain your thinking. Then check Micah's answer.

_____

_____

_____

_____

_____

19. Explain the Error To divide $14\frac{2}{3} \div 2\frac{3}{4}$, Erik multiplied $14\frac{2}{3} \times \frac{4}{3}$. Explain Erik's error.

_____

_____

_____

20. Analyze Relationships Explain how you can find the missing number in $3\frac{4}{5} \div \blacksquare = 2\frac{5}{7}$. Then find the missing number.

_____

_____

_____

Solving Multistep Problems with Fractions and Mixed Numbers

FL 6.NS.1.1

...Solve word problems involving division of fractions by fractions...

How can you solve word problems involving more than one fraction operation?

Solving Problems with Rational Numbers

Sometimes more than one operation will be needed to solve a multistep problem. You can use parentheses to group different operations. Recall that according to the **order of operations,** you perform operations in parentheses first.

Math On the Spot

my.hrw.com

EXAMPLE 1 Problem Solving

FL 6.NS.1.1

Jon is cooking enough lentils for lentil barley soup and lentil salad. The lentil barley soup recipe calls for $\frac{3}{4}$ cup of dried lentils. The lentil salad recipe calls for $1\frac{1}{2}$ cups of dried lentils. Jon has a $\frac{1}{8}$-cup scoop. How many scoops of dried lentils will Jon need to have enough for the soup and the salad?

 Analyze Information

Identify the important information.

- Jon needs $\frac{3}{4}$ cup of dried lentils for soup and $1\frac{1}{2}$ cups for salad.
- Jon has a $\frac{1}{8}$-cup scoop.
- You need to find the total number of many scoops of lentils he needs.

 Formulate a Plan

You can use the expression $\left(\frac{3}{4} + 1\frac{1}{2}\right) \div \frac{1}{8}$ to find the number of scoops of dried lentils Jon will need for the soup and the salad.

 Solve

Follow the order of operations. Perform the operations in parentheses first.

First add to find the total amount of dried lentils Jon will need.

$$\frac{3}{4} + 1\frac{1}{2} = \frac{3}{4} + \frac{3}{2}$$

$$= \frac{3}{4} + \frac{6}{4}$$

$$= \frac{9}{4}$$

$$= 2\frac{1}{4}$$

John needs $2\frac{1}{4}$ cups of lentils.

Jon needs $2\frac{1}{4}$ cups of dried lentils for both the soup and the salad.

To find how many $\frac{1}{8}$-cup scoops he needs, divide the total amount of dried lentils into groups of $\frac{1}{8}$.

$$2\frac{1}{4} \div \frac{1}{8} = \frac{9}{4} \div \frac{1}{8}$$

$$= \frac{9}{4} \times \frac{8}{1}$$

Simplify before multiplying using the GCF.

$$= \frac{9 \times \overset{2}{\cancel{8}}}{\underset{1}{\cancel{4}} \times 1}$$

$$= \frac{18}{1} = 18$$

Jon will need 18 scoops of dried lentils to have enough for both the lentil barley soup and the lentil salad.

 Justify and Evaluate

You added $\frac{3}{4}$ and $1\frac{1}{2}$ first to find the total number of cups of lentils. Then you divided the sum by $\frac{1}{8}$ to find the number of $\frac{1}{8}$-cup scoops.

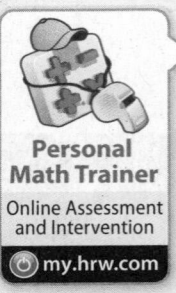

YOUR TURN

1. Before conducting some experiments, a scientist mixes $\frac{1}{2}$ gram of Substance A with $\frac{3}{4}$ gram of Substance B. If the scientist uses $\frac{1}{8}$ gram of the mixture for each experiment, how many experiments can be conducted? _____

Guided Practice

1. An art student uses a roll of wallpaper to decorate two gift boxes. The student will use $1\frac{1}{3}$ yards of paper for one box and $\frac{5}{6}$ yard of paper for the other box. The paper must be cut into pieces that are $\frac{1}{6}$ yard long. How many pieces will the student cut to use for the gift boxes? (Example 1) _____

 ESSENTIAL QUESTION CHECK-IN

2. How can you solve a multistep problem that involves fractions?

_____

Name_____ Class_____ Date_____

4.4 Independent Practice

 FL 6.NS.1.1

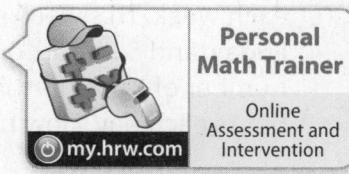

Personal Math Trainer

Online Assessment and Intervention

my.hrw.com

3. Naomi has earned $54 mowing lawns the past two days. She worked $2\frac{1}{2}$ hours yesterday and $4\frac{1}{4}$ hours today. If Naomi is paid the same amount for every hour she works, how much does she earn per hour to mow lawns?

_____

4. An art teacher has $1\frac{1}{2}$ pounds of red clay and $\frac{3}{4}$ pound of yellow clay. The teacher mixes the red clay and yellow clay together. Each student in the class needs $\frac{1}{8}$ pound of the clay mixture to finish the assigned art project for the class. How many students can get enough clay to finish the project?

_____

5. A hairstylist schedules $\frac{1}{4}$ hour to trim a customer's hair and $\frac{1}{6}$ hour to style the customer's hair. The hairstylist plans to work $3\frac{1}{3}$ hours each day for 5 days each week. How many appointments can the hairstylist schedule each week if each customer must be trimmed and styled?

6. A picture framer has a thin board $10\frac{1}{12}$ feet long. The framer notices that $2\frac{3}{8}$ feet of the board is scratched and cannot be used. The rest of the board will be used to make small picture frames. Each picture frame needs $1\frac{2}{3}$ feet of the board. At most, how many complete picture frames can be made?

_____

7. Jim's backyard is a rectangle that is $15\frac{5}{6}$ yards long and $10\frac{2}{5}$ yards wide. Jim buys sod in pieces that are $1\frac{1}{3}$ yards long and $1\frac{1}{3}$ yards wide. How many pieces of sod will Jim need to buy to cover his backyard with sod?

_____

8. Eva wants to make two pieces of pottery. She needs $\frac{3}{5}$ pound of clay for one piece and $\frac{7}{10}$ pound of clay for the other piece. She has three bags of clay that weigh $\frac{4}{5}$ pound each. How many bags of clay will Eva need to make both pieces of pottery? How many pounds of clay will she have left over?

_____

9. Mark wants to paint a mural. He has $1\frac{1}{3}$ gallons of yellow paint, $1\frac{1}{4}$ gallons of green paint, and $\frac{7}{8}$ gallon of blue paint. Mark plans to use $\frac{3}{4}$ gallon of each paint color. How many gallons of paint will he have left after painting the mural?

_____

© Houghton Mifflin Harcourt Publishing Company • Image Credits: Nicholas Eveleigh/The Image Bank/Getty Images

10. Trina works after school and on weekends. She always works three days each week. This week she worked $2\frac{3}{4}$ hours on Monday, $3\frac{3}{5}$ hours on Friday, and $5\frac{1}{2}$ hours on Saturday. Next week she plans to work the same number of hours as this week, but will work for the same number of hours each day. How many hours will she work on each day?

_____

 FOCUS ON HIGHER ORDER THINKING

11. Represent Real-World Problems Describe a real-world problem that can be solved using the expression $29 \div \left(\frac{3}{8} + \frac{5}{6}\right)$. Find the answer in the context of the situation.

_____

_____

_____

_____

_____

12. Justify Reasoning Indira and Jean begin their hike at 10 a.m. one morning. They plan to hike from the $2\frac{2}{5}$-mile marker to the $8\frac{1}{10}$-mile marker along the trail. They plan to hike at an average speed of 3 miles per hour. Will they reach the $8\frac{1}{10}$-mile marker by noon? Explain your reasoning.

_____

_____

_____

_____

13. Multiple Representations You are measuring walnuts for banana-walnut oatmeal and a spinach and walnut salad. You need $\frac{3}{8}$ cup of walnuts for the oatmeal and $\frac{3}{4}$ cup of walnuts for the salad. You have a $\frac{1}{4}$-cup scoop. Describe two different ways to find how many scoops of walnuts you will need.

_____

_____

_____

_____

_____

Ready to Go On?

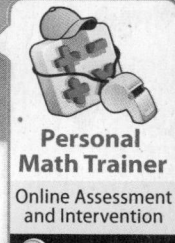

Personal Math Trainer

Online Assessment and Intervention

my.hrw.com

4.1 Applying GCF and LCM to Fraction Operations

Solve.

1. $\frac{4}{5} \times \frac{3}{4}$ _____

2. $\frac{5}{7} \times \frac{9}{10}$ _____

3. $\frac{3}{8} + 2\frac{1}{2}$ _____

4. $1\frac{3}{5} - \frac{5}{6}$ _____

4.2 Dividing Fractions

Divide.

5. $\frac{1}{3} \div \frac{7}{9}$ _____

6. $\frac{1}{3} \div \frac{5}{8}$ _____

7. Luci cuts a board that is $\frac{3}{4}$ yard long into pieces that are $\frac{3}{8}$ yard long. How many pieces does she cut? _____

4.3 Dividing Mixed Numbers

Divide.

8. $3\frac{1}{3} \div \frac{2}{3}$ _____

9. $1\frac{7}{8} \div 2\frac{2}{5}$ _____

10. $4\frac{1}{4} \div 4\frac{1}{2}$ _____

11. $8\frac{1}{3} \div 4\frac{2}{7}$ _____

4.4 Solving Multistep Problems with Fractions and Mixed Numbers

12. Jamal hiked on two trails. The first trail was $5\frac{1}{3}$ miles long, and the second trail was $1\frac{3}{4}$ times as long as the first trail. How many miles did Jamal hike? _____

 ESSENTIAL QUESTION

13. Describe a real-world situation that is modeled by dividing two fractions or mixed numbers.

_____

_____

_____

MODULE 4 MIXED REVIEW

Assessment Readiness

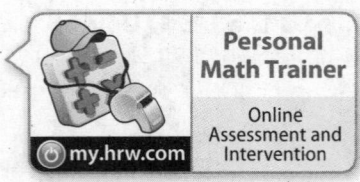

Personal
Math Trainer

Online
Assessment and
Intervention

my.hrw.com

Selected Response

1. Two sides of a rectangular fence are $5\frac{5}{8}$ feet long. The other two sides are $6\frac{1}{4}$ feet long. What is the perimeter?

(A) $11\frac{7}{8}$ feet (B) 13 feet

(C) $23\frac{3}{4}$ feet (D) $35\frac{5}{32}$ feet

2. Which shows the GCF of 18 and 24 with $\frac{18}{24}$ in simplest form?

(A) GCF: 3; $\frac{3}{4}$

(B) GCF: 3; $\frac{6}{8}$

(C) GCF: 6; $\frac{3}{4}$

(D) GCF: 6; $\frac{6}{8}$

3. A jar contains 133 pennies. A bigger jar contains $1\frac{2}{7}$ times as many pennies. What is the value of the pennies in the bigger jar?

(A) $1.49 (B) $1.52

(C) $1.68 (D) $1.71

4. Which of these is the same as $\frac{3}{5} \div \frac{4}{7}$?

(A) $\frac{3}{5} \div \frac{7}{4}$

(B) $\frac{4}{7} \div \frac{3}{5}$

(C) $\frac{3}{5} \times \frac{4}{7}$

(D) $\frac{3}{5} \times \frac{7}{4}$

5. Andy has $6\frac{2}{3}$ cups of juice. How many $\frac{2}{3}$-cup servings can he pour?

(A) $4\frac{4}{9}$ (B) 6

(C) 7 (D) 10

6. What is the reciprocal of $3\frac{3}{7}$?

(A) $\frac{7}{24}$ (B) $\frac{3}{7}$

(C) $\frac{7}{3}$ (D) $\frac{24}{7}$

7. A rectangular patio has a length of $12\frac{1}{2}$ feet and an area of $103\frac{1}{8}$ square feet. What is the width of the patio?

(A) $4\frac{1}{8}$ feet

(B) $8\frac{1}{4}$ feet

(C) $16\frac{1}{2}$ feet

(D) 33 feet

8. Which number is greater than the absolute value of $-\frac{3}{8}$?

(A) $-\frac{5}{8}$

(B) $-\frac{1}{8}$

(C) $\frac{1}{4}$

(D) 0.5

Mini-Task

9. Jodi is cutting out pieces of paper that measure $8\frac{1}{2}$ inches by 11 inches from a larger sheet of paper that has an area of 1,000 square inches

a. What is the area of each piece of paper that Jodi is cutting out?

_____

b. What is the greatest possible number of pieces of paper that Jodi can cut out of the larger sheet?

_____

Operations with Decimals

MODULE 5

ESSENTIAL QUESTION

How can you use operations with decimals to solve real-world problems?

LESSON 5.1
Dividing Whole Numbers
 FL 6.NS.2.2

LESSON 5.2
Adding and Subtracting Decimals
 FL 6.NS.2.3

LESSON 5.3
Multiplying Decimals
 FL 6.NS.2.3

LESSON 5.4
Dividing Decimals
FL 6.NS.2.3

LESSON 5.5
Applying Operations with Rational Numbers
 FL 6.NS.2.3

Real-World Video

The gravitational force on Earth's moon is less than the gravitational force on Earth. You can calculate your weight on the moon by multiplying your weight on Earth by a decimal.

my.hrw.com

GO DIGITAL
my.hrw.com

my.hrw.com

Go digital with your write-in student edition, accessible on any device.

Math On the Spot

Scan with your smart phone to jump directly to the online edition, video tutor, and more.

Animated Math

Interactively explore key concepts to see how math works.

Personal Math Trainer

Get immediate feedback and help as you work through practice sets.

Are YOU Ready?

Complete these exercises to review skills you will need for this module.

Personal Math Trainer

Online Assessment and Intervention

my.hrw.com

Represent Decimals

EXAMPLE

Think: 1 square = 1 of 100 equal parts
$= \frac{1}{100}$, or 0.01

10 squares = 10 of 100 equal parts
$= \frac{1}{10}$, or 0.1

So, 20 squares represent 2×0.1, or 0.2.

Write the decimal represented by the shaded square.

1.   2.   3.   4.

_____   _____   _____   _____

Multiply Decimals by Powers of 10

EXAMPLE 6.574×100 Count the zeros in 100: 2 zeros.

$6.574 \times 100 = 657.4$ Move the decimal point 2 places to the right.

Find the product.

5. 0.49×10 _____   6. $25.34 \times 1,000$ _____   7. 87×100 _____

Words for Operations

EXAMPLE   Write a numerical expression for the product of 5 and 9.
5×9 Think: *Product* means "to multiply."

Write 5 times 9.

Write a numerical expression for the word expression.

8. 20 decreased by 8 _____   9. the quotient of 14 and 7 _____

10. the difference between 72 and 16 _____   11. the sum of 19 and 3 _____

Reading Start-Up

Visualize Vocabulary

Use the ✔ words to complete the chart. You may put more than one word in each section.

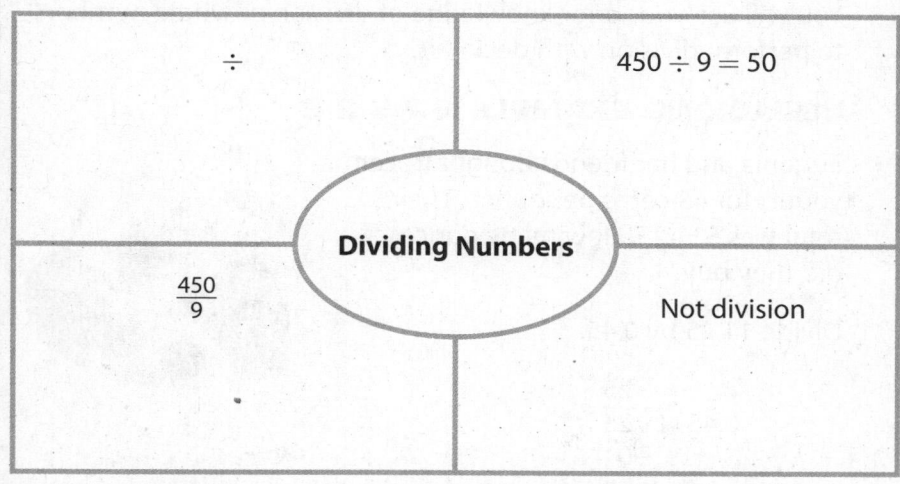

÷	450 ÷ 9 = 50
$\frac{450}{9}$	Not division

Dividing Numbers

Understand Vocabulary

Match the term on the left to the definition on the right.

1. divide   **A.** The bottom number in a fraction.

2. denominator   **B.** The top number in a fraction.

3. quotient   **C.** To split into equal groups.

4. numerator   **D.** The answer in a division problem.

Active Reading

Booklet Before beginning the module, create a booklet to help you learn the concepts in this module. Write the main idea of each lesson on its own page of the booklet. As you study each lesson, record examples that illustrate the main idea and make note of important details. Refer to your finished booklet as you work on assignments and study for tests.

Unpacking the Standards

Understanding the standards and the vocabulary terms in the standards will help you know exactly what you are expected to learn in this module.

 FL 6.NS.2.2

Fluently divide multi-digit numbers using the standard algorithm.

Key Vocabulary

quotient *(cociente)*
The result when one number is divided by another.

What It Means to You

You will use your prior knowledge of division of whole numbers to perform division with decimals.

UNPACKING EXAMPLE 6.NS.2.2

Eugenia and her friends bought frozen yogurt for 45 cents per ounce. Their total was $11.25. How many ounces did they buy?

Divide 11.25 by 0.45.

$$
\begin{array}{r}
25 \\
0.45\overline{)11.25} \\
\underline{90} \\
225 \\
\underline{225} \\
0
\end{array}
$$

They bought 25 ounces of frozen yogurt.

 FL 6.NS.2.3

Fluently add, subtract, multiply, and divide multi-digit decimals using the standard algorithm for each operation.

Key Vocabulary

algorithm *(algoritmo)*
A set of rules or a procedure for solving a mathematical problem in a finite number of steps.

What It Means to You

You will use your prior knowledge of operations with whole numbers to perform operations with decimals.

UNPACKING EXAMPLE 6.NS.2.3

Estimate and find the exact answer.

A. 3.25×4.8

$3 \times 5 = 15$

$$
\begin{array}{r}
3.25 \\
\times 4.8 \\
\hline
2600 \\
13000 \\
\hline
15.600
\end{array}
$$

B. $132.5 - 18.9$

$133 - 19 = 114$

$$
\begin{array}{r}
132.5 \\
-18.9 \\
\hline
113.6
\end{array}
$$

Visit **my.hrw.com** to see all **Florida Math Standards** unpacked.

 my.hrw.com

Dividing Whole Numbers

 FL 6.NS.2.2
...Divide multi-digit numbers using the standard algorithm....

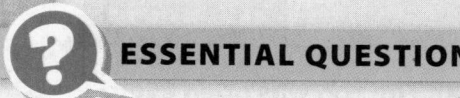

ESSENTIAL QUESTION

How do you divide multi-digit whole numbers?

EXPLORE ACTIVITY   FL 6.NS.2.2

Estimating Quotients

You can use estimation to predict the quotient of multi-digit whole numbers.

A local zoo had a total of 98,464 visitors last year. The zoo was open every day except for three holidays. On average, about how many visitors did the zoo have each day?

quotient
divisor⟌dividend

A To estimate the average number of visitors per day, you can divide the total number of visitors by the number of days. To estimate the quotient, first estimate the dividend by rounding the number of visitors to the nearest ten thousand.

98,464 rounded to the nearest ten thousand is _____.

B There were 365 days last year. How many

days was the petting zoo open? _____

C Estimate the divisor by rounding the number of days that the zoo was open to the nearest hundred.

_____ rounded to the nearest hundred is _____.

D Estimate the quotient. _____ ÷ _____ = _____

The average number of visitors per day last year was about _____.

Reflect

1. How can you check that your quotient is correct?

_____

_____

2. **Critical Thinking** Do you think that your estimate is greater than or less than the actual answer? Explain.

_____

© Houghton Mifflin Harcourt Publishing Company • Image Credits: ©John Coletti/ Getty Images

Using Long Division

The exact average number of visitors per day at the zoo in the Explore Activity is the quotient of 98,464 and 362. You can use long division to find this quotient.

EXAMPLE 1   FL 6.NS.2.2

A local zoo had a total of 98,464 visitors last year. The zoo was open every day except three holidays? On average, how many visitors did the zoo have each day?

Math Talk
Mathematical Practices

How does the estimate from the Explore Activity compare to the actual average number of visitors per day?

STEP 1 362 is greater than 9 and 98, so divide 984 by 362. Place the first digit in the quotient in the hundreds place. Multiply 2 by 362 and place the product under 984. Subtract.

$$
\begin{array}{r}
2 \\
362\overline{)\,98{,}464} \\
-72\ 4 \\
\hline
26\ 0
\end{array}
$$

STEP 2 Bring down the tens digit. Divide 2,606 by 362. Multiply 7 by 362 and place the product under 2,606. Subtract.

$$
\begin{array}{r}
27 \\
362\overline{)\,98{,}464} \\
-72\ 4\!\downarrow \\
\hline
26\ 06 \\
-25\ 34 \\
\hline
72
\end{array}
$$

STEP 3 Bring down the ones digit. Divide the ones.

$$
\begin{array}{r}
272 \\
362\overline{)\,98{,}464} \\
-72\ 4 \\
\hline
26\ 06 \\
-25\ 34\!\downarrow \\
\hline
724 \\
-724 \\
\hline
0
\end{array}
$$

The average number of visitors per day last year was 272.

YOUR TURN

Find each quotient.

3. 34,989 ÷ 321 _____

4. 73,375 ÷ 125 _____

Dividing with a Remainder

Suppose you and your friend want to divide 9 polished rocks between you so that you each get the same number of polished rocks. You will each get 4 rocks with 1 rock left over. You can say that the quotient 9 ÷ 2 has a remainder of 1.

Math On the Spot
my.hrw.com

EXAMPLE 2 FL 6.NS.2.2

My Notes

Callie has 1,850 books. She must pack them into boxes to ship to a bookstore. Each box holds 12 books. How many boxes will she need to pack all of the books?

Divide 1,850 by 12.

```
        154 R2
    12)1,850
      -12
        65
       -60
        50
       -48
         2
```

The quotient is 154, remainder 2. You can write 154 R2.

Reflect

5. **Interpret the Answer** What does the remainder mean in this situation?

    _____

    _____

6. **Interpret the Answer** How many boxes does Callie need to pack the books? Explain.

    _____

    _____

    _____

YOUR TURN

Divide.

7. 5,796 ÷ 25 _____   8. 67)3,098 _____

9. A museum gift shop manager wants to put 1,578 polished rocks into small bags to sell as souvenirs. If the shop manager wants to put 15 rocks in each bag, how many complete bags can be filled? How

    many rocks will be left over? _____

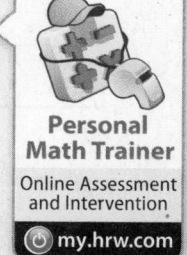

Personal
Math Trainer

Online Assessment
and Intervention

my.hrw.com

© Houghton Mifflin Harcourt Publishing Company

1. Estimate: 31,969 ÷ 488 (Explore Activity)

Round the numbers and then divide.

31,969 ÷ 488 = _____ ÷ _____ = _____

Divide. (Example 1, Example 2)

2. 3,072 ÷ 32 = _____

```
        9☐
32 )3, 0 7 2
  −☐☐☐
      1 9 2
  −☐☐☐
        ☐
```

3. 4,539 ÷ 51 = _____

```
     ☐☐
51 )4, 5 3 9
  −☐☐☐
      4 5 9
  −☐☐☐
        ☐
```

4. 9,317 ÷ 95 = _____

```
      ☐☐
95 )9, 3 1 7
  −☐☐☐
    ☐☐☐
  −☐☐☐
        ☐
```

5. 2,226 ÷ 53 = _____

6. Divide 4,514 by 74. _____

7. 3,493 ÷ 37 = _____

8. 2,001 ÷ 83 = _____

9. 39,751 ÷ 313 = _____

10. 35,506 ÷ 438 = _____

11. During a food drive, a local middle school collected 8,982 canned food items. Each of the 28 classrooms that participated in the drive donated about the same number of items. Estimate the number of items each classroom donated. (Explore Activity) _____

12. A theater has 1,120 seats in 35 equal rows. How many seats are in each row? (Example 1) _____

13. There are 1,012 souvenir paperweights that need to be packed in boxes. Each box will hold 12 paperweights. How many boxes will be needed? (Example 2) _____

? ESSENTIAL QUESTION CHECK-IN

14. What steps do you take to divide multi-digit whole numbers?

_____

_____

_____

_____

_____

5.1 Independent Practice

FL 6.NS.2.2

Personal Math Trainer

Online Assessment and Intervention

my.hrw.com

Divide.

15. 44,756 ÷ 167 = _____

16. 87,628 ÷ 931 = _____

17. 66,253 ÷ 317 = _____

18. 76,255 ÷ 309 = _____

19. 50,779 ÷ 590 = _____

20. 97,156 ÷ 107 = _____

21. 216,016 ÷ 368 = _____

22. 107,609 ÷ 72 = _____

23. Emilio has 8,450 trees to plant in rows on his tree farm. He will plant 125 trees per row. How many full rows of trees will he have? Explain.

_____

_____

24. Camilla makes and sells jewelry. She has 8,160 silver beads and 2,880 black beads to make necklaces. Each necklace will contain 85 silver beads and 30 black beads. How many necklaces can she make? _____

25. During a promotional weekend, a state fair gives a free admission to every 175th person who enters the fair. On Saturday, there were 6,742 people attending the fair. On Sunday, there were 5,487 people attending the fair. How many people received a free admission over the two days?

_____

26. How is the quotient 80,000 ÷ 2,000 different from the quotient 80,000 ÷ 200 or 80,000 ÷ 20?

_____

_____

27. Given that 9,554 ÷ 562 = 17, how can you find the quotient 95,540 ÷ 562?

_____

_____

28. **Earth Science** The diameter of the Moon is about 3,476 kilometers. The distance from Earth to the Moon is about 384,400 kilometers. About how many moons could be lined up in a row between Earth and the Moon? Round to the nearest whole number.

_____

Diameter 3,476 km

29. Vocabulary Explain how you could check the answer to a division question in which there is a remainder.

_____

_____

_____

30. Yolanda is buying a car with a base price of $16,750. She must also pay the options, fees, and taxes shown. The car dealership will give her 48 months to pay off the entire amount. Yolanda can only afford to pay $395 each month. Will she be able to buy the car? Explain.

Jackson Auto Dealer		
4-door sedan		
	base price	**$16,750**
	options	**$ 500**
	fees	**$ 370**
	taxes	**$ 1,425**

_____

_____

_____

H.O.T.   FOCUS ON HIGHER ORDER THINKING

Work Area

31. Check for Reasonableness Is 40 a reasonable estimate of a quotient for 78,114 ÷ 192? Explain your reasoning.

_____

_____

32. Critique Reasoning Harrison predicted that the actual quotient for 57,872 ÷ 305 will be less than the estimate 60,000 ÷ 300 = 200. Is Harrison correct? Explain how Harrison arrived at his prediction (without dividing the actual numbers).

_____

_____

_____

33. Make a Prediction In preparation for a storm, the town council buys 13,750 pounds of sand to fill sandbags. Volunteers are trying to decide whether to fill bags that can hold 25 pounds of sand or bags that can hold 50 pounds of sand. Will they have more or fewer sandbags if they fill the 25-pound bags? How many more or fewer? Explain your reasoning.

_____

_____

_____

LESSON
5.2 Adding and Subtracting Decimals

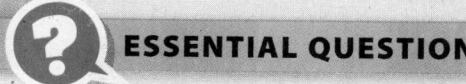

FL 6.NS.2.3
Fluently add [and] subtract...
decimals using the standard
algorithm....

 ESSENTIAL QUESTION

How do you add and subtract decimals?

EXPLORE ACTIVITY FL 6.NS.2.3

Modeling Decimal Addition

You have probably used decimal grids to model decimals. For example, the decimal 0.25, or $\frac{25}{100}$, can be modeled by shading 25 squares in a 10 × 10 grid. You can also use decimal grids to add decimal values.

A chemist combines 0.17 mL of water and 0.49 mL of hydrogen peroxide in a beaker. How much total liquid is in the beaker?

A How many grid squares should you shade to represent 0.17 mL of water? Why?

_____

B How many grid squares should you shade to represent 0.49 mL of hydrogen peroxide?

_____

C Use the grid at the right to model the addition. Use one color for 0.17 mL of water and another color for 0.49 mL of hydrogen peroxide.

D How much total liquid is in the beaker? 0.17 + 0.49 = _____ mL

Reflect

Multiple Representations **Show how to shade each grid to represent the sum. Then find the sum.**

1. 0.24 + 0.71 = _____

2. 0.08 + 0.65 = _____

Adding Decimals

Adding decimals is similar to adding whole numbers. First align the numbers by place value. Start adding at the right and regroup when necessary. Bring down the decimal point into your answer.

EXAMPLE 1   **FL** 6.NS.2.3

Susan rode her bicycle 3.12 miles on Monday and 4.7 miles on Tuesday. How many miles did she ride in all?

STEP 1 Align the decimal points.

STEP 2 Add zeros as placeholders when necessary.

	3	.	1	2
+	4	.	7	0
	7	.	8	2

STEP 3 Add from right to left.

Susan rode 7.82 miles in all.

STEP 4 Use estimation to check that the answer is reasonable. Round each decimal to the nearest whole number.

$$
\begin{array}{ccc}
3.12 & \longrightarrow & 3 \\
+\,4.70 & \longrightarrow & +\,5 \\
\hline
7.82 & & 8
\end{array}
$$

Since 8 is close to 7.82, the answer is reasonable.

Reflect

3. Why can you rewrite 4.7 as 4.70?

_____

_____

4. Why is it important to align the decimal points when adding?

_____

_____

© Houghton Mifflin Harcourt Publishing Company • Image Credits: Jacek Chabraszewski / Shutterstock

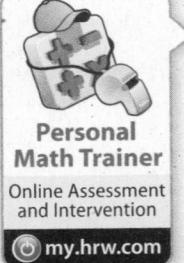
YOUR TURN

Add.

5. 0.42 + 0.27 = _____

6. 0.61 + 0.329 = _____

7. 3.25 + 4.6 = _____

8. 17.27 + 3.88 = _____

Subtracting Decimals

The procedure for subtracting decimals is similar to the procedure for adding decimals.

EXAMPLE 2   **FL** 6.NS.2.3

Math On the Spot
my.hrw.com

A Mia is 160.2 centimeters tall. Rosa is 165.1 centimeters tall. How much taller is Rosa than Mia?

STEP 1 Align the decimal points.

STEP 2 Add zeros as placeholders when necessary.

STEP 3 Subtract from right to left, regrouping when necessary.

	1	6	5⁴	.	1¹
−	1	6	0	.	2
			4	.	9

My Notes

Rosa is 4.9 centimeters taller than Mia.

To check that your answer is reasonable, you can estimate. Round each decimal to the nearest whole number.

$$
\begin{array}{c}
165.1 \longrightarrow 165 \\
-\ 160.2 \longrightarrow -\ 160 \\
\hline
4.9 \qquad\qquad 5
\end{array}
$$

Since 5 is close to 4.9, the answer is reasonable.

B Matthew throws a discus 58.7 meters. Zachary throws the discus 56.12 meters. How much farther did Matthew throw the discus?

STEP 1 Align the decimal points.

STEP 2 Add zeros as placeholders when necessary.

STEP 3 Subtract from right to left, regrouping when necessary.

	5	8	.	7⁶	0¹⁰
−	5	6	.	1	2
		2	.	5	8

Matthew threw the discus 2.58 meters farther than Zachary.

To check that your answer is reasonable, you can estimate. Round each decimal to the nearest whole number.

$$
\begin{array}{c}
58.7 \longrightarrow 59 \\
-\ 56.12 \longrightarrow -\ 56 \\
\hline
2.58 \qquad\qquad 3
\end{array}
$$

Math Talk
Mathematical Practices

How can you check a subtraction problem?

Since 3 is close to 2.58, the answer is reasonable.

© Houghton Mifflin Harcourt Publishing Company

Shade the grid to find each sum. (Explore Activity)

1. 0.72 + 0.19 = _____

2. 0.38 + 0.4 = _____

Add. Check that your answer is reasonable. (Example 1)

3.   54.87 ——→ 55
        + 7.48 ——→ + 7

4.   2.19 ——→ ☐
        + 34.92 ——→ + ☐

5.   0.215 ——→ ☐
        + 3.74 ——→ + ☐

Subtract. Check that your answer is reasonable. (Example 2)

6.   9.73 ——→ 10
        − 7.16 ——→ − 7

7.   18.419 ——→ ☐
        − 6.47 ——→ − ☐

8.   5.006 ——→ ☐
        − 3.2 ——→ − ☐

Add or subtract. (Example 1, Example 2)

9. 17.2 + 12.9 = _____

10. 28.341 + 37.5 = _____

11. 25.36 − 2.004 = _____

12. 15.52 − 8.17 = _____

13. 25.68 + 12 = _____

14. 150.25 − 78 = _____

15. Perry connects a blue garden hose and a green garden hose to make one long hose. The blue hose is 16.5 feet. The green hose is 14.75 feet. How long is the combined hose? (Example 1) _____

16. Keisha has $20.08 in her purse. She buys a book for $8.72. How much does she have left? (Example 2) _____

? ESSENTIAL QUESTION CHECK-IN

17. How is adding and subtracting decimals similar to adding and subtracting whole numbers?

_____

_____

5.2 Independent Practice

 FL 6.NS.2.3

Personal Math Trainer
Online Assessment and Intervention
my.hrw.com

Add or subtract.

18. $28.6 - 0.975 = $ _____

19. $5.6 - 0.105 = $ _____

20. $7.03 + 33.006 = $ _____

21. $57.42 + 4 + 1.602 = $ _____

22. $2.25 + 65.47 + 2.333 = $ _____

23. $18.419 - 6.47 = $ _____

24. $83 - 12.76 = $ _____

25. $102.01 - 95.602 = $ _____

26. **Multiple Representations** Ursula wrote the sum $5.815 + 6.021$ as a sum of two mixed numbers.

    a. What sum did she write? _____

    b. Compare the sum of the mixed numbers to the sum of the decimals. _____

Use the café menu to answer 27–29.

27. Stephen and Jahmya are having lunch. Stephen buys a garden salad, a veggie burger, and lemonade. Jahmya buys a fruit salad, a toasted cheese sandwich, and a bottle of water. Whose lunch cost more? How much more?

_____

28. Jahmya wants to leave $1.75 as a tip for her server. She has a $20 bill. How much change should she receive after paying for her food and leaving a tip?

_____

29. **What If?** In addition to his meal, Stephen orders a fruit salad for take-out, and wants to leave $2.25 as a tip for his server. He has a $10 bill and a $5 bill. How much change should he receive after paying for his lunch, the fruit salad, and the tip?

_____

30. A carpenter who is installing cabinets uses thin pieces of material called shims to fill gaps. The carpenter uses four shims to fill a gap that is 1.2 centimeters wide. Three of the shims are 0.75 centimeter, 0.125 centimeter, and 0.09 centimeter wide. What is the width of the fourth shim?

_____

> ### Café Menu
>
>
> Garden Salad **$2.29**
> Fruit Salad **$2.89**
>
> Veggie Burger **$4.75**
> Toasted Cheese Sandwich **$4.59**
>
> Bottle of Water **$1.39**
> Lemonade **$1.29**

31. A CD of classical guitar music contains 5 songs. The length of each song is shown in the table.

Track 1	Track 2	Track 3	Track 4	Track 5
6.5 minutes	8 minutes	3.93 minutes	4.1 minutes	5.05 minutes

a. Between each song is a 0.05-minute break. How long does it take to listen to the CD from the beginning of the first song to the end of the last song? _____

b. **What If?** Juan wants to buy the CD from an Internet music site. He downloads the CD onto a disc that can hold up to 60 minutes of music. How many more minutes of music can he still buy after downloading the CD? _____

 FOCUS ON HIGHER ORDER THINKING

32. **Analyze Relationships** Use the decimals 2.47, 9.57, and 7.1 to write two different addition facts and two different subtraction facts.

_____

_____

33. **Communicate Mathematical Ideas** The Commutative Property of Addition states that you can change the order of addends in a sum. The Associative Property of Addition states that you can change the grouping of addends in a sum. Use an example to show how the Commutative Property of Addition and the Associative Property of Addition apply to adding decimals.

_____

_____

_____

_____

_____

34. **Critique Reasoning** Indira predicts that the actual difference of $19 - 7.82$ will be greater than the estimate of $19 - 8 = 11$. Is Indira correct? Explain how Indira might have arrived at that prediction without subtracting the actual numbers.

_____

_____

_____

Work Area

© Houghton Mifflin Harcourt Publishing Company • Image Credits: ©Creatas/ Getty Images

LESSON
5.3 Multiplying Decimals

FL 6.NS.2.3
Fluently...multiply...
multi-digit decimals using
the standard algorithm....

? ESSENTIAL QUESTION

How do you multiply decimals?

EXPLORE ACTIVITY FL 6.NS.2.3

Modeling Decimal Multiplication

Use decimal grids or area models to find each product.

A **0.3 × 0.5**

0.3 × 0.5 represents 0.3 of 0.5. Shade 5 *rows* of the decimal grid to represent 0.5.

Shade 0.3 of each 0.1 that is already shaded

to represent 0.3 of _____.

_____ square(s) are double-shaded.

This represents _____ hundredth(s), or 0.15.

0.3 × 0.5 = _____

0.3

0.5

B **3.2 × 2.1**

Use an area model. In the model, the large squares represent wholes, the small rectangles along the right and lower edges represent tenths, and the small squares at the lower right represent hundredths. The model is 3 and 2 tenths units long, and 2 and 1 tenth unit wide.

The area of the model is

_____ whole(s) + _____ tenth(s) + _____ hundredth(s) square units.

3.2 × 2.1 = _____

3.2

2.1

Reflect

1. **Analyze Relationships** How are the products 2.1 × 3.2 and 21 × 32 alike? How are they different?

_____

_____

Math On the Spot
my.hrw.com

Multiplying Decimals

To multiply decimals, first multiply as you would with whole numbers. Then place the decimal point in the product. The number of decimal places in the product equals the sum of the number of decimal places in the factors.

EXAMPLE 1   **FL** 6.NS.2.3

Delia bought 3.8 pounds of peppers. The peppers cost $1.99 per pound. What was the total cost of Delia's peppers?

$$
\begin{array}{r}
1.99 \\
\times\ 3.8 \\
\hline
1592 \\
+\ 5970 \\
\hline
7.562
\end{array}
$$

← 2 decimal places
← + 1 decimal place

← 3 decimal places

The peppers cost $7.56.

> Round the answer to hundredths to show a dollar amount.

Reflect

1. **Communicate Mathematical Ideas** How can you use estimation to check that you have placed the decimal point correctly in your product?

_____

_____

_____

_____

_____

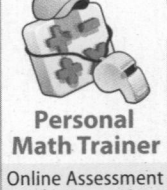

Personal Math Trainer
Online Assessment and Intervention
my.hrw.com

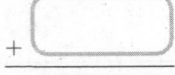 **YOUR TURN**

Multiply.

2. 12.6 ← ☐ decimal place(s)

    × 15.3 ← + ☐ decimal place(s)

    378

    ☐

    ☐

    + ☐

    ☐ ← ☐ decimal place(s)

3. 9.76 ← ☐ decimal place(s)

    × 0.46 ← + ☐ decimal place(s)

    ☐

    ☐

    + ☐

    ☐ ← ☐ decimal place(s)

Estimating to Check Reasonableness

In Example 1, you used estimation to check whether the decimal point was placed correctly in the product. You can also use estimation to check that your answer is reasonable.

EXAMPLE 2 Real World

FL 6.NS.2.3

Blades of grass grow 3.75 inches per month. If the grass continues to grow at this rate, how much will the grass grow in 6.25 months?

$$
\begin{array}{r}
3.75 \quad \leftarrow \quad \text{2 decimal places} \\
\times\ 6.25 \quad \leftarrow + \quad \text{2 decimal places} \\
\hline
1875 \\
7500 \\
+\ 225000 \\
\hline
23.4375 \quad \leftarrow \quad \text{4 decimal places}
\end{array}
$$

The grass will grow 23.4375 inches in 6.25 months.

Estimate to check whether your answer is reasonable.

Round 3.75 to the nearest whole number. _____

Round 6.25 to the nearest whole number. _____

Multiply the whole numbers. _____ × _____ = 24

The answer is reasonable because 24 is close to 23.4375.

My Notes

YOUR TURN

Multiply.

4.
$$
\begin{array}{r}
7.14 \\
\times\ 6.78 \\
\hline
5712 \\
\end{array}
$$

5.
$$
\begin{array}{r}
11.49 \\
\times\ 8.27 \\
\hline
\end{array}
$$

6. Rico bicycles at an average speed of 15.5 miles per hour.

   What distance will Rico bicycle in 2.4 hours? _____ miles

7. Use estimation to show that your answer to **7** is reasonable.

   _____

1. Use the grid to multiply 0.4 × 0.7.
(Explore Activity)

0.4 × 0.7 = _____

2. Draw an area model to multiply 1.1 × 2.4.
(Explore Activity)

1.1 × 2.4 = _____

Multiply. (Example 1 and Example 2)

3. 0.18 × 0.06 = _____

4. 35.15 × 3.7 = _____

5. 0.96 × 0.12 = _____

6. 62.19 × 32.5 = _____

7. 3.4 × 4.37 = _____

8. 3.762 × 0.66 = _____

9. Chan Hee bought 3.4 pounds of coffee that cost $6.95 per pound.

How much did he spend on coffee? $_____

10. Adita earns $9.40 per hour working at an animal shelter.

How much money will she earn for 18.5 hours of work? $_____

Catherine tracked her gas purchases for one month.

11. How much did Catherine spend on gas in week 2?

$_____

12. How much more did she spend in week 4 than

in week 1? $_____

Week	Gallons	Cost per gallon ($)
1	10.4	2.65
2	11.5	2.54
3	9.72	2.75
4	10.6	2.70

? ESSENTIAL QUESTION CHECK-IN

13. How can you check the answer to a decimal multiplication problem?

_____

_____

Name_____ Class_____ Date_____

5.3 Independent Practice

 FL 6.NS.2.3

Make a reasonable estimate for each situation.

14. A gallon of water weighs 8.354 pounds. Simon uses 11.81 gallons of water while taking a shower. About how many pounds of water did Simon use?

15. A snail moves at a speed of 2.394 inches per minute. If the snail keeps moving at this rate, about how many inches will it travel in 7.489 minutes?

16. Tricia's garden is 9.87 meters long and 1.09 meters wide. What is the area of her garden?

Kaylynn and Amanda both work at the same store. The table shows how much each person earns, and the number of hours each person works in a week.

	Wage	Hours worked per week
Kaylynn	$8.75 per hour	37.5
Amanda	$10.25 per hour	30.5

17. Estimate how much Kaylynn earns in a week.

18. Estimate how much Amanda earns in a week.

19. Calculate the exact difference between Kaylynn and Amanda's weekly salaries.

20. Victoria's printer can print 8.804 pages in one minute. If Victoria prints pages for 0.903 minutes, about how many pages will she have?

A taxi charges a flat fee of $4.00 plus $2.25 per mile.

21. How much will it cost to travel 8.7 miles? _____

22. **Multistep** How much will the taxi driver earn if he takes one passenger 4.8 miles and another passenger 7.3 miles? Explain your process.

_____

_____

_____

© Houghton Mifflin Harcourt Publishing Company

Kay goes for several bike rides one week. The table shows her speed and the number of hours spent per ride.

	Speed (in miles per hour)	Hours Spent on Bike
Monday	8.2	4.25
Tuesday	9.6	3.1
Wednesday	11.1	2.8
Thursday	10.75	1.9
Friday	8.8	3.75

23. How many miles did Kay bike on Thursday? _____

24. On which day did Kay bike a whole number of miles? _____

25. What is the difference in miles between Kay's longest bike ride and her shortest bike ride? _____

26. Check for Reasonableness Kay estimates that Wednesday's ride was about 3 miles longer than Tuesday's ride. Is her estimate reasonable? Explain.

_____

_____

_____

_____

 FOCUS ON HIGHER ORDER THINKING

Work Area

27. Explain the Error To estimate the product 3.48 × 7.33, Marisa multiplied 4 × 8 to get 32. Explain how she can make a closer estimate.

_____

28. Represent Real-World Problems A jeweler buys gold jewelry and resells the gold to a refinery. The jeweler buys gold for $1,235.55 per ounce, and then resells it for $1,376.44 per ounce. How much profit does the jeweler make from buying and reselling 73.5 ounces of gold?

_____

29. Problem Solving To find the weight of the gold in a 22 karat gold object, multiply the object's weight by 0.917. To find the weight of the gold in a 14 karat gold object, multiply the object's weight by 0.583. A 22 karat gold statue and a 14 karat gold statue both weigh 73.5 ounces. Which one contains more gold? How much more gold does it contain?

_____

5.4 Dividing Decimals

FL   6.NS.2.3
Fluently...divide multi-digit decimals using the standard algorithm....

ESSENTIAL QUESTION

How do you divide decimals?

EXPLORE ACTIVITY FL 6.NS.2.3

Modeling Decimal Division

Use decimal grids to find each quotient.

A 6.39 ÷ 3

Shade grids to model 6.39. Separate the model into 3 equal groups.

How many are in each group? _____

6.39 ÷ 3 = _____

B 6.39 ÷ 2.13

Shade grids to model 6.39. Separate the model into groups of 2.13.

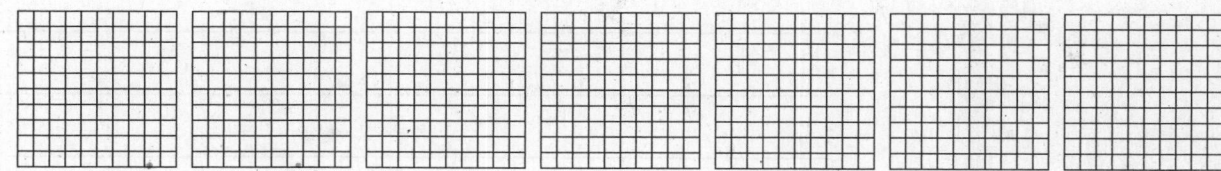

How many groups do you have? _____

6.39 ÷ 2.13 = _____

Reflect

1. **Multiple Representations** When using models to divide decimals, when might you want to use grids divided into tenths instead of hundredths?

_____

_____

Dividing Decimals by Whole Numbers

Dividing decimals is similar to dividing whole numbers. When you divide a decimal by a whole number, the placement of the decimal point in the quotient is determined by the placement of the decimal in the dividend.

EXAMPLE 1   FL 6.NS.2.3

A **A high school track is 9.76 meters wide. It is divided into 8 lanes of equal width for track and field events. How wide is each lane?**

Divide using long division as with whole numbers.

Place a decimal point in the quotient directly above the decimal point in the dividend.

Each lane is 1.22 meters wide.

$$\begin{array}{r} 1.22 \\ 8\overline{)9.76} \\ -8 \\ \hline 17 \\ -16 \\ \hline 16 \\ -16 \\ \hline 0 \end{array}$$

B **Aerobics classes cost $153.86 for 14 sessions. What is the fee for one session?**

Divide using long division as with whole numbers.

Place a decimal point in the quotient directly above the decimal point in the dividend.

The fee for one aerobics class is $10.99.

$$\begin{array}{r} 10.99 \\ 14\overline{)153.86} \\ -14 \\ \hline 13 \\ -0 \\ \hline 13\,8 \\ -12\,6 \\ \hline 1\,26 \\ -1\,26 \\ \hline 0 \end{array}$$

Reflect

2. **Check for Reasonableness** How can you estimate to check that your quotient in **A** is reasonable?

_____

_____

_____

_____

YOUR TURN

Divide.

3. $5\overline{)9.75}$

4. $7\overline{)6.44}$

Math Talk
Mathematical Practices

How can you check to see that the answer is correct?

My Notes

Math On the Spot
my.hrw.com

Personal Math Trainer
Online Assessment and Intervention
my.hrw.com

Dividing a Decimal by a Decimal

When dividing a decimal by a decimal, first change the divisor to a whole number by multiplying by a power of 10. Then multiply the dividend by the same power of 10.

EXAMPLE 2   **FL** 6.NS.2.3

A Ella uses 0.5 pound of raspberries in each raspberry cake that she makes. How many cakes can Ella make with 3.25 pounds of raspberries?

STEP 1 The divisor has one decimal place, so multiply both the dividend and the divisor by 10 so that the divisor is a whole number.

$0.5\overline{)3.25}$ $0.5\overline{)3.25}$

$0.5 \times 10 = 5$

$3.25 \times 10 = 32.5$

Ella can make 6 cakes.

STEP 2 Divide.

$$\begin{array}{r} 6.5 \\ 5\overline{)32.5} \\ -30 \\ \hline 2\ 5 \\ -2\ 5 \\ \hline 0 \end{array}$$

B Anthony spent $11.52 for some pens that were on sale for $0.72 each. How many pens did Anthony buy?

STEP 1 The divisor has two decimal places, so multiply both the dividend and the divisor by 100 so that the divisor is a whole number.

$0.72\overline{)11.52}$ $0.72\overline{)11.52}$

$0.72 \times 100 = 72$

$11.52 \times 100 = 1152$

Anthony bought 16 pens.

STEP 2 Divide.

$$\begin{array}{r} 16 \\ 72\overline{)1152} \\ -72 \\ \hline 432 \\ -432 \\ \hline 0 \end{array}$$

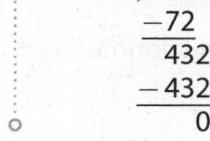

Math Talk
Mathematical Practices

The number of cakes Ella can make is not equal to the quotient. Why not?

YOUR TURN

Divide.

5. $0.5\overline{)4.25}$

6. $0.84\overline{)15.12}$

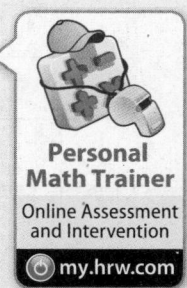

Personal Math Trainer

Online Assessment and Intervention

my.hrw.com

Guided Practice

Divide. (Explore Activity, Examples 1 and 2)

1. $4\overline{)29.5}$ _____

2. $3.1\overline{)10.261}$ _____

3. $2.4\overline{)16.8}$ _____

4. $0.96\overline{)0.144}$ _____

5. $38.5 \div 0.5 =$ _____

6. $23.85 \div 9 =$ _____

7. $5.6372 \div 0.17 =$ _____

8. $8.19 \div 4.2 =$ _____

9. $66.5 \div 3.5 =$ _____

10. $0.234 \div 0.78 =$ _____

11. $78.74 \div 12.7 =$ _____

12. $36.45 \div 0.09 =$ _____

13. $90 \div 0.36 =$ _____

14. $18.88 \div 1.6 =$ _____

15. Corrine has 9.6 pounds of trail mix to divide into 12 bags. How many pounds of trail mix will go in each bag? _____

16. Michael paid $11.48 for sliced cheese at the deli counter. The cheese cost $3.28 per pound. How much cheese did Michael buy? _____

17. A four-person relay team completed a race in 72.4 seconds. On average, what was each runner's time? _____

18. Elizabeth has a piece of ribbon that is 4.5 meters long. She wants to cut it into pieces that are 0.25 meter long. How many pieces of ribbon will she have? _____

19. Lisa paid $43.95 for 16.1 gallons of gasoline. What was the cost per gallon, rounded to the nearest hundredth? _____

20. One inch is equivalent to 2.54 centimeters. How many inches are there in 50.8 centimeters? _____

? ESSENTIAL QUESTION CHECK-IN

21. When you are dividing two decimals, how can you check whether you have divided the decimals correctly?

_____

_____

_____

_____

Name_____ Class_____ Date_____

5.4 Independent Practice

 FL 6.NS.2.3

Personal Math Trainer
my.hrw.com
Online Assessment and Intervention

Use the table for 22 and 23.

Custom Printing Costs				
Quantity	25	50	75	100
Mugs	$107.25	$195.51	$261.75	$329.00
T-shirts	$237.50	$441.00	$637.50	$829.00

22. What is the price per mug for 25 coffee mugs? _____

23. Find the price per T-shirt for 75 T-shirts. _____

A movie rental website charges $5.00 per month for membership and $1.25 per movie.

24. How many movies did Andrew rent this month if this month's bill was $16.25? _____

25. Marissa has $18.50 this month to spend on movie rentals.

    a. How many movies can she view this month? _____

    b. Critique Reasoning Marisa thinks she can afford 11 movies in one month. What mistake could she be making?

    _____

    _____

Victoria went shopping for ingredients to make a stew. The table shows the weight and the cost of each of the ingredients that she bought.

Ingredient	Weight (in pounds)	Cost
Potatoes	6.3	$7.56
Carrots	8.5	$15.30
Beef	4	$9.56
Bell peppers	2.50	$1.25

26. What is the price for one pound of bell peppers? _____

27. Which ingredient costs the most per pound? _____

28. What If? If carrots were $0.50 less per pound, how much would Victoria have paid for 8.5 pounds of carrots? _____

© Houghton Mifflin Harcourt Publishing Company

29. Brenda is planning her birthday party. She wants to have 10.92 liters of punch, 6.5 gallons of ice cream, 3.9 pounds of fudge, and 25 guests at the birthday party.

a. Brenda and each guest drink the same amount of punch. How many liters of punch will each person drink? _____

b. Brenda and each guest eat the same amount of ice cream. How many gallons of ice cream will each person eat? _____

c. Brenda and each guest eat the same amount of fudge. How many pounds of fudge will each person eat? _____

To make costumes for a play, Cassidy needs yellow and white fabric that she will cut into strips. The table shows how many yards of each fabric she needs, and how much she will pay for those yards.

Fabric	Yards	Cost
Yellow	12.8	$86.40
White	9.5	$45.60

30. Which costs more per yard, the yellow fabric or the white fabric? _____

31. Cassidy wants to cut the yellow fabric into strips that are 0.3 yards wide. How many strips of yellow fabric can Cassidy make? _____

 FOCUS ON HIGHER ORDER THINKING

32. Problem Solving Eight friends purchase various supplies for a camping trip and agree to share the total cost equally. They spend $85.43 on food, $32.75 on water, and $239.66 on other items. How much does each person owe? _____

33. Analyze Relationships Constance is saving money to buy a new bicycle that costs $195.75. She already has $40 saved and plans to save $8 each week. How many weeks will it take her to save enough money to purchase the bicycle? _____

34. Represent Real-World Problems A grocery store sells twelve bottles of water for $13.80. A convenience store sells ten bottles of water for $11.80. Which store has the better buy? Explain.

_____

_____

_____

LESSON 5.5 Applying Operations with Rational Numbers

FL 6.NS.2.3
Fluently add, subtract, multiply, and divide multi-digit decimals....

? ESSENTIAL QUESTION

How can you solve problems involving multiplication and division of fractions and decimals?

Interpreting a Word Problem

When you solve a word problem involving rational numbers, you often need to think about the problem to decide which operations to use.

EXAMPLE 1 Problem Solving **FL 6.NS.2.3**

Math On the Spot
my.hrw.com

Naomi earned $54 mowing lawns in two days. She worked 2.5 hours yesterday and 4.25 hours today. If Naomi was paid the same amount for every hour she works, how much did she earn per hour?

Analyze Information

Identify the important information.

• Naomi made $54 mowing lawns.

• Naomi worked 2.5 hours yesterday and 4.25 hours today.

• You are asked to find how much she earned per hour.

Formulate a Plan

• The total amount she earned divided by the total hours she worked gives the amount she earns per hour.

• Use the expression 54 ÷ (2.5 + 4.25) to find the amount she earned per hour.

Solve

Follow the order of operations.

(2.5 + 4.25) = 6.75   Add inside parentheses.

54 ÷ 6.75 = 8   Divide.

Naomi earned $8 per hour mowing lawns.

Justify and Evaluate

You added 2.5 and 4.25 first to find the total number of hours worked. Then you divided 54 by the sum to find the amount earned per hour.

© Houghton Mifflin Harcourt Publishing Company • Image Credits: Corbis Bridge / Alamy

Lesson 5.5 **131**

YOUR TURN

1. Casey buys 6.2 yards of blue fabric and 5.4 yards of red fabric. If the blue and red fabric cost the same amount per yard, and Casey pays $58 for all of the fabric, what is the cost per yard?

_____

Converting Fractions and Decimals to Solve Problems

Recall that you can use a number line to find equivalent fractions and decimals. If a fraction and a decimal are equivalent, they are represented by the same point on a number line.

EXAMPLE 2   **FL** 6.NS.2.3

Each part of a multipart question on a test is worth the same number of points. The whole question is worth 37.5 points. Roz got $\frac{1}{2}$ of the parts of a question correct. How many points did Roz receive?

Solution 1

STEP 1 Convert the decimal to a fraction greater than 1.

$$\frac{1}{2} \times 37.5 = \frac{1}{2} \times \frac{75}{2}$$ Write 37.5 as $37\frac{1}{2}$, or $\frac{75}{2}$.

STEP 2 Multiply. Write the product in simplest form.

$$\frac{1}{2} \times \frac{75}{2} = \frac{75}{4} = 18\frac{3}{4}$$ Roz received $18\frac{3}{4}$ points.

Solution 2

STEP 1 Convert the fraction to a decimal.

$$\frac{1}{2} \times 37.5 = 0.5 \times 37.5$$

STEP 2 Multiply.

$$0.5 \times 37.5 = 18.75$$ Roz received 18.75 points.

Math Talk

Mathematical Practices

Do the solutions give the same result? Explain.

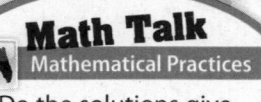

YOUR TURN

2. The bill for a pizza was $14.50. Charles paid for $\frac{3}{5}$ of the bill. Show two ways to find how much he paid.

_____

© Houghton Mifflin Harcourt Publishing Company

Name_____ Class_____ Date_____

5.5 Guided Practice

1. Bob and Cheryl are taking a road trip that is 188.3 miles. Bob drove $\frac{5}{7}$ of the total distance. How many miles did Bob drive? (Example 1) _____

2. The winner of a raffle will receive $\frac{3}{4}$ of the $530.40 raised from raffle ticket sales. How much money will the winner get? (Example 2) _____

5.5 Independent Practice

 FL 6.NS.2.3

Personal Math Trainer

Online Assessment and Intervention

⏻ my.hrw.com

3. Chanasia has 8.75 gallons of paint. She wants to use $\frac{2}{5}$ of the paint to paint her living room. How many gallons of paint will Chanasia use?

_____

4. Harold bought 3 pounds of red apples and 4.2 pounds of green apples from a grocery store, where both kinds of apples are $1.75 a pound. How much did Harold spend on apples?

_____

Samuel and Jason sell cans to a recycling center that pays $0.40 per pound of cans. The table shows the number of pounds of cans that they sold for several days.

Day	Samuel's cans (pounds)	Jason's cans (pounds)
Monday	16.2	11.5
Tuesday	11.8	10.7
Wednesday	12.5	7.1

5. Samuel wants to use his earnings from Monday and Tuesday to buy some batteries that cost $5.60 each. How many batteries can Samuel buy? Show your work.

_____

6. Jason wants to use his earnings from Monday and Tuesday for online movie rentals. The movies cost $2.96 each to rent. How many movies can Jason rent? Show your work.

_____

7. **Multistep** Samuel and Jason spend $\frac{3}{4}$ of their combined earnings from Wednesday to buy a gift. How much do they spend? Is there enough left over from Wednesday's earnings to buy a card that costs $3.25? Explain.

_____

_____

© Houghton Mifflin Harcourt Publishing Company • Image Credits: Photodisc/ Getty Images

8. Multiple Representations Give an example of a problem that could be solved using the expression 9.5 × (8 + 12.5). Solve your problem.

_____

_____

_____

_____

Tony and Alice are trying to reduce the amount of television they watch. For every hour they watch television, they have to put $2.50 into savings. The table shows how many hours of television Tony and Alice have watched in the past two months.

	Hours watched in February	Hours watched in March
Tony	35.4	18.2
Alice	21.8	26.6

9. Tony wants to use his savings at the end of March to buy video games. The games cost $35.75 each. How many games can Tony buy?

_____

10. Alice wants to use her savings at the end of the two months to buy concert tickets. If the tickets cost $17.50 each, how many can she buy?

_____

 FOCUS ON HIGHER ORDER THINKING

Work Area

11. Represent Real-World Problems A caterer prepares three times as many pizzas as she usually prepares for a large party. The caterer usually prepares 5 pizzas. The caterer also estimates that each party guest will eat $\frac{1}{3}$ of a pizza. Write an expression that represents this situation. How many party guests will the pizzas serve?

_____

Nadia charges $7.50 an hour for babysitting. She babysits 18.5 hours the first week of the month and 20 hours the second week of the month.

12. Explain the Error To find her total earnings for those two weeks, Nadia writes 7.5 × 18.5 + 20 = $158.75. Explain her error. Show the correct solution.

_____

_____

_____

13. What If? Suppose Nadia raises her rate by $0.75 an hour. How many hours would she need to work to earn the same amount of money she made in the first two weeks of the month? Explain.

_____

© Houghton Mifflin Harcourt Publishing Company

Ready to Go On?

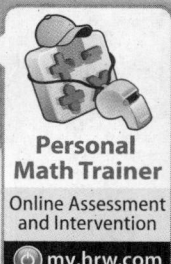

Personal Math Trainer
Online Assessment and Intervention
my.hrw.com

5.1 Dividing Whole Numbers

1. Landon is building new bookshelves for his bookstore's new mystery section. Each shelf can hold 34 books. There are 1,265 mystery books. How many shelves will he need to build? _____

5.2 Adding and Subtracting Decimals

2. On Saturday Keisha ran 3.218 kilometers. On Sunday she ran 2.41 kilometers. How much farther did she run on Saturday than on Sunday? _____

5.3 Multiplying Decimals

3. Marta walked at 3.9 miles per hour for 0.72 hours. How far did she walk? _____

Multiply.

4. 0.07×1.22 _____   **5.** 4.7×2.65 _____

5.4 Dividing Decimals

Divide.

6. $64 \div 0.4$ _____   **7.** $4.7398 \div 0.26$ _____

8. $26.73 \div 9$ _____   **9.** $4 \div 3.2$ _____

5.5 Applying Multiplication and Division of Rational Numbers

10. Doors for the small cabinets are 11.5 inches long. Doors for the large cabinets are 2.3 times as long as the doors for the small cabinets. How many large doors can be cut from a board that is $10\frac{1}{2}$ feet long? _____

? ESSENTIAL QUESTION

11. Describe a real-world situation that could be modeled by dividing two rational numbers.

_____

_____

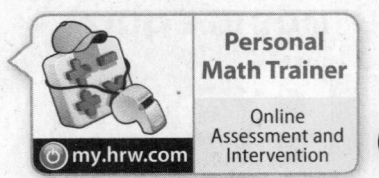

Personal
Math Trainer

Online
Assessment and
Intervention

my.hrw.com

Selected Response

1. Delia has 493 stamps in her stamp collection. She can put 16 stamps on each page of an album. How many pages can she fill completely?

Ⓐ 30 pages   Ⓒ 31 pages

Ⓑ 32 pages   Ⓓ 33 pages

2. Sumeet uses 0.4 gallon of gasoline each hour mowing lawns. How much gas does he use in 4.2 hours?

Ⓐ 1.68 gallons

Ⓑ 3.8 gallons

Ⓒ 13 gallons

Ⓓ 16 gallons

3. Sharon spent $3.45 on sunflower seeds. The price of sunflower seeds is $0.89 per pound. How many pounds of sunflower seeds did Sharon buy?

Ⓐ 3.07 pounds

Ⓑ 3.88 pounds

Ⓒ 4.15 pounds

Ⓓ 4.34 pounds

4. How many 0.4-liter glasses of water does it take to fill up a 3.4-liter pitcher?

Ⓐ 1.36 glasses   Ⓒ 8.2 glasses

Ⓑ 3.8 glasses   Ⓓ 8.5 glasses

5. Each paper clip is $\frac{3}{4}$ of an inch long and costs $0.02. Exactly enough paper clips are laid end to end to have a total length of 36 inches. What is the total cost of these paper clips?

Ⓐ $0.36   Ⓒ $0.96

Ⓑ $0.54   Ⓓ $1.20

6. Nelson Middle School raised $19,950 on ticket sales for its carnival fundraiser last year at $15 per ticket. If the school sells the same number of tickets this year but charges $20 per ticket, how much money will the school make?

Ⓐ $20,600   Ⓒ $26,600

Ⓑ $21,600   Ⓓ $30,600

7. Keri walks her dog every morning. The length of the walk is 0.55 kilometer on each weekday. On each weekend day, the walk is 1.4 times as long as a walk on a weekday. How many kilometers does Keri walk in one week?

Ⓐ 2.75 kilometers

Ⓑ 3.85 kilometers

Ⓒ 4.29 kilometers

Ⓓ 5.39 kilometers

Mini-Task

8. To prepare for a wedding, Aiden bought 60 candles. He paid $0.37 for each candle. His sister bought 170 candles at a sale where she paid $0.05 less for each candle than Aiden did.

a. How much did Aiden spend on candles?

_____

b. How much did Aiden's sister spend on candles?

_____

c. Who spent more on candles? How much more?

_____

Study Guide Review

MODULE 4 · Operations with Fractions

Key Vocabulary
reciprocals *(recíprocos)*

? ESSENTIAL QUESTION

How can you use operations with fractions to solve real-world problems?

EXAMPLE 1

Add.

$\frac{7}{9} + \frac{5}{12}$ The LCM of 9 and 12 is 36.

$\frac{7 \times 4}{9 \times 4} + \frac{5 \times 3}{12 \times 3}$ Use the LCM to make fractions with common denominators.

$\frac{28}{36} + \frac{15}{36} = \frac{43}{36}$ Simplify.

$\frac{43}{36} = 1\frac{7}{36}$

Subtract.

$\frac{9}{10} - \frac{5}{6}$ The LCM of 10 and 6 is 30.

$\frac{9 \times 3}{10 \times 3} - \frac{5 \times 5}{6 \times 5}$ Use the LCM to make fractions with common denominators.

$\frac{27}{30} - \frac{25}{30} = \frac{2}{30}$ Simplify.

$\frac{2}{30} = \frac{1}{15}$

EXAMPLE 2

Multiply.

A. $\frac{4}{5} \times \frac{1}{8}$

$\frac{4 \times 1}{5 \times 8} = \frac{4}{40}$ Multiply numerators.
Multiply denominators.

$\frac{4 \div 4}{40 \div 4} = \frac{1}{10}$ Simplify by dividing by the GCF.

B. $2\frac{1}{4} \times \frac{1}{5}$

$\frac{9}{4} \times \frac{1}{5}$ Rewrite the mixed number as a fraction greater than 1.

$\frac{9 \times 1}{4 \times 5} = \frac{9}{20}$ Multiply numerators.
Multiply denominators.

EXAMPLE 3

Divide.

A. $\frac{2}{7} \div \frac{1}{2}$

$\frac{2}{7} \times \frac{2}{1}$ Rewrite the problem as multiplication using the reciprocal of the second fraction.

$\frac{2 \times 2}{7 \times 1} = \frac{4}{7}$ Multiply numerators.
Multiply denominators.

B. $2\frac{1}{3} \div 1\frac{3}{4}$

$\frac{7}{3} \div \frac{7}{4}$ Write both mixed numbers as improper fractions.

$\frac{\cancel{7} \times 4}{3 \times \cancel{7}_1} = \frac{4}{3}$ Multiply by the reciprocal of the second fraction.

$1\frac{1}{3}$ Simplify: $\frac{4}{3} = 1\frac{1}{3}$

EXERCISES

Add. Write the answer in simplest form. (Lesson 4.1)

1. $\frac{3}{8} + \frac{4}{5}$ _____

2. $1\frac{9}{10} + \frac{3}{4}$ _____

3. $\frac{2}{8} + \frac{6}{12}$ _____

Subtract. Write the answer in simplest form. (Lesson 4.1)

4. $1\frac{3}{7} - \frac{4}{5}$ _____

5. $\frac{7}{8} - \frac{5}{12}$ _____

6. $3\frac{5}{10} - \frac{4}{8}$ _____

Multiply. Write the answer in simplest form. (Lesson 4.1)

7. $\frac{1}{7} \times \frac{4}{5}$ _____

8. $\frac{5}{6} \times \frac{2}{3}$ _____

9. $\frac{3}{7} \times \frac{14}{15}$ _____

10. $1\frac{1}{3} \times \frac{5}{8}$ _____

11. $1\frac{2}{9} \times 1\frac{1}{2}$ _____

12. $2\frac{1}{7} \times 3\frac{2}{3}$ _____

Divide. Write the answer in simplest form. (Lessons 4.2, 4.3)

13. $\frac{3}{7} \div \frac{2}{3}$ _____

14. $\frac{1}{8} \div \frac{3}{4}$ _____

15. $1\frac{1}{5} \div \frac{1}{4}$ _____

16. On his twelfth birthday, Ben was $4\frac{3}{4}$ feet tall. On his thirteenth birthday, Ben was $5\frac{3}{8}$ feet tall. How much did Ben grow between his twelfth and thirteenth birthdays? (Lesson 4.1)

_____

17. Ron had 20 apples. He used $\frac{2}{5}$ of the apples to make pies. How many apples did Ron use for pies? (Lesson 4.4)

_____

18. The area of a rectangular garden is $38\frac{1}{4}$ square meters. The width of the garden is $4\frac{1}{2}$ meters. Find the length of the garden. (Lesson 4.4)

_____

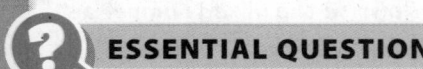
MODULE 5 # Operations with Decimals

Key Vocabulary
order of operations *(orden de las operaciones)*

? ESSENTIAL QUESTION

How can you use operations with decimals to solve real-world problems?

EXAMPLE 1

To prepare for a race, Lloyd ran every day for two weeks. He ran a total of 67,592 meters. Lloyd ran the same distance every day. He took a two-day rest and then started running again. The first day after his rest, he ran the same distance plus 1,607.87 meters more. How far did Lloyd run that day?

Step 1 Divide to see how far Lloyd ran every day during the two weeks.

$$\begin{array}{r} 4,828 \\ 14\overline{)67,592} \end{array}$$

Lloyd ran 4,828 meters a day.

Step 2 Add 1,607.87 to 4,828 to find out how far Lloyd ran the first day after his rest.

$$\begin{array}{r} 1,607.87 \\ +\ 4,828.00 \\ \hline 6,435.87 \end{array}$$

Lloyd ran 6,435.87 meters that day.

© Houghton Mifflin Harcourt Publishing Company

EXAMPLE 2

Rebecca bought 2.5 pounds of red apples. The apples cost $0.98 per pound. What was the total cost of Rebecca's apples?

$$
\begin{array}{r}
2.5 \quad \leftarrow \quad 1 \text{ decimal place} \\
\times\ .98 \quad \leftarrow\ +2 \text{ decimal places} \\
\hline
200 \\
+\ 2250 \\
\hline
2.450 \quad \leftarrow \quad 3 \text{ decimal places}
\end{array}
$$

The apples cost $2.45.

EXAMPLE 3

Rashid spent $37.29 on gas for his car. Gas was $3.39 per gallon. How many gallons did Rashid purchase?

Step 1 The divisor has two decimal places, so multiply both the dividend and the divisor by 100 so that the divisor is a whole number:

$$3.39\overline{)37.29} \qquad 339\overline{)3729}$$

Step 2 Divide:

$$
\begin{array}{r}
11 \\
339\overline{)3729} \\
-339 \\
\hline
339 \\
-339 \\
\hline
0
\end{array}
$$

Rashid purchased 11 gallons of gas.

EXERCISES

Add. (Lesson 5.2)

1. $12.24 + 3.9$ _____

2. $0.986 + 0.342$ _____

3. $2.479 + 0.31$ _____

Subtract. (Lesson 5.2)

4. $6.19 - 3.05$ _____

5. $7.285 - 0.975$ _____

6. $14.31 - 13.41$ _____

Multiply. (Lesson 5.3)

7. $\begin{array}{r} 12 \\ \times 0.4 \\ \hline \end{array}$ _____

8. $\begin{array}{r} 0.15 \\ \times\ 9.1 \\ \hline \end{array}$ _____

9. $\begin{array}{r} 3.12 \\ \times 0.25 \\ \hline \end{array}$ _____

Divide. (Lessons 5.1, 5.4)

10. $78,974 \div 21$ _____

11. $19,975 \div 25$ _____

12. $67,396 \div 123$ _____

13. $5\overline{)64.5}$ _____

14. $0.6\overline{)25.2}$ _____

15. $2.1\overline{)36.75}$ _____

16. A pound of rice crackers costs $2.88. Matthew purchased $\frac{1}{4}$ pound of crackers. How much did he pay for the crackers? (Lesson 5.5) _____

1. **CAREERS IN MATH** Chef Chef Alonso is creating a recipe called Spicy Italian Chicken with the following ingredients: $\frac{3}{4}$ pound chicken, $2\frac{1}{2}$ cups tomato sauce, 1 teaspoon oregano, and $\frac{1}{2}$ teaspoon of his special hot sauce.

   a. Chef Alonso wants each serving of the dish to include $\frac{1}{2}$ pound of chicken. How many $\frac{1}{2}$ pound servings does this recipe make?

   _____

   b. What is the number Chef Alonso should multiply the amount of chicken by so that the recipe will make 2 full servings, each with $\frac{1}{2}$ pound of chicken?

   _____

   c. Use the multiplier you found in part **b** to find the amount of all the ingredients in the new recipe.

   _____

   d. Chef Alonso only has three measuring spoons: 1 teaspoon, $\frac{1}{2}$ teaspoon, and $\frac{1}{4}$ teaspoon. Can he measure the new amounts of oregano and hot sauce exactly? Explain why or why not.

   _____

2. Amira is painting a rectangular banner $2\frac{1}{4}$ yards wide on a wall in the cafeteria. The banner will have a blue background. Amira has enough blue paint to cover $1\frac{1}{2}$ square yards of wall.

   a. Find the height of the banner if Amira uses all of the blue paint. Show your work.

   _____

   b. The school colors are blue and yellow, so Amira wants to add yellow rectangles on the left and right sides of the blue rectangle. The yellow rectangles will each be $\frac{3}{4}$ yard wide and the same height as the blue rectangle. What will be the total area of the two yellow rectangles? Explain how you found your answer.

   _____

   _____

   c. What are the dimensions of the banner plus yellow rectangles? What is the total area? Show your work.

   _____

   _____

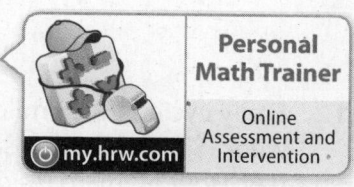

Selected Response

1. Each paper clip is $\frac{7}{8}$ of an inch long and costs $0.03. Exactly enough paper clips are laid end to end to have a total length of 56 inches. What is the total cost of these paper clips?

  Ⓐ $0.49   Ⓒ $1.47

  Ⓑ $0.64   Ⓓ $1.92

2. Which of these is the same as $\frac{8}{9} \div \frac{2}{3}$?

  Ⓐ $\frac{8}{9} \div \frac{3}{2}$ Ⓒ $\frac{8}{9} \times \frac{2}{3}$

  Ⓑ $\frac{2}{3} \div \frac{8}{9}$ Ⓓ $\frac{8}{9} \times \frac{3}{2}$

3. A rectangular tabletop has a length of $4\frac{3}{4}$ feet and an area of $11\frac{7}{8}$ square feet. What is the width of the tabletop?

  Ⓐ $1\frac{1}{16}$ feet

  Ⓑ $2\frac{1}{2}$ feet

  Ⓒ $4\frac{1}{4}$ feet

  Ⓓ $8\frac{1}{2}$ feet

4. Dorothy types 120 words per minute. How many words does Dorothy type in 1.75 minutes?

  Ⓐ 150 words

  Ⓑ 180 words

  Ⓒ 200 words

  Ⓓ 210 words

5. What is the opposite of 17?

  Ⓐ −17

  Ⓑ $-\frac{1}{17}$

  Ⓒ $\frac{1}{17}$

  Ⓓ 17

6. What is the absolute value of −36?

  Ⓐ −36

  Ⓑ 0

  Ⓒ 6

  Ⓓ 36

7. Noelle has $\frac{5}{6}$ of a yard of purple ribbon and $\frac{9}{10}$ of a yard of pink ribbon. How much ribbon does she have altogether?

  Ⓐ $1\frac{11}{15}$ yards   Ⓒ $2\frac{1}{5}$ yards

  Ⓑ $1\frac{4}{5}$ yards   Ⓓ $1\frac{14}{16}$ yards

8. Apples are on sale for $1.20 a pound. Logan bought $\frac{3}{4}$ of a pound. How much money did he spend on apples?

  Ⓐ $0.75   Ⓒ $0.90

  Ⓑ $0.80   Ⓓ $1.00

9. Samantha bought 4.5 pounds of pears. Each pound cost $1.68. How much did Samantha spend in all?

  Ⓐ $7.52   Ⓒ $8.40

  Ⓑ $7.56   Ⓓ $75.60

10. Gillian earns $7.50 an hour babysitting on the weekends. Last week she babysat for 2.2 hours on Saturday and 3.5 hours on Sunday. How much did Gillian earn?

  Ⓐ $4.25   Ⓒ $42.75

  Ⓑ $40.25   Ⓓ $427.50

11. Luis made some trail mix. He mixed $4\frac{2}{3}$ cups of popcorn, $1\frac{1}{4}$ cups of peanuts, $1\frac{1}{3}$ cups of raisins, and $\frac{3}{4}$ cup of sunflower seeds. He gave 5 of his friends an equal amount of trail mix each. How much did each friend get?

  Ⓐ $1\frac{3}{5}$ cups   Ⓒ $1\frac{3}{4}$ cups

  Ⓑ $1\frac{2}{3}$ cups   Ⓓ 2 cups

12. Emily cycled 20.25 miles over 4 days last week. She cycled the same amount each day. How many miles did Emily cycle each day to the nearest hundredth?

(A) 5.01 miles   (C) 5.60 miles

(B) 5.06 miles   (D) 5.65 miles

13. Landon drove 103.5 miles on Tuesday, 320.75 miles on Wednesday, and 186.30 miles on Thursday. How far did Landon drive all three days combined?

(A) 61.55 miles   (C) 610.55 miles

(B) 610.055 miles   (D) 6,105.5 miles

Mini Task

14. Carl earns $3.25 per hour walking his neighbor's dogs. He walks them $\frac{1}{3}$ of an hour in the morning and $\frac{1}{2}$ of an hour in the afternoon.

a. How much time does Carl spend dog walking every day?

_____

b. How much time does Carl spend dog walking in a week?

_____

c. Ten minutes is equal to $\frac{1}{6}$ of an hour. How many minutes does Carl work dog walking each week?

_____

d. How much money does Carl earn each week?

_____

15. The city zoo had an equal number of visitors on Saturday and Sunday. In all, 32,096 people visited the zoo that weekend. How many visited each day?

_____

a. On Saturday, $\frac{1}{8}$ of the people who visited were senior citizens, $\frac{1}{8}$ were infants, $\frac{1}{4}$ were children, and $\frac{1}{2}$ were adults. How many of each group visited the zoo on Saturday?

Senior Citizens: _____

Infants: _____

Children: _____

Adults: _____

b. On Sunday, $\frac{1}{16}$ of the people who visited were senior citizens, $\frac{3}{16}$ were infants, $\frac{3}{8}$ were children, and $\frac{3}{8}$ were adults. How many of each group visited the zoo on Sunday?

Senior Citizens: _____

Infants: _____

Children: _____

Adults: _____

c. The chart shows how much each type of ticket costs.

Type of Ticket	Cost
Infants	Free
Children Over 2	$4.50
Adults	$7.25
Senior Citizens	$5.75

d. How much money did the zoo make on Saturday? Show your work.

_____

_____

_____

_____

e. How much did the zoo make on Sunday?

_____

_____

_____

_____

© Houghton Mifflin Harcourt Publishing Company

Proportionality: Ratios and Rates

MODULE 6

Representing Ratios and Rates

🚩 FL 6.RP.1.1, 6.RP.1.2, 6.RP.1.3

MODULE 7

Applying Ratios and Rates

🚩 FL 6.RP.1.3, 6.RP.1.3a, 6.RP.1.3d

MODULE 8

Percents

🚩 FL 6.RP.1.3, 6.RP.1.3c

CAREERS IN MATH

Residential Builder A residential builder, also called a homebuilder, specializes in the construction of residences that range from single-family custom homes to buildings that contain multiple housing units, such as apartments and condominiums. Residential builders use math in numerous ways, such as blueprint reading, measuring and scaling, using ratios and rates to calculate the amounts of different building materials needed, and estimating costs for jobs.

If you are interested in a career as a residential builder, you should study these mathematical subjects:

- Algebra
- Geometry
- Business Math
- Technical Math

Research other careers that require using ratios and rates, and measuring and scaling.

Unit 3 Performance Task

At the end of the unit, check out how **residential builders** use math.

Vocabulary Preview

Use the puzzle to preview key vocabulary from this unit. Unscramble the circled letters within found words to answer the riddle at the bottom of the page.

Down

1. A rate that describes how much smaller or larger the scale drawing is than the real object. (Lesson 7.2)

4. A comparison by division of two quantities (Lesson 6.1)

5. Ratio of two quantities that have different units. (Lesson 6.2)

Across

1. Drawing that uses a scale to make an object proportionally smaller or larger than the real object. (Lesson 7.2)

2. A rate in which the second quantity is one unit. (Lesson 6.2)

3. A fraction that compares two equivalent measurements. (Lesson 7.3)

6. An equation that states two ratios are equivalent. (Lesson 7.2)

Q: Why was the draftsman excited that the raffle prize was a weighing device?

A: It was a ___ ___ ___ ___ ___ – ___ ___ ___ ___ ___ ___ ___ ___!

Representing Ratios and Rates

ESSENTIAL QUESTION

How can you use ratios and rates to solve real-world problems?

LESSON 6.1

Ratios

 FL 6.RP.1.1, 6.RP.1.3, 6.RP.1.3a

LESSON 6.2

Rates

 FL 6.RP.1.2, 6.RP.1.3, 6.RP.1.3b

LESSON 6.3

Using Ratios and Rates to Solve Problems

FL 6.RP.1.3, 6.RP.1.3a

Real-World Video

Scientists studying sand structures determined that the perfect sand and water mixture is equal to 1 bucket of water for every 100 buckets of sand. This recipe can be written as the ratio $\frac{1}{100}$.

© my.hrw.com

GO DIGITAL

my.hrw.com

my.hrw.com

Go digital with your write-in student edition, accessible on any device.

Math On the Spot

Scan with your smart phone to jump directly to the online edition, video tutor, and more.

Animated Math

Interactively explore key concepts to see how math works.

Personal Math Trainer

Get immediate feedback and help as you work through practice sets.

Are YOU Ready?

Complete these exercises to review skills you will need for this module.

Personal Math Trainer

Online Assessment and Intervention

my.hrw.com

Simplify Fractions

EXAMPLE Simplify $\frac{15}{24}$.

15: 1, ③, 5, 15
24: 1, 2, ③, 4, 6, 8, 12, 24

$\frac{15 \div 3}{24 \div 3} = \frac{5}{8}$

List all the factors of the numerator and denominator.

Circle the greatest common factor (GCF).

Divide the numerator and denominator by the GCF.

Write each fraction in simplest form.

1. $\frac{6}{9}$ _____

2. $\frac{4}{10}$ _____

3. $\frac{15}{20}$ _____

4. $\frac{20}{24}$ _____

5. $\frac{16}{56}$ _____

6. $\frac{45}{72}$ _____

7. $\frac{18}{60}$ _____

8. $\frac{32}{72}$ _____

Write Equivalent Fractions

EXAMPLE $\frac{6}{8} = \frac{6 \times 2}{8 \times 2}$

$= \frac{12}{16}$

$\frac{6}{8} = \frac{6 \div 2}{8 \div 2}$

$= \frac{3}{4}$

Multiply the numerator and denominator by the same number to find an equivalent fraction.

Divide the numerator and denominator by the same number to find an equivalent fraction.

Write the equivalent fraction.

9. $\frac{12}{15} = \frac{\boxed{}}{5}$

10. $\frac{5}{6} = \frac{\boxed{}}{30}$

11. $\frac{16}{24} = \frac{4}{\boxed{}}$

12. $\frac{3}{9} = \frac{21}{\boxed{}}$

13. $\frac{15}{40} = \frac{\boxed{}}{8}$

14. $\frac{18}{30} = \frac{\boxed{}}{10}$

15. $\frac{48}{64} = \frac{12}{\boxed{}}$

16. $\frac{2}{7} = \frac{18}{\boxed{}}$

Reading Start-Up

© Houghton Mifflin Harcourt Publishing Company

Visualize Vocabulary

Use the ✔ words to complete the chart. Choose the review words that describe multiplication and division.

Understanding Multiplication and Division		
Symbol	**Operation**	**Term for the answer**
×		
÷		

Understand Vocabulary

Match the term on the left to the definition on the right.

1. rate

2. ratio

3. unit rate

4. equivalent ratios

A. Rate in which the second quantity is one unit.

B. Comparison of two quantities by division.

C. Ratios that name the same comparison.

D. Ratio of two quantities that have different units.

Vocabulary

Review Words

colon (*dos puntos*)
denominator (*denominador*)
✔ divide (*dividir*)
fraction bar (*barra de fracciones*)
✔ multiply (*multiplicar*)
numerator (*numerador*)
✔ product (*producto*)
quantity (*cantidad*)
✔ quotient (*cociente*)
term (*término*)

Preview Words

equivalent ratios (*razones equivalentes*)
rate (*tasa*)
ratio (*razón*)
unit rate (*tasa unitaria*)

Active Reading

Two-Panel Flip Chart Create a two-panel flip chart, to help you understand the concepts in this module. Label one flap "Ratios" and the other flap "Rates." As you study each lesson, write important ideas under the appropriate flap. Include information about unit rates and any sample equations that will help you remember the concepts when you look back at your notes.

Unpacking the Standards

Understanding the standards and the vocabulary terms in the standards will help you know exactly what you are expected to learn in this module.

FL 6.RP.1.3

Use ratio and rate reasoning to solve real-world and mathematical problems, e.g., by reasoning about tables of equivalent ratios, tape diagrams, double number line diagrams, or equations.

Key Vocabulary

ratio *(razón)*
A comparison of two quantities by division.

rate *(tasa)*
A ratio that compares two quantities measured in different units.

equivalent ratios *(razones equivalentes)*
Ratios that name the same comparison.

What It Means to You

You will use equivalent ratios to solve real-world problems involving ratios and rates.

UNPACKING EXAMPLE 6.RP.1.3

A group of 10 friends is in line to see a movie. The table shows how much different groups will pay in all. Predict how much the group of 10 will pay.

Number in group	3	5	6	12
Amount paid ($)	15	25	30	60

The ratios are all the same.

$$\frac{3}{15} = \frac{1}{5} \qquad \frac{6}{30} = \frac{1}{5} \qquad \frac{5}{25} = \frac{1}{5} \qquad \frac{12}{60} = \frac{1}{5}$$

Find the denominator that gives a ratio equivalent to $\frac{1}{5}$ for a group of 10.

$$\frac{10}{?} = \frac{1}{5} \quad \rightarrow \quad \frac{10 \div 10}{50 \div 10} = \frac{1}{5} \quad \rightarrow \quad \frac{10}{50} = \frac{1}{5}$$

A group of 10 will pay $50.

FL 6.RP.1.3b

Solve unit rate problems including those involving unit pricing and constant speed.

Key Vocabulary

unit rate *(tasa unitaria)*
A rate in which the second quantity in the comparison is one unit.

What It Means to You

You will solve problems involving unit rates by division.

UNPACKING EXAMPLE 6.RP.1.3b

A 2-liter bottle of spring water costs $2.02. A 3-liter bottle of the same water costs $2.79. Which is the better deal?

2-liter bottle

$$\frac{\$2.02}{2 \text{ liters}}$$

$$\frac{\$2.02 \div 2}{2 \text{ liters} \div 2}$$

$$\frac{\$1.01}{1 \text{ liter}}$$

3-liter bottle

$$\frac{\$2.79}{3 \text{ liters}}$$

$$\frac{\$2.79 \div 3}{3 \text{ liters} \div 3}$$

$$\frac{\$0.93}{1 \text{ liter}}$$

The 3-liter bottle is the better deal.

Visit **my.hrw.com** to see all **Florida Math Standards** unpacked.

my.hrw.com

LESSON
6.1 Ratios

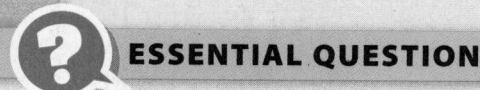

? ESSENTIAL QUESTION

How do you use ratios to compare two quantities?

EXPLORE ACTIVITY   6.RP.1.1

Representing Ratios with Models

A **ratio** is a comparison of two quantities. It shows how many times as great one quantity is than another.

For example, the ratio of star-shaped beads to moon-shaped beads in a bracelet is 3 to 1.

A Write the ratio of moon beads to star beads. _____

B Write the ratio of moon beads to all the beads. _____

C If the bracelet has 2 moon beads, how many star beads does it have? _____

D If the bracelet has 9 star beads, how many moon beads does it have? How do you know?

_____

_____

_____

Reflect

1. Make a Prediction Write a rule that you can use to find the number of star beads in a bracelet when you know the number of moon beads. Then write a rule that you can use to find the number of moon beads when you know the number of star beads.

_____

_____

_____

2. Make a Prediction Write a rule that you can use to find the total number of beads in a bracelet when you know the number of moon beads.

_____

Writing Ratios

The numbers in a ratio are called *terms*. A ratio can be written in several different ways.

5 dogs to 3 cats	5 to 3	5:3	$\frac{5}{3}$

A ratio can compare a part to a part, a part to the whole, or the whole to a part.

EXAMPLE 1 Real World   🏴 **FL**   **6.RP.1.1**

A Write the ratio of comedies to dramas in three different ways.

part to part

8:3 $\frac{8}{3}$ 8 comedies to 3 dramas

B Write the ratio of dramas to total videos in three different ways.

part to whole

3:14 $\frac{3}{14}$ 3 dramas to 14 total videos

Sam's Video Collection

🥸	Comedies	8
👁	Dramas	3
🐻	Cartoons	2
🛸	Science Fiction	1

The total number of videos is $8 + 3 + 2 + 1 = 14$.

Reflect

3. **Analyze Relationships** Describe the relationship between the drama videos and the science fiction videos.

_____

_____

4. **Analyze Relationships** The ratio of floor seats to balcony seats in a theater is 20:1. Does this theater have more floor seats or more balcony seats? How do you know?

_____

_____

YOUR TURN

Write each ratio in three different ways.

5. bagel chips to peanuts _____

6. total party mix to pretzels _____

7. cheese crackers to peanuts _____

Party Mix
Makes 8 cups
3 cups pretzels
3 cups bagel chips
1 cup cheese crackers
1 cup peanuts

Equivalent Ratios

Equivalent ratios are ratios that name the same comparison. You can find equivalent ratios by using a table or by multiplying or dividing both terms of a ratio by the same number. So, equivalent ratios have a multiplicative relationship.

Math On the Spot

my.hrw.com

A ratio with terms that have no common factors is said to be in simplest form.

EXAMPLE 2   **FL** 6.RP.1.3, 6.RP.1.3a

My Notes

You make 5 cups of punch by mixing 3 cups of cranberry juice with 2 cups of apple juice. How much cranberry juice and how much apple juice do you need to make four times the original recipe?

Method 1 Use a table.

STEP 1 Make a table comparing the number of cups of cranberry juice and apple juice needed to make two times, three times, and four times the original recipe.

> Multiply both terms of the original ratio by the same number to find an equivalent ratio.

$3 \times 2 \quad 3 \times 3 \quad 3 \times 4$

Cranberry Juice	3	6	9	12
Apple Juice	2	4	6	8

$2 \times 2 \quad 2 \times 3 \quad 2 \times 4$

STEP 2 Write the original ratio and the ratio that shows the amount of cranberry juice and apple juice needed to make four times the original recipe.

$$\frac{3}{2} = \frac{12}{8}$$

You will need 12 cups of cranberry juice and 8 cups of apple juice.

Method 2 Multiply both terms of the ratio by the same number.

STEP 1 Write the original ratio in fraction form.

$$\frac{3}{2}$$

STEP 2 Multiply the numerator and denominator by the same number.

To make four times the original recipe, multiply by 4.

To make four times the original recipe, you will need 12 cups of cranberry juice and 8 cups of apple juice.

Math Talk
Mathematical Practices

The ratio of apple juice to grape juice in a recipe is 8 cups to 10 cups. What is this ratio in simplest form? Explain.

YOUR TURN

Write three ratios equivalent to the given ratio.

8. $\frac{8}{10}$ _____

9. $\frac{5}{2}$ _____

Guided Practice

The number of dogs compared to the number of cats in an apartment complex is represented by the model shown. (Explore Activity)

1. Write a ratio that compares the number of dogs to the number of cats. _____

2. If there are 15 cats in the apartment complex, how many dogs are there?

15 ÷ _____ = _____ **dogs**

3. How many cats are there if there are 5 dogs in the apartment complex?

5 × _____ = _____ **cats**

4. The only pets in the apartment complex are cats and dogs. If there are 10 dogs, how many *pets* are there? _____

The contents of Dana's box of muffins are shown. Write each ratio in three different ways. (Example 1)

5. banana nut muffins to corn muffins _____

6. corn muffins to total muffins _____

Dana's Dozen Muffins
5 corn
4 bran
2 banana nut
1 blueberry

Vocabulary Write three equivalent ratios for the given ratio. Circle the simplest form of the ratio. (Example 2)

7. $\frac{10}{12}$ _____

8. $\frac{14}{2}$ _____

9. $\frac{4}{7}$ _____

❓ ESSENTIAL QUESTION CHECK-IN

10. Use an example to describe the multiplicative relationship between two equivalent ratios.

_____

_____

6.1 Independent Practice

  6.RP.1.1, 6.RP.1.3, 6.RP.1.3a

Personal Math Trainer

Online Assessment and Intervention

my.hrw.com

Write three ratios equivalent to the ratio described in each situation.

11. The ratio of cups of water to cups of milk in a recipe is 1 to 3.

_____

12. The ratio of boys to girls on the bus is $\frac{20}{15}$.

_____

13. In each bouquet of flowers, there are 4 roses and 6 white carnations. Complete the table to find how many roses and carnations there are in 4 bouquets of flowers.

Roses	4				
Carnations	6				

_____

14. Ed is using the recipe shown to make fruit salad. He wants to use 30 diced strawberries in his fruit salad. How many bananas, apples, and pears should Ed use in his fruit salad?

_____

Fruit Salad Recipe
4 bananas, diced
3 apples, diced
6 pears, diced
10 strawberries, diced

15. A collector has 120 movie posters and 100 band posters. She wants to sell 24 movie posters but still have her poster collection maintain the same ratio of 120:100. If she sells 24 movie posters, how many band posters should she sell? Explain.

_____

_____

_____

16. Bob needs to mix 2 cups of orange juice concentrate with 3.5 cups of water to make orange juice. Bob has 6 cups of concentrate. How much orange juice can he make? _____

17. Multistep The ratio of North American butterflies to South American butterflies at a butterfly park is 5:3. The ratio of South American butterflies to European butterflies is 3:2. There are 30 North American butterflies at the butterfly park.

a. How many South American butterflies are there? _____

b. How many European butterflies are there? _____

18. Sinea and Ren are going to the carnival next week. The table shows the amount that each person spent on snacks, games, and souvenirs the last time they went to the carnival.

	Snacks	Games	Souvenirs
Sinea	$5	$8	$12
Ren	$10	$8	$20

a. Sinea wants to spend money using the same ratios as on her last trip to the carnival. If she spends $26 on games, how much will she spend on souvenirs? _____

b. Ren wants to spend money using the same ratios as on his last trip to the carnival. If he spends $5 on souvenirs, how much will he spend on snacks? _____

c. **What If?** Suppose Sinea and Ren each spend $40 on snacks, and each person spends money using the same ratios as on their last trip. Who spends more on souvenirs? Explain.

_____

_____

_____

 FOCUS ON HIGHER ORDER THINKING

Work Area

19. **Multiple Representations** The diagram compares the ratio of girls in the chorus to boys in the chorus. What is the ratio of girls to boys? If there are 50 students in the chorus, how many are girls and how many are boys?

Girls

Boys

50

_____

20. **Analyze Relationships** How is the process of finding equivalent ratios like the process of finding equivalent fractions?

_____

_____

21. **Explain the Error** Tina says that 6:8 is equivalent to 36:64. What did Tina do wrong?

_____

_____

© Houghton Mifflin Harcourt Publishing Company

6.2 Rates

FL 6.RP.1.2
Understand the concept of a unit rate *a/b* associated with a ratio *a:b* with $b \neq 0$, and use rate language.... *Also 6.RP.1.3, 6.RP.1.3b*

? ESSENTIAL QUESTION

How do you use rates to compare quantities?

EXPLORE ACTIVITY   FL 6.RP.1.2, 6.RP.1.3b

Using Rates to Compare Prices

A **rate** is a comparison of two quantities that have different units.

Chris drove 107 miles in two hours. This can be expressed as the rate shown at the right. Notice that the units are different: miles and hours.   The rate is $\frac{107 \text{ miles}}{2 \text{ hours}}$.

Shana is at the grocery store comparing two brands of juice. Brand A costs $3.84 for a 16-ounce bottle. Brand B costs $4.50 for a 25-ounce bottle.

To compare the costs, Shana must compare prices for equal amounts of juice. How can she do this?

A Complete the tables.

Brand A

	Ounces	Price ($)	
÷ 2	16	3.84	÷ 2
÷ 2	8	1.92	÷ 2
÷ 2	4		÷ 2
÷ 2	2		÷ 2
	1		÷ 2

Brand B

	Ounces	Price ($)	
÷ 5	25	4.50	÷ 5
÷ 5	5		÷ 5
	1		

B Brand A costs $ _____ per ounce. Brand B costs $ _____ per ounce.

C Which brand is the better buy? Why? _____

Reflect

1. Analyze Relationships Describe another method to compare the costs.

_____

_____

Math On the Spot

my.hrw.com

Calculating Unit Rates

A **unit rate** is a rate in which the second quantity is one unit. When the first quantity in a unit rate is an amount of money, the unit rate is sometimes called a *unit price* or *unit cost*.

EXAMPLE 1   FL 6.RP.1.2

A Gerald pays $90 for 6 yoga classes. What is the cost per class?

Use the information in the problem to write a rate: $\dfrac{\$90}{6 \text{ classes}}$

To find the unit rate, divide both quantities in the rate by the same number so that the second quantity is 1.

$$\frac{\$90}{6 \text{ classes}} = \frac{\$15}{1 \text{ class}}$$

Gerald's yoga classes cost $15 per class.

B The cost of 2 cartons of milk is $5.50. What is the unit price?

The unit price is $2.75 per carton of milk.

$$\frac{\$5.50}{2 \text{ cartons}} = \frac{\$2.75}{1 \text{ carton}}$$

C A cruise ship travels 20 miles in 50 minutes. How far does the ship travel per minute?

The ship travels 0.4 mile per minute.

$$\frac{20 \text{ miles}}{50 \text{ minutes}} = \frac{0.4 \text{ mile}}{1 \text{ minute}}$$

> The first quantity in a unit rate can be less than 1.

Reflect

2. **Multiple Representations** Explain how you could use a diagram like the one shown below to find the unit rate in **A**. Then complete the diagram to find the unit rate.

_____

_____

_____

_____

Yoga Classes

This month's special:

6 classes for $90

© Houghton Mifflin Harcourt Publishing Company

156 Unit 3

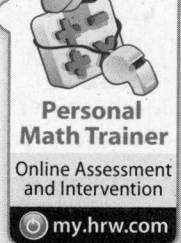

YOUR TURN

3. There are 156 players on 13 teams. How many players are on each

   team? _____ players per team

Problem Solving with Unit Rates

You can solve rate problems by using a unit rate or by using equivalent rates.

EXAMPLE 2 *Real World*   FL   6.RP.1.3, 6.RP.1.3b

At a summer camp, the campers are divided into groups. Each group has 16 campers and 2 cabins. How many cabins are needed for 112 campers?

Method 1   Find the unit rate. How many campers per cabin?

$$\frac{16\ \text{campers}}{2\ \text{cabins}} = \frac{8\ \text{campers}}{1\ \text{cabin}}$$

Divide to find the unit rate.

There are 8 campers per cabin.

$$\frac{112\ \text{campers}}{8\ \text{campers per cabin}} = 14\ \text{cabins}$$

Divide to find the number of cabins.

Method 2   Use equivalent rates.

$$\frac{16\ \text{campers}}{2\ \text{cabins}} = \frac{112\ \text{campers}}{14\ \text{cabins}}$$

The camp needs 14 cabins.

Check   Use a diagram to check the unit rate if there are 16 campers in 2 cabins. Then, use the unit rate to check if 14 cabins is a reasonable number for 112 campers.

16 campers

2 cabins

8 campers   8 campers

The unit rate of 8 campers per cabin is reasonable. You can multiply 14 cabins by 8 campers per cabin to find that there would be enough room for 112 campers.

© Houghton Mifflin Harcourt Publishing Company

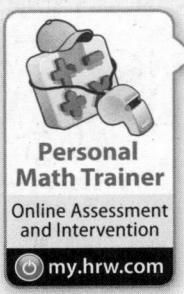

Personal Math Trainer

Online Assessment and Intervention

⏻ my.hrw.com

YOUR TURN

4. Petra jogs 3 miles in 27 minutes. At this rate, how long would it take her to jog 5 miles? Show your work.

_____

_____

Guided Practice

Mason's favorite brand of peanut butter is available in two sizes. Each size and its price are shown in the table. Use the table for 1 and 2. (Explore Activity)

1. What is the unit rate for each size of peanut butter?

   Regular: $ _____ per ounce

   Family size: $ _____ per ounce

	Size (oz)	Price ($)
Regular	16	3.36
Family Size	40	7.60

2. Which size is the better buy? _____

3. Martin charges $10 for every 5 bags of leaves he rakes. Last weekend, he raked 24 bags of leaves. How much money did he earn? (Example 1)

   _____ for 24 bags of leaves

$10

5 bags of leaves

1 bag of leaves

Find the unit rate. (Example 1)

4. Lisa walked 48 blocks in 3 hours.

   _____ blocks per hour

5. Gordon types 1,800 words in 25 minutes.

   _____ words per minute

6. A particular frozen yogurt has 75 calories in 2 ounces. How many calories are in 8 ounces of the yogurt? (Example 2) _____

7. The cost of 10 oranges is $1. What is the cost of 5 dozen oranges? (Example 2) _____

? **ESSENTIAL QUESTION CHECK-IN**

8. How can you use a rate to compare the costs of two boxes of cereal that are different sizes?

   _____

   _____

© Houghton Mifflin Harcourt Publishing Company

158 Unit 3

6.2 Independent Practice

  6.RP.1.2, 6.RP.1.3, 6.RP.1.3b

Personal Math Trainer

Online Assessment and Intervention ·

my.hrw.com

Taryn and Alastair both mow lawns. Each charges a flat fee to mow a lawn. The table shows the number of lawns mowed in the past week, the time spent mowing lawns, and the money earned.

	Number of Lawns Mowed	Time Spent Mowing Lawns (in hours)	Money Earned
Taryn	9	7.5	$112.50
Alastair	7	5	$122.50

9. How much does Taryn charge to mow a lawn? _____

10. How much does Alastair charge to mow a lawn? _____

11. Who earns more per hour, Taryn or Alastair? _____

12. What If? If Taryn and Alastair want to earn an additional $735 each, how many additional hours will each spend mowing lawns? Explain.

_____

_____

_____

_____

13. Multistep Tomas makes balloon sculptures at a circus. In 180 minutes, he uses 252 balloons to make 36 identical balloon sculptures.

a. How many minutes does it take to make one balloon sculpture? How many balloons are used in one sculpture? _____

b. What is Tomas's unit rate for balloons used per minute? _____

c. Complete the diagram to find out how many balloons he will use in 10 minutes. _____

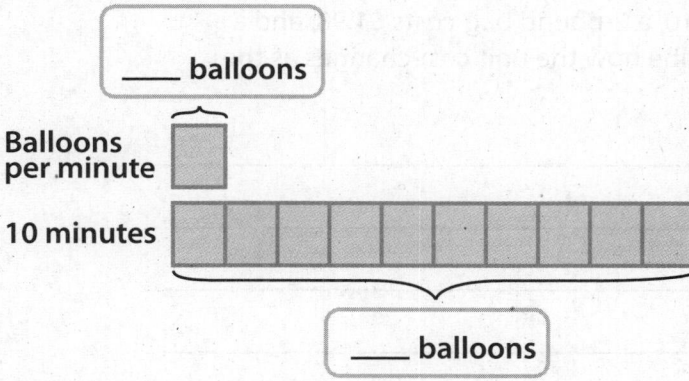

____ balloons

Balloons per minute

10 minutes

____ balloons

© Houghton Mifflin Harcourt Publishing Company

14. Abby can buy an 8-pound bag of dog food for $7.40 or a 4-pound bag of the same dog food for $5.38. Which is the better buy?

_____

15. A bakery offers a sale price of $3.50 for 4 muffins. What is the price per dozen?

_____

16. Mrs. Jacobsen wants to order toy instruments to give as prizes to her music students. The table shows the prices for various order sizes.

	25 items	50 items	80 items
Whistles	$21.25	$36.00	$60.00
Kazoos	$10.00	$18.50	$27.20

a. What is the difference between the highest unit price for whistles and the lowest unit price for whistles?

_____

b. What is the highest unit price per kazoo?

_____

c. **Persevere in Problem Solving** If Mrs. Jacobsen wants to buy the item with the lowest unit price, what item should she order and how many of that item should she order?

_____

 FOCUS ON HIGHER ORDER THINKING

Work Area

17. Draw Conclusions There are 2.54 centimeters in 1 inch. How many centimeters are there in 1 foot? in 1 yard? Explain your reasoning.

_____

_____

_____

18. Critique Reasoning A 2-pound box of spaghetti costs $2.50. Philip says that the unit cost is $\frac{2}{2.50} = \$0.80$ per pound. Explain his error.

_____

_____

_____

19. Look for a Pattern A grocery store sells three different quantities of sugar. A 1-pound bag costs $1.10, a 2-pound bag costs $1.98, and a 3-pound bag costs $2.85. Describe how the unit cost changes as the quantity of sugar increases.

_____

_____

_____

_____

Using Ratios and Rates to Solve Problems

 FL   6.RP.1.3

Use ratio and rate reasoning to solve... problems, e.g., by reasoning about tables... double number line diagrams... *Also 6.RP.1.3a*

? ESSENTIAL QUESTION

How can you use ratios and rates to make comparisons and predictions?

 EXPLORE ACTIVITY 1 Real World   FL   6.RP.1.3a

Using Tables to Compare Ratios

Anna's recipe for lemonade calls for 2 cups of lemonade concentrate and 3 cups of water. Bailey's recipe calls for 3 cups of lemonade concentrate and 5 cups of water.

A In Anna's recipe, the ratio of concentrate to water is _____.
Use equivalent ratios to complete the table.

2 × 2   2 × ⬜   2 × ⬜

Concentrate (c)	2	4		
Water (c)	3		9	15

3 × 2   3 × 3   3 × 5

B In Bailey's recipe, the ratio of concentrate to water is _____.
Use equivalent ratios to complete the table.

3 × 3   3 × 4   3 × ⬜

Concentrate (c)	3	9	12	
Water (c)	5			25

5 × 3   5 × ⬜   5 × ⬜

C Find two columns, one in each table, in which the amount of water is the same. Circle these two columns.

D Whose recipe makes stronger lemonade? How do you know?

_____

_____

E Compare the ratios: $\frac{10}{15}$ ◯ $\frac{9}{15}$ $\frac{2}{3}$ ◯ $\frac{3}{5}$

Reflect

1. **Analyze Relationships** Suppose each person pours herself one cup of the lemonade she made. How much concentrate is in each person's cup? How do you know?

_____

_____

_____

Comparing Ratios

You can use equivalent ratios to solve real-world problems.

EXAMPLE 1   FL   6.RP.1.3

A fruit and nut bar recipe calls for 4 cups of chopped nuts and 6 cups of dried fruit. When Tonya made a batch of these bars, she used 6 cups of chopped nuts and 9 cups of dried fruit. Did Tonya use the correct ratio of nuts to fruit?

STEP 1 Find the ratio of nuts to fruit in the recipe.

$\frac{4}{6}$ *4 cups of nuts to 6 cups of fruit*

STEP 2 Find the ratio of nuts to fruit that Tonya used.

$\frac{6}{9}$ *6 cups of nuts to 9 cups of fruit*

> 18 is a multiple of 6 and 9, so find equivalent ratios with 18 in the second term.

STEP 3 Find equivalent ratios that have the same second term.

$$\frac{4}{6} = \frac{12}{18} \qquad \frac{6}{9} = \frac{12}{18}$$

×3 ... ×3 ... ×2 ... ×2

$$\frac{12}{18} = \frac{12}{18}$$

The ratios $\frac{4}{6}$ and $\frac{6}{9}$ are equivalent. So, Tonya used the same ratio of nuts to fruit that was given in the recipe.

Math Talk
Mathematical Practices

Explain how you compare two ratios to check if they are equivalent.

YOUR TURN

2. In the science club, there are 2 sixth-graders for every 3 seventh-graders. At this year's science fair, there were 7 projects by sixth-graders for every 12 projects by seventh-graders. Is the ratio of sixth-graders to seventh-graders in the science club equivalent to the ratio of science fair projects by sixth-graders to projects by seventh-graders? Explain.

_____

Using Rates to Make Predictions

You can represent rates on a double number line to make predictions.

Janet drives from Clarkson to Humbolt in 2 hours. Suppose Janet drives for 10 hours. If she maintains the same driving rate, can she drive more than 600 miles? Justify your answer.

The double number line shows the number of miles Janet drives in various amounts of time.

A Explain how Janet's rate for two hours is represented on the double number line.

_____

_____

B Describe the relationship between Janet's rate for two hours and the other rates shown on the double number line.

_____

_____

C Complete the number line.

D At this rate, can Janet drive more than 600 miles in 10 hours? Explain.

_____

Reflect

3. In fifteen minutes, Lena can finish 2 math homework problems. How many math problems can she finish in 75 minutes? Use a double number line to find the answer.

_____

4. How is using a double number line similar to finding equivalent ratios?

_____

1. Celeste is making fruit baskets for her service club to take to a local hospital. The directions say to fill the boxes using 5 apples for every 6 oranges. Celeste is filling her baskets with 2 apples for every 3 oranges. (Explore Activity 1)

   a. Complete the tables to find equivalent ratios.

Apples	5			
Oranges	6			

Apples	2			
Oranges	3			

   b. Compare the ratios. Is Celeste using the correct ratio of apples to oranges?

   _____

   _____

2. Neha used 4 bananas and 5 oranges in her fruit salad. Daniel used 7 bananas and 9 oranges. Did Neha and Daniel use the same ratio of bananas to oranges? If not, who used the greater ratio of bananas to oranges? (Example 1)

   _____

   _____

3. Tim is a first grader and reads 28 words per minute. Assuming he maintains the same rate, use the double number line to find how many words he can read in 5 minutes. (Explore Activity 2.)

   _____

4. A cafeteria sells 30 drinks every 15 minutes. Predict how many drinks the cafeteria sells every hour. (Explore Activity 2)

   _____

© Houghton Mifflin Harcourt Publishing Company

? ESSENTIAL QUESTION CHECK-IN

5. Explain how to compare two ratios.

   _____

   _____

6.3 Independent Practice

FL 6.RP.1.3, 6.RP.1.3a

Personal Math Trainer

Online Assessment and Intervention

my.hrw.com

6. Gina's art teacher mixes 9 pints of yellow paint with 6 pints of blue paint to create green paint. Gina mixes 4 pints of yellow paint with 3 pints of blue paint. Did Gina use the same ratio of yellow paint to blue paint instructed by her teacher? Explain.

_____

_____

7. The Suarez family paid $15.75 for 3 movie tickets. How much would they have paid for 12 tickets?   _____

8. A grocery store sells snacks by weight. A six-ounce bag of mixed nuts costs $3.60. Predict the cost of a two-ounce bag.   _____

9. The Martin family's truck gets an average of 25 miles per gallon. Predict how many miles they can drive using 7 gallons of gas.   _____

10. Multistep The table shows two cell phone plans that offer free minutes for each given number of paid minutes used. Pablo has Plan A and Sam has Plan B.

a. What is Pablo's ratio of free to paid minutes?

_____

	Cell Phone Plans	
	Plan A	**Plan B**
Free minutes	2	8
Paid minutes	10	25

b. What is Sam's ratio of free to paid minutes?

_____

c. Does Pablo's cell phone plan offer the same ratio of free to paid minutes as Sam's? Explain.

_____

_____

11. Consumer Math A store has apples on sale for $3.00 for 2 pounds. How many pounds of apples can you buy for $9? If an apple is approximately 5 ounces, how many apples can you buy for $9? Explain your reasoning.

_____

_____

_____

12. Science Grass can grow up to six inches in a week depending on temperature, humidity, and time of year. At this rate, how tall will grass grow in 24 days?

_____

13. A town in east Texas received 10 inches of rain in two weeks. If it kept raining at this rate for a 31-day month, how much rain did the town receive?

_____

14. One patterned blue fabric sells for $15.00 every two yards, and another sells for $37.50 every 5 yards. Do these fabrics have the same unit cost? Explain.

_____

H.O.T. **FOCUS ON HIGHER ORDER THINKING**

15. Problem Solving Complete each ratio table.

	12	18	24
4.5			18

80.8	40.4		10.1
	512	256	

16. Represent Real-World Problems Write a real-world problem that compares the ratios 5 to 9 and 12 to 15.

_____

_____

_____

17. Analyze Relationships Explain how you can be sure that all the rates you have written on a double number line are correct.

_____

_____

_____

18. Paul can choose to be paid $50 for a job, or he can be paid $12.50 per hour. Under what circumstances should he choose the hourly wage? Explain.

_____

_____

_____

Ready to Go On?

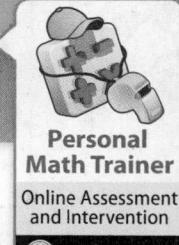

**Personal
Math Trainer**

Online Assessment
and Intervention

my.hrw.com

6.1 Ratios

Use the table to find each ratio.

1. white socks to brown socks _____

2. blue socks to nonblue socks _____

3. black socks to all of the socks _____

Color of socks	white	black	blue	brown
Number of socks	8	6	4	5

4. Find two ratios equivalent to the ratio in Exercise 1.

_____

6.2 Rates

Find each rate.

5. Earl runs 75 meters in 30 seconds. How many meters does Earl run per second? _____

6. The cost of 3 scarves is $26.25. What is the unit price? _____

6.3 Using Ratios and Rates to Solve Problems

7. Danny charges $35 for 3 hours of swimming lessons. Martin charges $24 for 2 hours of swimming lessons. Who offers a better deal? _____

8. There are 32 female performers in a dance recital. The ratio of men to women is 3:8. How many men are in the dance recital? _____

 ESSENTIAL QUESTION

9. How can you use ratios and rates to solve problems?

_____

_____

_____

_____

MODULE 6 MIXED REVIEW

Assessment Readiness

Personal
Math Trainer

⊙ my.hrw.com

Online
Assessment and
Intervention

Selected Response

1. Which ratio is **not** equivalent to the other three?

- (A) $\frac{2}{3}$
- (C) $\frac{12}{15}$
- (B) $\frac{6}{9}$
- (D) $\frac{18}{27}$

2. A lifeguard received 15 hours of first aid training and 10 hours of cardiopulmonary resuscitation (CPR) training. What is the ratio of hours of CPR training to hours of first aid training?

- (A) 15:10
- (C) 10:15
- (B) 15:25
- (D) 25:15

3. Jerry bought 4 DVDs for $25.20. What was the unit rate?

- (A) $3.15
- (C) $6.30
- (B) $4.20
- (D) $8.40

4. There are 1,920 fence posts used in a 12-kilometer stretch of fence. How many fence posts are used in 1 kilometer of fence?

- (A) 150
- (C) 155
- (B) 160
- (D) 180

5. Sheila can ride her bicycle 6,000 meters in 15 minutes. How far can she ride her bicycle in 2 minutes?

- (A) 400 meters
- (C) 800 meters
- (B) 600 meters
- (D) 1,000 meters

6. Lennon has a checking account. He withdrew $130 from an ATM Tuesday. Wednesday he deposited $240. Friday he wrote a check for $56. What was the total change in Lennon's account?

- (A) −$74
- (C) $184
- (B) $54
- (D) $226

7. Cheyenne is making a recipe that uses 5 cups of beans and 2 cups of carrots. Which combination below uses the same ratio of beans to carrots?

- (A) 10 cups of beans and 3 cups of carrots
- (B) 10 cups of beans and 4 cups of carrots
- (C) 12 cups of beans and 4 cups of carrots
- (D) 12 cups of beans and 5 cups of carrots

8. $\frac{5}{8}$ of the 64 musicians in a music contest are guitarists. Some of the guitarists play jazz solos, and the rest play classical solos. The ratio of the number of guitarists playing jazz solos to the total number of guitarists in the contest is 1:4. How many guitarists play classical solos in the contest?

- (A) 10
- (C) 16
- (B) 30
- (D) 48

Mini-Task

9. Mikaela is competing in a race in which she both runs and rides a bicycle. She runs 5 kilometers in 0.5 hour and rides her bicycle 20 kilometers in 0.8 hour.

a. At the rate given, how many kilometers can Mikaela run in 1 hour?

_____

b. At the rate given, how many kilometers can Mikaela bike in 1 hour?

_____

c. If Mikaela runs for 1 hour and bikes for 1 hour at the rates given, how far will she travel?

_____

Applying Ratios and Rates

ESSENTIAL QUESTION

How can you use ratios and rates to solve real-world problems?

LESSON 7.1

Ratios, Rates, Tables, and Graphs

 FL 6.RP.1.3, 6.RP.1.3a, 6.RP.1.3b

LESSON 7.2

Solving Problems with Proportions

 FL 6.RP.1.3, 6.RP.1.3b

LESSON 7.3

Converting Within Measurement Systems

FL 6.RP.1.3d

LESSON 7.4

Converting Between Measurement Systems

 FL 6.RP.1.3, 6.RP.1.3b, 6.RP.1.3d

Real-World Video

Chefs use lots of measurements when preparing meals. If a chef needs more or less of a dish, he can use ratios to scale the recipe up or down. Using proportional reasoning, the chef keeps the ratios of all ingredients constant.

 my.hrw.com

GO DIGITAL
my.hrw.com

my.hrw.com

Go digital with your write-in student edition, accessible on any device.

Math On the Spot

Scan with your smart phone to jump directly to the online edition, video tutor, and more.

Animated Math

Interactively explore key concepts to see how math works.

Personal Math Trainer

Get immediate feedback and help as you work through practice sets.

Are YOU Ready?

Complete these exercises to review skills you will need for this module.

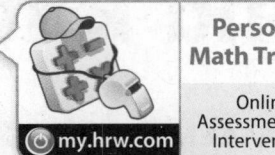

Graph Ordered Pairs (First Quadrant)

EXAMPLE

To graph A(2, 7), start at the origin.
Move 2 units right.
Then move 7 units up.
Graph point A(2, 7).

Graph each ordered pair on the coordinate plane above.

1. $B(9, 6)$
2. $C(0, 2)$
3. $D(6, 10)$
4. $E(3, 4)$

Write Equivalent Fractions

EXAMPLE $\dfrac{14}{21} = \dfrac{14 \times 2}{21 \times 2} = \dfrac{28}{42}$ Multiply the numerator and denominator by the same number to find an equivalent fraction.

$\dfrac{14}{21} = \dfrac{14 \div 7}{21 \div 7} = \dfrac{2}{3}$ Divide the numerator and denominator by the same number to find an equivalent fraction.

Write the equivalent fraction.

5. $\dfrac{6}{8} = \dfrac{\boxed{}}{32}$
6. $\dfrac{4}{6} = \dfrac{\boxed{}}{12}$
7. $\dfrac{1}{8} = \dfrac{\boxed{}}{56}$
8. $\dfrac{9}{12} = \dfrac{\boxed{}}{4}$

9. $\dfrac{5}{9} = \dfrac{25}{\boxed{}}$
10. $\dfrac{5}{6} = \dfrac{20}{\boxed{}}$
11. $\dfrac{36}{45} = \dfrac{12}{\boxed{}}$
12. $\dfrac{20}{36} = \dfrac{10}{\boxed{}}$

Multiples

EXAMPLE   List the first five multiples of 4.

$4 \times 1 = 4$
$4 \times 2 = 8$
$4 \times 3 = 12$ Multiply 4 by the numbers 1, 2, 3, 4, and 5.
$4 \times 4 = 16$
$4 \times 5 = 20$

List the first five multiples of each number.

13. 3 _____
14. 7 _____
15. 8 _____

Reading Start-Up

Visualize Vocabulary

Use the ✔ words to complete the graphic.

Comparing Unit Rates

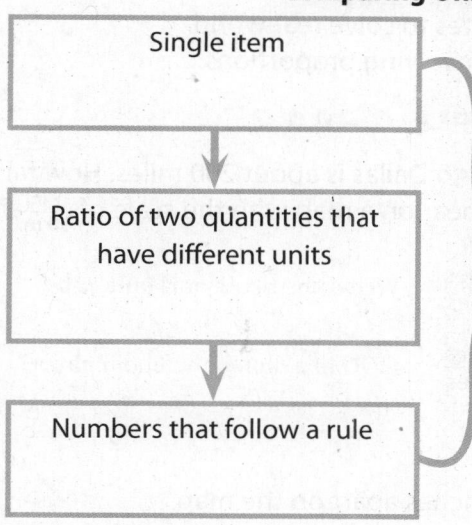

| Single item |

↓

| Ratio of two quantities that have different units |

↓

| Numbers that follow a rule |

| Rate in which the second quantity is one unit |

Understand Vocabulary

Complete the sentences using the preview words.

1. A _____ is a rate that compares two equivalent measurements.

2. In a scale drawing, the _____ describes how the dimensions in the actual object compare to the dimensions in the drawing.

Active Reading

Tri-Fold Before beginning the module, create a tri-fold to help you learn the concepts and vocabulary in this module. Fold the paper into three sections. Label one column "Rates and Ratios," the second column "Proportions," and the third column "Converting Measurements." Complete the tri-fold with important vocabulary, examples, and notes as you read the module.

Unpacking the Standards

Understanding the standards and the vocabulary terms in the standards will help you know exactly what you are expected to learn in this module.

 6.RP.1.3

Use ratio and rate reasoning to solve real-world and mathematical problems, e.g., by reasoning about tables of equivalent ratios, tape diagrams, double number line diagrams, or equations.

Key Vocabulary

ratio *(razón)*
A comparison of two quantities by division.

rate *(tasa)*
A ratio that compares two quantities measured in different units.

What It Means to You

You will use ratios and rates to solve real-world problems such as those involving proportions.

UNPACKING EXAMPLE 6.RP.1.3

The distance from Austin to Dallas is about 200 miles. How far apart will these cities appear on a map with the scale of $\frac{1 \text{ in.}}{50 \text{ mi}}$?

$$\frac{1 \text{ inch}}{50 \text{ miles}} = \frac{\blacksquare \text{ inches}}{200 \text{ miles}}$$ *Write the scale as a unit rate.*

$$\frac{1 \text{ inch} \times 4}{50 \text{ miles} \times 4} = \frac{\blacksquare \text{ inches}}{200 \text{ miles}}$$ *200 is a common denominator.*

$$\blacksquare = 4$$

Austin and Dallas are 4 inches apart on the map.

 6.RP.1.3d

Use ratio reasoning to convert measurement units; manipulate and transform units appropriately when multiplying or dividing quantities.

Key Vocabulary

unit rate *(tasa unitaria)*
A rate in which the second quantity in the comparison is one unit.

What It Means to You

You will use unit rates to convert measurement units.

UNPACKING EXAMPLE 6.RP.1.3D

The Washington Monument is about 185 yards tall. This height is almost equal to the length of two football fields. About how many feet is this?

$$185 \text{ yd} \cdot \frac{3 \text{ ft}}{1 \text{ yd}}$$

$$= \frac{185 \text{ yd}}{1} \cdot \frac{3 \text{ ft}}{1 \text{ yd}}$$

$$= 555 \text{ ft}$$

The Washington Monument is about 555 feet tall.

Visit **my.hrw.com** to see all **Florida Math Standards** unpacked.

my.hrw.com

Ratios, Rates, Tables, and Graphs

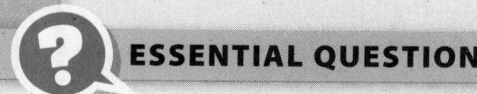

FL **6.RP.1.3a**
Make tables of equivalent ratios ..., find missing values in the tables, and plot the pairs of values on the coordinate plane. ... *Also 6.RP.1.3, 6.RP.1.3b*

? ESSENTIAL QUESTION

How can you represent real-world problems involving ratios and rates with tables and graphs?

EXPLORE ACTIVITY 1   FL **6.RP.1.3, 6.RP.1.3a**

Finding Ratios from Tables

Students in Mr. Webster's science classes are doing an experiment that requires 250 milliliters of distilled water for every 5 milliliters of ammonia. The table shows the amount of distilled water needed for various amounts of ammonia.

Ammonia (mL)	2	3	3.5		5
Distilled water (mL)	100			200	250

A Use the numbers in the first column of the table to write a ratio of distilled water to ammonia. _____

B How much distilled water is used for 1 milliliter of ammonia? _____
Use your answer to write another ratio of distilled water to ammonia.

_____

C The ratios in **A** and **B** are | **equivalent/not equivalent.** |

D How can you use your answer to **B** to find the amount of distilled water to add to a given amount of ammonia?

_____

_____

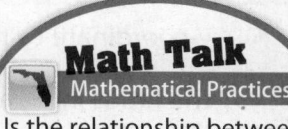
Math Talk
Mathematical Practices

Is the relationship between the amount of ammonia and the amount of distilled water additive or multiplicative? Explain.

E Complete the table. What are the equivalent ratios shown in the table?

$$\frac{100}{2} = \frac{\boxed{}}{3} = \frac{\boxed{}}{3.5} = \frac{200}{\boxed{}} = \frac{250}{5}$$

Reflect

1. Look for a Pattern When the amount of ammonia increases

by 1 milliliter, the amount of distilled water increases by _____

milliliters. So 6 milliliters of ammonia requires _____ milliliters of distilled water.

Graphing with Ratios

A Copy the table from Explore Activity 1 that shows the amounts of ammonia and distilled water.

Ammonia (mL)	2	3	3.5		5
Distilled water (mL)	100			200	250

B Write the information in the table as ordered pairs. Use the amount of ammonia as the *x*-coordinates and the amount of distilled water as the *y*-coordinates.

(2, _____) (3, _____), (3.5, _____), (_____, 200), (5, 250)

Graph the ordered pairs. Because fractions and decimals can represent amounts of chemicals, connect the points.

Describe your graph. _____

C For each ordered pair that you graphed, write the ratio of the

y-coordinate to the *x*-coordinate. _____

D The ratio of distilled water to ammonia is $\dfrac{\Box}{1}$. How are the ratios in

C related to this ratio? _____

E The point (2.5, 125) is on the graph but not in the table. The ratio of the

y-coordinate to the *x*-coordinate is _____. How is this ratio related to

the ratios in **C** and **D**? _____

2.5 milliliters of ammonia requires _____ milliliters of distilled water.

F **Conjecture** What do you think is true for every point on the graph?

_____

_____

Reflect

2. **Communicate Mathematical Ideas** How can you use the graph to find the amount of distilled water to use for 4.5 milliliters of ammonia?

_____

_____

(graph: Distilled Water (mL) on vertical axis marked 100, 200, 300; Ammonia (mL) on horizontal axis marked 2, 4, 6; point plotted at (5, 250))

Representing Rates with Tables and Graphs

You can use tables and graphs to represent real-world problems involving equivalent rates.

Math On the Spot
my.hrw.com

Animated Math
my.hrw.com

EXAMPLE 1   FL 6.RP.1.3a, 6.RP.1.3b

The Webster family is taking an express train to Washington, D.C. The train travels at a constant speed and makes the trip in 2 hours.

A Make a table to show the distance the train travels in various amounts of time.

STEP 1 Write a ratio of distance to time to find the rate.

$$\frac{\text{distance}}{\text{time}} = \frac{120 \text{ miles}}{2 \text{ hours}} = \frac{60 \text{ miles}}{1 \text{ hour}} = 60 \text{ miles per hour}$$

STEP 2 Use the unit rate to make a table.

Time (h)	2	3	3.5	4	5
Distance (mi)	120	180	210	240	300

B Graph the information from the table.

STEP 1 Write ordered pairs. Use Time as the x-coordinates and Distance as the y-coordinates.

(2, 120), (3, 180), (3.5, 210), (4, 240), (5, 300)

STEP 2 Graph the ordered pairs and connect the points.

YOUR TURN

3. A shower uses 12 gallons of water in 3 minutes. Complete the table and graph.

Time (min)	2	3	3.5		6.5
Water used (gal)			20		

Personal Math Trainer
Online Assessment and Intervention
my.hrw.com

© Houghton Mifflin Harcourt Publishing Company

1. The ratio of oxygen atoms to sulfur atoms in sulfur dioxide is always the same. The table shows the numbers of atoms in different quantities of sulfur dioxide. Complete the table. (Explore Activity 1)

Sulfur atoms	6	9	21	
Oxygen atoms	12			54

What are the equivalent ratios shown in the table?

_____

2. Use the table in Exercise 1 to graph the relationship between sulfur atoms and oxygen atoms. (Explore Activity 2)

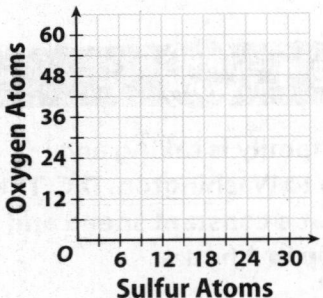

3. Stickers are made with the same ratio of width to length. A sticker 2 inches wide has a length of 4 inches. Complete the table. (Explore Activity 1)

Width (in.)	2	4	7	
Length (in.)				16

What are the equivalent ratios shown in the table?

_____

4. Graph the relationship between the width and the length of the stickers from Exercise 3. (Explore Activity 2)

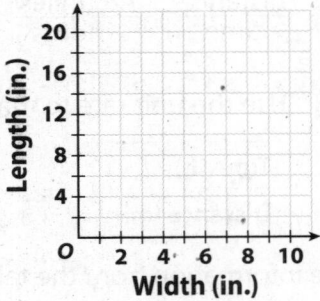

5. Five boxes of candles contain a total of 60 candles. Each box holds the same number of candles. Complete the table and graph the relationship. (Example 1)

Boxes	5	8	
Candles			120

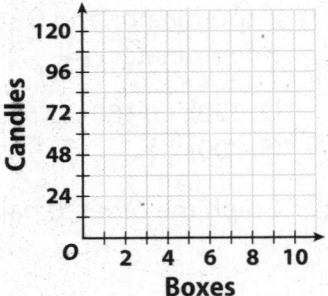

6. How do you represent real-world problems involving ratios and rates with tables and graphs?

_____

_____

_____

_____

© Houghton Mifflin Harcourt Publishing Company

7.1 Independent Practice

FL 6.RP.1.3, 6.RP.1.3a, 6.RP.1.3b

Personal Math Trainer

Online Assessment and Intervention

my.hrw.com

The table shows information about the number of sweatshirts sold and the money collected at a fundraiser for school athletic programs. For Exercises 7–12, use the table.

Sweatshirts sold	3	5	8		12
Money collected ($)	60			180	

7. Find the rate of money collected per sweatshirt sold. Show your work.

_____

_____

8. Use the unit rate to complete the table.

9. Explain how to graph information from the table.

_____

_____

_____

_____

10. Write the information in the table as ordered pairs. Graph the relationship from the table.

_____

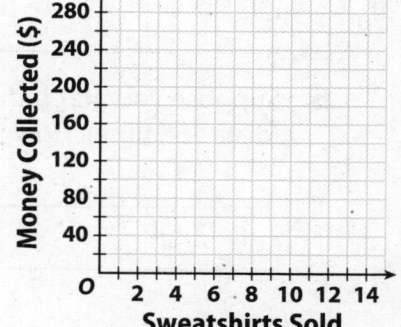

11. What If? How much money would be collected if 24 sweatshirts were sold? Show your work.

_____

_____

12. Analyze Relationships Does the point (5.5, 110) make sense in this context? Explain.

_____

_____

_____

13. Communicate Mathematical Ideas The table shows the distance Randy drove on one day of her vacation. Find the distance Randy would have gone if she had driven for one more hour at the same rate. Explain how you solved the problem.

Time (h)	1	2	3	4	5
Distance (mi)	55	110	165	220	275

_____

_____

Use the graph for Exercises 14–15.

14. Analyze Relationships How many weeks correspond to 56 days? Explain.

_____

15. Represent Real-World Problems What is a real-life relationship that might be described by the graph?

_____

_____

H.O.T. FOCUS ON HIGHER ORDER THINKING

Work Area

16. Make a Conjecture Complete the table. Then find the rates $\frac{distance}{time}$ and $\frac{time}{distance}$.

Time (min)	1	2	5	
Distance (m)			25	100

$\frac{distance}{time}$ = _____

$\frac{time}{distance}$ = _____

a. Are the $\frac{time}{distance}$ rates equivalent? Explain.

_____

b. Suppose you graph the points (time, distance) and your friend graphs (distance, time). How will your graphs be different?

_____

_____

_____

17. Communicate Mathematical Ideas To graph a rate or ratio from a table, how do you determine the scales to use on each axis?

_____

_____

_____

Solving Problems with Proportions

FL 6.RP.1.3
Use ratio and rate reasoning to solve real-world and mathematical problems, e.g., by reasoning about... equations. Also 6.RP.1.3b

Math On the Spot
my.hrw.com

? ESSENTIAL QUESTION

How can you solve problems with proportions?

Using Equivalent Ratios to Solve Proportions

A **proportion** is a statement that two ratios or rates are equivalent.

$\frac{1}{3}$ and $\frac{2}{6}$ are equivalent ratios. $\frac{1}{3} = \frac{2}{6}$ is a proportion.

EXAMPLE 1 Real World

FL 6.RP.1.3

Sheldon and Leonard are partners in a business. Sheldon makes $2 in profits for every $5 that Leonard makes. If Leonard makes $20 profit on the first item they sell, how much profit does Sheldon make?

STEP 1 Write a proportion.

> Sheldon's profit is unknown.

$$\text{Sheldon's profit} \rightarrow \frac{\$2}{\$5} = \frac{\blacksquare}{\$20} \leftarrow \text{Sheldon's profit}$$
$$\text{Leonard's profit} \rightarrow \qquad\qquad \leftarrow \text{Leonard's profit}$$

STEP 2 Use common denominators to write equivalent ratios.

$\frac{\$2 \times 4}{\$5 \times 4} = \frac{\blacksquare}{\$20}$ *20 is a common denominator.*

$\frac{\$8}{\$20} = \frac{\blacksquare}{\$20}$ *Equivalent ratios with the same denominators have the same numerators.*

$\blacksquare = \$8$

If Leonard makes $20 profit, Sheldon makes $8 profit.

> **Math Talk**
> **Mathematical Practices**
> For every dollar that Leonard makes, how much does Sheldon make? Explain.

YOUR TURN

1. The members of the PTA are ordering pizza for a meeting. They plan to order 2 cheese pizzas for every 3 pepperoni pizzas they order. How many cheese pizzas will they order if they order 15 pepperoni pizzas?

_____

_____

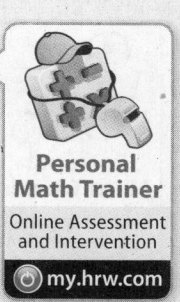
Personal Math Trainer
Online Assessment and Intervention
my.hrw.com

Using Unit Rates to Solve Proportions

You can also use equivalent rates to solve proportions. Finding a unit rate may help you write equivalent rates.

EXAMPLE 2 FL **6.RP.1.3b**

The distance Ali runs in 36 minutes is shown on the pedometer. At this rate, how far could he run in 60 minutes?

STEP 1 Write a proportion.

$$\frac{\text{time} \rightarrow}{\text{distance} \rightarrow} \frac{36 \text{ minutes}}{3 \text{ miles}} = \frac{60 \text{ minutes}}{\blacksquare \text{ miles}} \frac{\leftarrow \text{ time}}{\leftarrow \text{ distance}}$$

60 is not a multiple of 36. So, there is no whole number by which you can multiply 3 miles to find ▇.

STEP 2 Find the unit rate of the rate you know.

> You know that Ali runs 3 miles in 36 minutes.

$$\frac{36 \div 3}{3 \div 3} = \frac{12}{1}$$

The unit rate is 12 minutes per 1 mile.

STEP 3 Use the unit rate to write an equivalent rate that compares 60 miles to an unknown number of minutes.

Think: You can multiply $12 \times 5 = 60$. So multiply the denominator by the same number.

$$\frac{12 \times 5}{1 \times 5} = \frac{60}{\blacksquare}$$

Equivalent rates with the same numerators have the same denominators.

$$\frac{60}{5} = \frac{60}{\blacksquare}$$

$$\blacksquare = 5 \text{ miles}$$

At this rate, Ali can run 5 miles in 60 minutes.

Math Talk

Mathematical Practices

Compare the fractions $\frac{36}{3}$ and $\frac{60}{5}$ using <, > or =. Explain.

YOUR TURN

2. Ms. Reynold's sprinkler system has 9 stations that water all the parts of her front and back lawn. Each station runs for an equal amount of time. If it takes 48 minutes for the first 4 stations to water, how long

   does it take to water all parts of her lawn? _____

Using Proportional Relationships to Find Distance on a Map

A **scale drawing** is a drawing of a real object that is proportionally smaller or larger than the real object. A **scale** describes how the dimensions in the objects compare.

A map is a scale drawing. The measurements on a map are in proportion to the actual distances. If 1 inch on a map equals an actual distance of 2 miles, the scale is 1 inch = 2 miles. You can write a scale as a rate to solve problems.

EXAMPLE 3 FL 6.RP.1.3b

The distance between two schools on Lehigh Avenue is shown on the map. What is the actual distance between the schools?

Scale: 1 inch = 2 miles

STEP 1 Write a proportion.

$$\frac{2 \text{ miles}}{1 \text{ inch}} = \frac{\boxed{} \text{ miles}}{3 \text{ inches}}$$

Write the scale as a unit rate.

STEP 2 Write an equivalent rate to find the missing number.

$$\frac{2 \text{ miles} \times 3}{1 \text{ inch} \times 3} = \frac{6 \text{ miles}}{3 \text{ inches}}$$

So, in Step 1, the missing number is 6.

The actual distance between the two schools is 6 miles.

YOUR TURN

3. The distance between Sandville and Lewiston is shown on the map. What is the actual distance between the towns?

_____

Scale: 1 inch = 20 miles

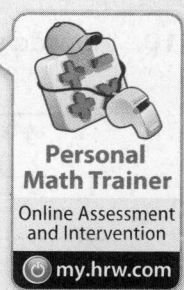

Find the unknown value in each proportion. (Example 1)

1. $\dfrac{3}{5} = \dfrac{\blacksquare}{30}$

   $\dfrac{3 \times \boxed{}}{5 \times \boxed{}} = \dfrac{\boxed{}}{30}$

2. $\dfrac{4}{10} = \dfrac{\blacksquare}{5}$

   $\dfrac{4 \div \boxed{}}{10 \div \boxed{}} = \dfrac{\boxed{}}{5}$

Solve using equivalent ratios. (Example 1)

3. Leila and Jo are two of the partners in a business. Leila makes $3 in profits for every $4 that Jo makes. If Jo makes $60 profit on the first item they sell, how much profit does Leila make? _____

4. Hendrick wants to enlarge a photo that is 4 inches wide and 6 inches tall. The enlarged photo keeps the same ratio. How tall is the enlarged photo if it is 12 inches wide? _____

Solve using unit rates. (Example 2)

5. A person on a moving sidewalk travels 21 feet in 7 seconds. The moving sidewalk has a length of 180 feet. How long will it take to move from one end of the sidewalk to the other?

   _____

6. In a repeating musical pattern, there are 56 beats in 7 measures. How many measures are there in 104 beats?

   _____

7. Contestants in a dance-a-thon rest for the same amount of time every hour. A couple rests for 25 minutes in 5 hours. How long did they rest in 8 hours?

   _____

8. Frances gets 6 paychecks in 12 weeks. How many paychecks does she get in 52 weeks?

   _____

9. What is the actual distance between Gendet and Montrose? (Example 3)

   _____

Scale: 1 centimeter = 16 kilometers

? ESSENTIAL QUESTION CHECK-IN

10. How do you solve problems with proportions?

_____

_____

_____

7.2 Independent Practice

FL 6.RP.1.3, 6.RP.1.3b

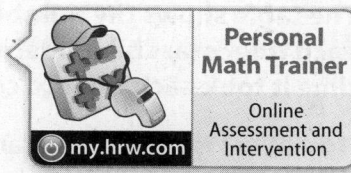

Personal Math Trainer

Online Assessment and Intervention

my.hrw.com

11. The scale of the map is missing. The actual distance from Liberty to West Quall is 72 miles, and it is 6 inches on the map.

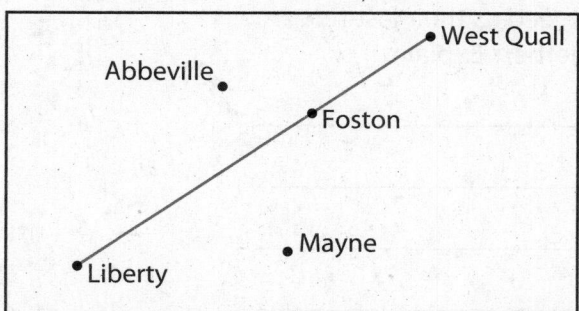

a. What is the scale of the map?

_____

b. Foston is between Liberty and West Quall and is 4 inches from Liberty on the map. How far is Foston from West Quall?

_____

12. A punch recipe says to mix 4 cups pineapple juice, 8 cups orange juice, and 12 cups seltzer in order to make 18 servings of punch.

a. How many cups of each ingredient do you need to make 108 cups of punch?

_____ cups pineapple juice

_____ cups orange juice

_____ cups seltzer

b. How many servings can be made from 108 cups of punch? _____

c. For every cup of seltzer you use, how much orange juice do you use?

_____

13. On an airplane, there are two seats on the left side in each row and three seats on the right side. There are 90 seats on the right side of the plane.

a. How many seats are on the left side of the plane? _____

b. How many seats are there altogether? _____

14. Carrie and Krystal are taking a road trip from Greenville to North Valley. Each person has her own map, and the scales on the maps are different.

a. On Carrie's map, Greenville and North Valley are 4.5 inches apart. The scale on her map is 1 inch = 20 miles. How far is Greenville from North Valley?

_____

b. The scale on Krystal's map is 1 inch = 18 miles. How far apart are Greenville and North Valley on Krystal's map?

_____

15. Multistep A machine can produce 27 inches of ribbon every 3 minutes. How many feet of ribbon can the machine make in one hour? Explain.

_____

_____

_____

_____

_____

Marta, Loribeth, and Ira all have bicycles. The table shows the number of miles of each rider's last bike ride, as well as the time it took each rider to complete the ride.

	Distance of Last Ride (in miles)	Time Spent on Last Bike Ride (in minutes)
Marta	8	80
Loribeth	6	42
Ira	15	75

16. What is Marta's unit rate, in minutes per mile? _____

17. Whose speed was the fastest on their last bike ride? _____

18. If all three riders travel for 3.5 hours at the same speed as their last ride, how many total miles will the 3 riders travel altogether? Explain.

_____

_____

_____

_____

19. **Critique Reasoning** Jason watched a caterpillar move 10 feet in 2 minutes. Jason says that the caterpillar's unit rate is 0.2 feet per minute. Is Jason correct? Explain.

_____

_____

 FOCUS ON HIGHER ORDER THINKING

Work Area

20. **Analyze Relationships** If the number in the numerator of a unit rate is 1, what does this indicate about the equivalent unit rates? Give an example.

_____

_____

21. **Multiple Representations** A boat travels at a constant speed. After 20 minutes, the boat has traveled 2.5 miles. The boat travels a total of 10 miles to a bridge.

a. Graph the relationship between the distance the boat travels and the time it takes.

b. How long does it take the boat to reach the bridge? Explain how you found it.

_____

_____

_____

Converting Within Measurement Systems

FL 6.RP.1.3d
Use ratio reasoning to convert measurement units; manipulate and transform units appropriately when multiplying or dividing quantities. *Also 6.RP.1.3*

? ESSENTIAL QUESTION

How do you convert units within a measurement system?

EXPLORE ACTIVITY   FL 6.RP.1.3d

Using a Model to Convert Units

The two most common systems of measurement are the customary system and the metric system. You can use a model to convert from one unit to another within the same measurement system.

STEP 1 Use the model to complete each statement below.

1 yard = 3 feet

2 yards = _____ feet

3 yards = _____ feet

4 yards = _____ feet

	3	6	9	12
feet				
yards	1	2	3	4

STEP 2 Rewrite your answers as ratios.

$$\frac{\boxed{}\text{ feet}}{2\text{ yards}} = \frac{3\text{ feet}}{1\text{ yard}} \qquad \frac{\boxed{}\text{ feet}}{3\text{ yards}} = \frac{3\text{ feet}}{1\text{ yard}} \qquad \frac{\boxed{}\text{ feet}}{4\text{ yards}} = \frac{3\text{ feet}}{1\text{ yard}}$$

Since 1 yard = 3 feet, the ratio of feet to yards in any measurement is always $\frac{3}{1}$. This means any ratio forming a proportion with $\frac{3}{1}$ can represent a ratio of feet to yards.

$\frac{3}{1} = \frac{12}{4}$, so 12 feet = _____ yards. $\frac{3}{1} = \frac{54}{18}$, so _____ feet = 18 yards.

Reflect

1. **Communicate Mathematical Ideas** How could you draw a model to show the relationship between feet and inches?

_____

_____

_____

Converting Units Using Proportions and Unit Rates

You can use ratios and proportions to convert both customary and metric units. Use the table below to convert from one unit to another within the same measurement system.

Customary Measurements		
Length	**Weight**	**Capacity**
1 ft = 12 in. 1 yd = 36 in. 1 yd = 3 ft 1 mi = 5,280 ft 1 mi = 1,760 yd	1 lb = 16 oz 1 T = 2,000 lb	1 c = 8 fl oz 1 pt = 2 c 1 qt = 2 pt 1 qt = 4 c 1 gal = 4 qt
Metric Measurements		
Length	**Mass**	**Capacity**
1 km = 1,000 m 1 m = 100 cm 1 cm = 10 mm	1 kg = 1,000 g 1 g = 1,000 mg	1 L = 1,000 mL

EXAMPLE 1 Real World

FL 6.RP.1.3d

My Notes

A What is the weight of a 3-pound human brain in ounces?

Use a proportion to convert 3 pounds to ounces.

Use $\frac{16 \text{ ounces}}{1 \text{ pound}}$ to convert pounds to ounces.

STEP 1 Write a proportion.

$$\frac{16 \text{ ounces}}{1 \text{ pound}} = \frac{\blacksquare \text{ ounces}}{3 \text{ pounds}}$$

STEP 2 Use common denominators to write equivalent ratios.

$$\frac{16 \times 3}{1 \times 3} = \frac{\blacksquare}{3}$$ 3 is a common denominator.

$$\frac{48}{3} = \frac{\blacksquare}{3}$$ Equivalent rates with the same denominators have the same numerators.

$$\blacksquare = 48 \text{ ounces}$$

The weight is 48 ounces.

B A moderate amount of daily sodium consumption is 2,000 milligrams. What is this mass in grams?

Use a proportion to convert 2,000 milligrams to grams.

Use $\frac{1,000 \text{ mg}}{1 \text{ g}}$ to convert milligrams to grams.

STEP 1 Write a proportion.

$$\frac{1{,}000 \text{ mg}}{1 \text{ g}} = \frac{2{,}000 \text{ mg}}{\blacksquare \text{ g}}$$

STEP 2 Write equivalent ratios.

Think: You can multiply $1{,}000 \times 2 = 2{,}000$. So multiply the denominator by the same number.

$$\frac{1{,}000 \times 2}{1 \times 2} = \frac{2{,}000}{\blacksquare}$$

$$\frac{2{,}000}{2} = \frac{2{,}000}{\blacksquare}$$ Equivalent ratios with the same numerators have the same denominators.

$$\blacksquare = 2 \text{ grams}$$

The mass is 2 grams.

Math Talk

Mathematical Practices

How would you convert 3 liters to milliliters?

YOUR TURN

2. The height of a doorway is 2 yards. What is the height of the doorway in inches? _____

Personal Math Trainer

Online Assessment and Intervention

my.hrw.com

Converting Units by Using Conversion Factors

Another way to convert measurements is by using a conversion factor. A **conversion factor** is a ratio comparing two equivalent measurements.

Math On the Spot

my.hrw.com

EXAMPLE 2 Real World   FL **6.RP.1.3d**

Elena wants to buy 2 gallons of milk but can only find quart containers for sale. How many quarts does she need?

> You are converting *to* quarts *from* gallons.

STEP 1 Find the conversion factor.

Write 4 quarts = 1 gallon as a ratio: $\dfrac{4 \text{ quarts}}{1 \text{ gallon}}$

STEP 2 Multiply the given measurement by the conversion factor.

$$2 \text{ gallons} \cdot \frac{4 \text{ quarts}}{1 \text{ gallon}} = \blacksquare \text{ quarts}$$

  $2 \text{ gallons} \cdot \dfrac{4 \text{ quarts}}{1 \text{ gallon}}$ $= 8 \text{ quarts}$ *Cancel the common unit.*

Elena needs 8 quarts of milk.

© Houghton Mifflin Harcourt Publishing Company

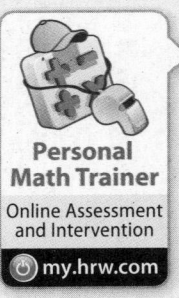
YOUR TURN

3. An oak tree is planted when it is 250 centimeters tall. What is this height in meters? _____

Guided Practice

Use the model below to complete each statement. (Explore Activity 1)

1. $\frac{4}{1} = \frac{12}{3}$, so 12 cups = _____ quarts

2. $\frac{4}{1} = \frac{48}{12}$, so _____ cups = 12 quarts

Use ratios and proportions to solve. (Example 1)

3. Mary Catherine makes 2 gallons of punch for her party. How many cups of punch did she make?

_____

4. An African elephant weighs 6 tons. What is the weight of the elephant in pounds?

_____

5. The distance from Jason's house to school is 0.5 kilometer. What is this distance in meters?

_____

6. The mass of a moon rock is 3.5 kilograms. What is the mass of the moon rock in grams?

_____

Use a conversion factor to solve. (Example 2)

7. 1.75 grams · $\frac{1,000 \text{ mg}}{1 \text{ g}}$ = _____

8. 27 millimeters · $\frac{1 \text{ cm}}{10 \text{ mm}}$ = _____

9. A package weighs 96 ounces. What is the weight of the package in pounds?

_____

10. A jet flies at an altitude of 52,800 feet. What is the height of the jet in miles?

_____

? **ESSENTIAL QUESTION CHECK-IN**

11. How do you convert units within a measurement system?

_____

_____

Name_____ Class_____ Date_____

7.3 Independent Practice

FL 6.RP.1.3, 6.RP.1.3d

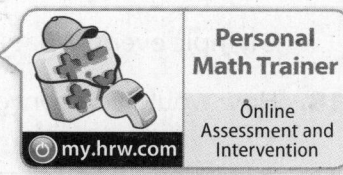

Personal Math Trainer

Online Assessment and Intervention

my.hrw.com

12. What is a conversion factor that you can use to convert gallons to pints? How did you find it?

_____

13. Three friends each have some ribbon. Carol has 42 inches of ribbon, Tino has 2.5 feet of ribbon, and Baxter has 1.5 yards of ribbon. Express the total length of ribbon the three friends have in inches, feet and yards.

_____ inches = _____ feet = _____ yards

14. Suzanna wants to measure a board, but she doesn't have a ruler to measure with. However, she does have several copies of a book that she knows is 17 centimeters tall.

a. Suzanna lays the books end to end and finds that the board is the same length as 21 books. How many centimeters long is the board?

_____

b. Suzanna needs a board that is at least 3.5 meters long. Is the board long enough? Explain.

_____

_____

Sheldon needs to buy 8 gallons of ice cream for a family reunion. The table shows the prices for different sizes of two brands of ice cream.

	Price of small size	Price of large size
Cold Farms	$2.50 for 1 pint	$4.50 for 1 quart
Cone Dreams	$4.25 for 1 quart	$9.50 for 1 gallon

15. Which size container of Cold Farm ice cream is the better deal for Sheldon? Explain.

_____

_____

_____

16. Multistep Which size and brand of ice cream is the best deal?

_____

© Houghton Mifflin Harcourt Publishing Company

17. In Beijing in 2008, the Women's 3,000 meter Steeplechase became an Olympic event. What is this distance in kilometers? _____

18. How would you convert 5 feet 6 inches to inches? _____

_____

London 2012

H.O.T. FOCUS ON HIGHER ORDER THINKING

19. Analyze Relationships A Class 4 truck weighs between 14,000 and 16,000 pounds.

  a. What is the weight range in tons? _____

  b. If the weight of a Class 4 truck is increased by 2 tons, will it still be classified as a Class 4 truck? Explain.

    _____

    _____

20. Persevere in Problem Solving A football field is shown at right.

  a. What are the dimensions of a football field in feet?

    _____

$53\frac{1}{3}$ yd

120 yd

  b. A chalk line is placed around the perimeter of the football field. What is the length of this line in feet?

    _____

  c. About how many laps around the perimeter of the field would equal 1 mile? Explain.

    _____

    _____

21. Look for a Pattern What is the result if you multiply a number of cups by $\frac{8 \text{ fl oz}}{1 \text{ cup}}$ and then multiply the result by $\frac{1 \text{ cup}}{8 \text{ fl oz}}$? Give an example.

_____

_____

22. Make a Conjecture 1 hour = 3,600 seconds and 1 mile = 5,280 feet. Make a conjecture about how you could convert a speed of 15 miles per hour to feet per second. Then convert.

_____

_____

_____

Work Area

LESSON 7.4 Converting Between Measurement Systems

FL 6.RP.1.3d

Use ratio reasoning to convert measurement units; manipulate and transform units appropriately when multiplying or dividing quantities. *Also 6.RP.1.3, 6.RP.1.3b*

? ESSENTIAL QUESTION

How can you use ratios and proportions to convert measurements?

EXPLORE ACTIVITY   FL 6.RP.1.3d

Converting Inches to Centimeters

Measurements are used when determining the length, weight, or capacity of an object. The two most common systems of measurement are the *customary system* and the *metric system*.

The table shows equivalencies between the customary and metric systems. You can use these equivalencies to convert a measurement in one system to a measurement in the other system.

Length	Weight/Mass	Capacity
1 inch = 2.54 centimeters 1 foot ≈ 0.305 meter 1 yard ≈ 0.914 meter 1 mile ≈ 1.61 kilometers	1 ounce ≈ 28.4 grams 1 pound ≈ 0.454 kilogram	1 fluid ounce ≈ 29.6 milliliters 1 quart ≈ 0.946 liter 1 gallon ≈ 3.79 liters

Most conversions are approximate, as indicated by the symbol ≈.

The length of a sheet of paper is 11 inches. What is this length in centimeters?

A You can use a bar diagram to solve this problem. Each part represents 1 inch.

1 inch = _____ centimeter(s)

11 in.

1 in.										

[____] cm

B How does the diagram help you solve the problem?

_____

C 11 inches = _____ centimeters

Reflect

1. **Communicate Mathematical Ideas** Suppose you wanted to use a diagram to convert ounces to grams. Which unit would the parts in your diagram represent?

_____

_____

Math On the Spot
⏻ my.hrw.com

Using Conversion Factors

Another way to convert measurements is by using a ratio called a *conversion factor*. A **conversion factor** is a ratio of two equivalent measurements. Since the two measurements in a conversion factor are equivalent, a conversion factor is equal to 1.

EXAMPLE 1   FL   6.RP.1.3d

While lifting weights, John adds 11.35 kilograms to his bar. About how many pounds does he add to his bar?

STEP 1 Find the conversion factor.

1 pound ≈ 0.454 kilogram

Write the conversion factor as a ratio: $\dfrac{1 \text{ pound}}{0.454 \text{ kilogram}}$

STEP 2 Convert the given measurement.

kilograms	×	conversion factor	=	pounds

11.35 kilograms × $\dfrac{1 \text{ pound}}{0.454 \text{ kilogram}}$ ≈ 25 pounds

John adds about 25 pounds to his bar.

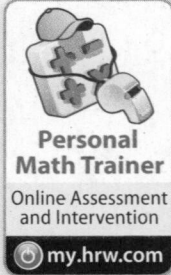

Personal Math Trainer

Online Assessment and Intervention

⏻ my.hrw.com

YOUR TURN

2. 6 quarts ≈ _____ liters   3. 14 feet ≈ _____ meters

4. 255.6 grams ≈ _____ ounces   5. 7 liters ≈ _____ quarts

Using Proportions to Convert Measurements

You can also convert a measurement from one unit to another by using a proportion. First write the conversion factor as a ratio, then multiply by a form of 1 to generate an equivalent ratio. Recall that two equal ratios form a proportion.

Proportions: $\dfrac{3 \text{ inches}}{2 \text{ feet}} = \dfrac{6 \text{ inches}}{4 \text{ feet}}$ $\dfrac{5}{10} = \dfrac{1}{2}$

EXAMPLE 2   FL 6.RP.1.3, 6.RP.1.3b, 6.RP.1.3d

My Notes

Bob's driveway is 45 feet long by 18 feet wide. He plans to pave the entire driveway. The asphalt paving costs $24 per square meter. What will be the total cost of the paving?

45 ft

18 ft

STEP 1 First find the dimensions of the driveway in meters.

Convert each measurement to meters.
Use 1 foot ≈ 0.305 meter.

$$\dfrac{1 \text{ foot}}{0.305 \text{ meter}} \overset{\times 45}{=} \dfrac{45 \text{ feet}}{13.725 \text{ meters}} \quad \times 45$$

Length ≈ 13.725 meters

$$\dfrac{1 \text{ foot}}{0.305 \text{ meter}} \overset{\times 18}{=} \dfrac{18 \text{ feet}}{5.49 \text{ meters}} \quad \times 18$$

Width ≈ 5.49 meters

> The length and width are approximate because the conversion between feet and meters is approximate.

STEP 2 Find the area in square meters.

Area = length × width

= 13.725 × 5.49

= 75.35 square meters

STEP 3 Now find the total cost of the paving.

square meters × cost per square meter = total cost
75.35   × $24   = $1,808.40

Math Talk
Mathematical Practices

How much does the paving cost per square foot? Explain.

Reflect

6. **Error Analysis** Yolanda found the area of Bob's driveway in square meters as shown. Explain why Yolanda's answer is incorrect.

> Area = 45 × 18 = 810 square feet
>
> 810 square feet × $\dfrac{0.305 \text{ meter}}{1 \text{ foot}}$ ≈ 247.1 square meters

_____

_____

YOUR TURN

7. A flower bed is 2 meters wide and 3 meters long. What is the area of the flower bed in square feet? Round your converted dimensions and your final answer to the nearest hundredth.

_____ square feet

Guided Practice

Complete each diagram to solve the problem. (Explore Activity)

1. Kate ran 5 miles. How far did she run in kilometers?

   5 miles = _____ kilometers

2. Alex filled a 5-gallon jug with water. How many liters of water are in the container?

   5 gallons ≈ _____ liters

Use a conversion factor to convert each measurement. (Example 1 and 2)

3. A ruler is 12 inches long. What is the length of this ruler in centimeters?

   _____ centimeters

4. A kitten weighs 4 pounds. What is the approximate mass of the kitten in kilograms?

   _____ kilograms

Use a proportion to convert each measurement. (Example 2)

5. 20 yards ≈ _____ meters

6. 12 ounces ≈ _____ grams

7. 5 quarts ≈ _____ liters

8. 400 meters ≈ _____ yards

9. 10 liters ≈ _____ gallons

10. 137.25 meters ≈ _____ feet

11. 165 centimeters ≈ _____ inches

12. 10,000 kilometers ≈ _____ miles

? ESSENTIAL QUESTION CHECK-IN

13. Write a proportion that you can use to convert 60 inches to centimeters.

_____

7.4 Independent Practice

FL 6.RP.1.3, 6.RP.1.3b, 6.RP.1.3d

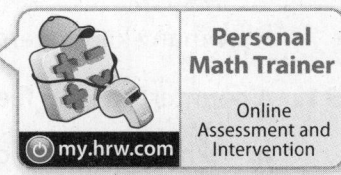

Personal Math Trainer

my.hrw.com

Online Assessment and Intervention

Tell which measure is greater.

14. Six feet or two meters _____

15. One inch or one centimeter _____

16. One yard or one meter _____

17. One mile or one kilometer _____

18. One ounce or one gram _____

19. One quart or one liter _____

20. 10 pounds or 10 kilograms _____

21. Four liters or one gallon _____

22. Two miles or three kilometers _____

23. What is the limit in kilograms?

weight limit for checked baggage: 50 pounds

_____

24. What is the speed limit in miles per hour?

_____

25. Which container holds more, a half-gallon milk jug or a 2-liter juice bottle?

_____

26. The label on a can of lemonade gives the volume as 12 fl oz, or 355 mL. Verify that these two measurements are nearly equivalent.

_____

27. The mass of a textbook is about 1.25 kilograms. About how many pounds is this?

_____

28. **Critique Reasoning** Michael estimated his mass as 8 kilograms. Is his estimate reasonable? Justify your answer.

_____

29. Your mother bought a three-liter bottle of water. When she got home, she discovered a small leak in the bottom and asked you to find a container to transfer the water into. All you could find were two half-gallon jugs.

a. Will your containers hold all of the water?

_____

_____

_____

b. **What If?** Suppose an entire liter of water leaked out in the car. In that case, would you be able to fit all of the remaining water into one of the half-gallon jugs?

_____

_____

_____

30. The track team ran a mile and a quarter during their practice.

How many kilometers did the team run? _____

31. A countertop is 16 feet long and 3 feet wide.

    a. What is the area of the countertop in square meters? _____

    b. Tile costs $28 per square meter. How much will it cost to cover the

       countertop with new tile? $ _____

32. At a school picnic, your teacher asks you to mark a field every ten yards so students can play football. The teacher accidentally gave you a meter stick instead of a yard stick. How far apart in meters should you mark the lines if you still want them to be in the right places?

_____

33. You weigh a gallon of 2% milk in science class and learn that it is approximately 8.4 pounds. You pass the milk to the next group, and then realize that your teacher wanted an answer in kilograms, not pounds. Explain how you can adjust your answer without weighing the milk again. Then give the weight in kilograms.

_____

H.O.T. FOCUS ON HIGHER ORDER THINKING

34. Analyze Relationships Annalisa, Keiko, and Stefan want to compare their heights. Annalisa is 64 inches tall. Stefan tells her, "I'm about 7.5 centimeters taller than you." Keiko knows she is 1.5 inches shorter than Stefan. Give the heights of all three people in both inches and centimeters to the nearest half unit.

_____

_____

_____

_____

35. Communicate Mathematical Ideas Mikhael wanted to rewrite the conversion factor "1 yard ≈ 0.914 meter" to create a conversion factor to convert meters to yards. He wrote "1 meter ≈ _____ ." Tell how Mikhael should finish his conversion, and explain how you know.

_____

_____

_____

Work Area

Ready to Go On?

Personal Math Trainer

Online Assessment and Intervention

my.hrw.com

7.1 Ratios, Rates, Tables, and Graphs

1. Charlie runs laps around a track. The table shows how long it takes him to run different numbers of laps. How long would it take Charlie to run 5 laps?

Number of Laps	2	4	6	8	10
Time (min)	10	20	30	40	50

_____

7.2 Solving Proportionality Problems

2. Emily is entering a bicycle race for charity. Her mother pledges $0.40 for every 0.25 mile she bikes. If Emily bikes 15 miles, how much will her

   mother donate? _____

3. Rob is saving to buy a new MP3 player. For every $15 he earns babysitting, he saves $6. On Saturday, Rob earned $75 babysitting.

   How much money did he save? _____

7.3 Within Measurement Systems

Convert each measurement.

4. 18 meters = _____ centimeters

5. 5 pounds = _____ ounces

6. 6 quarts = _____ fluid ounces

7. 9 liters = _____ milliliters

7.4 Converting Between Measurement Systems

Convert each measurement.

8. 5 inches = _____ centimeters

9. 198.9 grams ≈ _____ ounces

10. 8 gallons ≈ _____ liters

11. 12 feet ≈ _____ meters

 ESSENTIAL QUESTION

12. Write a real-world problem that could be solved using a proportion.

   _____

   _____

   _____

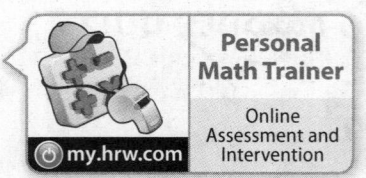

Personal Math Trainer

Online Assessment and Intervention

my.hrw.com

Selected Response

1. The graph below represents the distance Manuel walks over several hours.

Which is an ordered pair on the line?

(A) (2.5, 14)   (C) (2.25, 12)

(B) (1.25, 5)   (D) (1.5, 9)

2. Jonah's house and his grandparents' house are 8,046.72 meters apart. What is this distance in miles?

(A) 4 miles   (C) 7 miles

(B) 5 miles   (D) 8 miles

3. Megan is making bracelets to sell to earn money for the local animal shelter. It takes her $\frac{1}{4}$ hour to pick out all the beads and $\frac{1}{10}$ hour to string them. This week, she only has $5\frac{1}{4}$ hours to make bracelets. How many bracelets will Megan be able to make?

(A) 10 bracelets   (C) 15 bracelets

(B) 12 bracelets   (D) 21 bracelets

4. Rosa can run 4 miles in 56 minutes. How many miles does Rosa run if she runs for 42 minutes?

(A) 2 miles   (C) 3.5 miles

(B) 3 miles   (D) 5 miles

5. The table below shows the number of petals and leaves for different numbers of flowers.

Petals	5	10	15	20
Leaves	2	4	6	8

How many petals are present when there are 12 leaves?

(A) 25 petals   (C) 35 petals

(B) 30 petals   (D) 36 petals

6. A recipe calls for 3 cups of sugar and 9 cups of water. How many cups of water should be used with 2 cups of sugar?

(A) 3 cups   (C) 6 cups

(B) 4 cups   (D) 8 cups

Mini-Task

7. The unlabeled graph shows the relationship between two customary units of measure. Only two pairs of units can be represented by the graph.

a. Determine the possible pairs of units.

_____

_____

b. Describe the relationship for each pair.

_____

_____

© Houghton Mifflin Harcourt Publishing Company

Percents

ESSENTIAL QUESTION

How can you use percents to solve real-world problems?

MODULE 8

LESSON 8.1
Understanding Percent

FL 6.RP.1.3c

LESSON 8.2
Percents, Fractions, and Decimals

FL 6.RP.1.3

LESSON 8.3
Solving Percent Problems

FL 6.RP.1.3, 6.RP.1.3c

Real-World Video

When you eat at a restaurant, your bill will include sales tax for most items. It is customary to add a tip for your server in many restaurants. Both taxes and tips are calculated as a percent of the bill.

my.hrw.com

© Houghton Mifflin Harcourt Publishing Company

GO DIGITAL
my.hrw.com

my.hrw.com

Go digital with your write-in student edition, accessible on any device.

Math On the Spot

Scan with your smart phone to jump directly to the online edition, video tutor, and more.

Animated Math

Interactively explore key concepts to see how math works.

Personal Math Trainer

Get immediate feedback and help as you work through practice sets.

Are YOU Ready?

Complete these exercises to review skills you will need for this module.

Personal Math Trainer

Online Assessment and Intervention

Write Equivalent Fractions

EXAMPLE $\dfrac{9}{12} = \dfrac{9 \times 4}{12 \times 4} = \dfrac{36}{48}$ Multiply the numerator and denominator by the same number to find an equivalent fraction.

$\dfrac{9}{12} = \dfrac{9 \div 3}{12 \div 3} = \dfrac{3}{4}$ Divide the numerator and denominator by the same number to find an equivalent fraction.

Write the equivalent fraction.

1. $\dfrac{9}{18} = \dfrac{\boxed{}}{6}$

2. $\dfrac{4}{6} = \dfrac{\boxed{}}{18}$

3. $\dfrac{25}{30} = \dfrac{5}{\boxed{}}$

4. $\dfrac{12}{15} = \dfrac{36}{\boxed{}}$

5. $\dfrac{15}{24} = \dfrac{\boxed{}}{8}$

6. $\dfrac{24}{32} = \dfrac{\boxed{}}{8}$

7. $\dfrac{50}{60} = \dfrac{10}{\boxed{}}$

8. $\dfrac{5}{9} = \dfrac{20}{\boxed{}}$

Multiply Fractions

EXAMPLE $\dfrac{5}{12} \times \dfrac{3}{10} = \dfrac{\cancel{5}^1}{\cancel{12}_4} \times \dfrac{\cancel{3}^1}{\cancel{10}_2}$ Divide by the common factors.

$= \dfrac{1}{8}$ Simplify.

Multiply. Write each product in simplest form.

9. $\dfrac{3}{8} \times \dfrac{4}{11} =$ _____

10. $\dfrac{8}{15} \times \dfrac{5}{6} =$ _____

11. $\dfrac{7}{12} \times \dfrac{3}{14} =$ _____

12. $\dfrac{9}{20} \times \dfrac{4}{5} =$ _____

13. $\dfrac{7}{10} \times \dfrac{20}{21} =$ _____

14. $\dfrac{8}{18} \times \dfrac{9}{20} =$ _____

Decimal Operations (Multiplication)

EXAMPLE $\begin{array}{r} 1.6 \\ \times 0.3 \\ \hline 0.48 \end{array}$ Multiply as you would with whole numbers.
Count the total number of decimal places in the factors.
Place the decimal point that number of places in the product.

Multiply.

15. 20×0.25 _____

16. 0.3×16.99 _____

17. 0.2×75 _____

18. 5.5×1.1 _____

19. 11.99×0.8 _____

20. 7.25×0.5 _____

21. 4×0.75 _____

22. 0.15×12.50 _____

23. 6.5×0.7 _____

Reading Start-Up

Visualize Vocabulary

Use the ✔ words to complete the graphic. You may put more than one word in each box.

0.25	$\frac{3}{4}$, 3:4

Reviewing Fractions and Decimals

$\frac{2}{3} = \frac{6}{9}$	$\frac{4}{8} \rightarrow \frac{1}{2}$

Vocabulary

Review Words
✔ decimal *(decimal)*
✔ equivalent fractions *(fracciones equivalentes)*
 denominator *(denominador)*
✔ fraction *(fracción)*
 mixed number *(número mixto)*
 numerator *(numerador)*
✔ ratio *(razón)*
✔ simplest form *(mínima expresión)*

Preview Words
 equivalent decimals *(decimales equivalentes)*
 model *(modelo)*
 percent *(porcentaje)*
 proportional reasoning *(razonamiento proporcional)*

Understand Vocabulary

Match the term on the left to the correct expression on the right.

1. percent

2. model

3. equivalent decimals

A. A ratio that compares a number to 100.

B. Decimals that name the same amount.

C. Something that represents another thing.

Active Reading

Pyramid Before beginning the module, create a pyramid to help you organize what you learn. Label one side "Decimals," one side "Fractions," and the other side "Percents." As you study the module, write important vocabulary and other notes on the appropriate side.

Unpacking the Standards

Understanding the standards and the vocabulary terms in the standards will help you know exactly what you are expected to learn in this module.

 FL 6.RP.1.3c

Find a percent of a quantity as a rate per 100 (e.g., 30% of a quantity means $\frac{30}{100}$ times the quantity); solve problems involving finding the whole, given a part and the percent.

Key Vocabulary

percent *(porcentaje)*
   A ratio comparing a number to 100.

What It Means to You

You will learn to write numbers in various forms, including fractions, decimals, and percents.

UNPACKING EXAMPLE 6.RP.1.3c

Little brown bats flap their wings about $\frac{3}{4}$ as fast as pipistrelle bats do. How fast does the little brown bat flap its wings as a percent of the pipistrelle bat's wing flap rate?

$\frac{3}{4} = 3 \div 4 = 0.75$ Divide the numerator by the denominator.

$\quad\quad 0.75 = 75\%$ Move the decimal point 2 places to the right.

FL 6.RP.1.3c

Find a percent of a quantity as a rate per 100 (e.g., 30% of a quantity means $\frac{30}{100}$ times the quantity); solve problems involving finding the whole, given a part and the percent.

What It Means to You

You will solve problems involving percent.

UNPACKING EXAMPLE 6.RP.1.3c

About 67% of a person's total (100%) body weight is water. If Cameron weights 90 pounds, about how much of his weight is water?

67% of 90

$\quad \frac{67}{100} \cdot 90$

$= \frac{67}{100} \cdot \frac{90}{1}$

$= 60.3$

About 60.3 pounds of Cameron's weight is water.

Visit **my.hrw.com** to see all **Florida Math Standards** unpacked.

my.hrw.com

8.1 Understanding Percent

FL 6.RP.1.3c
Find a percent of a quantity as a rate per 100 (e.g., 30% of a quantity means 30/100 times the quantity); . . .

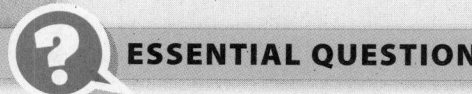

? ESSENTIAL QUESTION

How can you write a ratio as a percent?

EXPLORE ACTIVITY 1   FL 6.RP.1.3c

Using a Grid to Model Percents

A **percent** is a ratio that compares a number to 100. The symbol % is used to show a percent.

17% is equivalent to

- $\frac{17}{100}$
- 17 to 100
- 17:100

The free-throw ratios for three basketball players are shown.

Player 1: $\frac{17}{25}$ Player 2: $\frac{33}{50}$ Player 3: $\frac{14}{20}$

A Rewrite each ratio as a number compared to 100. Then shade the grid to represent the free-throw ratio.

Player 1: $\frac{17}{25} = \frac{\square}{100}$ Player 2: $\frac{33}{50} = \frac{\square}{100}$ Player 3: $\frac{14}{20} = \frac{\square}{100}$

B Which player has the greatest free-throw ratio? _____

How is this shown on the grids? _____

C Use a percent to describe each player's free-throw ratio. Write the percents in order from least to greatest.

_____

D How did you determine how many squares to shade on each grid?

_____

_____

Connecting Fractions and Percents

You can use a percent bar model to model a ratio expressed as a fraction and to find an equivalent percent.

A Use a percent bar model to find an equivalent percent for $\frac{1}{4}$.

Draw a model to represent 100 and divide it into fourths. Shade $\frac{1}{4}$.

0%   ☐ %   100%

$\frac{1}{4}$ of 100 = 25, so $\frac{1}{4}$ of 100% = _____

Tell which operation you can use to find $\frac{1}{4}$ of 100.

Then find $\frac{1}{4}$ of 100%. _____

B Use a percent bar model to find an equivalent percent for $\frac{1}{3}$.

Draw a model and divide it into thirds. Shade $\frac{1}{3}$.

0%   ☐ %   100%

$\frac{1}{3}$ of 100 = $33\frac{1}{3}$, so $\frac{1}{3}$ of 100% = _____ %

Tell which operation you can use to find $\frac{1}{3}$ of 100.

Then find $\frac{1}{3}$ of 100%. _____

Reflect

1. **Critique Reasoning** Jo says she can find the percent equivalent of $\frac{3}{4}$ by multiplying the percent equivalent of $\frac{1}{4}$ by 3. How can you use a percent bar model to support this claim?

_____

_____

_____

Using Benchmarks and Proportional Reasoning

You can use certain *benchmark* percents to write other percents and to estimate fractions.

The number line shows benchmark fractions $\frac{1}{10}$, $\frac{1}{4}$, $\frac{1}{3}$, $\frac{1}{2}$, $\frac{2}{3}$, $\frac{3}{4}$ from 0 to 1, and the corresponding percents 0, 10%, 25%, $33\frac{1}{3}\%$, 50%, $66\frac{2}{3}\%$, 75%, 100.

EXAMPLE 1   FL 6.RP.1.3c

A Find an equivalent percent for $\frac{3}{10}$.

STEP 1 Write $\frac{3}{10}$ as a multiple of a benchmark fraction.

$$\frac{3}{10} = 3 \cdot \frac{1}{10}$$ Think: $\frac{3}{10} = \frac{1}{10} + \frac{1}{10} + \frac{1}{10}$

STEP 2 Find an equivalent percent for $\frac{1}{10}$.

$$\frac{1}{10} = 10\%$$ Use the number lines to find the equivalent percent for $\frac{1}{10}$.

STEP 3 Multiply.

$$\frac{3}{10} = 3 \cdot \frac{1}{10} = 3 \cdot 10\% = 30\%$$

B 76% of the students at a middle school bring their own lunch. About what fraction of the students bring their own lunch?

STEP 1 Note that 76% is close to the benchmark 75%.

STEP 2 Find a fraction equivalent for 75%:

$$75\% = \frac{3}{4}$$

About $\frac{3}{4}$ of the students bring their own lunch.

> **Math Talk**
> Mathematical Practices
>
> Explain how you could use equivalent ratios to write $\frac{3}{10}$ as a percent.

YOUR TURN

Use a benchmark to find an equivalent percent for each fraction.

2. $\frac{9}{10}$ _____

3. $\frac{2}{5}$ _____

4. 64% of the animals at an animal shelter are dogs. About what fraction of the animals at the shelter are dogs?

_____

Guided Practice

1. Shade the grid to represent the ratio $\frac{9}{25}$. Then find a percent equivalent to the given ratio. (Explore Activity 1)

$$\frac{9 \times \boxed{}}{25 \times \boxed{}} = \frac{\boxed{}}{100} = \underline{\hspace{2cm}}$$

2. Use the percent bar model to find the missing percent. (Explore Activity 2)

| 0 | | $\frac{1}{5}$ | | 1 |

0%   100%

$\boxed{}$ %

Identify a benchmark you can use to find an equivalent percent for each ratio. Then find the equivalent percent. (Example 1)

3. $\frac{6}{10}$ Benchmark: $\dfrac{1}{\boxed{}}$

_____

4. $\frac{2}{4}$ Benchmark: $\dfrac{\boxed{}}{4}$

_____

5. $\frac{4}{5}$ Benchmark: $\dfrac{\boxed{}}{5}$

_____

6. 41% of the students at an art college want to be graphic designers. About what fraction of the students want to be graphic designers? (Example 1)

_____

? **ESSENTIAL QUESTION CHECK-IN**

7. How do you write a ratio as a percent?

_____

_____

8.1 Independent Practice

 FL 6.RP.1.3c

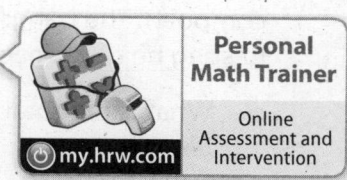

Shade the grid to represent the ratio. Then find the missing number.

8. $\frac{23}{50} = \frac{\boxed{}}{100}$

9. $\frac{11}{20} = \frac{\boxed{}}{100}$

10. Mark wants to use a grid like the ones in Exercises 1 and 2 to model the percent equivalent of the fraction $\frac{2}{3}$. How many grid squares should he shade? What percent would his model show?

_____

11. The ratios of saves for a baseball pitcher to the number of save opportunities are given for three relief pitchers: $\frac{9}{10}, \frac{4}{5}, \frac{17}{20}$. Write each ratio as a percent. Order the percents from least to greatest.

_____

Circle the greater quantity.

12. $\frac{1}{3}$ of a box of Corn Krinkles

50% of a box of Corn Krinkles

13. 30% of your minutes are used up

$\frac{1}{4}$ of your minutes are used up

14. **Multiple Representations** Explain how you could write 35% as the sum of two benchmark percents or as a multiple of a percent.

_____

15. Use the percent bar model to find the missing percent.

0    $\frac{1}{8}$ 1

0% $\boxed{}$%   100%

16. Multistep Carl buys songs and downloads them to his computer. The bar graph shows the numbers of each type of song he downloaded last year.

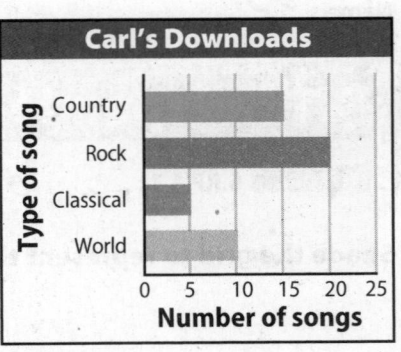

Carl's Downloads

(Type of song: Country, Rock, Classical, World; Number of songs: 0 5 10 15 20 25)

a. What is the total number of songs Carl downloaded last year?

_____

b. What fraction of the songs were country? Find the fraction for each type of song. Write each fraction in simplest form and give its percent equivalent.

_____

_____

_____

 FOCUS ON HIGHER ORDER THINKING

Work Area

17. Critique Reasoning Marcus bought a booklet of tickets to use at the amusement park. He used 50% of the tickets on rides, $\frac{1}{3}$ of the tickets on video games, and the rest of the tickets in the batting cage. Marcus says he used 10% of the tickets in the batting cage. Do you agree? Explain.

_____

_____

_____

_____

18. Look for a Pattern Complete the table.

Fraction	$\frac{1}{5}$	$\frac{2}{5}$	$\frac{3}{5}$	$\frac{4}{5}$	$\frac{5}{5}$	$\frac{6}{5}$
Percent	20%					

a. Analyze Relationships What is true when the numerator and denominator of the fraction are equal? What is true when the numerator is greater than the denominator?

_____

_____

b. Justify Reasoning What is the percent equivalent of $\frac{3}{2}$? Use a pattern like the one in the table to support your answer.

_____

_____

LESSON
8.2 Percents, Fractions, and Decimals

FL 6.RP.1.3
Use ratio and rate reasoning to solve real-world and mathematical problems,...

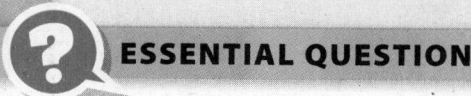 **ESSENTIAL QUESTION**

How can you write equivalent percents, fractions, and decimals?

Writing Percents as Decimals and Fractions

You can write a percent as an equivalent fraction or as an equivalent decimal. Equivalent percents, decimals, and fractions all represent equal parts of the same whole.

Math On the Spot
⏱ my.hrw.com

EXAMPLE 1 Real World
FL 6.RP.1.3

Lorenzo spends 35% of his budget on rent for his apartment. Write this percent as a fraction and as a decimal.

STEP 1 Write the percent as a fraction.

$35\% = \frac{35}{100}$ *Percent means per 100.*

STEP 2 Write the fraction in simplest form.

$$\frac{35}{100} = \frac{35}{100} = \frac{7}{20}$$
$$\div 5$$

Math Talk
Mathematical Practices
Explain why both the numerator and denominator in Step 2 are divided by 5.

STEP 3 Write the percent as a decimal.

$35\% = \frac{35}{100}$ *Write the fraction equivalent of 35%.*

$\quad\quad = 0.35$ *Write the decimal equivalent of $\frac{35}{100}$.*

So, 35% written as a fraction is $\frac{7}{20}$ and written as a decimal is 0.35.

 YOUR TURN

Write each percent as a fraction and as a decimal.

1. 15% _____

2. 48% _____

3. 80% _____

4. 75% _____

5. 36% _____

6. 40% _____

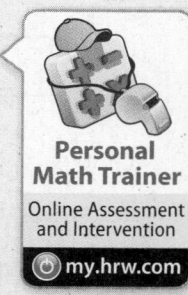
Personal Math Trainer
Online Assessment and Intervention
⏱ my.hrw.com

Modeling Decimal, Fraction, and Percent Equivalencies

Using models can help you understand how decimals, fractions, and percents are related.

A Model 0.78 by shading a 10-by-10 grid.

$0.78 = \dfrac{}{100}$,

_____ out of a hundred, or _____%.

B Model 1.42 by shading 10-by-10 grids.

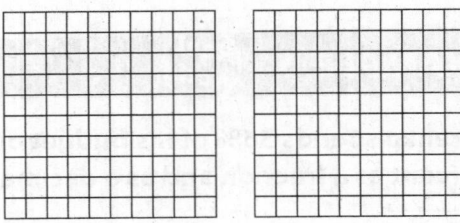

$1.42 = \dfrac{}{100} + \dfrac{}{100} = \dfrac{}{100} = 1\dfrac{}{100}$.

$1.42 = 100\% + _____\% = _____\%$

C Model 125% by shading 10-by-10 grids.

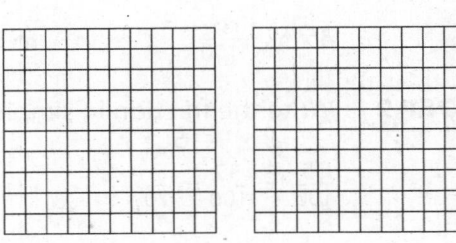

The model shows $100\% + _____\% = 125\%$.

$125\% = $ the decimal _____.

$125\% = \dfrac{}{100} + \dfrac{}{100} = \dfrac{}{100} = 1\dfrac{}{100} = 1\dfrac{}{}$.

Reflect

7. Multiple Representations What decimal, fraction, and percent equivalencies are shown in each model? Explain.

a. _____

_____

_____

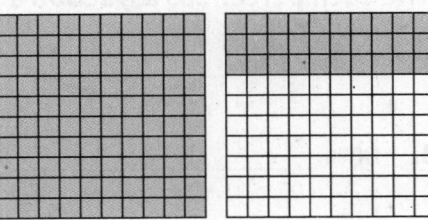

b. _____

_____

Writing Fractions as Decimals and Percents

You can write some fractions as percents by writing an equivalent fraction with a denominator of 100. This method is useful when the fraction has a denominator that is a factor or a multiple of 100. If a fraction does not have a denominator that is a factor or multiple of 100, you can use long division.

Math On the Spot
my.hrw.com

EXAMPLE 2 Real World FL 6.RP.1.3

A 96 out of 200 animals treated by a veterinarian are horses. Write $\frac{96}{200}$ as a decimal and as a percent.

> Notice that the denominator is a multiple of 100.

STEP 1 Write an equivalent fraction with a denominator of 100.

$$\frac{96}{200} = \frac{48}{100}$$ *Divide both the numerator and denominator by 2.*

STEP 2 Write the decimal equivalent.

$$\frac{48}{100} = 0.48$$

STEP 3 Write the percent equivalent.

$$\frac{48}{100} = 48\%$$ *Percent means per 100.*

> Notice that the denominator is not a factor or multiple of 100.

B $\frac{1}{8}$ of the animals treated by the veterinarian are dogs. Write $\frac{1}{8}$ as a decimal and as a percent.

STEP 1 Use long division to divide the numerator by the denominator.

$$\frac{1}{8} = 8)\overline{1.000}$$

$$\begin{array}{r} 0.125 \\ 8)\overline{1.000} \\ -8 \\ \hline 20 \\ -16 \\ \hline 40 \\ -40 \\ \hline 0 \end{array}$$

Add a decimal point and zeros to the right of the numerator as needed.

The decimal equivalent of $\frac{1}{8}$ is 0.125.

STEP 2 Write the decimal as a percent.

$$0.125 = \frac{125}{1,000}$$ *Write the fraction equivalent of the decimal.*

$$\frac{125}{1,000} \overset{\div 10}{=} \frac{12.5}{100} \underset{\div 10}{}$$ *Write an equivalent fraction with a denominator of 100.*

$$\frac{12.5}{100} = 12.5\%$$ *Write as a percent.*

The percent equivalent of $\frac{1}{8}$ is 12.5%.

YOUR TURN

Write each fraction as a decimal and as a percent.

8. $\frac{9}{25}$ _____

9. $\frac{7}{8}$ _____

Guided Practice

1. Helene spends 12% of her budget on transportation expenses. Write this percent as a fraction and as a decimal. (Example 1)

_____

Model the decimal. Then write percent and fraction equivalents.
(Explore Activity)

2. 0.53

_____

3. 1.07

_____

Write each fraction as a decimal and as a percent. (Example 2)

4. $\frac{7}{20}$ of the packages _____

5. $\frac{3}{8}$ of a pie _____

❓ ESSENTIAL QUESTION CHECK-IN

6. How does the definition of *percent* help you write fraction and decimal equivalents?

_____

_____

_____

_____

_____

8.2 Independent Practice

FL 6.RP.1.3

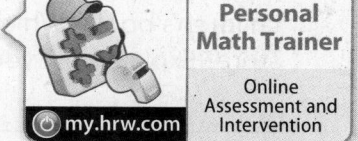

Personal Math Trainer

my.hrw.com Online Assessment and Intervention

Write each percent as a fraction and as a decimal.

7. 72% full

8. 25% successes

9. 500% increase

_____

_____

_____

10. 5% tax

11. 37% profit

12. 165% improvement

_____

_____

_____

Write each fraction as a decimal and as a percent.

13. $\frac{5}{8}$ of an inch

14. $\frac{258}{300}$ of the contestants

15. $\frac{350}{100}$ of the revenue

_____

_____

_____

16. The poster shows how many of its games the football team has won so far. Express this information as a fraction, a percent, and as a decimal.

GO TEAM!

12 out of 15 wins!

17. Justine answered 68 questions correctly on an 80-question test. Express this amount as a fraction, percent, and decimal.

_____

_____

Each diagram is made of smaller, identical pieces. Tell how many pieces you would shade to model the given percent.

18. 75% _____

19. 25% _____

20. Multiple Representations At Brian's Bookstore, 0.3 of the shelves hold mysteries, 25% of the shelves hold travel books, and $\frac{7}{20}$ of the shelves hold children's books. Which type of book covers the most shelf space in the store? Explain how you arrived at your answer.

_____

_____

FOCUS ON HIGHER ORDER THINKING

21. Critical Thinking A newspaper article reports the results of an election between two candidates. The article says that Smith received 60% of the votes and that Murphy received $\frac{1}{3}$ of the votes. A reader writes in to complain that the article cannot be accurate. What reason might the reader have to say this?

_____

_____

_____

22. Represent Real-World Problems Evan budgets $2,000 a month to spend on living expenses for his family. Complete the table to express the portion spent on each cost as a percent, fraction, and decimal.

	Food: $500	Rent: $1,200	Transportation: $300
Fraction			
Percent			
Decimal			

23. Communicate Mathematical Ideas Find the sum of each row in the table. Explain why these sums make sense.

_____

_____

_____

24. Explain the Error Your friend says that 14.5% is equivalent to the decimal 14.5. Explain why your friend is incorrect by comparing the fractional equivalents of 14.5% and 14.5.

_____

_____

LESSON
8.3 Solving Percent Problems

FL 6.RP.1.3c
Find a percent of a quantity
...; solve problems involving
finding the whole, given a
part and the percent. *Also*
6.RP.1.3

ESSENTIAL QUESTION

How do you use percents to solve problems?

EXPLORE ACTIVITY   FL 6.RP.1.3

Modeling a Percent Problem
You can use a model to solve a percent problem.

**A sports store received a shipment of 400 baseball gloves. 30% were
left-handed. How many left-handed gloves were in the shipment?**

A Use the diagram to solve this problem.

30% means 30 out of _____ .

There were _____ left-handed gloves
for every 100 baseball gloves.

Complete the diagram to model this situation.

B Describe how the diagram models the shipment of gloves.

_____

_____

_____

C Explain how you can use the diagram to find the total number of
left-handed gloves in the shipment.

_____

D Use a bar model to solve this problem. The bar represents 100%, or the
entire shipment of 400 gloves. The bar is divided into 10 equal parts.
Complete the labels along the bottom of the bar.

Reflect

1. **Justify Reasoning** How did you determine the labels along the bottom of the bar model in Step D?

   _____

   _____

2. **Communicate Mathematical Ideas** How can you use the bar model to find the number of left-handed gloves?

   _____

Math On the Spot

my.hrw.com

Finding a Percent of a Number

A percent is equivalent to the ratio of a part to a whole. To find a percent of a number, you can write a ratio to represent the percent, and find an equivalent ratio that compares the part to the whole.

To find 30% of 400, you can use:

> The word *of* indicates multiplication.

Proportional Reasoning

$$\frac{30}{100} = \frac{?}{400} \quad \begin{matrix} \leftarrow\text{part} \\ \leftarrow\text{whole} \end{matrix}$$

×4

$$= \frac{120}{400}$$

Multiplication

$$30\% \text{ of } 400 = \frac{30}{100} \text{ of } 400$$

$$= \frac{30}{100} \times 400$$

$$= 120$$

EXAMPLE 1

FL 6.RP.1.3c

A Use proportional reasoning to find 28% of 25.

Math Talk
Mathematical Practices

Could you also use the proportion $\frac{28}{100} = \frac{?}{25}$ to find 28% of 25? Explain.

STEP 1 Write a proportion comparing the percent to the ratio of part to whole.

$$\frac{?}{25} = \frac{28}{100}$$ *Notice that 25 is a factor of 100.*

STEP 2 Find the multiplication factor.

×4

$$\text{part} \rightarrow \quad \frac{?}{25} = \frac{28}{100} \quad \leftarrow \text{whole}$$

×4

Since 25 · 4 = 100, find what number times 4 equals 28.

STEP 3 Find the numerator.

$$\frac{7}{25} = \frac{28}{100}$$ *Since 4 · 7 = 28, 28% of 25 = 7.*

28% of 25 is 7.

B Multiply by a fraction to find 35% of 60.

STEP 1 Write the percent as a fraction.

$$35\% \text{ of } 60 = \frac{35}{100} \text{ of } 60$$

STEP 2 Multiply.

$$\frac{35}{100} \text{ of } 60 = \frac{35}{100} \times 60$$

$$= \frac{2,100}{100}$$

$$= 21 \quad \text{Simplify.}$$

35% of 60 is 21.

C Multiply by a decimal to find 5% of 180.

STEP 1 Write the percent as a decimal.

$$5\% = \frac{5}{100} = 0.05$$

STEP 2 Multiply.

$$180 \times 0.05 = 9$$

5% of 180 is 9.

Animated Math

⏻ my.hrw.com

Reflect

3. **Analyze Relationships** In **B**, the percent is 35%. What is the part and what is the whole?

_____

_____

4. **Communicate Mathematical Ideas** Explain how to use proportional reasoning to find 35% of 600.

_____

_____

_____

_____

Find the percent of each number.

5. 38% of 50 _____   **6.** 27% of 300 _____   **7.** 60% of 75 _____

Personal Math Trainer

Online Assessment and Intervention

⏻ my.hrw.com

Find a Percent Given a Part and a Whole

You can use proportional reasoning to solve problems in which you need to find a percent.

EXAMPLE 2   FL 6.RP.1.3

The school principal spent $2,000 to buy some new computer equipment. Of this money, $120 was used to buy some new keyboards. What percent of the money was spent on keyboards?

STEP 1 Since you want to know the part of the money spent on keyboards, compare the part to the whole.

part → $120
whole → $2,000

STEP 2 Write a proportion comparing the percent to the ratio of part to whole.

part → $\frac{?}{100} = \frac{120}{2,000}$ ← part
whole → ← whole

STEP 3 Find the multiplication factor.

$\frac{?}{100} = \frac{120}{2,000}$ ×20   Since $100 \times 20 = 2,000$, find what number times 20 equals 120.   ×20

STEP 4 Find the numerator.

$\frac{6}{100} = \frac{120}{2,000}$ Since $20 \times 6 = 120$, the percent is 6%.

The principal spent 6% of the money on keyboards.

Reflect

8. **Communicate Mathematical Ideas** Write 57% as a ratio. Which part of the ratio represents the part and which part represents the whole? Explain.

_____

_____

_____

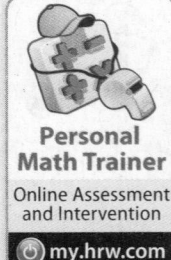
YOUR TURN

9. Out of the 25 students in Mrs. Green's class, 19 have a pet. What percent of the students in Mrs. Green's class have a pet? _____

© Houghton Mifflin Harcourt Publishing Company

Finding a Whole Given a Part and a Percent

You can use proportional reasoning to solve problems in which you know a part and a percent and need to find the whole.

EXAMPLE 3   **FL** 6.RP.1.3c

Twelve of the students in the school choir like to sing solos. These 12 students make up 24% of the choir. How many students are in the choir?

STEP 1 Since you want to know the total number of students in the choir, compare the part to the whole.

$$\text{part} \rightarrow \frac{12}{?} \leftarrow \text{whole}$$

STEP 2 Write a proportion comparing the percent to the ratio of part to whole.

$$\text{part} \rightarrow \frac{12}{?} = \frac{24}{100} \leftarrow \text{part} \atop \leftarrow \text{whole}$$

You know that 12 students represent 24%.

STEP 3 Find the multiplication factor.

$$\frac{12}{?} = \frac{24}{100}$$

×2

×2

Since 12 × 2 = 24, find what number times 2 equals 100.

STEP 4 Find the denominator.

$$\frac{12}{50} = \frac{24}{100}$$

Since 50 × 2 = 100, the denominator is 50.

There are 50 students in the choir.

Math Talk
Mathematical Practices

Suppose 10 more students join the choir. None of them are soloists. What percent are soloists now?

Reflect

10. **Check for Reasonableness** In Example 3, 24% is close to 25%. How could you use this fact to check that 50 is a reasonable number for the total number of students in the choir?

_____

_____

_____

_____

11. 6 is 30% of _____.

12. 15% of _____ is 75.

1. A store has 300 televisions on order, and 80% are high definition. How many televisions on order are high definition? Use the bar model and complete the bottom of the bar. (Explore Activity)

0% 10% 20% 30% 40% 50% 60% 70% 80% 90% 100%

0   30   300

_____

2. Use proportional reasoning to find 65% of 200. (Example 1)

part → ⬜ / 100 = ? / ⬜ ← part / ← whole

65% of 200 is _____.

3. Use multiplication to find 5% of 180. (Example 1)

$\frac{5}{100}$ of 180 = $\frac{5}{100}$ ⬜ 180

= ⬜ / 100 = ⬜

5% of 180 is _____.

4. Alana spent $21 of her $300 paycheck on a gift. What percent of her paycheck was spent on the gift? (Example 2)

part → ? / ⬜ = $ ⬜ / $ ⬜ ← part / ← whole

Alana spent _____ of her paycheck on the gift.

5. At Pizza Pi, 9% of the pizzas made last week had extra cheese. If 27 pizzas had extra cheese, how many pizzas in all were made last week? (Example 3)

part → ⬜ / 100 = 27 / ? ← part / ← whole

There were _____ pizzas made last week.

? ESSENTIAL QUESTION CHECK-IN

6. How can you use proportional reasoning to solve problems involving percent?

_____

_____

_____

_____

Name _____ Class _____ Date _____

8.3 Independent Practice

FL 6.RP.1.3, 6.RP.1.3c

Personal
Math Trainer

Online
Assessment and
Intervention

my.hrw.com

Find the percent of each number.

7. 64% of 75 tiles

_____

8. 20% of 70 plants

_____

9. 32% of 25 pages

_____

10. 85% of 40 e-mails

_____

11. 72% of 350 friends

_____

12. 5% of 220 files

_____

Complete each sentence.

13. 4 students is _____ % of 20 students.

14. 2 doctors is _____ % of 25 doctors.

15. _____ % of 50 shirts is 35 shirts.

16. _____ % of 200 miles is 150 miles.

17. 4% of _____ days is 56 days.

18. 60 minutes is 20% of _____ minutes.

19. 80% of _____ games is 32 games.

20. 360 kilometers is 24% of _____ kilometers.

21. 75% of _____ peaches is 15 peaches.

22. 9 stores is 3% of _____ stores.

23. At a shelter, 15% of the dogs are puppies. There are 60 dogs at the shelter.

How many are puppies? _____ puppies

24. Carl has 200 songs on his MP3 player. Of these songs, 24 are country songs. What percent of Carl's songs are country songs? _____

25. **Consumer Math** The sales tax in the town where Amanda lives is 7%. Amanda paid $35 in sales tax on a new stereo. What was the price of the stereo? _____

26. **Financial Literacy** Ashton is saving money to buy a new bike. He needs $120 but has only saved 60% so far. How much more money does Ashton need to buy the scooter? _____

27. **Consumer Math** Monica paid sales tax of $1.50 when she bought a new bike helmet. If the sales tax rate was 5%, how much did the store charge

for the helmet before tax? _____

28. Use the circle graph to determine how many hours per day Becky spends on each activity.

School: _____ hours

Eating: _____ hours

Sleep: _____ hours

Homework: _____ hours

Free time: _____ hours

Becky's Day

Eating 10%
Free time 15%
Homework 10%
Sleep 40%
School 25%

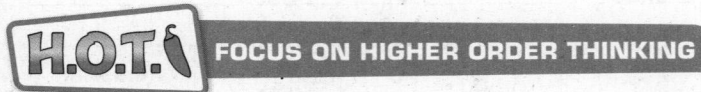

Work Area

29. Multistep Marc ordered a rug. He gave a deposit of 30% of the cost and will pay the rest when the rug is delivered. If the deposit was $75, how much more does Marc owe? Explain how you found your answer.

_____

_____

_____

_____

30. Earth Science Your weight on different planets is affected by gravity. An object that weighs 150 pounds on Earth weighs only 56.55 pounds on Mars. The same object weighs only 24.9 pounds on the Moon.

a. What percent of an object's Earth weight is its weight on Mars and on the Moon?

_____

b. Suppose x represents an object's weight on Earth. Write two expressions: one that you can use to find the object's weight on Mars and another that you can use to write the object's weight on the Moon.

_____

c. The space suit Neil Armstrong wore when he stepped on the Moon for the first time weighed about 180 pounds on Earth. How much did it weigh on the Moon?

_____

d. What If? If you could travel to Jupiter, your weight would be 236.4% of your Earth weight. How much would Neil Armstrong's space suit weigh on Jupiter?

_____

31. Explain the Error Your friend used the proportion $\frac{25}{100} = \frac{50}{?}$ to find 25% of 50 and says that the answer is 200. Explain why your friend is incorrect and find the correct answer.

_____

_____

_____

_____

Ready to Go On?

Personal Math Trainer

Online Assessment and Intervention

my.hrw.com

8.1 Understanding Percent

Shade the grid and write the equivalent percent for each fraction.

1. $\frac{19}{50}$ _____

2. $\frac{13}{20}$ _____

8.2 Percents, Fractions, and Decimals

Write each number in two equivalent forms.

3. $\frac{3}{5}$ _____

4. 62.5% _____

5. 0.24 _____

6. $\frac{31}{50}$ _____

7. Selma spent $\frac{7}{10}$ of her allowance on a new backpack. What percent of her allowance did she spend? _____

8.3 Solving Percent Problems

Complete each sentence.

8. 12 is 30% of _____.

9. 45% of 20 is _____.

10. 18 is _____ % of 30.

11. 56 is 80% of _____.

12. A pack of cinnamon-scented pencils sells for $4.00. What is the sales tax rate if the total cost of the pencils is $4.32? _____

? ESSENTIAL QUESTION

13. How can you solve problems involving percents?

_____

_____

_____

_____

Personal Math Trainer

Online Assessment and Intervention

my.hrw.com

Selected Response

1. What percent does this shaded grid represent?

Ⓐ 42%

Ⓑ 48%

Ⓒ 52%

Ⓓ 58%

2. Which expression is **not** equal to one fourth of 52?

Ⓐ 0.25 · 52

Ⓑ 4% of 52

Ⓒ 52 ÷ 4

Ⓓ $\frac{52}{4}$

3. Approximately $\frac{4}{5}$ of U.S. homeowners have a cell phone. What percent of homeowners do **not** have a cell phone?

Ⓐ 20%

Ⓑ 45%

Ⓒ 55%

Ⓓ 80%

4. The ratio of rock music to total CDs that Ella owns is $\frac{25}{40}$. Paolo has 50 rock music CDs. The ratio of rock music to total CDs in his collection is equivalent to the ratio of rock music to total CDs in Ella's collection. How many CDs do they own?

Ⓐ 65

Ⓒ 120

Ⓑ 80

Ⓓ 130

5. Gabriel saves 40% of his monthly paycheck for college. He earned $270 last month. How much money did Gabriel save for college?

Ⓐ $96

Ⓒ $162

Ⓑ $108

Ⓓ $180

6. Forty children from an after-school club went to the matinee. This is 25% of the children in the club. How many children are in the club?

Ⓐ 10

Ⓒ 200

Ⓑ 160

Ⓓ 900

7. Dominic answered 43 of the 50 questions on his spelling test correctly. Which decimal represents the fraction of problems he answered incorrectly?

Ⓐ 0.07

Ⓒ 0.86

Ⓑ 0.14

Ⓓ 0.93

Mini-Task

8. Jen bought some sesame bagels and some plain bagels. The ratio of the number of sesame bagels to the number of plain bagels is 1 : 3.

a. What fraction of the bagels are plain?

_____

b. What percent of the bagels are plain?

_____

c. If Jill bought 2 dozen bagels, how many of each type of bagel did she buy?

_____

MODULE 6 **Representing Ratios and Rates**

Key Vocabulary
equivalent ratios (*razones equivalentes*)
rate (*tasa*)
ratio (*razón*)
unit rate (*tasa unitaria*)

? ESSENTIAL QUESTION

How can you use ratios and rates to solve real-world problems?

EXAMPLE 1

Tina pays $45.50 for 13 boxes of wheat crackers. What is the unit price?

$\frac{\$45.50}{13 \text{ boxes}} = \frac{\$3.50}{1 \text{ box}}$ The unit price is $3.50 per box of crackers.

EXAMPLE 2

A trail mix recipe calls for 3 cups of raisins and 4 cups of peanuts. Mitt made trail mix for a party and used 5 cups of raisins and 6 cups of peanuts. Did Mitt use the correct ratio of raisins to peanuts?

$\frac{3 \text{ cups of raisins}}{4 \text{ cups of peanuts}}$ The ratio of raisins to peanuts in the recipe is $\frac{3}{4}$.

$\frac{5 \text{ cups of raisins}}{6 \text{ cups of peanuts}}$ Mitt used a ratio of $\frac{5}{6}$.

$\frac{3}{4} \times \frac{3}{3} = \frac{9}{12}$ $\frac{5}{6} \times \frac{2}{2} = \frac{10}{12}$ $\frac{9}{12} < \frac{10}{12}$

Mitt used a higher ratio of raisins to peanuts in his trail mix.

EXERCISES

Write three equivalent ratios for each ratio. (Lesson 7.1)

1. $\frac{18}{6}$ _____

2. $\frac{5}{45}$ _____

3. $\frac{3}{5}$ _____

4. To make a dark orange color, Ron mixes 3 ounces of red paint with 2 ounces of yellow paint. Write the ratio of red paint to yellow paint three ways. (Lesson 7.1) _____

5. A box of a dozen fruit tarts costs $15.00. What is the cost of one fruit tart?

(Lesson 7.2) _____

Compare the ratios. (Lesson 7.3)

6. $\frac{2}{5}$ ◯ $\frac{3}{4}$ **7.** $\frac{9}{2}$ ◯ $\frac{10}{7}$ **8.** $\frac{2}{11}$ ◯ $\frac{3}{12}$ **9.** $\frac{6}{7}$ ◯ $\frac{8}{9}$

Applying Ratios and Rates

Key Vocabulary

conversion factor (factor de conversión)

proportion (proporción)

scale (escala)

scale drawing (dibujo a escala)

? ESSENTIAL QUESTION

How can you use ratios and rates to solve real-world problems?

EXAMPLE 1

A. **Jessica earns $5 for each dog she walks. Complete the table, describe the rule, and tell whether the relationship is additive or multiplicative. Then graph the ordered pairs on a coordinate plane.**

Number of dogs	1	2	3	4	5
Profit ($)	5	10	15	20	25

Jessica's profit is the number of dogs walked multiplied by $5. The relationship is multiplicative.

B. **A veterinarian tells Lee that his dog should have a 35 centimeter collar. What is this measurement in inches?**

Use the conversion factor 1 inch = 2.54 centimeters, written as the rate $\frac{1 \text{ in.}}{2.54 \text{ cm}}$.

$35 \text{ cm} \cdot \frac{1 \text{ in.}}{2.54 \text{ cm}} \approx 13.78$

The collar should be about 14 inches.

EXERCISES

1. Thaddeus already has $5 saved. He wants to save more to buy a book. Complete the table, and graph the ordered pairs on the coordinate graph. (Lessons 8.1, 8.2)

New savings	4	6	8	10
Total savings	9			

2. There are 2 hydrogen atoms and 1 oxygen atom in a water molecule. Complete the table, and list the equivalent ratios shown on the table. (Lessons 8.1, 8.2)

Hydrogen atoms	8		16	20
Oxygen atoms		6		

3. Sam can solve 30 multiplication problems in 2 minutes. How many can he solve in 20 minutes? (Lesson 8.3)

4. A male Chihuahua weighs 5 pounds. How many ounces does he weigh? (Lesson 8.4)

_____

Percents

? ESSENTIAL QUESTION

How can you use percents to solve real-world problems?

EXAMPLE 1

Find an equivalent percent for $\frac{7}{10}$.

$$\frac{7}{10} = 7 \cdot \frac{1}{10} \qquad\qquad \frac{7}{10} = 7 \cdot 10\% \qquad\qquad \frac{7}{10} = 70\%$$

Find an equivalent percent for $\frac{1}{5}$.

$\frac{1}{5}$ of $100 = 20$, so $\frac{1}{5}$ of $100\% = 20\%$

$\frac{1}{5} = 20\%$

EXAMPLE 2

Thirteen of the 50 states in the United States do not touch the ocean. Write $\frac{13}{50}$ as a decimal and a percent.

$$\frac{13}{50} = \frac{26}{100} \qquad \frac{26}{100} = 0.26 \qquad 0.26 = 26\% \qquad \frac{13}{50} = 0.26 = 26\%$$

EXAMPLE 3

Buckner put $60 of his $400 paycheck into his savings account. Find the percent of his paycheck that Buckner saved.

$$\frac{60}{400} = \frac{?}{100} \qquad \frac{60 \div 4}{400 \div 4} = \frac{15}{100} \qquad$$ Buckner saved 15% of his paycheck.

EXERCISES

Write each fraction as a decimal and a percent. (Lessons 9.1, 9.2)

1. $\frac{3}{4}$ _____   **2.** $\frac{7}{20}$ _____   **3.** $\frac{8}{5}$ _____

Complete each statement. (Lessons 9.1, 9.2)

4. 25% of 200 is _____.   **5.** 16 is _____ of 20.   **6.** 21 is 70% of _____.

7. 42 of the 150 employees at Carlo's Car Repair wear contact lenses. What percent of the employees wear contact lenses? (Lesson 9.3) _____

8. Last week at Best Bargain, 75% of the computers sold were laptops. If 340 computers were sold last week, how many were laptops? (Lesson 9.3) _____

Unit 3 Performance Tasks

1. **CAREERS IN MATH** Residential Builder Kaylee, a residential builder, is working on a paint budget for a custom-designed home she is building. A gallon of paint costs $38.50, and its label says it covers about 350 square feet.

   a. Explain how to calculate the cost of paint per square foot. Find this value. Show your work.

   _____

   _____

   b. Kaylee measured the room she wants to paint and calculated a total area of 825 square feet. If the paint is only available in one-gallon cans, how many cans of paint should she buy? Justify your answer.

   _____

   _____

2. Davette wants to buy flannel sheets. She reads that a weight of at least 190 grams per square meter is considered high quality.

   a. Davette finds a sheet that has a weight of 920 grams for 5 square meters. Does this sheet satisfy the requirement for high-quality sheets? If not, what should the weight be for 5 square meters? Explain.

   _____

   b. Davette finds 3 more options for flannel sheets:

   Option 1: 1,100 g of flannel in 6 square meters, $45

   Option 2: 1,260 g of flannel in 6.6 square meters, $42

   Option 3: 1,300 g of flannel in 6.5 square meters, $52

   She would like to buy the sheet that meets her requirements for high quality and has the lowest price per square meter. Which option should she buy? Justify your answer.

   _____

   _____

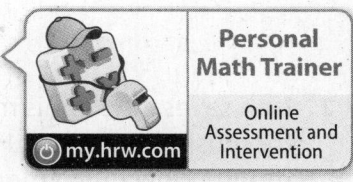

Personal Math Trainer

Online Assessment and Intervention

my.hrw.com

Selected Response

1. The deepest part of a swimming pool is 12 feet deep. The shallowest part of the pool is 3 feet deep. What is the ratio of the depth of the deepest part of the pool to the depth of the shallowest part of the pool?

Ⓐ 4:1

Ⓑ 12:15

Ⓒ 1:4

Ⓓ 15:12

2. How many centimeters are in 15 meters?

Ⓐ 0.15 centimeters

Ⓑ 1.5 centimeters

Ⓒ 150 centimeters

Ⓓ 1,500 centimeters

3. Barbara can walk 3,200 meters in 24 minutes. How far can she walk in 3 minutes?

Ⓐ 320 meters

Ⓑ 400 meters

Ⓒ 640 meters

Ⓓ 720 meters

4. The table below shows the number of windows and panes of glass in the windows.

Windows	2	3	4	5
Panes	12	18	24	30

Which represents the number of panes?

Ⓐ windows × 5

Ⓑ windows × 6

Ⓒ windows + 10

Ⓓ windows + 15

5. The graph below represents Donovan's speed while riding his bike.

Which would be an ordered pair on the line?

Ⓐ (1, 3)

Ⓑ (2, 2)

Ⓒ (6, 4)

Ⓓ (9, 3)

Read the graph or diagram as closely as you read the actual test question. These visual aids contain important information.

6. Which percent does this shaded grid represent?

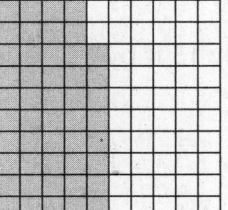

Ⓐ 42%

Ⓑ 48%

Ⓒ 52%

Ⓓ 58%

© Houghton Mifflin Harcourt Publishing Company

7. Ivan saves 20% of his monthly paycheck for music equipment. He earned $335 last month. How much money did Ivan save for music equipment?

Ⓐ $65

Ⓑ $67

Ⓒ $70

Ⓓ $75

8. How many 0.6-liter glasses can you fill up with a 4.5-liter pitcher?

Ⓐ 1.33 glasses

Ⓑ 3.9 glasses

Ⓒ 7.3 glasses

Ⓓ 7.5 glasses

9. Which shows the integers in order from greatest to least?

Ⓐ 22, 8, 7, 2, −11

Ⓑ 2, 7, 8, −11, 22

Ⓒ −11, 2, 7, 8, 22

Ⓓ 22, −11, 8, 7, 2

10. How do you convert 15 feet to centimeters?

Ⓐ Multiply 15 ft by $\frac{1 \text{ ft}}{12 \text{ in.}}$ and $\frac{2.54 \text{ cm}}{1 \text{ in.}}$.

Ⓑ Multiply 15 ft by $\frac{1 \text{ ft}}{12 \text{ in.}}$ and $\frac{1 \text{ in.}}{2.54 \text{ cm}}$.

Ⓒ Multiply 15 ft by $\frac{12 \text{ in.}}{1 \text{ ft}}$ and $\frac{2.54 \text{ cm}}{1 \text{ in.}}$.

Ⓓ Multiply 15 ft by $\frac{12 \text{ in.}}{1 \text{ ft}}$ and $\frac{1 \text{ cm}}{2.54 \text{ in.}}$.

Mini Task

11. Claire and Malia are training for a race.

a. Claire runs 10 km in 1 hour. How many kilometers does she run in half an hour? in $2\frac{1}{2}$ hours?

_____

b. Malia runs 5 miles in 1 hour. How many miles does she run in half an hour? in $2\frac{1}{2}$ hours?

_____

c. On Tuesday, Claire and Malia both ran for $2\frac{1}{2}$ hours. Who ran the farther distance?

_____

12. A department store is having a sale.

a. Malcolm bought 6 bowls for $13.20. What is the unit rate?

_____

b. The store is having a promotion. For every 8 glasses you buy, you get 3 free plates. Malcolm got 9 free plates. How many glasses did he buy?

_____

c. The unit rate of the glasses was $1.80 per glass. How much did Malcolm spend on glasses?

_____

13. A recipe calls for 6 cups of water and 4 cups of flour.

a. What is the ratio of water to flour?

_____

b. If the recipe is increased to use 6 cups of flour, how much water should be used?

_____

c. If the recipe is decreased to use 2 cups of water, how much flour should be used?

_____

Equivalent Expressions

MODULE **9**
Generating Equivalent Numerical Expressions
FL 6.EE.1.1

MODULE **10**
Generating Equivalent Algebraic Expressions
FL 6.EE.1.2a, 6.EE.1.2b, 6.EE.1.2c, 6.EE.1.3, 6.EE.1.4, 6.EE.2.6

CAREERS IN MATH

Freelance Computer Programmer
A computer programmer translates commands into code, a language that a computer understands. Programmers work on a variety of tasks, from creating computer games to testing software. A freelance programmer doesn't work for a specific company; this gives the freelancer more flexibility with his or her work schedule. Computer programmers use mathematical logic when writing or altering code.

If you are interested in a career as a computer programmer, you should study these mathematical subjects:
- Algebra
- Geometry
- Trigonometry
- Calculus
- Discrete Math

Research other careers that require the understanding of mathematical logic.

Unit 4 Performance Task

At the end of the unit, check out how a **freelance computer programmer** uses math.

Vocabulary Preview

Use the puzzle to preview key vocabulary from this unit. Unscramble the letters to create a key vocabulary term. Use the circled letters to answer the riddle at the bottom of the page.

1. **TEPNNEOX**

2. **EBSA**

3. **EPROW**

4. **RERDO FO SONPEOIRAT**

5. **CALIAGERB ENOXSPSRIE**

6. **ELTGNAVAIU**

7. **ELKI SEMRT**

8. **BVLIAREA**

1. Tells how many times the base appears in the expression. (Lesson 9.1)
2. A number that is multiplied. (Lesson 9.1)
3. The number formed by repeated multiplication by the same factor. (Lesson 9.1)
4. The rules which tell which calculations are done before others in an expression. (Lesson 9.3)
5. An expression that contains one or more variables. (Lesson 10.1)
6. Substituting a number for a variable in an expression and solving. (Lesson 10.2)
7. Terms with the same variables. (Lesson 10.3)
8. A letter or symbol used to represent an unknown number. (Lesson 10.1)

Q: Why does *n* always change its mind?

A: Because it's ___ ___ ___ ___ ___ ___ ___!

Generating Equivalent Numerical Expressions

MODULE 9

LESSON 9.1
Exponents
FL 6.EE.1.1

LESSON 9.2
Prime Factorization
FL 6.EE.1.1

LESSON 9.3
Order of Operations
FL 6.EE.1.1

ESSENTIAL QUESTION

How can you generate equivalent numerical expressions and use them to solve real-world problems?

my.hrw.com

Real-World Video

Assume that you post a video on the internet. Two of your friends view it, then two friends of each of those view it, and so on. The number of views is growing exponentially. Sometimes we say the video went viral.

GO DIGITAL
my.hrw.com

my.hrw.com

Go digital with your write-in student edition, accessible on any device.

Math On the Spot

Scan with your smart phone to jump directly to the online edition, video tutor, and more.

Animated Math

Interactively explore key concepts to see how math works.

Personal Math Trainer

Get immediate feedback and help as you work through practice sets.

Are YOU Ready?

Complete these exercises to review skills you will need for this module.

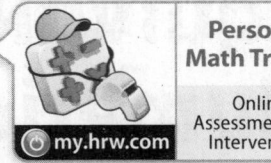

Personal Math Trainer

Online Assessment and Intervention

my.hrw.com

Whole Number Operations

EXAMPLE 270×83

```
    270
  × 83
    810    ← 3 × 270
+21,600    ← 80 × 270
 22,410    ← (3 × 270) + (80 × 270)
```

Find the product.

1. 992×16 **2.** 578×27 **3.** 839×65 **4.** 367×23

_____   _____   _____   _____

Use Repeated Multiplication

EXAMPLE $5 \times 5 \times 5 \times 5$ Multiply the first two factors.

$25 \quad \times \quad 5$ Multiply the result by the next factor.

$125 \quad \times \quad 5$ Multiply that result by the next factor.

625 Continue until there are no more factors to multiply.

Find the product.

5. $7 \times 7 \times 7$ **6.** $3 \times 3 \times 3 \times 3$ **7.** $6 \times 6 \times 6 \times 6 \times 6$ **8.** $2 \times 2 \times 2 \times 2 \times 2 \times 2$

_____   _____   _____   _____

Division Facts

EXAMPLE $54 \div 9 = $ ▆   Think: 9 times what number equals 54?
$9 \times 6 = 54$

$54 \div 9 = 6$ So, $54 \div 9 = 6$.

Divide.

9. $20 \div 4$ **10.** $21 \div 7$ **11.** $42 \div 7$ **12.** $56 \div 8$

_____   _____   _____   _____

Reading Start-Up

Vocabulary

Review Words
✔ factor *(factor)*
  factor tree *(árbol de factores)*
✔ integers *(entero)*
✔ numerical expression *(expresión numérica)*
✔ operations *(operaciones)*
✔ prime factorization *(factorización prima)*
  repeated multiplication *(multiplicación repetida)*
  simplified expression *(expresión simplificada)*

Preview Words
  base *(base)*
  exponent *(exponente)*
  order of operations *(orden de las operaciones)*
  power *(potencia)*

Visualize Vocabulary

Use the ✔ words to complete the graphic. You may put more than one word in each box.

Reviewing Factorization

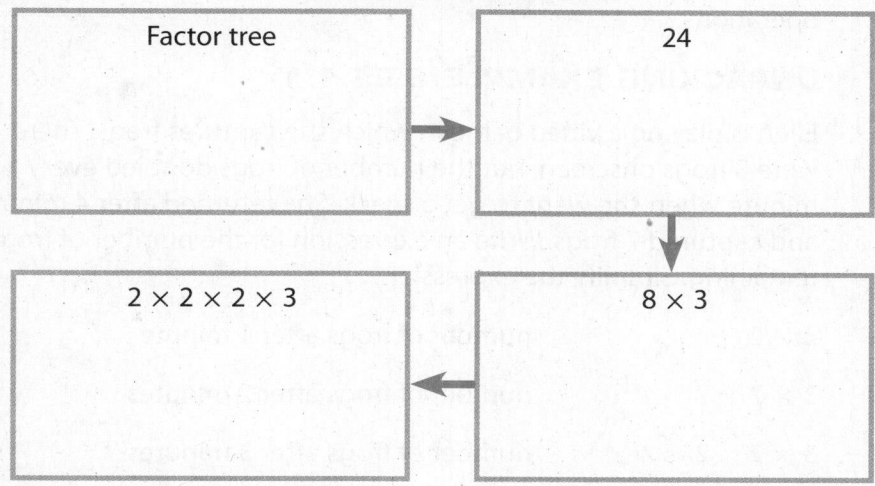

| Factor tree | → | 24 |

| 2 × 2 × 2 × 3 | ← | 8 × 3 |

Understand Vocabulary

Complete the sentences using the preview words.

1. A number that is formed by repeated multiplication by the same factor is a _____ .

2. A rule for simplifying expressions is _____ .

3. The _____ is a number that is multiplied. The number that indicates how many times this number is used as a factor is the _____ .

Active Reading

Three-Panel Flip Chart Before beginning the module, create a three-panel flip chart to help you organize what you learn. Label each flap with one of the lesson titles from this module. As you study each lesson, write important ideas like vocabulary, properties, and formulas under the appropriate flap.

Unpacking the Standards

Understanding the standards and the vocabulary terms in the standards will help you know exactly what you are expected to learn in this module.

© Houghton Mifflin Harcourt Publishing Company • Image Credits: Patrik Giardino/ Photodisc/Getty Images

 FL 6.EE.1.1

Write and evaluate numerical expressions involving whole-number exponents.

Key Vocabulary

exponent *(exponente)* The number that indicates how many times the base is used as a factor.

order of operations *(orden de las operaciones)* A rule for evaluating expressions: first perform the operations in parentheses, then compute powers and roots, then perform all multiplication and division from left to right, and then perform all addition and subtraction from left to right.

What It Means to You

You will simplify numerical expressions using the order of operations.

UNPACKING EXAMPLE 6.EE.1.1

Ellen is playing a video game in which she captures frogs. There were 3 frogs onscreen, but the number of frogs doubled every minute when she went to get a snack. She returned after 4 minutes and captured 7 frogs. Write an expression for the number of frogs remaining. Simplify the expression.

3×2	number of frogs after 1 minute
$3 \times 2 \times 2$	number of frogs after 2 minutes
$3 \times 2 \times 2 \times 2$	number of frogs after 3 minutes
$3 \times 2 \times 2 \times 2 \times 2$	number of frogs after 4 minutes

Since 3 and 2 are prime numbers, $3 \times 2 \times 2 \times 2 \times 2$ is the prime factorization of the number of frogs remaining.

$3 \times 2 \times 2 \times 2 \times 2$ can be written with exponents as 3×2^4.

The expression $3 \times 2^4 - 7$ is the number of frogs remaining after Ellen captured the 7 frogs.

Use the order of operations to simplify $3 \times 2^4 - 7$.

$$3 \times 2^4 - 7 = 3 \times 16 - 7$$
$$= 48 - 7$$
$$= 41$$

41 frogs remain.

9.1 Exponents

FL 6.EE.1.1

Write and evaluate ... expressions involving whole-number exponents.

? ESSENTIAL QUESTION

How do you use exponents to represent numbers?

EXPLORE ACTIVITY   FL 6.EE.1.1

Identifying Repeated Multiplication

A real-world problem may involve repeatedly multiplying a factor by itself.

A scientist observed the hourly growth of bacteria and recorded his observations in a table.

Time (h)	Total bacteria
0	1
1	2
2	$2 \times 2 = \boxed{}$
3	$2 \times 2 \times 2 = \boxed{}$
4	$2 \times 2 \times 2 \times 2 = \boxed{}$

> After 2 hours, there are $2 \cdot 2 = ?$ bacteria.

A Complete the table. What pattern(s) do you see in the Total bacteria column?

_____

_____

B Complete each statement.

At 2 hours, the total is equal to the product of two 2s.

At 3 hours, the total is equal to the product of _____ 2s.

At 4 hours, the total is equal to the product of _____ 2s.

Reflect

1. **Communicate Mathematical Ideas** How is the time, in hours, related to the number of times 2 is used as a factor?

_____

_____

Using Exponents

A number that is formed by repeated multiplication of the same factor is called a **power**. You can use an *exponent* and a *base* to write a power. For example, 7^3 means the product of three 7s:

$$7^3 = 7 \times 7 \times 7$$

The **base** is the number that is multiplied.

The **exponent** tells how many times the base appears in the expression.

Power	How to read the power
6^2	6 squared, 6 to the power of 2, 6 raised to the 2nd power
7^3	7 cubed, 7 to the power of 3, 7 raised to the 3rd power
9^4	9 to the power of 4, 9 raised to 4th power

EXAMPLE 1

 FL 6.EE.1.1

Use an exponent to write each expression.

A $3 \times 3 \times 3 \times 3 \times 3$

Find the base, or the number being multiplied. The base is 3.

Find the exponent by counting the number of 3s being multiplied. The exponent is 5.

$$\underbrace{3 \times 3 \times 3 \times 3 \times 3}_{5 \text{ factors of } 3} = 3^5$$

B $\frac{4}{5} \times \frac{4}{5} \times \frac{4}{5} \times \frac{4}{5}$

Find the base, or the number being multiplied. The base is $\frac{4}{5}$.

Find the exponent by counting the number of times $\frac{4}{5}$ appears in the expression. The exponent is 4.

$$\underbrace{\frac{4}{5} \times \frac{4}{5} \times \frac{4}{5} \times \frac{4}{5}}_{4 \text{ factors of } \frac{4}{5}} = \left(\frac{4}{5}\right)^4$$

Math Talk

Mathematical Practices

What is the value of a number raised to the power of 1?

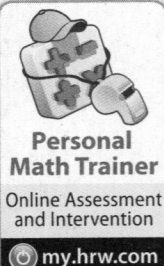

Personal Math Trainer

Online Assessment and Intervention

⏻ my.hrw.com

YOUR TURN

Use exponents to write each expression.

2. $4 \times 4 \times 4$ _____

3. 6 _____

4. $\frac{1}{8} \times \frac{1}{8}$ _____

5. $5 \times 5 \times 5 \times 5 \times 5 \times 5$ _____

Finding the Value of a Power

To find the value of a power, remember that the exponent indicates how many times to use the base as a factor.

> ## Property of Zero as an Exponent
>
> The value of any nonzero number raised to the power of 0 is 1.
>
> **Example:** $5^0 = 1$

EXAMPLE 2   FL 6.EE.1.1

Find the value of each power.

A 10^4

Identify the base and the exponent.
The base is 10, and the exponent is 4.

Evaluate: $10^4 = 10 \times 10 \times 10 \times 10 = 10,000$

B 0.4^3

Identify the base and the exponent.
The base is 0.4, and the exponent is 3.

Evaluate: $0.4^3 = 0.4 \times 0.4 \times 0.4 = 0.064$

C $\left(\frac{3}{5}\right)^0$

Identify the base and the exponent.
The base is $\frac{3}{5}$, and the exponent is 0.

Evaluate.

$\left(\frac{3}{5}\right)^0 = 1$ Any number raised to the power of 0 is 1.

D $\left(\frac{2}{3}\right)^2$

Identify the base and the exponent.
The base is $\frac{2}{3}$, and the exponent is 2.

Evaluate.

$\left(\frac{2}{3}\right)^2 = \left(\frac{2}{3}\right) \times \left(\frac{2}{3}\right) = \frac{4}{9}$

Math Talk
Mathematical Practices

Is the value of 2^3 the same as the value of 3^2? Explain.

YOUR TURN

Find the value of each power.

6. 3^4 _____

7. $(1)^9$ _____

8. $\left(\frac{2}{5}\right)^3$ _____

9. 12^2 _____

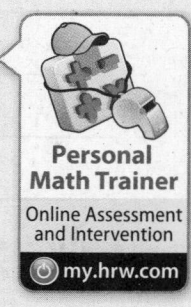
© Houghton Mifflin Harcourt Publishing Company

1. Complete the table. (Explore Activity 1)

Exponential form	Product	Simplified product
5^1	5	5
5^2	5×5	
5^3		125
	$5 \times 5 \times 5 \times 5$	
5^5		

Use an exponent to write each expression. (Example 1)

2. $6 \times 6 \times 6$ _____

___ factors of 6

3. $10 \times 10 \times 10 \times 10 \times 10 \times 10 \times 10$ _____

4. $\frac{3}{4} \times \frac{3}{4} \times \frac{3}{4} \times \frac{3}{4} \times \frac{3}{4}$ _____

5. $\frac{7}{9} \times \frac{7}{9} \times \frac{7}{9} \times \frac{7}{9} \times \frac{7}{9} \times \frac{7}{9} \times \frac{7}{9} \times \frac{7}{9}$ _____

Find the value of each power. (Example 2)

6. 8^3 _____

7. 7^4 _____

8. 10^3 _____

9. $\left(\frac{1}{4}\right)^2$ _____

10. $\left(\frac{1}{3}\right)^3$ _____

11. $\left(\frac{6}{7}\right)^2$ _____

12. 0.8^2 _____

13. 0.5^3 _____

14. 1.1^2 _____

15. 8^0 _____

16. 12^1 _____

17. $\left(\frac{1}{2}\right)^0$ _____

18. $(13)^2$ _____

19. $\left(\frac{2}{5}\right)^2$ _____

20. 0.9^2 _____

? ESSENTIAL QUESTION CHECK-IN

21. How do you use an exponent to represent a number such as 16?

_____

_____

_____

_____

_____

9.1 Independent Practice

 FL 6.EE.1.1

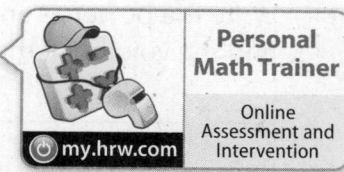

Write the missing exponent.

22. $100 = 10^{\boxed{}}$

23. $8 = 2^{\boxed{}}$

24. $25 = 5^{\boxed{}}$

25. $27 = 3^{\boxed{}}$

26. $\dfrac{1}{169} = \left(\dfrac{1}{13}\right)^{\boxed{}}$

27. $14 = 14^{\boxed{}}$

28. $32 = 2^{\boxed{}}$

29. $\dfrac{64}{81} = \left(\dfrac{8}{9}\right)^{\boxed{}}$

Write the missing base.

30. $1,000 = \boxed{}^{3}$

31. $256 = \boxed{}^{4}$

32. $16 = \boxed{}^{4}$

33. $9 = \boxed{}^{2}$

34. $\dfrac{1}{9} = \left(\boxed{}\right)^{2}$

35. $64 = \boxed{}^{2}$

36. $\dfrac{9}{16} = \left(\boxed{}\right)^{2}$

37. $729 = \boxed{}^{3}$

For Exercises 38–42, write the answer with and without using an exponent.

38. Hadley's softball team has a phone tree in case a game is canceled. The coach calls 3 players. Then each of those players calls 3 players, and so on. How many players will be notified during the third round of calls?

_____

39. Tim is reading a book. On Monday he reads 3 pages. On each day after that, he reads 3 times the number of pages that he read on the previous day. How many pages does he read on Thursday?

_____

40. The square tile shown has a side length of 10.5 inches. What power can you write to represent the area of the tile? Write the power as an expression with a base and an exponent, and then find the area of the square.

_____

41. Antonia is saving for a video game. On the first day, she saves two dollars in her piggy bank. Each day after that, she doubles the number of dollars she saved on the previous day. How many dollars does she save on the sixth day?

_____

42. A certain colony of bacteria triples in length every 10 minutes. Its length is now 1 millimeter. How long will it be in 40 minutes?

_____

43. Which power can you write to represent the volume of the cube shown? Write the power as an expression with a base and an exponent, and then find the volume of the cube.

$\frac{1}{3}$ in.

_____

44. Write a power represented with a positive base and a positive exponent whose value is less than the base.

_____

H.O.T. FOCUS ON HIGHER ORDER THINKING

45. Communicate Mathematical Ideas What is the value of 1 raised to the power of any exponent? What is the value of 0 raised to the power of any nonnegative nonzero exponent? Explain.

_____

_____

_____

46. Look for a Pattern Find the values of the powers in the following pattern: 10^1, 10^2, 10^3, 10^4…. Describe the pattern, and use it to evaluate 10^6 without using multiplication.

_____

_____

_____

47. Critical Thinking Some numbers can be written as powers of different bases. For example, $81 = 9^2$ and $81 = 3^4$. Write the number 64 using three different bases.

_____

48. Justify Reasoning Oman said that it is impossible to raise a number to the power of 2 and get a value less than the original number. Do you agree with Oman? Justify your reasoning.

_____

_____

_____

Work Area

LESSON
9.2 Prime Factorization

FL 6.EE.1.1
Write and evaluate numerical expressions involving whole-number exponents.

? ESSENTIAL QUESTION

How do you write the prime factorization of a number?

Finding Factors of a Number

Whole numbers that are multiplied to find a product are called factors of that product. A number is divisible by its factors. For example, 4 and 2 are factors of 8 because $4 \cdot 2 = 8$, and 8 is divisible by 4 and by 2.

EXAMPLE 1 Real World   FL Prep for 6.EE.1.1

Ana wants to build a rectangular garden with an area of 24 square feet. What are the possible whole number lengths and widths of the garden?

STEP 1 Recall that area = length · width. For Ana's garden,
24 ft^2 = length · width.

STEP 2 List the factors of 24 in pairs. List each pair only once.

$24 = 1 \cdot 24$
$24 = 2 \cdot 12$
$24 = 3 \cdot 8$
$24 = 4 \cdot 6$

$4 \cdot 6 = 6 \cdot 4$, so you only list $4 \cdot 6$.

You can also use a diagram to show the factor pairs.

1 2 3 4 6 8 12 24

The factors of 24 are 1, 2, 3, 4, 6, 8, 12, 24.

STEP 3 The possible lengths and widths are:

Length (ft)	24	12	8	6
Width (ft)	1	2	3	4

Math Talk
Mathematical Practices

Give an example of a whole number that has exactly two factors. What type of number has exactly two factors?

YOUR TURN

List all the factors of each number.

1. 21 _____

2. 37 _____

3. 42 _____

4. 30 _____

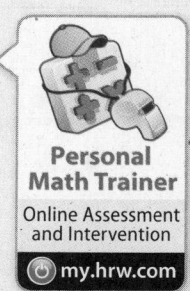

Personal Math Trainer

Online Assessment and Intervention

my.hrw.com

Finding the Prime Factorization of a Number

Animated Math

my.hrw.com

The prime factorization of a number is the number written as the product of its prime factors. For example, the prime factors of 12 are 3, 2, and 2.

The prime factorization of 12 is $2 \cdot 3 \cdot 2$ or $2^2 \cdot 3$.

> Use exponents to show repeated factors.

Use a factor tree to find the prime factorization of 240.

A List the factor pairs of 240.

_____

_____

240

· 48

B Choose any factor pair to begin the tree. If a number in this pair is prime, circle it. If a number in the pair can be written as a product of two factors, draw additional branches and write the factors.

C Continue adding branches until the factors at the ends of the branches are prime numbers.

D Write the prime factorization of 240.

_____

Then write the prime factorization using exponents.

_____

240

Reflect

5. **What If?** What will the factor tree for 240 look like if you start the tree with a different factor pair? Check your prediction by creating another factor tree for 240 that starts with a different factor pair.

_____

_____

_____

_____

Using a Ladder Diagram

A ladder diagram is another way to find the prime factorization of a number.

Use a ladder diagram to find the prime factorization of 132.

A Write 132 in the top "step" of the ladder. Choose a prime factor of 132 to write next to the step with 132. Choose 2. Divide 132 by 2 and write the quotient 66 in the next step of the ladder.

B Now choose a prime factor of 66. Write the prime factor next to the step with 66. Divide 66 by that prime factor and write the quotient in the next step of the ladder.

C Keep choosing prime factors, dividing, and adding to the ladder until you get a quotient of 1.

D What are the prime factors of 132? How can you tell from the ladder diagram?

_____

_____

E Write the prime factorization of 132 using exponents.

_____

Reflect

6. Complete a factor tree and a ladder diagram to find the prime factorization of 54.

54
/\

7. **Communicate Mathematical Ideas** If one person uses a ladder diagram and another uses a factor tree to write a prime factorization, will they get the same result? Explain.

_____

_____

Guided Practice

Use a diagram to list the factor pairs of each number. (Example 1)

1. 18

2. 52

_____

_____

3. Karl needs to build a stage that has an area of 72 square feet. The length of the stage should be longer than the width. What are the possible whole number measurements for the length and width of the stage? (Example 1)

Complete the table with possible measurements of the stage.

Length	72				
Width		2			

Use a factor tree to find the prime factorization of each number.
(Explore Activity 1)

4. 402

5. 36

_____

_____

Use a ladder diagram to find the prime factorization of each number.
(Explore Activity 2)

6. 64

7. 27

_____

_____

? ESSENTIAL QUESTION CHECK-IN

8. Tell how you know when you have found the prime factorization of a number.

_____

_____

9.2 Independent Practice

 FL 6.EE.1.1

Personal Math Trainer

Online
Assessment and
Intervention

🔵 my.hrw.com

9. **Multiple Representations** Use the grid to draw three different rectangles so that each has an area of 12 square units and they all have different widths. What are the dimensions of the rectangles?

_____

_____

10. Brandon has 32 stamps. He wants to display the stamps in rows, with the same number of stamps in each row. How many different ways can he display the stamps? Explain.

_____

_____

_____

11. **Communicate Mathematical Ideas** How is finding the factors of a number different from finding the prime factorization of a number?

_____

_____

_____

_____

Find the prime factorization of each number.

12. 891 _____   **13.** 504 _____

14. 23 _____   **15.** 230 _____

16. The number 2 is chosen to begin a ladder diagram to find the prime factorization of 66. What other numbers could have been used to start the ladder diagram for 66? How does starting with a different number change the diagram?

_____

_____

_____

17. **Critical Thinking** List five numbers that have 3, 5, and 7 as prime factors.

_____

© Houghton Mifflin Harcourt Publishing Company

18. In a game, you draw a card with three consecutive numbers on it. You can choose one of the numbers and find the sum of its prime factors. Then you can move that many spaces. You draw a card with the numbers 25, 26, 27. Which number should you choose if you want to move as many spaces as possible? Explain.

_____

_____

_____

_____

19. Explain the Error When asked to write the prime factorization of the number 27, a student wrote $9 \cdot 3$. Explain the error and write the correct answer.

_____

_____

 FOCUS ON HIGHER ORDER THINKING

20. Communicate Mathematical Ideas Explain why it is possible to draw more than two different rectangles with an area of 36 square units, but it is not possible to draw more than two different rectangles with an area of 15 square units. The sides of the rectangles are whole numbers.

_____

_____

_____

21. Critique Reasoning Alice wants to find all the prime factors of the number you get when you multiply $17 \cdot 11 \cdot 13 \cdot 7$. She thinks she has to use a calculator to perform all the multiplications and then find the prime factorization of the resulting number. Do you agree? Why or why not?

_____

_____

_____

22. Look for a Pattern Ryan wrote the prime factorizations shown below. If he continues this pattern, what prime factorization will he show for the number one million? What prime factorization will he show for one billion?

$10 = 5 \cdot 2$

$100 = 5^2 \cdot 2^2$

$1,000 = 5^3 \cdot 2^3 = 1,000$

_____

9.3 Order of Operations

FL 6.EE.1.1
Write and evaluate ...
expressions involving
whole-number exponents.

? ESSENTIAL QUESTION

How do you use the order of operations to simplify expressions with exponents?

EXPLORE ACTIVITY Real World FL 6.EE.1.1

Exploring the Order of Operations

Order of Operations

1. Perform operations in parentheses.
2. Find the value of numbers with exponents.
3. Multiply or divide from left to right.
4. Add or subtract from left to right.

Amy and three friends launch a new website. Each friend e-mails the web address to three new friends. These new friends forward the web address to three more friends. If no one receives the e-mail more than once, how many people will receive the web address in the second wave of e-mails?

Amy

1st wave →

2nd wave →

A Use a diagram to model the situation for Amy. Each dot represents one e-mail. Complete the diagram to show the second wave.

B Complete the table to show how many e-mails are sent in each wave of Amy's diagram.

Wave	Number of e-mails	Power of 3
1st		
2nd		

C Amy is just one of four friends initiating the first wave of e-mails. Write an expression for the total number of e-mails sent in the 2nd wave.

number of people × number of e-mails in 2nd wave written as a power

☐ × ☐

D Identify the computation that should be done first to simplify the expression in **C**. Then simplify the expression.

Multiply 4 and 3 / Find the value of 3^2

The value of the expression is $4 \times$ _____ = _____.

Reflect

1. In **B**, why does it makes sense to write the numbers of e-mails as powers? What is the pattern for the number of e-mails in each wave for Amy?

_____

_____

_____

Math On the Spot
my.hrw.com

Simplifying Numerical Expressions

A numerical expression is an expression involving numbers and operations. You can use the order of operations to simplify numerical expressions.

EXAMPLE 1

 FL 6.EE.1.1

Simplify each expression.

A $5 + 18 \div 3^2$

$5 + 18 \div 3^2 = 5 + 18 \div 9$	Evaluate 3^2.
$= 5 + 2$	Divide.
$= 7$	Add.

B $21 + \dfrac{3^2}{3}$

$21 + \dfrac{3^2}{3} = 21 + \dfrac{9}{3}$	Evaluate 3^2.
$= 21 + 3$	Divide.
$= 24$	Add.

C $6 \times 2^3 \div 3 + 1$

$6 \times 2^3 \div 3 + 1 = 6 \times 8 \div 3 + 1$	Evaluate 2^3.
$= 48 \div 3 + 1$	Multiply.
$= 16 + 1$	Divide.
$= 17$	Add.

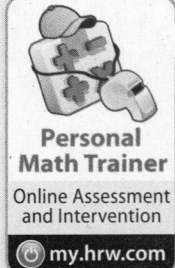

Personal Math Trainer

Online Assessment and Intervention
my.hrw.com

YOUR TURN

Simplify each expression using the order of operations.

2. $7 + 15 \times 9^2 =$ _____

3. $220 - 450 \div 3^2 =$ _____

Using Exponents with Grouping Symbols

Remember to perform operations inside parentheses first when you simplify expressions.

EXAMPLE 2   FL 6.EE.1.1

Simplify each expression using the order of operations.

My Notes

A $4 \times (9 \div 3)^2$

$4 \times (9 \div 3)^2 = 4 \times 3^2$	Perform operations inside parentheses.
$= 4 \times 9$	Evaluate 3^2.
$= 36$	Multiply.

B $5^3 + (12 - 2)^2$

$5^3 + (12 - 2)^2 = 5^3 + 10^2$	Perform operations inside parentheses.
$= 125 + 100$	Evaluate powers.
$= 225$	Add.

C $8 + \dfrac{(12 - 8)^2}{2}$

$8 + \dfrac{(12 - 8)^2}{2} = 8 + \dfrac{4^2}{2}$	Perform operations inside parentheses.
$= 8 + \dfrac{16}{2}$	Evaluate 4^2.
$= 8 + 8$	Divide.
$= 16$	Add.

Reflect

4. **Critique Reasoning** John wants to simplify the expression $(5 + 3)^2$. As a first step, he writes $5^2 + 3^2$. Will he get the correct value for the expression? If not, what should he do to simplify the expression?

_____

_____

_____

YOUR TURN

Simplify each expression using the order of operations.

5. $5 \times (20 \div 4)^2 =$ _____

6. $8^2 - (5 + 2)^2 =$ _____

7. $7 - \dfrac{(63 \div 9)^2}{7} =$ _____

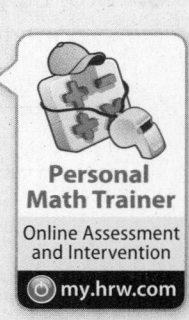
Personal Math Trainer

Online Assessment and Intervention

my.hrw.com

1. In a video game, a guppy that escapes a net turns into three goldfish. Each goldfish can turn into two betta fish. Each betta fish can turn into two angelfish. Complete the diagram and write the number of fish at each stage. Write and evaluate an expression for the number of angelfish that can be formed from one guppy. (Explore Activity)

1 guppy

3 goldfish

☐ × 2 betta fish

☐ × 2^☐ = ☐ angelfish

_____

Complete to simplify each expression. (Examples 1 and 2)

2. $89 - 4^2 \times 4 + 12 = 89 - \underline{\hspace{1cm}} \times 4 + 12$

$= 89 - \underline{\hspace{1cm}} + 12$

$= \underline{\hspace{1cm}} + 12$

$= \underline{\hspace{1cm}}$

3. $6 \times (36 \div 12)^2 + 8 = 6 \times (\underline{\hspace{1cm}})^2 + 8$

$= 6 \times \underline{\hspace{1cm}} + 8$

$= \underline{\hspace{1cm}} + 8$

$= \underline{\hspace{1cm}}$

4. $12 \times \left(\dfrac{(4+2)^2}{4} \right) - 7 = 12 \times \left(\dfrac{(\boxed{})^2}{4} \right) - 7$

$= 12 \times \left(\dfrac{\boxed{}}{4} \right) - 7$

$= 12 \times \underline{\hspace{1cm}} - 7$

$= \underline{\hspace{1cm}} - 7$

$= \underline{\hspace{1cm}}$

5. $320 \div \left(\dfrac{(11-9)^3}{2} \right) \times 8 = 320 \div \left(\dfrac{(\boxed{})^3}{2} \right) \times 8$

$= 320 \div \left(\dfrac{\boxed{}}{2} \right) \times 8$

$= 320 \div \underline{\hspace{1cm}} \times 8$

$= \underline{\hspace{1cm}} \times 8$

$= \underline{\hspace{1cm}}$

? ESSENTIAL QUESTION CHECK-IN

6. How do you use the order of operations to simplify expressions with exponents?

_____

_____

_____

9.3 Independent Practice

FL 6.EE.1.1

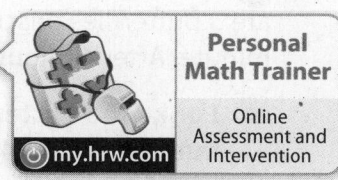

Personal Math Trainer

Online Assessment and Intervention

my.hrw.com

Simplify each expression using the order of operations.

7. $5 \times 2 + 3^2$ _____

8. $15 - 7 \times 2 + 2^3$ _____

9. $(11 - 8)^3 - 2 \times 6$ _____

10. $6 + 3(13 - 2) - 5^2$ _____

11. $12 + \frac{9^2}{3}$ _____

12. $\frac{8 + 6^2}{11} + 7 \times 2$ _____

13. **Explain the Error** Jay simplified the expression $3 \times (3 + 12 \div 3) - 4$. For his first step, he added $3 + 12$ to get 15. What was Jay's error? Find the correct answer.

_____

_____

14. **Multistep** A clothing store has the sign shown in the shop window. Pani sees the sign and wants to buy 3 shirts and 2 pairs of jeans. The cost of each shirt before the discount is $12, and the cost of each pair of jeans is $19 before the discount.

SALE Today ONLY $3 off every purchase!

a. Write and simplify an expression to find the amount Pani pays if a $3 discount is applied to her total.

_____

b. Pani says she should get a $3 discount on the price of each shirt and a $3 discount on the price of each pair of jeans. Write and simplify an expression to find the amount she would pay if this is true.

_____

c. **Analyze Relationships** Why are the amounts Pani pays in **a** and **b** different?

_____

_____

d. If you were the shop owner, how would you change the sign? Explain.

_____

_____

_____

15. Ellen is playing a video game in which she captures butterflies. There are 3 butterflies onscreen, but the number of butterflies doubles every minute. After 4 minutes, she was able to capture 7 of the butterflies.

   a. **Look for a Pattern** Write an expression for the number of butterflies after 4 minutes. Use a power of 2 in your answer.

   _____

   b. Write an expression for the number of butterflies remaining after Ellen captured the 7 butterflies. Simplify the expression.

   _____

16. Show how to write, evaluate and simplify an expression to represent and solve this problem: Jeff and his friend each text four classmates about a concert. Each classmate then texts four students from another school about the concert. If no one receives the message more than once, how many students from the other school receive a text about the concert?

   _____

H.O.T. **FOCUS ON HIGHER ORDER THINKING**

© Houghton Mifflin Harcourt Publishing Company • Image Credits: imagebroker/Alamy

Work Area

17. **Geometry** The figure shown is a rectangle. The green shape in the figure is a square. The blue and white shapes are rectangles, and the area of the blue rectangle is 24 square inches.

2 in.

6 in.

   a. Write an expression for the area of the entire figure that includes an exponent. Then find the area.

   _____

   b. Find the dimensions of the entire figure.

   _____

18. **Explain the Error** Rob and Lila try to simplify $18 \times 4^2 + (9 - 3)^2$. Rob simplifies the expression and gets 360. Lila simplifies it and gets 324. Which student is correct? What error did the other student make?

   _____

   _____

   _____

19. **Persevere in Problem Solving** Use parentheses to make this statement true: $8 \times 4 - 2 \times 3 + 8 \div 2 = 25$

   _____

Ready to Go On?

Personal Math Trainer
Online Assessment and Intervention
my.hrw.com

9.1 Exponents

Find the value of each power.

1. 7^3 _____

2. 9^2 _____

3. $\left(\frac{7}{9}\right)^2$ _____

4. $\left(\frac{1}{2}\right)^6$ _____

5. $\left(\frac{2}{3}\right)^3$ _____

6. $\left(\frac{1}{3}\right)^4$ _____

7. 12^0 _____

8. 1.4^2 _____

9.2 Prime Factorization

Find the factors of each number.

9. 96 _____

10. 120 _____

Find the prime factorization of each number.

11. 58 _____

12. 212 _____

13. 2,800 _____

14. 900 _____

9.3 Order of Operations

Simplify each expression using the order of operations.

15. $(21 - 3) \div 3^2$ _____

16. $7^2 \times (6 \div 3)$ _____

17. $17 + 15 \div 3 - 2^4$ _____

18. $(8 + 56) \div 4 - 3^2$ _____

19. The nature park has a pride of 7 adult lions and 4 cubs. The adults eat 6 pounds of meat each day and the cubs eat 3 pounds. Simplify $7 \times 6 + 4 \times 3$ to find the amount of meat consumed each day by the lions. _____

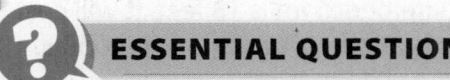 **ESSENTIAL QUESTION**

20. How do you use numerical expressions to solve real-world problems?

_____

_____

_____

_____

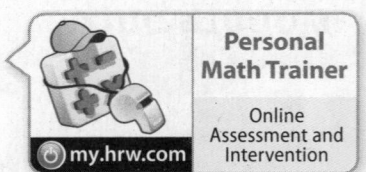
Selected Response

1. Which expression has a value that is less than the base of that expression?

(A) 2^3

(B) $\left(\frac{5}{6}\right)^2$

(C) 3^2

(D) 4^4

2. After the game the coach bought 9 chicken meals for $5 each and 15 burger meals for $6 each. What percent of the total amount the coach spent was used for the chicken meals?

(A) $33\frac{1}{3}\%$

(B) 45%

(C) $66\frac{2}{3}\%$

(D) 90%

3. Which operation should you perform first when you simplify $175 - (8 + 45 \div 3) \times 7$?

(A) addition

(B) division

(C) multiplication

(D) subtraction

4. For a game, three people are chosen in the first round. Each of those people chooses 3 people in the second round, and so on. How many people are chosen in the sixth round?

(A) 18

(B) 216

(C) 243

(D) 729

5. Which expression shows the prime factorization of 100?

(A) $2^2 \times 5^2$

(C) 10^{10}

(B) 10×10

(D) $2 \times 5 \times 10$

6. Which number has only two factors?

(A) 21

(C) 25

(B) 23

(D) 27

7. Which expression is equivalent to $3.6 \times 3.6 \times 3.6 \times 3.6$?

(A) 3.6×4

(C) $3^4 \times 6^4$

(B) 36^3

(D) 3.6^4

8. Which expression gives the prime factorization of 80?

(A) $2^4 \times 10$

(B) $2 \times 5 \times 8$

(C) $2^3 \times 5$

(D) $2^4 \times 5$

Mini-Task

9. George wants to put carpeting in a rectangular living room and a square bedroom. The length and width of the living room is 12 feet by 18 feet. One side of the square bedroom is 13 feet. It will cost $3.50 per square foot to carpet the rooms.

a. Write an expression that can be used to find the total amount George will pay for carpeting.

_____

b. Evaluate the expression. How much will George pay for the carpeting?

_____

Generating Equivalent Algebraic Expressions

? ESSENTIAL QUESTION

How can you generate equivalent algebraic expressions and use them to solve real-world problems?

LESSON 10.1

Modeling and Writing Expressions

FL 6.EE.1.2a, 6.EE.1.2b, 6.EE.1.4, 6.EE.2.6

LESSON 10.2

Evaluating Expressions

FL 6.EE.1.2c

LESSON 10.3

Generating Equivalent Expressions

FL 6.EE.1.2b, 6.EE.1.3, 6.EE.1.4

Real-World Video

Carpenters use formulas to calculate a project's materials supply. Sometimes formulas can be written in different forms. The perimeter of a rectangle can be written as $P = 2(l + w)$ or $P = 2l + 2w$.

my.hrw.com

GO DIGITAL
my.hrw.com

my.hrw.com

Go digital with your write-in student edition, accessible on any device.

Math On the Spot

Scan with your smart phone to jump directly to the online edition, video tutor, and more.

Animated Math

Interactively explore key concepts to see how math works.

Personal Math Trainer

Get immediate feedback and help as you work through practice sets.

Are YOU Ready?

Complete these exercises to review skills you will need for this module.

Use of Parentheses

EXAMPLE	$(6 + 4) \times (3 + 8 + 1) = 10 \times 12$	Do the operations inside parentheses first.
	$= 120$	Multiply.

Evaluate.

1. $11 + (20 - 13)$ _____

2. $(10 - 7) - (14 - 12)$ _____

3. $(4 + 17) - (16 - 9)$ _____

4. $(23 - 15) - (18 - 13)$ _____

5. $8 \times (4 + 5 + 7)$ _____

6. $(2 + 3) \times (11 - 5)$ _____

Words for Operations

EXAMPLE	Write a numerical expression for the quotient of 20 and 5.	Think: *Quotient* means to divide.
	$20 \div 5$	Write 20 divided by 5.

Write a numerical expression for the word expression.

7. the difference between 42 and 19 _____

8. the product of 7 and 12 _____

9. 30 more than 20 _____

10. 100 decreased by 77 _____

Evaluate Expressions

EXAMPLE	Evaluate $2(5) - 3^2$.	
	$2(5) - 3^2 = 2(5) - 9$	Evaluate exponents.
	$= 10 - 9$	Multiply.
	$= 1$	Subtract.

Evaluate the expression.

11. $3(8) - 15$ _____

12. $4(12) + 11$ _____

13. $3(7) - 4(2)$ _____

14. $4(2 + 3) - 12$ _____

15. $9(14 - 5) - 42$ _____

16. $7(8) - 5(8)$ _____

Reading Start-Up

Visualize Vocabulary

Use the review words to complete the graphic. You may put more than one word in each oval.

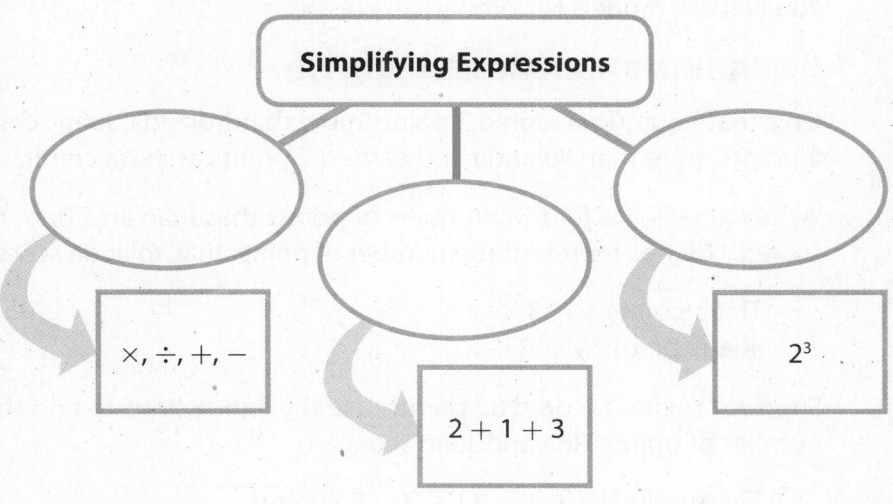

Simplifying Expressions

×, ÷, +, −

2 + 1 + 3

2^3

Understand Vocabulary

Complete the sentences using the preview words.

1. An expression that contains at least one variable is an
   _____

2. A part of an expression that is added or subtracted is a _____ .

3. A _____ is a specific number whose value does not change.

Active Reading

Key-Term Fold Before beginning the module, create a key-term fold to help you learn the vocabulary in this module. Write the highlighted vocabulary words on one side of the flap. Write the definition for each word on the other side of the flap. Use the key-term fold to quiz yourself on the definitions used in this module.

MODULE 10
Unpacking the Standards

Understanding the standards and the vocabulary terms in the standards will help you know exactly what you are expected to learn in this module.

© Houghton Mifflin Harcourt Publishing Company • Image Credits: Erik Dreyer/Getty Images

---

 FL 6.EE.1.2

Write, read, and evaluate expressions in which letters stand for numbers.

Key Vocabulary

expression (*expresión*)
A mathematical phrase that contains operations, numbers, and/or variables.

What It Means to You

You will use models to compare expressions.

UNPACKING EXAMPLE 6.EE.1.2

On a math quiz, Tina scored 3 points more than Yolanda. Juan scored 2 points more than Yolanda and earned 2 points as extra credit.

Write expressions for the numbers of points that Juan and Tina scored. Use y to represent the number of points that Yolanda scored.

> Tina's points: $y + 3$
> Juan's points: $y + 2 + 2$

Suppose Yolanda scored 82 points. Use the expressions to find the number of points Tina and Juan scored.

> Tina's points: $y + 3 = 82 + 3 = 85$ points
> Juan's points: $y + 2 + 2 = 82 + 2 + 2 = 86$ points

 FL 6.EE.1.3

Apply the properties of operations to generate equivalent expressions.

Key Vocabulary

equivalent expressions
(*expresión equivalente*)
Expressions that have the same value for all values of the variables.

What It Means to You

You will use the properties of operations to find an equivalent expression.

UNPACKING EXAMPLE 6.EE.1.3

William earns $13 an hour working at a movie theater. He worked h hours in concessions and three times as many hours at the ticket counter. Write and simplify an expression for the amount of money William earned.

$13 \cdot$ hours at concessions $+ \$13 \cdot$ hours at ticket counter

$13h + 13(3h)$

$13h + 39h$ Multiply $13 \cdot 3h$.

$h(13 + 39)$ Distributive Property

$52h$ Simplify.

Visit **my.hrw.com** to see all **Florida Math Standards** unpacked.

Modeling and Writing Expressions

FL 6.EE.1.2a

Write expressions that record operations with numbers and with letters standing for numbers. *Also 6.EE.1.2b, 6.EE.1.4, 6.EE.2.6*

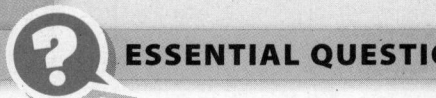 **ESSENTIAL QUESTION**

How can you model and write algebraic expressions?

Writing Algebraic Expressions

An **algebraic expression** is an expression that contains one or more variables and may also contain operation symbols, such as + or −.

A **variable** is a letter or symbol used to represent an unknown or unspecified number. The value of a variable may change.

A **constant** is a specific number whose value does not change.

> 150 is a constant and y is a variable.

Algebraic Expressions	x	$w + n$	$150 + y$

In algebraic expressions, multiplication and division are usually written without the symbols × and ÷.

- Write $3 \times n$ as $3n$, $3 \cdot n$, or $n \cdot 3$.
- Write $3 \div n$ as $\frac{3}{n}$.

There are several different ways to describe expressions with words.

Operation	Addition	Subtraction	Multiplication	Division
Words	• added to • plus • sum • more than	• subtracted from • minus • difference • less than	• times • multiplied by • product • groups of	• divided by • divided into • quotient

---

EXAMPLE 1 **FL** 6.EE.1.2a, 6.EE.1.2b

A **Write each phrase as an algebraic expression.**

The sum of 7 and x *The operation is addition.*

The algebraic expression is $7 + x$.

The quotient of z and 3   *The operation is division.*

The algebraic expression is $\frac{z}{3}$.

B Write a phrase for each expression.

$11x$ *The operation is multiplication.*

The product of 11 and x

$8 - y$ *The operation is subtraction.*

y less than 8

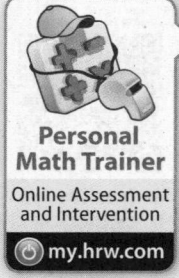

YOUR TURN

Write each phrase as an algebraic expression.

1. n times 7 _____   **2.** 4 minus y _____   **3.** 13 added to x _____

Write a phrase for each expression.

4. $\dfrac{x}{12}$ _____

5. $10y$ _____

6. $c + 3$ _____

Modeling Algebraic Expressions

Algebraic expressions can also be represented with models.

EXAMPLE 2   **FL** 6.EE.1.2a

Use a bar model to represent each expression.

A $7 + x$ *Combine 7 and x.*

B $\dfrac{z}{3}$ *Divide z into 3 equal parts.*

© Houghton Mifflin Harcourt Publishing Company

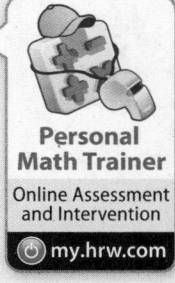

Personal Math Trainer

Online Assessment and Intervention

⏻ my.hrw.com

YOUR TURN

Draw a bar model to represent each expression.

7. $t - 2$

8. $4y$

Comparing Expressions Using Models

Algebraic expressions are *equivalent* if they are equal for all values of the variable. For example, $x + 2$ and $x + 1 + 1$ are equivalent.

Math On the Spot

⏻ my.hrw.com

EXAMPLE 3   **FL** 6.EE.1.4

Katriana and Andrew started the day with the same amount of money. Katriana spent 5 dollars on lunch. Andrew spent 3 dollars on lunch and 2 dollars on a snack after school. Do Katriana and Andrew have the same amount of money left?

My Notes

STEP 1 Write an algebraic expression to represent the money Katriana has left. Represent the expression with a model.

$x - 5$

The variable represents the amount of money both Katriana and Andrew have at the beginning of the day.

STEP 2 Write an algebraic expression to represent the money Andrew has left. Represent the expression with a model.

$x - 3 - 2$

STEP 3 Compare the models.

The models are equivalent, so the expressions are equivalent.

Andrew and Katriana have the same amount of money left.

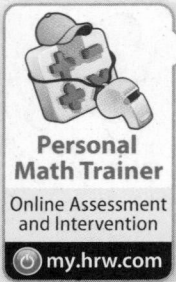
9. On a math quiz, Tina scored 3 points more than Julia. Juan scored 2 points more than Julia and earned 2 points in extra credit. Write an expression and draw a bar model to represent Tina's score and Juan's score. Did Tina and Juan make the same grade on the quiz? Explain.

Math On the Spot

⏻ my.hrw.com

Modeling Real-World Situations

You can use expressions to represent real-world situations.

EXAMPLE 4   **FL** 6.EE.2.6

A Tickets to the water park cost $53 per person. Write an expression to show the total cost of tickets for a group of people.

A group of is a clue to multiply. The ticket price of $53 is a constant. The number of people who need tickets is a variable.

Use *x* for the number of people.

The algebraic expression for the total cost of tickets is 53*x*.

B Genise has some savings. After babysitting, she adds $75 to her savings. How much money has Genise saved?

Adds is a clue to use addition. The $75 Genise added to her savings is a constant. The amount of money Genise had saved before is unknown, so use a variable.

Use *y* for Genise's savings before she adds the babysitting money.

The algebraic expression for Genise's total savings is $y + 75$.

Math Talk

Mathematical Practices

How do you know what operation to use to find the amount each niece receives?

10. Helen divides up some money to give equally to her four nieces. If *d* represents the total amount, write an expression to represent how much money each niece receives. _____

Write each phrase as an algebraic expression. (Example 1)

1. 3 less than y _____

2. The product of 2 and p _____

Write a phrase for each algebraic expression. (Example 1)

3. $y + 12$ _____

4. $\frac{p}{10}$ _____

5. Draw a bar model to represent the expression $m \div 4$. (Example 2)

At 6 p.m., the temperature in Phoenix, AZ, *t*, is the same as the temperature in Tucson, AZ. By 9 p.m., the temperature in Phoenix has dropped 2 degrees and in Tucson it has dropped 4 degrees. By 11 p.m., the temperature in Phoenix has dropped another 3 degrees. (Example 3)

6. Represent each city's temperature at 11 p.m. with an algebraic expression and a bar model.

7. Are the expressions that represent the temperatures in the two cities equivalent? Justify your answer.

_____

_____

8. Noelle bought some boxes of water bottles for a picnic. Each box contained 24 bottles of water. If c is the number of boxes, write an expression to show how many bottles of water Noelle bought. (Example 4)

_____

 ESSENTIAL QUESTION CHECK-IN

9. Give an example of a real-world situation that could be represented by an algebraic expression.

_____

_____

_____

10.1 Independent Practice

 FL 6.EE.1.2a, 6.EE.1.2b, 6.EE.1.4, 6.EE.2.6

Personal Math Trainer

Online Assessment and Intervention

my.hrw.com

10. Write an algebraic expression with the constant 7 and the variable *y*.

_____

Write each phrase as an algebraic expression.

11. *n* divided by 8 _____

12. *p* multiplied by 4 _____

13. *b* plus 14 _____

14. 90 times *x* _____

15. *a* take away 16 _____

16. *k* less than 24 _____

17. 3 groups of *w* _____

18. the sum of 1 and *q* _____

19. the quotient of 13 and *z* _____

20. *c* added to 45 _____

21. 8 less than *w* _____

Write a phrase in words for each algebraic expression.

22. $m + 83$ _____

23. $42s$ _____

24. $\dfrac{9}{d}$ _____

25. $t - 29$ _____

26. $2 + g$ _____

27. $11x$ _____

28. $\dfrac{h}{12}$ _____

29. $5 - k$ _____

Sarah and Noah work at Read On Bookstore and get paid the same hourly wage. The table shows their work schedule for last week.

Read On Bookstore Work Schedule (hours)			
	Monday	Tuesday	Wednesday
Sarah	5	3	
Noah			8

30. Write an expression that represents Sarah's total pay last week. Represent her hourly wage with *w*. _____

31. Write an expression that represents Noah's total pay last week. Represent his hourly wage with *w*. _____

32. Are the expressions equivalent? Did Sarah and Noah earn the same amount last week? Use models to justify your answer.

_____

33. Mia buys 3 gallons of gas that costs *d* dollars per gallon. Bob buys *g* gallons of gas that costs $3 per gallon.

a. Write an expression for the amount Mia pays for gas. _____

b. Write an expression for the amount Bob pays for gas. _____

c. What do the numeral and the variable represent in each expression?

_____

_____

_____

_____

34. The student council is asking people to donate money for the new park outside the school. Everyone who makes the suggested donation amount will be given a bracelet. If everyone donates the suggested amount, and *b* bracelets are given away, what algebraic expression represents the total amount collected in donations?

_____

35. Mr. Delgado has some young orange trees. He wants to plant them in 46 rows. If *t* is the total number of orange trees, write an algebraic expression to represent how many trees he can plant in each row.

_____

36. There are 15 violinists in the orchestra this year. Next year, two violinists will leave and some new violinists will join the orchestra. If *v* is the number of violinists who will join the orchestra, write an expression to represent the number of violinists in the orchestra next year.

_____

37. Jill, Meg, and Beth are sisters. Jill is 2 years younger than Meg. Beth is half as old as Meg. Let *m* represent Meg's age. Write two other algebraic expressions based on this situation. Tell what each expression represents, and what the variable stands for in each expression.

_____

_____

38. Multistep Will, Hector, and Lydia volunteered at the animal shelter in March and April. The table shows the number of hours Will and Hector volunteered in March. Let *x* represent the number of hours Lydia volunteered in March.

March Volunteering	
Will	3 hours
Hector	5 hours

a. Will's volunteer hours in April were equal to his March volunteer hours plus Lydia's March volunteer hours. Write an expression to represent Will's volunteer hours in April. _____

b. Hector's volunteer hours in April were equal to 2 hours less than his March volunteer hours plus Lydia's March volunteer hours. Write an expression to represent Hector's volunteer hours in April. _____

c. Did Will and Hector volunteer the same number of hours in April?

Explain. _____

39. The town of Rayburn received 6 more inches of snow than the town of Greenville. Let *g* represent the amount of snow in Greenville. Write an algebraic expression to represent the amount of snow in Rayburn. _____

40. Abby baked 48 dinner rolls and divided them evenly into bags. Let b represent the number of bags. Write an algebraic expression to represent the number of dinner rolls in each bag.

_____

41. Eli is driving at a speed of 55 miles per hour. Let h represent the number of hours that Eli drives at this speed. Write an algebraic expression to represent the number of miles that Eli travels during this time.

_____

 FOCUS ON HIGHER ORDER THINKING

42. Multistep Bob's Bagels offers two breakfast options, as shown.

   a. Let x represent the number of customers who order coffee and a bagel. How much money will Bob's Bagels make from these orders?

   _____

   b. Let y represent the number of customers who order tea and a breakfast sandwich. How much money will Bob's Bagels make from

   these orders? _____

   c. Write an algebraic expression for the total amount Bob's Bagels will make from all the coffee and bagel orders and from all the tea and

   breakfast sandwich orders. _____

43. Represent Real-World Problems The number of shoes in a closet is s.

   a. How many pairs of shoes are in the closet? Explain.

   _____

   b. What If? Suppose one of the pairs is missing a shoe. How many

   shoes are in the closet? _____

44. Problem Solving Write an expression that has three terms, two different

variables, and one constant. _____

45. Represent Real-World Problems Describe a situation that can be modeled by the expression $x - 8$.

_____

_____

46. Critique Reasoning Ricardo says that the expression $y + 4$ is equivalent to the expression $1y + 4$. Is he correct? Explain.

_____

_____

_____

Work Area

© Houghton Mifflin Harcourt Publishing Company

LESSON 10.2 Evaluating Expressions

FL 6.EE.1.2c

Evaluate expressions at specific values of their variables.

? ESSENTIAL QUESTION

How can you use the order of operations to evaluate algebraic expressions?

Evaluating Expressions

Recall that an algebraic expression contains one or more variables. You can substitute a number for that variable and then find the value of the expression. This is called **evaluating** the expression.

Math On the Spot

⏻ my.hrw.com

EXAMPLE 1

FL 6.EE.1.2c

Evaluate each expression for the given value of the variable.

My Notes

A $x - 9$; $x = 15$

$15 - 9$ Substitute 15 for x.

6 Subtract.

When $x = 15$, $x - 9 = 6$.

B $\frac{16}{n}$; $n = 8$

$\frac{16}{8}$ Substitute 8 for n.

2 Divide.

When $n = 8$, $\frac{16}{n} = 2$.

C $0.5y$; $y = 1.4$

$0.5(1.4)$ Substitute 1.4 for y.

0.7 Multiply.

When $y = 1.4$, $0.5y = 0.7$.

D $6k$; $k = \frac{1}{3}$

HINT: Think of 6 as $\frac{6}{1}$.

$6\left(\frac{1}{3}\right)$ Substitute $\frac{1}{3}$ for k.

2 Multiply.

When $k = \frac{1}{3}$, $6k = 2$.

© Houghton Mifflin Harcourt Publishing Company

Lesson 10.2 **269**

Evaluate each expression for the given value of the variable.

1. $4x; x = 8$ _____ **2.** $6.5 - n; n = 1.8$ _____ **3.** $\frac{m}{6}; m = 18$ _____

Using the Order of Operations

Expressions may have more than one operation or more than one variable. To evaluate these expressions, substitute the given value for each variable and then use the order of operations.

EXAMPLE 2   **FL** 6.EE.1.2c

Evaluate each expression for the given value of the variable.

A $4(x - 4); x = 7$

$4(7 - 4)$	Substitute 7 for x.
$4(3)$	Subtract inside the parentheses.
12	Multiply.

When $x = 7$, $4(x - 4) = 12$.

B $4x - 4; x = 7$

$4(7) - 4$	Substitute 7 for x.
$28 - 4$	Multiply.
24	Subtract.

When $x = 7$, $4x - 4 = 24$.

C $w - x + y; w = 6, x = 5, y = 3$

$(6) - (5) + (3)$	Substitute 6 for w, 5 for x, and 3 for y.
$1 + 3$	Subtract.
4	Add.

When $w = 6$, $x = 5$, $y = 3$, $w - x + y = 4$.

Math Talk

Mathematical Practices

Is $w - x + y$ equivalent to $w - y + x$? Explain any difference in the order the math operations are performed.

D $x^2 - x; x = 9$

$(9)^2 - (9)$	Substitute 9 for each x.
$81 - 9$	Evaluate exponents.
72	Subtract.

When $x = 9$, $x^2 - x = 72$.

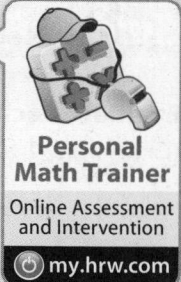

YOUR TURN

Evaluate each expression for $n = 5$.

4. $3(n + 1)$ _____   **5.** $4(n - 4) + 14$ _____   **6.** $6n + n^2$ _____

Evaluate each expression for $a = 3$, $b = 4$, and $c = 6$.

7. $ab - c$ _____   **8.** $bc + 5a$ _____   **9.** $a^3 - (b + c)$ _____

Evaluating Real-World Expressions

You can evaluate expressions to solve real-world problems.

EXAMPLE 3   FL 6.EE.1.2c

The expression $1.8c + 32$ gives the temperature in degrees Fahrenheit for a given temperature in degrees Celsius c. Find the temperature in degrees Fahrenheit that is equivalent to $30\,°C$.

STEP 1 Find the value of c.

$c = 30\,°C$

STEP 2 Substitute the value into the expression.

$1.8c + 32$

$1.8(30) + 32$ Substitute 30 for c.

$54 + 32$ Multiply.

86 Add.

$86\,°F$ is equivalent to $30\,°C$.

YOUR TURN

10. The expression $6x^2$ gives the surface area of a cube, and the expression x^3 gives the volume of a cube, where x is the length of one side of the cube. Find the surface area and the volume of a cube with a side length of 2 m.

$S =$ _____ m^2; $V =$ _____ m^3

11. The expression $60m$ gives the number of seconds in m minutes. How many seconds are there in 7 minutes?

_____ seconds

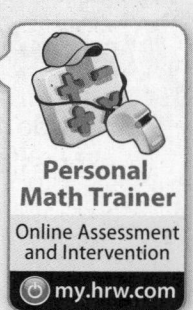

© Houghton Mifflin Harcourt Publishing Company

Guided Practice

Evaluate each expression for the given value(s) of the variable(s).
(Examples 1 and 2)

1. $x - 7; x = 23$ _____

2. $3a - b; a = 4, b = 6$ _____

3. $\frac{8}{t}; t = 4$ _____

4. $9 + m; m = 1.5$ _____

5. $\frac{1}{2}w + 2; w = \frac{1}{9}$ _____

6. $5(6.2 + z); z = 3.8$ _____

7. The table shows the prices for games in Bella's soccer league. Her parents and grandmother attended a soccer game. How much did they spend if they all went together in one car? (Example 3)

Women's Soccer Game Prices	
Student tickets	$6
Nonstudent tickets	$12
Parking	$5

  a. Write an expression that represents the cost of one carful of nonstudent soccer fans. Use x as the number of people who rode in the car and attended the game.

  _____ is an expression that represents the cost of one carful of nonstudent soccer fans.

  b. Since there are three attendees, evaluate the expression $12x + 5$ for $x = 3$.

  $12(\_\_\_) + 5 = \_\_\_\_\_ + 5 = \_\_\_\_\_$

  The family spent _____ to attend the game.

8. Stan wants to add trim all around the edge of a rectangular tablecloth that measures 5 feet long by 7 feet wide. The perimeter of the rectangular tablecloth is twice the length added to twice the width. How much trim does Stan need to buy? (Example 3)

  a. Write an expression that represents the perimeter of the rectangular tablecloth. Let l represent the length of the tablecloth and w represent its width. The expression would be _____.

  b. Evaluate the expression $P = 2w + 2l$ for $l = 5$ and $w = 7$.

  $2(\_\_\_\_\_) + 2(\_\_\_\_\_) = 14 + \_\_\_\_\_ = \_\_\_\_\_$

  Stan bought _____ of trim to sew onto the tablecloth.

? ESSENTIAL QUESTION CHECK-IN

9. How do you know the correct order in which to evaluate algebraic expressions?

_____

_____

© Houghton Mifflin Harcourt Publishing Company

10.2 Independent Practice

Personal Math Trainer

my.hrw.com Online Assessment and Intervention

10. The table shows ticket prices at the Movie 16 theater. Let a represent the number of adult tickets, c the number of children's tickets, and s the number of senior citizen tickets.

Movie 16 Ticket Prices	
Adults	$8.75
Children	$6.50
Seniors	$6.50

a. Write an expression for the total cost of the three types of tickets.

_____

_____

b. The Andrews family bought 2 adult tickets, 3 children's tickets, and 1 senior ticket. Evaluate your expression in part a to find the total cost of the tickets.

_____

_____

c. The Spencer family bought 4 adult tickets and 2 children's tickets. Did they spend the same as the Andrews family? Explain.

_____

11. The area of a triangular sail is given by the expression $\frac{1}{2}bh$, where b is the length of the base and h is the height. What is the area of a triangular sail in a model sailboat when $b = 12$ inches and $h = 7$ inches?

$A =$ _____ in.^{2}

12. Ramon wants to balance his checking account. He has $2,340 in the account. He writes a check for $140. He deposits a check for $268. How much does Ramon have left

in his checking account? _____

13. **Look for a Pattern** Evaluate the expression $6x - x^2$ for $x = 0, 1, 2, 3, 4, 5,$ and 6. Use your results to fill in the table and describe any pattern that you see.

x	0	1	2	3	4	5	6
$6x - x^2$							

_____

_____

_____

_____

_____

_____

_____

14. The kinetic energy (in joules) of a moving object can be calculated from the expression $\frac{1}{2}mv^2$, where m is the mass of the object in kilograms and v is its speed in meters per second. Find the kinetic energy of a 0.145-kg baseball that is thrown at a speed of 40 meters per second.

$E =$ _____ joules

15. The area of a square is given by x^2, where x is the length of one side. Mary's original garden was in the shape of a square. She has decided to double the area of her garden. Write an expression that represents the area of Mary's new garden. Evaluate the expression if the side length of Mary's original garden was 8 feet.

_____

_____

16. The volume of a pyramid with a square base is given by the expression $\frac{1}{3}s^2h$, where s is the length of a side of the base and h is the height. Find the volume of a pyramid with a square base of side length 24 feet and a height of 30 feet.

_____

 FOCUS ON HIGHER ORDER THINKING

17. Draw Conclusions Consider the expressions $3x(x - 2) + 2$ and $2x^2 + 3x - 12$.

a. Evaluate each expression for $x = 2$ and for $x = 7$. Based on your results, do you know whether the two expressions are equivalent? Explain.

_____

_____

_____

_____

_____

b. Evaluate each expression for $x = 5$. Based on your results, do you know whether the two expressions are equivalent? Explain.

_____

_____

_____

_____

_____

18. Critique Reasoning Marjorie evaluated the expression $3x + 2$ for $x = 5$ as shown:

$$3x + 2 = 35 + 2 = 37$$

What was Marjorie's mistake? What is the correct value of $3x + 2$ for $x = 5$?

_____

_____

_____

LESSON 10.3 Generating Equivalent Expressions

FL 6.EE.1.3

Apply the properties of operations to generate equivalent expressions. *Also 6.EE.1.2b, 6.EE.1.4*

❓ ESSENTIAL QUESTION

How can you identify and write equivalent expressions?

EXPLORE ACTIVITY 1 FL 6.EE.1.4

Identifying Equivalent Expressions

One way to test whether two expressions might be equivalent is to evaluate them for the same value of the variable.

Match the expressions in List A with their equivalent expressions in List B.

List A	List B
$5x + 65$	$5x + 1$
$5(x + 1)$	$5x + 5$
$1 + 5x$	$5(13 + x)$

A Evaluate each of the expressions in the lists for $x = 3$.

List A

$5(3) + 65 = \boxed{}$

$5(3 + 1) = \boxed{}$

$1 + 5(3) = \boxed{}$

List B

$5(3) + 1 = \boxed{}$

$5(3) + 5 = \boxed{}$

$5(13 + 3) = \boxed{}$

B Which pair(s) of expressions have the same value for $x = 3$?

_____

_____

C How could you further test whether the expressions in each pair are equivalent?

_____

D Do you think the expressions in each pair are equivalent? Why or why not?

_____

_____

© Houghton Mifflin Harcourt Publishing Company

Reflect

1. **Error Analysis** Lisa evaluated the expressions $2x$ and x^2 for $x = 2$ and found that both expressions were equal to 4. Lisa concluded that $2x$ and x^2 are equivalent expressions. How could you show Lisa that she is incorrect?

_____

_____

EXPLORE ACTIVITY 2   **FL** 6.EE.1.3

Modeling Equivalent Expressions

You can also use models to determine if two expressions are equivalent. *Algebra tiles* are one way to model expressions.

Algebra Tiles

$\boxed{+} = 1$

$\boxed{\ +\ } = x$

Determine if the expression $3(x + 2)$ is equivalent to $3x + 6$.

A Model each expression using algebra tiles.

$3(x + 2)$ $3x + 6$

B The model for $3(x + 2)$ has _____ x tiles and _____ 1 tiles.

The model for $3x + 6$ has _____ x tiles and _____ 1 tiles.

C Is the expression $3(x + 2)$ equivalent to $3x + 6$? Explain.

_____

_____

Reflect

2. Use algebra tiles to determine if $2(x + 3)$ is equivalent to $2x + 3$. Explain your answer.

_____

_____

Writing Equivalent Expressions Using Properties

> **Properties of operations can be used to identify equivalent expressions.**

Properties of Operations	Examples
Commutative Property of Addition: When adding, changing the order of the numbers does not change the sum.	$3 + 4 = 4 + 3$
Commutative Property of Multiplication: When multiplying, changing the order of the numbers does not change the product.	$2 \times 4 = 4 \times 2$
Associative Property of Addition: When adding more than two numbers, the grouping of the numbers does not change the sum.	$(3 + 4) + 5 = 3 + (4 + 5)$
Associative Property of Multiplication: When multiplying more than two numbers, the grouping of the numbers does not change the product.	$(2 \times 4) \times 3 = 2 \times (4 \times 3)$
Distributive Property: Multiplying a number by a sum or difference is the same as multiplying by each number in the sum or difference and then adding or subtracting.	$6(2 + 4) = 6(2) + 6(4)$ $8(5 - 3) = 8(5) - 8(3)$
Identity Property of Addition: Adding zero to a number does not change its value.	$9 + 0 = 9$
Identity Property of Multiplication: Multiplying a number by one does not change its value.	$1 \times 7 = 7$

EXAMPLE 1 FL 6.EE.1.3

Use a property to write an expression that is equivalent to $x + 3$.

The operation in the expression is addition.

You can use the Commutative Property of Addition to write an equivalent expression: $x + 3 = 3 + x$.

YOUR TURN

For each expression, use a property to write an equivalent expression. Tell which property you used.

3. $(ab)c =$ _____

4. $3y + 4y =$ _____

5. 6×7 _____

Personal Math Trainer

Online Assessment and Intervention

my.hrw.com

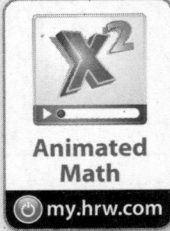

Identifying Equivalent Expressions Using Properties

EXAMPLE 2

 FL 6.EE.1.3

Use the properties of operations to determine if the expressions are equivalent.

A $3(x - 2)$; $3x - 6$

$3(x - 2) = 3x - 6$ — Distributive Property

$3(x - 2)$ and $3x - 6$ are equivalent expressions.

B $2 + x$; $\frac{1}{2}(4 + x)$

$\frac{1}{2}(x + 4) = \frac{1}{2}x + 2$ — Distributive Property

$= 2 + \frac{1}{2}x$ — Commutative Property

$2 + x$ does not equal $2 + \frac{1}{2}x$.

They are not equivalent expressions.

YOUR TURN

Use the properties of operations to determine if the expressions are equivalent.

6. $6x - 8$; $2(3x - 5)$

_____

_____

7. $2 - 2 + 5x$; $5x$

_____

_____

8. Jamal bought 2 packs of stickers and 8 individual stickers. Use x to represent the number of stickers in a pack of stickers and write an expression to represent the number of stickers Jamal bought. Is the expression equivalent to $2(4 + x)$? Check your answer with algebra tile models.

_____

_____

© Houghton Mifflin Harcourt Publishing Company

Generating Equivalent Expressions

Parts of an algebraic expression		
terms	The parts of the expression that are separated by + or − signs	$12 + 3y^2 + 4x + 2y^2 + 4$
coefficients	Numbers that are multiplied by at least one variable	$12 + 3y^2 + 4x + 2y^2 + 4$
like terms	Terms with the same variable(s) raised to the same power(s)	$12 + 3y^2 + 4x + 2y^2 + 4$

When an expression contains like terms, you can use properties to combine the like terms and write an equivalent expression.

EXAMPLE 3

FL   6.EE.1.3, 6.EE.1.2b

Combine like terms.

A $6x^2 - 4x^2$

> $6x^2$ and $4x^2$ are like terms.

$6x^2 - 4x^2 = x^2(6 - 4)$	Distributive Property
$= x^2(2)$	Subtract inside the parentheses.
$= 2x^2$	Commutative Property of Multiplication

$6x^2 - 4x^2 = 2x^2$

> **Math Talk**
> Mathematical Practices
> Write 2 terms that can be combined with $7y^4$.

B $3a + 2(b + 5a)$

$3a + 2(b + 5a) = 3a + 2b + 2(5a)$	Distributive Property
$= 3a + 2b + (2 \cdot 5)a$	Associative Property of Multiplication
$= 3a + 2b + 10a$	Multiply 2 and 5.
$= 3a + 10a + 2b$	Commutative Property of Addition
$= (3 + 10)a + 2b$	Distributive Property
$= 13a + 2b$	Add inside the parentheses.

$3a + 2(b + 5a) = 13a + 2b$

C $y + 11x + 7y - 7x$

> y and $7y$ are like terms; $11x$ and $7x$ are like terms.

$y + 11x + 7y - 7x = y + 7y + 11x - 7x$	Commutative Property
$= (1 + 7)y + (11 - 7)x$	Distributive Property
$= 8y + 4x$	Simplify inside parentheses.

$y + 11x + 7y - 7x = 8y + 4x$

YOUR TURN

Combine like terms.

9. $8y - 3y = $ _____

10. $6x^2 + 4(x^2 - 1) = $ _____

11. $4a^5 - 2a^5 + 4b + b = $

_____

12. $8m + 14 - 12 + 4n = $

_____

Guided Practice

1. Evaluate each of the expressions in the list for $y = 5$. Then, draw lines to match the expressions in List A with their equivalent expressions in List B. (Explore Activity 1)

List A	List B

List A

$4 + 4y = $ _____

$4(y - 1) = $ _____

$4y + 1 = $ _____

List B

$4y - 4 = $ _____

$4(y + 1) = $ _____

$1 + 4y = $ _____

2. Determine if the expressions are equivalent by comparing the models. (Explore Activity 2) _____

$x + 4$ $2(x + 2)$

For each expression, use a property to write an equivalent expression. Tell which property you used. (Example 1)

3. $ab = $ _____

_____

4. $5(3x - 2) = $ _____

_____

Use the properties of operations to determine if each pair of expressions is equivalent. (Example 2)

5. $\frac{1}{2}(4 - 2x); 2 - 2x$ _____

6. $\frac{1}{2}(6x - 2); 3 - x$ _____

Combine like terms. (Example 3)

7. $32y + 12y = $ _____

8. $12 + 3x - x - 12 = $ _____

? ESSENTIAL QUESTION CHECK-IN

9. Describe two ways to write equivalent algebraic expressions.

_____

_____

10.3 Independent Practice

Personal Math Trainer

Online Assessment and Intervention

my.hrw.com

FL 6.EE.1.2b, 6.EE.1.3, 6.EE.1.4

For each expression, use a property to write an equivalent expression. Tell which property you used.

10. $cd =$ _____

_____

11. $x + 13 =$ _____

_____

12. $4(2x - 3) =$ _____

_____

13. $2 + (a + b) =$ _____

_____

14. Draw algebra tile models to prove that $4 + 8x$ and $4(2x + 1)$ are equivalent.

_____   _____

Combine like terms.

15. $7x^4 - 5x^4 =$ _____

16. $32y + 5y =$ _____

17. $6b + 7b - 10 =$ _____

18. $2x + 3x + 4 =$ _____

19. $y + 4 + 3(y + 2) =$ _____

20. $7a^2 - a^2 + 16 =$ _____

21. $3y^2 + 3(4y^2 - 2) =$ _____

22. $z^2 + z + 4z^3 + 4z^2 =$ _____

23. $0.5(x^4 - 3) + 12 =$ _____

24. $\frac{1}{4}(16 + 4p) =$ _____

25. **Justify Reasoning** Determine whether $3x + 12 + x$ is equivalent to $4(3 + x)$. Use properties of operations to justify your answer.

_____

_____

26. William earns $13 an hour working at a movie theater. Last week he worked h hours at the concession stand and three times as many hours at the ticket counter. Write and simplify an expression for the amount of money William earned last week.

_____

© Houghton Mifflin Harcourt Publishing Company

27. Multiple Representations Use the information in the table to write and simplify an expression to find the total weight of the medals won by the top medal-winning nations in the 2012 London Olympic Games. The three types of medals have different weights.

2012 Summer Olympics			
	Gold	**Silver**	**Bronze**
United States	46	29	29
China	38	27	23
Great Britain	29	17	19

_____

_____

Write an expression for the perimeters of each given figure. Simplify the expression.

28. _____

$3x - 1$ mm

6 mm   6 mm

$3x - 1$ mm

29. _____

10.2 in.

$x + 4$ in. $x + 4$ in.

$x + 4$ in. $x + 4$ in.

10.2 in.

 FOCUS ON HIGHER ORDER THINKING

30. Problem Solving Examine the algebra tile model.

a. Write two equivalent expressions for the model. _____

b. What If? Suppose a third row of tiles identical to the ones above is added to the model. How does that change the two expressions?

_____

31. Communicate Mathematical Ideas Write an example of an expression that cannot be simplified, and explain how you know that it cannot be simplified.

_____

32. Problem Solving Write an expression that is equivalent to $8(2y + 4)$ that can be simplified.

_____

Work Area

Ready to Go On?

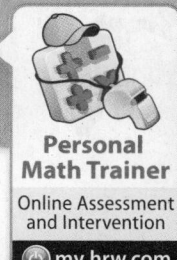

Personal Math Trainer
Online Assessment and Intervention

🔵 my.hrw.com

10.1 Modeling and Writing Expressions

Write each phrase as an algebraic expression.

1. p divided by 6 _____

2. 65 less than j _____

3. the sum of 185 and h _____

4. the product of 16 and g _____

5. Let x represent the number of television show episodes that are taped in a season. Write an expression for the number of episodes taped in

4 seasons. _____

10.2 Evaluating Expressions

Evaluate each expression for the given value of the variable.

6. $8p$; $p = 9$ _____

7. $11 + r$; $r = 7$ _____

8. $4(d + 7)$; $d = 2$ _____

9. $\frac{60}{m}$; $m = 5$ _____

10. To find the area of a triangle, you can use the expression $b \times h \div 2$, where b is the base of the triangle and h is its height. What is the area of

a triangle with a base of 6 and a height of 8? _____

10.3 Generating Equivalent Expressions

11. Draw lines to match the expressions in List A with their equivalent expressions in List B.

List A	List B
$7x + 14$	$7(1 + x)$
$7 + 7x$	$7x - 7$
$7(x - 1)$	$7(x + 2)$

? ESSENTIAL QUESTION

12. How can you solve problems involving equivalent expressions?

_____

_____

_____

_____

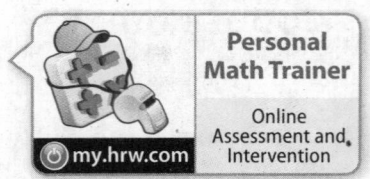
Selected Response

1. Which expression represents the product of 83 and x?

  Ⓐ $83 + x$

  Ⓑ $83 \div x$

  Ⓒ $83x$

  Ⓓ $83 - x$

2. Which phrase describes the algebraic expression $\frac{r}{9}$?

  Ⓐ the product of r and 9

  Ⓑ the quotient of r and 9

  Ⓒ 9 less than r

  Ⓓ r more than 9

3. Rhonda was organizing photos in a photo album. She took 60 photos and divided them evenly among p pages. Which algebraic expression represents the number of photos on each page?

  Ⓐ $p - 60$ Ⓒ $\frac{p}{60}$

  Ⓑ $60 - p$ Ⓓ $\frac{60}{p}$

4. Using the algebraic expression $4n + 6$, what is the greatest whole-number value of n that will give you a result less than 100?

  Ⓐ 22   Ⓒ 24

  Ⓑ 23   Ⓓ 25

5. Evaluate $7w - 14$ for $w = 9$.

  Ⓐ 2

  Ⓑ 18

  Ⓒ 49

  Ⓓ 77

6. Katie has read 32% of a book. If she has read 80 pages, how many more pages does Katie have left to read?

  Ⓐ 40

  Ⓑ 170

  Ⓒ 200

  Ⓓ 250

7. The expression $12(x + 4)$ represents the total number of CDs Mei bought in April and May at $12 each. Which property is applied to write the equivalent expression $12x + 48$?

  Ⓐ Associative Property of Addition

  Ⓑ Associative Property of Multiplication

  Ⓒ Commutative Property of Multiplication

  Ⓓ Distributive Property

Mini-Task

8. You can convert a temperature given in degrees Celsius to a Fahrenheit temperature by using the expression $9x \div 5 + 32$, where x is the Celsius temperature.

  a. Water freezes when the temperature is 0 °C. At what Fahrenheit temperature does water freeze? _____

  b. Water boils at 100 °C. At what temperature does water boil in degrees Fahrenheit? _____

  c. The temperature of some water is 15 °C. What is the Fahrenheit temperature? _____

MODULE 9 Generating Equivalent Numerical Expressions

? ESSENTIAL QUESTION

How can you generate equivalent numerical expressions and use them to solve real-world problems?

EXAMPLE 1

Find the value of each power.

A. 0.9^2

$0.9^2 = 0.9 \times 0.9 = 0.81$

B. 18^0

Any number raised to the power of 0 is 1.

$18^0 = 1$

C. $\left(\frac{1}{4}\right)^4$

$\left(\frac{1}{4}\right)^4 = \left(\frac{1}{4}\right)\left(\frac{1}{4}\right)\left(\frac{1}{4}\right)\left(\frac{1}{4}\right) = \frac{1}{256}$

EXAMPLE 2

Find the prime factorization of 60.

$$\begin{array}{r|r} 2 & 60 \\ 2 & 30 \\ 3 & 15 \\ 5 & 5 \\ & 1 \end{array}$$

$60 = 2 \times 2 \times 3 \times 5$

$60 = 2^2 \times 3 \times 5$

The prime factorization of 60 is $2^2 \times 3 \times 5$.

EXAMPLE 3

Simplify each expression.

A. $4 \times (2^3 + 5)$

$= 4 \times (8 + 5)$ $2^3 = 8$

$= 4 \times 13$ Add.

$= 52$ Multiply.

B. $27 \div 3^2 \times 6$

$= 27 \div 9 \times 6$ $3^2 = 9$

$= 3 \times 6$ Divide.

$= 18$ Multiply.

EXERCISES

Use an exponent to write each expression. (Lesson 9.1)

1. 3.6×3.6 _____

2. $9 \times 9 \times 9 \times 9$ _____

3. $\frac{4}{5} \times \frac{4}{5} \times \frac{4}{5}$ _____

Find the value of each power. (Lesson 9.1)

4. 12^0 _____

5. 13^2 _____

6. $\left(\frac{2}{7}\right)^3$ _____

7. 0.4^2 _____

8. $\left(\frac{4}{9}\right)^1$ _____

9. 0.7^3 _____

Find the prime factorization of each number. (Lesson 9.2)

10. 75 _____

11. 29 _____

12. 168 _____

13. Eduardo is building a sandbox that has an area of 84 square feet. What are the possible whole number measurements for the length and width of the sandbox? (Lesson 9.2)

_____

Simplify each expression. (Lesson 9.3)

14. $2 \times 5^2 - (4 + 1)$ _____

15. $\dfrac{22 - (3^2 + 4)}{12 \div 4}$ _____

MODULE 10 Generating Equivalent Algebraic Expressions

Key Vocabulary

algebraic expression
   (expresión algebraica)
coefficients *(coeficiente)*
constant *(contante)*
equivalent expressions
   (expresión equivalente)
evaluating *(evaluar)*
term *(término (en una
   expresión))*

? ESSENTIAL QUESTION

How can you generate equivalent algebraic expressions and use them to solve real-world problems?

EXAMPLE 1

Evaluate each expression for the given values of the variables.

A. $2(x^2 - 9)$; $x = 5$

$2(5^2 - 9)$ $5^2 = 25$

$= 2(16)$ Subtract.

$= 32$ Multiply.

When $x = 5$, $2(x^2 - 9) = 32$.

B. $w + y^2 + 3w$; $w = 2$, $y = 6$

$2 + 6^2 + 3(2)$ $6^2 = 36$

$= 2 + 36 + 6$ Multiply.

$= 44$ Add.

When $w = 2$ and $y = 6$, $w + y^2 + 3w = 44$.

EXAMPLE 2

Determine whether the algebraic expressions are equivalent:
$5(x + 2)$ and $10 + 5x$.

$5(x + 2) = 5x + 10$ Distributive Property

$= 10 + 5x$ Commutative Property

$5(x + 2)$ is equal to $10 + 5x$. They are equivalent expressions.

EXERCISES

Write each phrase as an algebraic expression. (Lesson 10.1)

1. x subtracted from 15 _____

2. 12 divided by t _____

3. 4 groups of y _____

4. the sum of z and 7 _____

Write a phrase for each algebraic expression. (Lesson 10.1)

5. $8p$ _____

6. $s + 7$ _____

Evaluate each expression for the given values of the variables.
(Lesson 10.2)

7. $8z + 3; z = 8$ _____

8. $3(7 + x^2); x = 2$ _____

9. $s - 5t + s^2; s = 4, t = -1$ _____

10. $x - y^3; x = -7, y = 3$ _____

11. The expression $\frac{1}{2}(h)(b_1 + b_2)$ gives the area of a trapezoid, with b_1 and b_2 representing the two base lengths of a trapezoid and h representing the height. Find the area of a trapezoid with base lengths 4 in. and 6 in. and a height of 8 in. (Lesson 10.2) _____

Determine if the expressions are equivalent. (Lesson 10.3)

12. $7 + 7x; 7\left(x + \frac{1}{7}\right)$ _____

13. $2.5(3 + x); 2.5x + 7.5$ _____

Combine like terms. (Lesson 10.3)

14. $3m - 6 + m^2 - 5m + 1$ _____

15. $7x + 4(2x - 6)$ _____

16. $b^2 + 3 + 2b^2 + 4 - 7$ _____

17. $3(p + 5) - 8 + 11p$ _____

Unit 4 Performance Tasks

1. **CAREERS IN MATH** | Freelance Computer Programmer

Antonio is a freelance computer programmer. In his work, he often uses the power of 2^n to find the number of ways bits (or units of information) can be arranged. The n often stands for the number of bits.

a. Antonio is working on programming a new video game called *Millie's Quest*. In the game, the main character, Millie, collects golden keys to help her in her quest. Antonio wants to write a formula to show that Millie can collect one less key than the highest number of bits that can be arranged in the system. What formula can he use?

_____

b. If Antonio is working with a 16-bit system, how many golden keys can Millie collect?

_____

c. Antonio is also working on a new spreadsheet program. The program takes up 14 bytes of memory. If each byte is equal to 8 bits, how many bits is Antonio's program? Show your work.

_____

2. Hannah just bought a new camera. In January she took 14 pictures. The number of pictures she took doubled each month for three months.

a. How many pictures did Hannah take in March? Write and solve an expression with an exponent to show how many pictures she took.

_____

b. In April, Hanna took half the number of pictures she took in March. Her brother Jack thinks she took the same number of pictures in April that she did in February. Hanna knew he was incorrect. Write and solve an expression to show why Hannah is right.

_____

_____

UNIT 4 MIXED REVIEW
Assessment Readiness

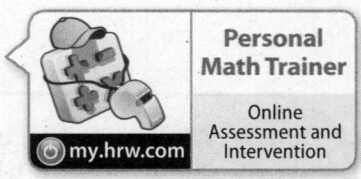

Personal Math Trainer

Online Assessment and Intervention

my.hrw.com

Selected Response

1. Which expression is equivalent to
$2.3 \times 2.3 \times 2.3 \times 2.3 \times 2.3$?

Ⓐ 2.3×5

Ⓑ 23^5

Ⓒ $2^5 \times 3^5$

Ⓓ 2.3^5

2. Which operation should you perform first when you simplify $63 - (2 + 54 \times 6) \div 5$?

Ⓐ addition

Ⓑ division

Ⓒ multiplication

Ⓓ subtraction

3. Sheena was organizing items in a scrapbook. She took 25 photos and divided them evenly between p pages. Which algebraic expression represents the number of photos on each page?

Ⓐ $p - 25$

Ⓑ $25 - p$

Ⓒ $\frac{p}{25}$

Ⓓ $\frac{25}{p}$

4. Which is another way to write
$7 \times 7 \times 7 \times 7$?

Ⓐ 7^4

Ⓑ $7(4)$

Ⓒ 28

Ⓓ 4^7

5. Angela earns x dollars an hour. On Friday, she worked 6 hours. On Saturday, she worked 8 hours. Which expression shows how much she earned both days?

Ⓐ $6x + 8$

Ⓑ $8x \times 6x$

Ⓒ $(6 + 8)x$

Ⓓ $\frac{6 + 8}{x}$

6. Marcus is doing a science experiment in which he measures the rate at which bacteria multiply. Every 15 seconds, the bacteria double in number. If there are 10 bacteria now, how many will there be in 2 minutes?

Ⓐ 160 bacteria

Ⓑ 256 bacteria

Ⓒ 1,280 bacteria

Ⓓ 2,560 bacteria

7. The prime factorization of which number is $2^5 \times 5$?

Ⓐ 50

Ⓑ 125

Ⓒ 160

Ⓓ 500

8. Which expression has a value of 36 when $x = 4$ and $y = 7$?

Ⓐ $2xy$

Ⓑ $2x + 4y$

Ⓒ $6y - x$

Ⓓ $12x - 2y$

© Houghton Mifflin Harcourt Publishing Company

9. What should you do first to simplify the expression $(4^3 + 9) \div 76 + 5$?

   (A) Add 4 and 9.

   (B) Add 76 and 5.

   (C) Multiply $4 \times 4 \times 4$.

   (D) Divide $(4^3 + 9)$ by 76.

10. Which ratio is equivalent to 4:10?

    (A) $\frac{2}{5}$

    (B) $\frac{8}{10}$

    (C) $\frac{12}{16}$

    (D) $\frac{16}{10}$

11. Travis and Paula went to lunch. Travis ordered a sandwich for $7.50, and Paula ordered a burger for $5.25. After lunch, they left a 15% tip for their waiter. How much money did they spend altogether?

    (A) $12.75

    (B) $14.66

    (C) $15.95

    (D) $16.00

12. Which shows the following numbers in order from greatest to least?

    $$1.5, \frac{2}{4}, \frac{4}{2}, 1.05$$

    (A) $\frac{4}{2}$, 1.5, 1.05, $\frac{2}{4}$

    (B) 1.05, 1.5, $\frac{2}{4}$, $\frac{4}{2}$

    (C) $\frac{4}{2}$, $\frac{2}{4}$, 1.5, 1.05

    (D) 1.05, $\frac{4}{2}$, $\frac{2}{4}$, 1.5

Mini-Tasks

13. For every bag of trail mix the local Scout Guide troop sells, they earn $0.45.

    a. Write an expression to represent this situation.

    _____

    b. Sarah sold 52 bags of trail mix. How much did she earn for her troop?

    _____

    c. Let x represent the total number of bags of trail mix sold by Sarah's troop. Write an expression to show what percentage of bags Sarah sold.

    _____

14. Robert is replacing sod in two square-shaped areas of his backyard. One side of the first area is 7.5 feet. One side of the other area is 5.7 feet. The sod costs y dollars per square foot.

    a. Write an expression to show how much Robert will spend on sod.

    _____

    b. If the sod costs $3.25 per square foot, about how much will Robert spend to put sod down in both areas of his backyard? Round to the nearest dollar.

    _____

15. Jose wants to find how many gallons of water he needs to fill his cube-shaped aquarium. One side of his aquarium is 4 feet long.

    a. Write and solve an expression to find the volume of Jose's aquarium.

    _____

    b. One cubic foot is equal to 7.48 gallons of water. How many gallons of water does Jose need to fill his aquarium? Round to the nearest gallon.

    _____

Equations and Inequalities

MODULE **11**
Equations and Relationships
FL   6.EE.2.5, 6.EE.2.7, 6.EE.2.8

MODULE **12**
Relationships in Two Variables
FL   6.NS.3.6c, 6.EE.3.9

CAREERS IN MATH

Botanist A botanist is a biologist who studies plants. Botanists use math to analyze data and create models of biological organisms and systems. They use these models to make predictions. They also use statistics to determine correlations. If you are interested in a career in botany, you should study these mathematical subjects:
- Algebra
- Trigonometry
- Probability and Statistics
- Calculus

Research other careers that require the analysis of data and use of mathematical models.

Unit 5 Performance Task

At the end of the unit, check out how **botanists** use math.

© Houghton Mifflin Harcourt Publishing Company • Image Credits: Andy Sotiriou/Photodisc/Getty Images

Vocabulary Preview

Use the puzzle to preview key vocabulary from this unit. Unscramble the circled letters within found words to answer the riddle at the bottom of the page.

- A word that describes a variable that depends on another variable. (Lesson 12.2)
- A value of the variable that makes the equation true. (Lesson 11.1)
- The numbers in an ordered pair. (Lesson 12.1)
- The point where the axes intersect to form the coordinate plane. (Lesson 12.1)
- One of the four regions into which the *x*- and *y*-axes divide the coordinate plane. (Lesson 12.1)
- The two number lines that intersect at right angles to form a coordinate plane. (Lesson 12.1)

Q: Why did the paper rip when the student tried to stretch out the horizontal axis of his graph?

A: Too much ___ – ___ ___ ___ ___ ___ ___ ___!

Equations and Relationships

LESSON 11.1
Writing Equations to Represent Situations
 FL 6.EE.2.5, 6.EE.2.6, 6.EE.2.7

LESSON 11.2
Addition and Subtraction Equations
 FL 6.EE.2.5, 6.EE.2.6, 6.EE.2.7

LESSON 11.3
Multiplication and Division Equations
 FL 6.EE.2.5, 6.EE.2.6, 6.EE.2.7

LESSON 11.4
Writing Inequalities
FL 6.EE.2.5, 6.EE.2.6, 6.EE.2.8

ESSENTIAL QUESTION

How can you use equations and relationships to solve real-world problems?

Real-World Video

Suppose a world weightlifting record is w pounds. To find how many more pounds m must be lifted to set a new record of n pounds, you can use the equation $n = w + m$.

my.hrw.com

GO DIGITAL
my.hrw.com

my.hrw.com

Go digital with your write-in student edition, accessible on any device.

Math On the Spot

Scan with your smart phone to jump directly to the online edition, video tutor, and more.

Animated Math

Interactively explore key concepts to see how math works.

Personal Math Trainer

Get immediate feedback and help as you work through practice sets.

Are YOU Ready?

Complete these exercises to review skills you will need for this module.

Evaluate Expressions

EXAMPLE   Evaluate $8(3+2) - 5^2$

$8(3+2) - 5^2 = 8(5) - 5^2$ Perform operations inside parentheses first.

$= 8(5) - 25$ Evaluate exponents.

$= 40 - 25$ Multiply.

$= 15$ Subtract.

Evaluate the expression.

1. $4(5 + 6) - 15$ _____

2. $8(2 + 4) + 16$ _____

3. $3(14 - 7) - 16$ _____

4. $6(8 - 3) + 3(7 - 4)$ _____

5. $10(6 - 5) - 3(9 - 6)$ _____

6. $7(4 + 5 + 2) - 6(3 + 5)$ _____

7. $2(8 + 3) + 4^2$ _____

8. $7(14 - 8) - 6^2$ _____

9. $8(2 + 1)^2 - 4^2$ _____

Connect Words and Equations

EXAMPLE   The product of a number and 4 is 32.

The product of x and 4 is 32.   Represent the unknown with a variable.

$4 \times x$ is 32.   Determine the operation.

$4 \times x = 32$.   Determine the placement of the equal sign.

Write an algebraic equation for the word sentence.

10. A number increased by 7.9 is 8.3. _____

11. 17 is the sum of a number and 6. _____

12. The quotient of a number and 8 is 4. _____

13. 81 is three times a number. _____

14. The difference between 31 and a number is 7. _____

15. Eight less than a number is 19. _____

Reading Start-Up

Visualize Vocabulary

Use the ✔ words to complete the graphic.

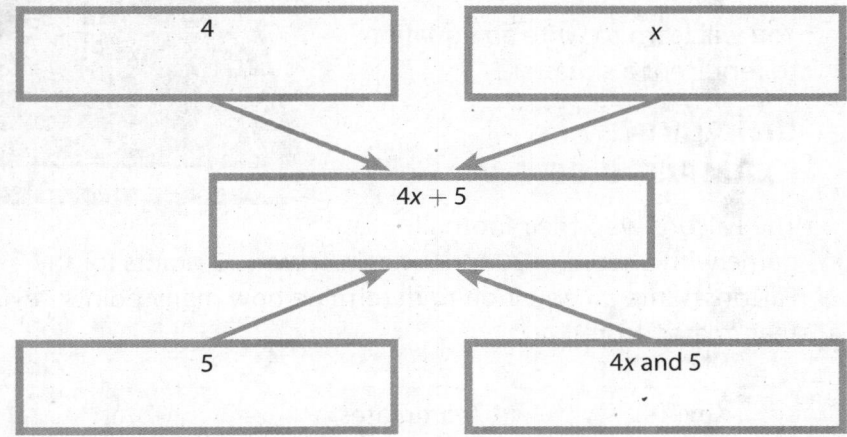

4		x

$4x + 5$

5		4x and 5

Understand Vocabulary

Match the term on the left to the correct expression on the right.

1. algebraic expression   **A.** A mathematical statement that two expressions are equal.

2. equation   **B.** A value of the variable that makes the statement true.

3. solution   **C.** A mathematical statement that includes one or more variables.

Active Reading

Booklet Before beginning the module, create a booklet to help you learn the concepts in this module. Write the main idea of each lesson on each page of the booklet. As you study each lesson, write important details that support the main idea, such as vocabulary and formulas. Refer to your finished booklet as you work on assignments and study for tests.

© Houghton Mifflin Harcourt Publishing Company

Vocabulary

Review Words
✔ algebraic expression *(expresión algebraica)*
✔ coefficient *(coeficiente)*
✔ constant *(constante)*
  equivalent expression *(expresión equivalente)*
  evaluating *(evaluar)*
  like terms *(términos semejantes)*
✔ term *(término, en una expresión)*
✔ variable *(variable)*

Preview Words
  equation *(ecuación)*
  properties of operations *(propiedades de las operaciones)*
  solution *(solución)*

Unpacking the Standards

Understanding the standards and the vocabulary terms in the standards will help you know exactly what you are expected to learn in this module.

 FL **6.EE.2.7**

Solve real-world and mathematical problems by writing and solving equations of the form $x + p = q$ and $px = q$ for cases in which p, q and x are all nonnegative rational numbers.

Key Vocabulary

equation *(ecuación)*
A mathematical sentence that shows that two expressions are equivalent.

What It Means to You

You will learn to write an equation to represent a situation.

UNPACKING EXAMPLE 6.EE.2.7

The Falcons won their football game with a score of 30 to 19. Kevin scored 12 points for the Falcons. Write an equation to determine how many points Kevin's teammates scored.

Kevin's points	+	Teammates' points	=	Total points
12	+	t	=	30

 FL **6.EE.2.5**

Understand solving an equation or inequality as a process of answering a question: which values from a specified set, if any, make the equation or inequality true? Use substitution to determine whether a given number in a specified set makes an equation or inequality true.

Key Vocabulary

inequality *(desigualdad)*
A mathematical sentence that shows the relationship between quantities that are not equal.

What It Means to You

You can substitute a given value for the variable in an equation or inequality to check if that value makes the equation or inequality true.

UNPACKING EXAMPLE 6.EE.2.5

Melanie has to buy 6 tickets to a play. She will pay at least $156 depending on the price of the seats. Write an inequality for this situation. Use it to decide if $20 and $30 are possible ticket prices.

Number of tickets bought	·	Price per ticket	≥	Total cost
6	·	p	≥	156

Substitute 20 and 30 for p to see if the inequality is true.

$$6p \geq 156$$
$$6 \cdot 20 \overset{?}{\geq} 156$$
$$120 \overset{?}{\geq} 156 \text{ ✗}$$

$$6p \geq 156$$
$$6 \cdot 30 \overset{?}{\geq} 156$$
$$180 \overset{?}{\geq} 156 \text{ ✓}$$

The price per ticket could be $30 but not $20.

Visit **my.hrw.com** to see all **Florida Math Standards** unpacked.

my.hrw.com

Writing Equations to Represent Situations

 FL 6.EE.2.7
Solve...problems by writing
...equations of the form
$x + p = q$ and $px = q$....
Also 6.EE.2.5, 6.EE.2.6

 ESSENTIAL QUESTION

How do you write equations and determine whether a number is a solution of an equation?

Determining Whether Values Are Solutions

An **equation** is a mathematical statement that two *expressions* are equal. An equation may or may not contain variables. For an equation that has a variable, a **solution** of the equation is a value of the variable that makes the equation true.

Math On the Spot
my.hrw.com

> An expression represents a single value.

> An equation represents a relationship between two values.

	Expression	Equation
Numerical	$5 + 4$	$5 + 4 = 9$
Words	a number *plus* 4	A number *plus* 4 *is* 9.
Algebraic	$n + 4$	$n + 4 = 9$

> An equation relates two expressions using symbols for *is* or *equals*.

EXAMPLE 1

 FL 6.EE.2.5

Determine whether the given value is a solution of the equation.

A $x + 9 = 15$; $x = 6$

$6 + 9 \overset{?}{=} 15$ Substitute 6 for x.

$15 \overset{?}{=} 15$ Add.

6 is a solution of $x + 9 = 15$.

B $\frac{y}{4} = 32$; $y = 8$

$\frac{8}{4} \overset{?}{=} 32$ Substitute 8 for y.

$2 \overset{?}{=} 32$ Divide.

8 is not a solution of the equation $\frac{y}{4} = 32$.

C $8x = 72$; $x = 9$

$8(9) \overset{?}{=} 72$ Substitute 9 for x.

$72 \overset{?}{=} 72$ Multiply.

9 is a solution of $8x = 72$.

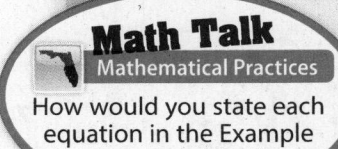
Math Talk
Mathematical Practices

How would you state each equation in the Example in words?

© Houghton Mifflin Harcourt Publishing Company

YOUR TURN

Determine whether the given value is a solution of the equation.

1. $11 = n + 6$; $n = 5$

_____

2. $y - 6 = 24$; $y = 18$

_____

3. $\frac{x}{9} = 4$; $x = 36$

_____

4. $15t = 100$; $t = 6$

_____

Writing Equations to Represent Situations

You can represent some real-world situations with an equation. Making a model first can help you organize the information.

EXAMPLE 2   FL 6.EE.2.6

Mark scored 17 points for the home team in a basketball game. His teammates as a group scored p points. Write an equation to represent this situation.

Mark's points	+	Teammates' points	=	Total points
↓		↓		↓
17	+	p	=	46

YOUR TURN

Write an equation to represent each situation.

5. Marilyn has a fish tank that contains 38 fish. There are 9 goldfish and f other fish.

_____

6. Juanita has 102 beads to make n necklaces. Each necklace will have 17 beads.

_____

7. Craig is c years old. His 12-year-old sister Kaitlin is 3 years younger than Craig.

_____

8. Kim rented skates for h hours. The rental fee was \$2 per hour and she paid a total of \$8.

_____

Writing an Equation and Checking Solutions

You can substitute a given value for the variable in a real-world equation to check if that value makes sense for the situation.

EXAMPLE 3   FL 6.EE.2.7

Sarah used a gift card to buy $47 worth of groceries. Now she has $18 left on her gift card. Write an equation to represent this situation. Use your equation to determine whether Sarah had $65 or $59 on the gift card before buying groceries.

STEP 1 Write a word equation based on the situation.

| Amount on card | − | Amount spent | = | Amount left on card |

STEP 2 Rewrite the equation using a variable for the unknown quantity and the given values for the known quantities.

Let x be the amount on the card.

| Amount on card | − | Amount spent | = | Amount left on card |
| x | − | 47 | = | 18 |

> The amount spent and the amount left on the card are the known quantities. Substitute those values in the equation.

STEP 3 Substitute 65 and 59 for x to see which equation is true.

$$x - 47 = 18 \qquad x - 47 = 18$$
$$65 - 47 \stackrel{?}{=} 18 \qquad 59 - 47 \stackrel{?}{=} 18$$
$$18 \stackrel{?}{=} 18 \qquad 12 \stackrel{?}{=} 18$$

The amount on Sarah's gift card before she bought groceries was $65.

Reflect

9. **What If?** Suppose Sarah has $12 left on her gift card. How would this change the equation and the final answer?

_____

_____

---

10. On Saturday morning, Owen earned $24. By the end of the afternoon he had earned a total of $62. Write an equation represent the situation. Determine whether Owen earned $38 or $31 on Saturday afternoon.

_____

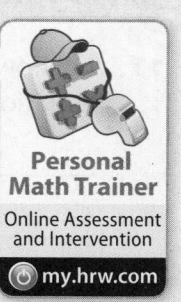
© Houghton Mifflin Harcourt Publishing Company

Determine whether the given value is a solution of the equation. (Example 1)

1. $23 = x - 9$; $x = 14$ _____

$23 \overset{?}{=} \boxed{} - 9$

$23 \overset{?}{=} \boxed{}$

2. $\frac{n}{13} = 4$; $n = 52$ _____

$\dfrac{\boxed{}}{13} \overset{?}{=} 4$

$\boxed{} \overset{?}{=} 4$

3. $14 + x = 46$; $x = 32$ _____

4. $17y = 85$; $y = 5$ _____

5. $25 = \frac{k}{5}$; $k = 5$ _____

6. $2.5n = 45$; $n = 18$ _____

7. $21 = m + 9$; $m = 11$ _____

8. $21 - h = 15$; $h = 6$ _____

9. $d - 4 = 19$; $d = 15$ _____

10. $5 + x = 47$; $x = 52$ _____

11. $w - 9 = 0$; $w = 9$ _____

12. $5q = 31$; $q = 13$ _____

13. Each floor of a hotel has r rooms. On 8 floors, there are a total of 256 rooms. Write an equation to represent this situation. (Example 2)

Number		Number of rooms		
_____	×	_____	=	_____

_____

14. In the school band, there are 5 trumpet players and f flute players. There are twice as many flute players as there are trumpet players. (Example 2)

_____

15. Pedro bought 8 tickets to a basketball game. He paid a total of $208. Write an equation to determine whether each ticket cost $26 or $28. (Example 3)

_____

16. The high temperature was 92 °F. This was 24 °F higher than the overnight low temperature. Write an equation to determine whether the low temperature was 62 °F or 68 °F. (Example 3)

_____

 ESSENTIAL QUESTION CHECK-IN

17. Tell how you can determine whether a number is a solution of an equation.

_____

_____

11.1 Independent Practice

FL 6.EE.2.5, 6.EE.2.6, 6.EE.2.7

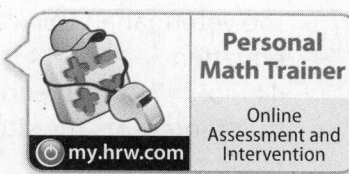

Personal Math Trainer

Online Assessment and Intervention

my.hrw.com

18. Andy is one-fourth as old as his grandfather, who is 76 years old. Write an equation to determine whether Andy is 19 or 22 years old.

_____

19. A sleeping bag weighs 8 pounds. Your backpack and sleeping bag together weigh 31 pounds. Write an equation to determine whether the backpack without the sleeping bag weighs 25 or 23 pounds.

_____

20. Halfway through a bus route, 23 students have been dropped off and 48 students remain on the bus. Write an equation to determine whether there are 61 or 71 students on the bus at the beginning of the route.

_____

21. Write an equation that involves multiplication, contains a variable, and has a solution of 5. Then write another equation that has the same solution and includes the same variable and numbers but uses division.

_____

_____

22. Vocabulary How are expressions and equations different?

_____

_____

_____

23. Multistep Alan has partially completed a table showing the distances between his town, Greenville, and two other towns.

Distance between Greenville and Nearby Towns (miles)	
Parker	29
Hadley	?

a. The distance between Hadley and Greenville is 13 miles less than the distance between Parker and Greenville. Write two equations that compare the distance between Hadley and Greenville and the distance between Parker and Greenville. Tell what your variable represents.

_____

_____

_____

b. Alan says the distance from Hadley to Greenville is 16 miles. Is he correct? Explain.

_____

_____

24. Explain the Error A problem states that Ursula earns $9 per hour. To write an expression that tells how much money Ursula earns for h hours, Joshua wrote $\frac{9}{h}$. Sarah wrote $9h$. Whose expression is correct and why?

_____

_____

_____

25. Communicate Mathematical Ideas A dog weighs 44 pounds and the veterinarian thinks it needs to lose 7 pounds. Mikala wrote the equation $x + 7 = 44$ to represent the situation. Kirk wrote the equation $44 - x = 7$. Which equation is correct? Can you write another equation that represents the situation?

_____

_____

26. Multiple Representations The table shows the ages of Cindy and her dad.

Dad's Age	Cindy's Age
28 years old	2 years old
36 years old	10 years old
?	18 years old

a. Write an equation that relates Cindy's age to her dad's age when Cindy is 18. Tell what the variable represents.

_____

b. Determine if 42 is a solution to the equation. Show your work.

_____

c. Explain the meaning of your answer in part **b.**

_____

 FOCUS ON HIGHER ORDER THINKING

27. Critical Thinking In the school band, there are 4 trumpet players and f flute players. The total number of trumpet and flute players is 12. Are there twice as many flute players as trumpet players? Explain.

_____

_____

28. Problem Solving Ronald paid $162 for 6 tickets to a basketball game. During the game he noticed that his friend paid $130 for 5 tickets. The price of each ticket was $26. Was Ronald overcharged? Explain.

_____

_____

29. Communicate Mathematical Ideas Tariq said you can write an equation by setting an expression equal to itself. Would an equation like this be true? Explain.

_____

_____

_____

Work Area

Addition and Subtraction Equations

FL 6.EE.2.7
Solve real-world and mathematical problems by writing and solving equations of the form $x + p = q$....
Also 6.EE.2.5, 6.EE.2.6

? ESSENTIAL QUESTION

How do you solve equations that contain addition or subtraction?

EXPLORE ACTIVITY

FL 6.EE.2.6, 6.EE.2.7

Modeling Equations

A puppy weighed 6 ounces at birth. After two weeks, the puppy weighed 14 ounces. How much weight did the puppy gain?

Let x represent the number of ounces gained.

| Weight at birth | + | Weight gained | = | Weight after 2 weeks |

$$6 \quad + \quad x \quad = \quad 14$$

To answer this question, you can solve the equation $6 + x = 14$.

Algebra tiles can model some equations. An equation mat represents the two sides of an equation. To solve the equation, remove the same number of tiles from both sides of the mat until the x tile is by itself on one side.

A Model $6 + x = 14$.

B How many 1 tiles must you remove on the left side so that the x tile is by itself? _____
Cross out these tiles on the equation mat.

$6 + x$ 14

C Whenever you remove tiles from one side of the mat, you must remove the same number of tiles from the other side of the mat. Cross out the tiles that should be removed on the right side of the mat.

D How many tiles remain on the right side of the mat? _____
This is the solution of the equation.

The puppy gained _____ ounces.

Math Talk
Mathematical Practices

Why did you remove tiles from each side of your model?

Reflect

1. **Communicate Mathematical Ideas** How do you know when the model shows the final solution? How do you read the solution?

_____

_____

Using Subtraction to Solve Equations

Removing the same number of tiles from each side of an equation mat models subtracting the same number from both sides of an equation.

> ### Subtraction Property of Equality
>
> You can subtract the same number from both sides of an equation, and the two sides will remain equal.

When an equation contains addition, solve by subtracting the same number from both sides.

EXAMPLE 1 FL 6.EE.2.5

Solve the equation $a + 15 = 26$. Graph the solution on a number line.

$a + 15 = 26$ Notice that the number 15 is added to a.

$$
\begin{array}{rl}
a + 15 = & 26 \\
\underline{-15 \quad -15} & \\
a \quad = & 11
\end{array}
$$

Subtract 15 from both sides of the equation.

Check: $a + 15 = 26$

$11 + 15 \overset{?}{=} 26$ Substitute 11 for a.

$26 \overset{?}{=} 26$ Add on the left side.

Graph the solution on a number line.

Reflect

2. Communicate Mathematical Ideas How do you decide which number to subtract from both sides?

_____

_____

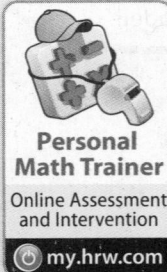
YOUR TURN

3. Solve the equation $5 = w + 1.5$.

Graph the solution on a number line.

$w = $ _____

© Houghton Mifflin Harcourt Publishing Company

Using Addition to Solve Equations

When an equation contains subtraction, solve by adding the same number to both sides.

Math On the Spot
⏻ my.hrw.com

> ### Addition Property of Equality
>
> You can add the same number to both sides of an equation, and the two sides will remain equal.

EXAMPLE 2 FL 6.EE.2.5

Solve the equation $y - 21 = 18$. Graph the solution on a number line.

$y - 21 = 18$ Notice that the number 21 is subtracted from y.

$$
\begin{aligned}
y - 21 &= 18 \\
+21 \quad &+21 \\
\hline
y \quad &= 39
\end{aligned}
$$

Add 21 to both sides of the equation.

Check: $y - 21 = 18$

$39 - 21 \overset{?}{=} 18$ Substitute 39 for y.

$18 \overset{?}{=} 18$ Subtract.

Graph the solution on a number line.

35 36 37 38 39 40 41 42 43 44 45

Reflect

4. **Communicate Mathematical Ideas** How do you know whether to add on both sides or subtract on both sides when solving an equation?

_____

_____

_____

YOUR TURN

5. Solve the equation $h - \frac{1}{2} = \frac{3}{4}$.

   Graph the solution on a number line.

   −2   −1   0   1   2

   $h =$ _____

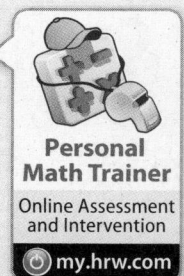

Personal Math Trainer
Online Assessment and Intervention
⏻ my.hrw.com

Solving Equations that Represent Geometric Concepts

You can write equations to represent geometric relationships.

Recall that a straight line has an angle measure of 180°. Two angles whose measures have a sum of 180° are called supplementary angles. Two angles whose measures have a sum of 90° are called complementary angles.

EXAMPLE 3

FL 6.EE.2.7, 6.EE.2.6

Find the measure of the unknown angle.

STEP 1   Write the information in the boxes.

Unknown angle	+	60°	=	180°

STEP 2   Write a description to represent the model. Include a question for the unknown angle.

The sum of an unknown angle and a 60° angle is 180°. What is the measure of the unknown angle?

STEP 3   Write an equation.

$x + 60° = 180°$

STEP 4   Solve the equation.

$$x + 60° = 180°$$
$$\underline{ -60° -60°}$$
$$x = 120°$$

Subtract 60 from each side.

The unknown angle measures 120°.

> The final answer includes units of degrees.

YOUR TURN

6.   Write and solve an equation to find the measure of the unknown angle.

_____

7.   Write and solve an equation to find the complement of an angle that measures 42°.

_____

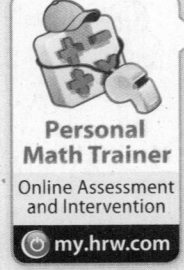
© Houghton Mifflin Harcourt Publishing Company

Writing Real-World Problems for a Given Equation

You can write a real-world problem for a given equation. Examine each number and mathematical operation in the equation.

EXAMPLE 4 FL 6.EE.2.7

Write a real-world problem for the equation 21.79 + x = 25. Then solve the equation.

21.79 + x = 25

STEP 1 Examine each part of the equation.

x is the unknown or quantity we are looking for.

21.79 is added to x.

= 25 means that after adding 21.79 and x, the result is 25.

STEP 2 Write a real-world situation that involves *adding* two quantities.

Joshua wants to buy his mother flowers and a card for Mother's Day. Joshua has $25 to spend and selects roses for $21.79. How much can he spend on a card?

Math Talk
Mathematical Practices

How is the question in a real-world problem related to its equation?

STEP 3 Solve the equation.

$$
\begin{array}{rcr}
21.79 + x & = & 25 \\
-21.79 & & -21.79 \\
\hline
x & = & 3.21
\end{array}
$$

The final answer includes units of money in dollars.

Joshua can spend $3.21 on a Mother's Day card.

Reflect

8. **What If?** How might the real-world problem change if the equation was x − 21.79 = 25 and you still used roses for $21.79?

_____

_____

_____

YOUR TURN

9. Write a real-world problem for the equation x − 100 = 40. Then solve the equation.

_____

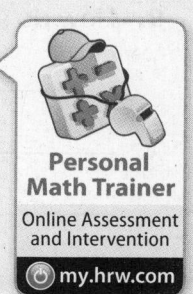

Personal Math Trainer

Online Assessment and Intervention

my.hrw.com

1. A total of 14 guests attended a birthday party. Three friends stayed after the party to help clean up. How many left when the party ended? (Explore Activity)

   a. Let x represent the _____

   b.

Number that		Number that		
	+		=	

    _____ + _____ = _____

   c. Draw algebra tiles to model the equation.

    _____ friends left when the party ended.

Solve each equation. Graph the solution on a number line. (Examples 1 and 2)

2. $2 = x - 3$ $x =$ _____

$$-5\ -4\ -3\ -2\ -1\ \ 0\ \ 1\ \ 2\ \ 3\ \ 4\ \ 5$$

3. $s + 12.5 = 14$ $s =$ _____

$$-5\ -4\ -3\ -2\ -1\ \ 0\ \ 1\ \ 2\ \ 3\ \ 4\ \ 5$$

Solve each equation. (Examples 1 and 2)

4. $h + 6.9 = 11.4$

   $h =$ _____

5. $82 + p = 122$

   $p =$ _____

6. $n + \frac{1}{2} = \frac{7}{4}$

   $n =$ _____

7. Write and solve an equation to find the measure of the unknown angle. (Example 3)

_____

8. Write a real-world problem for the equation $x - 75 = 200$. Then solve the equation. (Example 4)

_____

ESSENTIAL QUESTION CHECK-IN

9. How do you solve equations that contain addition or subtraction?

_____

_____

_____

11.2 Independent Practice

FL 6.EE.2.5, 6.EE.2.6, 6.EE.2.7

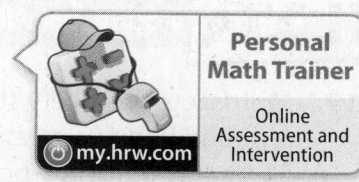

Personal Math Trainer

my.hrw.com

Online Assessment and Intervention

Write and solve an equation to answer each question.

10. A wildlife reserve had 8 elephant calves born during the summer and now has 31 total elephants. How many elephants were in the reserve before summer began?

_____

_____

11. My sister is 14 years old. My brother says that his age minus twelve is equal to my sister's age. How old is my brother?

_____

12. Kim bought a poster that cost $8.95 and some colored pencils. The total cost was $21.35. How much did the colored pencils cost?

_____

_____

13. The Acme Car Company sold 37 vehicles in June. How many compact cars were sold in June?

Acme Car Company — June Sales	
Type of car	Number sold
SUV	8
Compact	?

_____

_____

14. Sandra wants to buy a new MP3 player that is on sale for $95. She has saved $73. How much more money does she need?

_____

_____

15. Ronald spent $123.45 on school clothes. He counted his money and discovered that he had $36.55 left. How much money did he originally have?

_____

_____

16. Brita withdrew $225 from her bank account. After her withdrawal, there was $548 left in Brita's account. How much money did Brita have in her account before the withdrawal?

_____

_____

17. **Represent Real-World Problems** Write a real-world situation that can be represented by $15 + c = 17.50$. Then solve the equation and describe what your answer represents for the problem situation.

_____

_____

_____

18. **Critique Reasoning** Paula solved the equation $7 + x = 10$ and got 17, but she is not certain if she got the correct answer. How could you explain Paula's mistake to her?

_____

_____

_____

_____

19. Multistep A grocery store is having a sale this week. If you buy a 5-pound bag of apples for the regular price, you can get another bag for $1.49. If you buy a 5-pound bag of oranges at the regular price, you can get another bag for $2.49.

Grocery Prices	
	Regular price
5-pound bag of apples	$2.99
5-pound bag of oranges	$3.99

a. Write an equation to find the discount for each situation using a for the amount of the discount for apples and r for the amount of the discount for oranges.

_____

b. Which fruit has a greater discount? Explain.

_____

_____

20. Critical Thinking An orchestra has twice as many woodwind instruments as brass instruments. There are a total of 150 brass and woodwind instruments.

a. Write two different addition equations that describe this situation. Use w for woodwinds and b for brass.

_____

b. How many woodwinds and how many brass instruments satisfy the given information?

_____

21. Look for a Pattern Assume the following: $a + 1 = 2$, $b + 10 = 20$, $c + 100 = 200$, $d + 1,000 = 2,000$, ...

a. Solve each equation for each variable.

_____

b. What pattern do you notice between the variables?

_____

c. What would be the value of g if the pattern continues?

_____

11.3 Multiplication and Division Equations

FL 6.EE.2.5
Understand solving an equation...as a process of answering a question: which values...make the equation... true? *Also 6.EE.2.6, 6.EE.2.7*

ESSENTIAL QUESTION

How do you solve equations that contain multiplication or division?

EXPLORE ACTIVITY FL 6.EE.2.6

Modeling Equations

Deanna has a cookie recipe that requires 12 eggs to make 3 batches of cookies. How many eggs are needed per batch of cookies?

Let *x* represent the number of eggs needed per batch.

| Number of batches | · | Number of eggs per batch | = | Total eggs |

3 · *x* = 12

To answer this question, you can use algebra tiles to solve $3x = 12$.

A Model $3x = 12$.

3*x*   12

B There are 3 *x* tiles, so draw circles to separate the tiles into 3 equal groups. One group has been circled for you.

Math Talk
Mathematical Practices

Why is the solution to the equation the number of tiles in each group?

C How many 1 tiles are in each group? _____
This is the solution of the equation.

_____ eggs are needed per batch of cookies.

Reflect

1. Look for a Pattern Why does it make sense to arrange the twelve 1 tiles in 3 rows of 4 instead of any other arrangement of twelve 1 tiles, such as 2 rows of 6?

_____

Using Division to Solve Equations

Separating the tiles on both sides of an equation mat into an equal number of groups models dividing both sides of an equation by the same number.

> ### Division Property of Equality
>
> You can divide both sides of an equation by the same nonzero number, and the two sides will remain equal.

When an equation contains multiplication, solve by dividing both sides of the equation by the same nonzero number.

EXAMPLE 1   🏴 FL 6.EE.2.5

Solve each equation. Graph the solution on a number line.

A $9a = 54$

$9a = 54$	Notice that 9 is multiplied by a.
$\dfrac{9a}{9} = \dfrac{54}{9}$	Divide both sides of the equation by 9.
$a = 6$	

Check: $9a = 54$

$9(6) \overset{?}{=} 54$	Substitute 6 for a.
$54 \overset{?}{=} 54$	Multiply on the left side.

B $18 = 6d$

$18 = 6d$	Notice that 6 is multiplied by d.
$\dfrac{18}{6} = \dfrac{6d}{6}$	Divide both sides of the equation by 6.
$3 = d$	

Check: $18 = 6d$

$18 \overset{?}{=} 6(3)$	Substitute 3 for d.
$18 \overset{?}{=} 18$	Multiply on the right side.

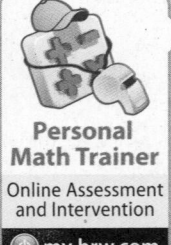
YOUR TURN

Solve the equation $3x = 21$. Graph the solution on a number line.

2. $x =$ _____

Using Multiplication to Solve Equations

When an equation contains division, solve by multiplying both sides of the equation by the same number.

Math On the Spot
⏻ my.hrw.com

> ## Multiplication Property of Equality
>
> You can multiply both sides of an equation by the same number, and the two sides will remain equal.

EXAMPLE 2
FL 6.EE.2.5

Solve each equation. Graph the solution on a number line.

A $\frac{x}{5} = 10$

$\frac{x}{5} = 10$ — Notice that x is divided by the number 5.

$5 \cdot \frac{x}{5} = 5 \cdot 10$ — Multiply both sides of the equation by 5.

$x = 50$

number line: 0 10 20 30 40 50 60 70 (point at 50)

Check: $\frac{x}{5} = 10$

$\frac{50}{5} \overset{?}{=} 10$ — Substitute 50 for x.

$10 \overset{?}{=} 10$ — Divide on the left side.

B $15 = \frac{r}{2}$

$15 = \frac{r}{2}$ — Notice that r is divided by the number 2.

$2 \cdot 15 = 2 \cdot \frac{r}{2}$ — Multiply both sides of the equation by 2.

$30 = r$

number line: 0 5 10 15 20 25 30 35 40 45 50 (point at 30)

Check: $15 = \frac{r}{2}$

$15 \overset{?}{=} \frac{30}{2}$ — Substitute 30 for r.

$15 \overset{?}{=} 15$ — Divide on the right side.

Math Talk
Mathematical Practices

How is solving a multiplication equation similar to solving a division equation? How is it different?

YOUR TURN

Solve the equation $\frac{y}{9} = 1$. Graph the solution on a number line.

3. $\frac{y}{9} = 1$

$y =$ _____

number line: 0 1 2 3 4 5 6 7 8 9 10

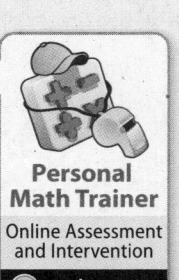

Personal Math Trainer

Online Assessment and Intervention

⏻ my.hrw.com

Math On the Spot

my.hrw.com

My Notes

Using Equations to Solve Problems

You can use equations to solve real-world problems.

EXAMPLE 3 Problem Solving

FL 6.EE.2.7

Juanita is scrapbooking. She usually completes about 9 pages per hour. One night last week she completed pages 23 through 47 in 2.5 hours. Did she work at her average rate?

 Analyze Information

Identify the important information.

- Worked for 2.5 hours
- Starting page: 23   Ending page: 47
- Scrapbooking rate: 9 pages per hour

Formulate a Plan

- Solve an equation to find the number of pages Juanita can expect to complete.

- Compare the number of pages Juanita can expect to complete with the number of pages she actually completed.

Solve

Let n represent the number of pages Juanita can expect to complete in 2.5 hours if she works at her average rate of 9 pages per hour.

Write an equation.

$\frac{n}{2.5} = 9$ Write the equation.

$2.5 \cdot \frac{n}{2.5} = 2.5 \cdot 9$ Multiply both sides by 2.5.

$n = 22.5$

Juanita can expect to complete 22.5 pages in 2.5 hours.

Juanita completed pages 23 through 47, a total of 25 pages. Because $25 > 22.5$, she worked faster than her expected rate.

 Justify and Evaluate

You used an equation to find the number of pages Juanita could expect to complete in 2.5 hours if she worked at her average rate. You found that she could complete 22.5 pages.

Since 22.5 pages is less than the 25 pages Juanita completed, she worked faster than her average rate.

The answer makes sense, because Juanita completed 25 pages in 2.5 hours, which is equivalent to a rate of 10 pages in 1 hour. Since $10 > 9$, you know that she worked faster than her average rate.

© Houghton Mifflin Harcourt Publishing Company

314 Unit 5

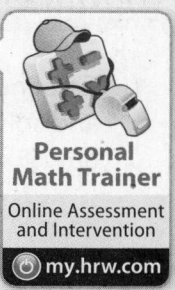

YOUR TURN

4. Roberto is dividing his baseball cards equally among himself, his brother, and his 3 friends. Roberto was left with 9 cards. How many cards did Roberto give away? Write and solve an equation to solve the problem.

_____

_____

Writing Real-World Problems

You can write a real-world problem for a given equation.

EXAMPLE 4   FL 6.EE.2.7

Write a real-world problem for the equation $8x = 72$. Then solve the problem.

STEP 1 Examine each part of the equation.

x is the unknown value you want to find.

8 is multiplied by x.

$= 72$ means that after multiplying 8 and x, the result is 72.

STEP 2 Write a real-world situation that involves multiplying two quantities.

A hot air balloon flew at 8 miles per hour. Write and solve a multiplication equation to find out how many hours the balloon traveled if it covered a distance of 72 miles.

STEP 3 Use the equation to solve the problem.

$8x = 72$

$\dfrac{8x}{8} = \dfrac{72}{8}$ Divide both sides by 8.

$x = 9$

The balloon traveled for 9 hours.

YOUR TURN

5. Write a real-world problem for the equation $11x = 385$. Then solve the problem.

_____

_____

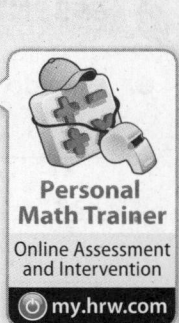

© Houghton Mifflin Harcourt Publishing Company

1. Caroline ran 15 miles in 5 days. She ran the same distance each day. Write and solve an equation to determine the number of miles she ran each day. (Explore Activity)

   a. Let x represent the _____.

   b.

Number of	.	Number of	=	

   _____ . _____ = _____

   c. Draw algebra tiles to model the equation.

   Caroline ran _____ miles each day.

Solve each equation. Graph the solution on a number line.
(Examples 1 and 2)

2. $x \div 3 = 3; x =$ _____

3. $4x = 32; x =$ _____

4. The area of the rectangle shown is 24 square inches. How much longer is its length than its width? (Example 3)

   6 in.

   w

   _____

   _____

5. Write a real-world problem for the equation $15w = 45$. Then solve the problem. (Example 4)

   _____

   _____

? ESSENTIAL QUESTION CHECK-IN

6. How do you solve equations that contain multiplication or division?

   _____

   _____

   _____

11.3 Independent Practice

 FL 6.EE.2.5, 6.EE.2.6, 6.EE.2.7

Personal Math Trainer

Online Assessment and Intervention

my.hrw.com

In 7–13, write and solve an equation to answer each question.

7. Jorge baked cookies for his math class's end-of-year party. There are 28 people in Jorge's math class including Jorge and his teacher. Jorge baked enough cookies for everyone to get 3 cookies each. How many cookies did Jorge bake?

_____

8. Sam divided a rectangle into 8 congruent rectangles that each have the area shown. What is the area of the rectangle before Sam divided it?

Area = 5 cm²			

_____

9. Carmen participated in a read-a-thon. Mr. Cole pledged $4.00 per book and gave Carmen $44. How many books did Carmen read?

_____

10. Lee drove 420 miles and used 15 gallons of gasoline. How many miles did Lee's car travel per gallon of gasoline?

_____

11. On some days, Melvin commutes 3.5 hours per day to the city for business meetings. Last week he commuted for a total of 14 hours. How many days did he commute to the city?

12. Dharmesh has a square garden with a perimeter of 132 feet. Is the area of the garden greater than 1,000 square feet?

```
      s
  ┌────────┐
  │        │
  │        │ s
  │        │
  └────────┘
```

_____

_____

_____

_____

13. Ingrid walked her dog and washed her car. The time she spent walking her dog was one-fourth the time it took her to wash her car. It took Ingrid 14 minutes to walk the dog. How long did it take Ingrid to wash her car?

_____

14. **Representing Real-World Problems** Write and solve a problem involving money that can be solved with a multiplication equation.

_____

_____

_____

_____

_____

_____

15. Representing Real-World Problems Write and solve a problem involving money that can be solved with a division equation and has a solution of 1,350.

_____

_____

_____

_____

_____

16. Communicating Mathematical Ideas Explain why $7 \cdot \frac{x}{7} = x$. How does your answer help you solve a division equation such as $\frac{x}{7} = 2$?

_____

_____

_____

_____

17. Critical Thinking A number tripled and tripled again is 729. What is the number? Show your work.

_____

_____

18. Multistep Andre has 4 times as many model cars as Peter, and Peter has one-third as many model cars as Jade. Andre has 36 model cars.

a. Write and solve an equation to find how many model cars Peter has.

_____

b. Using your answer from part **a**, write and solve an equation to find how many model cars Jade has.

_____

19. Persevere in Problem Solving The area of a rectangle is 42 square inches and one side is 12 inches long. Find the perimeter of the rectangle. Show your work.

_____

_____

_____

Work Area

© Houghton Mifflin Harcourt Publishing Company

11.4 Writing Inequalities

FL 6.EE.2.8

Write an inequality...to represent a constraint or condition in a real-world or mathematical problem....
Also 6.EE.2.5, 6.EE.2.6

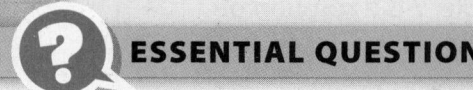
ESSENTIAL QUESTION

How can you use inequalities to represent real-world constraints or conditions?

EXPLORE ACTIVITY   FL 6.EE.2.8, 6.EE.2.5

Using Inequalities to Describe Quantities

You can use inequality symbols with variables to describe quantities that can have many values.

Symbol	Meaning	Word Phrases
$<$	Is less than	Fewer than, below
$>$	Is greater than	More than, above
$\leq$	Is less than or equal to	At most, no more than
$\geq$	Is greater than or equal to	At least, no less than

A The lowest temperature ever recorded in Florida was −2°F. Graph this temperature on the number line.

```
←—+——+——+——+——+——+——+——+——+——+——+——+——+——+——+——+——+→
 −8 −7 −6 −5 −4 −3 −2 −1  0  1  2  3  4  5  6  7  8
```

B The temperatures 0°F, 3°F, 6°F, 5°F, and −1°F have also been recorded in Florida. Graph these temperatures on the number line.

C How do the temperatures in **B** compare to −2? How can you see this relationship on the number line?

_____

_____

D How many other numbers have the same relationship to −2 as the temperatures in **B** ? Give some examples.

_____

E Suppose you could graph all of the possible answers to **D** on a number line. What would the graph look like?

_____

F Let *x* represent all the possible answers to **D** .

Complete this inequality: *x* ☐ −2

Graphing the Solutions of an Inequality

A **solution of an inequality** that contains a variable is any value of the variable that makes the inequality true. For example, 7 is a solution of $x > -2$, since $7 > -2$ is a true statement.

EXAMPLE 1

 FL 6.EE.2.5

Graph the solutions of each inequality. Check the solutions.

A $y \leq -3$

> **STEP 1** Draw a solid circle at -3 to show that -3 is a solution.

> **STEP 2** Shade the number line to the left of -3 to show that numbers less than -3 are solutions.

> *Use a solid circle for an inequality that uses $\geq$ or $\leq$.*

$$\xleftarrow{\hspace{1cm}} \begin{array}{ccccccccccc} -5 & -4 & -3 & -2 & -1 & 0 & 1 & 2 & 3 & 4 & 5 \end{array}$$

> **STEP 3** Check your solution.
>
> Choose a number that is on the shaded section of the number line, such as -4. Substitute -4 for y.
>
> $-4 \leq -3$ -4 is less than -3, so -4 is a solution.

B $1 < m$

> **STEP 1** Draw an empty circle at 1 to show that 1 is not a solution.

> **STEP 2** Shade the number line to the right of 1 to show that numbers greater than 1 are solutions.

> *Use an open circle for an inequality that uses $>$ or $<$.*

$$\xleftarrow{\hspace{1cm}} \begin{array}{ccccccccccc} -5 & -4 & -3 & -2 & -1 & 0 & 1 & 2 & 3 & 4 & 5 \end{array} \xrightarrow{\hspace{1cm}}$$

> **STEP 3** Check your answer.
> Substitute 2 for m.
>
> $1 < 2$ 1 is less than 2, so 2 is a solution.

Reflect

1. **Critique Reasoning** Inez says you can rewrite $1 < m$ as $m > 1$. Do you agree?

_____

2. **Analyze Relationships** How is $x < 5$ different from $x \leq 5$?

_____

_____

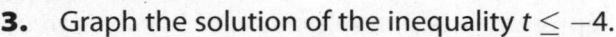

YOUR TURN

3. Graph the solution of the inequality $t \leq -4$.

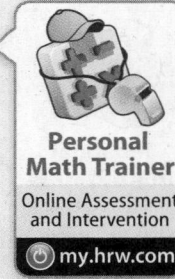

Personal Math Trainer
Online Assessment and Intervention
my.hrw.com

Writing Inequalities

You can write an inequality to model the relationship between an algebraic expression and a number. You can also write inequalities to represent certain real-world situations.

 EXAMPLE 2 **FL** 6.EE.2.8, 6.EE.2.6

Math On the Spot
my.hrw.com

A Write an inequality that represents the phrase *the sum of y and 2 is greater than 5*. Draw a graph to represent the inequality.

STEP 1 Write the inequality.

The sum of y and 2 is greater than 5.

$$y + 2 \qquad > \qquad 5$$

STEP 2 Graph the solution.

For $y + 2$ to have a value greater than 5, y must be a number greater than 3.

Use an open circle at 3 and shade to the right of 3.

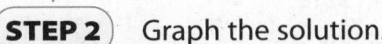

STEP 3 Check your solution by substituting a number greater than 3, such as 4, into the original inequality.

$4 + 2 > 5$ Substitute 4 for y.

$6 > 5$ 6 is greater than 5, so 4 is a solution.

B To test the temperature rating of a coat, a scientist keeps the temperature below 5°C. Write and graph an inequality to represent this situation.

STEP 1 Write the inequality. Let t represent the temperature in the lab.

$t < 5$ The temperature must be less than 5°C.

STEP 2 Graph the inequality.

Animated Math
my.hrw.com

My Notes

© Houghton Mifflin Harcourt Publishing Company

Lesson 11.4 **321**

YOUR TURN

4. Write an inequality that represents the phrase *the sum of 1 and y is greater than or equal to 3* . Check to see if $y = 1$ is a solution.

Write and graph an inequality to represent each situation.

5. The temperature in February was at most 6°F. _____

```
←—+—+—+—+—+—+—+—+—+—+—+—+—+→
   0  1  2  3  4  5  6  7  8  9 10 11 12
```

6. Each package must weigh more than 2 ounces. _____

```
←—+—+—+—+—+—+—+—+—+—+—+—+—+—+→
 −2 −1  0  1  2  3  4  5  6  7  8  9 10 11 12
```

Guided Practice

1. Graph $1 \leq x$. Use the graph to determine which of these numbers are solutions of the inequality: $-1, 3, 0, 1$ (*Explore Activity and Example 1*)

_____

2. Graph $-3 > z$. Check the graph using substitution. (*Example 1*)

3. Write an inequality that represents the phrase "the sum of 4 and *x* is greater than 6." Draw a graph that represents the inequality, and check your solution. (*Example 2*)

_____

4. During hibernation, a garter snake's body temperature never goes below 3°C. Write and graph an inequality that represents this situation. (*Example 2*)

_____

❓ ESSENTIAL QUESTION CHECK-IN

5. Write an inequality to represent this situation: Nina wants to take at least $15 to the movies. How did you decide which inequality symbol to use?

_____

_____

© Houghton Mifflin Harcourt Publishing Company

11.4 Independent Practice

FL   6.EE.2.5, 6.EE.2.6, 6.EE.2.8

Personal Math Trainer

Online Assessment and Intervention

my.hrw.com

6. Which of the following numbers are solutions to $x \geq 0$?

$-5, 0.03, -1, 0, 1.5, -6, \frac{1}{2}$ _____

Graph each inequality.

7. $t \leq 8$

8. $-7 < h$

9. $x \geq -9$

10. $n > 2.5$

11. $-4\frac{1}{2} > x$

Write an inequality that matches the number line model.

12. _____

13. _____

14. _____

15. _____

16. A child must be at least 48 inches tall to ride a roller coaster.

a. Write and graph an inequality to represent this situation.

_____

b. Can a child who is 46 inches tall ride the roller coaster? Explain.

_____

Write and graph an inequality to represent each situation.

17. The stock is worth at least $14.50. _____

18. The temperature is less than 3.5 °F. _____

19. The goal of the fundraiser is to make more than $150. _____

 FOCUS ON HIGHER ORDER THINKING

20. Communicate Mathematical Ideas Explain how to graph the inequality $8 \geq y$.

_____

_____

_____

_____

21. Represent Real-World Problems The number line shows an inequality. Describe a real-world situation that the inequality could represent.

_____

22. Critique Reasoning Natasha is trying to represent the following situation with a number line model: There are fewer than 5 students in the cafeteria. She has come up with two possible representations, shown below. Which is the better representation, and why?

_____

_____

_____

_____

© Houghton Mifflin Harcourt Publishing Company

Work Area

Ready to Go On?

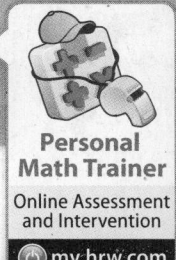

Personal Math Trainer

Online Assessment and Intervention

⏻ my.hrw.com

11.1 Writing Equations to Represent Situations

Determine whether the given value is a solution of the equation.

1. $\frac{b}{12} = 5$; $b = 60$ _____

2. $7w = 87$; $w = 12$ _____

Write an equation to represent the situation.

3. The number of eggs in the refrigerator e decreased by 5 equals 18.

_____

11.2 Addition and Subtraction Equations

Solve each equation.

4. $r - 38 = 9$ _____

5. $h + 17 = 40$ _____

6. $n + 75 = 155$ _____

7. $q - 17 = 18$ _____

11.3 Multiplication and Division Equations

Solve each equation.

8. $8z = 112$ _____

9. $\frac{d}{14} = 7$ _____

10. $\frac{f}{28} = 24$ _____

11. $3a = 57$ _____

11.4 Writing Inequalities

Write an inequality to represent each situation, then graph the solutions.

12. There are fewer than 8 gallons of gas in the tank. _____

13. There are at least 3 slices of bread left in the bag. _____

? ESSENTIAL QUESTION

14. How can you solve problems involving equations that contain addition, subtraction, multiplication, or division?

_____

_____

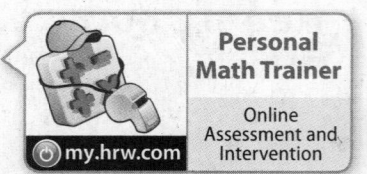

Selected Response

1. Kate has gone up to the chalkboard to do math problems 5 more times than Andre. Kate has gone up 11 times. Which equation represents this situation?

(A) $a - 11 = 5$

(B) $5a = 11$

(C) $a - 5 = 11$

(D) $a + 5 = 11$

2. For which equation is $y = 7$ a solution?

(A) $7y = 1$

(B) $18 = 11 + y$

(C) $y + 7 = 0$

(D) $\frac{y}{2} = 14$

3. Which is an equation?

(A) $17 + x$

(C) $20x = 200$

(B) $45 \div x$

(D) $90 - x$

4. The temperature never rose above 6 °F on Friday. Which number line could represent this situation?

(A)

(B)

(C)

(D)

5. Becca hit 7 more home runs than Beverly. Becca hit 21 home runs. How many home runs did Beverly hit?

(A) 3

(C) 21

(B) 14

(D) 28

6. Jeordie spreads out a rectangular picnic blanket with an area of 42 square feet. Its width is 6 feet. Which equation could you use to find its length?

(A) $6x = 42$

(C) $\frac{6}{x} = 42$

(B) $42 - x = 6$

(D) $6 + x = 42$

7. What is a solution to the equation $6t = 114$?

(A) $t = 19$

(C) $t = 120$

(B) $t = 108$

(D) $t = 684$

8. The area of a rectangular deck is 680 square feet. The deck's width is 17 feet. What is its perimeter?

(A) 40 feet

(C) 114 feet

(B) 57 feet

(D) 228 feet

Mini-Task

9. Sylvia earns $7 per hour at her afterschool job. After working one week, she received a paycheck for $91.

a. Write and solve an equation to find the number of hours Sylvia worked to earn $91.

_____

b. The greatest number of hours Sylvia can work in any week is 15. Write an inequality to represent this statement.

_____

c. What is the greatest amount of money Sylvia can earn in one week?

_____

Relationships in Two Variables

ESSENTIAL QUESTION

How can you use relationships in two variables to solve real-world problems?

LESSON 12.1

Graphing on the Coordinate Plane

FL   6.NS.3.6, 6.NS.3.6b, 6.NS.3.6c, 6.NS.3.8

LESSON 12.2

Independent and Dependent Variables in Tables and Graphs

FL   6.EE.3.9

LESSON 12.3

Writing Equations from Tables

FL   6.EE.3.9

LESSON 12.4

Representing Algebraic Relationships in Tables and Graphs

FL   6.EE.3.9

Real-World Video

A two-variable equation can represent an animal's distance over time. A graph can display the relationship between the variables. You can graph two or more animals' data to visually compare them.

my.hrw.com

GO DIGITAL

my.hrw.com

my.hrw.com

Go digital with your write-in student edition, accessible on any device.

Math On the Spot

Scan with your smart phone to jump directly to the online edition, video tutor, and more.

Animated Math

Interactively explore key concepts to see how math works.

Personal Math Trainer

Get immediate feedback and help as you work through practice sets.

Are YOU Ready?

Complete these exercises to review skills you will need for this module.

Multiplication Facts

EXAMPLE $8 \times 7 = $ ▮

Use a related fact you know.
$7 \times 7 = 49$
Think: $8 \times 7 = (7 \times 7) + 7$
$\qquad = 49 + 7$
$\qquad = 56$

Multiply.

1. 7×6 _____   **2.** 10×9 _____   **3.** 13×12 _____   **4.** 8×9 _____

Write the rule for each table.

5.

x	1	2	3	4
y	7	14	21	28

_____

6.

x	1	2	3	4
y	7	8	9	10

_____

7.

x	1	2	3	4
y	5	10	15	20

_____

8.

x	0	4	8	12
y	0	2	4	6

_____

Graph Ordered Pairs (First Quadrant)

EXAMPLE

Start at the origin.
Move 9 units right.
Then move 5 units up.
Graph point A(9, 5).

Graph each point on the coordinate grid above.

9. B (0, 8)   **10.** C (2, 3)   **11.** D (6, 7)   **12.** E (5, 0)

Reading Start-Up

Visualize Vocabulary

Use the ✔ words to complete the chart.

Parts of the Algebraic Expression $14 + 3x$		
Definition	Mathematical Representation	Review Word
A specific number whose value does not change	14	
A number that is multiplied by a variable in an algebraic expression	3	
A letter or symbol used to represent an unknown	x	

Understand Vocabulary

Complete the sentences using the preview words.

1. The numbers in an ordered pair are _____.

2. A _____ is formed by two number lines that intersect at right angles.

© Houghton Mifflin Harcourt Publishing Company

Vocabulary

Review Words

✔ coefficient *(coeficiente)*
✔ constant *(constante)*
  equation *(ecuación)*
  negative number *(número negativo)*
  positive number *(número positivo)*
  scale *(escala)*
✔ variable *(variable)*

Preview Words

  axes *(ejes)*
  coordinate plane *(plano cartesiano)*
  coordinates *(coordenadas)*
  dependent variable *(variable dependiente)*
  independent variable *(variable independiente)*
  ordered pair *(par ordenado)*
  origin *(origen)*
  quadrants *(cuadrante)*
  x-axis *(eje x)*
  x-coordinate *(coordenada x)*
  y-axis *(eje y)*
  y-coordinate *(coordenada y)*

Active Reading

Layered Book Before beginning the module, create a layered book to help you learn the concepts in this module. Label each flap with lesson titles from this module. As you study each lesson, write important ideas such as vocabulary and formulas under the appropriate flap. Refer to your finished layered book as you work on exercises from this module.

Unpacking the Standards

Understanding the standards and the vocabulary terms in the standards will help you know exactly what you are expected to learn in this module.

FL 6.EE.3.9

Use variables to represent two quantities in a real-world problem that change in relationship to one another; write an equation to express one quantity, thought of as the dependent variable, in terms of the other quantity, thought of as the independent variable. ...

Key Vocabulary

equation *(ecuación)*
A mathematical sentence that shows that two expressions are equivalent.

What It Means to You

You will learn to write an equation that represents the relationship in a table.

UNPACKING EXAMPLE 6.EE.3.9

Emily has a dog-walking service. She charges a daily fee of $7 to walk a dog twice a day. Create a table that shows how much Emily earns for walking 1, 6, 10, and 15 dogs. Write an equation that represents the situation.

Dogs walked	1	6	10	15
Earnings ($)	7	42	70	105

Earnings is 7 times the number of dogs walked. Let the variable e represent earnings and the variable d represent the number of dogs walked.

$$e = 7 \times d$$

FL 6.EE.3.9

...Analyze the relationship between the dependent and independent variables using graphs and tables, and relate these to the equation.

Key Vocabulary

coordinate plane
(plano cartesiano)
A plane formed by the intersection of a horizontal number line called the *x*-axis and a vertical number line called the *y*-axis.

Visit **my.hrw.com** to see all **Florida Math Standards** unpacked.

my.hrw.com

What It Means to You

You can use words, a table, a graph, or an equation to model the same mathematical relationship.

UNPACKING EXAMPLE 6.EE.3.9

The equation $y = 4x$ represents the total cost y for x games of miniature golf. Make a table of values and a graph for this situation.

Number of games, x	1	2	3	4
Total cost ($), y	4	8	12	16

12.1 Graphing on the Coordinate Plane

FL 6.NS.3.6c

...find and position pairs of integers and other rational numbers on a coordinate plane. *Also 6.NS.3.6, 6.NS.3.6b, 6.NS.3.8*

? ESSENTIAL QUESTION

How do you locate and name points in the coordinate plane?

Naming Points in the Coordinate Plane

A **coordinate plane** is formed by two number lines that intersect at right angles. The point of intersection is 0 on each number line.

Math On the Spot
my.hrw.com

- The two number lines are called the **axes**.

- The horizontal axis is called the **x-axis**.

- The vertical axis is called the **y-axis**.

- The point where the axes intersect is called the **origin**.

- The two axes divide the coordinate plane into four **quadrants**.

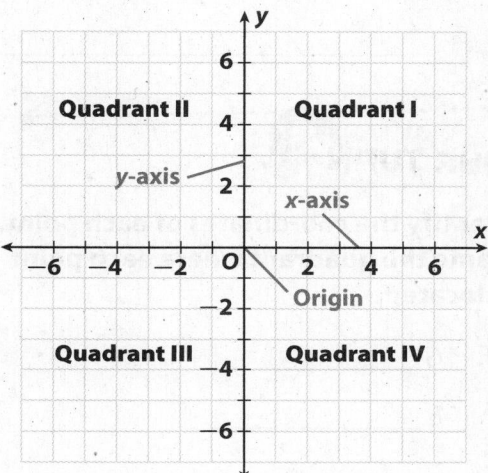

An **ordered pair** is a pair of numbers that gives the location of a point on a coordinate plane. The first number tells how far to the right (positive) or left (negative) the point is located from the origin. The second number tells how far up (positive) or down (negative) the point is located from the origin.

The numbers in an ordered pair are called **coordinates**. The first number is the **x-coordinate** and the second number is the **y-coordinate**.

EXAMPLE 1

FL 6.NS.3.6c, 6.NS.3.6b

Identify the coordinates of each point. Name the quadrant where each point is located.

Point *A* is 1 unit *left* of the origin, and 5 units *down*. It has *x*-coordinate -1 and *y*-coordinate -5, written $(-1, -5)$. It is located in Quadrant III.

Point *B* is 2 units *right* of the origin, and 3 units *up*. It has *x*-coordinate 2 and *y*-coordinate 3, written $(2, 3)$. It is located in Quadrant I.

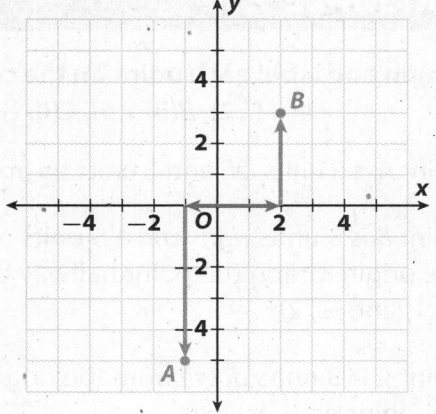

Reflect

1. If both coordinates of a point are negative, in which quadrant is the point located? _____

2. Describe the coordinates of all points in Quadrant I.

   _____

3. **Communicate Mathematical Ideas** Explain why (−3, 5) represents a different location than (3, 5).

   _____

   _____

   _____

YOUR TURN

Identify the coordinates of each point. Name the quadrant where each point is located.

4. G _____

   E _____

5. F _____

   H _____

Graphing Points in the Coordinate Plane

Points that are located on the axes are not located in any quadrant. Points on the x-axis have a y-coordinate of 0, and points on the y-axis have an x-coordinate of 0.

EXAMPLE 2

FL 6.NS.3.6c, 6.NS.3.6

Graph and label each point on the coordinate plane.
$A(−5, 2), B(3, 1.5), C(0, −3)$

Point A is 5 units *left* and 2 units *up* from the origin.

Point B is 3 units *right* and 1.5 units *up* from the origin. Graph the point halfway between (3, 1) and (3, 2).

Point C is 3 units *down* from the origin. Graph the point on the y-axis.

YOUR TURN

Graph and label each point on the coordinate plane.

6. $P(-4, 2)$

7. $Q(3, 2.5)$

8. $R(-4.5, -5)$

9. $S(4, -5)$

10. $T(-2.5, 0)$

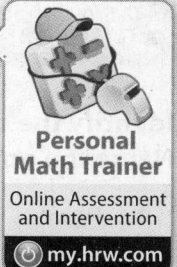

Personal Math Trainer

Online Assessment and Intervention

my.hrw.com

Reading Scales on Axes

The *scale* of an axis is the number of units that each grid line represents. So far, the graphs in this lesson have a scale of 1 unit, but graphs frequently use other units.

Math On the Spot

my.hrw.com

EXAMPLE 3   **FL** 6.NS.3.8

The graph shows the location of a city. It also shows the location of Gary's and Jen's houses. The scale on each axis represents miles.

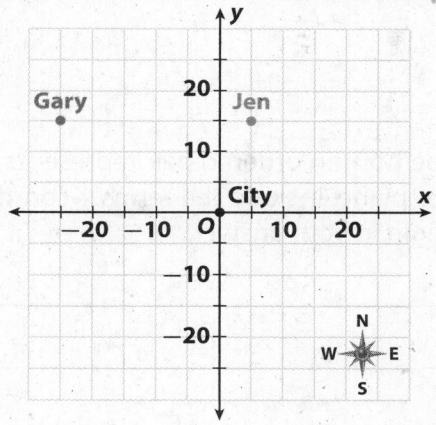

A Use the scale to describe Gary's location relative to the city.

Each grid square is 5 miles on a side.

Gary's house is at $(-25, 15)$, which is 25 miles west and 15 miles north of the city.

B Describe the location of Jen's house relative to Gary's house.

Jen's house is located 6 grid squares to the right of Gary's house. Since each grid square is 5 miles on a side, her house is $6 \cdot 5 = 30$ miles from Gary's.

Math Talk

Mathematical Practices

How are north, south, east, and west represented on the graph in Example 3?

YOUR TURN

Use the graph in the Example.

11. Ted lives 20 miles south and 20 miles west of the city represented on the graph in Example 3. His brother Ned lives 50 miles north of Ted's house. Give the coordinates of each brother's house.

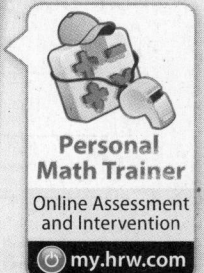

Personal Math Trainer

Online Assessment and Intervention

my.hrw.com

© Houghton Mifflin Harcourt Publishing Company

Lesson 12.1 **333**

Identify the coordinates of each point in the coordinate plane. Name the quadrant where each point is located. (Example 1)

1. Point *A* is 5 units _____ of the origin and

   1 unit _____ from the origin.

   Its coordinates are _____. It is in quadrant _____.

2. Point *B* is _____ units right of the origin

   and _____ units down from the origin.

   Its coordinates are _____. It is in quadrant _____.

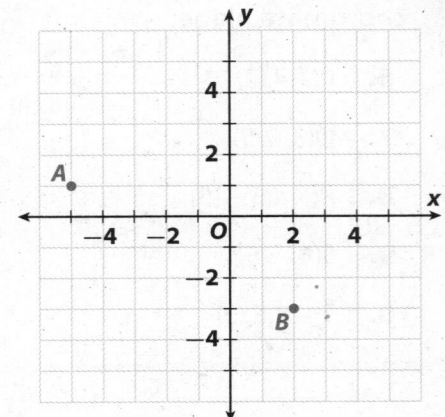

Graph and label each point on the coordinate plane above. (Example 2)

3. Point *C* at (−3.5, 3)   4. Point *D* at (5, 0)

For 5–7, use the coordinate plane shown. (Example 3)

5. Describe the scale of the graph.

   _____

6. Plot point *A* at $\left(-\frac{1}{2}, 2\right)$.

7. Plot point *B* at $\left(2\frac{1}{2}, -2\right)$.

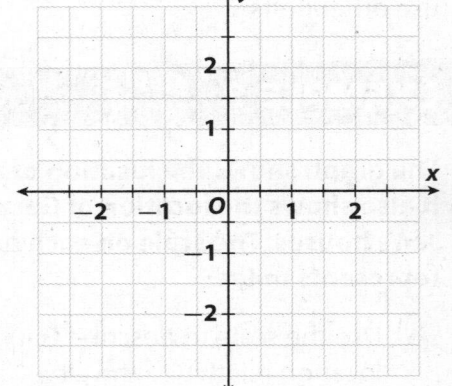

8. **Vocabulary** Describe how an ordered pair represents a point on a coordinate plane. Include the terms *x*-coordinate, *y*-coordinate, and origin in your answer.

   _____

   _____

   _____

   _____

? ESSENTIAL QUESTION CHECK-IN

9. Give the coordinates of one point in each of the four quadrants, one point on the *x*-axis, and one point on the *y*-axis.

   _____

   _____

   _____

12.1 Independent Practice

FL 6.NS.3.6, 6.NS.3.6b, 6.NS.3.6c, 6.NS.3.8

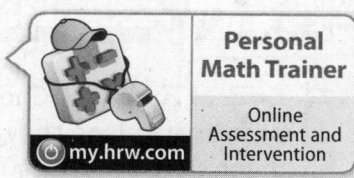

Personal Math Trainer

Online Assessment and Intervention

my.hrw.com

For 10–13, use the coordinate plane shown. Each unit represents 1 kilometer.

10. Write the ordered pairs that represent the location of Sam and the theater.

_____

11. Describe Sam's location relative to the theater.

_____

_____

12. Sam wants to meet his friend Beth at a restaurant before they go to the theater. The restaurant is 9 km south of the theater. Plot and label a point representing the restaurant. What are the coordinates of the point?

_____

13. Beth describes her current location: "I'm directly south of the theater, halfway to the restaurant." Plot and label a point representing Beth's location. What are the coordinates of the point?

_____

For 14–15, use the coordinate plane shown.

14. Find the coordinates of points *T*, *U*, and *V*.

_____

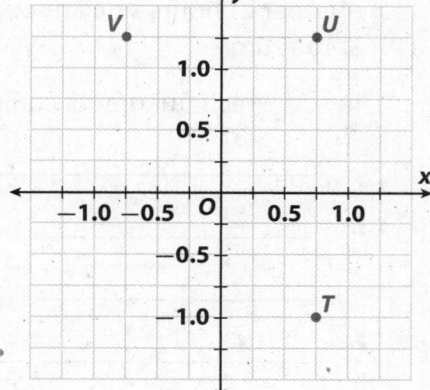

15. Points *T*, *U*, and *V* are the vertices of a rectangle. Point *W* is the fourth vertex. Plot point *W* and give its coordinates.

_____

16. **Explain the Error** Janine tells her friend that ordered pairs that have an *x*-coordinate of 0 lie on the *x*-axis. She uses the origin as an example. Describe Janine's error. Use a counterexample to explain why Janine's statement is false.

_____

_____

_____

17. Critical Thinking Choose scales for the coordinate plane shown so that you can graph the points $J(2, 40)$, $K(3, 10)$, $L(3, -40)$, $M(-4, 50)$, and $N(-5, -50)$. Explain why you chose the scale for each axis.

_____

_____

_____

_____

_____

_____

18. Communicate Mathematical Ideas Edgar wants to plot the ordered pair $(1.8, -1.2)$ on a coordinate plane. On each axis, one grid square equals 0.1. Starting at the origin, how can Edgar find $(1.8, -1.2)$?

_____

_____

_____

19. Represent Real-World Problems Zach graphs some ordered pairs in the coordinate plane. The x-values of the ordered pairs represent the number of hours since noon, and the y-values represent the temperature at that time.

a. In which quadrants could Zach graph points? Explain your thinking.

_____

_____

_____

_____

b. In what part of the world and at what time of year might Zach collect data so that the points he plots are in Quadrant IV?

_____

_____

Independent and Dependent Variables in Tables and Graphs

FL 6.EE.3.9

Use variables to represent two quantities in a real-world problem that change in relationship to one another; ... Analyze the relationship between the dependent and independent variables....

ESSENTIAL QUESTION

How can you identify independent and dependent quantities from tables and graphs?

EXPLORE ACTIVITY 1   FL 6.EE.3.9

Identifying Independent and Dependent Quantities from a Table

Many real-world situations involve two variable quantities in which one quantity depends on the other. The quantity that depends on the other quantity is called the **dependent variable**, and the quantity it depends on is called the **independent variable**.

A freight train moves at a constant speed. The distance _y_ in miles that the train has traveled after _x_ hours is shown in the table.

Time _x_ (h)	0	1	2	3
Distance _y_ (mi)	0	50	100	150

A What are the two quantities in this situation?

_____

Which of these quantities depends on the other?

_____

What is the independent variable? _____

What is the dependent variable? _____

B How far does the train travel each hour? _____

The relationship between the distance traveled by the train and the time in hours can be represented by an equation in two variables.

© Houghton Mifflin Harcourt Publishing Company

Reflect

1. **Analyze Relationships** Describe how the value of the independent variable is related to the value of the dependent variable. Is the relationship additive or multiplicative?

   _____

2. What are the units of the independent variable and of the dependent variable?

   _____

   _____

3. A rate is used in the equation. What is the rate?

   _____

EXPLORE ACTIVITY 2   FL 6.EE.3.9

Identifying Independent and Dependent Variables from a Graph

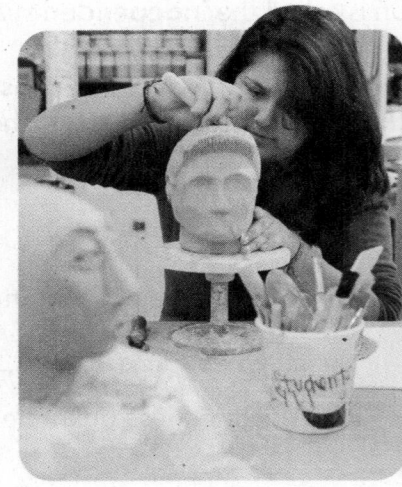

In Explore Activity 1, you used a table to represent a relationship between an independent variable (time) and a dependent variable (distance). You can also use a graph to show this relationship.

An art teacher has 20 pounds of clay but wants to buy more clay for her class. The amount of clay _x_ purchased by the teacher and the amount of clay _y_ available for the class are shown on the graph.

A If the teacher buys 10 more pounds of clay, how many

pounds will be available for the art class? _____ lb

If the art class has a total of 50 pounds of clay available, how many pounds of clay did the teacher buy?

How can you use the graph to find this information?

_____

_____

_____

Clay Used in Art Class

Clay bought
by teacher (lb)

B What are the two quantities in this situation?

_____

_____

Which of these quantities depends on the other?

_____

_____

What is the independent variable? _____

What is the dependent variable? _____

C The relationship between the amount of clay purchased by the teacher and the amount of clay available to the class can be represented by an equation in two variables.

Amount of clay available (pounds)	=	Current amount of clay (pounds)	+	Amount of clay purchased (pounds)
↓		↓		↓
y	=	20	+	x

D Describe in words how the value of the independent variable is related to the value of the dependent variable.

_____

_____

Reflect

4. In this situation, the same units are used for the independent and dependent variables. How is this different from the situation involving the train in the first Explore?

_____

_____

5. **Analyze Relationships** Tell whether the relationship between the independent variable and the dependent variable is a multiplicative or an additive relationship.

_____

6. What are the units of the independent variable, and what are the units of the dependent variable?

independent variable: _____; dependent variable: _____

Describing Relationships Between Independent and Dependent Variables

Thinking about how one quantity depends on another helps you identify which quantity is the independent variable and which quantity is the dependent variable. In a graph, the independent variable is usually shown on the horizontal axis and the dependent variable on the vertical axis.

EXAMPLE 1   FL 6.EE.3.9

A The table shows a relationship between two variables, x and y. Describe a possible situation the table could represent. Describe the independent and dependent variables in the situation.

Independent variable, x	0	1	2	3
Dependent variable, y	10	11	12	13

As x increases by 1, y increases by 1. The relationship is additive. The value of y is always 10 units greater than the value of x.

The table could represent Jina's savings if she starts with $10 and adds $1 to her savings every day.

The independent variable, x, is the number of days she has been adding money to her savings.
The dependent variable, y, is her savings after x days.

B The graph shows a relationship between two variables. Describe a possible situation that the graph could represent. Describe the independent and dependent variables.

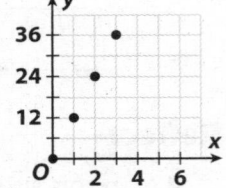

As x increases by 1, y increases by 12. The relationship is multiplicative. The value of y is always 12 times the value of x.

The graph could represent the number of eggs in cartons that each hold 12 eggs.

The independent variable, x, is the number of cartons.
The dependent variable, y, is the total number of eggs.

Reflect

7. What are other possible situations that the table and graph in the Examples could represent?

_____

_____

_____

_____

_____

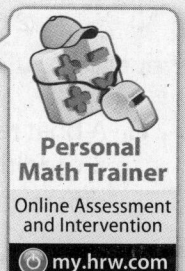
YOUR TURN

Describe real-world values that the variables could represent. Describe the relationship between the independent and dependent variables.

8.

x	0	1	2	3
y	15	16	17	18

_____

_____

_____

_____

_____

9.

x	0	1	2	3	4
y	0	16	32	48	64

_____

_____

_____

_____

_____

10.

_____

_____

_____

_____

_____

1. A boat rental shop rents paddleboats for a fee plus an additional cost per hour. The cost of renting for different numbers of hours is shown in the table.

Time (hours)	0	1	2	3
Cost ($)	10	11	12	13

What is the independent variable, and what is the dependent variable? How do you know? (Explore Activity 1)

_____

_____

_____

2. A car travels at a constant rate of 60 miles per hour. (Explore Activity 1)

Time x (h)	0	1	2	3
Distance y (mi)				

a. Complete the table.

b. What is the independent variable, and what is the dependent?

_____

_____

c. Describe how the value of the independent variable is related to the value of the dependent variable.

_____

Use the graph to answer the questions.

3. Describe in words how the value of the independent variable is related to the value of the dependent variable. (Explore Activity 2)

_____

_____

4. Describe a real-world situation that the graph could represent. (Example 1)

_____

_____

? ESSENTIAL QUESTION CHECK-IN

5. How can you identify the dependent and independent variables in a real-world situation modeled by a graph?

_____

_____

_____

12.2 Independent Practice

FL 6.EE.3.9

Personal Math Trainer

Online Assessment and Intervention

my.hrw.com

6. The graph shows the relationship between the hours a soccer team practiced after the season started and their total practice time for the year.

a. How many hours did the soccer team practice before the season began?

_____

b. What are the two quantities in this situation?

_____

_____

c. What are the dependent and independent variables?

_____

_____

d. Is the relationship between the variables additive or multiplicative? Explain.

_____

_____

e. Analyze Relationships Describe the relationship between the quantities in words.

_____

_____

Graph: Total practice time for year (hours) vs. Practice time during the season (hours)

7. Multistep Teresa is buying glitter markers to put in gift bags. The table shows the relationship between the number of gift bags and the number of glitter markers she needs to buy.

Number of gift bags, x	0	1	2	3
Number of markers, y	0	5	10	15

a. What is the dependent variable? _____

b. What is the independent variable? _____

c. Is the relationship additive or multiplicative? Explain.

_____

_____

d. Describe the relationship between the quantities in words.

_____

8. Ty borrowed $500 from his parents. The graph shows how much he owes them each month if he pays back a certain amount each month.

Ty's Loan Payments

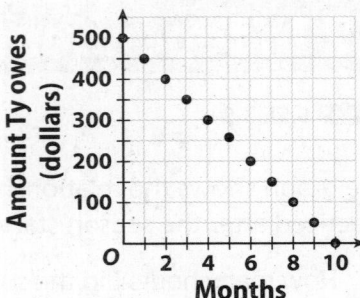

a. Describe the relationship between the number of months and the amount Ty owes. Identify an independent and dependent variable and explain your thinking.

_____

_____

_____

_____

_____

b. How long will it take Ty to pay back his parents?

_____

 FOCUS ON HIGHER ORDER THINKING

9. Error Analysis A discount store has a special: 8 cans of juice for a dollar. A shopper decides that since the number of cans purchased is 8 times the number of dollars spent, the cost is the independent variable and the number of cans is the dependent variable. Do you agree? Explain.

_____

_____

_____

_____

_____

10. Analyze Relationships Provide an example of a real-world relationship where there is no clear independent or dependent variable. Explain.

_____

_____

_____

_____

_____

_____

Work Area

Writing Equations from Tables

FL 6.EE.3.9
...write an equation to express one quantity, thought of as the dependent variable, in terms of the other quantity, thought of as the independent variable. ...

? ESSENTIAL QUESTION

How can you use an equation to show a relationship between two variables?

EXPLORE ACTIVITY Real World FL 6.EE.3.9

Writing an Equation to Represent a Real-World Relationship

Many real-world situations involve two variable quantities in which one quantity depends on the other. This type of relationship can be represented by a table. You can also use an equation to model the relationship.

The table shows how much Amanda earns for walking 1, 2, or 3 dogs. Use the table to determine how much Amanda earns per dog. Then write an equation that models the relationship between number of dogs walked and earnings. Use your equation to complete the table.

Dogs walked	1	2	3	5	10	20
Earnings	$8	$16	$24			

> For 1 dog, Amanda earns $1 \cdot 8 = \$8$.
> For 2 dogs, she earns $2 \cdot 8 = \$16$.

A For each column, compare the number of dogs walked and earnings. What is the pattern?

_____

_____

B Based on the pattern, Amanda earns $ _____ for each dog she walks.

C Write an equation that relates the number of dogs Amanda walks to the amount she earns. Let *e* represent earnings and *d* represent dogs.

_____

D Use your equation to complete the table for 5, 10, and 20 walked dogs.

E Amanda's earnings depend on _____.

Reflect

1. What If? If Amanda changed the amount earned per dog to $11, what equation could you write to model the relationship between number of

dogs walked and earnings? _____

Writing an Equation Based on a Table

The relationship between two variables where one variable depends on the other can be represented in a table or by an equation. An equation expresses the dependent variable in terms of the independent variable.

When there is no real-world situation to consider, we usually say *x* is the independent variable and *y* is the dependent variable. The value of *y* depends on the value of *x*.

EXAMPLE 1

 FL 6.EE.3.9

Write an equation that expresses *y* in terms of *x*.

A

x	1	2	3	4	5
y	0.5	1	1.5	2	2.5

STEP 1 Compare the *x*- and *y*-values to find a pattern.

Each *y*-value is $\frac{1}{2}$, or 0.5 times, the corresponding *x*-value.

STEP 2 Use the pattern to write an equation expressing *y* in terms of *x*.

$$y = 0.5x$$

B

x	2	4	6	8	10
y	5	7	9	11	13

STEP 1 Compare the *x*- and *y*-values to find a pattern.

Each *y*-value is 3 more than the corresponding *x*-value.

STEP 2 Use the pattern to write an equation expressing *y* in terms of *x*.

$$y = x + 3$$

Math Talk
Mathematical Practices

How can you check that your equations are correct?

 YOUR TURN

For each table, write an equation that expresses *y* in terms of *x*.

2.

x	12	11	10
y	10	9	8

_____

3.

x	10	12	14
y	25	30	35

_____

4.

x	5	4	3
y	10	9	8

_____

5.

x	0	1	2
y	0	2	4

_____

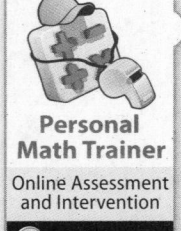

Using Tables and Equations to Solve Problems

You can use tables and equations to solve real-world problems.

EXAMPLE 2   Problem Solving   FL 6.EE.3.9

A certain percent of the sale price of paintings at a gallery will be donated to charity. The donation will be $50 if a painting sells for $200. The donation will be $75 if a painting sells for $300. Find the amount of the donation if a painting sells for $1,200.

Analyze Information

You know the donation amount when the sale price of a painting is $200 and $300. You need to find the donation amount if a painting sells for $1,200.

Formulate a Plan

You can make a table to help you determine the relationship between sale price and donation amount. Then you can write an equation that models the relationship. Use the equation to find the unknown donation amount.

Solve

Make a table.

Sale price ($)	200	300
Donation amount ($)	50	75

$$\frac{50}{200} = \frac{50 \div 2}{200 \div 2} = \frac{25}{100} = 25\% \qquad \frac{75}{300} = \frac{75 \div 3}{300 \div 3} = \frac{25}{100} = 25\%$$

> One way to determine the relationship between sale price and donation amount is to find the percent.

Write an equation. Let p represent the sale price of the painting. Let d represent the donation amount to charity.

The donation amount is equal to 25% of the sale price.

$$d = 0.25 \cdot p$$

> p is the independent variable; its value does not depend on any other value. d is the dependent variable; its value depends on the price of the painting.

Find the donation amount when the sale price is $1,200.

$d = 0.25 \cdot p$

$d = 0.25 \cdot 1{,}200$ Substitute $ 1,200 for the sale price of the painting.

$d = 300$ Simplify to find the donation amount.

When the sale price is $1,200, the donation to charity is $300.

Justify and Evaluate

Substitute values from the table for p and d to check that they are solutions of the equation $d = 0.25 \cdot p$. Then check your answer of $300 by substituting for d and solving for p.

$d = 0.25 \cdot p$	$d = 0.25 \cdot p$	$d = 0.25 \cdot p$
$d = 0.25 \cdot 200$	$d = 0.25 \cdot 300$	$300 = 0.25 \cdot p$
$d = 50$ ✓	$d = 75$ ✓	$p = 1{,}200$ ✓

YOUR TURN

6. When Ryan is 10, his brother Kyle is 15. When Ryan is 16, Kyle will be 21. When Ryan is 21, Kyle will be 26. Write and solve an equation to find Kyle's age when Ryan is 52.

_____

Guided Practice

Write an equation to express y in terms of x. (Explore Activity, Example 1)

1.
x	10	20	30	40
y	6	16	26	36

_____

2.
x	0	1	2	3
y	0	4	8	12

_____

3.
x	4	6	8	10
y	7	9	11	13

_____

4.
x	12	24	36	48
y	2	4	6	8

_____

5. Jameson downloaded one digital song for $1.35, two digital songs for $2.70, and 5 digital songs for $6.75. Write and solve an equation to find the cost to download 25 digital songs. (Example 2)

Songs downloaded	1	2	5	10
Total cost ($)	1.35			

Number of songs = n; Cost = _____

The total cost of 25 songs is _____

? ESSENTIAL QUESTION CHECK-IN

6. Explain how to use a table to write an equation that represents the relationship in the table.

_____

_____

© Houghton Mifflin Harcourt Publishing Company

12.3 Independent Practice

FL 6.EE.3.9

7. Vocabulary What does it mean for an equation to express y in terms of x?

_____

_____

_____

8. The length of a rectangle is 2 inches more than twice its width.

Write an equation relating the length l of the rectangle to its width w.

_____

9. Look for a Pattern Compare the y-values in the table to the corresponding x-values. What pattern do you see? How is this pattern used to write an equation that represents the relationship between the x- and y-values?

x	20	24	28	32
y	5	6	7	8

_____

_____

_____

10. Explain the Error A student modeled the relationship in the table with the equation $x = 4y$. Explain the student's error. Write an equation that correctly models the relationship.

x	2	4	6	8
y	8	16	24	32

_____

_____

11. Multistep Marvin earns $8.25 per hour at his summer job. He wants to buy a video game system that costs $206.25.

a. Write an equation to model the relationship between number of hours worked h and amount earned e.

_____

b. Solve your equation to find the number of hours Marvin needs to work in order to afford the video game system.

_____

12. Communicate Mathematical Ideas For every hour that Noah studies, his test score goes up 3 points. Explain which is the independent variable and which is the dependent variable. Write an equation modeling the relationship between hours studied h and the increase in Noah's test score s.

_____

_____

_____

13. Make a Conjecture Compare the y-values in the table to the corresponding x-values. Determine whether there is an additive relationship or a multiplicative relationship between x and y. If possible, write an equation modeling the relationship. If, not explain why.

x	1	3	5	7
y	3	6	8	21

_____

_____

14. Represent Real-World Problems Describe a real-world situation in which there is an additive or multiplicative relationship between two quantities. Make a table that includes at least three pairs of values. Then write an equation that models the relationship between the quantities.

_____

_____

_____

15. Critical Thinking Georgia knows that there is either an additive or multiplicative relationship between x and y. She only knows a single pair of data values. Explain whether Georgia has enough information to write an equation that models the relationship between x and y.

_____

_____

_____

_____

Work Area

Representing Algebraic Relationships in Tables and Graphs

 FL 6.EE.3.9
...Analyze the relationship between the dependent and independent variables using graphs and tables, and relate these to the equation.

? ESSENTIAL QUESTION

How can you use verbal descriptions, tables, and graphs to represent algebraic relationships?

EXPLORE ACTIVITY 1 *Real World* **FL** 6.EE.3.9

Representing Algebraic Relationships

Angie's walking speed is 5 kilometers per hour, and May's is 4 kilometers per hour. Show how the distance each girl walks is related to time.

A For each girl, make a table comparing time and distance.

Time (h)	0	1	2	3	4
Angie's distance (km)	0	5	10		

For every hour Angie walks, she travels 5 km.

Time (h)	0	1	2	3	4
May's distance (km)	0	4	8		

For every hour May walks, she travels 4 km.

B For each girl, make a graph showing her distance *y* as it depends on time *x*. Plot points from the table and connect them with a line. Write an equation for each girl that relates distance *y* to time *x*.

Math Talk
Mathematical Practices

Why does it make sense to connect the points in each graph?

Angie's equation: _____   May's equation: _____

Reflect

1. Analyze Relationships How can you use the tables to determine which girl is walking faster? How can you use the graphs?

_____

_____

Real World

FL 6.EE.3.9

Writing an Equation from a Graph

Cherise pays the entrance fee to visit a museum, then buys souvenirs at the gift shop. The graph shows the relationship between the total amount she spends at the museum and the amount she spends at the gift shop. Write an equation to represent the relationship.

A Read the ordered pairs from the graph. Use them to complete a table comparing total spent *y* to amount spent at the gift shop *x*.

Gift shop amount ($)	0	5	10	15	
Total amount ($)	5	10			

B What is the pattern in the table?

_____

_____

_____

C Write an equation that expresses the total amount spent, *y*, in terms of the amount spent at the gift shop, *x*.

_____

Reflect

2. Communicate Mathematical Ideas Identify the dependent and independent quantities in this situation.

_____

_____

_____

3. Multiple Representations Draw a line through the points on the graph. Find the point that represents Cherise spending $18 at the gift shop. Use this point to find the total she would spend if she spent $18 at the gift shop. Then use your equation from **c** to verify your answer.

_____

_____

Graphing an Equation

An ordered pair (x, y) that makes an equation like $y = x + 1$ true is called a **solution** of the equation. The graph of an equation represents all the ordered pairs that are solutions.

EXAMPLE 1

 FL 6.EE.3.9

Graph each equation.

A $y = x + 1$

STEP 1 Make a table of values. Choose some values for x and use the equation to find the corresponding values for y.

STEP 2 Plot the ordered pairs from the table.

STEP 3 Draw a line through the plotted points to represent all of the ordered pair solutions of the equation.

x	x + 1 = y	(x, y)
1	1 + 1 = 2	(1, 2)
2	2 + 1 = 3	(2, 3)
3	3 + 1 = 4	(3, 4)
4	4 + 1 = 5	(4, 5)
5	5 + 1 = 6	(5, 6)

Math Talk
Mathematical Practices

Is the ordered pair (3.5, 4.5) a solution of the equation $y = x + 1$? Explain.

B $y = 2x$

STEP 1 Make a table of values. Choose some values for x and use the equation to find the corresponding values for y.

STEP 2 Plot the ordered pairs from the table.

STEP 3 Draw a line through the plotted points to represent all of the ordered pair solutions of the equation.

x	2x = y	(x, y)
1	2 × 1 = 2	(1, 2)
2	2 × 2 = 4	(2, 4)
3	2 × 3 = 6	(3, 6)
4	2 × 4 = 8	(4, 8)
5	2 × 5 = 10	(5, 10)

Personal
Math Trainer
Online Assessment
and Intervention
my.hrw.com

4. Graph $y = x + 2.5$.

x	x + 2.5 = y	(x, y)

Guided Practice

Frank mows lawns in the summer to earn extra money. He can mow 3 lawns every hour he works. (Explore Activity 1 and Explore Activity 2)

1. Make a table to show the relationship between the number of hours Frank works, *x*, and the number of lawns he mows, *y*. Graph the relationship and write an equation. Label the axes of your graph.

Hours worked	Lawns mowed
0	
1	

_____

Graph $y = 1.5x$. (Example 1)

2. Make a table to show the relationship.

x				
y				

3. Plot the points and draw a line through them.

? **ESSENTIAL QUESTION CHECK-IN**

4. How can a table represent an algebraic relationship between two variables?

_____

_____

© Houghton Mifflin Harcourt Publishing Company

12.4 Independent Practice

FL 6.EE.3.9

Personal
Math Trainer

Online
Assessment and
Intervention

my.hrw.com

Students at Mills Middle School are required to work a certain number of community service hours. The table shows the numbers of additional hours several students worked beyond their required hours, as well as the total numbers of hours worked.

5. Read the ordered pairs from the graph to make a table.

Additional hours					
Total hours					

6. Write an equation that expresses the total hours in terms of the additional hours.

_____

7. Analyze Relationships How many community service hours are students required to work? Explain.

_____

_____

Beth is using a map. Let x represent a distance in centimeters on the map. To find an actual distance y in kilometers, Beth uses the equation $y = 8x$.

8. Make a table comparing a distance on the map to the actual distance.

Map distance (cm)				
Actual distance (km)				

9. Make a graph that compares the map distance to the actual distance. Label the axes of the graph.

10. Critical Thinking The actual distance between Town A and Town B is 64 kilometers. What is the distance on Beth's map? Did you use the graph or the equation to find the answer? Why?

_____

_____

_____

11. Multistep The equation $y = 9x$ represents the total cost y for x movie tickets. Label the axes of the graph.

a. Make a table and a graph to represent the relationship between x and y.

Number of tickets, x					
Total cost ($), y					

b. **Critical Thinking** In this situation, which quantity is dependent and which is independent? Justify your answer.

_____

_____

_____

c. **Multiple Representations** Eight friends want to go see a movie. Would you prefer to use an equation, a table, or a graph to find the cost of 8 movie tickets? Explain how you would use your chosen method to find the cost.

_____

_____

Work Area

12. Critical Thinking Suppose you graph $y = 5x$ and $y = x + 500$ on the same coordinate plane. Which line will be steeper? Why?

_____

_____

13. Persevere in Problem Solving Marcus plotted the points (0, 0), (6, 2), (18, 6), and (21, 7) on a graph. He wrote an equation for the relationship. Find another ordered pair that could be a solution of Marcus's equation. Justify your answer.

_____

_____

14. Error Analysis The cost of a personal pizza is $4. A drink costs $1. Anna wrote the equation $y = 4x + 1$ to represent the relationship between total cost y of buying x meals that include one personal pizza and one drink. Describe Anna's error and write the correct equation.

_____

_____

© Houghton Mifflin Harcourt Publishing Company

Ready to Go On?

Personal
Math Trainer

Online Assessment
and Intervention

my.hrw.com

12.1 Graphing on the Coordinate Plane

Graph each point on the coordinate plane.

1. $A(-2, 4)$ **2.** $B(3, 5)$

3. $C(6, -4)$ **4.** $D(-3, -5)$

5. $E(7, 2)$ **6.** $F(-4, 6)$

12.2 Independent and Dependent Variables in Tables and Graphs

7. Jon buys packages of pens for $5 each. Identify the independent and dependent variables in the situation.

_____

12.3 Writing Equations from Tables

Write an equation that represents the data in the table.

8.

x	3	5	8	10
y	21	35	56	70

9.

x	5	10	15	20
y	17	22	27	32

12.4 Representing Algebraic Relationships in Tables and Graphs

Graph each equation.

10. $y = x + 3$

11. $y = 5x$

? ESSENTIAL QUESTION

12. How can you write an equation in two variables to solve a problem?

_____

_____

MODULE 12 MIXED REVIEW

Assessment Readiness

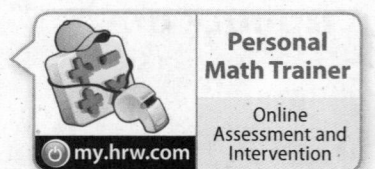

Personal
Math Trainer

Online
Assessment and
Intervention

my.hrw.com

Selected Response

1. What are the coordinates of point *G* on the coordinate grid below?

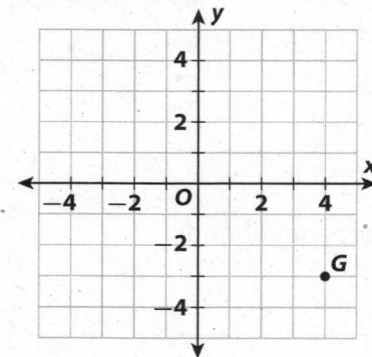

Ⓐ (4, 3)   Ⓒ (−4, 3)

Ⓑ (4, −3)   Ⓓ (−4, −3)

2. A point is located in quadrant II of a coordinate plane. Which of the following could be the coordinates of that point?

Ⓐ (−5, −7)   Ⓒ (−5, 7)

Ⓑ (5, 7)   Ⓓ (5, −7)

3. Matt had 5 library books. He checked 1 additional book out every week without returning any books. Which equation describes the number of books he has, *y*, after *x* weeks?

Ⓐ $y = 5x$ Ⓒ $y = 1 + 5x$

Ⓑ $y = 5 − x$ Ⓓ $y = 5 + x$

4. Stewart is playing a video game. He earns the same number of points for each prize he captures. He earned 1,200 points for 6 prizes, 2,000 points for 10 prizes, and 2,600 points for 13 prizes. Which is the dependent variable in the situation?

Ⓐ the number of prizes captured

Ⓑ the number of points earned

Ⓒ the number of hours

Ⓓ the number of prizes available

5. Which point is *not* on the graph of the equation $y = 10 + x$?

Ⓐ (0, 10)   Ⓒ (8, 2)

Ⓑ (3, 13)   Ⓓ (5, 15)

6. Amy gets paid by the hour. Her sister helps. As shown, Amy gives her sister part of her earnings. Which equation represents Amy's pay when her sister's pay is $13?

Amy's pay in dollars	10	20	30	40
Sister's pay in dollars	2	4	6	8

Ⓐ $y = \frac{13}{5}$ Ⓒ $5 = 13y$

Ⓑ $13 = \frac{x}{5}$ Ⓓ $13 = 5x$

Mini-Task

7. The table compares the ages, in years, of two cousins.

Ann's age, *x*	4	8	12
Tom's age, *y*	8	12	16

a. Write an equation that compares Tom's and Ann's ages.

_____

b. Draw a graph to represent the equation.

Study Guide Review

MODULE 11 ▶ Equations and Relationships

Key Vocabulary

equation *(ecuación)*

solution *(solución)*

solution of an inequality
(solución de una desigualdad)

? ESSENTIAL QUESTION

How can you use equations and relationships to solve real-world problems?

EXAMPLE 1

Determine if the given value is a solution of the equation.

A. $r - 5 = 17; r = 12$

$12 - 5 \overset{?}{=} 17$ Substitute.

$7 \neq 17$

12 is not a solution of $r - 5 = 17$.

B. $\frac{x}{6} = 7; x = 42$

$\frac{42}{6} \overset{?}{=} 7$ Substitute.

$7 = 7$

42 is a solution of $\frac{x}{6} = 7$.

EXAMPLE 2

Solve each equation. Check your answer.

A. $y - 12 = 10$

$\underline{+12 \quad +12}$ Add 12 to both sides.

$y = 22$

Check: $22 - 12 \overset{?}{=} 10$ Substitute.

$10 = 10$

B. $5p = 30$

$\frac{5p}{5} = \frac{30}{5}$ Divide both sides by 5.

$p = 6$

Check: $5(6) \overset{?}{=} 30$ Substitute.

$30 = 30$

EXAMPLE 3

Write and graph an inequality to represent each situation.

A. There are at least 5 gallons of water in an aquarium.

$g \geq 5$

B. The temperature today will be less than 35 °F.

$t < 35$

EXERCISES

Determine whether the given value is a solution of the equation. (Lesson 11.1)

1. $7x = 14; x = 3$ _____

2. $y + 13 = 17; y = 4$ _____

Write an equation to represent the situation. (Lesson 11.1)

3. Don has three times as much money as his brother, who has $25. _____

4. There are *s* students enrolled in Mr. Rodriguez's class. There are

6 students absent and 18 students present today. _____

Solve each equation. Check your answer. (Lessons 11.2, 11.3)

5. $p - 5 = 18$ _____ **6.** $9q = 18.9$ _____

7. $3.5 + x = 7$ _____ **8.** $\frac{2}{7} = 2x$ _____

9. Sonia used $12.50 to buy a new journal. She has $34.25 left in her savings account. How much money did Sonia have before she bought the journal? Write and solve an equation to solve

the problem. (Lesson 11.2) _____

Write and graph an inequality to represent each situation.
(Lesson 11.4)

10. The company's stock is worth less than

$2.50 per share. _____

11. Tina got a haircut, and her hair is still at least

15 inches long. _____

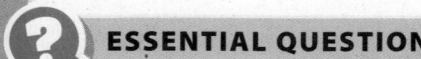

MODULE **12**   # Relationships in Two Variables

? ESSENTIAL QUESTION

How can you use relationships in two variables to solve real-world problems?

EXAMPLE 1

Graph the point (4, −2) and identify the quadrant where it is located.

(4, −2) is located 4 units
to the right of the origin and 2 units
down from the origin.

(4, −2) is in quadrant IV.

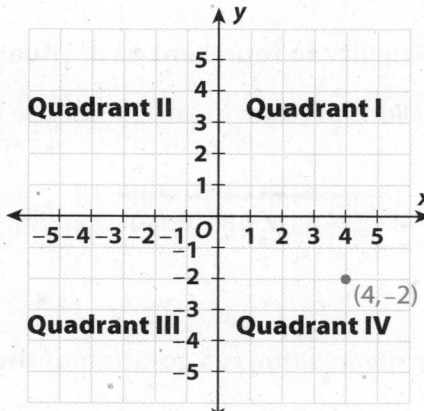

Key Vocabulary

axes *(ejes)*
coordinate plane *(plano cartesiano)*
coordinates *(coordenadas)*
ordered pair *(par ordenado)*
origin *(origen)*
quadrants *(cuadrantes)*
x-axis *(eje x)*

EXAMPLE 2

Tim is paid $8 more than the number of bags of peanuts he sells at the baseball stadium. The table shows the relationship between the money Tim earns and the number of bags of peanuts Tim sells. Identify the independent and dependent variables, and write an equation that represents the relationship.

Bags of peanuts, x	0	1	2	3
Money earned, y	8	9	10	11

The number of bags is the independent variable, and the money Tim earns is the dependent variable.

The equation $y = x + 8$ expresses the relationship between the number of bags Tim sells and the amount he earns.

EXERCISES

Graph and label each point on the coordinate plane. (Lesson 12.1)

1. (4, 4)

2. (−3, −1)

3. (−1, 4)

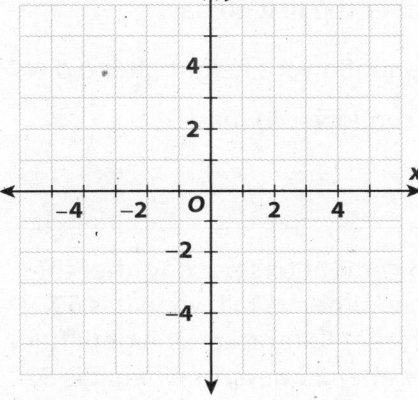

Use the graph to answer the questions. (Lesson 12.2)

4. What is the independent variable? _____

5. What is the dependent variable? _____

6. Describe the relationship between the independent variable and the dependent variable.

_____

7. Use the data in the table to write an equation to express *y* in terms of *x*. Then graph the equation.
(Lessons 12.3, 12.4)

x	0	1	2	3
y	4	5	6	7

_____

Unit 5 Performance Tasks

1. **CAREERS IN MATH** **Botanist** Dr. Adama is a botanist. She measures the daily height of a particular variety of sunflower, Sunny Yellow, beginning when the sunflower is 60 days old. At 60 days, the height of the sunflower is 205 centimeters. Dr. Adama finds that the growth rate of this sunflower is 2 centimeters per day after the first 60 days.

  a. Write an expression to represent the sunflower's height after *d* days. _____

  b. How many days does it take for the sunflower to reach 235 centimeters? Show your work.

  _____

  c. The Suntracker grows at a rate of 2.5 centimeters per day after the first 60 days. If this sunflower is 195 centimeters tall when it is 60 days old, write an expression to represent Suntracker's height after *d* days. Which sunflower will be taller after 22 days, or when it is 82 days old? Explain how you found your answer.

  _____

  _____

2. Vernon practiced soccer $5\frac{3}{4}$ hours this week. He practiced $4\frac{1}{3}$ hours on weekdays and the rest over the weekend.

  a. Write an equation that represents the situation. Define your variable.

  _____

  _____

  b. What is the least common multiple of the denominators of $5\frac{3}{4}$ and $4\frac{1}{3}$? Show your work.

  _____

  c. Solve the equation and interpret the solution. Show your work.

  _____

  _____

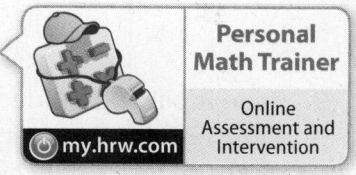

1. Using the expression $7x = 3y$, if y is 35, what is x?

(A) 15

(B) 21

(C) 35

(D) 105

2. Bruce has 97 sports cards. 34 of them are football cards. Which equation can be used to find the number of sports cards y that are not football cards?

(A) $97 + 34 = y$

(B) $y + 97 = 34$

(C) $34 + y = 97$

(D) $y - 97 = 34$

3. The overnight temperature in Tampa never reached below 40°F during November. Which inequality shows that?

(A) $x < 40$

(B) $x > 40$

(C) $x = 40$

(D) $x \geq 40$

4. Truman puts money into his savings account every time he gets paid. The table below shows how much he saves.

Amount Truman is paid	$15	$30	$45
Amount Truman saves	$1.50	$3	$4.50

Which of the following equations can be used to find the amount m Truman saves when he is paid $20?

(A) $m = 20(0.10)$

(C) $0.10m = 20$

(B) $20m = 0.10$

(D) $m = \frac{10}{20}$

5. No more than 7 copies of a newspaper are left in the newspaper rack. Which inequality represents this situation?

(A) $n < 7$

(B) $n \leq 7$

(C) $n > 7$

(D) $n \geq 7$

6. For which of the inequalities below is $v = 4$ a solution?

(A) $v + 5 \geq 9$

(B) $v + 5 > 9$

(C) $v + 5 \leq 8$

(D) $v + 5 < 8$

7. Sarah has read aloud in class 3 more times than Joel. Sarah has read 9 times. Which equation represents this situation?

(A) $j - 9 = 3$

(B) $3j = 9$

(C) $j - 3 = 9$

(D) $j + 3 = 9$

8. The number line below represents the solution to which inequality?

(A) $m > 4.4$

(B) $m > 5$

(C) $m < 4.4$

(D) $m < 4$

When possible, use logic to eliminate at least two answer choices.

© Houghton Mifflin Harcourt Publishing Company

9. Brian is playing a video game. He earns the same number of points for each star he picks up. He earned 2,400 points for 6 stars, 4,000 points for 10 stars, and 5,200 points for 13 stars. Which is the independent variable in the situation?

Ⓐ the number of stars picked up

Ⓑ the number of points earned

Ⓒ the number of hours played

Ⓓ the number of stars available

10. Which ratio is **not** equivalent to the other three?

Ⓐ $\frac{2}{5}$　　　　Ⓒ $\frac{6}{15}$

Ⓑ $\frac{12}{25}$　　　Ⓓ $\frac{18}{45}$

11. One inch is about 2.54 centimeters. About how many centimeters is 4.5 inches?

Ⓐ 1.8 centimeters

Ⓑ 11.4 centimeters

Ⓒ 13.7 centimeters

Ⓓ 114 centimeters

Mini-Tasks

12. Dana, Neil, and Frank are siblings. Dana is the oldest.

a. Frank's age is one-fourth of Dana's age. Write an equation to represent Frank's age *f* if Dana's age is *d* years.

_____

b. Neil's age is one-half of the difference between Dana's and Frank's ages. Write an equation to represent Neil's age *n* in terms of Dana's age *d*.

_____

c. Use the equations to find Neil's and Frank's ages if Dana is 16 years old.

_____

_____

13. Jillian is participating in a book reading contest to raise funds for her local library. For every book Jillian reads, her mother pledged to make a donation.

a. The table shows how much Jillian's mother will donate. Find the pattern, and finish the table.

Books Jillian reads	3	5	7	
Money Jillian's mother donates	$15	$25		

b. Write an equation showing the pattern from the table. Identify the variables.

_____

_____

_____

c. Graph the equation.

Relationships in Geometry

MODULE **13**
Area and Polygons
FL 6.G.1.1, 6.EE.2.7

MODULE **14**
Distance and Area in the Coordinate Plane
FL 6.NS.3.6b, 6.NS.3.8, 6.G.1.3

MODULE **15**
Surface Area and Volume of Solids
FL 6.G.1.2, 6.G.1.4, 6.EE.2.7

CAREERS IN MATH

Theater Set Construction A person who works in theater set construction works with the set designer to create scenery and needs technical precision when scaling and building sets based on the dimensions of the models.

If you are interested in a career in theater set construction, you should study these mathematical subjects:
- Geometry
- Algebra
- Trigonometry

Research other careers that require technical precision in scaling and building models.

Unit 6 Performance Task

At the end of the unit, check out how **theater set construction** workers use math.

Vocabulary Preview

Use the puzzle to preview key vocabulary from this unit. Unscramble the circled letters within found words to answer the riddle at the bottom of the page.

```
B Y W (P) R E V L P G E J Z V S
P Z O A V P R K L E B L F C U
D J M R Q W O E H Z B F Z O B
Z J W A (S) N B G L W W M C E M
K P O L G U I E G A G B Q S O
M N D L L R J V V E D J G H
Q E H Q L I F G S (I) S G Q (R)
Q T W L Y V D Y A O P M C N Q
O S O O E K B Z Z C B U D P B
Q B L G S K U E N E E L G C N
F H F R T S P L E C S A S I A
W Q F A T A L V D I (M) A R Y P
H L G M R I X G D Z F W W E W
X Y K T V A U P L V V J P C A
Z J H L K Q C A P I Q A D J L
```

- A quadrilateral where opposite sides are congruent and parallel. (Lesson 13.1)
- A quadrilateral in which all sides are congruent and opposite sides are parallel. (Lesson 13.1)
- A quadrilateral with exactly one pair of parallel sides. (Lesson 13.1)
- An arrangement of two-dimensional figures that can be folded to make a three-dimensional figure. (Lesson 15.1)
- A three-dimensional figure with a polygon base and where the other faces are triangles that all meet at a common vertex. (Lesson 15.1)
- The sum of the areas of the faces, or surfaces, of a three-dimensional figure. (Lesson 15.1)

Q: Where does a mathematician go when she commits a crime?

A: __ __ __ __ __!

Area and Polygons

ESSENTIAL QUESTION

How can you find the area of an irregular polygon using area formulas?

LESSON 13.1
Area of Quadrilaterals
 FL 6.G.1.1

LESSON 13.2
Area of Triangles
FL 6.G.1.1

LESSON 13.3
Solving Area Equations
 FL 6.G.1.1, 6.EE.2.7

LESSON 13.4
Area of Polygons
 FL 6.G.1.1

Real-World Video

Quilting, painting, and other art forms use familiar geometric shapes, such as triangles and rectangles. To buy enough supplies for a project, you need to find or estimate the areas of each shape in the project.

my.hrw.com

GO DIGITAL

my.hrw.com

my.hrw.com

Go digital with your write-in student edition, accessible on any device.

Math On the Spot

Scan with your smart phone to jump directly to the online edition, video tutor, and more.

Animated Math

Interactively explore key concepts to see how math works.

Personal Math Trainer

Get immediate feedback and help as you work through practice sets.

Are YOU Ready?

Complete these exercises to review skills you will need for this module.

Inverse Operations

EXAMPLES

$7k = 35$ k is multiplied by 7.
$\dfrac{7k}{7} = \dfrac{35}{7}$ Use the inverse operation, division.
$k = 5$

$k + 7 = 9$ 7 is added to k.
$k + 7 - 7 = 9 - 7$ Use the inverse operation, subtraction.
$k = 2$

Solve each equation using the inverse operation.

1. $9p = 54$ _____   **2.** $m - 15 = 9$ _____   **3.** $\dfrac{b}{8} = 4$ _____   **4.** $z + 17 = 23$ ____

Metric Units

EXAMPLE

$6\text{ m} = \blacksquare\text{ cm}$

$6\text{ m} = 600\text{ cm}$

Multiply to go from a larger unit to a smaller unit.

$4{,}000\text{ mL} = \blacksquare\text{ L}$

$4{,}000\text{ mL} = 4\text{ L}$

Divide to go from a smaller unit to a larger unit.

Convert to the given units.

5. $64\text{ m} =$ _____ cm   **6.** $500\text{ g} =$ _____ kg   **7.** $4.6\text{ kL} =$ _____ L

Area of Squares and Rectangles

EXAMPLE

7 ft

4 ft

Find the area of the rectangle.

$A = bh$
$= 7 \times 4$
$= 28$

Use the formula for the area of a rectangle. Substitute for base and height.

The area is 28 square feet.

8. Find the area of a rectangle with a base of 5 feet and a height

of $9\frac{1}{2}$ feet _____

Reading Start-Up

Visualize Vocabulary

Use the ✔ words to complete the graphic. You will put one word in each oval.

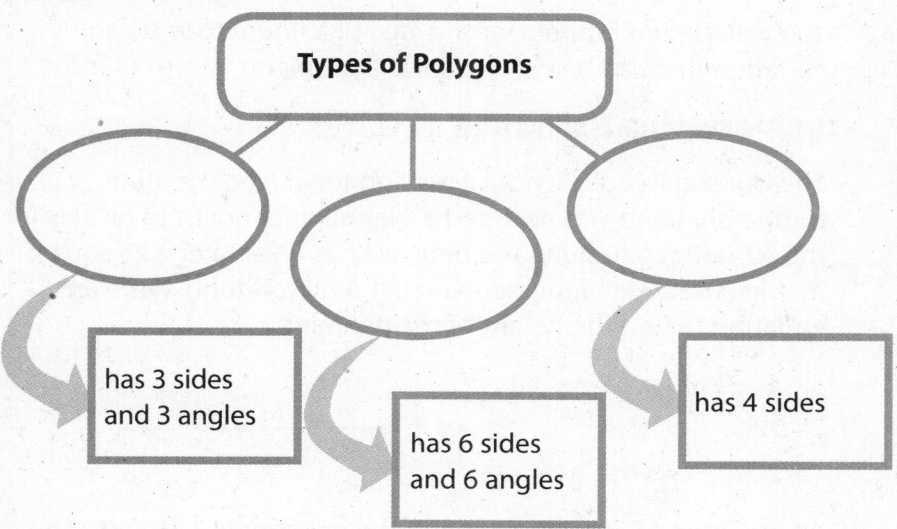

Types of Polygons

has 3 sides and 3 angles

has 6 sides and 6 angles

has 4 sides

Vocabulary

Review Words
- ✔ hexagon *(hexágono)*
- ✔ polygon *(polígono regular)*
- quadrilateral *(cuadrilátero)*
- rectangular prism *(prisma rectangular)*
- regular polygon *(polígono)*
- right triangle *(triángulo rectángulo)*
- ✔ triangle *(triángulo)*

Preview Words
- parallelogram *(paralelogramo)*
- rhombus *(rombo)*
- trapezoid *(trapecio)*

Understand Vocabulary

Match the term on the left to the correct expression on the right.

1. parallelogram   **A.** A quadrilateral in which all sides are congruent and opposite sides are parallel.

2. trapezoid   **B.** A quadrilateral in which opposite sides are parallel and congruent.

3. rhombus   **C.** A quadrilateral in which two sides are parallel.

Active Reading

Pyramid Before beginning the module, create a pyramid to help you organize what you learn. Label each side with one of the lesson titles from this module. As you study each lesson, write important ideas like vocabulary, properties, and formulas on the appropriate side.

Unpacking the Standards

Understanding the standards and the vocabulary terms in the standards will help you know exactly what you are expected to learn in this module.

FL 6.G.1.1

Find the area of right triangles, other triangles, special quadrilaterals, and polygons by composing into rectangles or decomposing into triangles and other shapes; apply these techniques in the context of solving real-world and mathematical problems.

What It Means to You

You will use the formula for the area of a figure to write an equation that can be used to solve a problem.

UNPACKING EXAMPLE 6.G.1.1

The Hudson Middle School wrestling team won the state tournament and was awarded a triangular pennant to display in the school gymnasium. The pennant has an area of 2.25 square meters. The base of the pennant is 1.5 meters long. Write an equation to find the height of the pennant.

$$A = \frac{1}{2}bh$$
$$2.25 = \frac{1}{2}(1.5)h$$
$$2.25 = 0.75h$$

1.5 m

An equation to find the height of the pennant is $2.25 = 0.75h$.

FL 6.G.1.1

Find the area of right triangles, other triangles, special quadrilaterals, and polygons by composing into rectangles or decomposing into triangles and other shapes; apply these techniques in the context of solving real-world and mathematical problems.

What It Means to You

You will use formulas to find the area of irregular polygons.

UNPACKING EXAMPLE 6.G.1.1

John is measuring his room for new carpet. Find the area of the room.

Find the area of the rectangle.

$A = bh = 15 \times 6 = 90$ ft²

Find the area of the square.

$A = s^2 = 6^2 = 36$ ft²

The total area is 90 ft² + 36 ft² = 126 ft².

6 ft

15 ft

6 ft

6 ft

Visit **my.hrw.com** to see all **Florida Math Standards** unpacked.

⏻ my.hrw.com

FL 6.G.1.1
Find the area of...special quadrilaterals, and polygons by composing into rectangles or decomposing into triangles and other shapes; ....

? **ESSENTIAL QUESTION**

How can you find the areas of parallelograms, rhombuses, and trapezoids?

EXPLORE ACTIVITY FL 6.G.1.1

Area of a Parallelogram

Recall that a rectangle is a special type of parallelogram.

A Draw a large parallelogram on grid paper. Cut out your parallelogram.

B Cut your parallelogram on the dashed line as shown. Then move the triangular piece to the other side of the parallelogram.

height (h)   base (b)   →   width (w)   length (l)

C What figure have you formed? _____

Does this figure have the same area as the parallelogram? _____

base of parallelogram = _____ of rectangle

height of parallelogram = _____ of rectangle

area of parallelogram = _____ of rectangle

What is the formula for the area of this figure? $A =$ _____

or · _____

D What is the formula for the area of a parallelogram? $A =$ _____

> **Math Talk**
> Mathematical Practices
>
> How is the relationship between the length and width of a rectangle similar to the relationship between the base and height of a parallelogram?

Area of a Parallelogram

The area A of a parallelogram is the product of its base b and its height h.

$$A = bh$$

h

b

Reflect

1. Find the area of the parallelogram.

A = _____

7 cm

14 cm

Math On the Spot

my.hrw.com

Finding the Area of a Trapezoid

To find the formula for the area of a trapezoid, notice that two copies of the same trapezoid fit together to form a parallelogram. Therefore, the area of the trapezoid is $\frac{1}{2}$ the area of the parallelogram.

h

b

The height of the parallelogram is the same as the height of the trapezoid. The base of the parallelogram is the sum of the two bases of the trapezoid.

$$A = \quad b \quad \cdot h$$
$$\downarrow$$
$$A = (b_1 + b_2) \cdot h$$

Area of a Trapezoid

The area of a trapezoid is half its height multiplied by the sum of the lengths of its two bases.

$$A = \frac{1}{2}h(b_1 + b_2)$$

b_1

h

b_2

EXAMPLE 1 Real World

FL 6.G.1.1

A section of a deck is in the shape of a trapezoid. What is the area of this section of the deck?

$b_1 = 17$ $b_2 = 39$ $h = 16$

17 ft

Use the formula for area of a trapezoid.

16 ft

39 ft

Math Talk

Mathematical Practices

Does it matter which of the trapezoid's bases is substituted for b_1 and which is substituted for b_2? Why or why not?

X^2

Animated Math

my.hrw.com

$A = \frac{1}{2}h(b_1 + b_2)$

$= \frac{1}{2} \cdot 16(17 + 39)$ Substitute.

$= \frac{1}{2} \cdot 16(56)$ Add inside the parentheses.

$= 8 \cdot 56$ Multiply $\frac{1}{2}$ and 16.

$= 448$ square feet   Multiply.

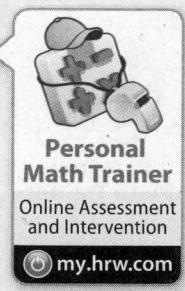

YOUR TURN

2. Another section of the deck is also shaped like a trapezoid. For this section, the length of one base is 27 feet, and the length of the other base is 34 feet. The height is 12 feet. What is the area of this section of the deck? $A =$ _____ ft²

Finding the Area of a Rhombus

A **rhombus** is a quadrilateral in which all sides are congruent and opposite sides are parallel. A rhombus can be divided into four triangles that can then be rearranged into a rectangle.

Math On the Spot

⊙ my.hrw.com

The base of the rectangle is the same length as one of the diagonals of the rhombus. The height of the rectangle is $\frac{1}{2}$ the length of the other diagonal.

$$A = b \cdot h$$
$$\downarrow \qquad \downarrow$$
$$A = d_1 \cdot \tfrac{1}{2}d_2$$

Area of a Rhombus

The area of a rhombus is half of the product of its two diagonals.

$$A = \frac{1}{2}d_1 d_2$$

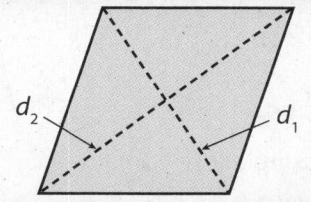

EXAMPLE 2   Real World   FL   6.G.1.1

Cedric is constructing a kite in the shape of a rhombus. The spars of the kite measure 15 inches and 24 inches. How much fabric will Cedric need for the kite?

To determine the amount of fabric needed, find the area of the kite.

$$d_1 = 15 \qquad d_2 = 24$$

Use the formula for area of a rhombus.

$$A = \frac{1}{2}d_1 d_2$$

$$= \frac{1}{2}(15)(24) \qquad \text{Substitute.}$$

$$= 180 \text{ square inches} \qquad \text{Multiply.}$$

15 in.

24 in.

YOUR TURN

Find the area of each rhombus.

3. $d_1 = 35$ m; $d_2 = 12$ m

   $A =$ _____ m²

4. $d_1 = 9.5$ in.; $d_2 = 14$ in.

   $A =$ _____ in²

5. $d_1 = 10$ m; $d_2 = 18$ m

   $A =$ _____ m²

6. $d_1 = 8\frac{1}{4}$ ft; $d_2 = 40$ ft

   $A =$ _____ ft²

Guided Practice

1. Find the area of the parallelogram. (Explore Activity)

   $A = bh$

   $= ($ _____ $)($ _____ $)$

   $=$ _____ in²

   9 in.

   13 in.

2. Find the area of the trapezoid. (Example 1)

   $A = \frac{1}{2}h(b_1 + b_2)$

   $= \frac{1}{2}\left(\bigcirc\right)\left(\bigcirc + \bigcirc\right)$

   $=$ _____ cm²

   9 cm

   14 cm

   15 cm

3. Find the area of the rhombus. (Example 2)

   $A = \frac{1}{2}d_1d_2$

   $= \frac{1}{2}\left(\bigcirc\right)\left(\bigcirc\right)$

   $=$ _____ in²

   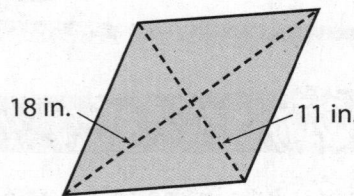

   18 in.   11 in.

? ESSENTIAL QUESTION CHECK-IN

4. How can you find the areas of parallelograms, rhombuses, and trapezoids?

   _____

   _____

   _____

   _____

13.1 Independent Practice

FL 6.G.1.1

Personal Math Trainer

Online Assessment and Intervention

my.hrw.com

5. Find the area of the parallelogram.

6 cm

14 cm

_____

6. What is the area of a parallelogram that has a base of $12\frac{3}{4}$ in. and a height of $2\frac{1}{2}$ in.?

_____

7. Find the area of the trapezoid.

42 in.

24 in.

36 in.

_____

8. The bases of a trapezoid are 11 meters and 14 meters. Its height is 10 meters. What is the area of the trapezoid?

_____

9. Find the area of the rhombus.

16 m   9 m

_____

10. The diagonals of a rhombus are 21 m and 32 m. What is the area of the rhombus?

_____

11. The seat of a bench is in the shape of a trapezoid with bases of 6 feet and 5 feet and a height of 1.5 feet. What is the area of the seat?

_____

12. A kite in the shape of a rhombus has diagonals that are 25 inches long and 15 inches long. What is the area of the kite?

_____

13. A window in the shape of a parallelogram has a base of 36 inches and a height of 45 inches. What is the area of the window?

_____

14. **Communicate Mathematical Ideas** Find the area of the figure. Explain how you found your answer.

10 ft

6 ft

12 ft

18 ft

_____

_____

_____

_____

_____

_____

_____

15. Multistep A parking space shaped like a parallelogram has a base of 17 feet and a height is 9 feet. A car parked in the space is 16 feet long and 6 feet wide. How much of the parking space is not covered by the car?

_____

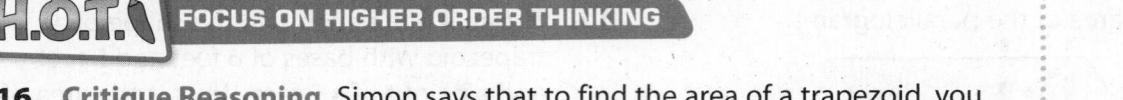

FOCUS ON HIGHER ORDER THINKING

© Houghton Mifflin Harcourt Publishing Company

Work Area

16. Critique Reasoning Simon says that to find the area of a trapezoid, you can multiply the height by the top base and the height by the bottom base. Then add the two products together and divide the sum by 2. Is Simon correct? Explain your answer.

_____

_____

_____

_____

17. Multistep The height of a trapezoid is 8 in. and its area is 96 in.^{2} One base of the trapezoid is 6 inches longer than the other base. What are the lengths of the bases? Explain how you found your answer.

_____

_____

_____

_____

_____

_____

18. Multiple Representations The diagonals of a rhombus are 12 in. and 16 in. long. The length of a side of the rhombus is 10 in. What is the height of the rhombus? Explain how you found your answer.

_____

_____

_____

_____

_____

_____

13.2 Area of Triangles

FL 6.G.1.1
Find the area of right triangles, other triangles, ... by composing into rectangles ...

? ESSENTIAL QUESTION

How do you find the area of a triangle?

EXPLORE ACTIVITY 1 FL 6.G.1.1

Area of a Right Triangle

A Draw a large rectangle on grid paper.

What is the formula for the area of a rectangle? $A = $ _____

B Draw one diagonal of your rectangle.

The diagonal divides the rectangle into _____.

Each one represents _____ of the rectangle.

Use this information and the formula for area of a rectangle to

write a formula for the area of a right triangle. $A = $ _____

Reflect

1. **Communicate Mathematical Ideas** In the formula for the area of a right triangle, what do b and h represent?

_____

EXPLORE ACTIVITY 2 FL 6.G.1.1

Area of a Triangle

A Draw a large triangle on grid paper. Do not draw a right triangle.

B Cut out your triangle. Then trace around it to make a copy of your triangle. Cut out the copy.

C Cut one of your triangles into two pieces by cutting through one angle directly across to the opposite side. Now you have three triangles — one large triangle and two smaller right triangles.

When added together, the areas of the two smaller triangles

equal the _____ of the large triangle.

D Arrange the three triangles into a rectangle.

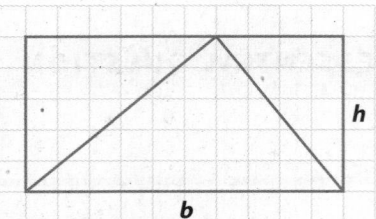

What fraction of the rectangle does the large

triangle represent? _____

The area of the rectangle is $A = bh$. What is the area

of the large triangle? $A =$ _____

How does this formula compare to the formula for the area
of a right triangle that you found in Explore Activity 1?

_____

Reflect

2. **Communicate Mathematical Ideas** What type of angle is formed by
   the base and height of a triangle?

   _____

Finding the Area of a Triangle

Area of a Triangle

The area A of a triangle is half the product
of its base b and its height h.

$$A = \tfrac{1}{2} bh$$

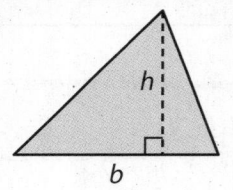

EXAMPLE 1

FL 6.G.1.1

Find the area of each triangle.

A

$b = 20$ meters $h = 8$ meters

$A = \tfrac{1}{2} bh$

$\quad = \tfrac{1}{2} (20 \text{ meters}) (8 \text{ meters})$ Substitute.

$\quad = 80$ square meters   Multiply.

Find the area of each triangle.

B

5 in.

12 in.

$b = 12$ inches $h = 5$ inches

$A = \frac{1}{2} bh$

$= \frac{1}{2}(12 \text{ inches})(5 \text{ inches})$ *Substitute.*

$= 30$ square inches   *Multiply.*

YOUR TURN

Find the area of the triangle.

3.

14 in.

8.5 in.

$A = \underline{\hspace{2cm}}$

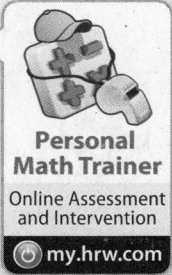

Personal Math Trainer

Online Assessment and Intervention

my.hrw.com

Math Talk

Mathematical Practices

Why can you also write the formula for the area of a triangle as $A = \frac{bh}{2}$?

Problem Solving Using Area of Triangles

You can use the formula for the area of a triangle to solve real-world problems.

Math On the Spot

my.hrw.com

EXAMPLE 2   Real World   FL 6.G.1.1

Each triangular face of the Pyramid of Peace in Kazakhstan is made up of 25 smaller equilateral triangles. These triangles have measurements as shown in the diagram. What is the area of one of the smaller equilateral triangles?

10.4 m

12 m

STEP 1   Identify the length of the base and the height of the triangle.

$b = 12$ m and $h = 10.4$ m

STEP 2   Use the formula to find the area of the triangle.

$A = \frac{1}{2} bh$ *Substitute.*

$= \frac{1}{2}(12)(10.4)$ *Multiply.*

$= 62.4$

The area of one small equilateral triangle is 62.4 m².

Reflect

4. Persevere in Problem Solving What is the total area of one face of the pyramid? What is the total surface area of the faces of the pyramid, not counting the bottom? (Hint: the bottom of the pyramid is a square.)

_____

_____

_____

Personal Math Trainer

Online Assessment and Intervention

⏱ my.hrw.com

YOUR TURN

5. Amy needs to order a shade for a triangular-shaped window that has a base of 6 feet and a height of 4 feet. What is the area of the shade?

_____

Guided Practice

Find the area of each triangle. (Explore Activities 1 and 2, Example 1)

1.

8 in.

14 in.

$A = \frac{1}{2} bh$

$= \frac{1}{2} (\underline{\hspace{1cm}}) (\underline{\hspace{1cm}})$

$= \underline{\hspace{1cm}}$ in^2

2. A pennant in the shape of a triangle has a base of 12 inches and a height of 30 inches. What is the area of the pennant? (Example 2)

$A = \frac{1}{2} bh$

$= \frac{1}{2} (\underline{\hspace{1cm}}) (\underline{\hspace{1cm}})$

$= \underline{\hspace{1cm}}$ in^2

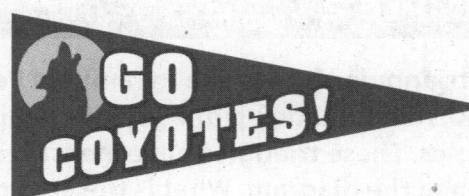

? ESSENTIAL QUESTION CHECK-IN

3. How do you find the area of a triangle?

_____

_____

_____

© Houghton Mifflin Harcourt Publishing Company

13.2 Independent Practice

FL 6.G.1.1

Personal Math Trainer

Online Assessment and Intervention

my.hrw.com

Find the area of each triangle.

4.

10 cm
15 cm

_____

5.

20 ft
24 ft

_____

6.

17 in.
12 in.

_____

7.

18 ft
32 ft

_____

8. What is the area of a triangle that has a base of $15\frac{1}{4}$ in. and a height of 18 in.?

_____

9. A right triangle has legs that are 11 in. and 13 in. long. What is the area of the triangle?

_____

10. A triangular plot of land has the dimensions shown in the diagram. What is the area of the land?

_____

11. The front part of a tent has the dimensions shown in the diagram. What is the area of this part of the tent?

_____

20 km
30 km

5 ft
8 ft

12. Multistep The sixth-grade art students are making a mosaic using tiles in the shape of right triangles. Each tile has leg measures of 3 centimeters and 5 centimeters. If there are 200 tiles in the mosaic, what is the area of the mosaic?

_____

13. Critique Reasoning Monica has a triangular piece of fabric. The height of the triangle is 15 inches and the triangle's base is 6 inches. Monica says that the area of the fabric is 90 in.^{2}. What error did Monica make? Explain your answer.

_____

_____

14. Multistep Wayne is going to paint the side of the house shown in the diagram. What is the area that will be painted? Explain how you found your answer.

_____

_____

_____

8 ft

12 ft

25 ft

Work Area

15. Communicate Mathematical Ideas Explain how the areas of a triangle and a parallelogram with the same base and height are related.

_____

_____

_____

_____

_____

16. Analyze Relationships A rectangle and a triangle have the same area. If their bases are the same lengths, how do their heights compare? Justify your answer.

_____

_____

_____

_____

_____

_____

17. What If? A right triangle has an area of 18 square inches.

a. If the triangle is an isosceles triangle, what are the lengths of the legs of the triangle?

_____

b. If the triangle is not an isosceles triangle, what are all the possible lengths of the legs, if the lengths are whole numbers?

_____

_____

LESSON 13.3 Solving Area Equations

FL 6.G.1.1

Find the area of right triangles, other triangles, special quadrilaterals, and polygons...; apply these techniques in the context of solving...problems. *Also 6.EE.2.7*

? ESSENTIAL QUESTION

How do you use equations to solve problems about area of rectangles, parallelograms, trapezoids, and triangles?

Problem Solving Using the Area of a Triangle

Recall that the formula for the area of a triangle is $A = \frac{1}{2}bh$. You can also use the formula to find missing dimensions if you know the area and one dimension.

Math On the Spot

⏻ my.hrw.com

EXAMPLE 1 Real World

FL 6.G.1.1, 6.EE.2.7

The Hudson High School wrestling team just won the state tournament and has been awarded a triangular pennant to hang on the wall in the school gymnasium. The base of the pennant is 1.5 feet long. It has an area of 2.25 square feet. What is the height of the pennant?

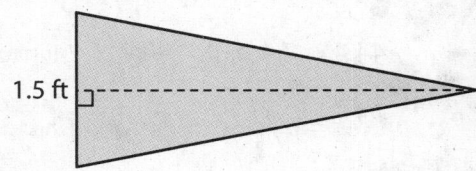

1.5 ft

$A = \frac{1}{2}bh$ Write the formula.

$2.25 = \frac{1}{2}(1.5)h$ Use the formula to write an equation.

$2.25 = 0.75h$ Multiply $\frac{1}{2}$ and 1.5.

$\dfrac{2.25}{0.75} = \dfrac{0.75h}{0.75}$ Divide both sides of the equation by 0.75.

$3 = h$

The height of the pennant is 3 feet.

Math Talk
Mathematical Practices

How can you use units in the formula to confirm that the units for the height are in feet?

© Houghton Mifflin Harcourt Publishing Company

YOUR TURN

1. Renee is sewing a quilt whose pattern contains right triangles. Each quilt piece has a height of 6 in. and an area of 24 in².

   How long is the base of each quilt piece? _____

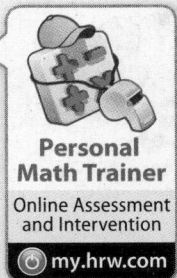

Personal Math Trainer

Online Assessment and Intervention

⏻ my.hrw.com

Writing Equations Using the Area of a Trapezoid

You can use the formula for area of a trapezoid to write an equation to solve a problem.

EXAMPLE 2   **FL** 6.G.1.1, 6.EE.2.7

A garden in the shape of a trapezoid has an area of 44.4 square meters. One base is 4.3 meters long and the other base is 10.5 meters long. The height of the trapezoid is the width of the garden. How wide is the garden?

4.3 m

10.5 m

$A = \frac{1}{2} h (b_1 + b_2)$ Write the formula.

$44.4 = \frac{1}{2} h (4.3 + 10.5)$ Use the formula to write an equation.

$44.4 = \frac{1}{2} h (14.8)$ Add inside parentheses.

$44.4 = 7.4 h$ Multiply $\frac{1}{2}$ and 14.8.

$\frac{44.4}{7.4} = \frac{7.4 h}{7.4}$ Divide both sides of the equation by 7.4.

$6 = h$

The garden is 6 meters wide.

Math Talk
Mathematical Practices
How can you check that the answer is reasonable?

Reflect

2. **Communicate Mathematical Ideas** Explain why the first step after substituting is addition.

_____

_____

_____

_____

YOUR TURN

3. The cross section of a water bin is shaped like a trapezoid. The bases of the trapezoid are 18 feet and 8 feet long. It has an area of 52 square feet. What is the height of the cross section?

_____

© Houghton Mifflin Harcourt Publishing Company

Solving Multistep Problems

You can write and solve equations that represent real-world problems related to relationships in geometry.

EXAMPLE 3 Problem Solving FL 6.G.1.1

John and Mary are using rolls of fabric to make a rectangular stage curtain for their class play. The rectangular piece of fabric on each roll measures 2.5 feet by 15 feet. If the area of the curtain is 200 square feet, what is the least number of rolls they need?

Analyze Information

Rewrite the question as a statement.

- Find the least number of rolls of fabric needed to cover an area of 200 ft^2.

List the important information.

- Each roll of fabric is a 2.5 foot by 15 foot rectangle.
- The area of the curtain is 200 square feet.

Formulate a Plan

Write an equation to find the area of each roll of fabric.

Use the area of the curtain and the area of each roll to write an equation to find the least number of rolls.

Solve

STEP 1 Write an equation to find the area of each roll of fabric.

$$A = lw$$
$$A = 15 \cdot 2.5$$
$$A = 37.5 \text{ ft}^2$$

STEP 2 Write an equation to find the least number of rolls.

$$n = 200 \div 37.5$$
$$n = 5\frac{1}{3}$$

STEP 3 The problem asks for the least number of rolls needed. Since 5 rolls will not be enough, they will need 6 rolls to make the curtain.

John and Mary will need 6 rolls of fabric to make the curtain.

Justify and Evaluate

The area of each roll is about 38 ft^2. Since 38 ft^2 · 6 = 228 ft^2, the answer is reasonable:

YOUR TURN

4. A parallelogram-shaped field in a park needs sod. The parallelogram has a base of 21.5 meters and a height of 18 meters. The sod is sold in pallets of 50 square meters. How many pallets of sod are needed to fill the field?

_____

Guided Practice

1. A triangular bandana has an area of 70 square inches. The height of the triangle is $8\frac{3}{4}$ inches. Write and solve an equation to find the length of the base of the triangle. (Example 1)

_____

2. The top of a desk is shaped like a trapezoid. The bases of the trapezoid are 26.5 and 30 centimeters long. The area of the desk is 791 square centimeters. The height of the trapezoid is the width of the desk. Write and solve an equation to find the width of the desk. (Example 2)

_____

3. Taylor wants to paint his rectangular deck that is 42 feet long and 28 feet wide. A gallon of paint covers about 350 square feet. How many gallons of paint will Taylor need to cover the entire deck? (Example 3)

Write an equation to find the _____ of the deck.

Write and solve the equation.

Write an equation to find the _____.

Write and solve the equation.

Taylor will need _____ gallons of paint.

? ESSENTIAL QUESTION CHECK-IN

4. How do you use equations to solve problems about area of rectangles, parallelograms, trapezoids, and triangles?

_____

13.3 Independent Practice

FL 6.G.1.1, 6.EE.2.7

Personal Math Trainer

Online
Assessment and
Intervention

my.hrw.com

5. A window shaped like a parallelogram has an area of $18\frac{1}{3}$ square feet. The height of the window is $3\frac{1}{3}$ feet. How long is the base of the window?

_____

6. A triangular sail has a base length of 2.5 meters. The area of the sail is 3.75 square meters. How tall is the sail?

_____

7. A section in a stained glass window is shaped like a trapezoid. The top base is 4 centimeters and the bottom base is 2.5 centimeters long. If the area of the section of glass is 3.9 square centimeters, how tall is the section?

_____

8. Multistep Amelia wants to paint three walls in her family room. Two walls are 26 feet long by 9 feet wide. The other wall is 18 feet long by 9 feet wide.

   a. What is the total area of the walls that Amelia wants to paint?

_____

   b. Each gallon of paint covers about 250 square feet. How many gallons of paint should Amelia buy to paint the walls?

_____

9. Critical Thinking The area of a triangular block is 64 square inches. If the base of the triangle is twice the height, how long are the base and the height of the triangle?

_____

10. Multistep Alex needs to varnish the top and the bottom of a dozen rectangular wooden planks. The planks are 8 feet long and 3 feet wide. Each pint of varnish covers about 125 square feet and costs $3.50.

   a. What is the total area that Alex needs to varnish?

_____

   b. How much will it cost Alex to varnish all the wooden planks?

_____

11. Multistep Leia cuts congruent triangular patches with an area of 45 square centimeters from a rectangular piece of fabric that is 18 centimeters long and 10 centimeters wide. How many of the patches can Leia cut from 32 pieces of the fabric?

12. Multistep A farmer needs to buy fertilizer for two fields. One field is shaped like a trapezoid, and the other is shaped like a triangle. The trapezoidal field has bases that are 35 and 48 yards and a height of 26 yards. The triangular field has the same height as the trapezoidal field and a base of 39 yards. Each bag of fertilizer covers 150 square yards. How many bags of fertilizer does the farmer need to buy?

_____

13. A tennis court for singles play is 78 feet long and 27 feet wide.

   a. The court for doubles play is 9 feet wider than the court for singles play. How much more area is covered by the tennis court used for doubles play?

     _____

   b. The junior court for players 8 and under is 36 feet long and 18 feet wide. How much more area is covered by the tennis court used for singles play?

     _____

   c. The court for players 10 and under is 18 feet shorter than the court for singles play. How much more area is covered by the tennis court used for singles play?

     _____

14. Draw Conclusions The cross section of a metal ingot is a trapezoid. The cross section has an area of 39 square centimeters. The top base of the cross section is 12 centimeters. The length of the bottom base is 2 centimeters greater than the top base. How tall is the metal ingot? Explain.

_____

_____

_____

 FOCUS ON HIGHER ORDER THINKING

Work Area

15. Analyze Relationships A mirror is made of two congruent parallelograms as shown in the diagram. The parallelograms have a combined area of $9\frac{1}{3}$ square yards. The height of each parallelogram is $1\frac{1}{3}$ yards.

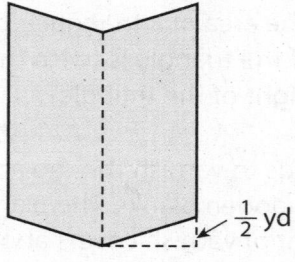

$\frac{1}{2}$ yd

   a. How long is the base of each parallelogram?

_____

   b. What is the area of the smallest *rectangle* of wall that the mirror could fit on?

_____

16. Persevere in Problem Solving
A watercolor painting is 20 inches long by 9 inches wide. Ramon makes a border around the watercolor painting by making a mat that adds 1 inch to each side of the length and the width. What is the area of the mat?

1 in.

20 in.

9 in.

_____

© Houghton Mifflin Harcourt Publishing Company

13.4 Area of Polygons

FL 6.G.1.1
Find the area of ... polygons by composing into rectangles or decomposing into triangles and other shapes ....

? ESSENTIAL QUESTION

How can you find the area of a polygon by breaking it into simpler shapes?

EXPLORE ACTIVITY **FL** 6.G.1.1

Finding Areas Using Tangrams

A tangram is a square that is divided into smaller shapes. The area of the small square is 1 square unit. Use a tangram to find the area of each of the other tangram pieces.

A Place one large triangle on top of the other large triangle. What is true about these two triangles? What does this mean about the areas of these two triangles?

_____

B Place the two small triangles on top of the square. What is the area of each small triangle? Write this area on the diagram. _____

C Arrange the square and one of the small triangles as shown.

What is the combined area? _____

Place the parallelogram and the other small triangle on top of the combined square and triangle. What is the area of the parallelogram? Explain.

_____

_____

_____

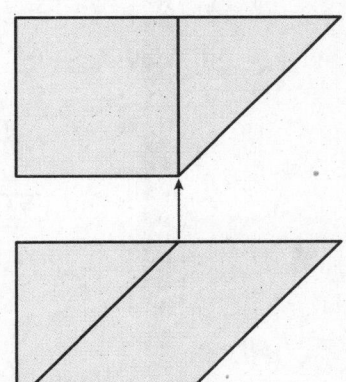

Reflect

1. Critical Thinking Complete the rest of the diagram by filling in the remaining areas. Explain how you found your answers.

_____

_____

© Houghton Mifflin Harcourt Publishing Company

Finding Areas of Polygons

You can find the areas of polygons by breaking the polygons into smaller shapes. Then you can apply area formulas you already know.

EXAMPLE 1   FL 6.G.1.1

Find the area of each polygon.

A **STEP 1** Draw a horizontal line segment on the diagram that divides the polygon into a rectangle and a triangle.

STEP 2 Find the area of the rectangle.

$A = bh = 16 \cdot 7 = \textbf{112}$ square centimeters

STEP 3 Find the area of the triangle.

$b = 16 - 8 = 8$ $h = 13 - 7 = 6$

$A = \frac{1}{2}bh = \frac{1}{2} \cdot 8 \cdot 6 = \textbf{24}$ square centimeters

STEP 4 Add the areas from Steps 2 and 3 to find the total area.

$A = \textbf{112} + \textbf{24} = 136$ square centimeters

B **STEP 1** Extend the top edge and the right edge of the polygon to form a square with side length 60 feet. Find the area of this square.

$60 \cdot 60 = \textbf{3600}$ square feet

STEP 2 Notice that the square you drew has a rectangular "missing piece." Find the area of this missing piece.

$b = 60 - 20 = 40$ $h = 60 - 30 = 30$

$A = bh = 40 \cdot 30 = \textbf{1200}$ square feet

STEP 3 Subtract the area in Step 2 from the area in Step 1.

$A = \textbf{3600} - \textbf{1200} = 2400$ square feet

Reflect

2. Describe another way to find the area of the polygon in **B**.

_____

_____

Math Talk
Mathematical Practices

What other shapes could you divide the polygon in **A** into? What formulas would you use?

Math On the Spot
my.hrw.com

© Houghton Mifflin Harcourt Publishing Company

YOUR TURN

Find the area of each polygon.

3.

4 m
3 m
6 m
8 m
3 m

$A =$ _____ square meters

4.

18 in.
9 in.
18 in.
18 in.
36 in.

$A =$ _____ square inches

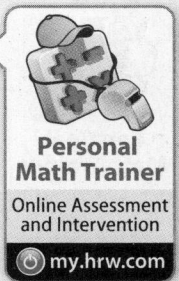

Personal Math Trainer

Online Assessment and Intervention

⏻ my.hrw.com

Solving Real-World Problems

You can apply the technique of dividing a shape into smaller shapes in problems that involve finding area.

EXAMPLE 2 Real World · FL · 6.G.1.1

Math On the Spot

⏻ my.hrw.com

The diagram shows the shape and dimensions of Teresa's rose garden.

15 ft
9 ft
18 ft
24 ft

My Notes

A Find the area of the garden.

STEP 1 Draw a horizontal line segment on the diagram that divides the polygon into two rectangles, one on top of the other.

STEP 2 Find the area of the smaller (top) rectangle.

$A = bh = 15 \cdot 9 = \mathbf{135}$ square feet

STEP 3 Find the area of the larger (bottom) rectangle.

The base of the larger rectangle is 24 feet.

The height is $18 - 9 = 9$ feet.

$A = bh = 24 \cdot 9 = \mathbf{216}$ square feet

STEP 4 Add the areas from Steps 2 and 3 to find the total area.

$A = \mathbf{135} + \mathbf{216} = 351$ square feet

The area of the garden is 351 square feet.

B Teresa wants to buy mulch for her garden. One bag of mulch covers 12 square feet. How many bags will she need?

$\dfrac{351 \text{ square feet}}{12 \text{ square feet}} = 29.25$ *Divide to find the number of bags needed.*

Teresa will need to buy 30 bags of mulch.

© Houghton Mifflin Harcourt Publishing Company

YOUR TURN

5. The diagram shows the floor plan of a hotel lobby. Carpet costs $3 per square foot. How much will it cost to carpet the lobby?

_____

30 ft

15.5 ft

42 ft

15.5 ft

30 ft

Guided Practice

1. In the diagram, the area of the large square is 1 square unit. Two diagonal segments divide the square into four equal-sized triangles. Two of these triangles are divided into smaller red and blue triangles that all have the same height and base length. Find the area of a red triangle. (Explore Activity)

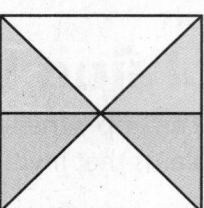

_____

Find the area of each polygon. (Example 1)

2.

4 ft

10 ft

14 ft

18 ft

$A =$ _____ square feet

3.

16 m

10 m

8 m

20 m

$A =$ _____ square meters

4. Jess is painting a giant arrow on a playground. Find the area of the giant arrow. If one can of paint covers 100 square feet, how many cans should Jess buy? (Example 2)

_____

5 ft

18 ft

24 ft

10 ft

5 ft

? ESSENTIAL QUESTION CHECK-IN

5. How can you find the area of a polygon that is not one for which you know an area formula?

_____

_____

_____

13.4 Independent Practice

  FL 6.G.1.1

6. Alice wants to put wall-to-wall carpeting in a small room with the floor plan shown.

   a. Alice says she can find the area of the room by dividing the floor plan into two trapezoids. Show how she can divide the floor plan. Then find the area using her method.

_____

   b. Describe another way to find the area.

_____

_____

   c. How much will Alice pay for carpet that costs $4.50 per square foot?

_____

7. Hal's backyard has a patio, a walkway, and a garden.

   a. About what percent of the total area of Hal's backyard is the area taken up by the patio, walkway, and garden? Round to the nearest whole percent.

_____

   b. One longer side of Hal's backyard lies next to the back of his house. Hal wants to build a fence that costs $9.75 per foot around the other three sides. How much will Hal spend on his new fence?

_____

8. The students in a furniture-making class make a tabletop shaped like the figure shown.

   a. What is the area of the tabletop?

_____

   b. One of the students wants to make a tabletop shaped like a right triangle. This tabletop will have the same area as the tabletop shown. What are a set of possible lengths for the sides of the tabletop that meet in a right angle? Explain.

_____

_____

_____

9. Multistep Cho is making banners shaped like triangles out of a rectangular piece of fabric. She cuts out two triangular banners as shown.

28 in.

21 in.

7 in.

a. What is the area of a triangular banner?

_____

b. What are the dimensions of the fabric left over after Cho cuts out the two banners?

_____

c. What is the maximum number of banners that Cho can cut out from the fabric? Will she use all the fabric?

_____

FOCUS ON HIGHER ORDER THINKING

10. Persevere in Problem Solving The base of a parallelogram is 8 units, and the height is 5 units. A segment divides the parallelogram into two identical trapezoids. The height of each trapezoid is 5 units. Draw the parallelogram and the two trapezoids on the grid shown. Then find the area of one of the trapezoids.

_____

11. Persevere in Problem Solving The figure shown is a square with a triangular hole cut into one side. The ratio of the height h of the triangle to a side length of the square is 7 to 8. The ratio of the base b of the triangle to the side length of the square is 1 to 2. If the area of the square is 64 square inches, what is the area of the shaded part of the square? Show your work.

b

h

_____

_____

_____

_____

_____

_____

_____

Work Area

Ready to Go On?

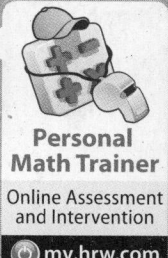

Personal
Math Trainer

Online Assessment
and Intervention

⏻ my.hrw.com

13.1 Area of Quadrilaterals

1. Find the area of the figure.

_____

$12\frac{1}{2}$ yd

$17\frac{1}{5}$ yd

13.2 Area of Triangles

2. Find the area of the triangle.

_____

14 ft

17 ft

13.3 Solving Area Equations

3. A triangular pane of glass has a height of 30 inches and an area of 270 square inches. What is the length of the base of the pane?

_____

4. A tabletop in the shape of a trapezoid has an area of 6,550 square centimeters. Its longer base measures 115 centimeters, and the shorter base is 85 centimeters. What is the height?

_____

13.4 Area of Polygons

5. Find the area of the polygon.

_____ square centimeters

5 cm

5 cm

8 cm

? ESSENTIAL QUESTION

6. How can you find the area of an irregular polygon using area formulas?

_____

_____

_____

_____

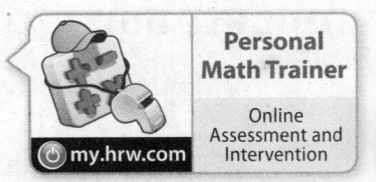

Selected Response

1. The lengths of the diagonals of the rhombus are given. What is the area of the rhombus?

23 in.

28 in.

Ⓐ 161 in²   Ⓒ 644 in²

Ⓑ 322 in²   Ⓓ 966 in²

2. In the triangle below, the value of h is $\frac{3}{4}$ the side length that is labeled on the figure. What is the area of the triangle?

h

4.8 mm

Ⓐ 3.6 mm²   Ⓒ 8.64 mm²

Ⓑ 6.4 mm²   Ⓓ 17.28 mm²

3. Tim is designing a logo. The logo is a polygon whose shape is a square attached to an equilateral triangle. The square and the equilateral triangle have side lengths of 2 centimeters, and the equilateral triangle has a height of about 1.7 cm. Find the area of the logo.

Ⓐ 1.7 cm²   Ⓒ 5.7 cm²

Ⓑ 4 cm²   Ⓓ 7.4 cm²

4. The trapezoid below has an area of 1,575 cm².

63 cm

27 cm

Which equation could you solve to find the height of the trapezoid?

Ⓐ $45h = 1{,}575$ Ⓒ $850.5h = 1{,}575$

Ⓑ $90h = 1{,}575$ Ⓓ $1{,}701h = 1{,}575$

Mini-Task

5. Cindy is designing a rectangular fountain in the middle of a courtyard. The rest of the courtyard will be covered in stone.

22 ft

6 ft

12 ft

Courtyard

Fountain

The part of the courtyard that will be covered in stone has an area of 246 square feet.

a. What is the width of the fountain?

_____

b. What fraction of the area of the courtyard will be occupied by the fountain?

_____

Distance and Area in the Coordinate Plane

LESSON 14.1
Distance in the Coordinate Plane
FL   6.NS.3.6b, 6.NS.3.8

LESSON 14.2
Polygons in the Coordinate Plane
FL   6.G.1.3

ESSENTIAL QUESTION

What steps might you take to solve a polygon problem given the coordinates of its vertices?

Real-World Video

Many cities are designed on a grid. You can use the lengths of blocks to calculate perimeters and areas just like on a coordinate plane.

⏻ my.hrw.com

GO DIGITAL

my.hrw.com

my.hrw.com

Go digital with your write-in student edition, accessible on any device.

Math On the Spot

Scan with your smart phone to jump directly to the online edition, video tutor, and more.

Animated Math

Interactively explore key concepts to see how math works.

Personal Math Trainer

Get immediate feedback and help as you work through practice sets.

Are YOU Ready?

Complete these exercises to review skills you will need for this module.

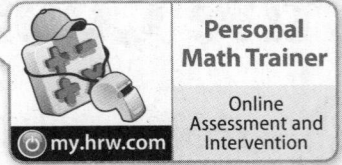
Graph Ordered Pairs

EXAMPLE Find the coordinates for Point A.

Start at O.
Count 8 units to the right and 2 units up from O.

The coordinates for Point A are (8, 2).

Write the ordered pair for each point shown on the graph.

1. Point V _____

2. Point W _____

3. Point X _____

4. Point Y _____

5. Point Z _____

Identify Polygons

EXAMPLE Name the type of polygon.

Count the number of sides.
Compare the sides.
Compare the angles.

There are 4 congruent sides and angles. The shape is a rhombus.

Name each figure. Choose from hexagon, isosceles triangle, right triangle, and trapezoid.

6. _____

7. _____

Reading Start-Up

Visualize Vocabulary

Use the ✔ words to complete the graphic.

Use the coordinates to find the distance from the origin on each _____ →

Add or subtract these to find the distance between two points on a coordinate plane _____

↓

If a rectangle is formed, multiply base and height to find _____ ←

If a shape is formed, add the sides to find _____

Understand Vocabulary

Complete the sentences using the preview words.

1. A corner of a rectangle is called a _____.

2. How an image would appear in a mirror is called a _____.

3. A two-dimensional shape with straight sides is

   a _____.

Active Reading

Two-Panel Flip Chart Create a two-panel flip chart to help you understand the concepts in Lesson 14.1. Label one flap "Reflection across the *x*-axis." Label the other flap "Reflection across the *y*-axis." Write important ideas about each type of reflection under the appropriate flap.

Unpacking the Standards

Understanding the standards and the vocabulary terms in the standards will help you know exactly what you are expected to learn in this module.

FL 6.NS.3.8

Solve real-world and mathematical problems by graphing points in all four quadrants of the coordinate plane. Include use of coordinates and absolute value to find distances between points with the same first coordinate or the same second coordinate.

What It Means to You

You will find the distance between two points on a coordinate plane.

UNPACKING EXAMPLE 6.NS.3.8

Find the distance between points A and B.

Add the absolute values of the y-coordinates.

$$= |3| + |-4|$$
$$= 3 + 4$$
$$= 7$$

The distance between points A and B is 7 units.

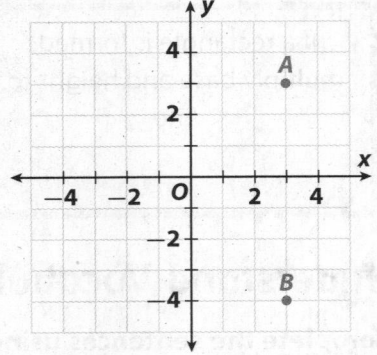

FL 6.G.1.3

Draw polygons in the coordinate plane given coordinates for the vertices; ...Apply these techniques in the context of solving real-world and mathematical problems.

What It Means to You

You can draw polygons on a coordinate plane by plotting the vertices and connecting them.

UNPACKING EXAMPLE 6.G.1.3

What type of polygon can you make by plotting these points?

Point A $(-4, 2)$
Point B $(2, 2)$
Point C $(-4, -2)$
Point D $(2, -2)$

Connect each point.

The points make a rectangle.

Visit **my.hrw.com** to see all **Florida Math Standards** unpacked.

my.hrw.com

LESSON 14.1 Distance in the Coordinate Plane

FL 6.NS.3.8

Solve...problems by graphing points....Include use of coordinates and absolute value to find distances between points.... *Also* 6.NS.3.6b

ESSENTIAL QUESTION

How can you use absolute value to find the distance between two points with the same *x*- or *y*-coordinates?

EXPLORE ACTIVITY 1   FL 6.NS.3.6b

Reflecting in the Coordinate Plane

A point on a coordinate plane can be *reflected* across an axis. The **reflection** is located on the opposite side of the axis, at the same distance from the axis.

> Hold your paper up to the light if necessary to see the reflection.

Draw a coordinate plane on graph paper. Label both axes from −10 to 10.

A Graph (3, −2). Then fold your coordinate plane along the *y*-axis and find the reflection of (3, −2). Record the coordinates of the new point in the table.

B Unfold your coordinate plane. Then fold it along the *x*-axis and find the reflection of (3, −2). Record the coordinates of the new point in the table.

C Choose three additional points and repeat **A** and **B**.

Point	Reflected across *y*-axis	Reflected across *x*-axis
(3, −2)		

Reflect

1. What is the relationship between the coordinates of a point and the coordinates of its reflection across each axis?

_____

_____

_____

2. **Conjecture** A point is reflected across the *y*-axis. Then the reflected point is reflected across the *x*-axis. How will the coordinates of the final point be related to the coordinates of the original point?

_____

_____

© Houghton Mifflin Harcourt Publishing Company

Finding Distances in the Coordinate Plane

You can also use absolute values to find distances between two points that have the same x-coordinates or the same y-coordinates on a coordinate plane.

EXAMPLE 1

FL 6.NS.3.6b

Find each distance.

A What is the distance between point A and point B?

> **STEP 1** Find the distance between point A and the x-axis.
>
> The y-coordinate is 3, so point A is $|3|$ units from the x-axis.

> **STEP 2** Find the distance between point B and the x-axis.
>
> The y-coordinate of B is -2, so point B is $|-2| = 2$ units from the x-axis.

> **STEP 3** Find the sum of the distances.
>
> Distance from A to B $= |3| + |-2| = 3 + 2 = 5$ units.

B What is the distance between point D and point C?

> **STEP 1** Find the distance between point D and the y-axis.
>
> Point D is $|-5| = 5$ units from the y-axis.

> **STEP 2** Find the distance between point C and the y-axis.
>
> Point C is $|-1| = 1$ unit from the y-axis.

> **STEP 3** Find the distance between C and D by finding this difference:
>
> Distance of D from the y-axis − distance of C from the y-axis
>
> $|-5| - |-1| = 4$ units

YOUR TURN

Personal Math Trainer

Online Assessment and Intervention

my.hrw.com

Find the distance between each pair of points.

3. $E(-4, 7)$ and $F(5, 7)$ _____

4. $G(0, -5)$ and $H(0, -10)$ _____

Solving Distance Problems

You can solve problems using the distance between points on a grid.

EXAMPLE 2 Problem Solving FL 6.NS.3.8

The coordinate plane represents a map. Each grid unit represents 20 miles. A retail company has warehouses at $M(-70, 10)$ and $N(50, 10)$. How long does it take a truck that drives 40 miles per hour to travel from warehouse M to warehouse N?

M (−70, 10)   N (50, 10)

Analyze Information

Identify the important information.

- One warehouse is located at $M(-70, 10)$. The other is at $N(50, 10)$.
- A truck drives from M to N at a speed of 40 miles per hour.

Formulate a Plan

- Find the distance between M and N by adding the absolute values of the x-coordinates of the points.
- Find the time it takes the truck to drive this distance by using the relationship, distance = rate · time.

Solve

Add the absolute values of the x-coordinates to find the distance between point M and point N on the grid.

$$|-70| + |50| = 70 + 50 = 120$$

The warehouses are 120 miles apart.

The truck drives 120 miles at 40 mi/h. Because $120 = 40(3)$, it takes the truck 3 hours to travel from M to N.

Justify and Evaluate

You found the sum of the absolute values of the x-coordinates to find the horizontal distance on the grid. Then you used distance = rate · time to find the time it takes to drive that distance.

© Houghton Mifflin Harcourt Publishing Company

YOUR TURN

5. A store is located at $P(50, -30)$. How long will it take a truck driving at 50 miles per hour to drive from warehouse N to this store?

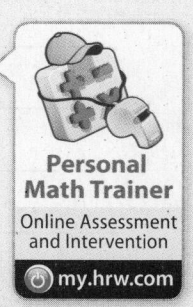

Personal Math Trainer

Online Assessment and Intervention

my.hrw.com

1. The point (5, −2) is reflected across the *x*-axis. What are the coordinates of the reflection? (Explore Activity)

_____

2. The point (−6, 8) is reflected across the *y*-axis. What are the coordinates of the reflection? (Explore Activity)

_____

Use the coordinate plane. (Example 1)

3. The distance between point *A* and point *B* is

| | + | | = ( ) + ( ) = ( ) units.

4. The distance between point *A* and point *C* is

| | − | | = ( ) − ( ) = ( ) units. .

5. Plot the reflection of point *C* across the *y*-axis. What is the distance between point *C* and its reflection? _____

6. Plot the reflection of point *A* across the *x*-axis. What is the distance of the reflection from the *x*-axis? _____

Use the map shown. Each grid on the map represents 1 city block.
(Example 2)

7. Yoko walks from the library to the mall. How many city blocks does she walk? _____

8. If Yoko walks 1 block in 3 minutes, how long does it take her to walk from the school to the library? How long does it take her to walk from home to school?

_____

? ESSENTIAL QUESTION CHECK-IN

9. How do you use absolute value to find the distance between two points that have the same *x*-coordinates but different *y*-coordinates?

_____

_____

_____

_____

Name _____ Class _____ Date _____

14.1 Independent Practice

6.NS.3.6b, 6.NS.3.8

Personal Math Trainer

Online Assessment and Intervention

my.hrw.com

Use the coordinate plane.

10. Plot the reflection of point A across the x-axis. What are the coordinates of the reflection of point A across the x-axis? What is the distance between point A and its reflection?

_____

11. How can you plot the reflection of point A across the y-axis? Give the coordinates of the reflection across the y-axis, and tell how many units the reflection is from point A.

_____

_____

_____

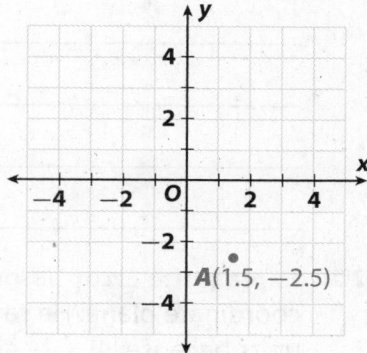
$A(1.5, -2.5)$

Find the coordinates of each point after the described reflection. Give the distance between each point and its reflection.

12. $R(-5, 8)$ is reflected across the x-axis. _____

13. $S(-7, -3)$ is reflected across the y-axis. _____

14. $T(8, 2)$ is reflected across the x-axis. _____

15. $U(2.4, -1)$ is reflected across the y-axis _____

Pedro uses a coordinate system to map the locations of some tourist locations in a large city. Each grid unit represents one mile.

16. The planetarium, which is not marked on the map, is halfway between the historic village and the science center. What are its coordinates?

_____

17. Pedro wants to walk from the historic village to the science center. Then he will walk from the science center to the museum. If he walks at a speed of $4\frac{1}{2}$ miles per hour, how long will it take him?

_____

18. Pedro is staying at a hotel whose location is a reflection across the x-axis of the museum's location. What are the coordinates of the location of Pedro's hotel?

_____

Historic Village $(-4\frac{1}{2}, 5\frac{1}{4})$ Water Park $(0, 5\frac{1}{4})$
Science Center $(-4\frac{1}{2}, -1\frac{3}{4})$ Museum $(2, -1\frac{3}{4})$

© Houghton Mifflin Harcourt Publishing Company

Lesson 14.1 **405**

19. **Communicate Mathematical Ideas** Deirdre plotted a point D in Quadrant IV. After she reflected the point across an axis, the reflection was in Quadrant III. Give possible coordinates for point D and its reflection, and tell why you chose these coordinates.

_____

_____

_____

_____

_____

20. **Explain the Error** Jason plotted the points $(4, 4)$ and $(-4, -4)$ on a coordinate plane. He says that the distance between the two points is 8 units because $|4| + |-4| = 8$. What mistake is Jason making?

_____

_____

_____

21. **Look for a Pattern** A point is reflected over the x-axis and then reflected again over the y-axis. Will the coordinates after these two reflections be the same or different if the point is first reflected over the y-axis and then over the x-axis? Use an example to support your answer.

_____

_____

_____

_____

_____

22. **Explain the Error** Bentley states that the distance between $R(-8, -3.5)$ and $S(-8, -12)$ is $|-12| + |-3.5| = 15.5$ units. Is Bentley correct? Explain your answer. If Bentley is not correct, explain how to find the correct distance between the points.

_____

_____

_____

_____

© Houghton Mifflin Harcourt Publishing Company

Polygons in the Coordinate Plane

FL 6.G.1.3

Draw polygons in the coordinate plane;...find the length of a side... in the context of solving... problems.

© Houghton Mifflin Harcourt Publishing Company • Image Credits: CVI Textures/Alamy

? ESSENTIAL QUESTION

How can you solve problems by drawing polygons in the coordinate plane?

EXPLORE ACTIVITY FL 6.G.1.3

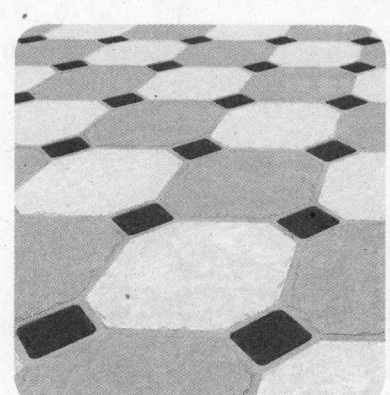

Polygons in the Coordinate Plane

A **polygon** is a closed plane figure formed by three or more line segments that meet only at their endpoints. A **vertex** is the point where two sides of a polygon meet. The *vertices* of a polygon can be represented as ordered pairs, and the polygon can then be drawn in the coordinate plane.

Sheila wants to make a pattern of two different tile shapes on a floor. She first graphs the shapes on a coordinate plane.

A Plot these points to form one of the tile shapes:

   $A(3, 5), B(4, 6), C(5, 5), D(4, 4)$

   Connect the points in order.

   The polygon formed is a(n) _____.

B Plot these points to form the other tile shape:

   $P(-5, 2), Q(-4, 3), R(0, 3), S(1, 2),$

   $T(1, -2), U(0, -3), V(-4, -3), W(-5, -2)$

   Connect the points in order.

   The polygon formed is a(n) _____.

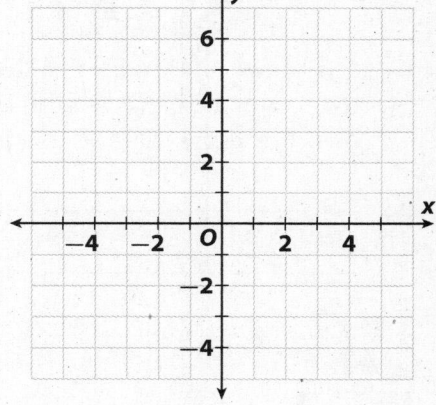

Reflect

1. How is the number of vertices related to the number of sides of the polygon and to the type of polygon? Give two examples.

_____

_____

_____

_____

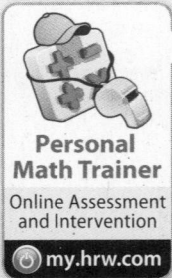
Finding Perimeter in the Coordinate Plane

You can use what you know about finding lengths in the coordinate plane to find the perimeter of a polygon.

EXAMPLE 1   **FL** 6.G.1.3

The grid shows the path Tommy followed when he walked from his home at (0, 0) to various locations and back home again. If each grid square represents one block, how many blocks did he walk?

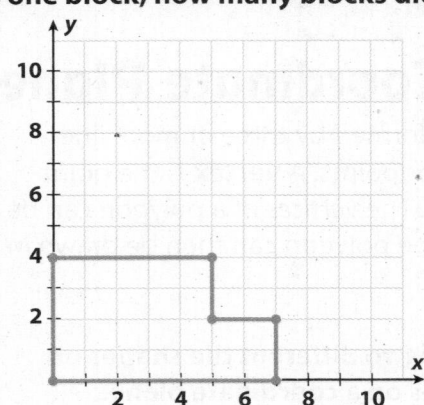

Home (0, 0)

Library (0, 4)

Park (5, 4)

Friend's house (5, 2)

Pond (7, 2)

Store (7, 0)

Math Talk
Mathematical Practices

How do you find the distance between two points in the same quadrant that have the same *x*-coordinate?

STEP 1 Find each distance. Each grid unit represents one block.

Tommy's home (0, 0) to the library (0, 4) is $|4| - 0 = 4 - 0 = 4$ blocks.

The library (0, 4) to the park (5, 4) is $|5| - 0 = 5 - 0 = 5$ blocks.

The park (5, 4) to Tommy's friend's house (5, 2) is $|4| - |2| = 4 - 2 = 2$ blocks.

Tommy's friend's house (5, 2) to the pond (7, 2) is $|7| - |5| = 7 - 5 = 2$ blocks.

The pond (7, 2) to the store (7, 0) is $|2| - 0 = 2 - 0 = 2$ blocks.

The store (7, 0) to Tommy's home (0, 0) is $|7| - 0 = 7 - 0 = 7$ blocks.

STEP 2 Find the sum of the distances.

Tommy walked $4 + 5 + 2 + 2 + 2 + 7 = 22$ blocks.

YOUR TURN

2. Suppose the next day Tommy walks from his home to the mall at (0, 8), and then walks to a movie theater at (7, 8). After leaving the theater Tommy walks to the store at (7, 0) before returning home.

   How far does he walk? _____ blocks

© Houghton Mifflin Harcourt Publishing Company

Finding Area in the Coordinate Plane

You can use familiar area formulas to find areas of polygons in the coordinate plane.

Math On the Spot
my.hrw.com

EXAMPLE 2   FL 6.G.1.3

Caleb is planning a new deck for his house. He graphs the deck as polygon *ABCDEF* on a coordinate plane in which each grid unit represents one foot. The vertices of the polygon are *A*(1, 0), *B*(3, 2), *C*(3, 5), *D*(8, 5), *E*(8, 2), and *F*(6, 0). What is the area of Caleb's deck?

STEP 1 Graph the vertices, and connect them in order.

Draw a horizontal dashed line segment to divide the polygon into two quadrilaterals—a rectangle and a parallelogram.

STEP 2 Find the area of the rectangle using the length of segment *BE* as the base *b* and the length of segment *BC* as the height *h*.

$b = |8| - |3| = 5$ feet $\qquad h = |5| - |2| = 3$ feet

$A = bh = 5 \cdot 3 = 15$ square feet

STEP 3 Find the area of the parallelogram using the length of segment *AF* as the base. Use the length of a segment from *F*(6, 0) to the point (6, 2) as the height *h*.

$b = |6| - |1| = 5$ feet $\qquad h = |2| - 0 = 2$ feet

$A = bh = 5 \cdot 2 = 10$ square feet

STEP 4 Add the areas to find the total area of the deck.

$A = 15 + 10 = 25$ square feet

YOUR TURN

3. The vertices of a polygon are
   L(1, 2), *M*(1, 6), *N*(7, 6), *O*(7, 2), *P*(5, 0),
   and *Q*(3, 0). Graph the polygon. Then find its area.

   $A = $ _____ square units

Personal Math Trainer
Online Assessment and Intervention
my.hrw.com

© Houghton Mifflin Harcourt Publishing Company • Image Credits: Dorling Kindersley/Getty Images

A gardener uses a coordinate grid to design a new garden. The gardener uses polygon *WXYZ* on the grid to represent the garden. The vertices of this polygon are *W*(3, 3), *X*(−3, 3), *Y*(−3, −3), and *Z*(3, −3). Each grid unit represents one yard.

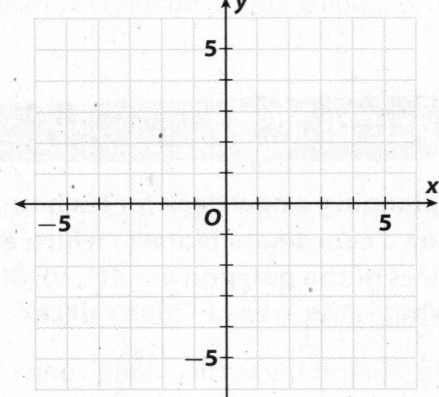

1. Graph the points, and connect them in order. What is the shape of the garden? (Explore Activity)

_____

2. How much fencing will the gardener need to enclose the garden? (Example 1)

Each side of the garden is _____ yards in length.

The gardener will need _____ yards of fencing to enclose the garden.

3. What is the area of the garden? (Example 2)

_____

4. A clothing designer makes letters for varsity jackets by graphing the letters as polygons on a coordinate plane. One of the letters is polygon *ABCDEF*. The vertices of this polygon are *A*(3, −2), *B*(3, −4), *C*(−3, −4), *D*(−3, 4), *E*(−1, 4), and *F*(−1, −2). Each grid unit represents one inch. Graph the points on the coordinate plane, and connect them in order. Identify the letter formed. Then find its area. (Example 2)

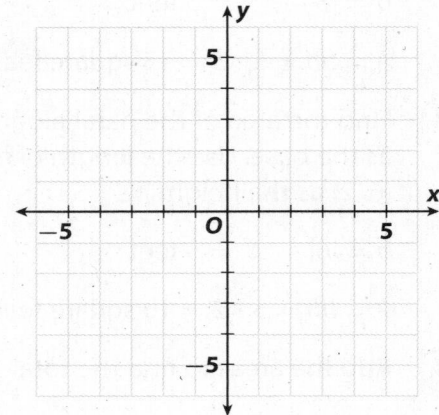

_____

? ESSENTIAL QUESTION CHECK-IN

5. How can you use a coordinate plane to solve perimeter and area problems?

_____

_____

_____

_____

14.2 Independent Practice

FL 6.G.1.3

Personal Math Trainer

Online Assessment and Intervention

my.hrw.com

6. A graphic designer creates letters for wall art by first graphing the letters as polygons on a coordinate plane. One of the letters is polygon *MNOPQRSTUV* with vertices *M*(2, 1), *N*(2, 9), *O*(7, 9), *P*(7, 7), *Q*(4, 7), *R*(4, 6), *S*(6, 6), *T*(6, 4), *U*(4, 4), and *V*(4, 1). Each grid unit represents one inch.

a. Graph the points on the coordinate plane, and connect them in order. What letter is formed? _____

b. The designer will use decorative tape to paint the outline of the letter on a wall. How many inches of tape are needed? _____

c. How much space does the letter cover on the wall? _____

d. How did you find your answer to c? Use the name(s) of shapes in your answer.

_____

_____

7. Vocabulary The polygon shown is a regular polygon since all sides have equal length and all angles have equal measure.

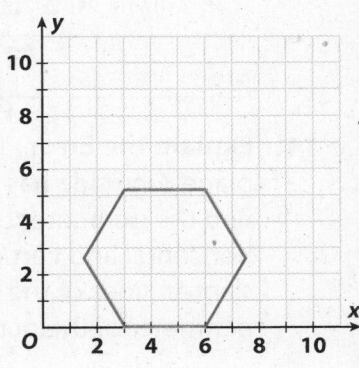

a. The polygon is a regular _____.

b. What is the perimeter of the polygon? _____

c. A line can divide the figure into two identical four-sided polygons. Each polygon has two bases, and one base is twice the length of the other base. Identify the polygon, and give its perimeter.

_____

8. Jean wants to put furniture in her clubhouse. She drew a floor plan of the clubhouse, as shown. Each grid unit represents one foot.

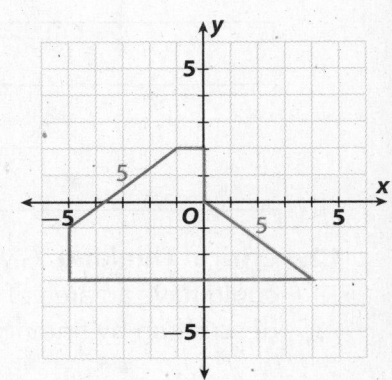

a. Which polygon names the shape of the floor?

_____

b. How many feet of baseboard are needed to go around the entire clubhouse?

_____

c. How much carpet is needed for the clubhouse floor?

_____

Work Area

9. Persevere in Problem Solving To find the area of triangle *ABC*, Jen first drew a square around the figure. Two sides of the square passed through the points *B* and *C*. The other two sides met at point *A*. Draw Jen's square, and explain how you can use it to find the area of triangle *ABC*.

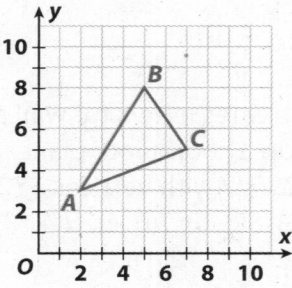

_____

_____

_____

_____

10. Communicate Mathematical Ideas The coordinates $A(5, -2)$, $B(3, -1)$, $C(-4, -4)$, $D(-3, 8)$, and $E(-1, 4)$ form the vertices of a polygon when they are connected in order from *A* through *E*. Classify the polygon without plotting the points. Explain your answer.

_____

_____

_____

_____

11. Explain the Error Josh's teacher draws a regular octagon on a coordinate plane. One side has endpoints at (1, 5) and (4, 5). Josh says he can't find the perimeter of the octagon because he can only find lengths of horizontal and vertical segments. He says he can't find the lengths of the slanted sides of the octagon. What mistake is Josh making? What is the perimeter of the octagon?

_____

_____

_____

_____

12. Critical Thinking Give coordinates for the vertices of a triangle that could have an area of 35 square units. Prove that your triangle fits the description by finding its area.

_____

_____

Ready to Go On?

14.1 Distance in the Coordinate Plane

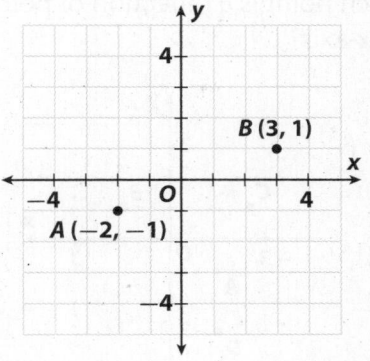

1. Reflect A across the x-axis. Label the reflection as N, and give its coordinates on the graph.

2. Reflect B across the x-axis. Label the reflection as M, and give its coordinates on the graph.

3. The distance between A and N is _____.

4. Suppose the graph represents a map in which each grid unit equals 1 mile. If a school is located at B and a library is located at N, what is the distance

between the school and the library? _____

Find the coordinates of the point for each reflection.

5. $(-5, 7)$ across the x-axis _____

6. $(2, 5.5)$ across the y-axis _____

Find the distance between each pair of points.

7. $(1, 1)$ and $(1, -2)$ _____ units

8. $(-2, 3)$ and $(-4, 3)$ _____ units

14.2 Polygons in the Coordinate Plane

9. On the coordinate plane shown, each grid unit represents 10 feet. Polygon QRST has vertices $Q(10, 20)$, $R(-10, 20)$, $S(-10, -10)$, and $T(10, -10)$, and represents the floor plan of a room. Find the perimeter and area of the room.

_____

_____

ESSENTIAL QUESTION

10. Suppose you are given the coordinates of the vertices of a polygon. What steps could you take to solve a problem involving the polygon's area?

_____

_____

_____

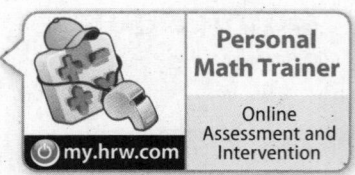

Selected Response

1. Which point is a reflection of point *R* across the *x*-axis?

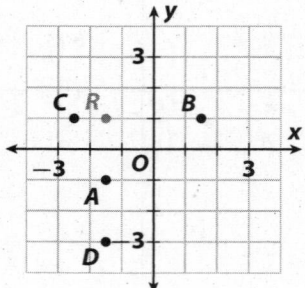

Ⓐ Point *A*   Ⓒ Point *C*

Ⓑ Point *B*   Ⓓ Point *D*

2. Which point is a reflection of $(12, -8)$ across the *y*-axis on a coordinate plane?

Ⓐ $(-12, -8)$ Ⓒ $(8, 12)$

Ⓑ $(-8, 12)$ Ⓓ $(12, 8)$

3. What is the distance between points *J* and *L* on the grid?

Ⓐ 1.5 units   Ⓒ 3 units

Ⓑ 2 units   Ⓓ 3.5 units

4. What is the greatest common factor of 12 and 30?

Ⓐ 2   Ⓒ 6

Ⓑ 3   Ⓓ 12

5. What is the distance between two points located at $(-6, 2)$ and $(-6, 8)$ on a coordinate plane?

Ⓐ 4 units   Ⓒ 10 units

Ⓑ 6 units   Ⓓ 12 units

6. Which is the sum of $\frac{1}{12} + \frac{3}{8}$?

Ⓐ $\frac{1}{6}$ Ⓒ $\frac{11}{48}$

Ⓑ $\frac{1}{5}$ Ⓓ $\frac{11}{24}$

Mini-Task

7. An artist is laying out the design for a wall hanging on a coordinate plane. She uses polygon *EFGH* with vertices *E*(4, 4), *F*(−4, 4), *G*(−4, −4), and *H*(4, −4) to represent the finished piece. Each unit on the grid represents two feet.

a. Plot the polygon on the grid, and classify its shape.

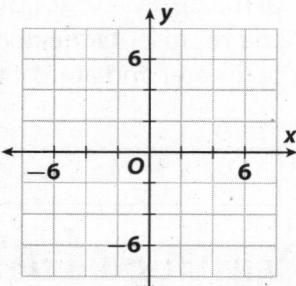

Name of Polygon: _____

b. How much area will the art cover on a wall? _____

Surface Area and Volume of Solids

MODULE **15**

ESSENTIAL QUESTION

How can a model help you to solve surface area and volume problems?

LESSON 15.1
Nets and Surface Area
FL 6.G.1.4

LESSON 15.2
Volume of Rectangular Prisms
FL 6.G.1.2

LESSON 15.3
Solving Volume Equations
FL 6.EE.2.7, 6.G.1.2

Real-World Video

Surface area and volume can be important considerations when constructing or repairing buildings or other structures.

my.hrw.com

GO DIGITAL
my.hrw.com

my.hrw.com

Go digital with your write-in student edition, accessible on any device.

Math On the Spot

Scan with your smart phone to jump directly to the online edition, video tutor, and more.

Animated Math

Interactively explore key concepts to see how math works.

Personal Math Trainer

Get immediate feedback and help as you work through practice sets.

Are YOU Ready?

Complete these exercises to review skills you will need for this module.

Use of Parentheses

EXAMPLE
$$\frac{1}{2}(14)(12 + 18) = \frac{1}{2}(14)(30) \quad \text{Perform operations inside parentheses first.}$$
$$= 7(30) \quad \text{Multiply left to right.}$$
$$= 210 \quad \text{Multiply again.}$$

Evaluate.

1. $\frac{1}{2}(3)(5 + 7)$ _____

2. $\frac{1}{2}(15)(13 + 17)$ _____

3. $\frac{1}{2}(10)(9.4 + 3.6)$ _____

4. $\frac{1}{2}(2.1)(3.5 + 5.7)$ _____

Area of Squares, Rectangles, Triangles

EXAMPLE Find the area of the rectangle.

8 ft

3 ft

$A = bh$ Use the formula for area of a rectangle.

$= 8 \cdot 3$ Substitute for base and height.

$= 24$ Multiply.

Area equals 24 square feet.

Find the area of each figure.

5. a triangle with base 6 in. and height 3 in. _____

6. a square with sides of 7.6 m _____

7. a rectangle with length $3\frac{1}{4}$ ft and width $2\frac{1}{2}$ ft _____

8. a triangle with base 8.2 cm and height 5.1 cm _____

Reading Start-Up

Visualize Vocabulary

Use review words to complete the graphic.

Shape	Area Formula
	$A = b \times \underline{\hspace{2cm}}$
	$A = \frac{1}{2} \times \underline{\hspace{2cm}} \times h$

© Houghton Mifflin Harcourt Publishing Company

Understand Vocabulary

Complete the sentences using the preview words.

1. The total area of all the faces of a three-dimensional figure is

   called the _____.

2. A model that looks like an unfolded three-dimensional figure is a

   _____.

3. A three-dimensional shape with a polygon for a base and triangles

   for sides is a _____.

Active Reading

Booklet Before beginning the module, create a booklet to help you learn the concepts in this module. Write the main idea of each lesson on each page of the booklet. As you study each lesson, write important details that support the main idea, such as vocabulary and important steps in solving problems. Refer to your finished booklet as you work on assignments and study for tests.

Vocabulary

Review Words
  area *(área)*
  base *(base)*
  height *(altura)*
  rectangular prism *(prisma rectangular)*
  volume *(volumen)*

Preview Words
  net *(plantilla)*
  pyramid *(pirámide)*
  surface area *(área total)*

Unpacking the Standards

Understanding the standards and the vocabulary terms in the standards will help you know exactly what you are expected to learn in this module.

FL 6.G.1.2

Find the volume of a right rectangular prism with fractional edge lengths by packing it with unit cubes of the appropriate unit fraction edge lengths, and show that the volume is the same as would be found by multiplying the edge lengths of the prism. Apply the formulas $V = lwh$ and $V = bh$ to find volumes of right rectangular prisms with fractional edge lengths in the context of solving real-world and mathematical problems.

What It Means to You

You will use the formula for the volume of a rectangular prism.

UNPACKING EXAMPLE 6.G.1.2

Jala has an aquarium in the shape of a rectangular prism. The dimensions of the base of the aquarium are $1\frac{1}{4}$ feet by $\frac{1}{2}$ foot, and the height is $\frac{3}{4}$ foot. Find the volume of the aquarium.

$$
\begin{aligned}
V &= l \cdot w \cdot h \\
&= 1\frac{1}{4} \cdot \frac{1}{2} \cdot \frac{3}{4} \\
&= \frac{5}{4} \cdot \frac{1}{2} \cdot \frac{3}{4} \\
&= \frac{15}{32}
\end{aligned}
$$

The volume of the aquarium is $\frac{15}{32}$ cubic foot.

FL 6.G.1.4

Represent three-dimensional figures using nets made up of rectangles and triangles, and use the nets to find the surface area of these figures. ...

What It Means to You

You will use a net to find the surface area of a square pyramid.

UNPACKING EXAMPLE 6.G.1.4

Meg drew a net to find the surface area of a square pyramid.

Square face: $A = b \times h = 16$ square inches

Triangular face: $A = \frac{1}{2} b \times h = 6$ square inches

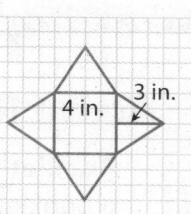

Total of the areas:
$16 + (4 \times 6) = 40$ square inches

The surface area is 40 square inches.

Visit **my.hrw.com** to see all **Florida Math Standards** unpacked.

my.hrw.com

Nets and Surface Area

FL 6.G.1.4
Represent three-dimensional figures using nets ... and use the nets to find...surface area.... *Also 6.EE.1.2c*

? ESSENTIAL QUESTION

How can you use nets to find surface areas?

EXPLORE ACTIVITY **FL 6.G.1.4**

Using a Net

A **net** is a two-dimensional pattern of shapes that can be folded into a three-dimensional figure. The shapes in the net become the faces of the three-dimensional figure.

A Copy each net on graph paper. Cut out each net along the blue lines.

Net A   Net B

One of these nets can be folded along the black lines to make a cube.

Which net will NOT make a cube? _____

B On your graph paper, draw a different net that you think will make a cube. Confirm by cutting out and folding your net. Compare results with several of your classmates. How many different nets for a cube did

you and your classmates find? _____

Reflect

How do you know that each net cannot be folded into a cube without actually cutting and folding it?

1.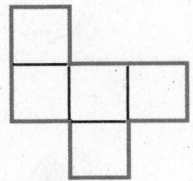

_____

_____

2.

_____

_____

3. What shapes will appear in a net for a rectangular prism that is not a cube? How many of these shapes will there be?

_____

Surface Area of a Pyramid

The **surface area** of a three-dimensional figure is the sum of the areas of its faces. A net can be helpful when finding surface area.

A **pyramid** is a three-dimensional figure whose base is a polygon and whose other faces are triangles that meet at a point. A pyramid is identified by the shape of its base.

EXAMPLE 1
FL 6.G.1.4

Make a net of this square pyramid, and use the net to find the surface area.

STEP 1   Make a net of the pyramid.

Draw the square base.

Draw a triangle on each side.

Label the dimensions.

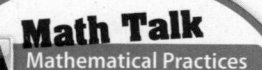

STEP 2   Use the net to find the surface area.

There are four triangles with base 16 in. and height 17 in.

The area of the 4 triangles is $4 \times \frac{1}{2}(16)(17) = 544$ in².

The area of the base is $16 \times 16 = 256$ in².

The surface area is $544 + 256 = 800$ in².

4. Use a net to find the surface area of the pyramid.

_____

Surface Area of a Prism

A **prism** is a three-dimensional figure with two identical and parallel bases that are polygons. The other faces are rectangles. A prism is identified by the shape of its base.

Math On the Spot
my.hrw.com

EXAMPLE 2   FL   6.G.1.4

A sculpture sits on pedestal in the shape of a square prism. The side lengths of a base of the prism are 3 feet. The height of the prism is 4 feet. The museum director wants to cover all but the underside of the pedestal with foil that costs $0.22 per square foot. How much will the foil cost?

My Notes

STEP 1 Use a net to show the faces that will be covered with foil.

Draw the top.

Draw the faces of the prism that are connected to the top.

You don't need to include the bottom of the pedestal.

```
        4 ft  Back  4 ft                Right
        4 ft   3 ft        4 ft          side
   ┌──────┬──────┬──────┐
   │ 3 ft │ Top  │ 3 ft │
   └──────┼──────┼──────┘
  Left     3 ft   4 ft
  side    Front  4 ft
```

STEP 2 Use the net to find the area that will be covered with foil.

Area of top = $3 \cdot 3 = 9 \text{ ft}^2$

The other four faces are identical.

Area of four faces = $4 \cdot 3 \cdot 4 = 48 \text{ ft}^2$

Area to be covered = $9 + 48 = 57 \text{ ft}^2$

STEP 3 Find the cost of the foil.

$57 \cdot \$0.22 = \$12.54$

The foil will cost $12.54.

Reflect

5. Critical Thinking What shapes would you see in the net of a triangular prism?

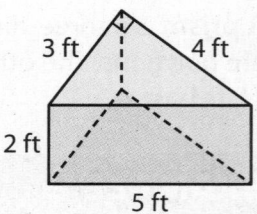

YOUR TURN

6. The figure shown is a triangular prism. How much would it cost to cover the bases and the other three faces with foil that costs $0.22 per square foot?

_____

3 ft   4 ft

2 ft

5 ft

Guided Practice

A square pyramid is shown.

1. The figure has _____ square base

   and _____ triangular faces.
   (Explore Activity)

2. Find the surface area. (Example 1)

   The area of the base is _____ square inches.

   The area of the four faces is _____ square inches.

   The surface area is _____ square inches.

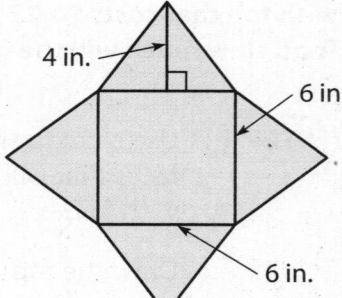

4 in.

6 in.

6 in.

6 in.

4 in.

6 in.

6 in.

3. Yolanda makes wooden boxes for a crafts fair. She makes 100 boxes like the one shown, and she wants to paint all the outside faces. (Example 2)

   a. Find the surface area of one box.

   _____

   b. Find the total surface area of 100 boxes.

   _____

   c. One can of paint will cover 14,000 square inches. How many cans of paint will Yolanda need to buy?

   _____

4 in.

6 in.

10 in.

? ESSENTIAL QUESTION CHECK-IN

4. How is a net useful when finding the surface area of prisms and pyramids?

_____

_____

_____

15.1 Independent Practice

FL 6.G.1.4

Personal Math Trainer

Online Assessment and Intervention

my.hrw.com

5. Use a net to find the surface area of the cereal box.

Total surface area: _____

6. Inez bought a shipping container at a packaging store. She measured the dimensions shown to the nearest tenth.

a. Sketch a net of the container, and label the dimensions.

b. Find the surface area of the shipping container.

_____

7. Raj builds a side table in the shape of a cube. Each edge of the cube measures 20 inches. Raj wants to cover the top and four sides of the table with ceramic tiles. Each tile has an edge length of 5 inches. How many tiles will he need?

_____

8. Santana wants to cover a gift box shaped like a rectangular prism with foil. The foil costs $0.03 per square inch. Santana has a choice between Box A which is 8 inches long, 3 inches wide, and 6 inches high, and Box B which is 10 inches long, 3 inches wide, and 4 inches high. Which box will be less expensive to cover with foil, and by how much?

_____

9. Vocabulary Name a three-dimensional shape that has four triangular faces and one rectangular face. Name a three-dimensional shape that has three rectangular faces and two triangular faces.

_____

10. Victor wrapped the gift box shown with adhesive paper (with no overlaps). How much paper did he use?

_____

11. Communicate Mathematical Ideas Describe how you approach a problem involving surface area. What do you do first? What are some strategies you can use?

_____

_____

_____

_____

Work Area

12. Persevere in Problem Solving A pedestal in a craft store is in the shape of a triangular prism. The bases are right triangles with side lengths of 12 centimeters, 16 centimeters, and 20 centimeters. The store owner wraps a piece of rectangular cloth around the pedestal, but does not cover the identical bases of the pedestal with cloth. The area of the cloth is 192 square centimeters.

a. What is the distance around the base of the pedestal? How do you know?

_____

_____

b. What is the height of the pedestal? How did you find your answer?

_____

_____

_____

13. Critique Reasoning Robert sketches two rectangular prisms, A and B. Prism A's side lengths are 5 centimeters, 6 centimeters, and 7 centimeters. Prism B's side lengths were twice those of prism A's: 10 centimeters, 12 centimeters, and 14 centimeters. Robert says the surface area of prism B is twice the surface area of prism A. Is he correct? If he is not, how many times as great as prism A's surface area is prism B's surface area? Show your work.

_____

_____

_____

_____

_____

LESSON
15.2 Volume of Rectangular Prisms

 FL 6.G.1.2
Find the volume of a right rectangular prism with fractional edge lengths....

ESSENTIAL QUESTION

How do you find the volume of a rectangular prism?

EXPLORE ACTIVITY FL 6.G.1.2

Using Fractional Edge Lengths

A cube with edge length 1 unit and volume 1 cubic unit is filled with smaller cubes as shown.

A How many small cubes are there? _____

How does the combined volume of the small cubes compare to the volume of the large cube?

1 unit

_____

Number of small cubes	·	Volume of one small cube	=	Volume of large cube

☐ · ? = ☐

What is the volume of one small cube? _____ cubic unit(s)

B Each edge of the large cube contains _____ small cubes.

Number of small cubes per edge	·	Edge length of one small cube	=	Edge length of large cube

☐ · ? = ☐

What is the edge length of one small cube? _____ unit(s)

C Complete:

Each small cube has edge length _____ unit(s) and

volume _____ cubic unit(s).

D The formula for volume of a cube with edge length ℓ is $V = \ell \cdot \ell \cdot \ell$, or $V = \ell^3$. Find the volume of one small cube using this formula.

$V =$ _____ $=$ _____

Reflect

1. Several of the small cubes in the Explore Activity are arranged into a medium-sized cube as shown.

   Show two different ways to find the volume of this cube.

   _____

   _____

   _____

   _____

Math On the Spot

my.hrw.com

Finding Volume

A rectangular prism has six faces. Any pair of opposite faces can be called the **bases** of the prism.

Volume of a Rectangular Prism

$V = \ell wh$, or $V = Bh$

(where B represents the area of the prism's base; $B = \ell w$)

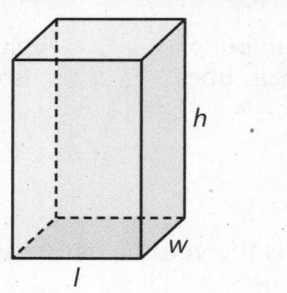

EXAMPLE 1

FL 6.G.1.2

Find the volume of the rectangular prism.

$\ell = 3$ meters $\qquad w = 2\frac{1}{4}$ meters $\qquad h = 4\frac{1}{2}$ meters

$V = \ell wh$

$= 3 \cdot 2\frac{1}{4} \cdot 4\frac{1}{2}$

$= 3 \cdot \dfrac{9}{4} \cdot \dfrac{9}{2}$ Write each mixed number as an improper fraction. Multiply.

$= \dfrac{243}{8}$

$= 30\frac{3}{8}$ cubic meters   Write as a mixed number in simplest form.

$4\frac{1}{2}$ m

$2\frac{1}{4}$ m

3 m

Math Talk

Mathematical Practices

Can you also use the formula $V = Bh$ to find the volume? Does it matter which face you choose as the base?

Find the volume of each rectangular prism.

2.
$2\frac{1}{2}$ in.

4 in.

$7\frac{1}{2}$ in.

3. length = $5\frac{1}{4}$ inches

width = $3\frac{1}{2}$ inches

height = 3 inches

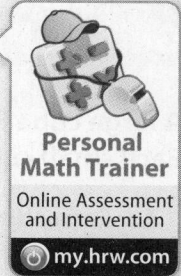

Personal Math Trainer
Online Assessment and Intervention
my.hrw.com

_____

_____

Solving Volume Problems

When you solve a real-world problem involving the volume of a prism, you can choose to use either of the volume formulas you know.

EXAMPLE 2 *Real World*   FL 6.G.1.2

A terrarium is shaped like a rectangular prism. The prism is $25\frac{1}{2}$ inches long, $13\frac{1}{2}$ inches wide, and 16 inches deep. What is the volume of the terrarium?

Math On the Spot
my.hrw.com

STEP 1 Choose one side to be the base, and find its area.

$B = 25\frac{1}{2} \times 13\frac{1}{2}$ *Use the $25\frac{1}{2}$-inch by $13\frac{1}{2}$-inch face as the base.*

$= \frac{51}{2} \times \frac{27}{2}$

$= \frac{1,377}{4}$

The area of the base is $\frac{1,377}{4}$ square inches. You need to perform another operation, so you don't need to write this value as a mixed number.

STEP 2 Find the volume.

$V = Bh$

$= \frac{1,377}{4} \times 16$ *Substitute $\frac{1,377}{4}$ for B and 16 for h.*

$= \frac{1,377}{{}_{1}4} \times \frac{\cancel{16}^{\,4}}{1}$ *Simplify before multiplying.*

$= 5,508$

The volume of the terrarium is 5,508 cubic inches.

4. A rectangular swimming pool is 15 meters long, $10\frac{1}{2}$ meters wide, and $2\frac{1}{2}$ meters deep. What is its volume?

Personal Math Trainer
Online Assessment and Intervention
my.hrw.com

_____

© Houghton Mifflin Harcourt Publishing Company

A large cube is made up of smaller unit cubes as shown on the right. Each small cube has an edge length of $\frac{1}{2}$ unit. (Explore Activity)

1. Each edge of the large cube is _____ units.

2. The volume of the large cube is _____ cubic units.

Find the volume of each prism. (Example 1)

3.

5 m
3.2 m
10 m

$V =$ _____ × _____ × _____

$=$ _____ cubic meters

4.

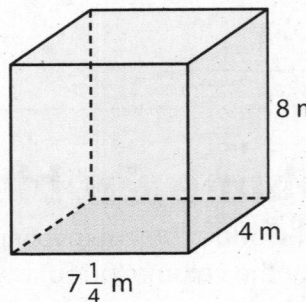

8 m
4 m
$7\frac{1}{4}$ m

$B =$ _____ × _____ $=$ _____ m²

$V =$ _____ cubic meters

5.

7.5 ft
4 ft
9.25 ft

$V =$ _____ cubic feet

6.

$6\frac{1}{2}$ in.
$4\frac{1}{2}$ in.
18 in.

$V =$ _____ cubic inches

7. A cereal box is $8\frac{1}{2}$ inches long, $3\frac{1}{2}$ inches wide, and 12 inches high.

What is the volume of the box? (Example 2) _____

? ESSENTIAL QUESTION CHECK-IN

8. Which two formulas can you use to find the volume of a rectangular prism? Why are these two formulas equivalent?

_____

_____

_____

15.2 Independent Practice

FL 6.G.1.2

Personal Math Trainer

Online Assessment and Intervention

my.hrw.com

9. A block of wood measures 4.5 inches by 3.5 inches by 7 inches. What is the volume of the block of wood?

_____

10. A restaurant buys a freezer in the shape of a rectangular prism. The dimensions of the freezer are shown. What is the volume of the freezer?

36 in.

$24\frac{1}{2}$ in.

$72\frac{1}{2}$ in.

_____

11. Rectangular prism A measures 6 inches by 4 inches by 5 inches. Rectangular prism B's dimensions are twice those of prism A. Find the volume of each prism. How many times as great is prism B's volume as prism A's volume?

_____

12. Leticia has a small paper weight in the shape of a rectangular prism. The dimensions of the paper weight are shown. What is the volume of the paper weight?

5 cm

$2\frac{3}{4}$ cm

$4\frac{1}{4}$ cm

_____

13. A company is designing a juice box. The box is in the shape of a rectangular prism. The base of the box is $6\frac{1}{2}$ inches by $2\frac{1}{2}$ inches, and the box is 4 inches high. If juice fills 90% of the box's volume, find the volume of juice in the box.

_____

14. **Science** Density is the amount of mass in a certain volume of an object. To find the density in grams per cubic centimeter of a substance you can use this relationship:

$$\text{Density} = \frac{\text{mass in grams}}{\text{volume in cubic centimeters}}$$

A gold bar that is 16 centimeters by 2.5 centimeters by 5 centimeters has a density of 19.3 grams per cubic centimeter. What is the mass of the gold bar?

_____

15. A suitcase is a rectangular prism whose dimensions are $1\frac{1}{4}$ feet by $1\frac{3}{4}$ feet by $1\frac{1}{4}$ feet. Find the volume of the suitcase.

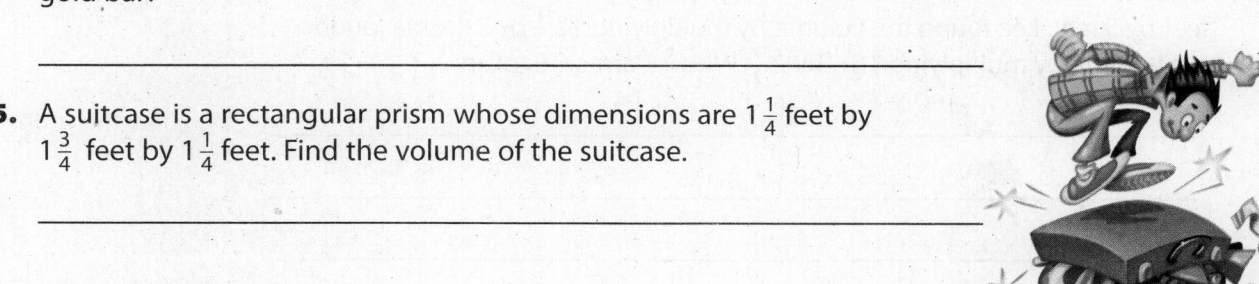

_____

16. The Smith family is moving and needs to decide on the size of the moving truck they should rent.

Inside Dimensions of Trucks			
Type	Length (ft)	Width (ft)	Height (ft)
Van	$10\frac{1}{2}$	6	6
Small Truck	12	8	$6\frac{3}{4}$
Large Truck	20	$8\frac{3}{4}$	$8\frac{1}{2}$

a. A moving van rents for $94.50 per day, and a small truck rents for $162 per day. Based on the amount of space inside the van or truck, which is the better deal? Explain your answer.

_____

_____

_____

b. How much greater is the volume of the large truck than the volume of the small truck?

_____

c. The family estimates that they need about 1,100 cubic feet to move their belongings. What should they rent?

_____

 FOCUS ON HIGHER ORDER THINKING

17. Persevere in Problem Solving A cube has a volume of $\frac{1}{512}$ cubic meter. What is the length of each side of the cube? Explain your thinking.

_____

_____

18. Communicate Mathematical Ideas Think about two rectangular prisms, one labeled prism P and one labeled prism Q.

a. Suppose the bases of the prisms have the same area, but the height of prism Q is twice the height of prism P. How do the volumes compare?

_____

b. Suppose the area of the base of prism Q is twice the area of the base of prism P. How do the volumes compare?

_____

19. Critical Thinking The dimensions of a rectangular prism are $3\frac{1}{4}$ feet by $2\frac{1}{2}$ feet by 5 feet. Lee found the volume by multiplying $12\frac{1}{2}$ by $3\frac{1}{4}$. Lola found the volume by multiplying $16\frac{1}{4}$ by $2\frac{1}{2}$. Who is correct? Explain.

_____

_____

_____

Work Area

LESSON 15.3 Solving Volume Equations

FL 6.G.1.2

... Apply the formulas $V = \ell wh$ and $V = bh$ ... in the context of solving real-world and mathematical problems. *Also 6.EE.2.7*

? **ESSENTIAL QUESTION**

How do you write equations to solve problems involving volume of rectangular prisms?

Writing Equations Using the Volume of a Rectangular Prism

You can use the formula for the volume of a rectangular prism to write an equation. Then solve the equation to find missing measurements for a prism.

Math On the Spot

my.hrw.com

EXAMPLE 1 **FL** 6.G.1.2, 6.EE.2.7

Samuel has an ant farm with a volume of 375 cubic inches. The width of the ant farm is 2.5 inches and the length is 15 inches. What is the height of Samuel's ant farm?

$V = \ell wh$ Write the formula.

$375 = 15 \cdot 2.5 \cdot h$ Use the formula to write an equation.

$375 = 37.5h$ Multiply.

$\dfrac{375}{37.5} = \dfrac{37.5h}{37.5}$ Divide both sides of the equation by 37.5.

$10 = h$

The height of the ant farm is 10 inches.

Reflect

1. **Communicate Mathematical Ideas** Explain how you would find the solution to Example 1 using the formula $V = Bh$.

_____

_____

YOUR TURN

2. Find the height of this rectangular prism, which has a volume of $\frac{15}{16}$ cubic feet.

_____

$\frac{3}{4}$ ft $\frac{1}{2}$ ft

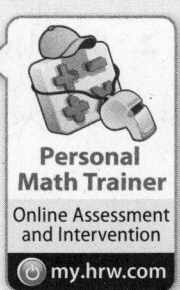

Personal Math Trainer

Online Assessment and Intervention

my.hrw.com

Math On the Spot
my.hrw.com

Solving Multistep Problems

One cubic foot of water equals approximately 7.5 gallons and weighs approximately 62.43 pounds.

EXAMPLE 2   **FL** 6.G.1.2, 6.EE.2.7

The classroom aquarium holds 30 gallons of water. It is 0.8 feet wide and has a height of 2 feet. Find the length of the aquarium.

STEP 1 Find the volume of the classroom aquarium in cubic feet.

> Divide the total number of gallons by the unit rate to find the number of cubic feet.

$$\frac{30 \text{ gallons}}{7.5 \text{ gallons per cubic foot}} = 4 \text{ cubic feet}$$

STEP 2 Find the length of the aquarium.

$4 = \ell \cdot 0.8 \cdot 2$	Use the formula $V = \ell wh$ to write an equation.
$4 = \ell(1.6)$	Multiply.
$\dfrac{4}{1.6} = \dfrac{\ell(1.6)}{1.6}$	Divide both sides of the equation by 1.6.
$2.5 = \ell$	

The length of the aquarium is 2.5 feet.

Math Talk
Mathematical Practices

How much does the water in the classroom aquarium weigh? Explain.

YOUR TURN

Personal Math Trainer
Online Assessment and Intervention
my.hrw.com

3. An aquarium holds 33.75 gallons of water. It has a length of 2 feet and a height of 1.5 feet. What is the width of the aquarium? _____

Guided Practice

1. Use an equation to find the width of the rectangular prism. (Example 1)

   _____

2. One clay brick weighs 5.76 pounds. The brick is 8 inches long and $2\frac{1}{4}$ inches wide. If the clay weighs 0.08 pounds per cubic inch, what is the volume of the brick? Find the height of the brick. (Example 2)

   _____

$V = 6{,}336 \text{ cm}^3$

18 cm

16 cm

? cm

15.3 Independent Practice

 FL 6.EE.2.7, 6.G.1.2

3. Jala has an aquarium in the shape of a rectangular prism with the dimensions shown. What is the height of the aquarium?

Height = _____

V = 3,758.75 cubic inches
12.5 in.
24.25 in.

4. The area of the base of a rectangular juice box is $4\frac{1}{2}$ square inches. If the volume of the box is 18 cubic inches, how tall is the box?

Height = _____

5. A box of cereal is shaped like a rectangular prism. The box is 20 centimeters long and 30 centimeters high. Its volume is 3,600 cubic centimeters. Find the width of the box.

Width = _____

6. About 7.5 gallons of water fill up 1 cubic foot of space. How many gallons of water will fill a goldfish pool shaped like the prism shown?

_____

$1\frac{1}{2}$ ft
$3\frac{1}{2}$ ft
3 ft

7. Physical Science A small bar of gold measures 40 mm by 25 mm by 2 mm. One cubic millimeter of gold weighs about 0.0005 ounce. Find the volume in cubic millimeters and the weight in ounces of this small bar of gold.

_____

_____

8. History A typical stone on the lowest level of the Great Pyramid in Egypt was a rectangular prism 5 feet long by 5 feet high by 6 feet deep and weighed 15 tons. What was the volume of the average stone? How much did one cubic foot of this stone weigh?

_____

9. Hank has cards that are 8 inches by 4 inches. A stack of these cards fits inside the box shown and uses up 32 cubic inches of volume. How tall is the stack of cards? What percent of the box's volume is taken up by the cards?

_____

4 in.
4 in.
8 in.

10. A freshwater fish is healthiest when there is at least 1 gallon of water for every inch of its body length. Roshel wants to put a goldfish that is about $2\frac{1}{2}$ inches long in her tank. Roshel's tank is 7 inches long, 5 inches wide, and 7 inches high. The volume of 1 gallon of water is about 231 cubic inches.

a. How many gallons of water would Roshel need for the fish? _____

b. What is the volume of Roshel's tank? _____

c. Is her fish tank large enough for the fish? Explain. _____

_____

H.O.T. FOCUS ON HIGHER ORDER THINKING

Work Area

11. Multistep Larry has a clay brick that is 7 inches long, 3.5 inches wide, and 1.75 inches thick, the same size as the gold stored in Fort Knox in the form of gold bars. Find the volume of this brick. If the weight of the clay in the brick is 0.1 pound per cubic inch and the weight of the gold is 0.7 pound per cubic inch, find the weight of the brick and the gold bar. Round all answers the nearest tenth.

Volume of the brick or bar = _____ cubic inches

Weight of the brick = _____ pounds

Weight of the gold bar = _____ pounds

12. Represent Real-World Problems Luisa's toaster oven, which is in the shape of a rectangular prism, has a base that is 55 cm long by 40 cm wide. It is 30 cm high. Luisa wants to buy a different oven with the same volume but a smaller length, so it will fit better on her kitchen counter. What is a possible set of dimensions for this different oven?

_____

_____

_____

_____

13. Multiple Representations Use the formula $V = Bh$ to write a different version of this formula that you could use to find the area of the base B of a rectangular prism if you know the height h and the volume V. Explain what you did to find this equation.

_____

_____

14. Communicate Mathematical Ideas The volume of a cube is 27 cubic inches. What is the length of an edge? Explain.

_____

Ready to Go On?

15.1 Nets and Surface Area

A square pyramid is shown sitting on its base.

1. Draw the net of the pyramid.

2. The surface area of the pyramid

is _____ square centimeters.

8 cm

12 cm   12 cm

15.2 Volume of Rectangular Prisms

Find the volume of each rectangular prism.

3.

$8\frac{1}{4}$ m

6 m

$8\frac{3}{8}$ m

$V =$ _____ cubic meters

4.

$2\frac{1}{4}$ ft

$6\frac{1}{2}$ ft

5 ft

$V =$ _____ cubic feet

15.3 Solving Volume Equations

Find the volume of each rectangular prism.

5. The volume inside a rectangular storage room is 2,025 cubic feet. The room is 9 feet high. Find the area of the floor. _____

6. An aquarium holds 11.25 cubic feet of water, and is 2.5 feet long and 1.5 feet wide. What is its depth? _____

? ESSENTIAL QUESTION

7. How can a model help you to solve surface area and volume problems?

_____

_____

_____

Assessment Readiness

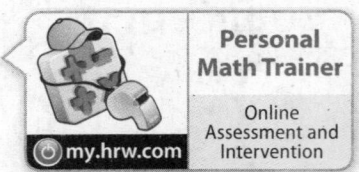

Personal
Math Trainer

Online
Assessment and
Intervention

Selected Response

1. Indira is wrapping the box below. How much wrapping paper does she need?

3 in.

6 in.

8 in.

Ⓐ 34 in.²   Ⓒ 144 in.²

Ⓑ 90 in.²   Ⓓ 180 in.²

2. Colin has an ice cube tray with 12 identical compartments. Each compartment is a prism that is 4 centimeters long, 3 centimeters wide, and 3 centimeters high. Given that 1 cubic centimeter holds 1 milliliter of water, how many milliliters of water can the tray hold?

Ⓐ 36 mL   Ⓒ 432 mL

Ⓑ 66 mL   Ⓓ 792 mL

3. A store manager set up a cardboard display to advertise a new brand of perfume. The display is a square pyramid whose base is 18 inches on each side. The height of each triangular face of the pyramid is 12 inches. How much cardboard was used to make the display?

Ⓐ 516 in²   Ⓒ 756 in²

Ⓑ 612 in²   Ⓓ 1,080 in²

4. Which expression is equivalent to $24 + 32$?

Ⓐ $8 \times (3 + 4)$

Ⓑ $8 \times (3 + 32)$

Ⓒ $6 \times (4 + 32)$

Ⓓ $6 \times (4 + 6)$

5. A bathtub in the shape of a rectangular prism is 5 feet long, $3\frac{1}{2}$ feet wide, and $4\frac{1}{4}$ feet high. How much water could the tub hold?

Ⓐ $14\frac{7}{8}$ ft³   Ⓒ $74\frac{3}{8}$ ft³

Ⓑ $25\frac{1}{2}$ ft³   Ⓓ $87\frac{1}{2}$ ft³

6. The point $(-1.5, 2)$ is reflected across the y-axis. What are the coordinates of the point after the reflection?

Ⓐ $(-1.5, -2)$ Ⓒ $(2, -1.5)$

Ⓑ $(1.5, 2)$ Ⓓ $(2, 1.5)$

Mini-Task

7. An cardboard box is open at one end and is shaped like a square prism missing one of its square bases. The volume of the prism is 810 cubic inches, and its height is 10 inches.

a. What is the length of each side of the base? _____

b. Draw a net of the box.

c. How much cardboard is used for the box?

_____

© Houghton Mifflin Harcourt Publishing Company

Study Guide Review

MODULE 13 — Area and Polygons

Key Vocabulary
parallelogram
(paralelogramo)
rhombus (rombo)
trapezoid (trapecio)

? ESSENTIAL QUESTION

How can you use area and volume equations to solve real-world problems?

EXAMPLE 1

Find the area of the trapezoid.

$A = \frac{1}{2}(h)(b_1 + b_2)$

$A = \frac{1}{2}(10)(7 + 4)$

$A = 55$ in^2

4 in.

10 in.

7 in.

EXAMPLE 2

Find the area of Jorge's backyard.

18 ft

11 ft

6 ft

6 ft

Find the area of the first rectangle.

$A = bh$

$A = 12(5)$

$A = 60$ square feet

Find the area of the second rectangle.

$A = bh$

$A = 6(11)$

$A = 66$ square feet

Total area of yard $= 60 + 66 = 126$ square feet

EXERCISES

Find the area of each figure. (Lessons 13.1, 13.2)

1.

24 in.

12 in.

_____

2.

5 cm

10 cm

10 cm

_____

Find the missing measurement. (Lesson 13.3)

3.

11 m

h $A = 62.5$ m^2

14 m

_____

4.

b

4 mm

$A = 26$ mm^2

_____

Distance and Area in the Coordinate Plane

Key Vocabulary

polygon (*polígono*)

reflection (*reflexión*)

vertex, vertices (*vértice, vértices*)

? ESSENTIAL QUESTION

What steps might you take to solve a polygon problem given the coordinates of its vertices?

EXAMPLE 1

Find the distance between points _A_ and _B_ on the coordinate plane.

Find the distance between point _A_ and the _x_-axis.

> The _y_-coordinate is −4. The absolute value represents the distance.
>
> $|-4| = 4$ The distance is 4 units.

Find the distance between point _B_ and the _x_-axis.

> The _y_-coordinate is 2. The distance is 2 units.

Add the two distances to find the distance between the two points.

> $4 + 2 = 6$ The distance between points _A_ and _B_ is 6 units.

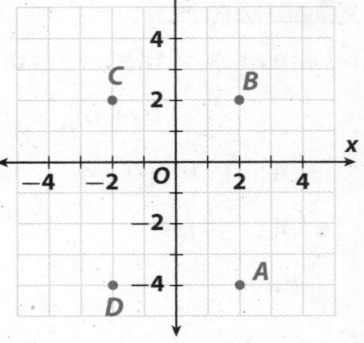

EXAMPLE 2

Find the area of the rectangle whose vertices are the points on the coordinate plane in Example 1.

Use the distance between points _A_ and _B_ in Example 1 as the height.

> height = 6 units

Find the distance between points _A_ and _D_ and use it as the base.

> Distance from _A_ to _D_ = $|-2| + 2 = 2 + 2 = 4$
>
> base = 4 units

Find the area.

> $A = bh = 4 \cdot 6 = 24$ square units

EXERCISES

Find the distance between the two points.

1. _Z_ and _Y_ _____

2. _X_ and _Y_ _____

3. _W_ and _X_ _____

4. Find the area of rectangle _XYZV_. _____

Surface Area and Volume of Solids

Key Vocabulary

net *(plantilla)*
pyramid *(pirámide)*
surface area *(área total)*

❓ ESSENTIAL QUESTION

How can a model help you solve surface area and volume problems?

EXAMPLE 1

Draw a net and find the surface area of the pyramid.

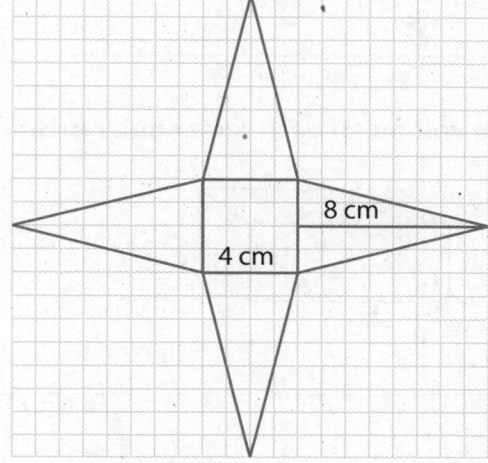

Find the area of the square base.

$A = bh$

$A = 4 \cdot 4$

$A = 16 \text{ cm}^2$

Find the area of one triangle and multiply by four.

$A = \frac{1}{2}bh$

$A = \frac{1}{2}(4 \cdot 8)$

$A = 16 \text{ cm}^2$

The area of the 4 triangles is $4 \cdot 16 = 64 \text{ cm}^2$.

The total surface area of the pyramid is $16 \text{ cm}^2 + 64 \text{ cm}^2 = 80 \text{ cm}^2$.

EXAMPLE 2

A cubic centimeter of gold weighs approximately 19.32 grams. Find the weight of a brick of gold that has a height of 6 centimeters, width of 3 centimeters, and length of 8 centimeters.

$V = lwh$

$V = 8 \, (3) \, (6)$

$V = 144 \text{ cm}^3$

The weight of the gold is 144×19.32 grams, which is 2,782.08 grams.

EXERCISES

Draw a net to find the surface area of each solid shape. (Lesson 15.1)

1.

5 in.   7 in.   3 in.

_____

2.

14 cm

8 cm

_____

Find the volume of each rectangular prism. (Lesson 15.2)

3.

6 in.
8 in.
20 in.

_____

4. A rectangular prism with a width of 7 units, a length of 8 units, and a height of 2 units _____

Unit 6 Performance Tasks

1. **CAREERS IN MATH** Theater Set Construction Ahmed and Karina are building scenery of the Egyptian pyramids out of plywood for a community play. The pyramids are represented by triangles on a rectangular base. The diagram shows the measurements of the piece of scenery.

1 ft   1.5 ft   0.75 ft

1.5 ft   2 ft   1 ft   0.75 ft

5 ft

a. How many square feet of plywood is in the scenery? Show your work.

_____

_____

b. The pyramids (the triangles) will be painted gray, and the base (the rectangle) will be painted black. How much of each paint color will they use, if one quart covers 45 square feet? Only one side of the model needs to be painted, but two coats of paint will be needed. Show your work. Round to the nearest hundredth of a square foot.

_____

_____

_____

Assessment Readiness

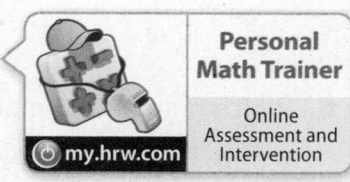

Personal Math Trainer

Online Assessment and Intervention

my.hrw.com

Selected Response

1. Jessie has a piece of cardboard that is 8.5 inches by 11 inches. She makes a picture frame with the cardboard by cutting out a 4 inch by 4 inch square from the center of the cardboard. What is the area of the frame?

   Ⓐ 16 in²
   Ⓑ 77.5 in²
   Ⓒ 93.5 in²
   Ⓓ 118.5 in²

2. Jermaine is ordering a piece of glass in the shape of a trapezoid to create a patio table top. Each square foot of glass costs $25. The trapezoid has base lengths of 5 feet and 3 feet and a height of 4 feet. What is the cost of the glass?

   Ⓐ $400
   Ⓑ $437.50
   Ⓒ $800
   Ⓓ $1,500

3. What is the area of a trapezoid that has bases measuring 19 centimeters and 23 centimeters, and a height of 14 centimeters?

   Ⓐ 105 square centimeters
   Ⓑ 266 square centimeters
   Ⓒ 294 square centimeters
   Ⓓ 322 square centimeters

4. What is the area of the triangle shown below?

17 in.   26 in.

   Ⓐ 110.5 square inches
   Ⓑ 221 square inches
   Ⓒ 442 square inches
   Ⓓ 884 square inches

5. The trapezoid below has an area of 475 square meters.

28 m

18 m

   Which equation could you solve to find the height of the trapezoid?

   Ⓐ $23h = 475$
   Ⓑ $252h = 475$
   Ⓒ $46h = 475$
   Ⓓ $504h = 475$

6. A rectangular prism has a volume of 1,500 cubic centimeters. It has a length of 34 centimeters and a width of 22 centimeters. Which equation could be solved to find the height of the rectangular prism?

   Ⓐ $374h = 1,500$
   Ⓑ $28h = 1,500$
   Ⓒ $748h = 1,500$
   Ⓓ $56h = 1,500$

7. Which expression represents the sum of 59 and x?

   Ⓐ $59 + x$
   Ⓑ $59 \div x$
   Ⓒ $59x$
   Ⓓ $59 - x$

8. Which number has more than two factors?

Ⓐ 19

Ⓑ 23

Ⓒ 25

Ⓓ 29

9. Which of the following statements about rational numbers is **not** correct?

Ⓐ All whole numbers are also rational numbers.

Ⓑ All integers are also rational numbers.

Ⓒ All rational numbers can be written in the form $\frac{a}{b}$.

Ⓓ Rational numbers cannot be negative.

Mini-Tasks

10. Lisa bought a tank for her hermit crab. The tank can hold 1,331 cubic inches of water and includes a top. The base of the aquarium is a square. The height of the aquarium is 11 inches.

a. What is the length of each side of the base of the tank?

_____

b. What shape is Lisa's tank?

_____

c. Draw a net of the tank.

d. What is the surface area of the tank?

_____

11. Chuck is making a map of his neighborhood. Each grid unit represents one city block. He uses the following coordinates, with north being the direction of the positive *y*-axis.

Library: $(-5, 5)$
Chuck's house: $(-5, -3)$
City Hall: $(3, -3)$

a. Plot each point on the coordinate grid below.

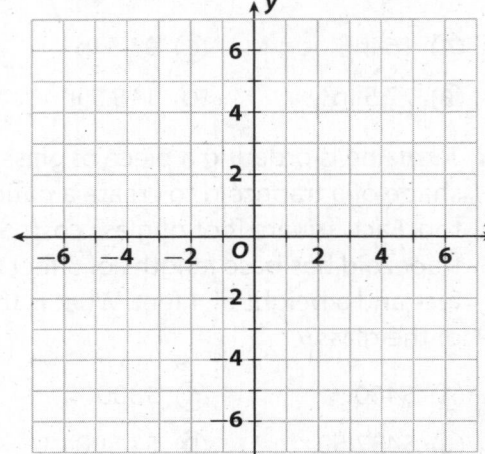

b. How far does Chuck live from the library and from City Hall?

_____

c. Chuck decided to add the post office to his map. The post office is 6 blocks east of the library. What are the coordinates of the post office? Plot the post office on the coordinate grid.

_____

d. If you connect the points on the map, what shape do you make?

_____

e. What is the area of the shape in **d**? Use square blocks as the unit.

_____

Measurement and Data

CAREERS IN MATH

Geneticist A geneticist is a scientist who studies and applies genetics, a branch of biology that focuses on heredity and variation in organisms. Geneticists analyze how different traits are passed from parents to offspring.

If you are interested in a career as a geneticist, you should study these mathematical subjects:
- Algebra
- Trigonometry
- Probability and Statistics
- Calculus

Research other careers that require the analysis of data.

Unit 7 Performance Task

At the end of the unit, check out how **geneticists** use math.

© Houghton Mifflin Harcourt Publishing Company •Image Credits: Don Mason/Blend Images/Corbis

Use the puzzle to preview key vocabulary from this unit. Unscramble the circled letters to answer the riddle at the bottom of the page.

1. **OBX LOTP**

2. **TOD TOLP**

3. **HOSTIARMG**

4. **NIADEM**

5. **PEPRU LAETURQI**

6. **NAME LATESBOL ANITVODIE**

1. A display that shows how the values in a data set are distributed. (Lesson 16.3)
2. A display in which each piece of data is represented by a dot above the number line. (Lesson 16.4)
3. A type of bar graph whose bars represent frequencies of numerical data within intervals. (Lesson 16.5)
4. The middle value of an ordered data set. (Lesson 16.1)
5. The median of the upper half of the data in a box plot. (Lesson 16.3)
6. The mean distance between each data value and the mean of the data set. (Lesson 16.2)

Q: What is a math teacher's favorite dessert?

A: ___ ___ ___ ___ ___ ___ ___ ___ ___ ___
___ ___ ___ ___ ___ ___ ___ ___ ___!

Displaying, Analyzing, and Summarizing Data

MODULE

16

ESSENTIAL QUESTION

How can you solve real-world problems by displaying, analyzing, and summarizing data?

LESSON 16.1
Measures of Center
 FL 6.SP.1.3, 6.SP.2.5, 6.SP.2.5a, 6.SP.2.5b, 6.SP.2.5c, 6.SP.2.5d

LESSON 16.2
Mean Absolute Deviation
 FL 6.SP.2.5c

LESSON 16.3
Box Plots
 FL 6.SP.2.4, 6.SP.2.5c

LESSON 16.4
Dot Plots and Data Distribution
 FL 6.SP.1.1, 6.SP.1.2, 6.SP.2.4, 6.SP.2.5c, 6.SP.2.5d

LESSON 16.5
Histograms
FL 6.SP.2.4, 6.SP.2.5

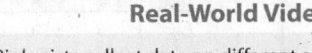
Real-World Video

Biologists collect data on different animals. They can describe the data using measures of center or spread, and by displaying the data in plots or graphs, they may see trends related to the animal population.

my.hrw.com

GO DIGITAL
my.hrw.com

my.hrw.com
Go digital with your write-in student edition, accessible on any device.

Math On the Spot
Scan with your smart phone to jump directly to the online edition, video tutor, and more.

Animated Math
Interactively explore key concepts to see how math works.

Personal Math Trainer
Get immediate feedback and help as you work through practice sets.

445

Are YOU Ready?

Complete these exercises to review skills you will need for this module.

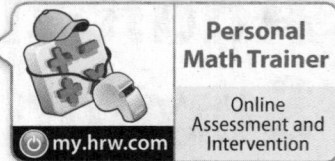

Remainders

EXAMPLE

$$
\begin{array}{r}
7.25 \\
12\overline{)87.00} \\
\underline{84} \\
30 \\
\underline{-24} \\
60 \\
\underline{-60} \\
0
\end{array}
$$

Write a decimal point and a zero in the dividend.

Place a decimal point in the quotient.

Add more zeros to the dividend if necessary.

Find the quotient. Write the remainder as a decimal.

1. $15\overline{)42}$ _____

2. $75\overline{)93}$ _____

3. $52\overline{)91}$ _____

4. $24\overline{)57}$ _____

Read Bar Graphs

EXAMPLE How many goals did Alec score?

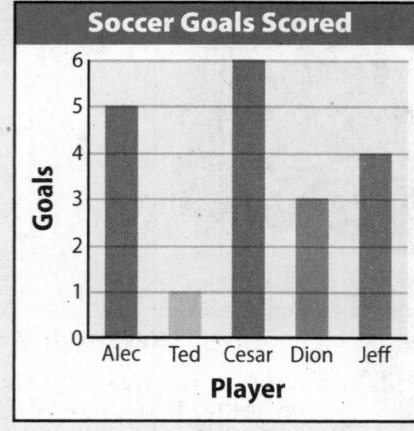

The first bar shows how many goals Alec scored.

The bar extends to a height of 5.

Alec scored 5 goals.

5. How many goals did Dion score? _____

6. Which two players together scored the same number of goals as Jeff? _____

7. How many fewer goals than Cesar did Alec score? _____

Reading Start-Up

Visualize Vocabulary

Use the review words to complete the chart.

Introduction to Statistics		
Definition	**Example**	**Review word**
A group of facts	The grades of all of the students in a school	
A tool used to gather information from individuals	A questionnaire given to all students to find the number of hours each student spends studying in 1 week	
A value that summarizes a set of unequal values, found by addition and division	Results of the survey show that students typically spend 5 hours a week studying	

Understand Vocabulary

Complete the sentences using the preview words.

1. The average of a data set is the _____.

2. The _____ is the middle value of a data set.

3. The number or category that occurs most frequently in a data set is the _____.

Vocabulary

Review Words

average *(promedio)*
data *(datos)*
survey *(encuesta)*

Preview Words

box plot *(diagrama de caja)*
categorical data *(datos categóricos)*
dot plot *(diagrama de puntos)*
histogram *(histograma)*
interquartile range *(rango entre cuartiles)*
lower quartile *(cuartil inferior)*
✔ mean *(media)*
mean absolute deviation (MAD) *(desviación absoluta media, (DAM))*
✔ median *(mediana)*
measure of center *(medida central)*
measure of spread *(medida de dispersión)*
✔ mode *(moda)*
range *(rango)*
statistical question *(pregunta estadística)*
upper quartile *(cuartil superior)*

Active Reading

Layered Book Before beginning the module, create a layered book to help you learn the concepts in this module. Label each flap with lesson titles from this module. As you study each lesson, write important ideas, such as vocabulary and formulas under the appropriate flap. Refer to your finished layered book as you work on exercises from this module.

MODULE 16
Unpacking the Standards

Understanding the standards and the vocabulary terms in the standards will help you know exactly what you are expected to learn in this module.

FL 6.SP.2.5C

Summarize numerical data sets in relation to their context, such as by giving quantitative measures of center (median and/or mean) and variability (interquartile range and/or mean absolute deviation), as well as describing any overall pattern and any striking deviations from the overall pattern with reference to the context in which the data were gathered.

What It Means to You

You will use measures of center to describe a data set.

UNPACKING EXAMPLE 6.SP.2.5C

Several students' scores on a history test are shown. Find the mean score and the median score. Which measure better describes the typical score for these students? Explain.

History Test Scores
73 48 88 90 90 81 83

Mean: $\dfrac{73 + 48 + 88 + 90 + 90 + 81 + 83}{7} = \dfrac{553}{7} = 79$

To find the median, write the data values in order from least to greatest and find the middle value.
Median: 48 73 81 83 88 90 90

The median better describes the typical score.
The mean is affected by the low score of 48.

FL 6.SP.2.4

Display numerical data in plots on a number line, including dot plots, histograms, and box plots.

What It Means to You

You will interpret the data from a dot plot, histogram, or box plot.

UNPACKING EXAMPLE 6.SP.2.4

Kim has started rating each movie she sees using a scale of 1 to 10 on an online site. She made a histogram that shows how she rated the movies. What does the shape of the distribution tell you about the movies Kim has rated?

Of the 15 movies that Kim rated, she rated almost half a 7 or an 8 and did not generally give extreme ratings.

 Visit **my.hrw.com** to see all **Florida Math Standards** unpacked.

my.hrw.com

448 Unit 7

LESSON

16.1 Measures of Center

FL 6.SP.2.5

Summarize numerical data sets in relation to their context, ... *Also 6.SP.1.3, 6.SP.2.5a, 6.SP.2.5b, 6.SP.2.5c, 6.SP.2.5d*

? ESSENTIAL QUESTION

How can you use measures of center to describe a data set?

EXPLORE ACTIVITY 1   FL 6.SP.2.5c, 6.SP.1.3, 6.SP.2.5a

Finding the Mean

A **measure of center** is a single number used to describe a set of numeric data. A measure of center describes a typical value from the data set.

One measure of center is the *mean*. The **mean**, or average, of a data set is the sum of the data values divided by the number of data values in the set.

Tami surveyed five of her friends to find out how many brothers and sisters they have. Her results are shown in the table.

Number of Siblings				
Amy	Ben	Cal	Don	Eva
2	3	1	1	3

A Model each person's response as a group of counters.

B Now rearrange the counters so that each group has the same number of counters.

Each group now has _____ counter(s). This value is the mean. This model demonstrates how the mean "evens out" the data values.

C Use numbers to calculate the mean.

The sum of the data values is $2 + 3 + $

How many data values are in the set? _____

© Houghton Mifflin Harcourt Publishing Company

Lesson 16.1 **449**

$$\text{Mean} = \frac{\text{sum of data values}}{\text{number of data values}} = \frac{\boxed{}}{\boxed{}} = \boxed{}$$

Math Talk
Mathematical Practices

Suppose you have a data set in which all of the values are 2. What is the mean?

Reflect

1. Can the mean be greater than the greatest value in a data set? Why or why not?

_____

_____

_____

Math On the Spot
ⓒ my.hrw.com

Finding the Median

Another measure of center is the *median*. The **median** represents the middle value of an ordered data set.

EXAMPLE 1 Real World   FL   6.SP.2.5c, 6.SP.2.5b

A A coach records the distances that some cross-country team members ran last week. Find the median.

Write the data values in order from least to greatest.

3 4 5 5 6 7 7 8 10 10 10

This value is the median.

Equal number of values on either side of the median

Distances Run	
Cara	3 mi
Rob	5 mi
Maria	7 mi
Olivia	10 mi
Paul	10 mi
Chris	4 mi
Amir	7 mi
Iris	5 mi
Alex	8 mi
Tara	10 mi
Ned	6 mi

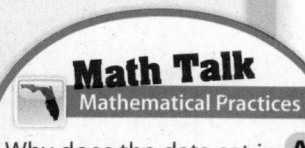
Math Talk
Mathematical Practices

Why does the data set in **A** have one middle value while the data set in **B** has two middle values?

The median is 7.

B Find the median of these test scores: 87, 90, 77, 83, 99, 94, 93, 90, 85, 83.

Write the data values in order from least to greatest.

77 83 83 85 87 90 90 93 94 99

This data set has two middle values: 87 and 90.

The median is the average of these two values:

$$\text{Median} = \frac{87 + 90}{2} = 88.5$$

The median is 88.5.

© Houghton Mifflin Harcourt Publishing Company

Reflect

2. **What If?** Which units are used for the data in ? If the coach had recorded some distances in kilometers and some in miles, can you still find the median of the data? Explain.

_____

_____

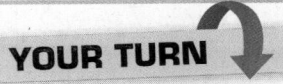 **YOUR TURN**

3. Charlotte recorded the number of minutes she spent exercising in the past ten days: 12, 4, 5, 6, 8, 7, 9, 8, 2, 1. Find the median of the data.

_____

Personal Math Trainer

Online Assessment and Intervention

my.hrw.com

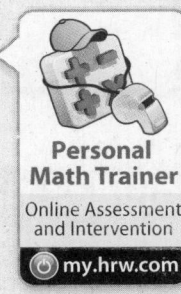

EXPLORE ACTIVITY 2 Real World

FL **6.SP.2.5d, 6.SP.2.5c**

Comparing the Mean and the Median

The mean and median of a data set may be equal, very close to each other, or very different from each other. For data sets where the mean and median differ greatly, one likely describes the data set better than the other.

The monthly earnings of several teenagers are $200, $320, $275, $250, $750, $350, and $310.

A Find the mean.

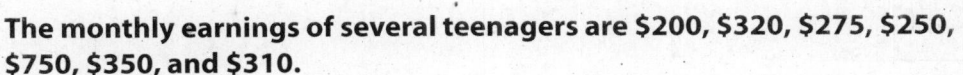

B Write the data values in order from least to greatest and find the median.

_____

C The mean and the median differ by about $_____. Why?

_____

_____

D Which measure of center better describes the typical monthly earnings for this group of teenagers—the mean or the median? Explain.

_____

_____

Reflect

4. **Communicate Mathematical Ideas** Luka's final exam scores for this semester are 70, 72, 99, 72, and 69. Find the mean and median. Which is a better description of Luka's typical exam score? Explain your thinking.

_____

_____

Guided Practice

1. Spencer surveyed five of his friends to find out how many pets they have. His results are shown in the table. What is the mean number of pets? (Explore Activity 1)

Number of Pets				
Lara	Cody	Sam	Ella	Maria
3	5	2	4	1

$$\text{Mean} = \frac{\text{sum of data values}}{\text{number of data values}} = \frac{\boxed{}}{\boxed{}} = \boxed{}$$

The mean number of pets is _____

2. The following are the weights, in pounds, of some dogs at a kennel: 36, 45, 29, 39, 51, 49. (Example 1)

   a. Find the median. _____

   b. Suppose one of the weights were given in kilograms. Can you still find the median? Explain.

   _____

3. a. Find the mean and the median of this data set: 9, 6, 5, 3, 28, 6, 4, 7. (Explore Activity 2)

   _____

   b. Which better describes the data set, the mean or the median? Explain.

   _____

   _____

? ESSENTIAL QUESTION CHECK-IN

4. How can you use measures of center to describe a data set?

_____

_____

16.1 Independent Practice

FL 6.SP.1.3, 6.SP.2.5, 6.SP.2.5a, 6.SP.2.5b, 6.SP.2.5c, 6.SP.2.5d

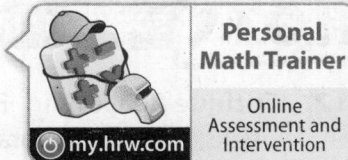

Personal Math Trainer

Online Assessment and Intervention

my.hrw.com

Several students in Ashton's class were randomly selected and asked how many text messages they sent yesterday. Their answers were 1, 0, 10, 7, 13, 2, 9, 15, 0, 3.

5. How many students were asked? How do you know?

_____

_____

_____

6. Find the mean and the median for these data.

Mean = _____   Median = _____

The points scored by a basketball team in its last 6 games are shown. Use these data for 7 and 8.

Points Scored					
73	77	85	84	37	115

7. Find the mean score and the median score.

Mean = _____   Median = _____

8. Which measure better describes the typical number of points scored? Explain.

_____

_____

_____

Some people were asked how long it takes them to commute to work. Use the data for 9–11.

9. What units are used for the data? What should you do before finding the mean and median number of minutes?

16 min	5 min
7 min	8 min
14 min	12 min
0.5 hr	1 hr

_____

10. Find the mean and median number of minutes.

Mean = _____   Median = _____

11. Which measure do you think is more typical of the data?

_____

_____

_____

12. Critique Reasoning For two weeks, the school librarian recorded the number of library books returned each morning. The data are shown in the dot plot. The librarian found the mean number of books returned each morning.

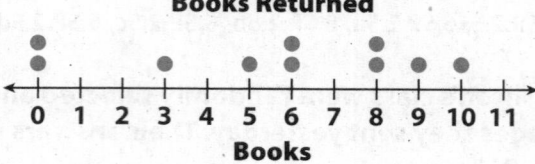

Books Returned

Books

$$\frac{8 + 6 + 10 + 5 + 9 + 8 + 3 + 6}{8} = \frac{55}{8} \approx 6.9$$

Is this the correct mean of this data set? If not, explain and correct the answer.

_____

_____

13. Critical Thinking Lauren's scores on her math tests are 93, 91, 98, 100, 95, 92, and 96. What score could Lauren get on her next math test so that the mean and median remain the same? Explain your answer.

_____

_____

_____

14. Persevere in Problem Solving Yuko wants to take a job selling cars. Since she will get a commission for every car she sells, she finds out the sale price of the last four cars sold at each company.

Company A: $16,000; $20,000; $25,000; $35,000;

Company B: $21,000, $23,000, $36,000, $48,000

a. Find the mean selling price at each company.

_____

b. Find the median selling price at each company.

_____

c. Communicate Mathematical Ideas At either company, Yuko will get paid a commission of 20% of the sale price of each car she sells. Based on the data, where do you recommend she take a job? Why?

_____

_____

_____

LESSON 16.2 Mean Absolute Deviation

FL 6.SP.2.5c
Summarize numerical data sets in relation to their context, such as by giving quantitative measures of ...variability (...mean absolute deviation)....

? **ESSENTIAL QUESTION**

How can you determine and use the mean absolute deviation of a set of data points?

EXPLORE ACTIVITY   FL 6.SP.2.5c

Understanding Mean Absolute Deviation

A **measure of variability** is a single number used to describe the spread of a data set. It can also be called a measure of spread. One measure of variability is the **mean absolute deviation (MAD)**, which is the mean of the distances between the data values and the mean of the data set.

The data represent the height, in feet, of various buildings. Find the mean absolute deviation for each data set.

A 60, 58, 54, 56, 63, 65, 62, 59, 56, 58

Calculate the mean. Round to the nearest whole number.

Complete the table.

Height (ft)	60	58	54	56	63	65	62	59	56	58
Distance from mean										

Calculate the MAD by finding the mean of the values in the second row of the table. Round to the nearest whole number.

B 46, 47, 56, 48, 46, 52, 57, 52, 45

Find the mean. Round to the nearest whole number.

Complete the table.

Height (ft)	46	47	56	48	46	52	57	52	45
Distance from mean									

Math Talk
Mathematical Practices
What is the difference between a measure of center and a measure of variability?

Calculate the MAD. Round to the nearest whole number.

Reflect

1. **Analyze Relationships** Compare the MADs. How do the MADs describe the distribution of the heights in each group?

_____

_____

Math On the Spot
my.hrw.com

Using Mean Absolute Deviation

The mean absolute deviation can be used to answer statistical questions in the real world. Many of these questions may have implications for the operation of various businesses.

EXAMPLE 1 Real World   FL 6.SP.2.5c

A chicken farmer wants her chickens to all have about the same weight. She is trying two types of feed to see which type produces the best results. All the chickens in Pen A are fed Premium Growth feed, and all the chickens in Pen B are fed Maximum Growth feed. The farmer records the weights of the chickens in each pen in the tables below. Which chicken feed produces less variability in weight?

Pen A: Premium Growth Weights (lb)									
5.8	6.1	5.5	6.6	7.3	5.9	6.3	5.7	6.8	7.1

Pen B: Maximum Growth Weights (lb)									
7.7	7.4	5.4	7.8	6.1	5.2	7.5	7.9	6.3	5.6

STEP 1 Find the mean weight of the chickens in each pen. Round your answers to the nearest tenth.

Pen A: $\dfrac{5.8 + 6.1 + 5.5 + 6.6 + 7.3 + 5.9 + 6.3 + 5.7 + 6.8 + 7.1}{10} \approx 6.3$

Pen B: $\dfrac{7.7 + 7.4 + 5.4 + 7.8 + 6.1 + 5.2 + 7.5 + 7.9 + 6.3 + 5.6}{10} \approx 6.7$

STEP 2 Find the distance from the mean for each of the weights.

The distances from the mean for Pen A are the distance of each weight from 6.3 lb.

Pen A: Premium Growth										
Weight (lb)	5.8	6.1	5.5	6.6	7.3	5.9	6.3	5.7	6.8	7.1
Distance from mean	0.5	0.2	0.8	0.3	1.0	0.4	0	0.6	0.5	0.8

The distances from the mean for Pen B are the distance of each weight from 6.7 lb.

Pen B: Maximum Growth										
Weight (lb)	7.7	7.4	5.4	7.8	6.1	5.2	7.5	7.9	6.3	5.6
Distance from mean	1.0	0.7	1.3	1.1	0.6	1.5	0.8	1.2	0.4	1.1

STEP 3 Calculate the MAD for the chickens in each pen. Round your answers to the nearest tenth.

Pen A: $\dfrac{0.5 + 0.2 + 0.8 + 0.3 + 1.0 + 0.4 + 0 + 0.6 + 0.5 + 0.8}{10} \approx 0.5$ lb

Pen B: $\dfrac{1.0 + 0.7 + 1.3 + 1.1 + 0.6 + 1.5 + 0.8 + 1.2 + 0.4 + 1.1}{10} \approx 1.0$ lb

Since Pen A's MAD is less, Premium Growth feed produces less variability in weight.

Animated Math
my.hrw.com

Math Talk
Mathematical Practices

Will a smaller mean always signal less variability?

 YOUR TURN

2. Two waiters at a cafe each served 10 large fruit smoothies. The amount in each large smoothie is shown below. Which waiter's smoothies showed less variability?

Amounts in Waiter A's Large Smoothies (oz)									
19.1	20.1	20.9	19.6	20.9	19.5	19.2	19.4	20.3	20.9

Amounts in Waiter B's Large Smoothies (oz)									
20.1	19.6	20.0	20.5	19.8	20.0	20.1	19.7	19.9	20.4

_____

_____

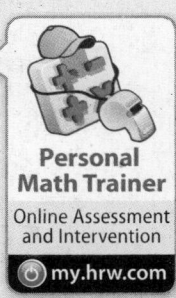

Personal Math Trainer

Online Assessment and Intervention

my.hrw.com

© Houghton Mifflin Harcourt Publishing Company

My Notes

Using a Spreadsheet to Find MAD

Spreadsheets can be used to find the mean absolute deviation of a data set.

EXAMPLE 2 FL 6.SP.2.5c

A paper mill is testing two paper-cutting machines. Both are set to produce pieces of paper with a width of 8.5 inches. The actual widths of 8 pieces of paper cut by each machine are shown. Use a spreadsheet to determine which machine has less variability and, thus, does a better job.

Widths of Pieces of Paper Cut by Machine A (in.)							
8.502	8.508	8.499	8.501	8.492	8.511	8.505	8.491

Widths of Pieces of Paper Cut by Machine B (in.)							
8.503	8.501	8.498	8.499	8.498	8.504	8.496	8.502

STEP 1 Enter the data values for Machine A into row 1 of a spreadsheet, using cells A to H.

	A	B	C	D	E	F	G	H
1	8.502	8.508	8.499	8.501	8.492	8.511	8.505	8.491
2								
3								

STEP 2 Enter "mean = " into cell A2 and the formula =AVERAGE(A1:H1) into cell B2.

	A	B	C	D	E	F	G	H
1	8.502	8.508	8.499	8.501	8.492	8.511	8.505	8.491
2	mean =	8.501125						
3								

STEP 3 Enter "MAD = " into cell A3 and the formula =AVEDEV(A1:H1) into cell B3.

	A	B	C	D	E	F	G	H
1	8.502	8.508	8.499	8.501	8.492	8.511	8.505	8.491
2	mean =	8.501125						
3	MAD =	0.005375						

The MAD for Machine A is about 0.0054 in.

STEP 4 Repeat Steps 1–3 with the data values for Machine B.

	A	B	C	D	E	F	G	H
1	8.503	8.501	8.498	8.499	8.498	8.504	8.496	8.502
2	mean =	8.500125						
3	MAD =	0.002375						

The MAD for Machine B is about 0.0024 in.

Machine B has less variability, so it does a better job.

3. Two aspirin-making devices are set to make tablets containing 0.35 gram of aspirin. The actual amounts in 8 tablets from each device are shown. Use a spreadsheet to determine which device has less variability.

Amounts of Aspirin in Tablets Made by Device A (g)							
0.353	0.351	0.350	0.352	0.349	0.348	0.350	0.346

Amounts of Aspirin in Tablets Made by Device B (g)							
0.349	0.341	0.347	0.358	0.359	0.354	0.339	0.343

Personal Math Trainer

Online Assessment and Intervention

my.hrw.com

Guided Practice

1. A bus route takes about 45 minutes. The company's goal is a MAD of less than 0.5 minute. One driver's times for 9 runs of the route are shown. Did the bus driver meet the goal? (Explore Activity and Example 1)

Times to Complete Bus Route (min)								
44.2	44.9	46.1	45.8	44.7	45.2	45.1	45.3	44.6

a. Calculate the mean of the bus times. _____

b. Calculate the MAD to the nearest tenth. _____

The bus driver **did / did not** meet the company's goal.

2. Below are a different driver's times on the same route. Find the mean and the MAD using a spreadsheet. Enter the data values into row 1 using cells A to I. Enter "mean = " into cell A2 and "MAD =" into cell A3. (Example 2)

Times to Complete Bus Route (min)								
44.4	43.8	45.6	45.9	44.1	45.6	44.0	44.9	45.8

The mean is _____ minutes, and the MAD is _____ minutes.

This time, the bus driver **did / did not** meet the company's goal.

ESSENTIAL QUESTION CHECK-IN

3. What is the mean absolute deviation and what does it tell you about data sets?

© Houghton Mifflin Harcourt Publishing Company

16.2 Independent Practice

FL 6.SP.2.5c

Frank wants to know how many people live in each household in his town. He conducts a random survey of 10 people and asks how many people live in their household. His results are shown in the table.

Number of People per Household									
1	6	2	4	4	3	5	5	2	8

4. Calculate the mean number of people per household. _____

5. Calculate the MAD of the number of people per household. _____

6. What conclusions can you draw about the "typical" number of people in each household? Explain.

_____

_____

_____

_____

Teachers are being trained to standardize the scores they give to students' essays. The same essay was scored by 10 different teachers at the beginning and at the end of their training. The results are shown in the tables.

Scores for Essay at Beginning of Teachers' Training									
76	81	85	79	89	86	84	80	88	79

Scores for Essay at End of Teachers' Training									
79	82	84	81	77	85	82	80	78	83

7. Calculate the MADs for the teachers' scores. Did the teachers make progress in standardizing their scores?

_____

_____

_____

8. What If? What would it mean if the teachers had a MAD of 0?

_____

_____

The annual rainfall for Austin, Texas, and San Antonio, Texas, in each of the years from 2002 to 2011 are shown in the tables. Use the data for 9–11.

Annual Rainfall for Austin, Texas (in.)									
36.00	21.41	52.27	22.33	34.70	46.95	16.07	31.38	37.76	19.68

Annual Rainfall for San Antonio, Texas (in.)									
46.27	28.45	45.32	16.54	21.34	47.25	13.76	30.69	37.39	17.58

9. Use a spreadsheet to find the mean for the two cities' annual rainfalls. In which city does it rain more in a year, on average?

_____

_____

_____

10. Use your spreadsheet to find the MADs. Use the MADs to compare the distribution of annual rainfall for the two cities.

_____

_____

_____

_____

11. **Make a Conjecture** Does the information allow you to predict how the future amounts of rainfall for the two cities will compare? Explain.

_____

_____

_____

12. **Critical Thinking** The life spans of 10 adult mayflies have a mean of 4 hours and a MAD of 2 hours. Fill in the table with possible values for the life spans. You can use the same value more than once.

Life Spans of Ten Mayflies (h)									

Can any one of the 10 mayflies in the group live for 1 full day? Justify your answer.

_____

_____

_____

13. Multistep In a spreadsheet, before entering any data values, first enter "mean =" into cell A2 and the formula =AVERAGE(A1:J1) into cell B2. Next, enter "MAD =" into cell A3 and the formula =AVEDEV(A1:J1) into cell B3. You should see #DIV/0! in cell B2 and #NUM! in cell B3 as shown. Now do the following:

	A	B
1		
2	mean =	#DIV/0!
3	MAD =	#NUM!

a. Enter "1" into cell A1. What do you get for the mean and the MAD of the data set? Explain why this makes sense.

_____

_____

_____

b. Enter "2" into cell B1. What do you get for the mean and the MAD of the data set this time? Explain why this makes sense.

_____

_____

_____

c. Enter the numbers 3 through 10 into cells C1 to J1 and watch the mean and the MAD change. Do they increase, decrease, or stay the same? Explain why this makes sense.

_____

_____

14. Make a Conjecture Each of the values in a data set is increased by 10. Does this affect the MAD of the data set? Why or why not?

_____

_____

_____

15. What If? Suppose a data set contains all whole numbers. Would the MAD for the data set also be a whole number? Explain.

_____

_____

_____

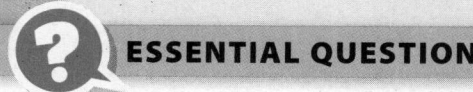

ESSENTIAL QUESTION

How can you use a box plot and measures of spread to describe a data set?

Using a Box Plot

A **box plot** is a display that shows how the values in a data set are distributed, or spread out.

To make a box plot, first find five values for the data set:

- the least value
- the **lower quartile** — the median of the lower half of the data
- the median
- the **upper quartile** — the median of the upper half of the data
- the greatest value

Math On the Spot

my.hrw.com

EXAMPLE 1 *Real World*

FL 6.SP.2.4

The heights of several students are shown. Make a box plot for the data.

Students' Heights (in.)					
60	58	54	56	63	61
65	61	62	59	56	58

STEP 1 Order the data and find the needed values.

54   56   56   58   58   59   60   61   61   62   63   65

Least value

Median = 59.5

Greatest value

Lower quartile = 57   Upper quartile = 61.5

STEP 2 Draw the box plot.

Draw a number line that includes all the data values.

On the number line, draw dots above the least value, the lower quartile, the median, the upper quartile, and the greatest value.

Math Talk
Mathematical Practices

How many data values are in the upper half of the data set? How many in the lower half?

Draw a segment connecting the least value to the lower quartile.

Draw a box whose ends pass through the lower and upper quartiles. Draw a vertical segment through the median.

Draw a segment connecting the upper quartile to the greatest value.

Students' Heights

54 55 56 57 58 59 60 61 62 63 64 65
Height (in.)

Reflect

1. In the example, what percent of the data values are included in the box portion? What percent are included in each of the "whiskers" on the

   ends of the box? _____

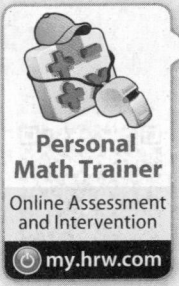

YOUR TURN

2. The daily high temperatures for some days last month are shown. Make a box plot of the data.

Daily High Temperatures (°F)					
85	78	92	88	78	84
80	94	89	75	79	83

Daily High Temperatures, °F

Finding the Interquartile Range

A **measure of spread** is a single number that describes the spread of a data set. One measure of spread is the *interquartile range*. The **interquartile range (IQR)** is the difference of the upper quartile and the lower quartile.

EXAMPLE 2 Real World   FL 6.SP.2.5c

The box plots compare the ages of dancers in two different dance troupes.

Dancers' Ages

A Find the IQR for each set of data.

Group A: IQR = Upper quartile − Lower quartile

= 24 − 20 = 4

Group B: IQR = Upper quartile − Lower quartile

= 26 − 21.5 = 4.5

B Compare the IQRs. How do the IQRs describe the distribution of the ages in each group?

The IQR of group B is slightly greater than the IQR of group A. The ages in the middle half of group B are slightly more spread out than in group A.

YOUR TURN

3. The box plots compare the weekly earnings of two groups of salespeople from different clothing stores. Find and compare the IQRs of the box plots.

Group A
Group B

Weekly Earnings ($)
1000 1500 2000

_____

_____

_____

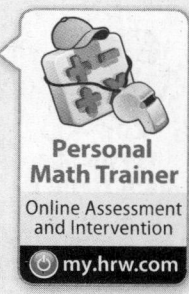
Finding the Range

Another measure that describes the spread of a set of data is the *range*. The **range** is the difference of the greatest value and the least value in a set of data.

 EXAMPLE 3 FL 6.SP.2.5c

The data sets show the ages of the players on two professional baseball teams. Find the range of each set of data.

Team A	36, 27, 28, 31, 39, 39, 28, 29, 24, 29, 30, 31, 29, 29, 28, 29, 31, 29, 32, 25, 37, 21, 26, 33, 29
Team B	25, 25, 26, 30, 27, 24, 29, 21, 27, 28, 26, 27, 25, 31, 22, 23, 29, 28, 25, 26, 28, 30, 23, 28, 29

STEP 1 Arrange the data sets in order from least to greatest.

Team A: 21, 24, 25, 26, 27, 28, 28, 28, 29, 29, 29, 29, 29, 29, 29, 30, 31, 31, 31, 32, 33, 36, 37, 39, 39

Team B: 21, 22, 23, 23, 24, 25, 25, 25, 25, 26, 26, 26, 27, 27, 27, 28, 28, 28, 28, 29, 29, 29, 30, 30, 31

STEP 2 Find the range of the data. Subtract the least value from the greatest value in each data set.

Team A: $39 - 21 = 18$

Team B: $31 - 21 = 10$

The range of ages for team A is 18 years, while the range of ages for team B is 10 years.

Math Talk
Mathematical Practices

How can you find the range of a set of data represented by a box plot?

Personal Math Trainer

Online Assessment and Intervention

⏻ my.hrw.com

YOUR TURN

4. Find the range of each set of data. Which city's data has a greater range?

Average Monthly High Temperature (°F)	
Miami, FL	76, 78, 80, 83, 87, 90, 91, 91, 89, 86, 82, 78, 84
Chicago, IL	31, 35, 47, 59, 70, 80, 84, 82, 75, 62, 48, 35, 59

_____

Guided Practice

The RBIs (runs batted in) for 15 players from the 2010 Seattle Mariners are shown. Use this data set for 1–7.

Mariners' RBIs
15 51 35 25 58 33 64
43 33 29 14 13 11 4 10

1. Order the data from least to greatest. (Example 1)

_____

2. Find the median. (Example 1) _____

3. Find the lower quartile. (Example 1) _____

4. Find the upper quartile. (Example 1) _____

5. Make a box plot for the data. (Example 1)

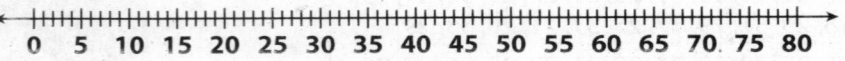

6. Find the IQR. (Example 2) _____

7. Find the range. (Example 3) _____

❓ ESSENTIAL QUESTION CHECK-IN

8. How is the range of a set of data different from the IQR?

_____

_____

_____

© Houghton Mifflin Harcourt Publishing Company

466 Unit 7

16.3 Independent Practice

 FL 6.SP.2.4, 6.SP.2.5c

Personal
Math Trainer

Online
Assessment and
Intervention

my.hrw.com

For 9–12, use the data set of the heights of several different students.

Students' Heights (in.)					
46	47	48	48	56	48
46	52	57	52	45	

9. Draw a box plot of the data.

45 46 47 48 49 50 51 52 53 54 55 56 57

10. How many students are included in the data set? _____

11. What method could have been used to collect the data?

_____

12. Represent Real-World Problems What other data could you collect from the students to create a box plot? Provide several examples with units of measurement, if applicable.

_____

For 13–15, use the box plots of the total precipitation for the same group of cities for the months of January and June.

January

June

1.2   1.4   1.6   1.8   2.0   2.2   2.4   2.6
Precipitation (in.)

13. Calculate the IQR for each month.

January = _____ inches   June = _____ inches

14. Calculate the range for each month.

January = _____ inches   June = _____ inches

15. Compare the IQRs. What can you conclude about the two data sets?

_____

_____

16. Compare the ranges. What can you conclude about the two data sets?

_____

Work Area

17. Analyze Relationships Can two box plots have the same range and IQR and yet represent completely different data? Explain.

_____

_____

_____

_____

18. Multiple Representations Matthew collected data about the ages of the actors in two different community theater groups. He drew a box plot for one of the sets of data.

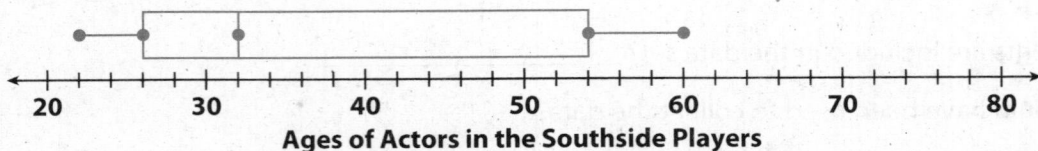

Ages of Actors in the Southside Players

Ages of Actors in the Northside Players	71, 62, 63, 21, 63, 39, 25, 26, 30

a. Find the median, range, and IQR for each set of data.

Theater Group	Median	Range	IQR
Northside Players			
Southside Players			

b. Suppose you were to draw a second box plot for the Northside Players using the same number line as for the Southside Players. Which box plot would be longer overall? Which would have the longest box portion?

_____

_____

_____

c. Critique Reasoning Mandy assumes that because nine data values are shown for the Northside Players, nine data values were used to make the box plot for the Southside Players. Explain why this is not necessarily true.

_____

_____

_____

LESSON
16.4
Dot Plots and Data Distribution

 FL 6.SP.2.4
Display numerical data in plots on a number line, including dot plots....
Also 6.SP.1.1, 6.SP.1.2, 6.SP.2.5c, 6.SP.2.5d

? ESSENTIAL QUESTION

How can you summarize and display numeric data?

EXPLORE ACTIVITY *Real World* **FL** 6.SP.1.1

Variable Data and Statistical Questions

The question "How much does a typical cat weigh?" is an example of a statistical question. A **statistical question** is a question that has many different, or variable, answers.

A Decide whether each of the situations below could yield variable data.

1. Your sister wants to know the typical weight for an adult cat.

   _____

2. You want to know how tall your friend is. _____

3. You want to know how far your house is from school. _____

4. A car owner wants to know how much money people usually pay

   for a new tire. _____

5. How many students were in line for lunch at the cafeteria today

   at 12:30? _____

B For which of the situations in part **A** can you write a statistical question? Write questions for these situations.

   _____

   _____

Reflect

1. Choose one of the questions you wrote in part **B**. How might you find answers to this question? What units would you use for the answers?

   _____

   _____

   _____

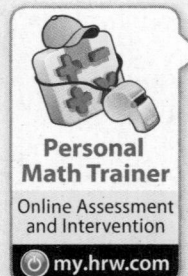
Making a Dot Plot

Statistical questions are answered by collecting and analyzing data. One way to understand a set of data is to make a visual display. A **dot plot** is a visual display in which each piece of data is represented by a dot above a number line. A dot plot shows the frequency of each data value.

EXAMPLE 1   **FL 6.SP.2.4**

A baseball team manager records the number of runs scored by the team in each game for several weeks. Use the data to make a dot plot.

1, 3, 1, 7, 2, 0, 11, 2, 2, 3, 1, 3, 4, 2, 2, 4, 5, 2, 6

> The team usually scores between 0 and 7 runs in a game, but in one game they scored 11 runs.

STEP 1 Make a number line.
Data values range from 0 to 11, so use a scale from 0 to 11.

STEP 2 Draw a dot above the number line for each data value.

Runs Scored

Reflect

2. How many games did the team play during the season? How can you tell from looking at the dot plot?

_____

_____

3. At how many games did the team score 2 runs or fewer? How do you know?

_____

_____

YOUR TURN

4. A different baseball team scores the following numbers of runs in its games for several weeks:
4, 4, 6, 1, 2, 4, 1, 2, 5, 3, 3, 5, 4, 2

Runs Scored

Use the data to make a dot plot. Tell how many games the team played, and identify the data value with the greatest frequency.

_____

_____

Interpreting a Dot Plot

A dot plot can give you a visual picture of the spread, center, and shape of a data distribution.

You can describe the spread of a data set by identifying the least and greatest values. You can also look for **outliers** which are data values that are either much greater or much less than the other data values.

You can describe the center and shape of a data set in terms of *peaks, clusters,* or *symmetry*. A symmetric distribution has approximately the same number of data values on either side of the center.

EXAMPLE 2

FL 6.SP.1.2

Describe the spread, center, and shape of each data distribution.

A The data values are spread out from 3 to 7 with no outliers.

The data has a cluster from 3 to 7 with one peak at 5, which is the center of the distribution.

The distribution is symmetric. The data values are clustered around the center of the distribution.

B The data values are spread out from 1 to 9. The data value 1 appears to be an outlier.

The data has a cluster from 6 to 9 with one peak at 9, which is the greatest value in the data set.

The distribution is not symmetric. The data values are clustered at one end of the distribution.

YOUR TURN

5. Describe the spread, center, and shape of the data distribution from Example 1.

_____

_____

_____

_____

My Notes

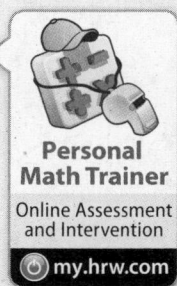
Personal Math Trainer
Online Assessment and Intervention
⊙ my.hrw.com

Finding Measures from a Dot Plot

You can also find and calculate measures of center and spread from a dot plot.

EXAMPLE 3 Real World   FL 6.SP.2.5d, 6.SP.2.5c

The dot plot shows the number of runs scored by a baseball team in each game for several weeks from Example 1.

Runs Scored

A Find the mean, median, and range of the data.

STEP 1 To find the mean, find the sum of the data values and divide by the number of data values.

$$\frac{1(0) + 3(1) + 6(2) + 3(3) + 2(4) + 1(5) + 1(6) + 1(7) + 1(11)}{19} = \frac{61}{19} \approx 3.2$$

The mean is about 3.2.

STEP 2 To find the median, count the dots from left to right until you find the middle value. You may need to find the mean of two middle values.

The median is 2.

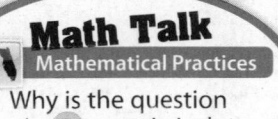

STEP 3 To find the range, read the least and greatest values from the dot plot. Subtract the least value from the greatest.

$11 - 0 = 11$

The range is 11.

B How many runs does the team typically score in a game? Explain.

The mean number of runs is 3.2. The median number of runs is 2.

The shape of the dot plot suggests that the outlier 11 may be affecting these measures of center. To see if that is the case, find the mean and median without including the outlier. Compare these values with the original values.

STEP 1 Find the mean without including the outlier.

$$\frac{1(0) + 3(1) + 6(2) + 3(3) + 2(4) + 1(5) + 1(6) + 1(7)}{18} = \frac{50}{18} \approx 2.8$$

Without the outlier, the mean is 2.8, which is less than the original mean of 3.2.

STEP 2 Find the median without including the outlier.

Counting from left to right, the median is still 2.

Given that it is not affected by the outlier, the median may be more typical of the data. The team typically scores two runs per game.

6. Find the mean, median, and range of the data from Your Turn question 4. What is the typical number of runs the team scores in a game? Justify your answer.

_____

_____

_____

Personal Math Trainer

Online Assessment and Intervention

🕐 my.hrw.com

Guided Practice

Tell whether the situation could yield variable data. If possible, write a statistical question. (Explore Activity)

1. The town council members want to know how much recyclable trash a typical household in town generates each week.

_____

_____

Kate asked some friends how many movies they saw last winter. Use her data for 2 and 3.

2. Make a dot plot of the data. (Example 1)

Movies Seen Last Winter
0, 1, 1, 2, 2, 3, 3, 3, 4, 4, 4, 4, 5, 5, 5, 5, 6, 6, 7, 7, 7, 8, 8, 9, 9, 17

Movies

3. Find the mean, median, and range of the data. (Example 3)

_____

4. Describe the spread, center, and shape of the data. (Example 2)

_____

_____

ESSENTIAL QUESTION CHECK-IN

5. What are some measures of center and spread that you can find from a dot plot? How can making a dot plot help you visualize a data distribution?

_____

_____

16.4 Independent Practice

FL 6.SP.1.1, 6.SP.1.2, 6.SP.2.4, 6.SP.2.5c, 6.SP.2.5d

Personal Math Trainer

Online Assessment and Intervention

my.hrw.com

6. **Vocabulary** Describe how a statistical question yields an answer with variability. Give an example.

_____

_____

_____

_____

For 7–10, determine whether the question is a statistical question. If it is a statistical question, identify the units for the answer.

7. An antique collector wants to know the age of a particular chair in a shop.

_____

8. How tall do the people in your immediate and extended family tend to be?

_____

_____

9. How tall is Sam?

_____

10. How much did your classmates typically spend on music downloads last year?

_____

For 11–14, use the following data. The data give the number of days of precipitation per month during one year in a city.

12   10   11   9   9   10   12   9   8   7   9   10

11. Make a dot plot of the data.

←—+—+—+—+—+—+—+—+—+—+—+—+—→

12. What does each dot represent? How many months are represented?

_____

_____

13. Describe the shape, center, and spread of the data distribution. Are there any outliers?

_____

_____

_____

14. Find the mean, median, and range of the data.

_____

_____

15. **What If?** During one month there were 7 days of precipitation. What if there had only been 3 days of precipitation that month? How would that change the measures of center?

_____

_____

_____

For 16–20, use the dot plot of the number of cars sold at a car dealership per week during the first half of the year.

Cars Sold

16. Find the mean, median, and range.

   Mean = _____   Median = _____

   Range = _____

17. The owner of the car dealership decides to treat the value 22 as an outlier. Which measure of center or spread is affected the most if the owner removes this outlier? Explain.

   _____

   _____

   _____

18. How many cars are sold in a typical week at the dealership? Explain.

   _____

   _____

19. Write an expression that represents the total number of cars sold during the first half of the year.

   _____

   _____

20. Describe the spread, center, and shape of the data distribution.

   _____

   _____

   _____

   _____

21. **Vocabulary** Explain how you can tell the frequency of a data value by looking at a dot plot.

   _____

   _____

For 22–26 use the following data. The data give the number of runs scored by opponents of the Boston Red Sox in June 2010.

   4, 4, 9, 0, 2, 4, 1, 2, 11, 8, 2, 2, 5, 3, 2, 5, 6, 4, 0

22. Make a dot plot for the data.

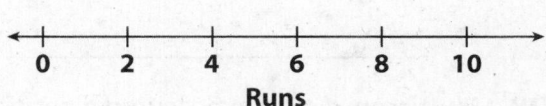

Runs

23. How many games did the Boston Red Sox play in June 2010? Explain.

   _____

24. Which data value in your dot plot has the greatest frequency? Explain what that frequency means for this data.

   _____

   _____

25. Find the mean, median, and range of the data.

   _____

   _____

26. What is a statistical question that you could answer using the dot plot? Answer your question and justify your response.

   _____

   _____

   _____

   _____

FOCUS ON HIGHER ORDER THINKING

 Work Area

27. A pediatrician records the ages of the patients seen in one day: 1, 2, 5, 7, 9, 17, 13, 16, 18, 12, 3, 5, 1.

a. **Explain the Error** Assuming that some of the patients are infants who are less than 1 year old, what information did the pediatrician forget to write down?

_____

b. **Critical Thinking** Can you make a dot plot of the pediatrician's data? Can you find the mean, median, and range? Why or why not?

_____

_____

_____

28. **Multistep** A nurse measured a patient's heart rate at different times over several days.

Heart Rate (beats per minute)
86, 87, 89, 87, 86, 88, 90, 85, 82, 86, 83, 85, 84, 86

a. Make a dot plot.

b. Describe the shape, center, and spread of the data. Then find the mean, median, range, and IQR for the data.

_____

_____

_____

c. **What If?** The nurse collected the data when the patient was resting. How might the dot plot and the measures change if the nurse collects the data when the patient is exercising?

_____

_____

476 Unit 7

16.5 Histograms

 FL 6.SP.2.4
Display numerical data in plots on a number line, including . . . histograms. . . .
Also 6.SP.2.5

? **ESSENTIAL QUESTION**

How can you display data in a histogram?

EXPLORE ACTIVITY   FL 6.SP.2.5, 6.SP.2.4

Grouping Data in Intervals

The members of the high-school basketball team practice free throws. Each player attempts 50 free throws. The number of free throws made by each player is listed below.

25, 29, 29, 30, 33, 34, 35, 35, 36, 39, 42, 44

A Use a dot plot to represent the data.

25 26 27 28 29 30 31 32 33 34 35 36 37 38 39 40 41 42 43 44 45

B On your dot plot, circle the dots that are in each interval of the frequency table below. Then complete the frequency table.

Interval	Frequency
20–29	
30–39	
40–49	

> Enter the number of data values for the interval 30–39.

C Analyze the data. How were the data collected? How many data values are there? What are the mean, median, range, and IQR of the data?

_____

_____

_____

_____

Reflect

1. Can you use the dot plot to find the mean and the median of the data? Can you use the frequency table? Why or why not?

_____

_____

_____

_____

2. How do you find the number of data values in a data set from a dot plot? How can you find the number of data values from a frequency table?

_____

Math On the Spot

⊙ my.hrw.com

Using a Histogram

A **histogram** is a type of bar graph whose bars represent the frequencies of numeric data within intervals.

EXAMPLE 1 Real World FL 6.SP.2.4, 6.SP.2.5

A birdwatcher counts and records the number of birds at a birdfeeder every morning at 9:00 for several days.

12, 3, 8, 1, 1, 6, 10, 14, 3, 6, 2, 1, 3, 2, 7

Make a histogram of the data.

STEP 1 Make a frequency table.

Divide the data into equal-sized intervals of 4. Make a frequency table.

Interval	Frequency
1–4	8
5–8	4
9–12	2
13–16	1

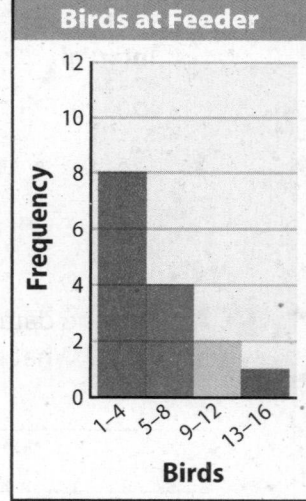

Birds at Feeder

STEP 2 Make a histogram.

The intervals are listed along the horizontal axis. The vertical axis shows the frequencies. For each interval, draw a bar to show the number of days in that interval. The bars should have equal widths. They should touch but not overlap.

Math Talk
Mathematical Practices

How does the histogram show the total number of days the birdwatcher counted birds?

Reflect

3. **What If?** Suppose the birdwatcher continues his observation for three more days and collects these new data values: 5, 18, and 2. How could you change the histogram to include the data?

_____

_____

_____

YOUR TURN

4. Kim has started rating each movie she sees using a scale of 1 to 10 on an online site. Here are her ratings so far:

6, 9, 8, 5, 7, 4, 8, 8, 3, 7, 8, 7, 5, 1, 10

Make a histogram of the data.

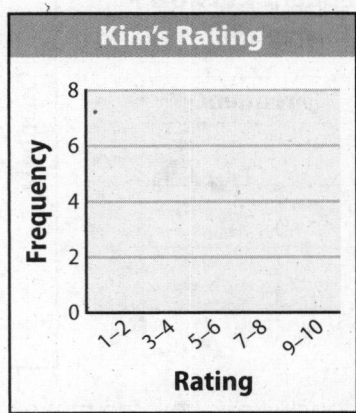

Kim's Rating

Frequency / Rating

Analyzing a Histogram

By grouping data in intervals, a histogram gives a picture of the distribution of a data set.

EXAMPLE 2 Real World   FL 6.SP.2.5

Use the histogram from Example 1. What are some conclusions about the data that can you make from the shape of the distribution?

The highest bar is for the interval 1–4, which means that on more than half the days (8 out of 15), the birdwatcher saw only 1–4 birds. The bars decrease in height from left to right, showing that it was more likely for the birdwatcher to see a small number of birds rather than a large number on any given day.

YOUR TURN

5. Use your histogram from Your Turn 4. What are some conclusions you can make about Kim's movie ratings from the shape of the distribution?

_____

_____

1. Wendy kept track of the number of text messages she sent each day for three weeks. Complete the frequency table.
   (Explore Activity)

   0, 5, 5, 7, 11, 12, 15, 20, 22, 24, 25,
   25, 27, 27, 29, 29, 32, 33, 34, 35, 35

Interval	Frequency
0–9	

Ed counted the number of seats available in each cafe in his town. Use his data for 2–3.

18, 20, 22, 26, 10, 12, 16, 18, 7, 8

2. Complete the frequency table and the histogram. (Example 1)

Interval	Frequency
1–7	
8–14	
15–21	
22–28	

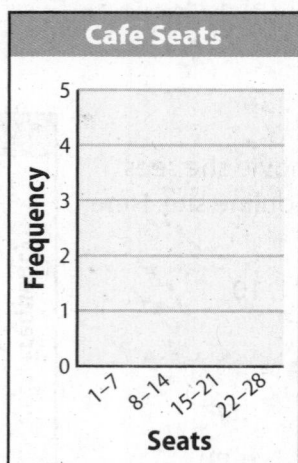

3. What are some conclusions you can make about the distribution of the data? (Example 2)

_____

_____

_____

_____

? ESSENTIAL QUESTION CHECK-IN

4. How can you display data in a histogram?

_____

_____

_____

16.5 Independent Practice

FL 6.SP.2.4, 6.SP.2.5

Personal Math Trainer

my.hrw.com

Online Assessment and Intervention

An amusement park employee records the ages of the people who ride the new roller coaster during a fifteen–minute period.

Ages of riders: 47, 16, 16, 35, 45, 43, 11, 29, 31, 50, 23, 18, 18, 20, 29, 17, 18, 48, 56, 24, 18, 21, 38, 12, 23.

5. Complete the frequency table. Then make a histogram of the data.

Interval	Frequency
10–19	

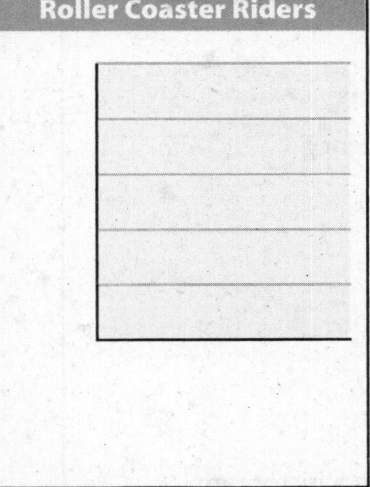

Roller Coaster Riders

6. Describe two things you know about the riders who are represented by the data.

_____

_____

_____

7. **Multiple Representations** West Middle School has classes of many different sizes during first period. The number of students in each class is shown.

9, 23, 18, 14, 20, 26, 14, 18, 18, 12, 8, 13, 21, 22, 28, 10, 7, 19, 24, 20

a. Hank made a histogram using intervals of 6–10, 11–15, and so on. How many bars did his histogram

have? What was the height of the highest bar? _____

b. Lisa made a histogram using intervals of 0–9, 10–19, and so on. How many bars did her histogram have?

What was the height of the highest bar? _____

c. Besides a histogram, what are some other ways you could display these data?

_____

Work Area

8. Communicate Mathematical Ideas Can you find the mean or median of a set of data from a histogram? Explain.

_____

_____

9. Multistep A theater owner keeps track of how many people come to see movies on 21 different Saturdays.

Saturday Moviegoers

Interval	Frequency
60–69	1
70–79	3
80–89	10
90–99	7

Saturday Moviegoers

a. Use the data to make a histogram.

b. Make a Prediction The theater owner asks, "How many moviegoers come to the theater on a typical Saturday?" What would you tell the theater owner? Use your histogram to support your answer.

_____

_____

_____

c. Communicate Mathematical Ideas Is the theater owner's question a statistical question? Why or why not?

_____

10. Explain the Error Irina says she can find the range of a set of data from a histogram. Is she correct? Justify your answer.

_____

_____

_____

Ready to Go On?

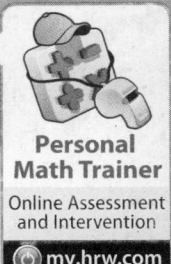

Personal Math Trainer

Online Assessment and Intervention

(○) my.hrw.com

16.1 Measures of Center

1. Find the mean and median of these data: 2, 5, 9, 11, 17, 19. _____

16.2 Mean Absolute Deviation

2. Find the distance of each data value in Exercise 1 from the mean. Then find the

mean absolute deviation of the data. _____

16.3 Box Plots

3. Make a box plot for the data set.

| 36 42 44 52 61 70 78 |

16.4 Dot Plots and Data Distribution

A baseball team scored the following number of runs over a 10-game period:
6, 6, 8, 5, 4, 6, 4, 3, 8, 4

4. Make a dot plot for the data.

5. Find the mean, median, and range.

_____

_____

16.5 Histograms

6. Make a histogram for the data set.

23	45	62	19
48	10	39	54
39	16	48	12
25	32	18	4

 ESSENTIAL QUESTION

7. How can you represent and summarize data in a dot plot?

_____

_____

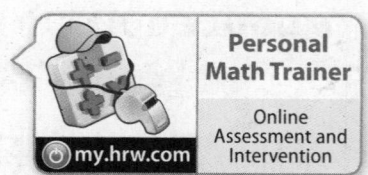

Selected Response

1. What is the interquartile range of the data represented by the box plot shown below?

Ⓐ 15   Ⓒ 35

Ⓑ 20   Ⓓ 40

The dot plot shows the ages of quiz show contestants.

2. What is the median of the data?

Ⓐ 21   Ⓒ 22

Ⓑ 21.5   Ⓓ 25

3. Which inequalities describe the possible ages of the contestants in the dot plot?

Ⓐ $a > 20$ and $a < 25$

Ⓑ $a \geq 20$ and $a \leq 25$

Ⓒ $a < 20$ and $a > 25$

Ⓓ $a \leq 20$ and $a \geq 25$

4. Suppose a new data value, 30, is included in the dot plot. Which statement describes the effect on the median?

Ⓐ The median would increase.

Ⓑ The median would decrease.

Ⓒ The median would stay the same.

Ⓓ The median would equal the mean.

5. Andrea recorded the points she scored in her last eight basketball games. What is the mean absolute deviation of the scores?

28, 32, 47, 16, 40, 35, 38, 54

Ⓐ 8.5   Ⓒ 17.75

Ⓑ 36.25   Ⓓ 38

Mini-Task

6. The frequency table shows data about how many tickets were sold by students.

Tickets Sold	Frequency
0–9	2
10–19	4
20–29	3
30–39	1

a. Use the frequency table to make a histogram.

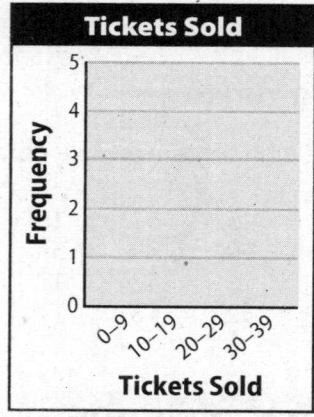

b. How many students sold tickets?

_____

c. What percent of the students sold 20 or more tickets?

_____

MODULE 16 Displaying, Analyzing, and Summarizing Data

Key Vocabulary

box plot (*diagrama de caja*)
categorical data (*datos categóricos*)
dot plot (*diagrama de puntos*)
histogram (*histograma*)
interquartile range (*rango entre cuartiles*)
lower quartile (*cuartil inferior*)
mean (*media*)
mean absolute deviation (MAD) (*desviación absoluta media, (DAM)*)
measure of center (*medida central*)
measure of spread (*medida de dispersión*)
median (*mediana*)
mode (*moda*)
range (*rango*)
statistical question (*pregunta estadística*)
upper quartile (*cuartil superior*)

? ESSENTIAL QUESTION

How can you solve real-world problems by displaying, analyzing, and summarizing data?

EXAMPLE 1

The ages of Thomas's neighbors are shown.

Ages of Thomas's Neighbors
30, 48, 31, 45, 42, 32, 32, 38, 34, 50, 49, 48

Make a box plot of the data.

30   31   <u>32   32</u>   34   <u>38   42</u>   45   <u>48   48</u>   49   50

Lower quartile = 32   Median = 40   Upper quartile = 48

30 32 34 36 38 40 42 44 46 48 50

EXAMPLE 2

Find the mean, median, and range of the data shown on the dot plot.

9 10 11 12 13 14 15 16 17

The mean is 13. $\dfrac{2(9) + 4(13) + 5(14) + 16}{12} = 13$

The median is 13.5.   9, 9, 13, 13, 13, <u>13, 14</u>, 14, 14, 14, 14, 16

The range is 7. $16 - 9 = 7$

EXAMPLE 3

Find the mean absolute deviation (MAD) of the data in Example 2. Round to the nearest tenth.

The MAD is the mean distance of each of the 12 data points from the mean, 13.

$$\frac{4 + 4 + 0 + 0 + 0 + 0 + 1 + 1 + 1 + 1 + 1 + 3}{12} = \frac{16}{12} \approx 1.3$$

The mean absolute deviation is approximately 1.3.

EXERCISES

1. The number of goals for the 13 players on a soccer team are 4, 9, 0, 1, 1, 2, 0, 0, 2, 8, 8, 3, 1. Find the median, lower quartile, and upper quartile. Then make a box plot for the data. (Lesson 16.3) _____

2. The coach recorded the time it took 14 students to run a mile. The times are as follows: 9:23, 8:15, 9:23, 9:01, 6:45, 6:55, 7:20, 9:14, 6:21, 7:12, 7:34, 6:10, 9:15, 9:18. (Lesson 16.5)

Use the data to complete the frequency table. Then use the table to make a histogram.

Interval	Frequency
6–6:59	

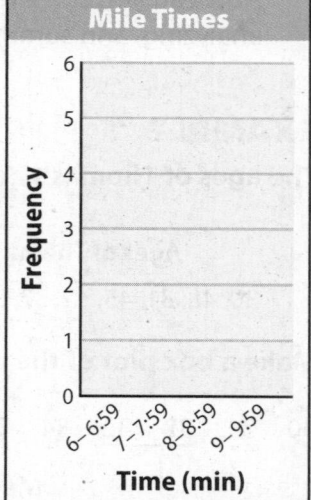

3. Find the mean and mean absolute deviation of the set of data. Round to the nearest hundredth. (Lesson 16.2)

Distance per day (mi) driven by Juan						
12	9	7	7	11	10	7

Mean: _____   Mean absolute deviation: _____

Unit 7 Performance Tasks

1. **CAREERS IN MATH** | Geneticist Kinesha collects data about the heights of students in her science class. What measures of center and variation are appropriate for the data? Which of the data displays that you learned about in this unit could Keisha use to display the data? Which could be used to show the measures of center and variation you named? Explain.

_____

_____

_____

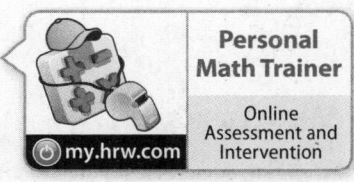
Selected Response

1. Over 6 days, Jim jogged 6.5 miles, 5 miles, 3 miles, 2 miles, 3.5 miles, and 4 miles. What is the mean distance that Jim jogged?

 Ⓐ 3.75 miles   Ⓒ 4.5 miles

 Ⓑ 4 miles   Ⓓ 6.5 miles

Use the data set below for 2–3.

26	30	45	43	26
14	28	33	56	29

2. What is the mean of the data set?

 Ⓐ 14   Ⓒ 33

 Ⓑ 26   Ⓓ 46

3. What is the mean absolute deviation?

 Ⓐ 2

 Ⓑ 4

 Ⓒ 6

 Ⓓ 9

4. The ages of the volunteers at a local food bank are shown below.

  34, 25, 24, 50, 18, 46, 43, 36, 32

What is the median of this set of data?

 Ⓐ 32   Ⓒ 34

 Ⓑ 33.1   Ⓓ 50

5. Which expression shows the prime factorization of 120?

 Ⓐ $2^3 \times 3 \times 5$

 Ⓑ $2 \times 3 \times 5$

 Ⓒ 10^{12}

 Ⓓ $2 \times 5 \times 12$

6. The dot plot shows the number of participants in each age group in a science fair.

11 12 13 14 15 16 17

Which of the following is **not** supported by the dot plot?

 Ⓐ The range is 6.

 Ⓑ The mean of the ages is about 14.4.

 Ⓒ The mode of the ages is 13.

 Ⓓ The median of the ages is 15.

7. Sarita recorded the distances she ran for 5 days: 5 miles, 4 miles, 5.5 miles, 4.5 miles, and 5.5 miles. What is the mean distance Sarita ran?

 Ⓐ 4.9 miles

 Ⓑ 5 miles

 Ⓒ 5.1 miles

 Ⓓ 5.5 miles

8. On a map of the city, 1 centimeter represents 2.5 miles. What distance on the map would represent 20 miles?

 Ⓐ 6 centimeters

 Ⓑ 8 centimeters

 Ⓒ 12 centimeters

 Ⓓ 18 centimeters

9. The ratio of the number of male lions to female lions in the animal reserve is 21:20. If there are 123 lions in the animal reserve, how many of the lions are female?

 Ⓐ 40   Ⓒ 60

 Ⓑ 50   Ⓓ 70

Mini-Tasks

10. The students in Ms. Lorenzo's class collected the following numbers of bottle caps:

10, 20, 40, 50, 30, 10, 60, 10, 20
40, 30, 30, 50, 70, 50, 70, 60, 30

a. Make a dot plot for the data.

10 20 30 40 50 60 70

b. What is the median?

_____

c. What is the mean?

_____

11. The heights in inches of 8 students are 50, 53, 52, 68, 54, 49, 55, and 51.

a. What is the mean of the students' heights?

_____

b. Is there an outlier in the data set? If so, which number is the outlier?

_____

c. What is the mean height if the outlier is removed from the data?

_____

Read a graph or diagram as closely as you read the actual test question. These visual aids contain important information.

12. The data show the latest math test scores in Mr. White's class.

98	76	76	85	43
90	85	76	98	100
75	84	95	87	98
100	57	92	67	73
56	97	100	75	100

a. Draw a histogram of the data.

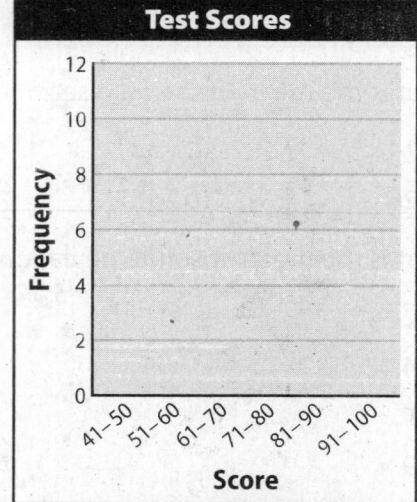

b. What is the outlier? Would removing the outlier change how the chart looks?

_____

_____

_____

UNIT 8

The Number System

MODULE 17

Adding and Subtracting Integers

 FL 7.NS.1.1, 7.NS.1.1b, 7.NS.1.1c, 7.NS.1.1d, 7.NS.1.3, 7.EE.2.3

MODULE 18

Multiplying and Dividing Integers

 FL 7.NS.1.2, 7.NS.1.2a, 7.NS.1.2c, 7.NS.1.2b, 7.NS.1.3, 7.EE.2.3

MODULE 19

Rational Numbers

 FL 7.NS.1.1, 7.NS.1.1a, 7.NS.1.1b, 7.NS.1.1c, 7.NS.1.1d, 7.NS.1.2, 7.NS.1.2a, 7.NS.1.2b, 7.NS.1.2c, 7.NS.1.2d, 7.NS.1.3, 7.EE.1.1, 7.EE.1.2, 7.EE.2.3

© Houghton Mifflin Harcourt Publishing Company

CAREERS IN MATH

Urban Planner An urban planner creates plans for urban, suburban, and rural communities and makes recommendations about locations for infrastructure, such as buildings, roads, and sewer and water pipes. Urban planners perform cost-benefit analysis of projects, use measurement and geometry when they design the layout of infrastructure, and use statistics and mathematical models to predict the growth and future needs of a population.

If you are interested in a career as an urban planner, you should study these mathematical subjects:
- Algebra
- Geometry
- Trigonometry
- Statistics

Research other careers that require using measurement, geometry, and mathematical modeling.

Unit 8 Performance Task

At the end of the unit, check out how **urban planners** use math.

Use the puzzle to preview key vocabulary from this unit. Unscramble the circled letters within found words to answer the riddle at the bottom of the page.

1. NIOARLTA
   MURNEB

2. GREITEN

3. PIRGENAET
   CMSEADIL

4. EADITIVD
   SENEIRV

5. TIIRANGTNEM
   SAELIDMC

1. Any number that can be written as a ratio of two integers. (Lesson 19.1)
2. A member of the set of whole numbers and their opposites. (Lesson 17.1)
3. Decimals in which one or more digits repeat infinitely. (Lesson 19.1)
4. The opposite of any number. (Lesson 17.2)
5. Decimals that have a finite number of digits. (Lesson 19.1)

Q: Why were the two fractions able to settle their differences peacefully?

A: They were both ___ ___ ___ ___ ___ ___ ___ ___!

Adding and Subtracting Integers

 ESSENTIAL QUESTION

How can you use addition and subtraction of integers to solve real-world problems?

LESSON 17.1
Adding Integers with the Same Sign

 FL   7.NS.1.1, 7.NS.1.1b, 7.NS.1.1d

LESSON 17.2
Adding Integers with Different Signs

 FL   7.NS.1.1, 7.NS.1.1b

LESSON 17.3
Subtracting Integers

FL   7.NS.1.1, 7.NS.1.1c

LESSON 17.4
Applying Addition and Subtraction of Integers

 FL   7.NS.1.1, 7.NS.1.1d, 7.NS.1.3, 7.EE.2.3

Real-World Video

Death Valley contains the lowest point in North America, elevation −282 feet. The top of Mt. McKinley, elevation 20,320 feet, is the highest point in North America. To find the difference between these elevations, you can subtract integers.

ⓜ my.hrw.com

© Houghton Mifflin Harcourt Publishing Company • Image Credits: ©Peter Haigh/ Digital Vision/Getty Images

GO DIGITAL
my.hrw.com

 my.hrw.com
Go digital with your write-in student edition, accessible on any device.

 Math On the Spot
Scan with your smart phone to jump directly to the online edition, video tutor, and more.

 Animated Math
Interactively explore key concepts to see how math works.

 Personal Math Trainer
Get immediate feedback and help as you work through practice sets.

Are YOU Ready?

Complete these exercises to review skills you will need for this module.

Understand Integers

> **EXAMPLE**   A diver descended 20 meters.
>
> −20
>
> Decide whether the integer is positive or negative:
>
> *descended → negative*
>
> Write the integer.

Write an integer to represent each situation.

1. an elevator ride down 27 stories

2. a $700 profit

3. 46 degrees below zero

4. a gain of 12 yards

_____   _____   _____   _____

Whole Number Operations

> **EXAMPLE** $245 - 28$
>
> $245 - 28 = 217$
>
> $$\begin{array}{r} \overset{3\ 15}{2\cancel{4}\cancel{5}} \\ -\ 2\ 8 \\ \hline 2\ 1\ 7 \end{array}$$
>
> Think:
> $8 > 5$
> Regroup 1 ten as 10 ones.
> 1 ten + 5 ones = 15 ones
> Subtract: $15 - 8 = 7$

Find the sum or difference.

5. $\begin{array}{r} 183 \\ +\ 78 \\ \hline \end{array}$

6. $\begin{array}{r} 677 \\ -288 \\ \hline \end{array}$

7. $\begin{array}{r} 1{,}188 \\ +\ 902 \\ \hline \end{array}$

8. $\begin{array}{r} 2{,}647 \\ -1{,}885 \\ \hline \end{array}$

Locate Points on a Number Line

> **EXAMPLE**
>
>
>
> Graph $+2$ by starting at 0 and counting 2 units to the *right*.
> Graph -5 by starting at 0 and counting 5 units to the *left*.

Graph each number on the number line.

9. 7   **10.** −4   **11.** −9   **12.** 4

© Houghton Mifflin Harcourt Publishing Company

Reading Start-Up

Visualize Vocabulary

Use the ✔ words to fill in the ovals on the graphic. You may put more than one word in each oval.

Understanding Integers

50

−50

−50, 50

Vocabulary

Review Words
   difference *(diferencia)*
   integers *(enteros)*
✔ negative number *(número negativo)*
✔ opposites *(opuestos)*
✔ positive number *(número positivo)*
   sum *(suma)*
✔ whole number *(número entero)*

Preview Words
   absolute value *(valor absoluto)*
   additive inverse *(inverso aditivo)*
   expression *(expresión)*
   model *(modelo)*

Understand Vocabulary

Complete the sentences using the preview words.

1. The _____ of a number gives its distance from zero.

2. The sum of a number and its _____ is zero.

Active Reading

Booklet Before beginning the module, create a booklet to help you learn the concepts in this module. Write the main idea of each lesson on each page of the booklet. As you study each lesson, write important details that support the main idea, such as vocabulary and processes. Refer to your finished booklet as you work on assignments and study for tests.

MODULE 17
Unpacking the Standards

Understanding the standards and the vocabulary terms in the standards will help you know exactly what you are expected to learn in this module.

FL 7.NS.1.1

Apply and extend previous understandings of addition and subtraction to add and subtract rational numbers; represent addition and subtraction on a horizontal or vertical number line diagram.

Key Vocabulary

additive inverse *(inverso aditivo)*
The opposite of a number.

What It Means to You

You will learn how to use models to add and subtract integers with the same sign and with different signs.

UNPACKING EXAMPLE 7.NS.1.1

You will learn how to use models to add and subtract integers with the same sign and with different signs.

$4 + (-7)$

Start at 0.
Move right 4 units.
Then move left 7 units.

$4 + (-7) = -3$

FL 7.NS.1.1c

Understand subtraction of rational numbers as adding the additive inverse, $p - q = p + (-q)$. Show that the distance between two rational numbers on the number line is the absolute value of their difference, and apply this principle in real-world contexts.

Key Vocabulary

integer *(entero)*
A member of the set of whole numbers and their opposites.

What It Means to You

You will learn that subtracting an integer is the same as adding its additive inverse.

UNPACKING EXAMPLE 7.NS.1.1c

Find the difference between 3,000 °F and −250 °F, the temperatures the space shuttle must endure.

$$3,000 - (-250)$$

$$3,000 + 250 = 3,250$$

The difference in temperatures the shuttle must endure is 3,250 °F.

Visit **my.hrw.com** to see all **Florida Math Standards** unpacked.

⏻ my.hrw.com

Adding Integers with the Same Sign

 FL   7.NS.1.1

Apply and extend previous understandings of addition and subtraction to add... rational numbers; represent addition... on a...vertical number line diagram: *Also 7.NS.1.1b, 7.NS.1.1d*

? **ESSENTIAL QUESTION**

How do you add integers with the same sign?

EXPLORE ACTIVITY 1 FL   7.NS.1.1

Modeling Sums of Integers with the Same Sign

You can use colored counters to add positive integers and to add negative integers.

○ = 1
● = −1

Model with two-color counters.

A $3 + 4$

3 positive counters ○ ○ ○
4 positive counters ○ ○ ○ ○ } total number of counters

How many counters are there in total? _____

What is the sum and how do you find it?

_____

_____

B $-5 + (-3)$

5 negative counters ● ● ● ● ●
3 negative counters ● ● ● } total number of counters

How many counters are there in total? _____

Since the counters are negative integers, what is the sum? _____

Math Talk
Mathematical Practices

What does the color of each row of counters represent?

Reflect

1. **Communicate Mathematical Ideas** When adding two numbers with the same sign, what sign do you use for the sum?

_____

Adding on a Number Line

Just as you can add positive integers on a number line, you can add negative integers.

The temperature was 2 °F below zero. The temperature drops by 5 °F. What is the temperature now?

Temperature (°F)

A What is the initial temperature written as an integer?

_____

B Mark the initial temperature on the number line.

C A drop in temperature of 5° is like adding −5° to the temperature.

Count on the number line to find the final temperature. Mark the temperature now on the number line.

D What is the temperature written as an integer?

_____

The temperature is _____

| **above / below** | zero.

Reflect

2. **What If?** Suppose the temperature is −1 °F and drops by 3 °F. Explain how to use the number line to find the new temperature.

_____

_____

3. **Communicate Mathematical Ideas** How would using a number line to find the sum 2 + 5 be different from using a number line to find the sum − 2 + (− 5)?

_____

_____

4. **Analyze Relationships** What are two other negative integers that have the same sum as − 2 and − 5?

_____

Adding Integers with a Common Sign

To add integers with the same sign, add the absolute values of the integers and use the sign of the integers for the sum.

EXAMPLE 1

FL 7.NS.1.1, 7.NS.1.1d

Add $-7 + (-6)$.   The signs of both integers are the same.

STEP 1 Find the absolute values.

$|-7| = 7$ $|-6| = 6$ The absolute value is always positive or zero.

STEP 2 Find the sum of the absolute values: $7 + 6 = 13$

STEP 3 Use the sign of the integers to write the sum.

$-7 + (-6) = -13$ The sign of each integer is negative.

Math Talk
Mathematical Practices

Can you use the same procedure you use to find the sum of two negative integers to find the sum of two *positive* numbers? Explain.

Reflect

5. **Communicate Mathematical Ideas** Does the Commutative Property of Addition apply when you add two negative integers? Explain.

_____

_____

6. **Critical Thinking** Choose any two negative integers. Is the sum of the integers less than or greater than the value of either of the integers? Will this be true no matter which integers you choose? Explain.

_____

_____

_____

_____

YOUR TURN

Find each sum.

7. $-8 + (-1) =$ _____

8. $-3 + (-7) =$ _____

9. $-48 + (-12) =$ _____

10. $-32 + (-38) =$ _____

11. $109 + 191 =$ _____

12. $-40 + (-105) =$ _____

13. $-150 + (-1500) =$ _____

14. $-200 + (-800) =$ _____

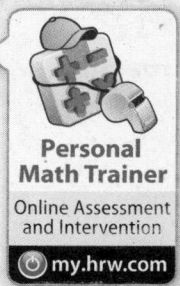
Personal Math Trainer
Online Assessment and Intervention
my.hrw.com

Find each sum. (Explore Activity 1)

1. $-5 + (-1)$

    a. How many counters are there? _____

    b. Do the counters represent positive or

      negative numbers? _____

    c. $-5 + (-1) =$ _____

2. $-2 + (-7)$

    a. How many counters are there? _____

    b. Do the counters represent positive or

      negative numbers? _____

    c. $-2 + (-7) =$ _____

Model each addition problem on the number line to find each sum.
(Explore Activity 2)

3. $-5 + (-2) =$ _____

4. $-1 + (-3) =$ _____

5. $-3 + (-7) =$ _____

6. $-4 + (-1) =$ _____

7. $-2 + (-2) =$ _____

8. $-6 + (-8) =$ _____

Find each sum. (Example 1)

9. $-5 + (-4) =$ _____

10. $-1 + (-10) =$ _____

11. $-9 + (-1) =$ _____

12. $-90 + (-20) =$ _____

13. $-52 + (-48) =$ _____

14. $5 + 198 =$ _____

15. $-4 + (-5) + (-6) =$ _____

16. $-50 + (-175) + (-345) =$ _____

? ESSENTIAL QUESTION CHECK-IN

17. How do you add integers with the same sign?

_____

_____

© Houghton Mifflin Harcourt Publishing Company

17.1 Independent Practice

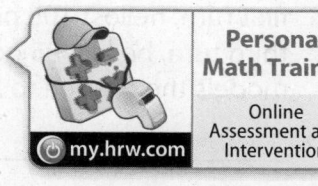

Personal Math Trainer

Online Assessment and Intervention

my.hrw.com

18. Represent Real-World Problems Jane and Sarah both dive down from the surface of a pool. Jane first dives down 5 feet, and then dives down 3 more feet. Sarah first dives down 3 feet, and then dives down 5 more feet.

a. Multiple Representations Use the number line to model the equation $-5 + (-3) = -3 + (-5)$.

b. Does the order in which you add two integers with the same sign affect the sum? Explain.

_____

_____

19. A golfer has the following scores for a 4-day tournament.

Day	1	2	3	4
Score	−3	−1	−5	−2

What was the golfer's total score for the tournament?

_____

20. A football team loses 3 yards on one play and 6 yards on another play. Write a sum of negative integers to represent this situation. Find the sum and explain how it is related to the problem.

_____

_____

21. When the quarterback is sacked, the team loses yards. In one game, the quarterback was sacked four times. What was the total sack yardage?

Sack	1	2	3	4
Sack yardage	−14	−5	−12	−23

_____

22. Multistep The temperature in Jonestown and Cooperville was the same at 1:00. By 2:00, the temperature in Jonestown dropped 10 degrees, and the temperature in Cooperville dropped 6 degrees. By 3:00, the temperature in Jonestown dropped 8 more degrees, and the temperature in Cooperville dropped 2 more degrees.

a. Write an equation that models the change to the temperature in Jonestown since 1:00.

_____

b. Write an equation that models the change to the temperature in Cooperville since 1:00.

_____

c. Where is it colder at 3:00, Jonestown or Cooperville?

_____

23. Represent Real-World Problems Julio is playing a trivia game. On his first turn, he lost 100 points. On his second turn, he lost 75 points. On his third turn, he lost 85 points. Write a sum of three negative integers that models the change to Julio's score after his first three turns.

_____

 FOCUS ON HIGHER ORDER THINKING

Work Area

24. Multistep On Monday, Jan made withdrawals of $25, $45, and $75 from her savings account. On the same day, her twin sister Julie made withdrawals of $35, $55, and $65 from *her* savings account.

a. Write a sum of negative integers to show Jan's withdrawals on Monday. Find the total amount Jan withdrew.

_____

b. Write a sum of negative integers to show Julie's withdrawals on Monday. Find the total amount Julie withdrew.

_____

c. Julie and Jan's brother also withdrew money from his savings account on Monday. He made three withdrawals and withdrew $10 more than Julie did. What are three possible amounts he could have withdrawn?

_____

25. Communicate Mathematical Ideas Why might you want to use the Commutative Property to change the order of the integers in the following sum before adding?

$$-80 + (-173) + (-20)$$

_____

_____

26. Critique Reasoning The absolute value of the sum of two different integers with the same sign is 8. Pat says there are three pairs of integers that match this description. Do you agree? Explain.

_____

_____

_____

_____

© Houghton Mifflin Harcourt Publishing Company

LESSON
17.2

Adding Integers with Different Signs

  FL **7.NS.1.1**
Apply and extend previous understandings of addition and subtraction to add... rational numbers; represent addition... on a horizontal... number line diagram. *Also 7.NS.1.1b*

? **ESSENTIAL QUESTION**

How do you add integers with different signs?

EXPLORE ACTIVITY 1 **FL** **7.NS.1.1, 7.NS.1.1b**

Adding on a Number Line

To find the sum of integers with the same sign, such as $3 + 2$, you can start at 3 and move $|2| = 2$ units in the positive direction.

To find the sum of integers with different signs, such as $3 + (-2)$, you can start at 3 and move $|-2| = 2$ units in the negative direction.

$3 + 2 = 5$ −3 −2 −1 0 1 2 3 4 5 $3 + (-2) = 1$ −3 −2 −1 0 1 2 3 4 5

Model each sum on a number line.

A Model $4 + (-3)$.

Start at 4. Move 3 units to the left, or in the negative direction.   0 1 2 3 4 5 6 7 8

$4 + (-3) = \underline{\hspace{2cm}}$

B Model $-7 + 5$.

Start at \underline{\hspace{1.5cm}}. Move 5 units to the \underline{\hspace{1.5cm}},   −8 −7 −6 −5 −4 −3 −2 −1 0

or in the \underline{\hspace{1.5cm}} direction.

$-7 + 5 = \underline{\hspace{2cm}}$

C Model $6 + (-6)$.

Start at \underline{\hspace{1cm}}. Move \underline{\hspace{1.5cm}} units to   0 1 2 3 4 5 6 7 8

the \underline{\hspace{1.5cm}}, or in the \underline{\hspace{1.5cm}} direction.

$6 + (-6) = \underline{\hspace{2cm}}$

Reflect

1. **Make a Prediction** Predict the sum of $-2 + 2$. Explain your prediction and check it using the number line.   −5 −4 −3 −2 −1 0 1 2 3

\underline{\hspace{13cm}}

Modeling Sums of Integers with Different Signs

You can use colored counters to model adding integers with different signs. When you add a positive integer (yellow counter) and a negative integer (red counter), the result is 0. One red and one yellow counter form a *zero pair*.

$1 + (-1) = 0$

Model and find each sum using counters. Part A is modeled for you. For Part B, follow the steps to model and find the sum using counters.

A Model $3 + (-2)$.

Start with 3 positive counters to represent 3.

Add 2 negative counters to represent adding −2.

Form zero pairs.

> The value of a zero pair is 0. Adding or subtracting 0 to any number does not change its value.

What is left when you remove the zero pairs?

_____ counter

Find the sum: $3 + (-2) =$ _____

B Model $-6 + 3$.

Start with _____ counters to represent _____.

Add _____ counters to represent adding _____.

Form zero pairs.

What is left when you remove the zero pairs?

_____ counters

Find the sum: $-6 + 3 =$ _____

Reflect

2. **Make a Prediction** Kyle models a sum of two integers. He uses more negative (red) counters than positive (yellow) counters. What do you predict about the sign of the sum? Explain.

_____

_____

YOUR TURN

Model and find each sum using counters.

3. $5 + (-1)$ _____

4. $4 + (-6)$ _____

5. $1 + (-7)$ _____

6. $3 + (-4)$ _____

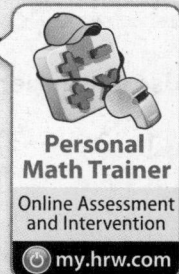

Personal
Math Trainer

Online Assessment
and Intervention

🔵 my.hrw.com

Adding Integers

You have learned how to add integers with the same signs and how to add integers with different signs. The table below summarizes the rules for adding integers.

Math On the Spot

🔵 my.hrw.com

Adding Integers		Examples
Same signs	Add the absolute values of the integers. Use the common sign for the sum.	$3 + 5 = 8$ $-2 + (-7) = -9$
Different signs	Subtract the lesser absolute value from the greater absolute value. Use the sign of the integer with the greater absolute value for the sum.	$3 + (-5) = -2$ $-10 + 1 = -9$
A number and its opposite	The sum is 0. The opposite of any number is called its **additive inverse**.	$4 + (-4) = 0$ $-11 + 11 = 0$

EXAMPLE 1   FL 7.NS.1.1, 7.NS.1.1b

Find each sum.

Ⓐ $-11 + 6$

$|-11| - |6| = 5$ Subtract the lesser absolute value from the greater.

$-11 + 6 = -5$ Use the sign of the number with the greater absolute value.

Ⓑ $(-37) + 37$

$(-37) + 37 = 0$ The sum of a number and its opposite is 0.

Math Talk

Mathematical Practices

Give an example of two integers with different signs whose sum is a positive number. How did you choose the integers?

YOUR TURN

Find each sum.

7. $-51 + 23 =$ _____

8. $10 + (-18) =$ _____

9. $13 + (-13) =$ _____

10. $25 + (-26) =$ _____

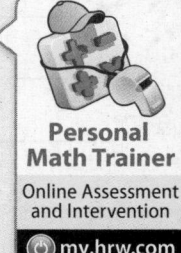

Personal
Math Trainer

Online Assessment
and Intervention

🔵 my.hrw.com

© Houghton Mifflin Harcourt Publishing Company

Lesson 17.2 **503**

Use a number line to find each sum. (Explore Activity 1)

1. $9 + (-3) =$ _____

2. $-2 + 7 =$ _____

3. $-15 + 4 =$ _____

4. $1 + (-4) =$ _____

Circle the zero pairs in each model. Find the sum. (Explore Activity 2)

5. $-4 + 5 =$ _____

6. $-6 + 6 =$ _____

7. $2 + (-5) =$ _____

8. $-3 + 7 =$ _____

Find each sum. (Example 1)

9. $-8 + 14 =$ _____

10. $7 + (-5) =$ _____

11. $5 + (-21) =$ _____

12. $14 + (-14) =$ _____

13. $0 + (-5) =$ _____

14. $32 + (-8) =$ _____

? ESSENTIAL QUESTION CHECK-IN

15. Describe how to find the sums $-4 + 2$ and $-4 + (-2)$ on a number line.

_____

_____

_____

17.2 Independent Practice

FL 7.NS.1.1, 7.NS.1.1b

Personal Math Trainer

Online Assessment and Intervention

my.hrw.com

Find each sum.

16. $-15 + 71 =$ _____

17. $-53 + 45 =$ _____

18. $-79 + 79 =$ _____

19. $-25 + 50 =$ _____

20. $18 + (-32) =$ _____

21. $5 + (-100) =$ _____

22. $-12 + 8 + 7 =$ _____

23. $-8 + (-2) + 3 =$ _____

24. $15 + (-15) + 200 =$ _____

25. $-500 + (-600) + 1200 =$ _____

26. A football team gained 9 yards on one play and then lost 22 yards on the next. Write a sum of integers to find the overall change in field position. Explain your answer.

_____

27. A soccer team is having a car wash. The team spent $55 on supplies. They earned $275, including tips. The team's profit is the amount the team made after paying for supplies. Write a sum of integers that represents the team's profit.

_____

28. As shown in the illustration, Alexa had a negative balance in her checking account before depositing a $47.00 check. What is the new balance of Alexa's checking account?

_____

Accounts   Regular Checking   Sign Out

Search transactions

Available Balance
−$47.00

29. The sum of two integers with different signs is 8. Give two possible integers that fit this description.

_____

30. **Multistep** Bart and Sam played a game in which each player earns or loses points in each turn. A player's total score after two turns is the sum of his points earned or lost. The player with the greater score after two turns wins. Bart earned 123 points and lost 180 points. Sam earned 185 points and lost 255 points. Which person won the game? Explain.

_____

_____

FOCUS ON HIGHER ORDER THINKING

© Houghton Mifflin Harcourt Publishing Company

Work Area

31. Critical Thinking Explain how you could use a number line to show that $-4 + 3$ and $3 + (-4)$ have the same value. Which property of addition states that these sums are equivalent?

_____

_____

_____

_____

32. Represent Real-World Problems Jim is standing beside a pool. He drops a weight from 4 feet above the surface of the water in the pool. The weight travels a total distance of 12 feet down before landing on the bottom of the pool. Explain how you can write a sum of integers to find the depth of the water.

_____

_____

_____

_____

_____

33. Communicate Mathematical Ideas Use counters to model two integers with different signs whose sum is positive. Explain how you know the sum is positive.

_____

_____

_____

_____

34. Analyze Relationships You know that the sum of -5 and another integer is a positive integer. What can you conclude about the sign of the other integer? What can you conclude about the value of the other integer? Explain.

_____

_____

_____

_____

17.3 Subtracting Integers

FL 7.NS.1.1c

Understand subtraction of rational numbers as adding the additive inverse, $p - q = p + (-q)$. . . . Also 7.NS.1

? ESSENTIAL QUESTION

How do you subtract integers?

EXPLORE ACTIVITY 1 FL 7.NS.1.1

Modeling Integer Subtraction

You can use counters to find the difference of two integers. In some cases, you may need to add zero pairs.

$1 + (-1) = 0$

Model and find each difference using counters.

A Model $-4 - (-3)$.

Start with 4 negative counters to represent -4.

Take away 3 negative counters to represent subtracting -3.

What is left? _____

Find the difference: $-4 - (-3) = $ _____

B Model $6 - (-3)$.

Start with 6 positive counters to represent 6.

You need to take away 3 negative counters, so add 3 zero pairs.

Take away 3 negative counters to represent subtracting -3.

What is left? _____

Find the difference: $6 - (-3) = $ _____

C Model $-2 - (-5)$.

Start with _____ counters.

You need to take away _____ counters, so add _____ zero pairs.

Take away _____ counters.

What is left? _____

Find the difference: $-2 - (-5) = $ _____

Reflect

1. **Communicate Mathematical Ideas** Suppose you want to model the difference $-4 - 7$. Do you need to add zero pairs? If so, why? How many should you add? What is the difference?

    _____

    _____

    _____

EXPLORE ACTIVITY 2 FL 7.NS.1.1, 7.NS.1.1c

Subtracting on a Number Line

To model the difference $5 - 3$ on a number line, you start at 5 and move 3 units to the left. Notice that you model the sum $5 + (-3)$ in the same way. Subtracting 3 is the same as adding its opposite, -3.

You can use the fact that subtracting a number is the same as adding its opposite to find a difference of two integers.

Find each difference on a number line.

A Find $-1 - 5$ on a number line.

Rewrite subtraction as addition of the opposite.

$-1 - 5 = -1 +$ _____

Start at _____ and move _____ units to the left.

The difference is _____

B Find $-7 - (-3)$.

Rewrite subtraction as addition of the opposite.

$-7 - (-3) = -7 +$ _____

Start at _____ and move _____ units to the _____.

The difference is _____

Reflect

2. **Communicate Mathematical Ideas** Describe how to find $5 - (-8)$ on a number line. If you found the difference using counters, would you get the same result? Explain.

_____

_____

_____

_____

_____

Subtracting Integers by Adding the Opposite

You can use the fact that subtracting an integer is the same as adding its opposite to solve problems.

Math On the Spot
my.hrw.com

EXAMPLE 1   FL 7.NS.1.1c, 7.NS.1.1

The temperature on Monday was −5 °C. By Tuesday the temperature rose to −2 °C. Find the change in temperature.

STEP 1 Write a subtraction expression.

final temperature − Monday's temperature = change in temperature

$-2\,°C - (-5\,°C)$

Animated Math
my.hrw.com

STEP 2 Find the difference.

$-2 - (-5) = -2 + 5$ *To subtract −5, add its opposite, 5.*

$-2 + 5 = 3$ *Use the rule for adding integers.*

The temperature increased by 3 °C.

Math Talk
Mathematical Practices

Why does it make sense that the change in temperature is a positive number?

Reflect

3. **What If?** In Example 1, the temperature rose by 3 °C. Suppose it fell from −2 °C to −10 °C. Predict whether the change in temperature would be positive or negative. Then subtract to find the change.

_____

_____

YOUR TURN

Find each difference.

4. $-7 - 2 =$ _____

5. $-1 - (-3) =$ _____

6. $3 - 5 =$ _____

7. $-8 - (-4) =$ _____

Guided Practice

Explain how to find each difference using counters. (Explore Activity 1)

1. $5 - 8 =$ _____

_____

_____

_____

_____

2. $-5 - (-3) =$ _____

_____

_____

_____

_____

Use a number line to find each difference. (Explore Activity 2)

3. $-4 - 5 = -4 +$ _____ $=$ _____

4. $1 - 4 = 1 +$ _____ $=$ _____

Solve. (Example 1)

5. $8 - 11 =$ _____

6. $-3 - (-5) =$ _____

7. $15 - 21 =$ _____

8. $-17 - 1 =$ _____

9. $0 - (-5) =$ _____

10. $1 - (-18) =$ _____

11. $15 - 1 =$ _____

12. $-3 - (-45) =$ _____

13. $19 - (-19) =$ _____

14. $-87 - (-87) =$ _____

❓ ESSENTIAL QUESTION CHECK-IN

15. How do you subtract an integer from another integer without using a number line or counters? Give an example.

_____

_____

Personal Math Trainer

my.hrw.com

Online Assessment and Intervention

16. Theo had a balance of −$4 in his savings account. After making a deposit, he has $25 in his account. What is the overall change to his account?

_____

17. As shown, Suzi starts her hike at an elevation below sea level. When she reaches the end of the hike, she is still below sea level at −127 feet. What was the change in elevation from the beginning of Suzi's hike to the end of the hike?

Current Elevation: −225 feet

_____

18. The record high January temperature in Austin, Texas, is 90 °F. The record low January temperature is −2 °F. Find the difference between the high and low temperatures.

_____

19. Cheyenne is playing a board game. Her score was −275 at the start of her turn, and at the end of her turn her score was −425. What was the change in Cheyenne's score from the start of her turn to the end of her turn?

_____

20. A scientist conducts three experiments in which she records the temperature of some gases that are being heated. The table shows the initial temperature and the final temperature for each gas.

Gas	Initial Temperature	Final Temperature
A	−21 °C	−8 °C
B	−12 °C	12 °C
C	−19 °C	−15 °C

a. Write a difference of integers to find the overall temperature change for each gas.

Gas A: _____

_____

Gas B: _____

_____

Gas C: _____

_____

b. **What If?** Suppose the scientist performs an experiment in which she cools the three gases. Will the changes in temperature be positive or negative for this experiment? Why?

_____

_____

_____

_____

_____

_____

_____

21. Analyze Relationships For two months, Nell feeds her cat Diet Chow brand cat food. Then for the next two months, she feeds her cat Kitty Diet brand cat food. The table shows the cat's change in weight over 4 months.

	Cat's Weight Change (oz)
Diet Chow, Month 1	−8
Diet Chow, Month 2	−18
Kitty Diet, Month 3	3
Kitty Diet, Month 4	−19

Which brand of cat food resulted in the greatest weight loss for Nell's cat? Explain.

_____

_____

_____

  FOCUS ON HIGHER ORDER THINKING

Work Area

22. Represent Real-World Problems Write and solve a word problem that can be modeled by the difference −4 − 10.

_____

_____

_____

23. Explain the Error When Tom found the difference −11 − (−4), he got −15. What might Tom have done wrong?

_____

_____

24. Draw Conclusions When you subtract one negative integer from another, will your answer be greater than or less than the integer you started with? Explain your reasoning and give an example.

_____

_____

_____

25. Look for a Pattern Find the next three terms in the pattern 9, 4, −1, −6, −11, … . Then describe the pattern.

_____

LESSON
17.4 Applying Addition and Subtraction of Integers

FL 7.NS.1.3
Solve real-world and mathematical problems involving the four operations with rational numbers. *Also 7.NS.1.1, 7.NS.1.1d, 7.EE.2.3*

? ESSENTIAL QUESTION

How do you solve multistep problems involving addition and subtraction of integers?

Solving a Multistep Problem

You can use what you know about adding and subtracting integers to solve a multistep problem.

EXAMPLE 1   FL 7.NS.1.3, 7.NS.1.1

Math On the Spot
my.hrw.com

A seal is swimming in the ocean 5 feet below sea level. It dives down 12 feet to catch some fish. Then, the seal swims 8 feet up towards the surface with its catch. What is the seal's final elevation relative to sea level?

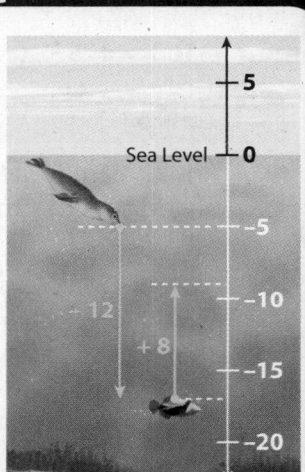

STEP 1   Write an expression.

- The seal starts at 5 feet below the surface, so its initial position is −5 ft.

Starts	−	Dives down	+	Swims up
−5	−	12	+	8

STEP 2   Add or subtract from left to right to find the value of the expression.

$$-5 - 12 + 8 = -17 + 8$$
$$= -9$$

> This is reasonable because the seal swam farther down than up.

The seal's final elevation is 9 feet below sea level.

1. Anna is in a cave 40 feet below the cave entrance. She descends 13 feet, then ascends 18 feet. Find her new position relative to the cave entrance.

_____

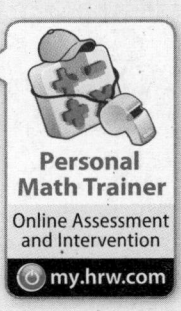

Personal Math Trainer

Online Assessment and Intervention

my.hrw.com

© Houghton Mifflin Harcourt Publishing Company

Applying Properties to Solve Problems

You can use properties of addition to solve problems involving integers.

EXAMPLE 2 Problem Solving **FL** 7.NS.1.1d, 7.NS.1.3, 7.EE.2.3

Irene has a checking account. On Monday she writes a $160 check for groceries. Then she deposits $125. Finally she writes another check for $40. What was the total change in the amount in Irene's account?

 Analyze Information

When Irene deposits money, she adds that amount to the account. When she writes a check, that money is deducted from the account.

 Formulate a Plan

Use a positive integer for the amount Irene added to the account. Use negative integers for the checks she wrote. Find the sum.

$$-160 + 125 + (-40)$$

 Solve

Add the amounts to find the total change in the account. Use properties of addition to simplify calculations.

$$-160 + 125 + (-40) = -160 + (-40) + 125 \qquad \textit{Commutative Property}$$
$$= -200 + 125 \qquad \textit{Associative Property}$$
$$= -75$$

The amount in the account decreased by $75.

 Justify and Evaluate

Irene's account has $75 less than it did before Monday. This is reasonable because she wrote checks for $200 but only deposited $125.

Reflect

2. **Communicative Mathematical Ideas** Describe a different way to find the change in Irene's account.

_____

_____

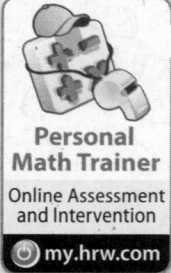
YOUR TURN

3. Alex wrote checks on Tuesday for $35 and $45. He also made a deposit in his checking account of $180. Find the overall change in the amount in his checking account.

_____

© Houghton Mifflin Harcourt Publishing Company

Comparing Values of Expressions

Sometimes you may want to compare values obtained by adding and subtracting integers.

Math On the Spot

my.hrw.com

EXAMPLE 3   Problem Solving   FL 7.NS.1.3, 7.EE.2.3

The Tigers, a football team, must gain 10 yards in the next four plays to keep possession of the ball. The Tigers lose 12 yards, gain 5 yards, lose 8 yards, and gain 14 yards. Do the Tigers maintain possession of the ball?

 Analyze Information

When the team gains yards, add that distance.

When the team loses yards, subtract that distance.

If the total change in yards is greater than or equal to 10, the team keeps possession of the ball.

 Formulate a Plan

$-12 + 5 - 8 + 14$

 Solve

$-12 + 5 - 8 + 14$

$-12 + 5 + (-8) + 14$ To subtract, add the opposite.

$-12 + (-8) + 5 + 14$ Commutative Property

$(-12 + (-8)) + (5 + 14)$ Associative Property

$-20 + 19 = -1$

$-1 < 10$ Compare to 10 yards

The Tigers gained less than 10 yards, so they do not maintain possession.

 Justify and Evaluate

The football team gained 19 yards and lost 20 yards for a total of -1 yard.

> **Math Talk**
> Mathematical Practices
>
> What does it mean that the football team had a total of -1 yard over four plays?

4. Jim and Carla are scuba diving. Jim started out 10 feet below the surface. He descended 18 feet, rose 5 feet, and descended 12 more feet. Then he rested. Carla started out at the surface. She descended 20 feet, rose 5 feet, and descended another 18 feet. Then she rested. Which person rested at a greater depth? Explain.

_____

_____

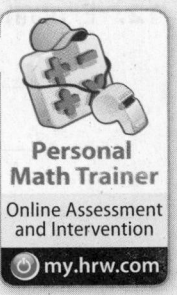

Personal Math Trainer

Online Assessment and Intervention

my.hrw.com

Guided Practice

Write an expression. Then find the value of the expression.
(Examples 1, 2, 3)

1. Tomas works as an underwater photographer. He starts at a position that is 15 feet below sea level. He rises 9 feet, then descends 12 feet to take a photo of a coral reef. Write and evaluate an expression to find his position relative to sea level when he took the photo.

   _____

2. The temperature on a winter night was -23 °F. The temperature rose by 5 °F when the sun came up. When the sun set again, the temperature dropped by 7 °F. Write and evaluate an expression to find the temperature after the sun set.

   _____

3. Jose earned 50 points in a video game. He lost 40 points, earned 87 points, then lost 30 more points. Write and evaluate an expression to find his final score in the video game.

   _____

Find the value of each expression. (Example 2)

4. $-6 + 15 + 15 = $ _____

5. $9 - 4 - 17 = $ _____

6. $50 - 42 + 10 = $ _____

7. $6 + 13 + 7 - 5 = $ _____

8. $65 + 43 - 11 = $ _____

9. $-35 - 14 + 45 + 31 = $ _____

Determine which expression has a greater value. (Example 3)

10. $-12 + 6 - 4$ or $-34 - 3 + 39$

    _____

11. $21 - 3 + 8$ or $-14 + 31 - 6$

    _____

? ESSENTIAL QUESTION CHECK-IN

12. Explain how you can find the value of the expression $-5 + 12 + 10 - 7$.

    _____

    _____

17.4 Independent Practice

FL 7.NS.1.1, 7.NS.1.1d, 7.NS.1.3, 7.EE.2.3

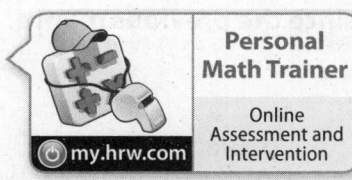

Personal Math Trainer

my.hrw.com Online Assessment and Intervention

13. Sports Cameron is playing 9 holes of golf. He needs to score a total of at most 15 over par on the last four holes to beat his best golf score. On the last four holes, he scores 5 over par, 1 under par, 6 over par, and 1 under par.

a. Write and find the value of an expression that gives Cameron's score for 4 holes of golf.

_____

b. Is Cameron's score on the last four holes over or under par?

_____

c. Did Cameron beat his best golf score?

_____

14. Herman is standing on a ladder that is partly in a hole. He starts out on a rung that is 6 feet under ground, climbs up 14 feet, then climbs down 11 feet. What is Herman's final position, relative to ground level?

_____

15. Explain the Error Jerome tries to find the value of the expression $3 - 6 + 5$ by first applying the Commutative Property. He rewrites the expression as $3 - 5 + 6$. Explain what is wrong with Jerome's approach.

_____
_____
_____
_____

16. Lee and Barry play a trivia game in which questions are worth different numbers of points. If a question is answered correctly, a player earns points. If a question is answered incorrectly, the player loses points. Lee currently has −350 points.

a. Before the game ends, Lee answers a 275-point question correctly, a 70-point question correctly, and a 50-point question incorrectly. Write and find the value of an expression to find Lee's final score.

_____

b. Barry's final score is 45. Which player had the greater final score?

_____

17. Multistep Rob collects data about how many customers enter and leave a store every hour. He records a positive number for customers entering the store each hour and a negative number for customers leaving the store each hour.

	Entering	Leaving
1:00 to 2:00	30	−12
2:00 to 3:00	14	−8
3:00 to 4:00	18	−30

a. During which hour did more customers leave than arrive?

_____

b. There were 75 customers in the store at 1:00. The store must be emptied of customers when it closes at 5:00. How many customers must leave the store between 4:00 and 5:00?

_____

The table shows the changes in the values of two friends' savings accounts since the previous month.

	June	July	August
Carla	−18	22	−53
Leta	−17	−22	18

18. Carla had $100 in her account in May. How much money does she have in her account in August? _____

19. Leta had $45 in her account in May. How much money does she have in her account in August? _____

20. **Analyze Relationships** Whose account had the greatest decrease in value from May to August? _____

  FOCUS ON HIGHER ORDER THINKING

21. **Represent Real-World Problems** Write and solve a word problem that matches the diagram shown.

_____

_____

_____

22. **Critical Thinking** Mary has $10 in savings. She owes her parents $50. She does some chores and her parents pay her $12. She also gets $25 for her birthday from her grandmother. Does Mary have enough money to pay her parents what she owes them? If not, how much more money does she need? Explain.

_____

_____

23. **Draw Conclusions** An expression involves subtracting two numbers from a positive number. Under what circumstances will the value of the expression be negative? Give an example.

_____

_____

_____

_____

Ready to Go On?

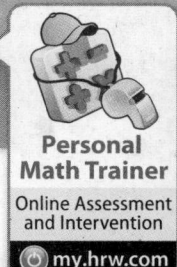

Personal Math Trainer

Online Assessment and Intervention

⏱ my.hrw.com

17.1 Adding Integers with the Same Sign

Add.

1. $-8 + (-6)$ _____

2. $-4 + (-7)$ _____

3. $-9 + (-12)$ _____

17.2 Adding Integers with Different Signs

Add.

4. $5 + (-2)$ _____

5. $-8 + 4$ _____

6. $15 + (-8)$ _____

17.3 Subtracting Integers

Subtract.

7. $2 - 9$ _____

8. $-3 - (-4)$ _____

9. $11 - (-12)$ _____

17.4 Applying Addition and Subtraction of Integers

10. A bus makes a stop at 2:30, letting off 15 people and letting on 9. The bus makes another stop ten minutes later to let off 4 more people. How many more or fewer people are on the bus after the second stop compared to the number of people on the bus before the 2:30 stop?

_____

11. Cate and Elena were playing a card game. The stack of cards in the middle had 24 cards in it to begin with. Cate added 8 cards to the stack. Elena then took 12 cards from the stack. Finally, Cate took 9 cards from the stack. How many cards were left in the stack? _____

 ESSENTIAL QUESTION

12. Write and solve a word problem that can be modeled by addition of two negative integers.

_____

_____

_____

Assessment Readiness

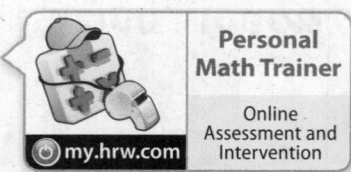

Personal Math Trainer
my.hrw.com
Online Assessment and Intervention

Selected Response

1. Which expression has the same value as $-3 + (-5)$?

- (A) $-3 - (-5)$
- (B) $-3 + 5$
- (C) $-5 + (-3)$
- (D) $-5 - (-3)$

2. A diver's elevation is -30 feet relative to sea level. She dives down 12 feet. What is her elevation after the dive?

- (A) 12 feet
- (B) 18 feet
- (C) -30 feet
- (D) -42 feet

3. Which number line models the expression $-3 + 5$?

- (A)
- (B)
- (C)
- (D)

4. Which number can you add to 5 to get a sum of 0?

- (A) -10
- (B) -5
- (C) 0
- (D) 5

5. The temperature in the morning was $-3\,°F$. The temperature dropped 11 degrees by night. What was the temperature at night?

- (A) $-14\,°F$
- (B) $-8\,°F$
- (C) $8\,°F$
- (D) $14\,°F$

6. Which of the following expressions has the greatest value?

- (A) $3 - 7 + (-10)$
- (B) $3 + 7 - (-10)$
- (C) $3 - 7 - (-10)$
- (D) $3 + 7 + (-10)$

Mini-Task

7. At the end of one day, the value of a share of a certain stock was $12. Over the next three days, the change in the value of the share was $-$1$, then, $-$1$, and then $3.

a. Write an expression that describes the situation.

_____

b. Evaluate the expression. _____

c. What does your answer to part **b** mean in the context of the problem?

_____

_____

Multiplying and Dividing Integers

MODULE **18**

ESSENTIAL QUESTION

How can you use multiplication and division of integers to solve real-world problems?

LESSON 18.1
Multiplying Integers
FL 7.NS.1.2 , 7.NS.1.2a

LESSON 18.2
Dividing Integers
 FL 7.NS.1.2, 7.NS.1.2b, 7.NS.1.3

LESSON 18.3
Applying Integer Operations
 FL 7.NS.1.2a, 7.NS.1.2c, 7.NS.1.3, 7.EE.2.3

Real-World Video

The giant panda is an endangered animal. For some endangered species, the population has made a steady decline. This can be represented by multiplying integers with different signs.

⏻ my.hrw.com

GO DIGITAL
my.hrw.com

my.hrw.com

Go digital with your write-in student edition, accessible on any device.

Math On the Spot

Scan with your smart phone to jump directly to the online edition, video tutor, and more.

Animated Math

Interactively explore key concepts to see how math works.

Personal Math Trainer

Get immediate feedback and help as you work through practice sets.

521

Are YOU Ready?

Complete these exercises to review skills you will need for this module.

Personal Math Trainer

Online Assessment and Intervention

Multiplication Facts

Multiply.

1. 9×3 _____   **2.** 7×10 _____   **3.** 9×8 _____   **4.** 15×10 _____

5. 6×9 _____   **6.** 10×23 _____   **7.** 9×9 _____   **8.** 10×20 _____

Division Facts

EXAMPLE $48 \div 6 = $ ■   Think: 6 times what number equals 48?

$6 \times 8 = 48$

$48 \div 6 = 8$ So, $48 \div 6 = 8$

Divide.

9. $54 \div 9$ _____ **10.** $42 \div 6$ _____ **11.** $24 \div 3$ _____ **12.** $64 \div 8$ _____

13. $90 \div 10$ _____ **14.** $56 \div 7$ _____ **15.** $81 \div 9$ _____ **16.** $110 \div 11$ _____

Order of Operations

EXAMPLE $32 - 2(10 - 7)^2$

$32 - 2(3)^2$ To evaluate, first operate within parentheses.

$32 - 2(9)$ Next, simplify exponents.

$32 - 18$ Then multiply and divide from left to right.

14 Finally add and subtract from left to right.

Evaluate each expression.

17. $12 + 8 \div 2$ _____   **18.** $15 - (4 + 3) \times 2$ _____   **19.** $18 - (8 - 5)^2$ _____

20. $6 + 7 \times 3 - 5$ _____   **21.** $9 + (2^2 + 3)^2 \times 2$ _____   **22.** $6 + 5 - 4 \times 3 \div 2$ _____

© Houghton Mifflin Harcourt Publishing Company

Reading Start-Up

Visualize Vocabulary

Use the ✔ words to complete the chart. You may put more than one word in each box.

÷, or put into equal groups		×, or repeated addition

Multiplying and Dividing Whole Numbers

$4 \times 1 = 4$		$32 \div 4 = 8$

Vocabulary

Review Words
- ✔ divide (*dividir*)
- ✔ dividend (*dividendo*)
- ✔ divisor (*divisor*)
- integers (*enteros*)
- ✔ multiply (*multiplicar*)
- negative number (*número negativo*)
- operation (*operación*)
- opposites (*opuestos*)
- positive number (*número positivo*)
- ✔ product (*producto*)
- ✔ quotient (*cociente*)

Understand Vocabulary

Complete the sentences using the review words.

1. A _____ is a number that is less than 0. A _____ is a number that is greater than 0.

2. Division problems have three parts. The part you want to divide into groups is called

   the _____. The number that is divided into another number is called

   the _____. The answer to a division problem is called the _____.

3. _____ are all whole numbers and their opposites.

Active Reading

Double-Door Fold Create a double-door fold to help you understand the concepts in this module. Label one flap "Multiplying Integers" and the other flap "Dividing Integers." As you study each lesson, write important ideas under the appropriate flap. Include information that will help you remember the concepts later when you look back at your notes.

MODULE 18
Unpacking the Standards

Understanding the standards and the vocabulary terms in the standards will help you know exactly what you are expected to learn in this module.

 FL **7.NS.1.2a**

Understand that multiplication is extended from fractions to rational numbers by requiring that operations continue to satisfy the properties of operations, particularly the distributive property, leading to products such as $(-1)(-1) = 1$ and the rules for multiplying signed numbers. Interpret products of rational numbers by describing real-world contexts.

Key Vocabulary
integer *(entero)*
   A member of the set of whole numbers and their opposites.

What It Means to You

You will use your knowledge of multiplication of whole numbers and addition of negative numbers to multiply integers.

UNPACKING EXAMPLE 7.NS.1.2a

Show that $(-1)(-1) = 1$.

$0 = -1(0)$	*Multiplication property of 0*
$0 = -1(-1 + 1)$	*Addition property of opposites*
$0 = (-1)(-1) + (-1)(1)$	*Distributive Property*
$0 = (-1)(-1) + (-1)$	*Multiplication property of 1*
So, $(-1)(-1) = 1$.	*Definition of opposites*

In general, a negative number times a negative number is always a positive number.

 FL **7.NS.1.2b**

Understand that integers can be divided, provided that the divisor is not zero, and every quotient of integers (with non-zero divisor) is a rational number. If p and q are integers, then $-\left(\frac{p}{q}\right) = \frac{(-p)}{q} = \frac{p}{(-q)}$. Interpret quotients of rational numbers by describing real-world contexts.

What It Means to You

You will use your knowledge of division of whole numbers and multiplication of integers to divide integers.

UNPACKING EXAMPLE 7.NS.1.2b

The temperature in Fairbanks, Alaska, dropped over four consecutive hours from $0°$ F to $-44°$F. If the temperature dropped the same amount each hour, how much did the temperature change each hour?

$$\frac{-44}{4} = -11$$

The quotient of -44 and 4 is the same as the negative quotient of 44 and 4.

A negative number divided by a positive number is negative.

Visit **my.hrw.com** to see all **Florida Math Standards** unpacked.

my.hrw.com

© Houghton Mifflin Harcourt Publishing Company • Image Credits: Carol Falcetta/Flickr/Getty Images

LESSON

18.1 Multiplying Integers

FL 7.NS.1.2

Apply and extend previous understandings of multiplication and division... to multiply ... rational numbers. *Also 7.NS.1.2a*

? ESSENTIAL QUESTION

How do you multiply integers?

EXPLORE ACTIVITY 1   FL 7.NS.1.2, 7.NS.1.2a

Multiplying Integers Using a Number Line

You can use a number line to see what happens when you multiply a positive number by a negative number.

A Henry made three withdrawals of $2 each from his savings account. What was the change in his balance?

Find 3(−2).

To graph −2, you would start at 0 and move _____ units to the left.

3(−2) means (_____) + (_____) + (_____).

To graph 3(−2), start at 0 and move

2 units to the left _____ times.

The result is _____.

$+(-2) +(-2) +(-2)$

−8 −7 −6 −5 −4 −3 −2 −1 0

The change in Henry's balance was _____

B Lisa plays a video game in which she loses points. She loses 3 points 2 times. What is her score?

Find 2(−3).

2(−3) means (_____) + (_____).
Show this on the number line.

Lisa has a score of _____.

−8 −7 −6 −5 −4 −3 −2 −1 0

Reflect

1. What do you notice about the product of two integers with different signs?

_____

_____

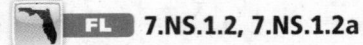

Modeling Integer Multiplication

Counters representing positive and negative numbers can help you understand how to find the product of two negative integers.

○ = +1
● = −1

Find the product of −3 and −4.

Write $(-3)(-4)$ as $-3(-4)$, which means the *opposite* of $3(-4)$.

STEP 1   Use negative counters to model $3(-4)$.

3 groups of −4

STEP 2   Make the same model using positive counters to find the *opposite* of $3(-4)$.

The *opposite* of 3 groups of −4

STEP 3   Translate the model into a mathematical expression:

$(-3)(-4) = $ _____

The product of −3 and −4 is _____.

Reflect

2. What do you notice about the sign of the product of two negative integers?

_____

_____

3. **Make a Conjecture** What can you conclude about the sign of the product of two integers with the same sign?

_____

_____

_____

_____

Multiplying Integers

The product of two integers with opposite signs is negative. The product of two integers with the same sign is positive. The product of 0 and any other integer is 0.

Math On the Spot
my.hrw.com

EXAMPLE 1

 FL 7.NS.1.2

A Multiply: (13)(−3):

STEP 1 Determine the sign of the product.

13 is positive and −3 is negative. Since the numbers have opposite signs, the product will be negative.

STEP 2 Find the absolute values of the numbers and multiply them.

$|13| = 13$ $\qquad$ $|-3| = 3$

$13 \times 3 = 39$

STEP 3 Assign the correct sign to the product.

$13(-3) = -39$ $\quad$ *The product is −39.*

B Multiply: (−5)(−8).

STEP 1 Determine the sign of the product.

−5 is negative and −8 is negative. Since the numbers have the same sign, the product will be positive.

STEP 2 Find the absolute values of the numbers and multiply them.

$|-5| = 5$ $\qquad$ $|-8| = 8$

$5 \times 8 = 40$

STEP 3 Assign the correct sign to the product.

$(-5)(-8) = 40$ $\quad$ *The product is 40.*

C Multiply: (−10)(0).

$(-10)(0) = 0$ $\quad$ *One of the factors is 0, so the product is 0.*

Animated Math
my.hrw.com

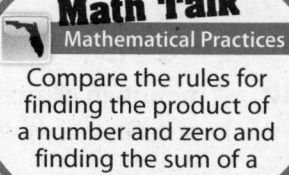

Math Talk
Mathematical Practices

Compare the rules for finding the product of a number and zero and finding the sum of a number and 0.

YOUR TURN

Find each product.

4. −3(5) _____

5. (−10)(−2) _____

6. 7(−6) _____

7. 0(−22) _____

8. (−15)(−3) _____

9. 8(4) _____

Personal Math Trainer

Online Assessment and Intervention

my.hrw.com

Find each product. (Explore Activity 2 and Example 1)

1. −1(9) _____

2. 14(−2) _____

3. (−9)(−6) _____

4. (−2)(50) _____

5. (−4)(15) _____

6. −18(0) _____

7. (−7)(−7) _____

8. −15(9) _____

9. (8)(−12) _____

10. −3(−100) _____

11. 0(−153) _____

12. −6(32) _____

13. Flora made 7 withdrawals of $75 each from her bank account. What was the overall change in her account? (Example 1)

_____

14. A football team lost 5 yards on each of 3 plays. Explain how you could use a number line to find the team's change in field position after the 3 plays. (Explore Activity 1)

_____

_____

15. The temperature dropped 2 °F every hour for 6 hours. What was the total number of degrees the temperature changed in the 6 hours? (Explore Activity 1)

_____

16. The price of one share of Acme Company declined $5 per day for 4 days in a row. How much did the price of one share change in total after the 4 days? (Explore Activity 1)

_____

17. A mountain climber climbed down a cliff 50 feet at a time. He did this 5 times in one day. What was the overall change in his elevation? (Explore Activity 1)

_____

? ESSENTIAL QUESTION CHECK-IN

18. Explain the process for finding the product of two integers.

_____

_____

_____

_____

18.1 Independent Practice

FL **7.NS.1.2**

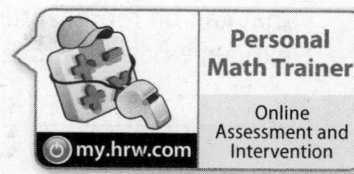
19. Critique Reasoning Lisa used a number line to model −2(3). Does her number line make sense? Explain why or why not.

$+(-3)$ $+(-3)$

−8 −7 −6 −5 −4 −3 −2 −1 0

_____

_____

_____

20. Represent Real-World Problems Mike got on an elevator and went down 3 floors. He meant to go to a lower level, so he stayed on the elevator and went down 3 more floors. How many floors did Mike go down altogether?

_____

Solve. Show your work.

21. When Brooke buys lunch at the cafeteria, money is withdrawn from a lunch account. The table shows amounts withdrawn in one week. By how much did the amount in Brooke's lunch account change by the end of that week?

Lunch Account			
Week 1	**Lunch**	**Cost**	**Balance**
			$28
Monday	Pizza	$4	
Tuesday	Fish Tacos	$4	
Wednesday	Spaghetti	$4	
Thursday	Sandwich	$4	
Friday	Chicken	$4	

_____

22. Adam is scuba diving. He descends 5 feet below sea level. He descends the same distance 4 more times. What is Adam's final elevation?

_____

_____

_____

23. The price of jeans was reduced $6 per week for 7 weeks. By how much did the price of the jeans change over the 7 weeks?

_____

_____

_____

24. Casey uses some of his savings on batting practice. The cost of renting a batting cage for 1 hour is $6. He rents a cage for 9 hours in each of two months. What is the change in Casey's savings after two months?

_____

_____

_____

25. Volunteers at Sam's school use some of the student council's savings for a special project. They buy 7 backpacks for $8 each and fill each backpack with paper and pens that cost $5. By how much did the student council's savings change because of this project?

_____

_____

_____

26. Communicate Mathematical Ideas Describe a real-world situation that can be represented by the product 8(−20). Then find the product and explain what the product means in terms of the real-world situation.

_____

_____

_____

27. What If? The rules for multiplying two integers can be extended to a product of 3 or more integers. Find the following products by using the Associative Property to multiply 2 numbers at a time.

a. 3(3)(−3) _____   **b.** 3(−3)(−3) _____   **c.** −3(−3)(−3) _____

d. 3(3)(3)(−3) _____   **e.** 3(3)(−3)(−3) _____   **f.** 3(−3)(−3)(−3) _____

g. Make a Conjecture Based on your results, complete the following statements:

When a product of integers has an odd number of negative factors,

then the sign of the product is _____.

When a product of integers has an even number of negative factors,

then the sign of the product is _____.

H.O.T. FOCUS ON HIGHER ORDER THINKING

28. Multiple Representations The product of three integers is −3. Determine all of the possible values for the three factors.

_____

29. Analyze Relationships When is the product of two nonzero integers less than or equal to both of the two factors?

_____

_____

30. Justify Reasoning The sign of the product of two integers with the same sign is positive. What is the sign of the product of three integers with the same sign? Explain your thinking.

_____

_____

_____

_____

Work Area

LESSON
18.2 Dividing Integers

FL 7.NS.1.2
Apply and extend previous understandings of multiplication and division... to. . .divide rational numbers. *Also 7.NS.1.2b, 7.NS.1.3*

? **ESSENTIAL QUESTION**

How do you divide integers?

EXPLORE ACTIVITY   **FL** 7.NS.1.2, 7.NS.1.3

A diver needs to descend to a depth of 100 feet. She wants to do it in 5 equal descents. How far should she travel in each descent?

A Use the number line at the right to find how far the diver should travel in each of the 5 descents.

_____

B To solve this problem, you can set up a division problem: $\dfrac{-100}{\boxed{}} = ?$

C Rewrite the division problem as a multiplication problem. Think: Some number multiplied by 5 equals −100.

_____ × ? = −100

D Remember the rules for integer multiplication. If the product is negative, one of the factors must be negative. Since _____ is positive, the unknown factor must be **positive / negative.**

E You know that 5 × _____ = 100. So, using the rules for integer multiplication you can say that 5 × _____ = −100.

The diver should descend _____ feet in each descent.

F Use the process you just learned to find each of the quotients below.

$\dfrac{14}{-7} =$ _____ $\dfrac{-36}{-9} =$ _____ $\dfrac{-55}{11} =$ _____ $\dfrac{-45}{-5} =$ _____

Number line (right side):
0
−10
−20
−30
−40
−50
−60
−70
−80
−90
−100
−110

Reflect

1. **Make a Conjecture** Make a conjecture about the quotient of two integers with different signs. Make a conjecture about the quotient of two integers with the same sign.

_____

_____

© Houghton Mifflin Harcourt Publishing Company

Dividing Integers

You used the relationship between multiplication and division to make conjectures about the signs of quotients of integers. You can use multiplication to understand why division by zero is not possible.

Think about the division problem below and its related multiplication problem.

$$5 \div 0 = ? \qquad 0 \times ? = 5$$

The multiplication sentence says that there is some number times 0 that equals 5. You already know that 0 times any number equals 0. This means division by 0 is not possible, so we say that division by 0 is undefined.

My Notes

EXAMPLE 1

FL   7.NS.1.2

A Divide: $24 \div (-3)$

STEP 1 Determine the sign of the quotient.

24 is positive and -3 is negative. Since the numbers have opposite signs, the quotient will be negative.

STEP 2 Divide.

$24 \div (-3) = -8$

B Divide: $-6 \div (-2)$

STEP 1 Determine the sign of the quotient.

-6 is negative and -2 is negative. Since the numbers have the same sign, the quotient will be positive.

STEP 2 Divide: $-6 \div (-2) = 3$

C Divide: $0 \div (-9)$

STEP 1 Determine the sign of the quotient.

The dividend is 0 and the divisor is not 0. So, the quotient is 0.

STEP 2 Divide: $0 \div (-9) = 0$

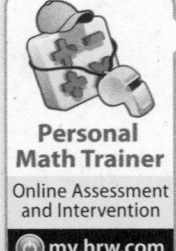
YOUR TURN

Find each quotient.

2. $0 \div (-6)$ _____

3. $38 \div (-19)$ _____

4. $-13 \div (-1)$ _____

© Houghton Mifflin Harcourt Publishing Company

Using Integer Division to Solve Problems

You can use integer division to solve real-world problems. For some problems, you may need to perform more than one step. Be sure to check that the sign of the quotient makes sense for the situation.

Math On the Spot

my.hrw.com

EXAMPLE 2   **FL** 7.NS.1.3, 7.NS.1.2

Jake answers questions in two different online Olympic trivia quizzes. In each quiz, he loses points when he gives an incorrect answer. The table shows the points lost for each wrong answer in each quiz and Jake's total points lost in each quiz. In which quiz did he have more wrong answers?

Olympic Trivia Quiz	Points lost for each wrong answer	Total points lost
Winter Quiz	−3 points	−33 points
Summer Quiz	−7 points	−56 points

STEP 1 Find the number of incorrect answers in the winter quiz.

$-33 \div (-3) = 11$ *Divide the total points lost by the number of points lost per wrong answer.*

STEP 2 Find the number of incorrect answers Jake gave in the summer quiz.

$-56 \div (-7) = 8$ *Divide the total points lost by the number of points lost per wrong answer.*

STEP 3 Compare the numbers of wrong answers.

$11 > 8$, so Jake had more wrong answers in the winter quiz.

> **Math Talk**
> **Mathematical Practices**
>
> What is the sign of each quotient in Steps 1 and 2? Why does this make sense for the situation?

YOUR TURN

5. A penalty in Meteor-Mania is −5 seconds. A penalty in Cosmic Calamity is −7 seconds. Yolanda had penalties totaling −25 seconds in a game of Meteor-Mania and −35 seconds in a game of Cosmic Calamity. In which game did Yolanda receive more penalties? Justify your answer.

_____

_____

_____

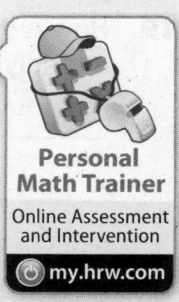

Personal Math Trainer

Online Assessment and Intervention

my.hrw.com

© Houghton Mifflin Harcourt Publishing Company

Guided Practice

Find each quotient. (Example 1)

1. $\dfrac{-14}{2}$ _____

2. $21 \div (-3)$ _____

3. $\dfrac{26}{-13}$ _____

4. $0 \div (-4)$ _____

5. $\dfrac{-45}{-5}$ _____

6. $-30 \div (10)$ _____

7. $\dfrac{-11}{-1}$ _____

8. $-31 \div (-31)$ _____

9. $\dfrac{0}{-7}$ _____

10. $\dfrac{-121}{-11}$ _____

11. $84 \div (-7)$ _____

12. $\dfrac{500}{-25}$ _____

13. $-6 \div (0)$ _____

14. $\dfrac{-63}{-21}$ _____

Write a division expression for each problem. Then find the value of the expression. (Example 2)

15. Clark made four of his truck payments late and was fined four late fees. The total change to his savings from late fees was −$40. How much was one late fee?

_____

16. Jan received −22 points on her exam. She got 11 questions wrong out of 50 questions. How much was Jan penalized for each wrong answer?

_____

17. Allen's score in a video game was changed by −75 points because he missed some targets. He got −15 points for each missed target. How many targets did he miss?

_____

18. Louisa's savings change by −$9 each time she goes bowling. In all, it changed by −$99 during the summer. How many times did she go bowling in the summer?

_____

? ESSENTIAL QUESTION CHECK-IN

19. How is the process of dividing integers similar to the process of multiplying integers?

_____

_____

_____

18.2 Independent Practice

FL 7.NS.1.2, 7.NS.1.2b, 7.NS.1.3

Personal Math Trainer

my.hrw.com

Online Assessment and Intervention

20. Walter buys a bus pass for $30. Every time he rides the bus, money is deducted from the value of the pass. He rode 12 times and $24 was deducted from the value of the pass. How much does each bus ride cost? _____

21. Analyze Relationships Elisa withdrew $20 at a time from her bank account and withdrew a total of $140. Francis withdrew $45 at a time from his bank account and withdrew a total of $270. Who made the greater number of withdrawals? Justify your answer.

_____

_____

_____

22. Multistep At 7 p.m. last night, the temperature was 10°F. At 7 a.m. the next morning, the temperature was −2°F.

a. By how much did the temperature change from 7 p.m. to 7 a.m.?

_____

b. The temperature changed by a steady amount overnight. By how much did it change each hour?

_____

_____

23. Analyze Relationships Nola hiked down a trail at a steady rate for 10 minutes. Her change in elevation was −200 feet. Then she continued to hike down for another 20 minutes at a different rate. Her change in elevation for this part of the hike was −300 feet. During which portion of the hike did she walk down at a faster rate? Explain your reasoning.

_____

_____

_____

24. Write a real world description to fit the expression −50 ÷ 5.

_____

_____

25. Communicate Mathematical Ideas Two integers, a and b, have different signs. The absolute value of integer a is divisible by the absolute value of integer b. Find two integers that fit this description. Then decide if the product of the integers is greater than or less than the quotient of the integers. Show your work.

_____

_____

_____

Determine if each statement is true or false. Justify your answer.

26. For any two nonzero integers, the product and quotient have the same sign.

_____

_____

_____

27. Any nonzero integer divided by 0 equals 0.

_____

_____

H.O.T. FOCUS ON HIGHER ORDER THINKING

Work Area

28. Multi-step A perfect score on a test with 25 questions is 100. Each question is worth the same number of points.

a. How many points is each question on the test worth? _____

b. Fred got a score of 84 on the test. Write a division sentence using negative numbers where the quotient represents the number of questions Fred answered incorrectly. _____

29. Persevere in Problem Solving Colleen divided integer a by -3 and got 8. Then she divided 8 by integer b and got -4. Find the quotient of integer a and integer b. _____

30. Justify Reasoning The quotient of two negative integers results in an integer. How does the value of the quotient compare to the value of the original two integers? Explain.

_____

_____

_____

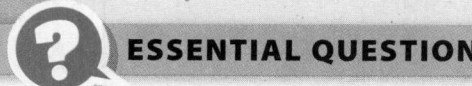
18.3 Applying Integer Operations

FL **7.NS.1.3**
Solve real-world and
mathematical problems
involving the four operations
with rational numbers. *Also
7.NS.1.2a, 7.NS.1.2c,
7.EE.2.3*

? ESSENTIAL QUESTION

How can you use integer operations to solve real-world problems?

Using the Order of Operations with Integers

The order of operations applies to integer operations as well as positive number operations. Perform multiplication and division first, and then addition and subtraction. Work from left to right in the expression.

Math On the Spot
⏻ my.hrw.com

EXAMPLE 1 *Problem Solving* FL **7.NS.1.2c, 7.NS.1.2a**

Hannah made four withdrawals of $20 from her checking account. She also wrote a check for $215. By how much did the amount in her checking account change?

 Analyze Information

You need to find the total *change* in Hannah's account. Since withdrawals and writing a check represent a decrease in her account, use negative numbers to represent these amounts.

 Formulate a Plan

Write a product to represent the four withdrawals.

$$-20 + (-20) + (-20) + (-20) = 4(-20)$$

Add −215 to represent the check that Hannah wrote.

$$4(-20) + (-215)$$

 Solve

Evaluate the expression to find by how much the amount in the account changed.

$$4(-20) - 215 = -80 - 215 \qquad \text{Multiply first.}$$
$$= -295 \qquad \text{Then subtract.}$$

The amount in the account decreased by $295.

 Justify and Evaluate

The value −295 represents a decrease of 295 dollars. This makes sense, since withdrawals and writing checks remove money from the checking account.

YOUR TURN

1. Reggie lost 3 spaceships in level 3 of a video game. He lost 30 points for each spaceship. When he completed level 3, he earned a bonus of 200 points. By how much did his score change?

_____

_____

2. Simplify: $-6(13) - 21$ _____

Math On the Spot

🕙 my.hrw.com

Using Negative Integers to Represent Quantities

You can use positive and negative integers to solve problems involving amounts that increase or decrease. Sometimes you may need to use more than one operation.

EXAMPLE 2   **FL** 7.NS.1.3, 7.EE.2.3

Three brothers each have their own savings. They borrow \$72 from their parents for concert tickets. Each brother must pay back an equal share of this amount. Also, the youngest brother owes his parents \$15. By how much will the youngest brother's savings change after he pays his parents?

STEP 1 Determine the signs of the values and the operations you will use. Write an expression.

Since the money is being paid back, it will *decrease* the amount in each brother's savings. Use -72 and -15.

Since an *equal share* of the \$72 will be paid back, use division to determine 3 equal parts of -72. Then add -15 to one of these equal parts.

Change to youngest brother's savings $= (-72) \div 3 + (-15)$

STEP 2 Evaluate the expression.

$(-72) \div 3 + (-15) = -24 + (-15)$ *Divide.*

$ = -39$ *Add.*

The youngest brother's savings will decrease by \$39.

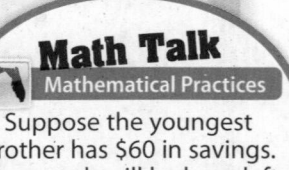

Math Talk

Mathematical Practices

Suppose the youngest brother has \$60 in savings. How much will he have left after he pays his parents what he owes?

Reflect

3. **What If?** Suppose there were four brothers in Example 2. How much would the youngest brother need to pay?

_____

© Houghton Mifflin Harcourt Publishing Company

YOUR TURN

Simplify each expression.

4. $(-12) \div 6 + 2$ _____

5. $-87 \div (-3) - 9$ _____

6. $40 \div (-5) + 30$ _____

7. $-39 \div 3 - 15$ _____

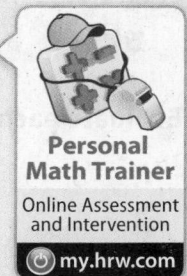

Personal Math Trainer

Online Assessment and Intervention

⏵ my.hrw.com

Comparing Values of Expressions

Often, problem situations require making comparisons between two values. Use integer operations to calculate values. Then compare the values.

Math On the Spot

⏵ my.hrw.com

EXAMPLE 3 **FL** 7.NS.1.3, 7.EE.2.3

Jill and Tony play a board game in which they move counters along a board. Jill moves her counter back 3 spaces four times, and then moves her counter forward 6 spaces. Tony moves his counter back 2 spaces three times, and then moves his player forward 3 spaces one time. Find each player's overall change in position. Who moved farther?

STEP 1 Find each player's overall change in position.

Jill: $4(-3) + 6 = -12 + 6 = -6$ *Jill moves back 6 spaces.*

Tony: $3(-2) + 3 = -6 + 3 = -3$ *Tony moves back 3 spaces.*

STEP 2 Compare the numbers of spaces moved by the players.

$|-6| > |-3|$ *Compare absolute values.*

Jill moves farther back than Tony.

Math Talk
Mathematical Practices

Why do you compare absolute values in Step 2?

YOUR TURN

8. Amber and Will are in line together to buy tickets. Amber moves back by 3 places three times to talk to friends. She then is invited to move 5 places up in line. Will moved back by 4 places twice, and then moved up in line by 3 places. Overall, who moved farther back in line?

_____

Evaluate each expression. Circle the expression with the greater value.

9. $(-10) \div 2 - 2 =$ _____

$(-28) \div 4 + 1 =$ _____

10. $42 \div (-3) + 9 =$ _____

$(-36) \div 9 - 2 =$ _____

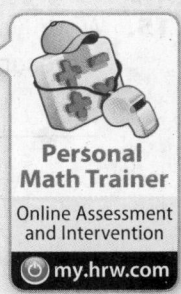

Personal Math Trainer

Online Assessment and Intervention

⏵ my.hrw.com

© Houghton Mifflin Harcourt Publishing Company

Lesson 18.3 **539**

Guided Practice

Evaluate each expression. (Example 1)

1. $-6(-5) + 12$ _____

2. $3(-6) - 3$ _____

3. $-2(8) + 7$ _____

4. $4(-13) + 20$ _____

5. $(-4)(0) - 4$ _____

6. $-3(-5) - 16$ _____

Write an expression to represent the situation. Evaluate the expression and answer the question. (Example 2)

7. Bella pays 7 payments of $5 each to a game store. She returns one game and receives $20 back. What is the change to the amount of money she has?

_____

8. Ron lost 10 points seven times playing a video game. He then lost an additional 100 points for going over the time limit. What was the total change in his score?

_____

9. Ned took a test with 25 questions. He lost 4 points for each of the 6 questions he got wrong and earned an additional 10 points for answering a bonus question correctly. How many points did Ned receive or lose overall?

_____

10. Mr. Harris has some money in his wallet. He pays the babysitter $12 an hour for 4 hours of babysitting. His wife gives him $10, and he puts the money in his wallet. By how much does the amount in his wallet change?

_____

Compare the values of the two expressions using $<$, $=$, or $>$. (Example 3)

11. $-3(-2) + 3$ _____ $3(-4) + 9$

12. $-8(-2) - 20$ _____ $3(-2) + 2$

13. $-7(5) - 9$ _____ $-3(20) + 10$

14. $-16(0) - 3$ _____ $-8(-2) - 3$

? ESSENTIAL QUESTION CHECK-IN

15. When you solve a problem involving money, what can a negative answer represent?

_____

_____

_____

© Houghton Mifflin Harcourt Publishing Company

18.3 Independent Practice

FL 7.NS.1.2a, 7.NS.1.2c, 7.NS.1.3, 7.EE.2.3

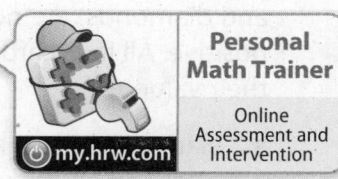

Personal Math Trainer

Online Assessment and Intervention

my.hrw.com

Evaluate each expression.

16. $-12(-3) + 7$ _____

17. $-42 \div (-6) + 5 - 8$ _____

18. $10(-60) - 18$ _____

19. $(-11)(-7) + 5 - 82$ _____

20. $35 \div (-7) + 6$ _____

21. $-13(-2) - 16 - 8$ _____

22. Multistep Lily and Rose are playing a game. In the game, each player starts with 0 points and the player with the most points at the end wins. Lily gains 5 points two times, loses 12 points, and then gains 3 points. Rose loses 3 points two times, loses 1 point, gains 6 points, and then gains 7 points.

a. Write and evaluate an expression to find Lily's score.

_____

b. Write and evaluate an expression to find Rose's score.

_____

c. Who won the game?

_____

Write an expression from the description. Then evaluate the expression.

23. 8 less than the product of 5 and −4

_____

24. 9 more than the quotient of −36 and −4.

_____

25. Multistep Arleen has a gift card for a local lawn and garden store. She uses the gift card to rent a tiller for 4 days. It costs $35 per day to rent the tiller. She also buys a rake for $9.

a. Find the change to the value on her gift card.

_____

b. The original amount on the gift card was $200. Does Arleen have enough left on the card to buy a wheelbarrow for $50? Explain.

_____

_____

26. Carlos made up a game where, in a deck of cards, the red cards (hearts and diamonds) are negative and the black cards (spades and clubs) are positive. All face cards are worth 10 points, and number cards are worth their value.

   a. Samantha has a king of hearts, a jack of diamonds, and a 3 of spades. Write an expression to find the value of her cards.

      _____

   b. Warren has a 7 of clubs, a 2 of spades, and a 7 of hearts. Write an expression to find the value of his cards.

      _____

   c. If the greater score wins, who won?

      _____

   d. If a player always gets three cards, describe two different ways to receive a score of 7.

      _____

      _____

 FOCUS ON HIGHER ORDER THINKING

Work Area

27. Represent Real-World Problems Write a problem that the expression $3(-7) - 10 + 25 = -6$ could represent.

_____

_____

_____

28. Critique Reasoning Jim found the quotient of two integers and got a positive integer. He added another integer to the quotient and got a positive integer. His sister Kim says that all the integers Jim used to get this result must be positive. Do you agree? Explain.

_____

_____

_____

29. Persevere in Problem Solving Lisa is standing on a dock beside a lake. She drops a rock from her hand into the lake. After the rock hits the surface of the lake, the rock's distance from the lake's surface changes at a rate of −5 inches per second. If Lisa holds her hand 5 feet above the lake's surface, how far from Lisa's hand is the rock 4 seconds after it hits the surface?

_____

Ready to Go On?

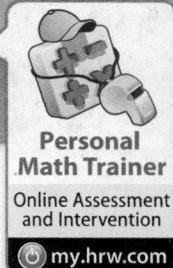

Personal Math Trainer

Online Assessment and Intervention

⊙ my.hrw.com

18.1 Multiplying Integers

Find each product.

1. $(-2)(3)$ _____

2. $(-5)(-7)$ _____

3. $(8)(-11)$ _____

4. $(-3)(2)(-2)$ _____

5. The temperature dropped 3 °C every hour for 5 hours. Write an integer that represents the change in temperature. _____

18.2 Dividing Integers

Find each quotient.

6. $\frac{-63}{7}$ _____

7. $\frac{-15}{-3}$ _____

8. $0 \div (-15)$ _____

9. $96 \div (-12)$ _____

10. An elephant at the zoo lost 24 pounds over 6 months. The elephant lost the same amount of weight each month. Write an integer that represents the change in the elephant's weight each month. _____

18.3 Applying Integer Operations

Evaluate each expression.

11. $(-4)(5) + 8$ _____

12. $(-3)(-6) - 7$ _____

13. $-27 \div 9 - 11$ _____

14. $\frac{-24}{-3} - (-2)$ _____

? ESSENTIAL QUESTION

15. Write and solve a real-world problem that can be represented by the expression $(-3)(5) + 10$.

_____

_____

_____

_____

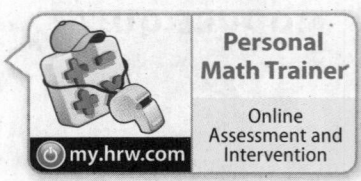

Selected Response

1. A diver is at an elevation of −18 feet relative to sea level. The diver descends to an undersea cave that is 4 times as far from the surface. What is the elevation of the cave?

   (A) −72 feet

   (B) −22 feet

   (C) −18 feet

   (D) −14 feet

2. The football team lost 4 yards on 2 plays in a row. Which of the following could represent the change in field position?

   (A) −12 yards

   (B) −8 yards

   (C) −6 yards

   (D) −2 yards

3. Clayton climbed down 50 meters. He climbed down in 10-meter intervals. In how many intervals did Clayton make his climb?

   (A) 5

   (B) 10

   (C) 40

   (D) 500

4. Which expression results in a negative answer?

   (A) a negative number divided by a negative number

   (B) a positive number divided by a negative number

   (C) a negative number multiplied by a negative number

   (D) a positive number multiplied by a positive number

5. Clara played a video game before she left the house to go on a walk. She started with 0 points, lost 6 points 3 times, won 4 points, and then lost 2 points. How many points did she have when she left the house to go on the walk?

   (A) −20

   (C) 12

   (B) −16

   (D) 20

6. Which expression is equal to 0?

   (A) $\frac{-24}{6} - 4$

   (B) $\frac{-24}{-6} + 4$

   (C) $\frac{24}{6} + 4$

   (D) $\frac{-24}{-6} - 4$

Mini-Task

7. Rochelle and Denae started with the same amount of money in their bank accounts. Rochelle made three withdrawals of $25 and then wrote a $100 check. Denae deposited $5 and then wrote a $200 check.

   a. Find the total change in the amount of money in Rochelle's account.

   _____

   b. Find the total change in the amount of money in Denae's account.

   _____

   c. Compare the amounts of money the two women have in their accounts now.

   _____

   _____

   _____

Rational Numbers

ESSENTIAL QUESTION

How can you use rational numbers to solve real-world problems?

LESSON 19.1
Rational Numbers and Decimals
FL   7.NS.1.2b, 7.NS.1.2d

LESSON 19.2
Adding Rational Numbers
FL   7.NS.1.1a, 7.NS.1.1b, 7.NS.1.1d, 7.NS.1.3

LESSON 19.3
Subtracting Rational Numbers
FL   7.NS.1.1, 7.NS.1.1c

LESSON 19.4
Multiplying Rational Numbers
FL   7.NS.1.2, 7.NS.1.2a, 7.NS.1.2c

LESSON 19.5
Dividing Rational Numbers
FL   7.NS.1.2, 7.NS.1.2b, 7.NS.1.2c

LESSON 19.6
Applying Rational Number Operations
FL   7.NS.1.3, 7.EE.2.3

LESSON 19.7
Algebraic Expressions
FL   7.EE.1.1, 7.EE.1.2

Real-World Video

In many competitive sports, scores are given as decimals. For some events, the judges' scores are averaged to give the athlete's final score.

my.hrw.com

GO DIGITAL

my.hrw.com

my.hrw.com

Go digital with your write-in student edition, accessible on any device.

Math On the Spot

Scan with your smart phone to jump directly to the online edition, video tutor, and more.

Animated Math

Interactively explore key concepts to see how math works.

Personal Math Trainer

Get immediate feedback and help as you work through practice sets.

Are YOU Ready?

Complete these exercises to review skills you will need for this module.

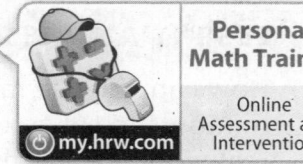

Multiply Fractions

EXAMPLE $\dfrac{3}{8} \times \dfrac{4}{9}$ $\dfrac{3}{8} \times \dfrac{4}{9} = \dfrac{\overset{1}{\cancel{3}}}{\underset{2}{\cancel{8}}} \times \dfrac{\overset{1}{\cancel{4}}}{\underset{3}{\cancel{9}}}$ Divide by the common factors.

$\qquad\qquad\qquad\qquad\qquad = \dfrac{1}{6}$ Simplify.

Multiply. Write the product in simplest form.

1. $\dfrac{9}{14} \times \dfrac{7}{6}$ _____   **2.** $\dfrac{3}{5} \times \dfrac{4}{7}$ _____   **3.** $\dfrac{11}{8} \times \dfrac{10}{33}$ _____   **4.** $\dfrac{4}{9} \times 3$ _____

Operations with Fractions

EXAMPLE $\dfrac{2}{5} \div \dfrac{7}{10} = \dfrac{2}{5} \times \dfrac{10}{7}$ Multiply by the reciprocal of the divisor.

$\qquad\qquad\qquad\qquad = \dfrac{2}{\underset{1}{\cancel{5}}} \times \dfrac{\overset{2}{\cancel{10}}}{7}$ Divide by the common factors.

$\qquad\qquad\qquad\qquad = \dfrac{4}{7}$ Simplify.

Divide.

5. $\dfrac{1}{2} \div \dfrac{1}{4}$ _____   **6.** $\dfrac{3}{8} \div \dfrac{13}{16}$ _____   **7.** $\dfrac{2}{5} \div \dfrac{14}{15}$ _____   **8.** $\dfrac{4}{9} \div \dfrac{16}{27}$ _____

9. $\dfrac{3}{5} \div \dfrac{5}{6}$ _____   **10.** $\dfrac{1}{4} \div \dfrac{23}{24}$ _____   **11.** $6 \div \dfrac{3}{5}$ _____   **12.** $\dfrac{4}{5} \div 10$ _____

Order of Operations

EXAMPLE $50 - 3(3 + 1)^2$ To evaluate, first operate within parentheses.

$\qquad\qquad$ $50 - 3(4)^2$ Next simplify exponents.

$\qquad\qquad$ $50 - 3(16)$ Then multiply and divide from left to right.

$\qquad\qquad$ $50 - 48$ Finally add and subtract from left to right.

$\qquad\qquad$ 2

Evaluate each expression.

13. $21 - 6 \div 3$ ____   **14.** $18 + (7 - 4) \times 3$ ____   **15.** $5 + (8 - 3)^2$ ____

16. $9 + 18 \div 3 + 10$ ____   **17.** $60 - (3 - 1)^4 \times 3$ ____   **18.** $10 - 16 \div 4 \times 2 + 6$ ___

Reading Start-Up

Visualize Vocabulary

Use the ✔ words to complete the graphic. You can put more than one word in each section of the triangle.

Integers

45

2, 24, 108

−2, −24, −108

Vocabulary

Review Words

integers *(enteros)*

✔ negative numbers *(números negativos)*

pattern *(patrón)*

✔ positive numbers *(números positivos)*

✔ whole numbers *(números enteros)*

Preview Words

additive inverse *(inverso aditivo)*

opposite *(opuesto)*

rational number *(número racional)*

repeating decimal *(decimal periódico)*

terminating decimal *(decimal finito)*

Understand Vocabulary

Complete the sentences using the preview words.

1. A decimal number for which the decimals come to an end is a

   _____ decimal.

2. The _____ , or _____ , of a number is the same distance from 0 on a number line as the original number, but on the other side of 0.

Active Reading

Layered Book Before beginning the module, create a layered book to help you learn the concepts in this module. At the top of the first flap, write the title of the module, "Rational Numbers." Label the other flaps "Adding," "Subtracting," "Multiplying," and "Dividing." As you study each lesson, write important ideas, such as vocabulary and processes, on the appropriate flap.

MODULE 19

Unpacking the Standards

Understanding the Standards and the vocabulary terms in the Standards will help you know exactly what you are expected to learn in this module.

FL 7.NS.1.3

Solve real-world and mathematical problems involving the four operations with rational numbers.

Key Vocabulary

rational number *(número racional)*
Any number that can be expressed as a ratio of two integers.

What It Means to You

You will add, subtract, multiply, and divide rational numbers.

UNPACKING EXAMPLE 7.NS.1.3

$$-15 \cdot \frac{2}{3} - 12 \div 1\frac{1}{3}$$

$$-\frac{15}{1} \cdot \frac{2}{3} - \frac{12}{1} \div \frac{4}{3}$$ Write as fractions.

$$-\frac{15}{1} \cdot \frac{2}{3} - \frac{12}{1} \cdot \frac{3}{4}$$ To divide, multiply by the reciprocal.

$$-\frac{\overset{5}{\cancel{15}} \cdot 2}{1 \cdot \underset{1}{\cancel{3}}} - \frac{\overset{3}{\cancel{12}} \cdot 3}{1 \cdot \underset{1}{\cancel{4}}}$$ Simplify.

$$-\frac{10}{1} - \frac{9}{1} = -10 - 9 = -19$$ Multiply.

FL 7.NS.1.3

Solve real-world and mathematical problems involving the four operations with rational numbers.

What It Means to You

You will solve real-world and mathematical problems involving the four operations with rational numbers.

UNPACKING EXAMPLE 7.NS.1.3

In 1954, the Sunshine Skyway Bridge toll for a car was $1.75. In 2012, the toll was $\frac{5}{7}$ of the toll in 1954. What was the toll in 2012?

$$1.75 \cdot \frac{5}{7} = 1\frac{3}{4} \cdot \frac{5}{7}$$ Write the decimal as a fraction.

$$= \frac{7}{4} \cdot \frac{5}{7}$$ Write the mixed number as an improper fraction.

$$= \frac{\overset{1}{\cancel{7}} \cdot 5}{4 \cdot \underset{1}{\cancel{7}}}$$ Simplify.

$$= \frac{5}{4} = 1.25$$ Multiply, then write as a decimal.

The Sunshine Skyway Bridge toll for a car was $1.25 in 2012.

Visit **my.hrw.com** to see all **Florida Math Standards** unpacked.

⏻ my.hrw.com

LESSON 19.1 Rational Numbers and Decimals

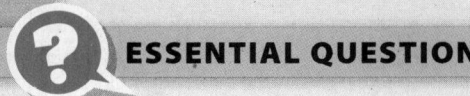

FL 7.NS.1.2d

Convert a rational number to a decimal using long division; know that the decimal form of a rational number terminates in 0s or eventually repeats.
Also 7.NS.1.2b

? ESSENTIAL QUESTION

How can you convert a rational number to a decimal?

EXPLORE ACTIVITY **FL** 7.NS.1.2b, 7.NS.1.2d

Describing Decimal Forms of Rational Numbers

A **rational number** is a number that can be written as a ratio of two integers a and b, where b is not zero. For example, $\frac{4}{7}$ is a rational number, as is 0.37 because it can be written as the fraction $\frac{37}{100}$.

A Use a calculator to find the equivalent decimal form of each fraction. Remember that numbers that repeat can be written as 0.333... or $0.\overline{3}$.

Fraction	$\frac{1}{4}$	$\frac{5}{8}$	$\frac{2}{3}$	$\frac{2}{9}$	$\frac{12}{5}$		
Decimal Equivalent						0.2	0.875

B Now find the corresponding fraction of the decimal equivalents given in the last two columns in the table. Write the fractions in simplest form.

C **Conjecture** What do you notice about the digits after the decimal point in the decimal forms of the fractions? Compare notes with your neighbor and refine your conjecture if necessary.

_____

Reflect

1. Consider the decimal 0.101001000100001000001…. Do you think this decimal represents a rational number? Why or why not?

_____

_____

2. Do you think a negative sign affects whether or not a number is a rational number? Use $-\frac{8}{5}$ as an example.

_____

_____

© Houghton Mifflin Harcourt Publishing Company

Lesson 19.1 **549**

3. Do you think a mixed number is a rational number? Explain.

_____

_____

_____

Math On the Spot

Writing Rational Numbers as Decimals

You can convert a rational number to a decimal using long division. Some decimals are **terminating decimals** because the decimals come to an end. Other decimals are **repeating decimals** because one or more digits repeat infinitely.

EXAMPLE 1 FL 7.NS.1.2d

Write each rational number as a decimal.

A $\frac{5}{16}$

Divide 5 by 16.
Add a zero after the decimal point.
Subtract 48 from 50.
Use the grid to help you complete the long division.

Add zeros in the dividend and continue dividing until the remainder is 0.

The decimal equivalent of $\frac{5}{16}$ is 0.3125.

```
        0. 3 1 2 5
  1 6 ) 5. 0 0 0 0
      - 4 8
          2 0
        - 1 6
            4 0
          - 3 2
              8 0
            - 8 0
                0
```

B $\frac{13}{33}$

Divide 13 by 33.
Add a zero after the decimal point.
Subtract 99 from 130.
Use the grid to help you complete the long division.

You can stop dividing once you discover a repeating pattern in the quotient.

Write the quotient with its repeating pattern and indicate that the repeating numbers continue.

The decimal equivalent of $\frac{13}{33}$ is 0.3939…, or $0.\overline{39}$.

```
          0. 3 9 3 9
  3 3 ) 1 3. 0 0 0 0
        - 9 9
          3 1 0
        - 2 9 7
            1 3 0
            - 9 9
              3 1 0
            - 2 9 7
                1 3
```

Math Talk

Mathematical Practices

Do you think that decimals that have repeating patterns always have the same number of digits in their pattern? Explain.

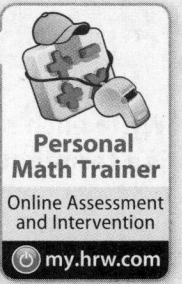
Write each rational number as a decimal.

4. $\frac{4}{7}$ _____   5. $\frac{1}{3}$ _____   6. $\frac{9}{20}$ _____

Writing Mixed Numbers as Decimals

You can convert a mixed number to a decimal by rewriting the fractional part of the number as a decimal.

EXAMPLE 2   **FL** 7.NS.1.2d

Shawn rode his bike $6\frac{3}{4}$ miles to the science museum. Write $6\frac{3}{4}$ as a decimal.

STEP 1 Rewrite the fractional part of the number as a decimal.

$$\begin{array}{r} 0.75 \\ 4\overline{)3.00} \\ -28 \\ \hline 20 \\ -20 \\ \hline 0 \end{array}$$

Divide the numerator by the denominator.

$6\frac{3}{4}$ mi

STEP 2 Rewrite the mixed number as the sum of the whole part and the decimal part.

$$6\frac{3}{4} = 6 + \frac{3}{4}$$
$$= 6 + 0.75$$
$$= 6.75$$

7. Yvonne made $2\frac{3}{4}$ quarts of punch. Write $2\frac{3}{4}$ as a decimal. $2\frac{3}{4} =$ _____

   Is the decimal equivalent a terminating or repeating decimal

   _____

8. Yvonne bought a watermelon that weighed $7\frac{1}{3}$ pounds. Write $7\frac{1}{3}$ as

   a decimal. $7\frac{1}{3} =$ _____

   Is the decimal equivalent a terminating or repeating decimal?

   _____

My Notes

Guided Practice

Write each rational number as a decimal. Then tell whether each decimal is a terminating or a repeating decimal. (Explore Activity and Example 1)

1. $\frac{3}{5} =$ _____

   _____

2. $\frac{89}{100} =$ _____

   _____

3. $\frac{4}{12} =$ _____

   _____

4. $\frac{25}{99} =$ _____

   _____

5. $\frac{7}{9} =$ _____

   _____

6. $\frac{9}{25} =$ _____

   _____

7. $\frac{1}{25} =$ _____

   _____

8. $\frac{25}{176} =$ _____

   _____

9. $\frac{12}{1,000} =$ _____

   _____

Write each mixed number as a decimal. (Example 2)

10. $11\frac{1}{6} =$ _____

11. $2\frac{9}{10} =$ _____

12. $8\frac{23}{100} =$ _____

13. $7\frac{3}{15} =$ _____

14. $54\frac{3}{11} =$ _____

15. $3\frac{1}{18} =$ _____

16. Maggie bought $3\frac{2}{3}$ lb of apples to make some apple pies. What is the weight of the apples written as a decimal? (Example 2)

    $3\frac{2}{3} =$ _____

17. Harry's dog weighs $12\frac{7}{8}$ pounds. What is the weight of Harry's dog written as a decimal? (Example 2)

    $12\frac{7}{8} =$ _____

? ESSENTIAL QUESTION CHECK-IN

18. Tom is trying to write $\frac{3}{47}$ as a decimal. He used long division and divided until he got the quotient 0.0638297872, at which point he stopped. Since the decimal doesn't seem to terminate or repeat, he concluded that $\frac{3}{47}$ is not rational. Do you agree or disagree? Why?

_____

_____

_____

_____

_____

19.1 Independent Practice

FL 7.NS.1.2b, 7.NS.1.2d

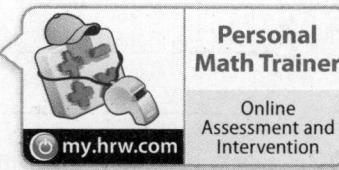
Use the table for 19–23. Write each ratio in the form $\frac{a}{b}$ and then as a decimal. Tell whether each decimal is a terminating or a repeating decimal.

Team Sports	
Sport	**Number of Players**
Baseball	9
Basketball	5
Football	11
Hockey	6
Lacrosse	10
Polo	4
Rugby	15
Soccer	11

19. basketball players to football players

_____

20. hockey players to lacrosse players

_____

21. polo players to football players

_____

22. lacrosse players to rugby players

_____

23. football players to soccer players

_____

24. **Look for a Pattern** Beth said that the ratio of the number of players in any sport to the number of players on a lacrosse team must always be a terminating decimal. Do you agree or disagree? Why?

_____

_____

_____

25. Yvonne bought $4\frac{7}{8}$ yards of material to make a dress.

a. What is $4\frac{7}{8}$ written as an improper fraction? _____

b. What is $4\frac{7}{8}$ written as a decimal? _____

c. **Communicate Mathematical Ideas** If Yvonne wanted to make 3 dresses that use $4\frac{7}{8}$ yd of fabric each, explain how she could use estimation to make sure she has enough fabric for all of them.

_____

_____

_____

26. Vocabulary A rational number can be written as the ratio of one

_____ to another and can be represented by a repeating

or _____ decimal.

27. Problem Solving Marcus is $5\frac{7}{24}$ feet tall. Ben is $5\frac{5}{16}$ feet tall. Which of the two boys is taller? Justify your answer.

_____

28. Represent Real-World Problems If one store is selling $\frac{3}{4}$ of a bushel of apples for $9, and another store is selling $\frac{2}{3}$ of a bushel of apples for $9, which store has the better deal? Explain your answer.

_____

_____

_____

_____

H.O.T. FOCUS ON HIGHER ORDER THINKING

29. Analyze Relationships You are given a fraction in simplest form. The numerator is not zero. When you write the fraction as a decimal, it is a repeating decimal. Which numbers from 1 to 10 could be the denominator?

_____

_____

30. Communicate Mathematical Ideas Julie got 21 of the 23 questions on her math test correct. She got 29 of the 32 questions on her science test correct. On which test did she get a higher score? Can you compare the fractions $\frac{21}{23}$ and $\frac{29}{32}$ by comparing 29 and 21? Explain. How can Julie compare her scores?

_____

_____

_____

_____

31. Look for a Pattern Look at the decimal 0.121122111222.... If the pattern continues, is this a repeating decimal? Explain.

_____

_____

_____

Adding Rational Numbers

FL **7.NS.1.1d**

Apply properties of operations as strategies to add and subtract rational numbers. *Also 7.NS.1.1a, 7.NS.1.1b, 7.NS.1.3*

 ESSENTIAL QUESTION

How can you add rational numbers?

Adding Rational Numbers with the Same Sign

To add rational numbers with the same sign, apply the rules for adding integers. The sum has the same sign as the sign of the rational numbers.

Math On the Spot
my.hrw.com

EXAMPLE 1 (Real World)   **FL** **7.NS.1.1b**

A **Malachi hikes for 2.5 miles and stops for lunch. Then he hikes for 1.5 more miles. How many miles did he hike altogether?**

STEP 1 Use positive numbers to represent the distance Malachi hiked.

STEP 2 Find $2.5 + 1.5$.

STEP 3 Start at 2.5.

STEP 4 Move 1.5 units to the *right* because the second addend is *positive*.

The result is 4.

Malachi hiked 4 miles.

B **Kyle pours out $\frac{3}{4}$ liter of liquid from a beaker. Then he pours out another $\frac{1}{2}$ liter of liquid. What is the overall change in the amount of liquid in the beaker?**

STEP 1 Use negative numbers to represent the amount of change each time Kyle pours liquid from the beaker.

STEP 2 Find $-\frac{3}{4} + \left(-\frac{1}{2}\right)$.

STEP 3 Start at $-\frac{3}{4}$.

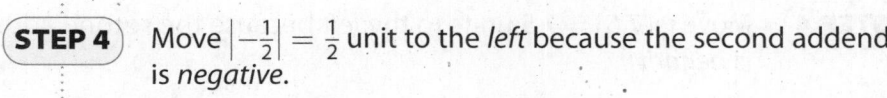

STEP 4 Move $\left|-\frac{1}{2}\right| = \frac{1}{2}$ unit to the *left* because the second addend is *negative*.

The result is $-1\frac{1}{4}$.

The amount of liquid in the beaker has decreased by $1\frac{1}{4}$ liters.

Reflect

1. Explain how to determine whether to move right or left on the number line when adding rational numbers.

_____

_____

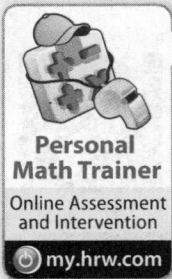
YOUR TURN

Use a number line to find each sum.

2. $3 + 1\frac{1}{2} =$ _____

$\begin{array}{ccccccc} 0 & 1 & 2 & 3 & 4 & 5 \end{array}$

3. $-2.5 + (-4.5) =$ _____

$\begin{array}{ccccccccc} -7 & -6 & -5 & -4 & -3 & -2 & -1 & 0 \end{array}$

Adding Rational Numbers with Different Signs

To add rational numbers with different signs, find the difference of their absolute values. Then use the sign of the rational number with the greater absolute value.

EXAMPLE 2 Real World   FL 7.NS.1.1b

A During the day, the temperature increases by 4.5 degrees. At night, the temperature decreases by 7.5 degrees. What is the overall change in temperature?

STEP 1 Use a positive number to represent the increase in temperature and a negative number to represent a decrease in temperature.

STEP 2 Find $4.5 + (-7.5)$.

STEP 3 Start at 4.5.

$\begin{array}{ccccccccccc} -5 & -4 & -3 & -2 & -1 & 0 & 1 & 2 & 3 & 4 & 5 \end{array}$

STEP 4 Move $|-7.5| = 7.5$ units to the *left* because the second addend is *negative*.

The result is -3.

The temperature decreased by 3 degrees overall.

© Houghton Mifflin Harcourt Publishing Company

556 Unit 8

B Ernesto writes a check for $2.50. Then he deposits $6 in his checking account. What is the overall increase or decrease in the account balance?

Animated Math

⏻ my.hrw.com

STEP 1 Use a positive number to represent a deposit and a negative number to represent a withdrawal or a check.

STEP 2 Find $-2.5 + 6$.

STEP 3 Start at -2.5.

<-5 -4 -3 -2 -1 0 1 2 3 4 5->

STEP 4 Move $|6| = 6$ units to the *right* because the second addend is *positive*.

The result is 3.5.

The account balance will increase by $3.50.

My Notes

Reflect

4. Do $-3 + 2$ and $2 + (-3)$ have the same sum? Does it matter if the negative number is the first addend or the second addend?

_____

_____

_____

5. Make a Conjecture Do you think the sum of a negative number and a positive number will always be negative? Explain your reasoning.

_____

_____

_____

YOUR TURN

Use a number line to find each sum.

6. $-8 + 5 =$ _____

<-8 -7 -6 -5 -4 -3 -2 -1 0 1 2->

7. $\frac{1}{2} + \left(-\frac{3}{4}\right) =$ _____

8. $-1 + 7 =$ _____

Personal Math Trainer

Online Assessment and Intervention

⏻ my.hrw.com

© Houghton Mifflin Harcourt Publishing Company

Finding the Additive Inverse

The **opposite**, or **additive inverse**, of a number is the same distance from 0 on a number line as the original number, but on the other side of 0. The sum of a number and its additive inverse is 0. Zero is its own additive inverse.

EXAMPLE 3   **FL** 7.NS.1.1a, 7.NS.1.1b, 7.NS.1.1d

A A football team loses 3.5 yards on their first play. On the next play, they gain 3.5 yards. What is the overall increase or decrease in yards?

STEP 1 Use a positive number to represent the gain in yards and a negative number to represent the loss in yards.

STEP 2 Find $-3.5 + 3.5$.

STEP 3 Start at -3.5.

STEP 4 Move $|3.5| = 3.5$ units to the *right*, because the second addend is *positive*.

The result is 0. This means the overall change is 0 yards.

B Kendrick adds $\frac{3}{4}$ cup of chicken stock to a pot. Then he takes $\frac{3}{4}$ cup of stock out of the pot. What is the overall increase or decrease in the amount of chicken stock in the pot?

STEP 1 Use a positive number to represent chicken stock added to the pot and a negative number to represent chicken stock taken out of the pot.

STEP 2 Find $\frac{3}{4} + \left(-\frac{3}{4}\right)$.

STEP 3 Start at $\frac{3}{4}$.

STEP 4 Move $\left|-\frac{3}{4}\right| = \frac{3}{4}$ units to the *left* because the second addend is *negative*.

The result is 0. This means the overall change is 0 cups.

Math Talk
Mathematical Practices

Explain how to use a number line to find the additive inverse, or opposite, of -3.5.

My Notes

YOUR TURN

Use a number line to find each sum.

9. $2\frac{1}{2} + \left(-2\frac{1}{2}\right) =$ _____

10. $-4.5 + 4.5 =$ _____

Personal
Math Trainer

Online Assessment
and Intervention

my.hrw.com

558 Unit 8

© Houghton Mifflin Harcourt Publishing Company

Adding Three or More Rational Numbers

Recall that the Associative Property of Addition states that you are adding more than two numbers, you can group any of the numbers together. This property can help you add numbers with different signs.

EXAMPLE 4   FL 7.NS.1.1d, 7.NS.1.3

Tina spent $5.25 on craft supplies to make friendship bracelets. She made $3.75 on Monday. On Tuesday, she sold an additional $4.50 worth of bracelets. What was Tina's overall profit or loss?

STEP 1   Use *negative* numbers to represent the amount Tina *spent* and *positive* numbers to represent the money Tina *earned*.

> Profit means the difference between income and costs is positive.

STEP 2   Find $-5.25 + 3.75 + 4.50$.

STEP 3   Group numbers with the same sign.

$-5.25 + (3.75 + 4.50)$ Associative Property

STEP 4 $-5.25 + 8.25$ Add the numbers inside the parentheses.

Find the difference of the absolute values: $8.25 - 5.25$.

3

Use the sign of the number with the greater absolute value. The sum is positive.

Tina earned a profit of $3.00.

YOUR TURN

Find each sum.

11. $-1.5 + 3.5 + 2 =$ _____

12. $3\frac{1}{4} + (-2) + \left(-2\frac{1}{4}\right) =$ _____

13. $-2.75 + (-3.25) + 5 =$ _____

14. $15 + 8 + (-3) =$ _____

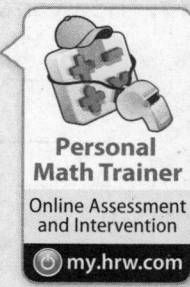
Personal Math Trainer
Online Assessment and Intervention
my.hrw.com

Guided Practice

Use a number line to find each sum. (Example 1 and Example 2)

1. $-3 + (-1.5) =$ _____

2. $1.5 + 3.5 =$ _____

3. $\frac{1}{4} + \frac{1}{2} =$ _____

$$\overset{\longleftarrow}{\underset{-1 \quad -0.5 \quad\quad 0 \quad\quad 0.5 \quad\quad 1}{\mid\mid\mid\mid\mid\mid\mid\mid\mid\mid\mid}}\overset{\longrightarrow}{}$$

4. $-1\frac{1}{2} + \left(-1\frac{1}{2}\right) =$ _____

5. $3 + (-5) =$ _____

$$\overset{\longleftarrow}{\underset{-5\,-4\,-3\,-2\,-1\ \ 0\ \ 1\ \ 2\ \ 3\ \ 4\ \ 5}{\mid\mid\mid\mid\mid\mid\mid\mid\mid\mid\mid}}\overset{\longrightarrow}{}$$

6. $-1.5 + 4 =$ _____

$$\overset{\longleftarrow}{\underset{-5\,-4\,-3\,-2\,-1\ \ 0\ \ 1\ \ 2\ \ 3\ \ 4\ \ 5}{\mid\mid\mid\mid\mid\mid\mid\mid\mid\mid\mid}}\overset{\longrightarrow}{}$$

7. Victor borrowed $21.50 from his mother to go to the theater. A week later, he paid her $21.50 back. How much does he still owe her? (Example 3)

_____

8. Sandra used her debit card to buy lunch for $8.74 on Monday. On Tuesday, she deposited $8.74 back into her account. What is the overall increase or decrease in her bank account? (Example 3)

_____

Find each sum without using a number line. (Example 4)

9. $2.75 + (-2) + (-5.25) =$ _____

10. $-3 + \left(1\frac{1}{2}\right) + \left(2\frac{1}{2}\right) =$ _____

11. $-12.4 + 9.2 + 1 =$ _____

12. $-12 + 8 + 13 =$ _____

13. $4.5 + (-12) + (-4.5) =$ _____

14. $\frac{1}{4} + \left(-\frac{3}{4}\right) =$ _____

15. $-4\frac{1}{2} + 2 =$ _____

16. $-8 + \left(-1\frac{1}{8}\right) =$ _____

? **ESSENTIAL QUESTION CHECK-IN**

17. How can you use a number line to find the sum of -4 and 6?

_____

_____

19.2 Independent Practice

FL 7.NS.1.1a, 7.NS.1.1b, 7.NS.1.1d, 7.NS.1.3

Personal
Math Trainer

Online
Assessment and
Intervention

my.hrw.com

18. Samuel walks forward 19 steps. He represents this movement with a positive 19. How would he represent the opposite of this number?

_____

19. Julia spends $2.25 on gas for her lawn mower. She earns $15.00 mowing her neighbor's yard. What is Julia's profit?

_____

20. A submarine submerged at a depth of -35.25 meters dives an additional 8.5 meters. What is the new depth of the submarine?

_____

21. Renee hiked for $4\frac{3}{4}$ miles. After resting, Renee hiked back along the same route for $3\frac{1}{4}$ miles. How many more miles does Renee need to hike to return to the place where she started?

_____

22. **Geography** The average elevation of the city of New Orleans, Louisiana, is 0.5 m below sea level. The highest point in Louisiana is Driskill Mountain at about 163.5 m higher than New Orleans. How high is Driskill Mountain?

_____

23. **Problem Solving** A contestant on a game show has 30 points. She answers a question correctly to win 15 points. Then she answers a question incorrectly and loses 25 points. What is the contestant's final score?

_____

Financial Literacy **Use the table for 24–26. Kameh owns a bakery. He recorded the bakery income and expenses in a table.**

Month	Income ($)	Expenses ($)
January	1,205	1,290.60
February	1,183	1,345.44
March	1,664	1,664.00
June	2,413	2,106.23
July	2,260	1,958.50
August	2,183	1,845.12

24. In which months were the expenses greater than the income? Name the month and find how much money

was lost. _____

25. In which months was the income greater than the expenses? Name the months and find how much money was gained.

_____

26. **Communicate Mathematical Ideas** If the bakery started with an extra $250 from the profits in December, describe how to use the information in the table to figure out the profit or loss of money at the bakery by the end of August. Then calculate the profit or loss.

_____

_____

_____

_____

27. Vocabulary −2 is the _____ of 2.

28. The basketball coach made up a game to play where each player takes 10 shots at the basket. For every basket made, the player gains 10 points. For every basket missed, the player loses 15 points.

   a. The player with the highest score sank 7 baskets and missed 3. What was the highest score?

   _____

   b. The player with the lowest score sank 2 baskets and missed 8. What was the lowest score?

   _____

   c. Write an expression using addition to find out what the score would be if a player sank 5 baskets and missed 5 baskets.

   _____

 FOCUS ON HIGHER ORDER THINKING

29. Communicate Mathematical Ideas Explain the different ways it is possible to add two rational numbers and get a negative number.

_____

_____

_____

30. Explain the Error A student evaluated $-4 + x$ for $x = -9\frac{1}{2}$ and got an answer of $5\frac{1}{2}$. What might the student have done wrong?

_____

_____

31. Draw Conclusions Can you find the sum $[5.5 + (-2.3)] + (-5.5 + 2.3)$ without performing any additions?

_____

_____

_____

Subtracting Rational Numbers

FL 7.NS.1.1c
Understand subtraction... as adding the additive inverse.... Show that the distance between two rational numbers...is the absolute value of their difference.... *Also 7.NS.1.1*

ESSENTIAL QUESTION

How do you subtract rational numbers?

Subtracting Positive Rational Numbers

To subtract rational numbers, you can apply the same rules you use to subtract integers.

EXAMPLE 1 Real World   FL 7.NS.1.1

The temperature on an outdoor thermometer on Monday was 5.5 °C. The temperature on Thursday was 7.25 degrees less than the temperature on Monday. What was the temperature on Thursday?

Subtract to find the temperature on Thursday.

STEP 1 Find $5.5 - 7.25$.

STEP 2 Start at 5.5.

$$-6\ -5\ -4\ -3\ -2\ -1\ \ 0\ \ 1\ \ 2\ \ 3\ \ 4\ \ 5\ \ 6$$

STEP 3 Move $|7.25| = 7.25$ units to the *left* because you are subtracting a *positive number*.

The result is -1.75.

The temperature on Thursday was -1.75 °C.

Math On the Spot
my.hrw.com

YOUR TURN

Use a number line to find each difference.

1. $-6.5 - 2 = $ _____

$$-9\ \ -8.5\ \ -8\ \ -7.5\ \ -7\ \ -6.5\ \ -6\ \ -5.5\ \ -5\ \ -4.5\ \ -4$$

2. $1\frac{1}{2} - 2 = $ _____

$$-1\ \ \ \ 0\ \ \ \ 1\ \ \ \ 2\ \ \ \ 3\ \ \ \ 4$$

3. $-2.25 - 5.5 = $ _____

$$-10\ -9\ \ -8\ \ -7\ \ -6\ \ -5\ \ -4\ \ -3\ \ -2\ \ -1\ \ \ 0$$

Personal Math Trainer
Online Assessment and Intervention
my.hrw.com

Subtracting Negative Rational Numbers

To subtract negative rational numbers, move in the opposite direction on the number line.

EXAMPLE 2

 FL 7.NS.1.1

During the hottest week of the summer, the water level of the Muskrat River was $\frac{5}{6}$ foot below normal. The following week, the level was $\frac{1}{3}$ foot below normal. What is the overall change in the water level?

Subtract to find the difference in water levels.

STEP 1 Find $-\frac{1}{3} - \left(-\frac{5}{6}\right)$.

STEP 2 Start at $-\frac{1}{3}$.

STEP 3 Move $\left|-\frac{5}{6}\right| = \frac{5}{6}$ to the *right* because you are subtracting a *negative* number.

The result is $\frac{1}{2}$.

So, the water level changed $\frac{1}{2}$ foot.

Reflect

4. Work with other students to compare addition of negative numbers on a number line to subtraction of negative numbers on a number line.

_____

_____

5. Compare the methods used to solve Example 1 and Example 2.

_____

_____

_____

_____

YOUR TURN

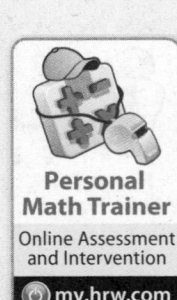
Use a number line to find each difference.

6. $0.25 - (-1.50) = $ _____

7. $-\frac{1}{2} - \left(-\frac{3}{4}\right) = $ _____

Adding the Opposite

Joe is diving $2\frac{1}{2}$ feet below sea level. He decides to descend $7\frac{1}{2}$ more feet.
How many feet below sea level is he?

STEP 1 Use negative numbers to represent the number of feet below
sea level.

STEP 2 Find $-2\frac{1}{2} - 7\frac{1}{2}$.

STEP 3 Start at $-2\frac{1}{2}$.

STEP 4 Move $\left|7\frac{1}{2}\right| = 7\frac{1}{2}$ units to the _____

because you are subtracting a _____ number.

The result is -10.

Joe is _____ sea level.

> You move left on a number line to add a negative number. You move the same direction to subtract a positive number.

Reflect

8. Use a number line to find each difference or sum.

a. $-3 - 3 = $ _____

b. $-3 + (-3) = $ _____

9. **Make a Conjecture** Work with other students to make a conjecture
about how to change a subtraction problem into an addition
problem.

_____

_____

_____

Math Talk
Mathematical Practices

Compare the results from
8a and **8b**.

Adding the Opposite

To subtract a number, add its opposite. This can also be written
as $p - q = p + (-q)$.

EXPLORE ACTIVITY 2   FL 7.NS.1.1c

Finding the Distance between Two Numbers

A cave explorer climbed from an elevation of −11 meters to an elevation of −5 meters. What vertical distance did the explorer climb?

There are two ways to find the vertical distance.

A Start at _____.

Count the number of units on the vertical number line up to −5.

The explorer climbed _____ meters.

This means that the vertical distance between

−11 meters and −5 meters is _____ meters.

B Find the difference between the two elevations and use absolute value to find the distance.

$-11 - (-5) = $ _____

Take the absolute value of the difference because distance traveled is always a nonnegative number.

$|-11 - (-5)| = $ _____

The vertical distance is _____ meters.

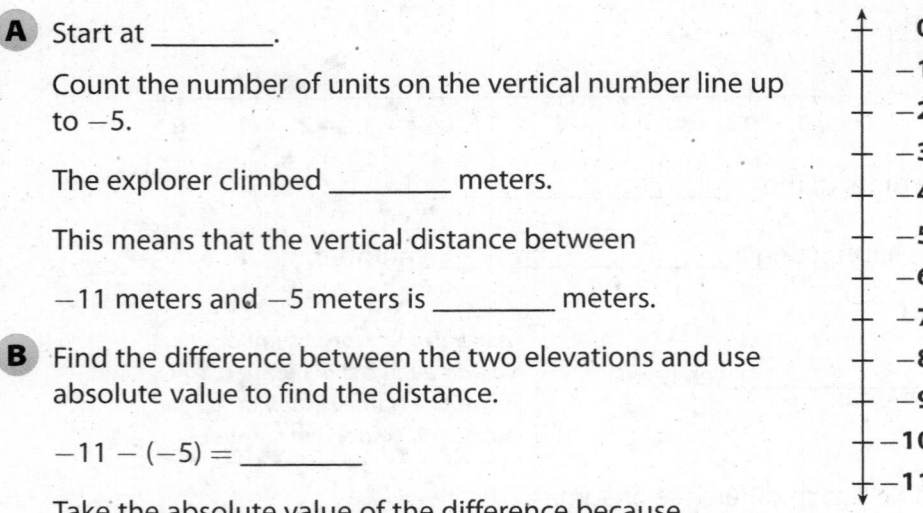

Reflect

10. Does it matter which way you subtract the values when finding distance? Explain.

_____

_____

11. Would the same methods work if both the numbers were positive? What if one of the numbers were positive and the other negative?

_____

Distance Between Two Numbers

The distance between two values a and b on a number line is represented by the absolute value of the difference of a and b.

Distance between a and $b = |a - b|$ or $|b - a|$.

Use a number line to find each difference. (Example 1, Example 2 and Explore Activity 1)

1. $5 - (-8) =$ _____

2. $-3\frac{1}{2} - 4\frac{1}{2} =$ _____

3. $-7 - 4 =$ _____

4. $-0.5 - 3.5 =$ _____

Find each difference. (Explore Activity 1)

5. $-14 - 22 =$ _____   **6.** $-12.5 - (-4.8) =$ _____   **7.** $\frac{1}{3} - \left(-\frac{2}{3}\right) =$ _____

8. $65 - (-14) =$ _____   **9.** $-\frac{2}{9} - (-3) =$ _____   **10.** $24\frac{3}{8} - \left(-54\frac{1}{8}\right) =$ _____

11. A girl is snorkeling 1 meter below sea level and then dives down another 0.5 meter. How far below sea level is the girl? (Explore Activity 1) _____

12. The first play of a football game resulted in a loss of $12\frac{1}{2}$ yards. Then a penalty resulted in another loss of 5 yards. What is the total loss or gain? (Explore Activity 1) _____

13. A climber starts descending from 533 feet above sea level and keeps going until she reaches 10 feet below sea level. How many feet did she descend? (Explore Activity 2) _____

14. Eleni withdrew $45.00 from her savings account. She then used her debit card to buy groceries for $30.15. What was the total amount Eleni took out of her account? (Explore Activity 1) _____

? ESSENTIAL QUESTION CHECK-IN

15. Mandy is trying to subtract $4 - 12$, and she has asked you for help. How would you explain the process of solving the problem to Mandy, using a number line?

_____

_____

_____

19.3 Independent Practice

FL 7.NS.1.1, 7.NS.1.1c

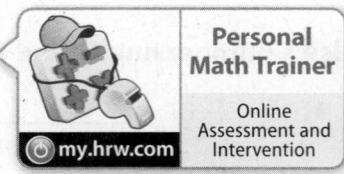

Personal
Math Trainer

Online
Assessment and
Intervention

my.hrw.com

16. **Science** At the beginning of a laboratory experiment, the temperature of a substance is −12.6 °C. During the experiment, the temperature of the substance decreases 7.5 °C. What is the final temperature of the substance?

_____

17. A diver went 25.65 feet below the surface of the ocean, and then 16.5 feet further down, he then rose 12.45 feet. Write and solve an expression to find the diver's new depth.

_____

_____

18. A city known for its temperature extremes started the day at −5 degrees Fahrenheit. The temperature increased by 78 degrees Fahrenheit by midday, and then dropped 32 degrees by nightfall.

a. What expression can you write to find the temperature at nightfall? _____

b. What expression can you write to describe the overall change in temperature? *Hint*: Do not include the temperature at the beginning of the day since you only want to know about how much the temperature changed. _____

c. What is the final temperature at nightfall? What is the overall change in temperature? _____

19. **Financial Literacy** On Monday, your bank account balance was −$12.58. Because you didn't realize this, you wrote a check for $30.72 for groceries.

a. What is the new balance in your checking account? _____

b. The bank charges a $25 fee for paying a check on a negative balance. What is the balance in your checking account after this fee? _____

c. How much money do you need to deposit to bring your account balance back up to $0 after the fee? _____

Astronomy **Use the table for problems 20–21.**

20. How much deeper is the deepest canyon on Mars than the deepest canyon on Venus?

_____

Elevations on Planets		
	Lowest (ft)	Highest (ft)
Earth	−36,198	29,035
Mars	−26,000	70,000
Venus	−9,500	35,000

21. Persevere in Problem Solving What is the difference between Earth's highest mountain and its deepest ocean canyon? What is the difference between Mars' highest mountain and its deepest canyon? Which difference is greater? How much greater is it?

_____

_____

_____

22. Pamela wants to make some friendship bracelets for her friends. Each friendship bracelet needs 5.2 inches of string.

   a. If Pamela has 20 inches of string, does she have enough to make bracelets for 4 of her friends?

   _____

   _____

   b. If so, how much string would she had left over? If not, how much more string would she need?

   _____

23. Jeremy is practicing some tricks on his skateboard. One trick takes him forward 5 feet, then he flips around and moves backwards 7.2 feet, then he moves forward again for 2.2 feet.

   a. What expression could be used to find how far Jeremy is from his starting position when he finishes the trick?

   _____

   b. How far from his starting point is he when he finishes the trick? Explain

   _____

   _____

24. Esteban has $20 from his allowance. There is a comic book he wishes to buy that costs $4.25, a cereal bar that costs $0.89, and a small remote control car that costs $10.99.

   a. Does Esteban have enough to buy everything?

   _____

   b. If so, how much will he have left over? If not, how much does he still need?

   _____

   _____

25. **Look for a Pattern** Show how you could use the Commutative Property to simplify the evaluation of the expression $-\frac{7}{16} - \frac{1}{4} - \frac{5}{16}$.

_____

_____

_____

26. **Problem Solving** The temperatures for five days in Kaktovik, Alaska, are given below.

$-19.6\,°F$, $-22.5\,°F$, $-20.9\,°F$, $-19.5\,°F$, $-22.4\,°F$

Temperatures for the following week are expected to be twelve degrees lower every day. What are the highest and lowest temperatures expected for the corresponding 5 days next week?

_____

_____

27. **Make a Conjecture** Must the difference between two rational numbers be a rational number? Explain.

_____

_____

_____

_____

_____

28. **Look for a Pattern** Evan said that the difference between two negative numbers must be negative. Was he right? Use examples to illustrate your answer.

_____

_____

_____

_____

Multiplying Rational Numbers

FL   7.NS.1.2

Apply and extend previous understandings of multiplication...and of fractions to multiply ...rational numbers. *Also 7.NS.1.2a, 7.NS.1.2c*

 ESSENTIAL QUESTION

How do you multiply rational numbers?

Multiplying Rational Numbers with Different Signs

The rules for the signs of products of rational numbers with different signs are summarized below. Let p and q be rational numbers.

Math On the Spot
my.hrw.com

Products of Rational Numbers

Sign of Factor p	Sign of Factor q	Sign of Product pq
+	−	−
−	+	−

You can also use the fact that multiplication is repeated addition.

EXAMPLE 1   **FL   7.NS.1.2, 7.NS.1.2a**

Gina hiked down a canyon and stopped each time she descended $\frac{1}{2}$ mile to rest. She hiked a total of 4 sections. What is her overall change in elevation?

STEP 1 Use a negative number to represent the change in elevation.

STEP 2 Find $4\left(-\frac{1}{2}\right)$.

STEP 3 Start at 0. Move $\frac{1}{2}$ unit to the left 4 times.

The result is −2.

The overall change is −2 miles.

   −3   −2   −1   0

Check: Use the rules for multiplying rational numbers.

$$4\left(-\frac{1}{2}\right) = \left(-\frac{4}{2}\right)$$ A negative times a positive equals a negative.

$$= -2 \checkmark$$ Simplify.

YOUR TURN

1. Use a number line to find 2(−3.5). _____

−8   −7   −6   −5   −4   −3   −2   −1   0

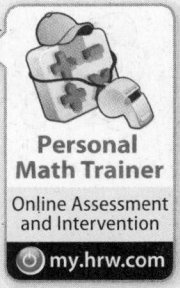

Personal Math Trainer

Online Assessment and Intervention

my.hrw.com

© Houghton Mifflin Harcourt Publishing Company • Image Credits: ©Sebastien Fremont/Fotolia

Multiplying Rational Numbers with the Same Sign

The rules for the signs of products with the same signs are summarized below.

Products of Rational Numbers

Sign of Factor *p*	Sign of Factor *q*	Sign of Product *pq*
+	+	+
−	−	+

You can also use a number line to find the product of rational numbers with the same signs.

My Notes

 EXAMPLE 2   FL   7.NS.1.2, 7.NS.1.2a

Multiply −2(−3.5).

STEP 1   First, find the product 2(−3.5).

STEP 2   Start at 0. Move 3.5 units to the left two times.

STEP 3   The result is −7.

STEP 4   This shows that 2 groups of −3.5 equals −7.

So, −2 groups of −3.5 must equal the *opposite* of −7.

STEP 5   −2(−3.5) = 7

Check: Use the rules for multiplying rational numbers.

−2(−3.5) = 7   *A negative times a negative equals a positive.*

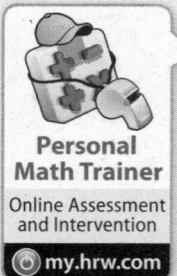
YOUR TURN

2.   Find −3(−1.25). _____

© Houghton Mifflin Harcourt Publishing Company

Multiplying More Than Two Rational Numbers

Math On the Spot
my.hrw.com

If you multiply three or more rational numbers, you can use a pattern to find the sign of the product.

EXAMPLE 3

 FL 7.NS.1.2, 7.NS.1.2c

Multiply $\left(-\frac{2}{3}\right)\left(-\frac{1}{2}\right)\left(-\frac{3}{5}\right)$.

STEP 1 First, find the product of the first two factors. Both factors are negative, so their product will be positive.

STEP 2 $\left(-\frac{2}{3}\right)\left(-\frac{1}{2}\right) = +\left(\frac{2}{3} \cdot \frac{1}{2}\right)$.

$\qquad = \frac{1}{3}$

STEP 3 Now, multiply the result, which is positive, by the third factor, which is negative. The product will be negative.

STEP 4 $\frac{1}{3}\left(-\frac{3}{5}\right) = \frac{1}{3}\left(-\frac{3}{5}\right)$

STEP 5 $\left(-\frac{2}{3}\right)\left(-\frac{1}{2}\right)\left(-\frac{3}{5}\right) = -\frac{1}{5}$

Reflect

3. Look for a Pattern You know that the product of two negative numbers is positive, and the product of three negative numbers is negative. Write a rule for finding the sign of the product of *n* negative numbers.

_____

_____

_____

Math Talk
Mathematical Practices

Suppose you find the product of several rational numbers, one of which is zero. What can you say about the product?

YOUR TURN

Find each product.

4. $\left(-\frac{3}{4}\right)\left(-\frac{4}{7}\right)\left(-\frac{2}{3}\right)$ _____

5. $\left(-\frac{2}{3}\right)\left(-\frac{3}{4}\right)\left(\frac{4}{5}\right)$ _____

6. $\left(\frac{2}{3}\right)\left(-\frac{9}{10}\right)\left(\frac{5}{6}\right)$ _____

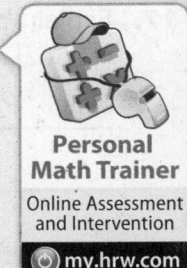

Personal Math Trainer
Online Assessment and Intervention
my.hrw.com

Use a number line to find each product. (Example 1 and Example 2)

1. $5\left(-\frac{2}{3}\right) =$ _____

2. $3\left(-\frac{1}{4}\right) =$ _____

3. $-3\left(-\frac{4}{7}\right) =$ _____

4. $-\frac{3}{4}(-4) =$ _____

5. $4(-3) =$ _____

6. $-1.8(5) =$ _____

7. $-2(-3.4) =$ _____

8. $0.54(8) =$ _____

9. $-5(-1.2) =$ _____

10. $-2.4(3) =$ _____

Multiply. (Example 3)

11. $\frac{1}{2} \times \frac{2}{3} \times \frac{3}{4} = \boxed{} \times \frac{3}{4} =$ _____

12. $-\frac{4}{7}\left(-\frac{3}{5}\right)\left(-\frac{7}{3}\right) = \left(\boxed{}\right) \times \left(-\frac{7}{3}\right) =$ _____

13. $-\frac{1}{8} \times 5 \times \frac{2}{3} =$ _____

14. $-\frac{2}{3}\left(\frac{1}{2}\right)\left(-\frac{6}{7}\right) =$ _____

15. The price of one share of Acme Company declined $3.50 per day for 4 days in a row. What was the overall change in the price of one share? (Example 1)

_____

16. In one day, 18 people each withdrew $100 from an ATM machine. What was the overall change in the amount of money in the ATM machine? (Example 1)

_____

? **ESSENTIAL QUESTION CHECK-IN**

17. Explain how you can find the sign of the product of two or more rational numbers.

_____

_____

_____

19.4 Independent Practice

FL 7.NS.1.2, 7.NS.1.2a, 7.NS.1.2c

Personal Math Trainer

Online Assessment and Intervention

my.hrw.com

18. **Financial Literacy** Sandy has $200 in her bank account.

  a. If she writes 6 checks for exactly $19.98, what expression describes the change in her bank account?

  _____

  b. What is her account balance after the checks are cashed?

  _____

19. **Communicating Mathematical Ideas** Explain, in words, how to find the product of −4(−1.5) using a number line. Where do you end up?

_____
_____
_____
_____
_____

20. Greg sets his watch for the correct time on Wednesday. Exactly one week later, he finds that his watch has lost $3\frac{1}{4}$ minutes. If his watch continues to lose time at the same rate, what will be the overall change in time after 8 weeks?

_____

21. A submarine dives below the surface, heading downward in three moves. If each move downward was 325 feet, where is the submarine after it is finished diving?

_____
_____

22. **Multistep** For Home Economics class, Sandra has 5 cups of flour. She made 3 batches of cookies that each used 1.5 cups of flour. Write and solve an expression to find the amount of flour Sandra has left after making the 3 batches of cookies.

_____
_____

23. **Critique Reasoning** In class, Matthew stated, "I think that a negative is like an opposite. That is why multiplying a negative times a negative equals a positive. The opposite of negative is positive, so it is just like multiplying the opposite of a negative twice, which is two positives." Do you agree or disagree with his reasoning? What would you say in response to him?

_____
_____
_____
_____
_____
_____
_____
_____
_____

24. Kaitlin is on a long car trip. Every time she stops to buy gas, she loses 15 minutes of travel time. If she has to stop 5 times, how late will she be getting to her destination?

_____
_____

25. The table shows the scoring system for quarterbacks in Jeremy's fantasy football league. In one game, Jeremy's quarterback had 2 touchdown passes, 16 complete passes, 7 incomplete passes, and 2 interceptions. How many total points did Jeremy's quarterback score?

Quarterback Scoring	
Action	**Points**
Touchdown pass	6
Complete pass	0.5
Incomplete pass	−0.5
Interception	−1.5

_____

 FOCUS ON HIGHER ORDER THINKING

26. Represent Real-World Problems The ground temperature at Brigham Airport is 12°C. The temperature decreases by 6.8 °C for every increase of 1 kilometer above the ground. What is the temperature outside a plane flying at an altitude of 5 kilometers above Brigham Airport?

_____

27. Identify Patterns The product of four numbers, a, b, c, and d, is a negative number. The table shows one combination of positive and negative signs of the four numbers that could produce a negative product. Complete the table to show the seven other possible combinations.

a	b	c	d
+	+	+	−

28. Reason Abstractly Find two integers whose sum is −7 and whose product is 12. Explain how you found the numbers.

_____

_____

_____

_____

LESSON
19.5

FL 7.NS.1.2

Apply and extend previous understandings of multiplication and division and of fractions to...divide rational numbers. *Also* 7.NS.1.2b, 7.NS.1.2c

Dividing Rational Numbers

© Houghton Mifflin Harcourt Publishing Company • Image Credits: ©JUPITERIMAGES/Comstock Images/Alamy

 ESSENTIAL QUESTION

How do you divide rational numbers?

EXPLORE ACTIVITY 1 Real World **FL** 7.NS.1.2, 7.NS.1.2b

Dividing Rational Numbers

A diver needs to descend to a depth of 100 feet below sea level. She wants to do it in 5 equal descents. How far should she travel in each descent?

A To solve this problem, you can set up a division problem: $\dfrac{-100}{\boxed{}} = ?$

B Rewrite the division problem as a multiplication problem. Think: Some number multiplied by 5 equals -100.

_____ × ? = -100

C Remember the rules for integer multiplication. If the product is negative, one of the factors must be negative. Since _____ is positive, the unknown factor must be **positive / negative.**

D You know that $5 \times$ _____ $= 100$. So, using the rules for integer multiplication you can say that $5 \times$ _____ $= -100$.

The diver should descend _____ feet in each descent.

Reflect

1. What do you notice about the quotient of two rational numbers with different signs?

_____

_____

2. What do you notice about the quotient of two rational numbers with the same sign? Does it matter if both signs are positive or both are negative?

_____

_____

Let p and q be rational numbers.

Quotients of Rational Numbers

Sign of Dividend p	Sign of Divisor q	Sign of Quotient $\frac{p}{q}$
+	−	−
−	+	−
+	+	+
−	−	+

Also, $-\left(\dfrac{p}{q}\right) = \dfrac{-p}{q} = \dfrac{p}{-q}$, for q not zero.

EXPLORE ACTIVITY 2 FL 7.NS.1.2b

Placement of Negative Signs in Quotients

Quotients can have negative signs in different places.

Are the rational numbers $\dfrac{12}{-4}$, $\dfrac{-12}{4}$, and $-\left(\dfrac{12}{4}\right)$ equivalent?

A Find each quotient. Then use the rules you found in Explore Activity 1 to make sure the sign of the quotient is correct.

$\dfrac{12}{-4} =$ _____ $\dfrac{-12}{4} =$ _____ $-\left(\dfrac{12}{4}\right) =$ _____

B What do you notice about each quotient?

_____

C The rational numbers $\boxed{\text{are / are not}}$ equivalent.

D **Conjecture** Explain how the placement of the negative sign in the rational number affects the sign of the quotients.

_____

_____

Reflect

Write two equivalent expressions for each quotient.

3. $\dfrac{14}{-7}$ _____ , _____   **4.** $\dfrac{-32}{-8}$ _____ , _____

Quotients of Rational Numbers

The rules for dividing rational numbers are the same as dividing integers.

EXAMPLE 1   **FL** 7.NS.1.2c

A Over 5 months, Carlos wrote 5 checks for a total of $323.75 to pay for his cable TV service. His cable bill is the same amount each month. What was the change in Carlos' bank account each month to pay for cable?

Find the quotient: $\frac{-323.75}{5}$

STEP 1 Use a negative number to represent the withdrawal from his account each month.

STEP 2 Find $\frac{-323.75}{5}$.

STEP 3 Determine the sign of the quotient.

The quotient will be negative because the signs are different.

STEP 4 Divide.

$$\frac{-323.75}{5} = -64.75$$

Carlos withdrew $64.75 each month to pay for cable TV.

B Find $\frac{\frac{7}{10}}{-\frac{1}{5}}$.

STEP 1 Determine the sign of the quotient.
The quotient will be negative because the signs are different.

STEP 2 Write the complex fraction as division: $\frac{\frac{7}{10}}{-\frac{1}{5}} = \frac{7}{10} \div -\frac{1}{5}$

STEP 3 Rewrite using multiplication: $\frac{7}{10} \times \left(-\frac{5}{1}\right)$ Multiply by the reciprocal.

STEP 4 $\frac{7}{10} \times \left(-\frac{5}{1}\right) = -\frac{35}{10}$ Multiply.

$$= -\frac{7}{2}$$ Simplify.

$$\frac{\frac{7}{10}}{-\frac{1}{5}} = -\frac{7}{2}$$

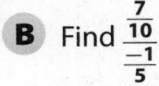 **YOUR TURN**

Find each quotient.

5. $\frac{2.8}{-4} =$ _____

6. $\frac{-\frac{5}{8}}{\frac{6}{7}} =$ _____

7. $-\frac{5.5}{0.5} =$ _____

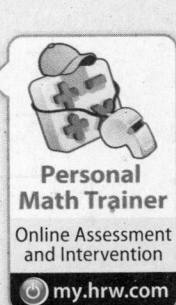
Personal Math Trainer
Online Assessment and Intervention
my.hrw.com

Guided Practice

Find each quotient. (Explore Activity 1 and 2, Example 1)

1. $\dfrac{0.72}{-0.9} =$ _____

2. $\left(-\dfrac{\frac{1}{5}}{\frac{7}{5}}\right) =$ _____

3. $\dfrac{56}{-7} =$ _____

4. $\dfrac{251}{4} \div \left(-\dfrac{3}{8}\right) =$ _____

5. $\dfrac{75}{-\frac{1}{5}} =$ _____

6. $\dfrac{-91}{-13} =$ _____

7. $\dfrac{-\frac{3}{7}}{\frac{9}{4}} =$ _____

8. $-\dfrac{12}{0.03} =$ _____

9. A water pail in your backyard has a small hole in it. You notice that it has drained a total of 3.5 liters in 4 days. What is the average change in water volume each day? (Example 1)

_____

10. The price of one share of ABC Company declined a total of $45.75 in 5 days. What was the average change of the price of one share per day? (Example 1)

_____

11. To avoid a storm, a passenger-jet pilot descended 0.44 mile in 0.8 minute. What was the plane's average change of altitude per minute? (Example 1)

_____

? ESSENTIAL QUESTION CHECK-IN

12. Explain how you would find the sign of the quotient $\dfrac{32 \div (-2)}{-16 \div 4}$.

_____

_____

_____

_____

_____

_____

19.5 Independent Practice

FL 7.NS.1.2, 7.NS.1.2b, 7.NS.1.2c

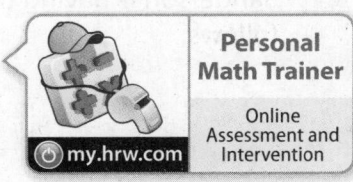

Personal
Math Trainer

Online
Assessment and
Intervention

my.hrw.com

13. $\dfrac{\frac{5}{2}}{-\frac{2}{8}} = $ _____

14. $5\frac{1}{3} \div \left(-1\frac{1}{2}\right) = $ _____

15. $\dfrac{-120}{-6} = $ _____

16. $\dfrac{\frac{4}{5}}{-\frac{2}{3}} = $ _____

17. $1.03 \div (-10.3) = $ _____

18. $\dfrac{-0.4}{80} = $ _____

19. $1 \div \dfrac{9}{5} = $ _____

20. $\dfrac{-\frac{1}{4}}{\frac{23}{24}} = $ _____

21. $\dfrac{-10.35}{-2.3} = $ _____

22. Alex usually runs for 21 hours a week, training for a marathon. If he is unable to run for 3 days, describe how to find out how many hours of training time he loses, and write the appropriate integer to describe how it affects his time.

_____

_____

_____

_____

_____

_____

23. The running back for the Bulldogs football team carried the ball 9 times for a total loss of $15\frac{3}{4}$ yards. Find the average change in field position on each run.

_____

24. The 6:00 a.m. temperatures for four consecutive days in the town of Lincoln were $-12.1\,°C$, $-7.8\,°C$, $-14.3\,°C$, and $-7.2\,°C$. What was the average 6:00 a.m. temperature for the four days?

_____

25. **Multistep** A seafood restaurant claims an increase of $1,750.00 over its average profit during a week where it introduced a special of baked clams.

a. If this is true, how much extra profit did it receive per day?

_____

b. If it had, instead, lost $150 per day, how much money would it have lost for the week?

_____

c. If its total loss was $490 for the week, what was its average daily change?

_____

26. A hot air balloon descended 99.6 meters in 12 seconds. What was the balloon's average rate of descent in meters per second?

_____

_____

27. Sanderson is having trouble with his assignment. His shown work is as follows:

$$\frac{-\frac{3}{4}}{\frac{4}{3}} = -\frac{3}{4} \times \frac{4}{3} = -\frac{12}{12} = -1$$

However, his answer does not match the answer that his teacher gives him. What is Sanderson's mistake? Find the correct answer.

_____

_____

_____

_____

28. Science Beginning in 1996, a glacier lost an average of 3.7 meters of thickness each year. Find the total change in its thickness by the end of 2012.

_____

 FOCUS ON HIGHER ORDER THINKING

29. Represent Real-World Problems Describe a real-world situation that can be represented by the quotient $-85 \div 15$. Then find the quotient and explain what the quotient means in terms of the real-world situation.

_____

_____

_____

_____

30. Construct an Argument Divide 5 by 4. Is your answer a rational number? Explain.

_____

_____

_____

31. Critical Thinking Should the quotient of an integer divided by a nonzero integer always be a rational number? Why or why not?

_____

_____

_____

LESSON 19.6 Applying Rational Number Operations

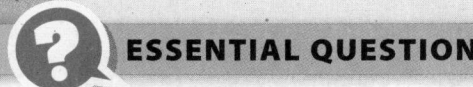

FL 7.EE.2.3

Solve ... problems ... with positive and negative rational numbers in any form ... using tools strategically. *Also 7.NS.1.3*

? ESSENTIAL QUESTION

How do you use different forms of rational numbers and strategically choose tools to solve problems?

Assessing Reasonableness of Answers

Even when you understand how to solve a problem, you might make a careless solving error. You should always check your answer to make sure that it is reasonable.

Math On the Spot
⊙ my.hrw.com

EXAMPLE 1 *Real World*   **FL** 7.EE.2.3, 7.NS.1.3

Jon is hanging a picture. He wants to center it horizontally on the wall. The picture is $32\frac{1}{2}$ inches long, and the wall is $120\frac{3}{4}$ inches long. How far from each edge of the wall should he place the picture?

STEP 1 Find the total length of the wall not covered by the picture.

$120\frac{3}{4} - 32\frac{1}{2} = 88\frac{1}{4}$ in.   *Subtract the whole number parts and then the fractional parts.*

STEP 2 Find the length of the wall on each side of the picture.

$\frac{1}{2}\left(88\frac{1}{4}\right) = 44\frac{1}{8}$ in.

Jon should place the picture $44\frac{1}{8}$ inches from each edge of the wall.

STEP 3 Check the answer for reasonableness.

The wall is about 120 inches long. The picture is about 30 inches long. The length of wall space left for *both* sides of the picture is about $120 - 30 = 90$ inches. The length left for *each* side is about $\frac{1}{2}(90) = 45$ inches.

The answer is reasonable because it is close to the estimate.

YOUR TURN

1. A 30-minute TV program consists of three commercials, each $2\frac{1}{2}$ minutes long, and four equal-length entertainment segments. How long is each entertainment segment? _____

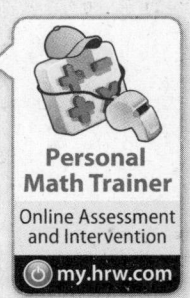

Personal Math Trainer

Online Assessment and Intervention

⊙ my.hrw.com

© Houghton Mifflin Harcourt Publishing Company

Using Rational Numbers in Any Form

You have solved problems using integers, positive and negative fractions, and positive and negative decimals. A single problem may involve rational numbers in two or more of those forms.

My Notes

EXAMPLE 2 Problem Solving   **FL**   7.EE.2.3, 7.NS.1.3

Alana uses $1\frac{1}{4}$ cups of flour for each batch of blueberry muffins she makes. She has a 5-pound bag of flour that cost \$4.49 and contains seventy-six $\frac{1}{4}$-cup servings. How many batches can Alana make if she uses all the flour? How much does the flour for one batch cost?

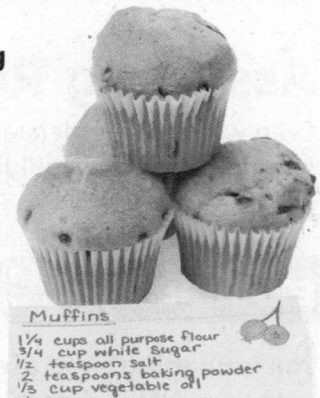

Muffins
1¼ cups all purpose flour
3/4 cup white sugar
½ teaspoon salt
2 teaspoons baking powder
⅓ cup vegetable oil
1 egg
⅕ cup milk
1 cup fresh blueberries

 Analyze Information

Identify the important information.
- Each batch uses $1\frac{1}{4}$ cups of flour.
- Seventy-six $\frac{1}{4}$-cup servings of flour cost \$4.49.

 Formulate a Plan

Use logical reasoning to solve the problem. Find the number of cups of flour that Alana has. Use that information to find the number of batches she can make. Use that information to find the cost of flour for each batch.

 Solve

Number of cups of flour in bag:

76 servings $\times \frac{1}{4}$ cup per serving = 19 cups

Number of batches Alana can make:

> Write $1\frac{1}{4}$ as a decimal.

$$\text{total cups of flour} \div \frac{\text{cups of flour}}{\text{batch}} = 19 \text{ cups} \div \frac{1.25 \text{ cups}}{1 \text{ batch}}$$
$$= 19 \div 1.25$$
$$= 15.2$$

Alana cannot make 0.2 batch. The recipe calls for one egg, and she cannot divide one egg into tenths. So, she can make 15 batches.

Cost of flour for each batch: \$4.49 ÷ 15 = \$0.299, or about \$0.30.

 Justify and Evaluate

A bag contains about 80 quarter cups, or about 20 cups. Each batch uses about 1 cup of flour, so there is enough flour for about 20 batches. A bag costs about \$5.00, so the flour for each batch costs about \$5.00 ÷ 20 = \$0.25. The answers are close to the estimates, so the answers are reasonable.

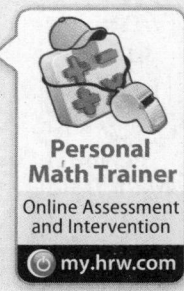

Personal
Math Trainer
Online Assessment
and Intervention
🌐 my.hrw.com

2. A 4-pound bag of sugar contains 454 one-teaspoon servings and costs $3.49. A batch of muffins uses $\frac{3}{4}$ cup of sugar. How many batches can you make if you use all the sugar? What is the cost of sugar for each batch? (1 cup = 48 teaspoons) _____

Using Tools Strategically

A wide variety of tools are available to help you solve problems. Rulers, models, calculators, protractors, and software are some of the tools you can use in addition to paper and pencil. Choosing tools wisely can help you solve problems and increase your understanding of mathematical concepts.

Math On the Spot
🌐 my.hrw.com

EXAMPLE 3 Real World   **FL** 7.EE.2.3, 7.NS.1.3

The depth of Golden Trout Lake has been decreasing in recent years. Two years ago, the depth of the lake was 186.73 meters. Since then the depth has been changing at an average rate of $-1\frac{3}{4}$% per year. What is the depth of the lake today?

STEP 1 Convert the percent to a decimal.

$-1\frac{3}{4}\% = -1.75\%$ *Write the fraction as a decimal.*

$= -0.0175$ *Move the decimal point two places left.*

STEP 2 Find the depth of the lake after one year. Use a calculator to simplify the computations.

$186.73 \times (-0.0175) \approx -3.27$ meters   *Find the change in depth.*

$186.73 - 3.27 = 183.46$ meters   *Find the new depth.*

STEP 3 Find the depth of the lake after two years.

$183.46 \times (-0.0175) \approx -3.21$ meters   *Find the change in depth.*

$183.46 - 3.21 = 180.25$ meters   *Find the new depth.*

STEP 4 Check the answer for reasonableness.

The original depth was about 190 meters. The depth changed by about −2% per year. Because $(-0.02)(190) = -3.8$, the depth changed by about −4 meters per year or about −8 meters over two years. So, the new depth was about 182 meters. The answer is close to the estimate, so it is reasonable.

Math Talk
Mathematical Practices

How could you write a single expression for calculating the depth after 1 year? after 2 years?

YOUR TURN

3. Three years ago, Jolene bought $750 worth of stock in a software company. Since then the value of her purchase has been increasing at an average rate of $12\frac{3}{5}$% per year. How much is the stock worth now? _____

Guided Practice

1. Mike hiked to Big Bear Lake in 4.5 hours at an average rate of $3\frac{1}{5}$ miles per hour. Pedro hiked the same distance at a rate of $3\frac{3}{5}$ miles per hour. How long did it take Pedro to reach the lake? (Example 1 and Example 2)

   STEP 1 Find the distance Mike hiked.

   4.5 h × [   ] miles per hour = [   ] miles

   STEP 2 Find Pedro's time to hike the same distance.

   [   ] miles ÷ [   ] miles per hour = [   ] hours

2. Until this year, Greenville had averaged 25.68 inches of rainfall per year for more than a century. This year's total rainfall showed a change of $-2\frac{3}{8}$% with respect to the previous average. How much rain fell this year? (Example 3)

   STEP 1 Use a calculator to find this year's decrease to the nearest hundredth.

   [   ] inches × [   ] ≈ [   ] inches

   STEP 2 Find this year's total rainfall.

   [   ] inches − [   ] inches ≈ [   ] inches

? **ESSENTIAL QUESTION CHECK-IN**

3. Why is it important to consider using tools when you are solving a problem?

   _____

   _____

   _____

19.6 Independent Practice

FL 7.NS.1.3, 7.EE.2.3

Personal Math Trainer

Online Assessment and Intervention

my.hrw.com

Solve, using appropriate tools.

4. Three rock climbers started a climb with each person carrying 7.8 kilograms of climbing equipment. A fourth climber with no equipment joined the group. The group divided the total weight of climbing equipment equally among the four climbers. How much

   did each climber carry? _____

5. Foster is centering a photo that is $3\frac{1}{2}$ inches wide on a scrapbook page that is 12 inches wide. How far from each side of the page

   should he put the picture? _____

6. Diane serves breakfast to two groups of children at a daycare center. One box of Oaties contains 12 cups of cereal. She needs $\frac{1}{3}$ cup for each younger child and $\frac{3}{4}$ cup for each older child. Today's group includes 11 younger children and 10 older children. Is one box of Oaties enough for everyone?

   Explain. _____

7. The figure shows how the yard lines on a football field are numbered. The goal lines are labeled G. A referee was standing on a certain yard line as the first quarter ended. He walked $41\frac{3}{4}$ yards to a yard line with the same number as the one he had just left. How far was the referee from the nearest goal

   line? _____

In 8–10, a teacher gave a test with 50 questions, each worth the same number of points. Donovan got 39 out of 50 questions right. Marci's score was 10 percentage points higher than Donovan's.

8. What was Marci's score? Explain.

   _____

9. How many more questions did Marci answer correctly? Explain.

   _____

10. Explain how you can check your answers for reasonableness.

    _____

    _____

    _____

For 11–13, use the expression $1.43 \times \left(-\frac{19}{37}\right)$.

11. Critique Reasoning Jamie says the value of the expression is close to −0.75. Does Jamie's estimate seem reasonable? Explain.

_____

12. Find the product. Explain your method.

_____

_____

13. Does your answer to Exercise 12 justify your answer to Exercise 11?

_____

 FOCUS ON HIGHER ORDER THINKING

Work Area

14. Persevere in Problem Solving A scuba diver dove from the surface of the ocean to an elevation of $-79\frac{9}{10}$ feet at a rate of −18.8 feet per minute. After spending 12.75 minutes at that elevation, the diver ascended to an elevation of $-28\frac{9}{10}$ feet. The total time for the dive so far was $19\frac{1}{8}$ minutes. What was

the rate of change in the diver's elevation during the ascent? _____

15. Analyze Relationships Describe two ways you could evaluate 37% of the sum of $27\frac{3}{5}$ and 15.9. Tell which method you would use and why.

_____

_____

_____

_____

_____

_____

16. Represent Real-World Problems Describe a real-world problem you could solve with the help of a yardstick and a calculator.

_____

_____

_____

_____

_____

_____

FL 7.EE.1.1
Apply properties of operations as strategies to add, subtract, factor, and expand linear expressions with rational coefficients. *Also 7.EE.1.2*

ESSENTIAL QUESTION

How do you add, subtract, factor, and multiply algebraic expressions?

Adding and Subtracting Expressions

You can use the properties of addition along with the Distributive Property to add and subtract algebraic expressions.

Math On the Spot
my.hrw.com

EXAMPLE 1

FL 7.EE.1.1, 7.EE.1.2

Jill and Kyle get paid per project. Jill is paid a project fee of $25 plus $10 per hour. Kyle is paid a project fee of $18 plus $14 per hour. Write an expression to represent how much a company will pay to hire both to work the same number of hours on a project.

STEP 1 Write expressions for how much the company will pay each person. Let h represent the number of hours they will work on the project.

Jill: $\$25 + \$10h$ Kyle: $\$18 + \$14h$

Fee + Hourly rate × Hours   Fee + Hourly rate × Hours

STEP 2 Add the expressions to represent the amount the company will pay to hire both.

$25 + 10h + 18 + 14h$ Combine their pay.

$= 25 + 18 + 10h + 14h$ Use the Commutative Property.

$= 43 + 24h$ Combine like terms.

The company will pay $43 + 24h$ dollars to hire both Jill and Kyle.

Reflect

1. **Critical Thinking** What can you read directly from the expression $43 + 24h$ that you cannot read directly from the equivalent expression $25 + 10h + 18 + 14h$?

_____

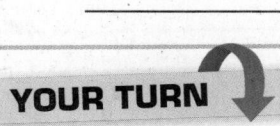

Simplify each expression.

2. $\left(3x + \dfrac{1}{2}\right) + \left(7x - 4\dfrac{1}{2}\right)$

_____

3. $(-0.25x - 3) - (1.5x + 1.4)$

_____

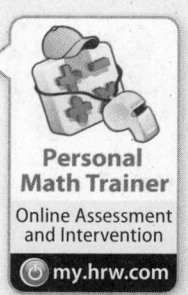

Personal Math Trainer

Online Assessment and Intervention

my.hrw.com

Using the Distributive Property

You can use the Distributive Property to remove the parentheses from an algebraic expression like $3(x + 5)$. Sometimes this is called "simplifying" or "expanding" the expression. Multiply the quantity in front of parentheses by each term within parentheses: $3(x + 5) = 3 \cdot x + 3 \cdot 5 = 3x + 15$.

EXAMPLE 2

Marc is selling tickets for a high school band concert. The band gets to keep 25% of the money he collects from ticket sales to put toward new uniforms. Write an expression to represent how much the band gets to keep.

Let a represent the number of adult tickets he sells.

Let y represent the number of youth tickets he sells.

The expression $16.60a + 12.20y$ represents the amount of money Marc collects from ticket sales.

Write 25% as a decimal: 0.25

Write an expression to represent 25% of the money he collects:

0.25	×	(16.60a	+	12.20y)
25%	of	adult ticket sales	and	youth ticket sales

Use the Distributive Property to simplify the expression.

$0.25(16.60a) + 0.25(12.20y) = 4.15a + 3.05y$

Reflect

4. **Analyze Relationships** Instead of using the Distributive Property to expand $0.25 \times (16.60a + 12.20y)$, could you have first found the sum $16.60a + 12.20y$? Explain.

_____

_____

YOUR TURN

Simplify each expression.

5. $7(9k + 6m)$

6. $0.2(3b - 15c)$

7. $\frac{2}{3}(6e + 9f - 21g)$

_____   _____   _____

Factoring Expressions

A factor is a number that is multiplied by another number to get a product.
To **factor** is to write a number or an algebraic expression as a product.

Factor $4x + 8$.

A Model the expression with algebra tiles.

Use _____ positive x tiles and _____ $+1$-tiles.

B Arrange the tiles to form a rectangle. The total area represents $4x + 8$.

C Since the length multiplied by the width equals the area, the length and the width of the rectangle are the factors of $4x + 8$. Find the length and width.

The length is
__ x tile and
__ $+1$-tiles, or
_____ .

← The width is __ $+1$-tiles, or __.

D Use the expressions for the length and width of the rectangle

to write the area of the rectangle, $4x + 8$, in factored form. _____

Reflect

8. **Communicate Mathematical Ideas** How could you use the Distributive Property to check your factoring?

_____

YOUR TURN

Factor each expression.

9. $2x + 2$ **10.** $3x + 9$ **11.** $5x + 15$ **12.** $4x + 16$

_____   _____   _____   _____

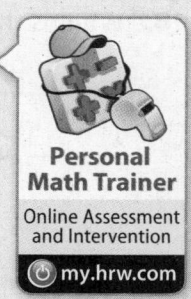

Personal Math Trainer

Online Assessment and Intervention

my.hrw.com

1. The manager of a summer camp has 14 baseballs and 23 tennis balls.
   The manager buys some boxes of baseballs with 12 baseballs to a
   box and an equal number of boxes of tennis balls with 16 tennis balls
   to a box. Write an expression to represent the total number of balls.
   (Example 1)

   STEP 1 Write expressions for the total number of baseballs and tennis balls.
           Let n represent the number of boxes of each type.

           baseballs: _____ + (_____)n tennis balls: _____ + (_____)n

   STEP 2 Find an expression for the total number of balls.

           _____ + _____ + _____ + _____   Combine the two expressions.

           _____ + _____ + _____ + _____   Use the Commutative Property.

           _____ + _____   Combine like terms.

           So, the total number of baseballs and tennis balls is _____ + _____.

2. Use the expression you found above to find the total number of baseballs
   and tennis balls if the manager bought 9 boxes of each type. (Example 1) _____

Use the Distributive Property to expand each expression. (Example 2)

3. $0.5(12m - 22n)$

   $0.5(12m - 22n) = 0.5(\underline{\hspace{1cm}}) - 0.5(\underline{\hspace{1cm}})$ Distribute 0.5 to both terms in parentheses.

   $ = \underline{\hspace{1cm}} - \underline{\hspace{1cm}}$ Multiply.

4. $\frac{2}{3}(18x + 6z)$

   $\frac{2}{3}(\underline{\hspace{1cm}}) + \frac{2}{3}(\underline{\hspace{1cm}}) = \underline{\hspace{1cm}} + \underline{\hspace{1cm}}$

Factor each expression. (Example 3)

5. $2x + 12$ 6. $12x + 24$ 7. $7x + 35$

   _____   _____   _____

? ESSENTIAL QUESTION CHECK-IN

8. What is the relationship between multiplying and factoring?

   _____

   _____

   _____

19.7 Independent Practice

FL 7.EE.1.1, 7.EE.1.2

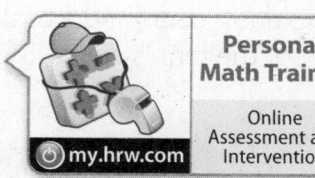

Personal Math Trainer

Online Assessment and Intervention

my.hrw.com

Write and simplify an expression for each situation.

9. A company rents out 15 food booths and 20 game booths at the county fair. The fee for a food booth is $100 plus $5 per day. The fee for a game booth is $50 plus $7 per day. The fair lasts for d days, and all the booths are rented for the entire time. Write and simplify an expression for the amount in dollars that the company is paid.

_____

10. A rug maker is using a pattern that is a rectangle with a length of 96 inches and a width of 60 inches. The rug maker wants to increase each dimension by a different amount. Let ℓ and w be the increases in inches of the length and width. Write and simplify an expression for the perimeter of the new pattern.

_____

In 11–12, identify the two factors that were multiplied together to form the array of tiles. Then identify the product of the two factors.

11.   _____

12.   _____

13. Explain how the figure illustrates that $6(9) = 6(5) + 6(4)$.

_____

_____

_____

_____

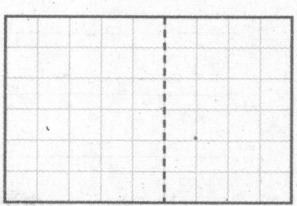

In 14–15, the perimeter of the figure is given. Find the length of the indicated side.

14.

$x + 3$ $2x + 4$

?

Perimeter = $6x$ _____

15.

?

$3x - 3$

Perimeter = $10x + 6$ _____

16. Persevere in Problem Solving The figures show the dimensions of a tennis court and a basketball court given in terms of the width x in feet of the tennis court.

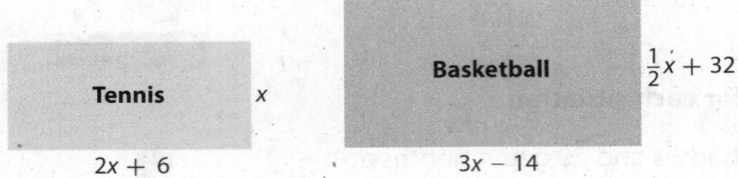

Tennis x

2x + 6

Basketball $\frac{1}{2}x + 32$

3x − 14

a. Write an expression for the perimeter of each court. _____

b. Write an expression that describes how much greater the perimeter of the basketball court is than the perimeter of the

tennis court. _____

c. Suppose the tennis court is 36 feet wide. Find all dimensions of the

two courts. _____

 FOCUS ON HIGHER ORDER THINKING

Work Area

17. Draw Conclusions Use the figure to find the product $(x + 3)(x + 2)$. (*Hint*: Find the area of each small square or rectangle, then add.)

x 1   1   1

x

1

1

$(x + 3)(x + 2) =$ _____

18. Communicate Mathematical Ideas Desmond claims that the product shown at the right illustrates the Distributive Property. Do you agree? Explain why or why not.

```
    58
  × 23
   174
  1160
 1,334
```

_____

_____

_____

_____

19. Justify Reasoning Describe two different ways that you could find the product 8×997 using mental math. Find the product and explain why your methods work.

_____

_____

_____

_____

Ready to Go On?

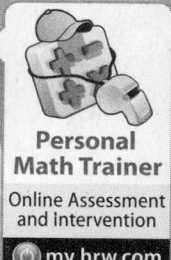

Personal Math Trainer

Online Assessment and Intervention

my.hrw.com

19.1 Rational Numbers and Decimals

Write each mixed number as a decimal.

1. $4\frac{1}{5}$ _____

2. $12\frac{14}{15}$ _____

3. $5\frac{5}{32}$ _____

19.2 Adding Rational Numbers

4. $4.5 + 7.1 =$ _____

5. $5\frac{1}{6} + \left(-3\frac{5}{6}\right) =$ _____

19.3 Subtracting Rational Numbers

6. $-\frac{1}{8} - \left(6\frac{7}{8}\right) =$ _____

7. $14.2 - (-4.9) =$ _____

19.4 Multiplying Rational Numbers

8. $-4\left(\frac{7}{10}\right) =$ _____

9. $-3.2(-5.6)(4) =$ _____

19.5 Dividing Rational Numbers

10. $-\frac{19}{2} \div \frac{38}{7} =$ _____

11. $\frac{-32.01}{-3.3} =$ _____

19.6 Applying Rational Number Operations

12. Luis bought stock at $83.60. The next day, the price changed by $-4\frac{3}{4}\%$. What was the final stock price?

_____

19.7 Algebraic Expressions

13. $4y + 36 =$ _____

14. $11d - 88 =$ _____

? ESSENTIAL QUESTION

15. How can you use negative numbers to represent real-world problems?

_____

_____

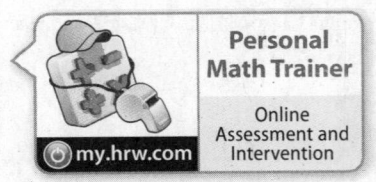
Selected Response

1. What is $-7\frac{5}{12}$ written as a decimal?

  Ⓐ -7.25

  Ⓑ $-7.333\ldots$

  Ⓒ $-7.41666\ldots$

  Ⓓ -7.512

2. Glenda began the day with a golf score of -6 and ended with a score of -10. Which statement represents her golf score for that day?

  Ⓐ $-6 - (-10) = 4$

  Ⓑ $-10 - (-6) = -4$

  Ⓒ $-6 + (-10) = -16$

  Ⓓ $-10 + (-6) = -16$

3. A submersible vessel at an elevation of -95 feet descends to 5 times that elevation. What is the vessel's new elevation?

  Ⓐ -475 ft   Ⓒ 19 ft

  Ⓑ -19 ft   Ⓓ 475 ft

4. The temperature at 7 P.M. at a weather station in Minnesota was $-5\,°F$. The temperature began changing at the rate of $-2.5\,°F$ per hour. What was the temperature at 10 P.M.?

  Ⓐ $-15\,°F$ Ⓒ $2.5\,°F$

  Ⓑ $-12.5\,°F$ Ⓓ $5\,°F$

5. How is $7x + 721$ factored?

  Ⓐ $7x + 7(103)$ Ⓒ $-7(x - 103)$

  Ⓑ $x(7 + 103)$ Ⓓ $7(x + 103)$

6. On Sunday, the wind chill temperature reached $-36\,°F$. On Monday, the wind chill temperature only reached $\frac{1}{4}$ of Sunday's wind chill temperature. What was the lowest wind chill temperature on Monday?

  Ⓐ $-9\,°F$ Ⓒ $-40\,°F$

  Ⓑ $-36\frac{1}{4}\,°F$ Ⓓ $-144\,°F$

7. The level of a lake was 8 inches below normal. It decreased $1\frac{1}{4}$ inches in June and $2\frac{3}{8}$ inches more in July. What was the new level with respect to the normal level?

  Ⓐ $-11\frac{5}{8}$ in.   Ⓒ $-9\frac{1}{8}$ in.

  Ⓑ $-10\frac{5}{8}$ in.   Ⓓ $-5\frac{3}{8}$ in.

Mini-Task

8. The average annual rainfall for a town is 43.2 inches.

  a. What is the average *monthly* rainfall?

    _____

  b. The difference of a given month's rainfall from the average monthly rainfall is called the *deviation*. What is the deviation for each month shown?

Town's Rainfall in Last Three Months			
Month	May	June	July
Rain (in.)	$2\frac{3}{5}$	$\frac{7}{8}$	$4\frac{1}{4}$

    _____

  c. The average monthly rainfall for the previous 9 months was 4 inches. Did the town exceed its average annual rainfall? If so, by how much?

    _____

MODULE 17 Adding and Subtracting Integers

Key Vocabulary
additive inverse *(inverso aditivo)*

? ESSENTIAL QUESTION

How can you use addition and subtraction of integers to solve real-world problems?

EXAMPLE 1

Add.

A. $-8 + (-7)$	The signs of both integers are the same.
$8 + 7 = 15$	Find the sum of the absolute values.
$-8 + (-7) = -15$	Use the sign of integers to write the sum.
B. $-5 + 11$	The signs of the integers are different.
$|11| - |-5| = 6$	Greater absolute value – lesser absolute value.
$-5 + 11 = 6$	11 has the greater absolute value, so the sum is positive.

EXAMPLE 2

The temperature Tuesday afternoon was 3 °C. Tuesday night, the temperature was −6 °C. Find the change in temperature.

Find the difference $-6 - 3$.

Rewrite as $-6 + (-3)$.   *−3 is the opposite of 3.*

$-6 + (-3) = -9$

The temperature decreased 9 °C.

EXERCISES

Add. (Lessons 17.1, 17.2)

1. $-10 + (-5)$ _____   **2.** $9 + (-20)$ _____   **3.** $-13 + 32$ _____

Subtract. (Lesson 17.3)

4. $-12 - 5$ _____   **5.** $25 - (-4)$ _____   **6.** $-3 - (-40)$ _____

7. Antoine has $13 in his checking account. He buys some school supplies and ends up with $5 in his account. What was the overall change in Antoine's account? (Lesson 17.4) _____

Multiplying and Dividing Integers

ESSENTIAL QUESTION

How can you use multiplication and division of integers to solve real-world problems?

EXAMPLE 1

Multiply.

A. $(13)(-3)$

Find the sign of the product. The numbers have different signs, so the product will be negative. Multiply the absolute values. Assign the correct sign to the product.

$$13(-3) = -39$$

B. $(-5)(-8)$

Find the sign of the product. The numbers have the same sign, so the product will be positive. Multiply the absolute values. Assign the correct sign to the product.

$$(-5)(-8) = 40$$

EXAMPLE 2

Christine received -25 points on her exam for 5 wrong answers. How many points did Christine receive for each wrong answer?

Divide -25 by 5.

$$-25 \div 5 = -5$$ The signs are different.
The quotient is negative.

Christine received -5 points for each wrong answer.

EXAMPLE 3

Simplify: $15 + (-3) \times 8$

$15 + (-24)$ Multiply first.

-9 Add.

EXERCISES

Multiply or divide. (Lessons 18.1, 18.2)

1. $-9 \times (-5)$ _____

2. $0 \times (-10)$ _____

3. $12 \times (-4)$ _____

4. $-32 \div 8$ _____

5. $-9 \div (-1)$ _____

6. $-56 \div 8$ _____

Simplify. (Lesson 18.3)

7. $-14 \div 2 - 3$ _____

8. $8 + (-20) \times 3$ _____

9. $36 \div (-6) - 15$ _____

10. Tony bought 3 packs of pencils for $4 each and a pencil box for $7. Mario bought 4 binders for $6 each and used a coupon for $6 off. Write and evaluate expressions to find who spent more money. (Lesson 18.3)

_____

? ESSENTIAL QUESTION

How can you use rational numbers to solve real-world problems?

EXAMPLE 1

Eddie walked $1\frac{2}{3}$ miles on a hiking trail. Write $1\frac{2}{3}$ as a decimal. Use the decimal to classify $1\frac{2}{3}$ according to the number group(s) to which it belongs.

$1\frac{2}{3} = \frac{5}{3}$ Write $1\frac{2}{3}$ as an improper fraction.

$$
\begin{array}{r}
1.66 \\
3\overline{)5.00} \\
-3 \\
\hline
2\,0 \\
-1\,8 \\
\hline
20 \\
-18 \\
\hline
2
\end{array}
$$

Divide the numerator by the denominator.

The decimal equivalent of $1\frac{2}{3}$ is 1.66…, or $1.\overline{6}$. It is a repeating decimal, and therefore can be classified as a rational number.

EXAMPLE 2

Find each sum or difference.

A. $-2 + 4.5$

Start at -2 and move 4.5 units to the right: $-2 + 4.5 = 2.5$.

B. $-\frac{2}{5} - \left(-\frac{4}{5}\right)$

Start at $-\frac{2}{5}$. Move $\left|-\frac{4}{5}\right| = \frac{4}{5}$ unit to the right because you are subtracting a negative number: $-\frac{2}{5} - \left(-\frac{4}{5}\right) = \frac{2}{5}$.

EXAMPLE 3

Find the product: $3\left(-\frac{1}{6}\right)\left(-\frac{2}{5}\right)$.

$3\left(-\frac{1}{6}\right) = -\frac{1}{2}$ Find the product of the first two factors. One is positive and one is negative, so the product is negative.

$-\frac{1}{2}\left(-\frac{2}{5}\right) = \frac{1}{5}$ Multiply the result by the third factor. Both are negative, so the product is positive.

$3\left(-\frac{1}{6}\right)\left(-\frac{2}{5}\right) = \frac{1}{5}$

EXAMPLE 4

Find the quotient: $\frac{15.2}{-2}$.

$\frac{15.2}{-2} = -7.6$ The quotient is negative because the signs are different.

EXAMPLE 5

A lake's level dropped an average of $3\frac{4}{5}$ inches per day for 21 days. A heavy rain then raised the level 8.25 feet, after which it dropped $9\frac{1}{2}$ inches per day for 4 days. Jayden says that overall, the lake level changed about $-1\frac{1}{2}$ feet. Is this answer reasonable?

Yes; the lake drops about 4 inches, or $\frac{1}{3}$ foot, per day for 21 days, rises about 8 feet, then falls about $\frac{3}{4}$ foot for 4 days:
$$-\frac{1}{3}(21) + 8 - \frac{3}{4}(4) = -7 + 8 - 3 = -2 \text{ feet.}$$

EXAMPLE 6

Cole receives an allowance of \$10 a week plus \$1 for every chore he completes. Finn gets \$15 a week plus \$0.75 per chore he completes. If c represents the number of chores, write an expression to represent how much they both will be paid if each completes the same number of chores.

Cole: \$10 + \$1c Finn: \$15 + \$0.75c	*Base pay + chore rate*
$10 + 1c + 15 + 0.75c$	*Combine the rates.*
$10 + 15 + 1c + 0.75c$	*Use the Commutative Property.*
$25 + 1.75c$	*Combine like terms.*

EXERCISES

Write each mixed number as a whole number or decimal. Classify each number according to the group(s) to which it belongs: rational numbers, integers, or whole numbers. (Lesson 19.1)

1. $\frac{3}{4}$ _____

2. $\frac{8}{2}$ _____

Find each sum or difference. (Lessons 19.2, 19.3)

3. $-5 + 9.5$ _____

4. $\frac{1}{6} + \left(-\frac{5}{6}\right)$ _____

5. $-0.5 + (-8.5)$ _____

Find each product or quotient. (Lessons 19.4, 19.5)

6. $-9 \times (-5)$ _____

7. $\frac{-130}{-5}$ _____

8. $\left(\frac{1}{5}\right)\left(-\frac{5}{7}\right)\left(\frac{3}{4}\right)$ _____

9. Dan is cutting 4.75 foot lengths of twine from a 240 foot spool of twine. He needs to cut 42 lengths, and says that 40.5 feet of twine will remain. Show that this is reasonable.

_____

Write an expression. (Lesson 19.6)

10. The drama club is selling tickets to the Spring play. Adult tickets a cost \$10 and youth tickets y cost \$7.50. The drama club keeps 35% of each ticket sold. Write an expression to show how much the drama club makes on the Spring play.

_____

© Houghton Mifflin Harcourt Publishing Company

1. **CAREERS IN MATH** Urban Planner Armand is an urban planner, and he has proposed a site for a new town library. The site is between City Hall and the post office on Main Street.

City Hall   Library site   Post office

The distance between City Hall and the post office is $6\frac{1}{2}$ miles. City Hall is $1\frac{1}{4}$ miles closer to the library site than it is to the post office.

   a. Write $6\frac{1}{2}$ miles and $1\frac{1}{4}$ miles as decimals.

   _____

   b. Let d represent the distance from City Hall to the library site. Write an expression for the distance from the library site to the post office.

   _____

   c. Write an equation that represents the following statement: The distance from City Hall to the library site plus the distance from the library site to the post office is equal to the distance from City Hall to the post office.

   _____

   d. Solve your equation from part **c** to determine the distance from City Hall to the library site, and the distance from the post office to the library site.

   _____

   _____

2. Sumaya is reading a book with 288 pages. She has already read 90 pages. She plans to read 20 more pages each day until she finishes the book.

   a. Sumaya writes the equation $378 = -20d$ to find the number of days she will need to finish the book. Identify the errors that Sumaya made.

   _____

   _____

   b. Write and solve an equation to determine how many days Sumaya will need to finish the book. In your answer, count part of a day as a full day. Show that your answer is reasonable.

   _____

   _____

c. Estimate how many days you would need to read a book about the same length as Sumaya's book. What information did you use to find the estimate?

_____

_____

_____

3. Jackson works as a veterinary technician and earns $12.20 per hour.

a. Jackson normally works 40 hours a week. In a normal week, what is his total pay before taxes and other deductions?

_____

b. Last week, Jackson was ill and missed some work. His total pay before deductions was $372.10. Write and solve an equation to find the number of hours Jackson worked.

_____

c. Jackson records his hours each day on a time sheet. Last week when he was ill, his time sheet was incomplete. How many hours are missing? Show your work. Then show that your answer is reasonable.

Mon	Tues	Wed	Thurs	Fri
8	$7\frac{1}{4}$	$8\frac{1}{2}$		

_____

_____

_____

d. When Jackson works more than 40 hours in a week, he earns 1.5 times his normal hourly rate for each of the extra hours. Jackson worked 43 hours one week. What was his total pay before deductions? Justify your answer.

_____

_____

e. Jackson's sister works with him as a pet groomer. She makes $9 an hour. When she works more than 40 hours a week, she earns 1.25 times her normal hourly rate for each of the extra hours. If *h* represents hours worked, write an expression to show how much Jackson and his sister will be paid if they both work extra hours this week.

_____

_____

© Houghton Mifflin Harcourt Publishing Company

UNIT 8 MIXED REVIEW
Assessment Readiness

Personal
Math Trainer

my.hrw.com

Online
Assessment and
Intervention

Selected Response

1. What is $-6\frac{9}{16}$ written as a decimal?

①(A) -6.625

②(B) -6.5625

③(C) -6.4375

④(D) -6.125

2. Working together, 6 friends pick $14\frac{2}{5}$ pounds of pecans at a pecan farm. They divide the pecans equally among themselves. How many pounds does each friend get?

(A) $20\frac{2}{5}$ pounds

(B) $8\frac{2}{5}$ pounds

(C) $2\frac{3}{5}$ pounds

(D) $2\frac{2}{5}$ pounds

3. What is the value of $(-3.25)(-1.56)$?

(A) -5.85

(B) -5.07

(C) 5.07

(D) 5.85

4. Mrs. Rodriguez is going to use $6\frac{1}{3}$ yards of material to make two dresses. The larger dress requires $3\frac{2}{3}$ yards of material. How much material will Mrs. Rodriguez have left to use on the smaller dress?

(A) $1\frac{2}{3}$ yards

(B) $2\frac{1}{3}$ yards

(C) $2\frac{2}{3}$ yards

(D) $3\frac{1}{3}$ yards

5. Jaime had $37 in his bank account on Sunday. The table shows his account activity for the next four days. What was the balance in Jaime's account after his deposit on Thursday?

Jamie's Bank Account		
Day	Deposit	Withdrawal
Monday	$17.42	none
Tuesday	none	$-$12.60
Wednesday	none	$-$9.62
Thursday	$62.29	none

(A) $57.49

(B) $59.65

(C) $94.49

(D) $138.93

6. A used motorcycle is on sale for $3,600. Erik makes an offer equal to $\frac{3}{4}$ of this price. How much does Erik offer for the motorcycle?

(A) $4,800

(B) $2,700

(C) $2,400

(D) $900

7. Ruby ate $\frac{1}{3}$ of a pizza, and Angie ate $\frac{1}{5}$ of the pizza. How much of the pizza did they eat in all?

(A) $\frac{1}{15}$ of the pizza

(B) $\frac{1}{8}$ of the pizza

(C) $\frac{3}{8}$ of the pizza

(D) $\frac{8}{15}$ of the pizza

8. Winslow buys 1.2 pounds of bananas. The bananas cost $1.29 per pound. To the nearest cent, how much does Winslow pay for the bananas?

Ⓐ $1.08

Ⓑ $1.20

Ⓒ $1.55

Ⓓ $2.49

9. The temperature was $-10\,°F$ and dropped by $16\,°F$. Which statement represents the resulting temperature in degrees Fahrenheit?

Ⓐ $-10 - (-16) = -6$

Ⓑ $-10 - 16 = -26$

Ⓒ $10 - (-16) = 26$

Ⓓ $-10 + 16 = 6$

10. A scuba diver at a depth of -12 ft (12 ft below sea level), dives down to a coral reef that is 3.5 times the diver's original depth. What is the diver's new depth?

Ⓐ -420 ft

Ⓑ -42 ft

Ⓒ 42 ft

Ⓓ about 3.4 ft

11. The school Drama Club keeps $\frac{1}{5}$ of the money from tickets sold at the spring play. Adult tickets a cost $15 each and children's tickets c cost $10 each. Which expression represents how much money the Drama Club will make?

Ⓐ $\frac{1}{5}a + \frac{1}{5}c$

Ⓑ $\frac{1}{5}(15a + 10a)$

Ⓒ $\frac{1}{5}(\$15a + \$10c)$

Ⓓ $(a + c)(0.20)$

12. Lila graphed the points -2 and 2 on a number line. What does the distance between these two points represent?

Ⓐ the sum of -2 and 2

Ⓑ the difference of 2 and -2

Ⓒ the difference of -2 and 2

Ⓓ the product of -2 and 2

 Some answer choices, called distracters, may seem correct because they are based on common errors.

13. What is a reasonable estimate of $-3\frac{4}{5} + (-5.25)$ and the actual value?

Ⓐ $-4 + (-5) = -9;\ -9\frac{1}{20}$

Ⓑ $-3 + (-5) = -8;\ -8\frac{1}{20}$

Ⓒ $-4 + (-5) = -1;\ -8\frac{9}{20}$

Ⓓ $-3 + (-5) = 8;\ 8\frac{1}{20}$

Mini-Task

14. Juanita is watering her lawn using the water stored in her rainwater tank. The water level in the tank drops $\frac{1}{3}$ inch every 10 minutes she waters.

a. What is the change in the tank's water level after 1 hour?

_____

b. What is the expected change in the tank's water level after 2.25 hours?

_____

c. If the tank's water level is 4 feet, how many days can Juanita water if she waters for 15 minutes each day?

_____

Ratios and Proportional Relationships

MODULE **20**

Rates and Proportionality

FL 7.RP.1.1, 7.RP.1.2,
7.RP.1.2a, 7.RP.1.2b,
7.RP.1.2c, 7.RP.1.2d

MODULE **21**

Proportions and Percents

FL 7.RP.1.3, 7.EE.1.2,
7.EE.2.3

CAREERS IN MATH

Bicycle Tour Operator A bike tour operator organizes cycling trips for tourists all over the world. Bike tour operators use math to calculate expenses, determine rates, and compute payroll information for their employees. If tours include travel in another country, operators must understand how to calculate currency exchange rates.

If you are interested in a career as a bicycle tour operator, you should study these mathematical subjects:
• Basic Math
• Business Math

Research other careers that require the understanding of business mathematics.

Unit 9 Performance Task

At the end of the unit, check out how **bicycle tour operators** use math.

© Houghton Mifflin Harcourt Publishing Company • Image Credits: KAREN BLEIER/AFP/Getty Images

Vocabulary Preview

Use the puzzle to preview key vocabulary from this unit. Unscramble the circled letters within found words to answer the riddle at the bottom of the page.

1. A relationship between two quantities in which the rate of change or the ratio of one quantity to the other is constant. (Lesson 20.3)

◯__ ◯__ __ __ __ __ __ __ __ __ __

◯__ __ __ __ __ ◯__ __ __ __ __ __

2. Describes how much a quantity decreases in comparison to the original

amount. (Lesson 21.1) __ __ ◯__ __ __ __ __

__ __ __ __ __ __ __ __ __

3. A fixed percent of the principal. (Lesson 21.3)

__ __ __ __ __ __   __ __ ◯__ __ __ __ ◯__

4. The quantity *k* in a relationship described by an equation of the form *y = kx*. (Lesson 20.3)

__ ◯__ __ __ __ __ __ __ __   __ __

__ __ __ __ __ __ __ __ ◯__ __ __

5. A ratio that compares the amount of change in the dependent variable to the amount of change in the independent variable. (Lesson 20.2)

◯__ __ __ ◯__ __   __ __ __ __ __ __

Q: What did the athlete order when he needed a huge helping of mashed potatoes?

A: __ __ __ __ __ - __ __ __ __ __ __ __ !

Rates and Proportionality

ESSENTIAL QUESTION

How can you use rates and proportionality to solve real-world problems?

LESSON 20.1
Unit Rates
 FL 7.RP.1.1

LESSON 20.2
Constant Rates of Change
FL 7.RP.1.2, 7.RP.1.2a, 7.RP.1.2b, 7.RP.1.2c

LESSON 20.3
Proportional Relationships and Graphs
FL 7.RP.1.2a, 7.RP.1.2b, 7.RP.1.2c, 7.RP.1.2d

Real-World Video

You can use rates to describe lots of real-world situations. A cyclist can compute rates such as miles per hour or rotations per minute.

my.hrw.com

GO DIGITAL
my.hrw.com

my.hrw.com

Go digital with your write-in student edition, accessible on any device.

Math On the Spot

Scan with your smart phone to jump directly to the online edition, video tutor, and more.

Animated Math

Interactively explore key concepts to see how math works.

Personal Math Trainer

Get immediate feedback and help as you work through practice sets.

607

Are YOU Ready?

Complete these exercises to review skills you will need for this module.

Operations with Fractions

EXAMPLE $\dfrac{3}{10} \div \dfrac{5}{8} = \dfrac{3}{10} \times \dfrac{8}{5}$ Multiply by the reciprocal of the divisor.

$= \dfrac{3}{\overset{}{10}_5} \times \dfrac{\overset{4}{8}}{5}$ Divide by the common factors.

$= \dfrac{12}{25}$ Simplify.

Divide.

1. $\dfrac{3}{4} \div \dfrac{4}{5}$ _____

2. $\dfrac{5}{9} \div \dfrac{10}{11}$ _____

3. $\dfrac{3}{8} \div \dfrac{1}{2}$ _____

4. $\dfrac{16}{21} \div \dfrac{8}{9}$ _____

Ordered Pairs

EXAMPLE

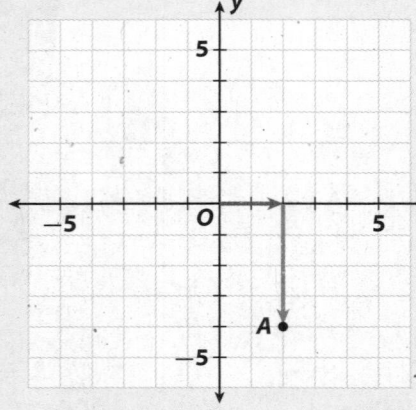

To write the ordered pair for A, start at the origin.
Move 2 units right.
Then move 4 units down.
The ordered pair for point A is (2, −4).

Write the ordered pair for each point.

5. B _____

6. C _____

7. D _____

8. E _____

9. F _____

10. G _____

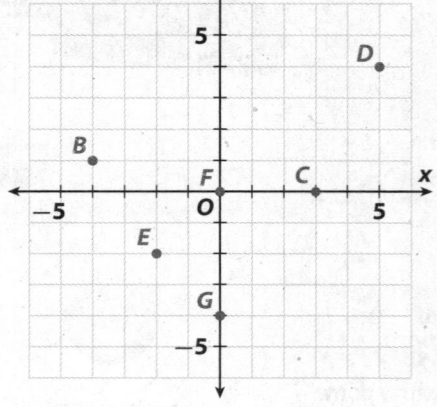

Reading Start-Up

Visualize Vocabulary

Use the ✔ words to complete the graphic. You can put more than one word in each bubble.

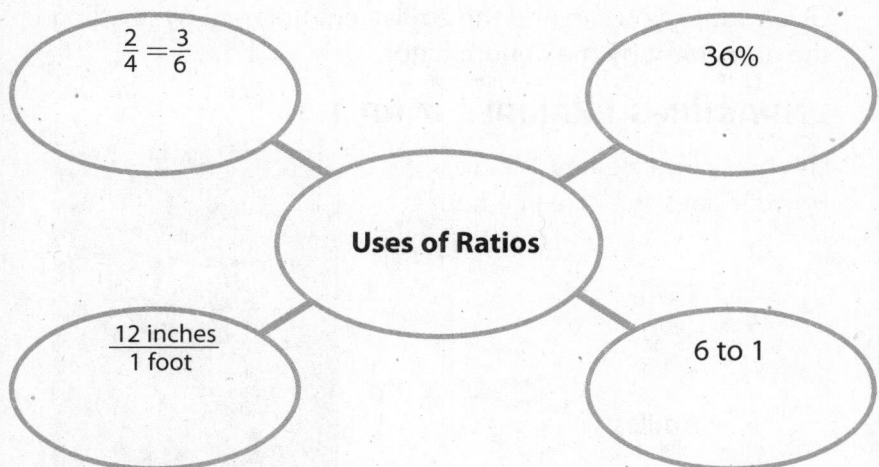

$\frac{2}{4} = \frac{3}{6}$

36%

Uses of Ratios

$\frac{12 \text{ inches}}{1 \text{ foot}}$

6 to 1

Vocabulary

Review Words

constant *(constante)*

✔ conversion factor *(factor de conversión)*

✔ equivalent ratios *(razones equivalentes)*

✔ percent *(porcentaje)*

rate *(tasa)*

✔ ratio *(razón)*

Preview Words

complex fraction *(fracción compleja)*

constant of proportionality *(constante de proporcionalidad)*

proportion *(proporción)*

proportional relationship *(relación proporcional)*

rate of change *(tasa de cambio)*

unit rates *(tasas unitarias)*

Understand Vocabulary

Match the term on the left to the definition on the right.

1. rate of change

2. proportion

3. unit rate

A. Statement that two rates or ratios are equivalent.

B. A rate that describes how one quantity changes in relation to another quantity.

C. Rate in which the second quantity is one unit.

Active Reading

Three-Panel Flip Chart Before beginning the module, create a three-panel flip chart to help you organize what you learn. Label each flap with one of the lesson titles from this module. As you study each lesson, write important ideas like vocabulary, properties, and formulas under the appropriate flap.

Unpacking the Standards

Understanding the standards and the vocabulary terms in the standards will help you know exactly what you are expected to learn in this module.

FL 7.RP.1.1

Compute unit rates associated with ratios of fractions, including ratios of lengths, areas and other quantities measured in like or different units.

Key Vocabulary

rate *(tasa)*
A ratio that compares two quantities measured in different units.

unit rate *(tasa unitaria)*
A rate in which the second quantity in the comparison is one unit.

What It Means to You

Given a rate, you can find the equivalent unit rate by dividing the numerator by the denominator.

UNPACKING EXAMPLE 7.RP.1.1

Lisa hikes $\frac{1}{3}$ mile every $\frac{1}{6}$ hour. How far does she hike in 1 hour?

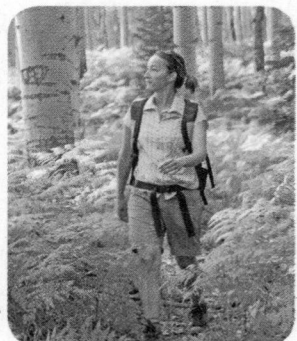

$$\frac{\frac{1}{3}}{\frac{1}{6}} = \frac{1}{3} \div \frac{1}{6}$$

$$= \frac{1}{3} \cdot \frac{\overset{2}{\cancel{6}}}{1}$$

$$= 2 \text{ miles}$$

FL 7.RP.1.2b

Identify the constant of proportionality (unit rate) in tables, graphs, equations, diagrams, and verbal descriptions of proportional relationships.

Key Vocabulary

constant *(constante)*
A value that does not change.

constant of proportionality *(constante de proporcionalidad)*
A constant ratio of two variables related proportionally.

What It Means to You

You will determine the constant of proportionality for proportional relationships.

UNPACKING EXAMPLE 7.RP.1.2b

The graph shows the distance a bicyclist travels over time. How fast does the bicyclist travel?

$$\text{slope (speed)} = \frac{\text{rise (distance)}}{\text{run (time)}}$$

$$= \frac{15}{1}$$

The bicyclist travels at 15 miles per hour.

The bicyclist's speed is a unit rate. It is indicated on the graphed line by the point (1, 15).

Visit **my.hrw.com** to see all **Florida Math Standards** unpacked.

my.hrw.com

LESSON
20.1 Unit Rates

  FL 7.RP.1.1

Compute unit rates associated with ratios of fractions, including ratios of lengths, areas and other quantities measured in like or different units.

? ESSENTIAL QUESTION

How do you find and use unit rates?

EXPLORE ACTIVITY Real World   **FL 7.RP.1.1**

Exploring Rates

Commonly used rates like miles per hour make it easy to understand and compare rates.

Jeff hikes $\frac{1}{2}$ mile every 15 minutes, or $\frac{1}{4}$ hour. Lisa hikes $\frac{1}{3}$ mile every 10 minutes, or $\frac{1}{6}$ hour. How far do they each hike in 1 hour? 2 hours?

A Use the bar diagram to help you determine how many miles Jeff hikes. How many $\frac{1}{4}$-hours are in 1 hour? How far does Jeff hike in 1 hour?

? miles

| $\frac{1}{4}$ hour | $\frac{1}{4}$ hour | $\frac{1}{4}$ hour | $\frac{1}{4}$ hour |

$\frac{1}{2}$ mile

_____

B Complete the table for Jeff's hike.

Distance (mi)	$\frac{1}{2}$				
Time (h)	$\frac{1}{4}$	$\frac{1}{2}$	$\frac{3}{4}$	1	2

C Complete the bar diagram to help you determine how far Lisa hikes. How many miles does she hike in 1 hour?

| $\frac{1}{6}$ hour | $\frac{1}{6}$ hour | $\frac{1}{6}$ hour | $\frac{1}{6}$ hour | $\frac{1}{6}$ hour | $\frac{1}{6}$ hour |

_____

D Complete the table for Lisa's hike.

Distance (mi)	$\frac{1}{3}$				
Time (h)	$\frac{1}{6}$	$\frac{1}{3}$	$\frac{1}{2}$	1	2

© Houghton Mifflin Harcourt Publishing Company

Reflect

1. How did you find Jeff's distance for $\frac{3}{4}$ hour?

_____

2. Which hiker walks farther in one hour? Which is faster?

_____

Math On the Spot

my.hrw.com

Finding Unit Rates

A rate is a comparison of two quantities that have different units, such as miles and hours. Rates are often expressed as **unit rates**, that is, with a denominator of 1 unit.

$$\frac{60 \text{ miles} \div 2}{2 \text{ hours} \div 2} = \frac{30 \text{ miles}}{1 \text{ hour}}$$ This means 30 miles per hour.

When the two quantities being compared in the rate are both fractions, the rate is expressed as a *complex fraction*. A **complex fraction** is a fraction that has a fraction in its numerator, denominator, or both.

$$\frac{\frac{a}{b}}{\frac{c}{d}} = \frac{a}{b} \div \frac{c}{d}$$

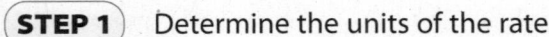

EXAMPLE 1   Real World   FL 7.RP.1.1

While remodeling her kitchen, Angela is repainting. She estimates that she paints 55 square feet every half-hour. How many square feet does Angela paint per hour?

STEP 1   Determine the units of the rate.

The rate is **area in square feet** per **time in hours**.

STEP 2   Find Angela's rate of painting in area painted per time.

area painted: 55 sq ft   **time:** $\frac{1}{2}$ hour

$$\frac{\text{area painted}}{\text{time}} = \frac{55 \text{ square feet}}{\frac{1}{2} \text{ hour}}$$

> The fraction represents area in square feet per time in hours.

STEP 3   Find Angela's unit rate of painting in square feet per hour.

$$\frac{55}{\frac{1}{2}} = 55 \div \frac{1}{2}$$ Rewrite the fraction as division.

$$= \frac{55}{1} \times \frac{2}{1}$$ Multiply by the reciprocal.

$$= \frac{110 \text{ square feet}}{1 \text{ hour}}$$

> The unit rate has a denominator of 1.

Angela paints 110 square feet per hour.

YOUR TURN

3. Paige mows $\frac{1}{6}$ acre in $\frac{1}{4}$ hour. How many acres does Paige mow per hour?

   _____

4. Greta uses 3 ounces of pasta to make $\frac{3}{4}$ of a serving of pasta. How many

   ounces of pasta are there per serving? _____

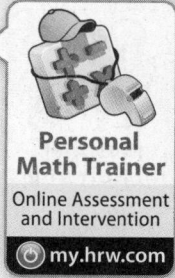
Using Unit Rates

You can use unit rates to simplify rates and ratios that appear complicated, such as those containing fractions in both the numerator and denominator.

EXAMPLE 2 Real World   🏴 FL   7.RP.1.1

Two pools are leaking. After 15 minutes, pool A has leaked $\frac{2}{3}$ gallon. After 20 minutes, pool B has leaked $\frac{3}{4}$ gallon. Which pool is leaking faster?

My Notes

STEP 1 Find the rate in volume (gallons) per time (hours) at which each pool is leaking. First convert minutes to hours.

Pool A

$$\frac{\frac{2}{3}\text{ gal}}{15\text{ min}} = \frac{\frac{2}{3}\text{ gal}}{\frac{1}{4}\text{ h}}$$

$15\text{ min} = \frac{1}{4}\text{ h}$

Pool B

$$\frac{\frac{3}{4}\text{ gal}}{20\text{ min}} = \frac{\frac{3}{4}\text{ gal}}{\frac{1}{3}\text{ h}}$$

$20\text{ min} = \frac{1}{3}\text{ h}$

STEP 2 To find the unit rates, first rewrite the fractions.

Pool A

$$\frac{\frac{2}{3}\text{ gal}}{\frac{1}{4}\text{ h}} = \frac{2}{3} \div \frac{1}{4}$$

Pool B

$$\frac{\frac{3}{4}\text{ gal}}{\frac{1}{3}\text{ h}} = \frac{3}{4} \div \frac{1}{3}$$

STEP 3 To divide, multiply by the reciprocal.

Pool A

$$\frac{2}{3} \div \frac{1}{4} = \frac{2}{3} \times \frac{4}{1}$$
$$= \frac{8}{3}, \text{ or } 2\frac{2}{3}\text{ gal per h}$$

Pool B

$$\frac{3}{4} \div \frac{1}{3} = \frac{3}{4} \times \frac{3}{1}$$
$$= \frac{9}{4}, \text{ or } 2\frac{1}{4}\text{ gal per h}$$

STEP 4 Compare the unit rates.

Pool A   Pool B

$$2\frac{2}{3} \ > \ 2\frac{1}{4}$$

So, Pool A is leaking faster.

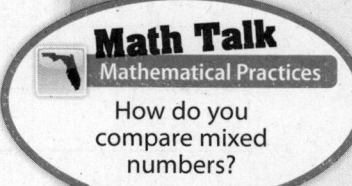

Math Talk

Mathematical Practices

How do you compare mixed numbers?

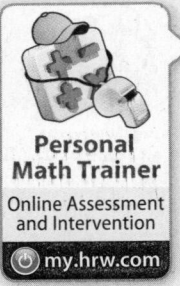
YOUR TURN

5. One tank is filling at a rate of $\frac{3}{4}$ gallon per $\frac{2}{3}$ minute. A second tank is filling at a rate of $\frac{5}{8}$ gallon per $\frac{1}{2}$ minute. Which tank is filling faster?

_____

Guided Practice

1. Brandon enters bike races. He bikes $8\frac{1}{2}$ miles every $\frac{1}{2}$ hour. Complete the table to find how far Brandon bikes for each time interval. (Explore Activity)

Distance (mi)	$8\frac{1}{2}$				
Time (h)	$\frac{1}{2}$	1	$1\frac{1}{2}$	2	$2\frac{1}{2}$

Find each unit rate. (Example 1)

2. Julio walks $3\frac{1}{2}$ miles in $1\frac{1}{4}$ hours.

_____

3. Kenny reads $\frac{5}{8}$ page in $\frac{2}{3}$ minute.

_____

4. A garden snail moves $\frac{1}{6}$ foot in $\frac{1}{3}$ hour.

_____

5. A machine covers $\frac{5}{8}$ square foot in $\frac{1}{4}$ hour.

_____

Find each unit rate. Determine which is lower. (Example 2)

6. Brand A: 240 mg sodium for $\frac{1}{3}$ pickle
or Brand B: 325 mg sodium for $\frac{1}{2}$ pickle

_____

_____

_____

7. Ingredient C: $\frac{1}{4}$ cup for $\frac{2}{3}$ serving
or Ingredient D: $\frac{1}{3}$ cup for $\frac{3}{4}$ serving

_____

_____

_____

 ESSENTIAL QUESTION CHECK-IN

8. How can you find a unit rate when given a rate?

_____

_____

_____

_____

20.1 Independent Practice

9. The information for two pay-as-you-go cell phone companies is given.

On Call	Talk Time
3.5 hours: $10	$\frac{1}{2}$ hour: $1.25

a. What is the unit rate in dollars per hour for each company?

_____

_____

b. **Analyze Relationships** Which company offers the best deal? Explain your answer.

_____

c. **What If?** Another company offers a rate of $0.05 per minute. How would you find the unit rate per hour?

_____

_____

d. **Draw Conclusions** Is the rate in part **c** a better deal than On Call or Talk Time? Explain.

_____

_____

10. **Represent Real-World Problems** Your teacher asks you to find a recipe that includes two ingredients with a rate of $\frac{2 \text{ units}}{3 \text{ units}}$.

a. Give an example of two ingredients in a recipe that would meet this requirement.

_____

_____

b. If you needed to triple the recipe, would the rate change? Explain.

_____

_____

_____

_____

11. A radio station requires DJs to play 2 commercials for every 10 songs they play. What is the unit rate of songs to commercials?

_____

12. **Multistep** Terrance and Jesse are training for a long-distance race. Terrance trains at a rate of 6 miles every half hour, and Jesse trains at a rate of 2 miles every 15 minutes.

a. What is the unit rate in miles per hour for each runner?

_____

_____

b. How long will each person take to run a total of 50 miles at the given rates?

_____

_____

c. Sandra runs at a rate of 8 miles in 45 minutes. How does her unit rate compare to Terrance's and to Jesse's?

_____

_____

_____

13. Analyze Relationships Eli takes a typing test and types all 300 words in $\frac{1}{10}$ hour. He takes the test a second time and types the words in $\frac{1}{12}$ hour. Was he faster or slower on the second attempt? Explain.

_____

_____

Work Area

14. Justify Reasoning An online retailer sells two packages of protein bars.

Package	10-pack of 2.1 ounce bars	12-pack of 1.4 ounce bars
Cost ($)	15.37	15.35

a. Which package has the better price per bar?

_____

_____

_____

b. Which package has the better price per ounce?

_____

_____

_____

c. Which package do you think is a better buy? Justify your reasoning.

_____

_____

15. Check for Reasonableness A painter painted about half a room in half a day. Coley estimated the painter would paint 7 rooms in 7 days. Is Coley's estimate reasonable? Explain.

_____

_____

16. Communicate Mathematical Ideas If you know the rate of a water leak in gallons per hour, how can you find the number of hours it takes for 1 gallon to leak out? Justify your answer.

_____

_____

_____

Constant Rates of Change

FL   7.RP.1.2

Recognize and represent
proportional relationships
between quantities. *Also*
7.RP.1.2a, 7.RP.1.2b,
7.RP.1.2c

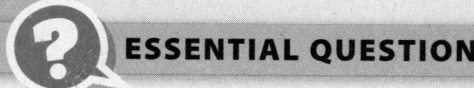

? ESSENTIAL QUESTION

How can you identify and represent proportional relationships?

EXPLORE ACTIVITY   FL   7.RP.1.2a

Discovering Proportional Relationships

Many real-world situations can be described by *proportional relationships*.
Proportional relationships have special characteristics.

**A giant tortoise moves at a slow but steady pace. It takes the
giant tortoise 3 seconds to travel 10.5 inches.**

A Use the bar diagram to help you determine
how many inches a tortoise travels in 1 second.
What operation did you use to find the answer?

_____

B Complete the table.

Time (sec)	1	2	3	4	5
Distance (in.)			10.5		

C For each column of the table, find the distance and the time. Write
each fraction as a decimal. Put distance in the numerator and time in
the denominator.

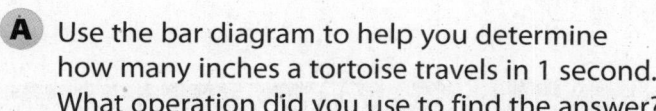

D What do you notice about the decimal forms of the fractions?

_____

E **Conjecture** How do you think the distance a tortoise travels is related
to the time?

_____

Reflect

1. Suppose the tortoise travels for 12 seconds. Explain how you could find the distance the tortoise travels.

_____

2. How would you describe the rate of speed at which a tortoise travels?

_____

Math On the Spot

🔵 my.hrw.com

Proportional Relationships

A **rate of change** is a rate that describes how one quantity changes in relation to another quantity. A **proportional relationship** between two quantities is one in which the rate of change is constant, or one in which the ratio of one quantity to the other is constant.

Any two rates or ratios based on a given proportional relationship can be used to form a *proportion*. A **proportion** is a statement that two rates or ratios are equivalent, for example, $\frac{6 \text{ mi}}{2 \text{ h}} = \frac{3 \text{ mi}}{1 \text{ h}}$, or $\frac{2}{4} = \frac{1}{2}$.

My Notes

EXAMPLE 1 (Real World)   FL   7.RP.1.2a, 7.RP.1.2b

Callie earns money by dog sitting. Based on the table, is the relationship between the amount Callie earns and the number of days a proportional relationship?

Number of Days	1	2	3	4	5
Amount Earned ($)	16	32	48	64	80

STEP 1 Write the rates.

$\dfrac{\text{Amount earned}}{\text{Number of days}} = \dfrac{\$16}{1 \text{ day}}$ Put the amount earned in the numerator and the number of days in the denominator.

$\dfrac{\$32}{2 \text{ days}} = \dfrac{\$16}{1 \text{ day}}$

$\dfrac{\$48}{3 \text{ days}} = \dfrac{\$16}{1 \text{ day}}$ Each rate is equal to $\frac{\$16}{1 \text{ day}}$, or $16 per day.

$\dfrac{\$64}{4 \text{ days}} = \dfrac{\$16}{1 \text{ day}}$

$\dfrac{\$80}{5 \text{ days}} = \dfrac{\$16}{1 \text{ day}}$

Math Talk

Mathematical Practices

How can you use the constant rate to find how much Callie earns for 10 days of dog sitting?

STEP 2 Compare the rates. The rates are all equal. This means the rate is constant, so the relationship is proportional.

The constant rate of change is $16 per day.

YOUR TURN

3. The table shows the distance Allison drove on one day of her vacation. Is the relationship between the distance and the time a proportional relationship? Did she drive at a constant speed? Explain.

Time (h)	1	2	3	4	5
Distance (mi)	65	120	195	220	300

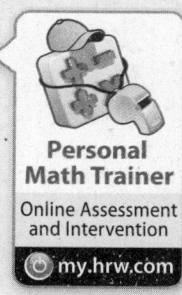
Writing an Equation for a Proportional Relationship

If there is a proportional relationship between x and y, you can describe that relationship using the equation $y = kx$. The variable k is called the **constant of proportionality**, and it represents the constant rate of change or constant ratio between x and y. The value of k is represented by the equation $k = \frac{y}{x}$.

Math On the Spot

my.hrw.com

EXAMPLE 2

 FL 7.RP.1.2c, 7.RP.1.2b

Two pounds of cashews shown cost $19, and 8 pounds cost $76. Show that the relationship between the number of pounds of cashews and the cost is a proportional relationship. Then write an equation for the relationship.

STEP 1 Make a table relating cost in dollars to pounds.

Number of Pounds	2	3	8
Cost ($)	19	28.50	76

STEP 2 Write the rates. Put cost in the numerator and pounds in the denominator. Then simplify each rate.

$$\frac{\text{Cost}}{\text{Number of Pounds}} \longrightarrow \quad \frac{19}{2} = 9.50 \qquad \frac{28.50}{3} = 9.50 \qquad \frac{76}{8} = 9.50$$

The rates are all equal to $9.50 per pound. They are constant, so the relationship is proportional. The constant rate of change is $9.50 per pound.

STEP 3 To write an equation, first tell what the variables represent.

- Let x represent the number of pounds of cashews.
- Let y represent the cost in dollars.
- Use the numerical part of the constant rate of change as the constant of proportionality.

So, the equation for the relationship is $y = 9.5x$.

Math Talk
Mathematical Practices

How can you use your equation to find the cost of 6 pounds of cashews?

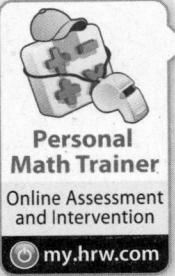
YOUR TURN

4. For a school field trip, there must be 1 adult to accompany 12 students, 3 adults to accompany 36 students, and 5 adults to accompany 60 students. Show that the relationship between the number of adults and the number of students is a proportional relationship. Then write an equation for the relationship.

Number of students	12	36	60
Number of adults	1	3	5

_____

_____

Guided Practice

1. Based on the information in the table, is the relationship between time and the number of words typed a proportional relationship? (Explore Activity and Example 1)

Time (min)	1	2	3	4
Number of words	45	90	135	180

$\dfrac{\text{Number of words}}{\text{Minutes}}$: $\dfrac{45}{1} = \boxed{}$ $\dfrac{\boxed{}}{\boxed{}} = \boxed{}$ $\dfrac{\boxed{}}{\boxed{}} = \boxed{}$ $\dfrac{\boxed{}}{\boxed{}} = \boxed{}$

The relationship   **is / is not**   proportional.

Find the constant of proportionality k. Then write an equation for the relationship between x and y. (Example 2)

2.

x	2	4	6	8
y	10	20	30	40

3.

x	8	16	24	32
y	2	4	6	8

_____

_____

? ESSENTIAL QUESTION CHECK-IN

4. How can you represent a proportional relationship using an equation?

_____

_____

20.2 Independent Practice

FL 7.RP.1.2, 7.RP.1.2a, 7.RP.1.2b, 7.RP.1.2c

Personal Math Trainer

Online Assessment and Intervention

ⓑ my.hrw.com

Information on three car-rental companies is given.

5. Write an equation that gives the cost *y* of renting a car for *x* days from Rent-All. _____

6. What is the cost per day of renting a car from A-1? _____

7. Analyze Relationships Which company offers the best deal? Why?

_____

_____

Rent-All				
Days	3	4	5	6
Total Cost ($)	55.50	74.00	92.50	111.00

A-1 Rentals	**Car Town**
The cost *y* of renting a car for *x* days is $10.99 for each half day.	The cost of renting a car from us is just $19.25 per day!

8. Critique Reasoning A skydiver jumps out of an airplane. After 0.8 second, she has fallen 100 feet. After 3.1 seconds, she has fallen 500 feet. Emtiaz says that the skydiver should fall about 187.5 feet in 1.5 seconds. Is his answer reasonable? Explain.

_____

_____

_____

Steven earns extra money babysitting. He charges $31.25 for 5 hours and $50 for 8 hours.

9. Explain why the relationship between how much Steven charges and time is a proportional relationship.

_____

10. Interpret the Answer Explain what the constant rate of change means in the context.

_____

11. Write an equation to represent the relationship. Tell what the variables represent.

_____

_____

12. How much would Steven charge for 3 hours? _____

A submarine dives 300 feet every 2 minutes, and 6,750 feet every 45 minutes.

13. Find the constant rate at which the submarine dives. Give your answer in feet per minute and in feet per hour.

_____

14. Let *x* represent the time of the dive. Let *y* represent the depth of the submarine. Write an equation for the proportional relationship using the rate in feet per minute.

_____

15. **Draw Conclusions** If you wanted to find the depth of a submarine during a dive, would it be more reasonable to use an equation with the rate in feet per minute or feet per hour? Explain your reasoning.

_____

_____

 FOCUS ON HIGHER ORDER THINKING

16. **Make a Conjecture** There is a proportional relationship between your distance from a thunderstorm and the time from when you see lightning and hear thunder. If there are 9 seconds between lightning and thunder, the storm is about 3 kilometers away. If you double the amount of time between lightning and thunder, do you think the distance in kilometers also double? justify your reasoning.

_____

_____

_____

_____

17. **Communicate Mathematical Ideas** A store sells 3 ears of corn for $1. They round prices to the nearest cent as shown in the table. Tell whether you would describe the relationship between cost and number of ears of corn as a proportional relationship. Justify your answer.

Ears of corn	1	2	3	4
Amount charged ($)	0.33	0.67	1.00	1.34

_____

_____

_____

_____

Work Area

LESSON 20.3 Proportional Relationships and Graphs

Decide whether two quantities are in a proportional relationship, e.g., by...graphing on a coordinate plane and observing whether the graph is a straight line through the origin. *Also 7.RP.1.2b, 7.RP.1.2c, 7.RP.1.2d*

? **ESSENTIAL QUESTION**

How can you use graphs to represent and analyze proportional relationships?

EXPLORE ACTIVITY   FL 7.RP.1.2a

Graphing Proportional Relationships

You can use a graph to explore proportional relationships.

Most showerheads that were manufactured before 1994 use 5 gallons of water per minute. Is the relationship between the number of gallons of water and the number of minutes a proportional relationship?

> Each minute, 5 gallons of water are used. So for 2 minutes, 2 · 5 gallons are used.

A Complete the table.

Time (min)	1	2	3		10
Water Used (gal)	5			35	

B Based on the table, is this a proportional relationship? Explain your answer.

_____

C Write the data in the table as ordered pairs (time, water used).

(1, 5), (2, ___), (3, ___), (__ , 35), (10, ___)

D Plot the ordered pairs.

E If the showerhead is used for 0 minutes, how many gallons of water will be used? What ordered pair represents this situation? What is this location called?

_____

F **Draw Conclusions** If you continued the table to include 23 minutes, would the point (23, 125) be on this graph? Why or why not?

_____

_____

Water Use

Identifying Proportional Relationships

In addition to using a table to determine if a relationship is proportional, you also can use a graph. A relationship is a proportional relationship if its graph is a straight line through the origin.

EXAMPLE 1   FL   7.RP.1.2a, 7.RP.1.2d

A house cleaning company charges $45 per hour. Is the relationship a proportional relationship? Explain.

STEP 1 Make a table.

> Each hour costs $45. So for 2 hours, the cost is 2 · $45 = $90.

Time (h)	1	2	3	5	8
Total cost ($)	45	90	135	225	360

STEP 2 Write the data in the table as ordered pairs (time, cost).

(1, 45), (2, 90), (3, 135), (5, 225), (8, 360)

STEP 3 Graph the ordered pairs.

Place time on the x-axis and total cost on the y-axis.

Plot each point.

Connect the points with a line.

The graph is a line that goes through the origin.

So, the relationship is proportional. The point (1, 45) on the graph shows that the unit rate is $45 for 1 hour.

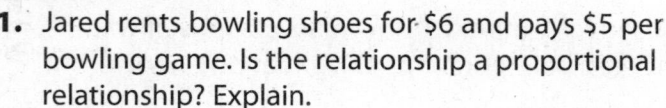

YOUR TURN

1. Jared rents bowling shoes for $6 and pays $5 per bowling game. Is the relationship a proportional relationship? Explain.

Games	1	2	3	4
Total Cost ($)	11	16	21	26

_____

_____

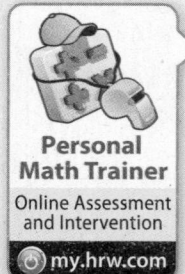
© Houghton Mifflin Harcourt Publishing Company

Analyzing Graphs

Recall that you can describe a proportional relationship with the equation $y = kx$. The constant of proportionality k tells you how steep the graph of the relationship is. The greater the absolute value of k, the steeper the line.

EXAMPLE 2   FL 7.RP.1.2d, 7.RP.1.2b, 7.RP.1.2c

The graph shows the relationship between time in minutes and the number of miles Damon runs. Write an equation for this relationship.

STEP 1 Choose a point on the graph and tell what the point represents.

The point (25, 2.5) represents the distance (2.5 miles) that Damon runs in 25 minutes.

STEP 2 What is the constant of proportionality?

Because $\frac{\text{distance}}{\text{time}} = \frac{2.5 \text{ mi}}{25 \text{ min}} = \frac{1}{10}$, the constant of proportionality is $\frac{1}{10}$.

STEP 3 Write an equation in the form $y = kx$.

$$y = \frac{1}{10} x$$

> The points appear to form a line through the origin so the relationship is proportional.

Reflect

2. **Communicate Mathematical Ideas** What does the point (0, 0) on the graph represent?

_____

3. **What If?** Suppose you drew a graph representing the relationship $y = \frac{1}{8} x$ between time in minutes and the number of miles Esther runs. How would the graph compare to the one for Damon? Explain.

_____

Math Talk
Mathematical Practices

What is the meaning of the point on the graph in Exercise 4 with x-coordinate 1?

YOUR TURN

4. The graph shows the relationship between the distance a bicyclist travels and the time in hours.

   a. What does the point (4, 60) represent?

   _____

   b. What is the constant of proportionality? _____

   c. Write an equation in the form $y = kx$ for this relationship. _____

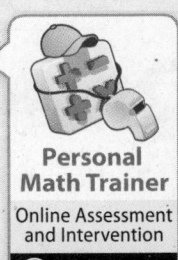

© Houghton Mifflin Harcourt Publishing Company

Complete each table. Tell whether the relationship is a proportional relationship. Explain why or why not. (Explore Activity)

1. A student reads 65 pages per hour.

Time (h)	3	5		10
Pages			585	

_____

_____

2. A babysitter makes $7.50 per hour.

Time (h)	2		5	
Amount ($)		22.50		60

_____

_____

Tell whether the relationship is a proportional relationship. Explain why or why not. (Explore Activity and Example 1)

3.   Chores

_____

_____

4.   Movie Rentals

_____

_____

Write an equation of the form $y = kx$ for the relationship shown in each graph. (Example 2)

5.

_____

6.

_____

? ESSENTIAL QUESTION CHECK-IN

7. How does a graph show a proportional relationship?

_____

20.3 Independent Practice

FL 7.RP.1.2a, 7.RP.1.2b, 7.RP.1.2c, 7.RP.1.2d

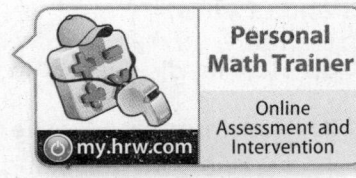

Personal Math Trainer

Online Assessment and Intervention

my.hrw.com

For Exercises 8–12, the graph shows the relationship between time and distance run by two horses.

8. Explain the meaning of the point (0, 0).

_____

_____

9. How long does it take each horse to run a mile?

_____

_____

10. Multiple Representations Write an equation for the relationship between time and distance for each horse.

_____

11. Draw Conclusions At the given rates, how far would each horse run in 12 minutes?

_____

_____

12. Analyze Relationships Draw a line on the graph representing a horse than runs faster than horses A and B.

_____

13. A bullet train can travel at 170 miles per hour. Will a graph representing distance in miles compared to time in hours show a proportional relationship? Explain.

_____

_____

_____

_____

14. Critical Thinking When would it be more useful to represent a proportional relationship with a graph rather than an equation?

_____

_____

_____

15. Multiple Representations Bargain DVDs cost $5 each at Mega Movie.

a. Graph the proportional relationship that gives the cost *y* in dollars of buying *x* bargain DVDs.

b. Give an ordered pair on the graph and explain its meaning in the real world context.

_____

_____

© Houghton Mifflin Harcourt Publishing Company

The graph shows the relationship between distance and time as Glenda swims.

16. How far did Glenda swim in 4 seconds? _____

17. **Communicate Mathematical Ideas** Is this a proportional relationship? Explain your reasoning.

_____

18. **Multiple Representations** Write an equation that shows the relationship

between time and distance. _____

 FOCUS ON HIGHER ORDER THINKING

19. **Make a Conjecture** If you know that a relationship is proportional and are given one ordered pair that is not (0, 0), how can you find another pair?

_____

_____

_____

The tables show the distance traveled by three cars.

Car 1	
Time (h)	Distance (mi)
0	0
2	120
3	180
5	300
6	360

Car 2	
Time (h)	Distance (mi)
0	0
5	200
10	400
15	600
20	800

Car 3	
Time (h)	Distance (mi)
0	0
1	65
2	85
3	105
4	125

20. **Communicate Mathematical Ideas** Which car is not traveling at a constant speed? Explain your reasoning.

_____

_____

21. **Make a Conjecture** Car 4 is traveling at twice the rate of speed of car 2. How will the table values for car 4 compare to the table values for car 2?

_____

_____

_____

Work Area

Ready to Go On?

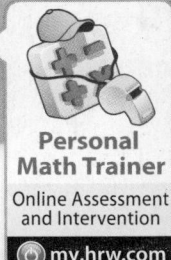

Personal Math Trainer

Online Assessment and Intervention

my.hrw.com

20.1 Unit Rates

Find each unit rate. Round to the nearest hundredth, if necessary.

1. $140 for 18 ft² _____

2. 14 lb for $2.99 _____

Circle the better deal in each pair. Then give the unit rate for the better deal.

3. $\frac{\$56}{25\,gal}$ or $\frac{\$32.05}{15\,gal}$ _____

4. $\frac{\$160}{5\,g}$ or $\frac{\$315}{9\,g}$ _____

20.2 Constant Rates of Change

5. The table shows the amount of money Tyler earns for mowing lawns. Is the relationship a proportional relationship? Why or why not?

Number of Lawns	1	2	3	4
Amount Earned ($)	15	30	48	64

_____

6. On a recent day, 8 euros were worth $9 and 24 euros were worth $27. Write an equation of the form $y = kx$ to show the relationship between the number of euros and the value in dollars.

_____ , where y is dollars and x is euros

20.3 Proportional Relationships and Graphs

7. The graph shows the number of servings in different amounts of frozen yogurt listed on a carton. Write an equation that gives the number of servings y in x pints.

_____

8. A refreshment stand makes 2 large servings of frozen yogurt from 3 pints. Add the line to the graph and write its equation.

_____

Frozen Yogurt

ESSENTIAL QUESTION

9. How can you use rates to determine whether a situation is a proportional relationship?

_____

_____

MODULE 20 MIXED REVIEW
Assessment Readiness

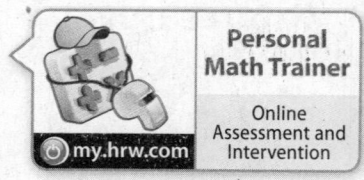

Personal Math Trainer

Online Assessment and Intervention

my.hrw.com

Selected Response

1. Kori spent $46.20 on 12 gallons of gasoline. What was the price per gallon?

(A) $8.35   (C) $2.59

(B) $3.85   (D) $0.26

2. A rabbit can run short distances at a rate of 35 miles per hour. A fox can run short distances at a rate of 21 miles per half hour. Which animal is faster, and by how much?

(A) The rabbit; 7 miles per hour

(B) The fox; 7 miles per hour

(C) The rabbit; 14 miles per hour

(D) The fox; 14 miles per hour

3. A pet survey found that the ratio of dogs to cats is $\frac{2}{5}$. Which proportion shows the number of dogs if the number of cats is 140?

(A) $\frac{2 \text{ dogs}}{5 \text{ cats}} = \frac{140 \text{ dogs}}{350 \text{ cats}}$

(B) $\frac{2 \text{ dogs}}{5 \text{ cats}} = \frac{140 \text{ cats}}{350 \text{ dogs}}$

(C) $\frac{2 \text{ dogs}}{5 \text{ cats}} = \frac{28 \text{ dogs}}{140 \text{ cats}}$

(D) $\frac{2 \text{ dogs}}{5 \text{ cats}} = \frac{56 \text{ dogs}}{140 \text{ cats}}$

4. What is the cost of 2 kilograms of flour if 3 kilograms cost $4.86 and the unit price for each package of flour is the same?

(A) $0.81   (C) $3.24

(B) $2.86   (D) $9.72

5. One gallon of paint covers about 450 square feet. How many square feet will 1.5 gallons of paint cover?

(A) 300 ft²   (C) 675 ft²

(B) 451.5 ft²   (D) 900 ft²

6. The graph shows the relationship between the late fines the library charges and the number of days late.

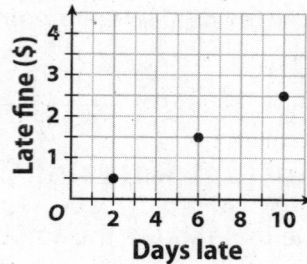

What is an equation for the relationship?

(A) $y = 0.25x$ (C) $y = 0.50x$

(B) $y = 0.40x$ (D) $y = 0.75x$

Mini-Task

7. School is 2 miles from home along a straight road. The table shows your distance from home as you walk home at a constant rate.

Time (min)	10	20	30
Distance from home (mi)	1.5	1	0.5

a. Is the relationship in the table proportional?

_____

b. Find your distance from school for each time in the table.

_____

c. Write an equation representing the relationship between the distance from school and time walking.

_____

© Houghton Mifflin Harcourt Publishing Company

Proportions and Percent

ESSENTIAL QUESTION

How can you use proportions and percent to solve real-world problems?

LESSON 21.1

Percent Increase and Decrease

 FL 7.RP.1.3

LESSON 21.2

Rewriting Percent Expressions

FL 7.RP.1.3, 7.EE.1.2, 7.EE.2.3

LESSON 21.3

Applications of Percent

FL 7.RP.1.3, 7.EE.2.3

Real-World Video

A store may have a sale with deep discounts on some items. They can still make a profit because they first markup the wholesale price by as much as 400%, then markdown the retail price.

my.hrw.com

GO DIGITAL
my.hrw.com

my.hrw.com

Go digital with your write-in student edition, accessible on any device.

Math On the Spot

Scan with your smart phone to jump directly to the online edition, video tutor, and more.

Animated Math

Interactively explore key concepts to see how math works.

Personal Math Trainer

Get immediate feedback and help as you work through practice sets.

© Houghton Mifflin Harcourt Publishing Company

631

Are YOU Ready?

Complete these exercises to review skills you will need for this module.

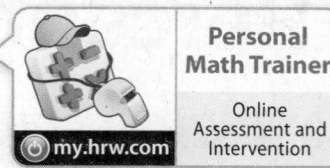

Percents and Decimals

EXAMPLE

$147\% = 100\% + 47\%$ Write the percent as the sum of 1 whole and a percent remainder.

$= \frac{100}{100} + \frac{47}{100}$ Write the percents as fractions.

$= 1 + 0.47$ Write the fractions as decimals.

$= 1.47$ Simplify.

Write each percent as a decimal.

1. 22% _____ **2.** 75% _____ **3.** 6% _____ **4.** 189% _____

Write each decimal as a percent.

5. 0.59 _____ **6.** 0.98 _____ **7.** 0.02 _____ **8.** 1.33 _____

Find the Percent of a Number

EXAMPLE

30% of 45 = ?

$30\% = 0.30$ Write the percent as a decimal.

$\begin{array}{r} 45 \\ \times 0.3 \\ \hline 13.5 \end{array}$ Multiply.

Find the percent of each number.

9. 50% of 64 _____ **10.** 7% of 30 _____ **11.** 15% of 160 _____

12. 32% of 62 _____ **13.** 120% of 4 _____ **14.** 6% of 1,000 _____

Reading Start-Up

Visualize Vocabulary

Use the ✔ words to complete the triangle. Write the review word that fits the description in each section of the triangle.

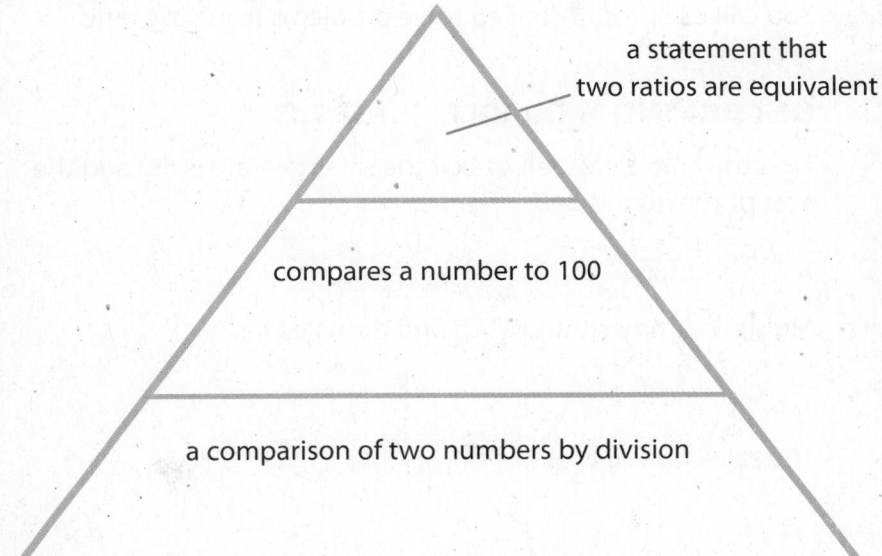

a statement that two ratios are equivalent

compares a number to 100

a comparison of two numbers by division

Vocabulary

Review Words
✔ proportion *(proporción)*
✔ percent *(porcentaje)*
  rate *(tasa)*
✔ ratio *(razón)*
  unit rate *(tasa unitaria)*

Preview Words
  percent decrease *(porcentaje de disminución)*
  percent increase *(porcentaje de aumento)*
  principal *(capital)*
  simple interest *(interés simple)*

Understand Vocabulary

Complete the sentences using the preview words.

1. A fixed percent of the principal is _____.

2. The original amount of money deposited or borrowed is the _____.

3. A _____ is the amount of increase divided by the original amount.

Active Reading

Tri-Fold Before beginning the module, create a tri-fold to help you learn the concepts and vocabulary in this module. Fold the paper into three sections. Label the columns "What I Know," "What I Need to Know," and "What I Learned." Complete the first two columns before you read. After studying the module, complete the third.

Unpacking the Standards

Understanding the Standards and the vocabulary terms in the Standards will help you know exactly what you are expected to learn in this module.

FL 7.RP.1.3

Use proportional relationships to solve multistep ratio and percent problems.

Key Vocabulary

proportion *(proporción)*
An equation that states that two ratios are equivalent.

ratio *(razón)*
A comparison of two quantities by division.

percent *(porcentaje)*
A ratio that compares a part to the whole using 100.

What It Means to You

You will use proportions to solve problems involving ratio and percent.

UNPACKING EXAMPLE 7.RP.1.3

Find the amount of sales tax if the sales tax rate is 5% and the cost of the item is $40.

$$5\% = \frac{5}{100} = \frac{1}{20}$$

Multiply $\frac{1}{20}$ times the cost to find the sales tax.

$$\frac{1}{20} \times 40 = 2$$

The sales tax is $2.

FL 7.EE.1.2

Understand that rewriting an expression in different forms in a problem context can shed light on the problem and how the quantities in it are related.

Key Vocabulary

expression *(expresión)*
A mathematical phrase containing variables, constants and operation symbols.

What It Means to You

You will find helpful ways to rewrite an expression in an equivalent form.

UNPACKING EXAMPLE 7.EE.1.2

A store advertises that all bicycle helmets will be sold at 10% off the regular price. Find two expressions that represent the value of the sale price p for the helmets that are on sale.

Sale price = original price minus 10% of the price

$$= p - 0.10p$$

Equivalently,

$$p - 0.10p = p(1 - 0.10) = 0.90p$$

Visit **my.hrw.com** to see all **Florida Math Standards** unpacked.

my.hrw.com

Percent Increase and Decrease

FL 7.RP.1.3
Use proportional relationships to solve multistep ratio and percent problems.

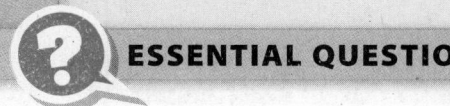

How do you use percents to describe change?

Finding Percent Increase

Percents can be used to describe how an amount changes.

$$\text{Percent Change} = \frac{\text{Amount of Change}}{\text{Original Amount}}$$

The change may be an increase or a decrease. **Percent increase** describes how much a quantity increases in comparison to the original amount.

Math On the Spot
my.hrw.com

EXAMPLE 1 FL 7.RP.1.3

Amber got a raise, and her hourly wage increased from $8 to $9.50. What is the percent increase?

STEP 1 Find the amount of change.

Amount of Change = Greater Value − Lesser Value

$= 9.50 − 8.00$ Substitute values.

$= 1.50$ Subtract.

STEP 2 Find the percent increase. Round to the nearest percent.

$$\text{Percent Change} = \frac{\text{Amount of Change}}{\text{Original Amount}}$$

$= \dfrac{1.50}{8.00}$ Substitute values.

$= 0.1875$ Divide.

$\approx 19\%$ Write as a percent and round.

Reflect

1. What does a 100% increase mean?

_____

_____

 YOUR TURN

2. The price of a pair of shoes increases from $52 to $64. What is the

percent increase to the nearest percent? _____

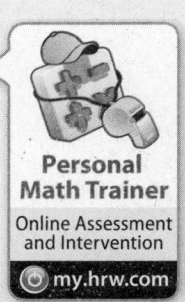

Personal Math Trainer

Online Assessment and Intervention

my.hrw.com

My Notes

Finding Percent Decrease

When the change in the amount decreases, you can use a similar approach to find percent decrease. **Percent decrease** describes how much a quantity decreases in comparison to the original amount.

EXAMPLE 2

David moved from a house that is 89 miles away from his workplace to a house that is 51 miles away from his workplace. What is the percent decrease in the distance from his home to his workplace?

STEP 1   Find the amount of change.

Amount of Change = Greater Value − Lesser Value

$= 89 - 51$ Substitute values.

$= 38$ Subtract.

STEP 2   Find the percent decrease. Round to the nearest percent.

$$\text{Percent Change} = \frac{\text{Amount of Change}}{\text{Original Amount}}$$

$= \frac{38}{89}$ Substitute values.

≈ 0.427 Divide.

$= 43\%$ Write as a percent and round.

Reflect

3. **Critique Reasoning**   David considered moving even closer to his workplace. He claims that if he had done so, the percent of decrease would have been more than 100%. Is David correct? Explain your reasoning.

_____

_____

_____

YOUR TURN

4.   The number of students in a chess club decreased from 18 to 12. What is the percent decrease? Round to the nearest percent. _____

5.   Officer Brimberry wrote 16 tickets for traffic violations last week, but only 10 tickets this week. What is the percent decrease? _____

Using Percent of Change

Given an original amount and a percent increase or decrease, you can use the percent of change to find the new amount.

EXAMPLE 3   **FL 7.RP.1.3**

The grizzly bear population in Yellowstone National Park in 1970 was about 270. Over the next 35 years, it increased by about 115%. What was the population in 2005?

STEP 1 Find the amount of change.

$1.15 \times 270 = 310.5$ Find 115% of 270. Write 115% as a decimal.

≈ 311 Round to the nearest whole number.

STEP 2 Find the new amount.

New Amount = Original Amount + Amount of Change

$= 270 + 311$ Substitute values.

$= 581$ Add.

The population in 2005 was about 581 grizzly bears.

> Add the amount of change because the population increased.

Reflect

6. Why will the percent of change always be represented by a positive number?

_____

_____

_____

7. **Draw Conclusions** If an amount of $100 in a savings account increases by 10%, then increases by 10% again, is that the same as increasing by 20%? Explain.

_____

_____

_____

A TV has an original price of $499. Find the new price after the given percent of change.

8. 10% increase _____

9. 30% decrease _____

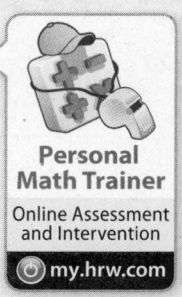

Personal
Math Trainer

Online Assessment
and Intervention

my.hrw.com

Find each percent increase. Round to the nearest percent. (Example 1)

1. From $5 to $8 _____

2. From 20 students to 30 students _____

3. From 86 books to 150 books _____

4. From $3.49 to $3.89 _____

5. From 13 friends to 14 friends _____

6. From 5 miles to 16 miles _____

7. Nathan usually drinks 36 ounces of water per day. He read that he should drink 64 ounces of water per day. If he starts drinking 64 ounces, what is the percent increase? Round to the nearest percent. (Example 1) _____

Find each percent decrease. Round to the nearest percent. (Example 2)

8. From $80 to $64 _____

9. From 95°F to 68°F _____

10. From 90 points to 45 points _____

11. From 145 pounds to 132 pounds _____

12. From 64 photos to 21 photos _____

13. From 16 bagels to 0 bagels _____

14. Over the summer, Jackie played video games 3 hours per day. When school began in the fall, she was only allowed to play video games for half an hour per day. What is the percent decrease? Round to the nearest percent. (Example 2) _____

Find the new amount given the original amount and the percent of change. (Example 3)

15. $9; 10% increase _____

16. 48 cookies; 25% decrease _____

17. 340 pages; 20% decrease _____

18. 28 members; 50% increase _____

19. $29,000; 4% decrease _____

20. 810 songs; 130% increase _____

21. Adam currently runs about 20 miles per week, and he wants to increase his weekly mileage by 30%. How many miles will Adam run per week? (Example 3) _____

? ESSENTIAL QUESTION CHECK-IN

22. What process do you use to find the percent change of a quantity?

_____

_____

21.1 Independent Practice

 FL 7.RP.1.3

23. Complete the table.

Item	Original Price	New Price	Percent Change	Increase or Decrease
Bike	$110	$96		
Scooter	$45	$56		
Tennis Racket	$79		5%	Increase
Skis	$580		25%	Decrease

24. Multiple Representations The bar graph shows the number of hurricanes in the Atlantic Basin from 2006–2011.

a. Find the amount of change and the percent of decrease in the number of hurricanes from 2008 to 2009 and from 2010 to 2011. Compare the amounts of change and percents of decrease.

_____

_____

_____

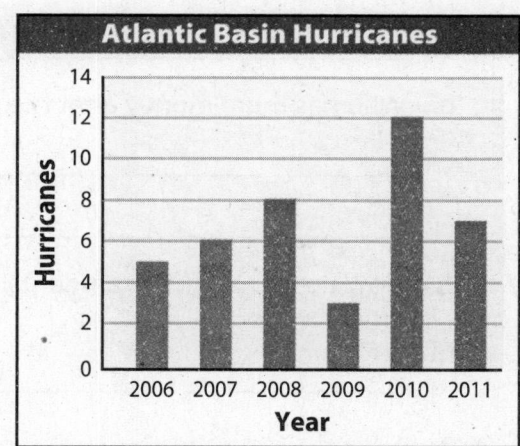

b. Between which two years was the percent of change the greatest? What was the percent of change during that period?

_____

25. Represent Real-World Problems Cheese sticks that were previously priced at "5 for $1" are now "4 for $1". Find each percent of change and show your work.

a. Find the percent decrease in the number of cheese sticks you can buy for $1.

_____

b. Find the percent increase in the price per cheese stick.

_____

_____

26. Percent error calculations are used to determine how close to the true values, or how accurate, experimental values really are. The formula is similar to finding percent of change.

$$\text{Percent Error} = \frac{|\text{Experimental Value} - \text{Actual Value}|}{\text{Actual Value}} \times 100$$

In chemistry class, Charlie records the volume of a liquid as 13.3 milliliters. The actual volume is 13.6 milliliters. What is his percent error? Round to

the nearest percent. _____

 FOCUS ON HIGHER ORDER THINKING

27. **Look for a Pattern** Leroi and Sylvia both put $100 in a savings account. Leroi decides he will put in an additional $10 each week. Sylvia decides to put in an additional 10% of the amount in the account each week.

a. Who has more money after the first additional deposit? Explain.

_____

_____

b. Who has more money after the second additional deposit? Explain.

_____

_____

c. How do you think the amounts in the two accounts will compare after a month? A year?

_____

_____

_____

28. **Critical Thinking** Suppose an amount increases by 100%, then decreases by 100%. Find the final amount. Would the situation change if the original increase was 150%? Explain your reasoning.

_____

_____

29. **Look for a Pattern** Ariel deposited $100 into a bank account. Each Friday she will withdraw 10% of the money in the account to spend. Ariel thinks her account will be empty after 10 withdrawals. Do you agree? Explain.

_____

_____

_____

© Houghton Mifflin Harcourt Publishing Company

Work Area

Rewriting Percent Expressions

FL 7.EE.1.2
Understand that rewriting an expression in different forms in a problem context can shed light on the problem and how the quantities in it are related. *Also 7.RP.1.3, 7.EE.2.3*

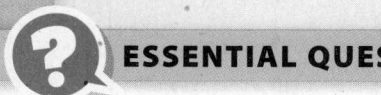

? ESSENTIAL QUESTION

How can you rewrite expressions to help you solve markup and markdown problems?

Calculating Markups

A *markup* is one kind of percent increase. You can use a bar model to represent the *retail price* of an item, that is, the total price including the markup.

Math On the Spot
my.hrw.com

EXAMPLE 1 *Real World*   FL 7.EE.1.2, 7.RP.1.3, 7.EE.2.3

To make a profit, stores mark up the prices on the items they sell. A sports store buys skateboards from a supplier for *s* dollars. What is the retail price for skateboards that the manager buys for $35 and $56 after a 42% markup?

STEP 1 Use a bar model.

Draw a bar for the cost of the skateboard *s*.

Then draw a bar that shows the markup: 42% of *s*, or 0.42*s*.

$$s$$

$$0.42s \longrightarrow$$

$$s + 0.42s$$

These bars together represent the cost plus the markup, $s + 0.42s$.

STEP 2 Retail price = Original cost + Markup

$$= \quad s \quad + \quad 0.42s$$
$$= \quad 1s \quad + \quad 0.42s$$
$$= \quad\quad 1.42s$$

Math Talk
Mathematical Practices

Why write the retail price as the sum of two terms? as one term?

STEP 3 Use the expression to find the retail price of each skateboard.

$s = \$35 \longrightarrow$ Retail price $= 1.42(\$35) = \$49.70$

$s = \$56 \longrightarrow$ Retail price $= 1.42(\$56) = \$79.52$

Reflect

1. **What If?** The markup is changed to 34%; how does the expression for the retail price change?

YOUR TURN

2. Rick buys remote control cars to resell. He applies a markup of 10%.

   a. Write two expressions that represent the retail price of the cars.

   _____

   b. If Rick buys a remote control car for $28.00, what is his selling price?

   _____

3. An exclusive clothing boutique triples the price of the items it purchases for resale.

   a. What is the boutique's markup percent? _____

   b. Write two expressions that represent the retail price of the clothes.

   _____

Calculating Markdowns

An example of a percent decrease is a *discount*, or *markdown*. A price after a markdown may be called a sale price. You can also use a bar model to represent the price of an item including the markdown.

EXAMPLE 2   **FL** 7.EE.1.2, 7.RP.1.3, 7.EE.2.3

A discount store marks down all of its holiday merchandise by 20% off the regular selling price. Find the discounted price of decorations that regularly sell for $16 and $23.

STEP 1   Use a bar model.

       Draw a bar for the regular price p.

       Then draw a bar that shows the discount: 20% of p, or $0.2p$.

       The difference between these two bars represents the price minus the discount, $p - 0.2p$.

STEP 2 Sale price = Original price − Markdown

$$= \quad p \quad − \quad 0.2p$$

$$= \quad 1p \quad − \quad 0.2p$$

$$= \quad 0.8p$$

STEP 3 Use the expression to find the sale price of each decoration.

$p = \$16 \longrightarrow$ Retail price $= 0.8(\$16) = \$12.80$

$p = \$23 \longrightarrow$ Retail price $= 0.8(\$23) = \$18.40$

Reflect

4. **Conjecture** Compare the single term expression for retail price after a markup from Example 1 and the single term expression for sale price after a markdown from Example 2. What do you notice about the coefficients in the two expressions?

_____

_____

Math Talk

Mathematical Practices

Is a 20% markup equal to a 20% markdown? Explain.

YOUR TURN

5. A bicycle shop marks down each bicycle's selling price *b* by 24% for a holiday sale.

   a. Draw a bar model to represent the problem.

   b. What is a single term expression for the sale price? _____

6. Jane sells pillows. For a sale, she marks them down 5%.

   a. Write two expressions that represent the sale price of the pillows.

   _____

   b. If the original price of a pillow is $15.00, what is the sale price?

   _____

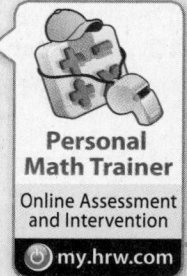

Personal Math Trainer

Online Assessment and Intervention

my.hrw.com

© Houghton Mifflin Harcourt Publishing Company

1. Dana buys dress shirts from a clothing manufacturer for *s* dollars each, and then sells the dress shirts in her retail clothing store at a 35% markup. (Example 1)

   a. Write the markup as a decimal. _____

   b. Write an expression for the retail price of the dress shirt. _____

   c. What is the retail price of a dress shirt that Dana purchased for $32.00? _____

   d. How much was added to the original price of the dress shirt? _____

List the markup and retail price of each item. Round to two decimal places when necessary. (Example 1)

	Item	Price	Markup %	Markup	Retail Price
2.	Hat	$18	15%		
3.	Book	$22.50	42%		
4.	Shirt	$33.75	75%		
5.	Shoes	$74.99	33%		
6.	Clock	$48.60	100%		
7.	Painting	$185.00	125%		

Find the sale price of each item. Round to two decimal places when necessary. (Example 2)

8. Original price: $45.00; Markdown: 22%

   _____

9. Original price: $89.00; Markdown: 33%

   _____

10. Original price: $23.99; Markdown: 44%

    _____

11. Original price: $279.99, Markdown: 75%

    _____

? ESSENTIAL QUESTION CHECK-IN

12. How can you determine the sale price if you are given the regular price and the percent of markdown?

    _____

    _____

© Houghton Mifflin Harcourt Publishing Company

21.2 Independent Practice

FL 7.RP.1.3, 7.EE,1.2, 7.EE.2.3

Personal Math Trainer

Online Assessment and Intervention

my.hrw.com

13. A bookstore manager marks down the price of older hardcover books, which originally sell for *b* dollars, by 46%.

   a. Write the markdown as a decimal. _____

   b. Write an expression for the sale price of the hardcover book.

   _____

   c. What is the sale price of a hardcover book for which the original retail

   price was $29.00? _____

   d. If you buy the book in part **c**, how much do you save by paying the

   sale price? _____

14. Raquela's coworker made price tags for several items that are to be marked down by 35%. Match each Regular Price to the correct Sale Price, if possible. Not all sales tags match an item.

Regular Price $3.29	Regular Price $4.19	Regular Price $2.79	Regular Price $3.09	Regular Price $3.77

Sale Price $2.01	Sale Price $2.45	Sale Price $1.15	Sale Price $2.72	Sale Price $2.24

15. **Communicate Mathematical Ideas** For each situation, give an example that includes the original price and final price after markup or markdown.

   a. A markdown that is greater than 99% but less than 100%

   _____

   b. A markdown that is less than 1%

   _____

   c. A markup that is more than 200%

   _____

16. Represent Real-World Problems Harold works at a men's clothing store, which marks up its retail clothing by 27%. The store purchases pants for $74.00, suit jackets for $325.00, and dress shirts for $48.00. How much will Harold charge a customer for two pairs of pants, three dress shirts, and a suit jacket?

_____

17. Analyze Relationships Your family needs a set of 4 tires. Which of the following deals would you prefer? Explain.

(I) Buy 3, get one free   **(II)** 20% off   **(III)** $\frac{1}{4}$ off

_____

_____

 FOCUS ON HIGHER ORDER THINKING

18. Critique Reasoning Margo purchases bulk teas from a warehouse and marks up those prices by 20% for retail sale. When teas go unsold for more than two months, Margo marks down the retail price by 20%. She says that she is _breaking even_, that is, she is getting the same price for the tea that she paid for it. Is she correct? Explain.

_____

_____

_____

19. Problem Solving Grady marks down some $2.49 pens to $1.99 for a week and then marks them back up to $2.49. Find the percent of increase and the percent of decrease to the nearest tenth. Are the percents of change the same for both price changes? If not, which is a greater change?

_____

_____

20. Persevere in Problem Solving At Danielle's clothing boutique, if an item does not sell for eight weeks, she marks it down by 15%. If it remains unsold after that, she marks it down an additional 5% each week until she can no longer make a profit. Then she donates it to charity.

Rafael wants to buy a coat originally priced $150, but he can't afford more than $110. If Danielle paid $100 for the coat, during which week(s) could Rafael buy the coat within his budget? Justify your answer.

_____

_____

_____

Work Area

Applications of Percent

Math On the Spot
my.hrw.com

? ESSENTIAL QUESTION

How do you use percents to solve problems?

Finding Total Cost

Sales tax, which is the tax on the sale of an item or service, is a percent of the purchase price that is collected by the seller.

EXAMPLE 1   FL   7.RP.1.3, 7.EE.2.3

Marcus buys a varsity jacket from a clothing store in Arlington. The price of the jacket is $80 and the sales tax is 8%. What is the total cost of the jacket?

STEP 1   Use a bar model to find the amount of the tax.

Draw a bar for the price of the jacket, $80. Divide it into 10 equal parts. Each part represents 10% of $80, or $8.

Then draw a bar that shows the sales tax: 8% of $80.

$80

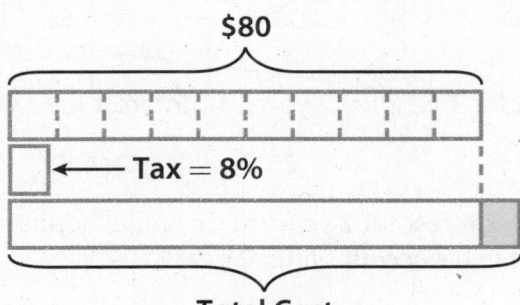

⟵ Tax = 8%

Total Cost

Because 8% is $\frac{4}{5}$ of 10%, the tax is $\frac{4}{5}$ of one part of the whole bar.

Each part of the whole bar is $8.

So, the sales tax is $\frac{4}{5}$ of $8.

$\frac{4}{5} \times \$8 = \$6.40$

The sales tax is $6.40.

Math Talk
Mathematical Practices

How could you find the tax without drawing a model of the situation?

STEP 2   To find the total cost of the jacket, add the price of the jacket and the sales tax.

Jacket price + Sales tax = Total cost

    $80 $6.40   = $86.40

1. Sharon wants to buy a shirt that costs $20. The sales tax is 5%. How much is the sales tax? What is her total cost for the shirt? _____

Finding Simple Interest

When you deposit money in a savings account, your money usually earns interest. When you borrow money, you must pay back the original amount of the loan plus interest. **Simple interest** is a fixed percent of the *principal*. The **principal** is the original amount of money deposited or borrowed.

EXAMPLE 2   FL 7.RP.1.3, 7.EE.2.3

My Notes

Terry deposits $200 into a bank account that earns 3% simple interest per year. What is the total amount in the account after 2 years?

STEP 1 Find the amount of interest earned in one year. Then calculate the amount of interest for 2 years.

Write 3% as a decimal: *0.03*

Interest Rate × Initial Deposit = Interest for 1 year

   0.03   × $200   = $6

Interest for 1 year × 2 years = Interest for 2 years

   $6   ×   2   = $12

STEP 2 Add the interest for 2 years to the initial deposit to find the total amount in his account after 2 years.

Initial deposit + Interest for 2 years = Total

   $200   + $12   = $212

The total amount in the account after 2 years is $212.

Reflect

2. Write an expression you can use to find the total amount in Terry's account.

_____

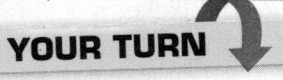

3. Ariane borrows $400 on a 4-year loan. She is charged 5% simple interest per year. How much interest is she charged for 4 years? What is the total amount she has to pay back? _____

Using Multiple Percents

Math On the Spot
my.hrw.com

Some situations require applying more than one percent to a problem. For example, when you dine at a restaurant, you might pay a tax on the meal, and pay a tip to the wait staff. The tip is usually paid on the amount before tax. When you pay tax on a sale item, you pay tax only on the discounted price.

EXAMPLE 3   **FL** 7.EE.2.3, 7.RP.1.3

The Maxwell family goes out for dinner, and the price of the meal is $60. The sales tax on the meal is 7%, and they also want to leave a 15% tip. What is the total cost of the meal?

 Analyze Information

Identify the important information.
- The bill for the meal is $60.
- The sales tax is 7%, or 0.07.
- The tip is 15%, or 0.15.

The total cost will be the sum of the bill for the meal, the sales tax, and the tip.

 Formulate a Plan

Calculate the sales tax separately, then calculate the tip, and then add the products to the bill for the meal to find the total.

 Solve

Sales tax: $0.07 \times \$60 = \$4.20$ Tip: $0.15 \times \$60 = \$9.00$

Meal + Sales tax + Tip = Total cost

$60 + $4.20 + $9 = $73.20

The total cost is $73.20.

 Justify and Evaluate

Estimate the sales tax and tip. Sales tax is about 10% plus 15% for tip gives 25%. Find 25% of the bill: $0.25 \times \$60 = \$15$. Add this to the bill: $60 + $15 = $75. The total cost should be about $75.

 YOUR TURN

4. Samuel orders four DVDs from an online music store. Each DVD costs $9.99. He has a 20% discount code, and sales tax is 6.75%. What is the total cost of his order?

_____

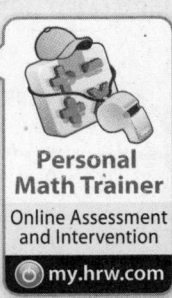

Personal Math Trainer
Online Assessment and Intervention
my.hrw.com

1. 5% of $30 = _____

2. 15% of $70 = _____

3. 0.4% of $100 = _____

4. 150% of $22 = _____

5. 1% of $80 = _____

6. 200% of $5 = _____

7. Brandon buys a radio for $43.99 in a state where the sales tax is 7%. (Example 1)

   a. How much does he pay in taxes? _____

   b. What is the total Brandon pays for the radio? _____

8. Luisa's restaurant bill comes to $75.50, and she leaves a 15% tip. What is Luisa's total restaurant bill? (Example 1)

   _____

9. Joe borrowed $2,000 from the bank at a rate of 7% simple interest per year. How much interest did he pay in 5 years? (Example 2)

   _____

10. You have $550 in a savings account that earns 3% simple interest each year. How much will be in your account in 10 years? (Example 2)

    _____

11. Martin finds a shirt on sale for 10% off at a department store. The original price was $20. Martin must also pay 8.5% sales tax. (Example 3)

    a. How much is the shirt before taxes are applied? _____

    b. How much is the shirt after taxes are applied? _____

12. Teresa's restaurant bill comes to $29.99 before tax. If the sales tax is 6.25% and she tips the waiter 20%, what is the total cost of the meal? (Example 3)

    _____

? ESSENTIAL QUESTION CHECK-IN

13. How can you determine the total cost of an item including tax if you know the price of the item and the tax rate?

    _____

    _____

21.3 Independent Practice

FL 7.RP.1.3, 7.EE.2.3

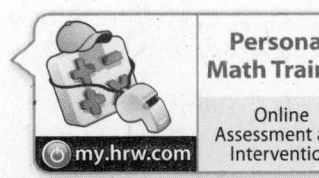

14. Emily's meal costs $32.75 and Darren's meal costs $39.88. Emily treats Darren by paying for both meals, and leaves a 14% tip. Find the total cost.

_____

15. The Jayden family eats at a restaurant that is having a 15% discount promotion. Their meal costs $78.65, and they leave a 20% tip. If the tip applies to the cost of the meal before the discount, what is the total cost of the meal?

_____

16. A jeweler buys a ring from a jewelry maker for $125. He marks up the price by 135% for sale in his store. What is the selling price of the ring with 7.5% sales tax?

_____

17. Luis wants to buy a skateboard that usually sells for $79.99. All merchandise is discounted by 12%. What is the total cost of the skateboard if Luis has to pay a state sales tax of 6.75%?

_____

18. Kedar earns a monthly salary of $2,200 plus a 3.75% *commission* on the amount of his sales at a men's clothing store. What would he earn this month if he sold $4,500 in clothing? Round to the nearest cent.

_____

19. Danielle earns a 7.25% commission on everything she sells at the electronics store where she works. She also earns a base salary of $750 per week. How much did she earn last week if she sold $4,500 in electronics merchandise? Round to the nearest cent.

_____

20. Francois earns a weekly salary of $475 plus a 5.5% commission on sales at a gift shop. How much would he earn in a week if he sold $700 in goods? Round to the nearest cent.

_____

21. Sandra is 4 feet tall. Pablo is 10% taller than Sandra, and Michaela is 8% taller than Pablo.

a. Explain how to find Michaela's height with the given information.

_____

_____

_____

_____

_____

_____

b. What is Michaela's approximate height in feet and inches?

_____

22. Eugene wants to buy jeans at a store that is giving $10 off everything. The tag on the jeans is marked 50% off. The original price is $49.98.

a. Find the total cost if the 50% discount is applied before the $10 discount.

_____

b. Find the total cost if the $10 discount is applied before the 50% discount.

_____

23. Multistep Eric downloads the coupon shown and goes shopping at Gadgets Galore, where he buys a digital camera for $95 and an extra battery for $15.99.

a. What is the total cost if the coupon is applied to the digital camera?

_____

b. What is the total cost if the coupon is applied to the extra battery?

_____

c. To which item should Eric apply the discount? Explain.

_____

d. Eric has to pay 8% sales tax after the coupon is applied. How much is his total bill?

_____

24. Two stores are having sales on the same shirts. The sale at Store 1 is "2 shirts for $22" and the sale at Store 2 is "Each $12.99 shirt is 10% off".

a. Explain how much will you save by buying at Store 1.

_____

_____

b. If Store 3 has shirts originally priced at $20.98 on sale for 55% off, does it have a better deal than the other stores? Justify your answer.

_____

![H.O.T.] **FOCUS ON HIGHER ORDER THINKING**

25. Analyze Relationships Marcus can choose between a monthly salary of $1,500 plus 5.5% of sales or $2,400 plus 3% of sales. He expects sales between $5,000 and $10,000 a month. Which salary option should he choose? Explain.

_____

_____

_____

26. Multistep In chemistry class, Bob recorded the volume of a liquid as 13.2 mL. The actual volume was 13.7 mL. Use the formula to find percent error of Bob's measurement to the nearest tenth of a percent.

$$\text{Percent Error} = \frac{|\text{Experimental Value} - \text{Actual Value}|}{\text{Actual Value}} \times 100$$

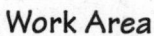

_____

Work Area

Ready to Go On?

Personal Math Trainer

Online Assessment and Intervention

my.hrw.com

21.1 Percent Increase and Decrease

Find the percent change from the first value to the second.

1. 36; 63 _____

2. 50; 35 _____

3. 40; 72 _____

4. 92; 69 _____

21.2 Markup and Markdown

Use the original price and the markdown or markup to find the retail price.

5. Original price: $60; Markup: 15%; Retail price: _____

6. Original price: $32; Markup: 12.5%; Retail price: _____

7. Original price: $50; Markdown: 22%; Retail price: _____

8. Original price: $125; Markdown: 30%; Retail price: _____

21.3 Applications of Percent

9. Mae Ling earns a weekly salary of $325 plus a 6.5% commission on sales at a gift shop. How much would she make in a work week if she sold $4,800 worth of merchandise? _____

10. Ramon earns $1,735 each month and pays $53.10 for electricity. To the nearest tenth of a percent, what percent of Ramon's earnings are spent on electricity each month? _____

11. James, Priya, and Siobhan work in a grocery store. James makes $7.00 per hour. Priya makes 20% more than James, and Siobhan makes 5% less than Priya. How much does Siobhan make per hour? _____

12. The Hu family goes out for lunch, and the price of the meal is $45. The sales tax on the meal is 6%, and the family also leaves a 20% tip on the pre-tax amount. What is the total cost of the meal? _____

ESSENTIAL QUESTION

13. Give three examples of how percents are used in the real-world. Tell whether each situation represents a percent increase or a percent decrease.

_____

_____

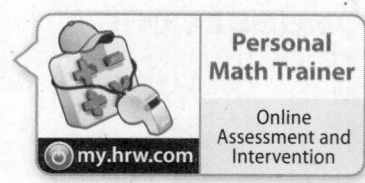

Selected Response

1. Zalmon walks $\frac{3}{4}$ of a mile in $\frac{3}{10}$ of an hour. What is his speed in miles per hour?

   Ⓐ 0.225 miles per hour

   Ⓑ 2.3 miles per hour

   Ⓒ 2.5 miles per hour

   Ⓓ 2.6 miles per hour

2. Find the percent change from 70 to 56.

   Ⓐ 20% decrease   Ⓒ 25% decrease

   Ⓑ 20% increase   Ⓓ 25% increase

3. The rainfall total two years ago was 10.2 inches. Last year's total was 20% greater. What was last year's rainfall total?

   Ⓐ 8.16 inches   Ⓒ 12.24 inches

   Ⓑ 11.22 inches   Ⓓ 20.4 inches

4. A pair of basketball shoes was originally priced at $80, but was marked up 37.5%. What was the retail price of the shoes?

   Ⓐ $50   Ⓒ $110

   Ⓑ $83   Ⓓ $130

5. The sales tax rate in Jan's town is 7.5%. If she buys 3 lamps for $23.59 each and a sofa for $769.99, how much sales tax does she owe?

   Ⓐ $58.85   Ⓒ $67.26

   Ⓑ $63.06   Ⓓ $71.46

6. The day after a national holiday, decorations were marked down 40%. Before the holiday, a patriotic banner cost $5.75. How much did the banner cost after the holiday?

   Ⓐ $1.15   Ⓒ $3.45

   Ⓑ $2.30   Ⓓ $8.05

7. Dustin makes $2,330 each month and pays $840 for rent. To the nearest tenth of a percent, what percent of Dustin's earnings are spent on rent?

   Ⓐ 84.0%   Ⓒ 56.4%

   Ⓑ 63.9%   Ⓓ 36.1%

8. A scuba diver is positioned at −30 feet. How many feet will she have to rise to change her position to −12 feet?

   Ⓐ −42 ft   Ⓒ 18 ft

   Ⓑ −18 ft   Ⓓ 42 ft

9. A bank offers an annual simple interest rate of 8% on home improvement loans. Tobias borrowed $17,000 over a period of 2 years. How much did he repay altogether?

   Ⓐ $1,360   Ⓒ $18,360

   Ⓑ $2,720   Ⓓ $19,720

Mini-Task

10. The granola Summer buys used to cost $6.00 per pound, but it has been marked up 15%.

    a. How much did it cost Summer to buy 2.6 pounds of granola at the old price?

    _____

    b. How much does it cost her to buy 2.6 pounds of granola at the new price?

    _____

    c. Suppose Summer buys 3.5 pounds of granola. How much more does it cost at the new price than at the old price?

    _____

UNIT 9

Study Guide Review

MODULE 20 — Rates and Proportionality

Key Vocabulary
- complex fraction (*fracción compleja*)
- constant of proportionality (*constante de proporcionalidad*)
- proportion (*proporción*)
- proportional relationship (*relación proporcional*)
- rate of change (*tasa de cambio*)
- unit rate (*tasa unitaria*)

ESSENTIAL QUESTION

How can you use rates and proportionality to solve real-world problems?

EXAMPLE 1

A store sells onions by the pound. Is the relationship between the cost of an amount of onions and the number of pounds proportional? If so, write an equation for the relationship, and represent the relationship on a graph.

Number of pounds	2	5	6
Cost ($)	3.00	7.50	9.00

Write the rates.

$$\frac{\text{cost}}{\text{number of pounds}} : \frac{\$3.00}{2 \text{ pounds}} = \frac{\$1.50}{1 \text{ pound}}$$

$$\frac{\$7.50}{5 \text{ pounds}} = \frac{\$1.50}{1 \text{ pound}}$$

$$\frac{\$9.00}{6 \text{ pounds}} = \frac{\$1.50}{1 \text{ pound}}$$

The rates are constant, so the relationship is proportional.

The constant rate of change is $1.50 per pound, so the constant of proportionality is 1.5. Let x represent the number of pounds and y represent the cost.

The equation for the relationship is $y = 1.5x$.

Plot the ordered pairs (pounds, cost): (2, 3), (5, 7.5), and (6, 9).

Connect the points with a line.

Cost of Onions

EXERCISES

1. Steve uses $\frac{8}{9}$ gallon of paint to paint 4 identical birdhouses. How many gallons of paint does he use for each birdhouse?

   (Lesson 20.1) _____

2. Ron walks 0.5 mile on the track in 10 minutes. Stevie walks 0.25 mile on the track in 6 minutes. Find the unit rate for each walker in miles per hour. Who is the faster walker?

   (Lesson 20.1) _____

   _____

3. The table below shows the proportional relationship between Juan's pay and the hours he works. Complete the table. Plot the data and connect the points with a line. (Lessons 20.2, 21.3)

Hours worked	2		5	6
Pay ($)	40	80		

Juan's Pay

MODULE **21** # Proportions and Percent

? ESSENTIAL QUESTION

How can you use proportions and percent to solve real-world problems?

EXAMPLE 1

Donata had a 25-minute commute from home to work. Her company moved, and now her commute to work is 33 minutes long. Does this situation represent an increase or a decrease? Find the percent increase or decrease in her commute to work.

This situation represents an increase. Find the percent increase.

amount of change = greater value − lesser value

$33 - 25 = 8$

$$\text{percent increase} = \frac{\text{amount of change}}{\text{original amount}}$$

$\frac{8}{25} = 0.32 = 32\%$

Donata's commute increased by 32%.

1. Michelle purchased 25 audio files in January. In February she purchased 40 audio files. Find the percent increase. (Lesson 21.1) _____

2. Sam's dog weighs 72 pounds. The vet suggests that for the dog's health, its weight should decrease by 12.5 percent. According to the vet, what is a healthy weight for the dog? (Lesson 21.1) _____

3. The original price of a barbecue grill is $79.50. The grill is marked down 15%. What is the sale price of the grill? (Lesson 21.2) _____

4. A sporting goods store marks up the cost *s* of soccer balls by 250%. Write an expression that represents the retail cost of the soccer balls. The store buys soccer balls for $5.00 each. What is the retail price of the soccer balls? (Lesson 21.2) _____

1. **CAREERS IN MATH** **Bicycle Tour Operator** Viktor is a bike tour operator and needs to replace two of his touring bikes. He orders two bikes from the sporting goods store for a total of $2,000 and pays using his credit card. When the bill arrives, he reads the following information:

> **Balance:** $2,000
> **Annual interest rate:** 14.9%
> **Minimum payment due:** $40
> **Late fee:** $10 if payment not received by 3/1/2013

a. To keep his good credit, Viktor promptly sends in a minimum payment of $40. When the next bill arrives, it looks a lot like the previous bill.

> Balance: $1,984.34
> Annual interest rate: 14.9%
> Minimum payment due: $40
> Late fee: $10 if payment not received by 4/1/2013

Explain how the credit card company calculated the new balance. Notice that the given interest rate is annual, but the payment is monthly.

_____

_____

_____

b. Viktor was upset about the new bill, so he decided to send in $150 for his April payment. The minimum payment on his bill is calculated as 2% of the balance (rounded to the nearest dollar) or $20, whichever is greater. Fill out the details for Viktor's new bill.

> **Balance:** _____
>
> **Annual interest rate:** _____
>
> **Minimum payment due:** _____
>
> **Late fee: $10 if payment not received by** _____

c. Viktor's bank offers a credit card with an introductory annual interest rate of 9.9%. He can transfer his current balance for a fee of $40. After one year, the rate will return to the bank's normal rate, which is 13.9%. The bank charges a late fee of $15. Give two reasons why Viktor should transfer the balance, and two reasons why he should not.

_____

_____

_____

_____

2. The table below shows how far several animals can travel at their maximum speeds in a given time.

Animal Distances		
Animal	**Distance traveled (ft)**	**Time (s)**
elk	33	$\frac{1}{2}$
giraffe	115	$2\frac{1}{2}$
zebra	117	2

a. Write each animal's speed as a unit rate in feet per second.

_____

_____

_____

b. Which animal has the fastest speed?

_____

c. How many miles could the fastest animal travel in 2 hours if it maintained the speed you calculated in part **a**? Use the formula $d = rt$ and round your answer to the nearest tenth of a mile. Show your work.

_____

_____

_____

d. The data in the table represents how fast each animal can travel at its maximum speed. Is it reasonable to expect the animal from part **b** to travel that distance in 2 hours? Explain why or why not.

_____

_____

_____

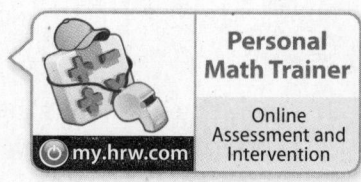
Selected Response

1. If the relationship between distance y in feet and time x in seconds is proportional, which rate is represented by $\frac{y}{x} = 0.6$?

Ⓐ 3 feet in 5 s

Ⓑ 3 feet in 9 s

Ⓒ 10 feet in 6 s

Ⓓ 18 feet in 3 s

2. The Baghrams make regular monthly deposits in a savings account. The graph shows the relationship between the number x of months and the amount y in dollars in the account.

Account Balance

What is the equation for the deposit?

Ⓐ $\frac{y}{x} = \$25$/month

Ⓑ $\frac{y}{x} = \$40$/month

Ⓒ $\frac{y}{x} = \$50$/month

Ⓓ $\frac{y}{x} = \$75$/month

Hot Tip!

Read graphs and diagrams carefully. Look at the labels for important information.

3. What is the decimal form of $-4\frac{7}{8}$?

Ⓐ -4.9375

Ⓑ -4.875

Ⓒ -4.75

Ⓓ -4.625

4. Find the percent change from 72 to 90.

Ⓐ 20% decrease

Ⓑ 20% increase

Ⓒ 25% decrease

Ⓓ 25% increase

5. A store had a sale on art supplies. The price p of each item was marked down 60%. Which expression represents the new price?

Ⓐ $0.4p$ Ⓒ $1.4p$

Ⓑ $0.6p$ Ⓓ $1.6p$

6. Clarke borrows $16,000 to buy a car. He pays simple interest at an annual rate of 6% over a period of 3.5 years. How much does he pay altogether?

Ⓐ $18,800

Ⓑ $19,360

Ⓒ $19,920

Ⓓ $20,480

7. To which set or sets does the number 37 belong?

Ⓐ integers only

Ⓑ rational numbers only

Ⓒ integers and rational numbers only

Ⓓ whole numbers, integers, and rational numbers

8. In which equation is the constant of proportionality 5?

Ⓐ $x = 5y$

Ⓑ $y = 5x$

Ⓒ $y = x + 5$

Ⓓ $y = 5 - x$

9. Suri earns extra money by dog walking. She charges $6.25 to walk a dog once a day 5 days a week and $8.75 to walk a dog once a day 7 days a week. Which equation represents this relationship?

Ⓐ $y = 7x$

Ⓑ $y = 5x$

Ⓒ $y = 2.50x$

Ⓓ $y = 1.25x$

10. Randy walks $\frac{1}{2}$ mile in each $\frac{1}{5}$ hour. How far will Randy walk in one hour?

Ⓐ $\frac{1}{2}$ miles

Ⓑ 2 miles

Ⓒ $2\frac{1}{2}$ miles

Ⓓ 5 miles

11. On a trip to Spain, Sheila bought a piece of jewelry that cost $56.75. She paid for it with her credit card, which charges a foreign transaction fee of 3%. How much was the foreign transaction fee?

Ⓐ $0.17

Ⓑ $1.07

Ⓒ $1.70

Ⓓ $17.00

12. A baker is looking for a recipe that has the lowest unit rate for flour per batch of muffins. Which recipe should she use?

Ⓐ $\frac{1}{2}$ cup flour for $\frac{2}{3}$ batch

Ⓑ $\frac{2}{3}$ cup flour for $\frac{1}{2}$ batch

Ⓒ $\frac{3}{4}$ cup flour for $\frac{2}{3}$ batch

Ⓓ $\frac{1}{3}$ cup flour for $\frac{1}{4}$ batch

Mini-Task

13. Kevin was able to type 2 pages in 5 minutes, 3 pages in 7.5 minutes, and 5 pages in 12.5 minutes.

a. Make a table of the data.

b. Graph the relationship between the number of pages typed and the number of minutes.

c. Explain how to use the graph to find the unit rate.

_____

_____

_____

_____

_____

_____

LESSON
A1 Ratios and Pi

FL 6.RP.1.3e

Understand the concept of Pi as the ratio of the circumference of a circle to its diameter.

ESSENTIAL QUESTION

What is the relationship between the circumference of a circle and its diameter?

EXPLORE ACTIVITY   **FL** 6.RP.1.3

Exploring Circumference

A circle is a set of points in a plane that are a fixed distance from the center.

A **radius** is a line segment with one endpoint at the center of the circle and the other endpoint on the circle. The length of a radius is called the radius of the circle.

A **diameter** of a circle is a line segment that passes through the center of the circle and whose endpoints lie on the circle. The length of the diameter is twice the length of the radius. The length of a diameter is called the diameter of the circle.

The **circumference** of a circle is the distance around the circle.

A Use a measuring tape to find the circumference of five circular objects. Then measure the distance across each item to find its diameter. Record the measurements of each object in the table below.

Object	Circumference C	Diameter d	$\frac{C}{d}$

B Divide the circumference of each object by its diameter. Round your answer to the nearest hundredth.

Reflect

1. **Make a Conjecture** Describe what you notice about the ratio $\frac{C}{d}$ in your table.

_____

© Houghton Mifflin Harcourt Publishing Company

Lesson A1 **661**

Determining Proportionality in Circles

The ratio of the circumference to the diameter $\frac{C}{d}$ of any circle is the same for all circles. This ratio $\frac{C}{d}$ is represented by the Greek letter π, called **pi**. As you calculated in the Explore Activity, the value of π is close to 3. You can approximate π as 3.14 or $\frac{22}{7}$.

Later, you can use this ratio to find a formula for circumference. Circles do not have sides and angles, but every circle has a radius and diameter whose lengths you can measure and compare.

EXAMPLE 1 FL · 6.RP.1.3

Determine if the radius and diameter of the two circles are proportional.

STEP 1 Find the radius and diameter of each circle.

Larger circle		Smaller circle
$r = 5$ in.	The radius is given.	$r = 3$ in.
$d = 10$ in.	To find the diameter, multiply the radius by 2.	$d = 6$ in.

> The diameter is 2 times the length of the radius.

STEP 2 Set up a proportion using the corresponding lengths of the radius and diameter.

$\frac{r}{r} = \frac{d}{d}$ Set up a proportion.

$\frac{5}{3} \overset{?}{=} \frac{10}{6}$ Substitute the values for r and d.

$\frac{5}{3} \overset{?}{=} \frac{10 \div 2}{6 \div 2}$ Simplify.

$\frac{5}{3} = \frac{5}{3}$ ✓   The two ratios are equal so the corresponding lengths are proportional.

The radius and diameter of the two circles are proportional.

$r = 5$ in.

$r = 3$ in.

Reflect

2. In every circle, what is the ratio of the radius to the diameter? What is the ratio of the circumference to the diameter?

_____

_____

3. **Draw Conclusions** Based on the ratios of the radius to diameter and circumference to diameter, are all circles proportional? Is the ratio of circumference to the diameter of any circle the same for all circles?

_____

_____

_____

YOUR TURN

4. Determine if the radius and diameter of the two circles are proportional.

8 ft   9 ft

_____

Finding Missing Parts of a Circle

You know that $\frac{C}{d} = \pi$ for all circles. You can use this ratio to find unknown measures.

EXAMPLE 2

   FL 6.RP.1.3

My Notes

A The circumference of the larger circle is approximately 94 cm. Use a proportion to find the approximate circumference of the smaller circle.

30 cm   15 cm

Set up a proportion using the given information for the larger and smaller circles.

$$\frac{C}{d} = \frac{C}{d}$$ Set up a proportion.

$$\frac{94}{30} = \frac{C}{15}$$ Substitute the given values.

$$\frac{94 \div 2}{30 \div 2} = \frac{C}{15}$$ Since 30 divided by 2 is 15, divide 94 by 2 to find the value of C.

$$\frac{94}{30} = \frac{47}{15}$$

$$C = 47$$

The circumference of the smaller circle is approximately 47 cm.

B A larger circle has a circumference of 50.24 cm and a diameter of 16 cm. The circumference of a smaller circle is 25.12 cm. Use a proportion to find the diameter of the smaller circle.

$$\frac{C}{d} = \frac{C}{d}$$ Set up a proportion.

$$\frac{50.24}{16} = \frac{25.12}{d}$$ Substitute the given values.

$$\frac{50.24 \div 2}{16 \div 2} = \frac{25.12}{d}$$ Since 50.24 divided by 2 is 25.12, divide 16 by 2 to find the value of d.

$$\frac{50.24}{16} = \frac{25.12}{8}$$

$$d = 8$$

The diameter of the smaller circle is 8 cm.

© Houghton Mifflin Harcourt Publishing Company

YOUR TURN

5. The circumference of the larger circle is approximately 44 meters and the circumference of the smaller circle is approximately 11 meters. Use a proportion to find the approximate

   diameter of the smaller circle. _____

Guided Practice

Fill in the blanks. (Explore Activity)

1. **Vocabulary** In any circle, the ratio of the _____ to the diameter is pi.

2. **Vocabulary** In any circle, the ratio of the _____ to the radius is 2.

3. You can use the decimal number _____ or the fraction _____ as an approximation for pi.

4. Determine if the radius and diameter of a circle with a diameter of 100 mm and a circle with a diameter of 10 mm are proportional. (Example 1)

   _____ = _____

5. Is the circle represented by a penny similar to the one of a quarter? Explain. (Example 1)

   _____

   _____

6. The circumference of the larger circle is about 18.8 centimeters and the circumference of the smaller circle is about 6.3 centimeters. Find the approximate diameter of the smaller circle.

   (Example 2) _____

ESSENTIAL QUESTION CHECK-IN

7. What is the result of dividing the distance around a circle by the distance across the same circle? What number can you use as an approximate value for this ratio?

   _____

A1 Independent Practice

 FL 6.RP.1.3

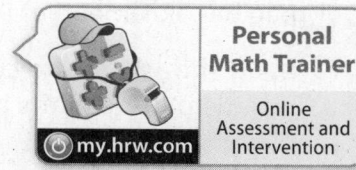
8. Measurement Jillian measured the distance around a small fishpond as 27 yards. Which would be a good estimate for the distance across the pond, 14 yards, 9 yards, or 7 yards? Explain how you decided.

_____

_____

_____

_____

9. A rotating wind turbine has a diameter of about 185 feet and its circumference is about 580 feet. A smaller model of the turbine has a circumference of about 10 feet. What will the diameter of the model be?

_____

10. Multistep Andrew has a flying disc with a radius of 10 centimeters. What is the circumference of the disc? (Remember $\frac{C}{d} = 3.14$.)

_____

11. Mandie wants to put some lace trim around the outside of a round tablecloth she expanded. The original tablecloth had a radius of 2 feet and a circumference of 12.56 feet. If the tablecloth now has a radius of 3 feet, is 15 feet of lace enough? Explain.

_____

_____

_____

12. Marta is making two different charms for a necklace. One charm has a 1 centimeter diameter and a 3.14 centimeter circumference. A similar charm has a diameter of 4 centimeters. What is the circumference?

_____

13. Randy is putting bricks around the outside of his round flower bed to protect the plants.

a. If the diameter of his flower bed is 100 inches, what is the distance around the garden? (Remember $\frac{C}{d} = 3.14$.)

_____

b. If the curved bricks he wants to buy are each half a foot long, how many will he need to put around the outside of the garden? Explain.

_____

_____

c. If each brick costs $0.68, and he can only buy whole bricks, how much will it cost him to get the material to put around the outside of his garden?

_____

d. If his mother decides he can only have half of that diameter for his flower bed, how will the cost of the bricks be affected? Explain?

_____

_____

_____

_____

14. Your grandmother is teaching you how to make a homemade pie. The pie pan has a diameter of 9 inches.

   a. If she asks you to cut a strip of pie crust long enough to go around the outside of the pan, how long does it need to be? (Remember $\frac{C}{d} = 3.14$.)

   _____

   b. If another pie pan is 8 inches across the diameter, how long does that piece of crust need to be?

   _____

 FOCUS ON HIGHER ORDER THINKING

Work Area

15. **Make a Conjecture** You know that all squares are similar and all circles are similar. An equilateral triangle has 3 equal sides and 3 angles of 60 degrees each. Are all equilateral triangles similar?

_____

_____

16. **Multiple Representations** You know three different number representations for pi that you can use to approximate the answer to a problem. Describe a situation when you might choose to use $\frac{22}{7}$.

_____

_____

17. **Represent Real-World Problems** Describe an example in your daily life where you might be able to measure around something but could not measure across it.

_____

_____

18. **Critical Thinking** Every morning Jesse runs 3 laps on a circular track. One morning the track is closed, but the straight path from one side of the track to the other is open. How many times should Jesse run across the path if he wants to run his usual distance? Explain your answer.

_____

_____

_____

Selected Answers

LESSON 1.1

Your Turn

6.
−5   0   5

8. −10 **9.** 5 **10.** 0 **11.** 6

Guided Practice

2.
−5   0   5

4.
−5   0   5

5. −4 **6.** 11 **7.** −3 **8.** 3 **9.** 0
10. −22

Independent Practice
13. 17 **15.** 2 **17.** 12 **19a.** gain
b. Tino **c.** Tino and Luis **d.** −6
e. No; −6 pound change means
Frankie lost 6 pounds. **21.** 4 units
23. 14 units **25.** −9; it is 9 units
away from 0 on a number line, and
6 is only 6 units away from 0.

LESSON 1.2

Your Turn

2. 4, 2, 0, −3, −5, −6
−6   0   4

3. 9, 8, 5, 2, 0, −1, −6, −10
4. < **5.** < **6.** >
7. −2 > −18; −18 < −2
8. −39 < 39; 39 > −39

Guided Practice

1b. A **c.** B **2.** −9, −6, −3, 0, 1, 4, 8
3. −65, −13, −7, 7, 34, 55, 62
4. −17 > −22; −22 < −17 **5.** <
6. < **7.** > **8.** > **9.** > **10.** < **11.** <
12. > **13a.** −3 < 2 **b.** 0 > −4

Independent Practice

15b. E. Simpson **17.** 167 > −65
19b. −5, −2, 2, 4, 7 **21.** 377 > 249
23. Argentina **25.** No; −12 °F <
−3 °F, so it was getting colder
outside. **27.** −10, −3, 5, 16 and
−3, 5, −10, 16

LESSON 1.3

Your Turn

4. The temperature at night
reached 13 °F below zero.
5. 12 **6.** 91 **7.** 55 **8.** 0 **9.** 88 **10.** 1

Guided Practice

1. negative **2a.** −$10; it is a fee, so
it represents a change of −$10 in
the amount of money Ryan has.
b. | −10 | = 10

−10   0

3a. more than 100 **b.** less than
Leo **c.** more than 50

Independent Practice

5. The first week his balance
changed by +$80. The second
week his balance changed by
−$85. **7b.** April **9a.** −5, 4, −1, 3,
−2 **b.** The spinner landing on red
results in a change of −$5 to
Lisa's amount of money. **13.** No;
−| −4 | = −4, and | −(−4) | =
| 4 | = 4.

LESSON 2.1

Your Turn

3. 7 **4.** 4 **5.** 8 teams; 4 girls,
5 boys

Guided Practice

1. Common factors: 1, 2, 4, 8;
Possible numbers of vests: 1, 2, 4,
8; GCF = 8; greatest number of
vests = 8 **2.** 9; 9; 4; 9; 5; 9; 4; 5
3. 15; 15; 5; 15; 6; 15; 5; 6

Independent Practice

5. 1, 2, 3, 4, 6, 12 **7.** 1, 3, 13, 39
9. 8 **11.** 5 **13.** 1 **15.** 12 **17.** 4
19. 1, 2, 4, or 8 shelves
21. 6 groups; 2 coaches and 7
players **23.** 8 × (7 + 8) = 8 × 15
25. 6 × (5 + 9) = 6 × 14
27. 11 × (5 + 6) 11 × 11
29. 5 × (8 + 5) 8 × 13

31. 1 is a factor of all whole
numbers. Some pairs of whole
numbers have no common
factors other than 1. For example,
7 and 16 have no common factors
other than 1. **33.** Find the factors
of all three numbers, and take the
greatest factor that is common to
all three. For example, for the GCF
of 6, 9, and 12, the factors of 6 are
1, 2, 3, and 6; the factors of 9 are 1,
3, and 9; and the factors of 12 are
1, 2, 3, 4, 6, and 12. So, the GCF is 3.

LESSON 2.2

Your Turn

2. 36; 4, 8, 12, 16, 20, 24, 28, 32,
36, 40; 9, 18, 27, 36, 45, 54, 63, 72,
81, 90

Guided Practice

1. 36th and 72nd visits; 36th visit

Independent Practice

3. 56 **5.** 60 **7.** 48 **9.** 45
11a. February 15 **b.** No; there are
only 28 or 29 days in February,
and the next common multiple
of 3 and 5 is 30. **13.** 40 **15.** 120
17. The LCM is the greater of the
two numbers. **19.** 5 and 12.

LESSON 3.1

Your Turn

3. $\frac{-15}{1}$ **4.** $\frac{31}{100}$ **5.** $\frac{41}{9}$ **6.** $\frac{62}{1}$
9. rational numbers **10.** rational
numbers **11.** integers and
rational numbers **12.** whole
numbers, integers, and rational
numbers

© Houghton Mifflin Harcourt Publishing Company

Guided Practice

1a. 4 rolls of ribbon divided evenly among the 5 friends. $4 \div 5$.
b. $\frac{4}{5}$ roll **2.** $\frac{7}{10}$ **3.** $\frac{-29}{1}$ **4.** $\frac{25}{3}$
5. integers, rational numbers
6. rational numbers

Independent Practice

11. $\frac{22}{5}$, or $4.40 **13.** Venn **15.** $\frac{35}{2}$, rational numbers **17.** $\frac{8}{15}$ cup

LESSON 3.2

Your Turn

2. -7, 3.5, -2.25, and $-9\frac{1}{3}$. **4.** 4.5
5. $1\frac{1}{2}$ **6.** 4 **7.** $3\frac{1}{4}$

Guided Practice

5. -3.78 **6.** $7\frac{5}{12}$ **7.** 0 **8.** -4.2
9. -12.1 **10.** -2.6 **11.** They are the same distance from 0 on the number line. **12.** 5.23 **13.** $4\frac{2}{11}$
14. 0 **15.** $6\frac{3}{5}$ **16.** 2.12 **17.** 8.2

Independent Practice

19a. Girardi $85.23, Lewis $-$$20.44, Stein $116.33, Yuan $-$$13.50, Wenner $9.85
b. Wenner **c.** Stein **23.** to the left
25a. $-25,344$ ft **b.** -5 and -4
c.

```
<-----•-|-|-|-|-|-|-|-|-|-|->
     -5        0        5
```

LESSON 3.3

Your Turn

3. 0.15, $\frac{3}{5}$, $\frac{7}{10}$, 0.85 **5.** -1.8, -1.25, 1, $1\frac{2}{5}$, $1\frac{9}{10}$

Guided Practice

1. $\frac{3}{5}$ **2.** 0.25 **3.** $\frac{9}{10}$ **4.** $\frac{1}{10}$ **5.** 0.3
6. $1\frac{2}{5}$ **7.** 0.8 **8.** $\frac{2}{5}$ **9.** 0.75
10. $\frac{1}{5}$, 0.4, $\frac{1}{2}$, 0.75 **11.** $12\frac{3}{4}$, 12.7, $12\frac{3}{5}$

12. 2.3, 2.6, $2\frac{4}{5}$ **13.** $\frac{5}{48}$, $\frac{3}{16}$, 0.5, 0.75
14. $\frac{1}{5}$, 0.35, $\frac{12}{25}$, 0.5, $\frac{4}{5}$ **15.** $-\frac{3}{4}$, $-\frac{7}{10}$, $\frac{3}{4}$, $\frac{8}{10}$ **16.** -0.65, $-\frac{3}{8}$, $\frac{5}{16}$, $\frac{2}{4}$ **17.** $-2\frac{4}{5}$, -2.6, -2.3 **18.** -0.72, $-\frac{5}{8}$, -0.6, $-\frac{7}{12}$
19. 1.2, $1\frac{1}{3}$, 1.45, $1\frac{1}{2}$ **20.** -0.35, -0.3, 0.5, 0.55

Independent Practice

23a. $6\frac{1}{6}$, 5.5, $4\frac{3}{8}$, 4.3, $\frac{15}{4}$ **b.** Claire, Peter, Brenda, and Jim; Micah
c. Yes; the smallest donation is $\frac{15}{4}$ pounds. $\frac{1}{2}$ is equal to $\frac{2}{4}$ pound. $\frac{15}{4} + \frac{2}{4} = \frac{17}{4} = 4\frac{1}{4} = 4.25$ pounds, which is enough to win a free movie coupon.

UNIT 2 Selected Answers

LESSON 4.1

Your Turn

1. $\frac{1}{10}$ **2.** $\frac{7}{12}$ **3.** $\frac{2}{7}$ **4.** $\frac{8}{35}$ **5.** $\frac{4}{15}$ **6.** $\frac{1}{7}$
8. 15 **9.** 12 **10.** $\frac{8}{3}$ **11.** $\frac{7}{2}$ **12.** $25\frac{9}{10}$
13. 23 **15.** $\frac{11}{21}$ **16.** $\frac{4}{15}$ **17.** $\frac{1}{24}$
18. $1\frac{11}{20}$ **19.** $6\frac{13}{15}$ **20.** $3\frac{1}{42}$

Guided Practice

1. $\frac{5}{16}$ **2.** $\frac{1}{3}$ **3.** $\frac{3}{20}$ **4.** 38 **5.** $\frac{3}{4}$ **6.** 6
7. 3 **8.** 16 **9.** 24 **10.** 15 **11.** $\frac{7}{12}$
12. $\frac{7}{15}$ **13.** $\frac{1}{5}$ **14.** $\frac{24}{35}$ **15.** $3\frac{19}{24}$
16. $5\frac{19}{45}$

Independent Practice

19a. 10 pounds **b.** 5 more bags
21a. oranges $= 1\frac{1}{2}$, apples $= 1\frac{4}{5}$,
blueberries $= \frac{3}{4}$ cup, peaches $= 2$
b. Sample answer: If you triple
3, it becomes 9. If you triple $\frac{1}{2}$, it
becomes $1\frac{1}{2}$. Add $9 + 1\frac{1}{2} = 10\frac{1}{2}$.
23a. $22\frac{1}{2}$ minutes **b.** Yes, there
is enough time; 15 min for the
teacher's introduction + 15 min
for students to get ready +
$22\frac{1}{2}$ min for speeches $= 52\frac{1}{2}$ min
25. Cameron divided a factor in
one of the numerators by the GCF
but did not divide a factor in one
of the denominators by the GCF.
He should have simplified $\frac{4}{9}$ to $\frac{4}{3}$
and multiplied $\frac{1}{7}$ and $\frac{4}{3}$ to find the
product $\frac{4}{21}$.

LESSON 4.2

Your Turn

5. $\frac{8}{7}$ **6.** $\frac{1}{9}$ **7.** 11 **10.** $2\frac{1}{4}$ **11.** $1\frac{1}{2}$

Guided Practice

1. $\frac{5}{2}$ **2.** 9 **3.** $\frac{3}{10}$ **4.** $\frac{4}{5}$ **5.** $\frac{3}{8}$ **6.** $1\frac{1}{4}$

Independent Practice

9. 4 runners will be needed.
11. $\frac{1}{10}$ pound **13.** 9 bags
15. 8 **17.** 2; $\frac{1}{12}$ meter
19. Greater than $\frac{1}{2}$ **21.** Robyn

LESSON 4.3

Your Turn

6. 9; $10\frac{1}{2} \div 1\frac{1}{4} = 8\frac{2}{5}$; She will need
9 containers. **8.** $4\frac{1}{2}$ meters
9. $3\frac{1}{4}$ yards

Guided Practice

1. 17; 17; 4; 3; $5\frac{2}{3}$ **2.** 3; 9; 3; 4; 9; $\frac{2}{3}$
3. $3\frac{5}{9}$ **4.** $2\frac{4}{5}$ **5.** $3\frac{1}{3}$ **6.** 4 **7.** $26 \div 5\frac{1}{2}$;
The width is $4\frac{8}{11}$ feet. **8.** $230 \div 12\frac{1}{2}$;
$18\frac{2}{5}$ feet

Independent Practice

13a. No **b.** $\frac{11}{20}$ of a cup; $5\frac{1}{2}$ cups $\div$
10 people $= \frac{11}{2} \times \frac{1}{10} = \frac{11}{20}$
c. She would need $7\frac{1}{2}$ cups total,
so she would need 2 more cups
of trail mix. **15.** yes because the
height is $4\frac{1}{4}$ feet **17.** $5\frac{1}{4}$ feet
19. He used the reciprocal of $\frac{3}{4}$
instead of the reciprocal of $2\frac{3}{4}$.

LESSON 4.4

Your Turn

1. 10

Guided Practice

1. 13

Independent Practice

3. $8 per hour
5. 40 appointments
7. 93 pieces **9.** $1\frac{5}{24}$ gallons
11. Sample answer: A person
taking a test averages $\frac{3}{8}$ minute
to read a question and $\frac{5}{6}$ minute
to answer the question. It takes
the person 29 minutes to answer
all of the questions. How many
questions are on the test?
24 questions

LESSON 5.1

Your Turn

3. 109 **4.** 587 **7.** 231 R21
8. 46 R16 **9.** 105 bags; 3 rocks
left over

Guided Practice

1. 30,000; 500; 60 **2.** 96 **3.** 89
4. 98 R7 **5.** 42 **6.** 61 **7.** 94 R15
8. 24 R9 **9.** 127 **10.** 81 R28
11. 300 items **12.** 32 seats
13. 85 boxes

Independent Practice

15. 268 **17.** 209
19. 86 R39 **21.** 587
23. 67 rows; $8,450 \div 125 =$
67 R75 so he will have 67 full rows
and one partial row of 75 trees.
25. 69 people **29.** Multiply the
quotient and the divisor, then add
the remainder to the product. If
the division was done correctly,
the result will equal the dividend.
31. No; 78,114 is about 80,000 and
192 is about 200; $80,000 \div 200 =$
400, and 40 isn't close to 400.
33. More; the whole amount is
divided into smaller portions, so
there will be more bags; since 25
is half of 50, they will have twice
as many bags.

LESSON 5.2

Your Turn

5. 0.69 **6.** 0.939 **7.** 7.85 **8.** 21.15

Guided Practice

1. 0.91 **2.** 0.78 **3.** 62.35
4. 37.11 **5.** 3.955 **6.** 2.57
7. 11.949 **8.** 1.806 **9.** 30.1
10. 65.841 **11.** 23.356
12. 7.35 **13.** 37.68 **14.** 72.25
15. 31.25 feet **16.** $11.36

© Houghton Mifflin Harcourt Publishing Company

Independent Practice

19. 5.495 **21.** 63.022
23. 11.949 **25.** 6.408
27. Jahmya; $0.54 more
29. $1.53 **31a.** 27.78 minutes
b. 32.22 minutes
33. Sample answer: The sum
$2.55 + (3.72 + 1.45) =$
$2.55 + 5.17 = 7.72$. Using the
Commutative Property, the
sum can be written as $2.55 +$
$(1.45 + 3.72) = 7.72$, and using
the Associative Property, the sum
can be written as $(2.55 + 1.45) +$
$3.72 = 7.72$.

LESSON 5.3

Your Turn

3. 1; 1; 6300; 12600; 192.78; 2
4. 2; 2; 5856; 39040; 4.4896; 4
5. 49980; 428400; 48.4092
6. 8043; 22980; 919200; 95.0223
7. 37.2
8. Sample answer: Round 15.5 to
16 and 2.4 to 2; $16 \times 2 = 32$; 32 is
close to 37.2.

Guided Practice

1. 0.28

2. 2.64

3. 0.0108 **4.** 130.055 **5.** 0.1152
6. 2,021.175 **7.** 14.858 **8.** 2.48292
9. 23.63 **10.** 173.90 **11.** 29.21
12. 1.06

Independent Practice

15. 14 inches **17.** $342 **19.** $15.50
21. $23.58 **23.** 20.425 miles
25. 14.125 miles **27.** 3.48 is
closer to 3 and 7.33 is closer to 7;
$3 \times 7 = 21$ **29.** The 22-karat gold
statue; 24.549 ounces

LESSON 5.4

Your Turn

3. 1.95 **4.** 0.92 **5.** 8.5 **6.** 18

Guided Practice

1. 7.375 **2.** 3.31 **3.** 7 **4.** 0.15
5. 77 **6.** 2.65 **7.** 33.16 **8.** 1.95
9. 19 **10.** 0.3 **11.** 6.2 **12.** 405
13. 250 **14.** 11.8 **15.** 0.8 pound
16. 3.5 pounds **17.** 18.1 seconds
18. 18 **19.** $2.73 per gallon
20. 20 inches

Independent Practice

23. $8.50 **25a.** 10 movies
27. beef **29a.** 0.42 **b.** 0.25
c. 0.15 **31.** 42 **33.** 20 weeks

LESSON 5.5

Your Turn

2. He paid $\frac{29}{2} \times \frac{3}{5} = 8\frac{7}{10}$ dollars or
$14.5 \times 0.6 = \$8.70$

Guided Practice

1. $134\frac{1}{2}$ miles **2.** $397.80

Independent Practice

3. $3\frac{1}{2}$ gallons **5.** 2 batteries
7. $5.88; No. They earned $7.84
on Wednesday. $7.84 - 5.88 = 1.96$,
so they don't have enough money.
9. 3 games **13.** 35.

MODULE **6**

LESSON 6.1

Your Turn

5. 3 : 1; 3 to 1; $\frac{3}{1}$ **6.** 8 : 3; 8 to 3; $\frac{8}{3}$
7. 1 : 1; 1 to 1; $\frac{1}{1}$ **8.** $\frac{4}{5}, \frac{16}{20}, \frac{12}{15}$ **9.** $\frac{10}{4}$,
$\frac{15}{6}, \frac{20}{8}$

Guided Practice

1. 1 to 5 **2.** 5; 3 **3.** 5; 25
4. 60 pets **5.** 2 to 5; 2 : 5; $\frac{2}{5}$
6. 5 to 12; 5 : 12; $\frac{5}{12}$
7. Sample answer: $\frac{5}{6}, \frac{20}{24}, \frac{25}{30}$.
8. Sample answer: $\frac{7}{1}, \frac{21}{3}, \frac{28}{4}$.
9. Sample answer: $\frac{8}{14}, \frac{12}{21}, \frac{16}{28}$.

Independent Practice

11. 2 to 6, 3 to 9, 4 to 12
13. 16 roses and 24 carnations
15. 20; her current ratio of movie posters to band posters is 120 : 100. If she sells 24 movie posters, she will have 96 left. 120 : 100 = 96 : 80, so she should sell 20 movie posters. **17a.** 18 **b.** 12
19. 3 : 2; 30 girls and 20 boys
21. Tina multiplied 6 by 6 to get 36 and 8 by 8 to get 64. She should have multiplied both terms by the same number.

LESSON 6.2

Your Turn

3. 12
4. 45 minutes, $\frac{27 \text{ minutes} \div 3}{3 \text{ miles} \div 3} =$
$\frac{9 \text{ minutes}}{1 \text{ mile}}$. The unit rate is 9 minutes per mile. $\frac{9 \text{ minutes} \times 5}{1 \text{ mile} \times 5} = \frac{45 \text{ minutes}}{5 \text{ miles}}$

Guided Practice

1. 0.21; 0.19 **2.** family size **3.** $48
4. 16 **5.** 72 **6.** 300 calories **7.** $6

Independent Practice

9. $12.50 per lawn **11.** Alastair
13a. 5 minutes; 7 balloons
b. $1\frac{2}{5}$ balloons per minute
c. 14 balloons

15. $10.50
17. There are 12 inches in 1 foot, and 2.54 × 12 = 30.48 centimeters per foot; there are 3 feet per yard, so 30.48 cm × 3 = 91.44 centimeters per yard.
19. The unit costs are $1.10 per pound for a 1-pound bag, $0.99 per pound for a 2-pound bag, and $0.95 per pound for a 3-pound bag. The unit cost decreases as the quantity of sugar increases.

LESSON 6.3

Your Turn

1. Anna: $\frac{2}{5}$ cup; Bailey: $\frac{3}{8}$ cup; ratio of concentrate to total cups of lemonade is 2 to 5 for Anna and 3 to 8 for Bailey. So, Anna has $\frac{2}{5}$ cup of concentrate in 1 cup of lemonade, and Bailey has $\frac{3}{8}$ cup. **2.** No, the ratios are not equivalent. $\frac{2 \times 4}{3 \times 4} = \frac{8}{12}$ $\frac{8}{12} > \frac{7}{12}$

Guided Practice

1b. $\frac{5}{6} > \frac{4}{6}$; No Celeste is not using the correct ratio of apples to oranges **2.** No; Neha used the greater ratio of bananas to oranges. **3.** Tim can read 140 words in 5 minutes.
4. On average, the cafeteria sells 120 drinks per hour.

Independent Practice

7. $63 **9.** 175 miles
11. 6 pounds; 19 apples
13. approximately 22 inches
17. All of the rates should be equivalent to each other. One way to check that they are equivalent is to divide the top term by the bottom term. All of the quotients will be equal if the rates are all correct.

MODULE **7**

LESSON 7.1

Your Turn

3.

Time (min)	2	3	3.5	5	6.5
Water used (gal)	8	12	14	20	26

Guided Practice

1. $\frac{6}{12} = \frac{9}{18} = \frac{21}{42} = \frac{27}{54}$
2.

3. $\frac{2}{4} = \frac{4}{8} = \frac{7}{14} = \frac{8}{16}$
4.

© Houghton Mifflin Harcourt Publishing Company

5.

Boxes	5	8	10
Candles	60	96	120

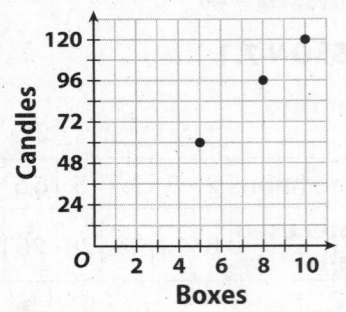

Independent Practice

7. $\frac{\text{money collected}}{\text{sweatshirts sold}} = \frac{\$60}{3 \text{ sweatshirts}} = \frac{\$20}{1 \text{ sweatshirt}} = \$20$ per sweatshirt sold **11.** $480 **13.** 330 mi

LESSON 7.2

Your Turn

1. 10 cheese pizzas
2. 108 minutes **3.** 50 miles

Guided Practice

1. 6; 6; 18 **2.** 2; 2; 2 **3.** $45
4. 18 inches tall **5.** 60 seconds
6. 13 measures **7.** 40 minutes
8. 26 paychecks **9.** 24 kilometers

Independent Practice

11a. 1 inch = 12 miles **b.** 24 miles
13a. 60 seats **b.** 150 seats
15. 45 ft **17.** Ira **19.** No, the caterpillar's unit rate should be 5 feet per minute.
21a. b. 80 minutes

LESSON 7.3

Your Turn

2. 72 inches **3.** 2.5 meters

Guided Practice

1. 3 **2.** 48 **3.** 32 cups
4. 12,000 pounds
5. 500 meters **6.** 3,500 grams
7. 1,750 mg **8.** 2.7 cm
9. 6 pounds **10.** 10 miles

Independent Practice

13. 126; 10.5; 3.5 **15.** The large size **17.** 3 kilometers
19a. between 7 tons and 8 tons **b.** No **21.** You get the original number.

LESSON 7.4

Your Turn

2. 5.676 **3.** 4.27 **4.** 9 **5.** 7.40
7. 64.55

Guided Practice

1. 8.05; 5 miles; 1.61 km **2.** 18.95; 5 gallons; 3.79 L **3.** 30.48 **4.** 1.816
5. 18.28 **6.** 339.6 **7.** 4.73 **8.** 437.64
9. 2.64 **10.** 450 **11.** 64.96 **12.** 6,211

Independent Practice

15. one inch **17.** one mile
19. one liter **21.** 4 liters **23.** 22.7 kg **25.** 2-liter juice bottle **27.** 2.75 pounds **29a.** Yes; Two half-gallon containers will hold one gallon, which is about 3.79 liters. **b.** No; A gallon jug can hold 3.79 liters, so a half-gallon jug would hold half of that, which is only 1.895 liters.
33. Multiply the number of pounds by 0.454; 3.8 kg

LESSON 8.1

Your Turn

2. 90% **3.** 40% **4.** about $\frac{2}{3}$

Guided Practice

1. 4; 4; 36; 36%
2.

0 — $\frac{1}{5}$ — — — **1**

0% 20% 100%

3. 10; 60% **4.** 1: 50% **5.** 1; 80%
6. about $\frac{2}{5}$

Independent Practice

9. 55 **11.** $\frac{9}{10} = 90\%, \frac{4}{5} = 80\%,$ $\frac{17}{20} = 85\%,$ 80%, 85%, 90%
13. 30% of your minutes are used up **17.** No

LESSON 8.2

Your Turn

1. $\frac{3}{20}$, 0.15 **2.** $\frac{12}{25}$, 0.48 **3.** $\frac{4}{5}$, 0.8
4. $\frac{3}{4}$, 0.75 **5.** $\frac{9}{25}$, 0.36 **6.** $\frac{2}{5}$, 0.4
8. 0.36, 36% **9.** 0.875, 87.5%

Guided Practice

1. $\frac{3}{25}$, 0.12 **2.** 53%, $\frac{53}{100}$ **3.** 107%; $\frac{107}{100}, 1\frac{7}{100}$ **4.** 0.35; 35% **5.** 0.375; 37.5%

Independent Practice

7. $\frac{18}{25}$, 0.72 **9.** $\frac{500}{100}, \frac{5}{1} = \frac{5}{1}$, 5 **11.** $\frac{37}{100}$; 0.37 **13.** 0.625, 62.5% **15.** 3.5, 350% **17.** $\frac{68}{80} = \frac{17}{20}$; 85%; 0.85
19. 6 **23.** 1, 100%, 1

LESSON 8.3

Your Turn

5. 19 **6.** 81 **7.** 45 **9.** 76%
11. 20 **12.** 500

Guided Practice

1. 240 televisions are high definition. **2.** 65; 200; 130
3. ×; 900; 9; 9 **4.** 21; 100; 300; 7%
5. 9; 300

Independent Practice

7. 48 tiles **9.** 8 pages **11.** 252 friends **13.** 20 **15.** 70 **17.** 1,400
19. 40 **21.** 20 **23.** 9 **25.** $500
27. $30 **29.** $175 **31.** $\frac{25}{100} = \frac{?}{50}$. 25% of 50 is 12.5.

UNIT 4 Selected Answers

MODULE 9

LESSON 9.1

Your Turn

2. 4^3 **3.** 6^1 **4.** $\left(\frac{1}{8}\right)^2$ **5.** 5^6 **6.** 81
7. 1 **8.** $\frac{8}{125}$ **9.** 144

Guided Practice

2. 6^3 **3.** 10^7 **4.** $\left(\frac{3}{4}\right)^5$ **5.** $\left(\frac{7}{9}\right)^8$ **6.** 512
7. $2{,}401$ **8.** $1{,}000$ **9.** $\frac{1}{16}$ **10.** $\frac{1}{27}$
11. $\frac{36}{49}$ **12.** 0.64 **13.** 0.125
14. 1.21 **15.** 1 **16.** 12 **17.** 1
18. 169 **19.** $\frac{4}{25}$ **20.** 0.81

Independent Practice

23. 3 **25.** 3 **27.** 1 **29.** 2 **31.** 4
33. 3 **35.** 8 **37.** 9 **39.** 3^4 pages, or
81 pages **41.** 2^6 dollars, or $\$64$
47. 2^6, 4^3, and 8^2

LESSON 9.2

1. $1, 3, 7, 21$ **2.** $1, 37$ **3.** $1, 2, 3, 6, 7,$
$14, 21, 42$ **4.** $1, 2, 3, 5, 6, 10, 15, 30$

Guided Practice

1. $1, 2, 3, 6, 9, 18$ **2.** $1, 2, 4, 13, 26,$
52 **4.** $2 \cdot 3 \cdot 67$ **5.** $2^2 \cdot 3^2$ **6.** 2^5
7. $3 \cdot 3 \cdot 3$ or 3^3

Independent Practice

9. 1×12; 2×6; 3×4
13. $2^3 \cdot 3^2 \cdot 7$ **15.** $2 \cdot 5 \cdot 23$
19. prime factorization of $27 = 3^3$

LESSON 9.3

Your Turn

2. $1{,}222$ **3.** 170 **5.** 125 **6.** 15
7. 0

Guided Practice

1. $3 \times 2^2 = 12$ angelfish **2.** 16; 64;
76; 13 **3.** 3; 9; 54; 62 **4.** 6; 36; 9;
108; 101 **5.** 2; 8; 4; 32; 10

Independent Practice

7. 19 **9.** 15 **11.** 39
15a. $3 \times 2 \times 2 \times 2 \times 2 = 3 \times 2^4$
b. $3 \times 2^4 - 7 = 3 \times 16 - 7 =$
$48 - 7 = 41$ butterflies

17a. $6^2 + 2 \times 6 + 24 = 72$ square
inches **b.** 8 in. by 9 in.
19. $8 \times 4 - (2 \times 3 + 8) \div 2$

MODULE 10

LESSON 10.1

Your Turn

1. $7n$ **2.** $4 - y$ **3.** $x + 13$
4. Sample answer: the quotient of
x and 12 **5.** Sample answer:
10 multiplied by y **6.** Sample
answer: c plus 3
7.

8.

9. No; the expressions are not
equivalent. **10.** $\frac{d}{4}$

Guided Practice

1. $y - 3$ **2.** $2p$ **3.** Sample answer:
12 added to y **4.** Sample answer:
10 divided into p
5.

6.

7. No **8.** $24c$

Independent Practice

11. $\frac{n}{8}$ **13.** $b + 14$ **15.** $a - 16$
17. $3w$ **19.** $\frac{13}{z}$ **21.** $w - 8$
23. Sample answer: 83 added to m
25. Sample answer: t minus 29
27. Sample answer: the product
of 11 and x **29.** Sample answer:
k less than 5 **31.** $8w$ **33a.** $3d$
b. $3g$ **c.** In Mia's expression, the
numeral is the number of gallons
and variable is the cost per gallon;
in Bob's, the numeral is the
cost per gallon and the variable
is the number of gallons he
buys. **41.** $55h$ **43a.** $\frac{s}{2}$
b. $\frac{s}{2} - 1$ shoes

LESSON 10.2

Your Turn

1. 32 **2.** 4.7 **3.** 3 **4.** 18 **5.** 18
6. 55 **7.** 6 **8.** 39 **9.** 17
10. 24; 8 **11.** 420

Guided Practice

1. 16 **2.** 6 **3.** 2 **4.** 10.5 **5.** $2\frac{1}{18}$
6. 50 **7a.** $12x + 5$ **b.** 3; 36; 41;
$\$41$ **8a.** $2w + 2l$ **b.** 7; 5; 10; 24;
24 feet

Independent Practice

11. 42 **15.** $2(x^2)$; $2(64) =$
128 square feet

LESSON 10.3

Your Turn

3. Sample answer: $a(bc)$; Associative Property of Multiplication **4.** Sample answer: $(3 + 4)y$; Distributive Property **5.** Sample answer: 7×6; Commutative Property of Addition **6.** $2(3x - 5) = 6x - 10$; not equivalent **7.** $2 - 2 + 5x = 5x$; equivalent **8.** Jamal bought $2x + 8$ stickers. $2(4 + x) = 8 + 2x = 2x + 8$; yes **9.** $5y$ **10.** $10x^2 - 4$ **11.** $2a^5 + 5b$ **12.** $8m + 2 + 4n$

Guided Practice

2. not equivalent **3.** Sample answer: ba; Commutative Prop. of Mult. **4.** Sample answer: $5(3x) - 5(2)$; Distributive Prop. **5.** not equivalent **6.** not equivalent **7.** $44y$ **8.** $2x$

Independent Practice

11. Sample answer: $13 + x$; Commutative Prop. of Addition **13.** Sample answer: $(2 + a) + b$; Associative Prop. of Addition **15.** $2x^4$ **17.** $13b - 10$ **19.** $4y + 10$ **21.** $15y^2 - 6$ **23.** $0.5x^4 + 10.5$

25. $3x + 12 + x$ is equivalent to $4(3 + x)$. **27.** $(46 + 38 + 29)g + (29 + 27 + 17)s + (29 + 23 + 19)b$; $113g + 73s + 71b$ **29.** $36.4 + 4x$ in. **31.** $3x^2 - 4x + 7$; It does not have any like terms.

MODULE 11

LESSON 11.1

Your Turn

1. yes **2.** no **3.** yes **4.** no
5. $f + 9 = 38$ **6.** $17n = 102$
7. $c - 3 = 12$ **8.** $2h = 8$
10. Sample equation: $x + 24 = 62$; $38

Guided Practice

1. no; 14; 5 **2.** yes; 52; 4 **3.** yes
4. yes **5.** no **6.** yes **7.** no
8. yes **9.** no **10.** no **11.** yes
12. no **13.** $8r = 256$ **14.** Sample answer: $\frac{f}{2} = 5$ **15.** Sample equation: $8x = 208$; $26
16. Sample equation: $x + 24 = 92$; $68\,^{\circ}F$

Independent Practice

19. $x + 8 = 31$; 23 pounds
21. Sample answer: $4x = 20$; Yes: $20 \div x = 4$ or $x = 20 \div 4$
23a. $29 - 13 = x$; $13 + x = 29$; the distance between Hadley and Greenville. **b.** Yes; 16 is a solution of the equations in a. **25.** Both equations are correct. Another correct equation is $44 - 7 = x$.
27. Yes, because $4 + f = 12$ means there are 8 flute players, and 8 is twice 4. **29.** Yes

LESSON 11.2

Your Turn

4. 3.5

5. $\frac{5}{4}$; or $1\frac{1}{4}$

6. $x + 65 = 90$; $x = 25^{\circ}$
7. $x + 42 = 90$; $x = 48^{\circ}$

Guided Practice

1a. number of guests who left when the party ended. **c.** 11 **2.** 5

3. 1.5

4. 4.5 **5.** 40 **6.** $\frac{5}{4}$ **7.** $x + 45 = 180$; $x = 135^{\circ}$ **8.** $x = 275$

Independent Practice

11. Sample answer: $14 = b - 12$; $b = 26$ **13.** Sample answer: $x + 8 = 37$; 29 compact cars **15.** Sample answer: $m - 123.45 = 36.55$; $160 **17.** $c = 2.50$ **19a.** $1.49 + a = 2.99$; $2.49 + r = 3.99$ **b.** Both a and r are equal to $1.50, so the discount is the same.

LESSON 11.3

Your Turn

2. 7

3. 9

4. Sample answer: $\frac{x}{5} = 9$; $x = 45$; Roberto gave away $45 - 9 = 36$ cards. **5.** $x = 35$

Guided Practice

1a. number of miles run each day **b.** 5; x; 15 **c.** 3 **2.** 9

3. 8

4. $24 = 6w$; $w = 4$ inches; length is 2 inches longer than the width
5. Sample problem: The area of a rectangle is 45 cm², and the length is 15 cm. What is the width?; $w = 3$

Independent Practice

7. $\frac{c}{28} = 3$; 84 cookies **9.** $4k = 44$; 11 books **11.** $3.5d = 14$; 4 days
13. $\frac{w}{4} = 14$; 56 minutes **17.** 81
19. 31 inches

LESSON 11.4

Your Turn

3.

4. $1 + y \geq 3$; $y = 1$ is not a solution because $1 + 1$ is not greater than or equal to 3. **5.** $t \leq 6$

6. $w > 2$

Guided Practice

1. 3, 1

2.

3. $4 + x < 6$

4. Let t be temperature in °C; $t \geq 3$

Independent Practice

7.

11.

13. $x \leq -3$ **15.** $x \geq -3.5$
19. $g > 150$

Selected Answers

MODULE 12

LESSON 12.1

Your Turn

4. $G(4, -4)$; IV; $E(-2, 4)$; II
5. $F(3, 2)$; I; $H(-1, -3)$; III
6–10.

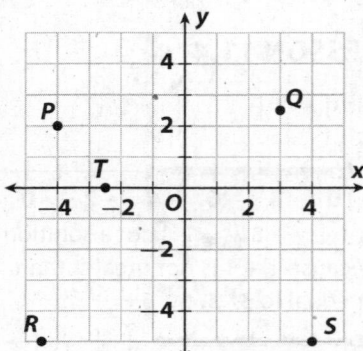

11. Ted $(-20, -20)$, Ned $(-20, 30)$

Guided Practice

1. left; up; $(-5, 1)$; II **2.** 2; 3; $(2, -3)$; IV
3–4.

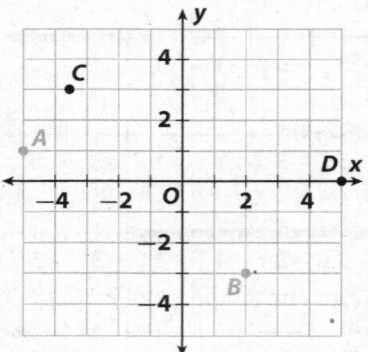

5. Each grid square is $\frac{1}{2}$ unit on a side.
6–7.

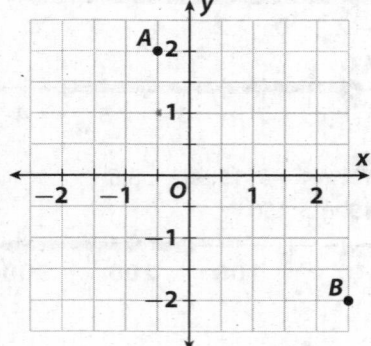

Independent Practice

11. Sam is 3 km south and 7 km east of the theater.
13. $(-3, 0.5)$ **15.** $W(-0.75, -1.0)$

LESSON 12.2

Your Turn

8. Sample answer: Bridget's grandmother gave her a collection of 15 perfume bottles. Bridget adds one bottle per week to the collection. The independent variable is the number of weeks. The dependent variable is the number of perfume bottles in her collection. The value of y is always 15 units greater than the value of x.
9. Sample answer: Colin created a website to sell T-shirts that are printed with funny slogans. He makes $16 per T-shirt. The independent variable is the number of T-shirts he sells, and the dependent variable is his profit in dollars. As the independent variable increases by 1, the dependent variable increases by 16. **10.** Sample answer: Tickets to the school musical cost $3 each. The independent variable is the number of tickets purchased, and the dependent variable is the total cost. The value of y is always 3 times the value of x.

Guided Practice

1. Time is the independent variable and cost is the dependent variable.
2a.

Time x (h)	0	1	2	2
Distance y (mi)	0	60	120	180

b. Time is the independent variable and distance is the dependent variable. **c.** The value of y is always 60 times the value of x. **3.** The value of the

dependent variable is 5 times the value of the independent variable.

Independent Practice

7a. number of markers **b.** number of gift bags **c.** The relationship is multiplicative because y increases by a factor of 5 as x increases by 1.
d. The number of glitter markers is 5 times the number of gift bags.

LESSON 12.3

Your Turn

2. $y = x - 2$ **3.** $y = 2.5x$ **4.** $y = x + 5$
5. $y = 2x$ **6.** $k = r + 5$; 57 years old

Guided Practice

1. $y = x - 4$ **2.** $y = 4x$ **3.** $y = x + 3$
4. $y = \frac{x}{6}$
5. $c = 1.35n$; $33.75

Independent Practice

9. The y-value is $\frac{1}{4}$ of the x-value.
11a. $e = 8.25h$ **b.** $206.25 = 8.25h$; $25 = h$; 25 hours **13.** Not possible; there is no consistent pattern between the y-values and corresponding x-values.
15. No

LESSON 12.4

Your Turn

4.

x	$x + 2.5 = y$	(x, y)
0	$0 + 2.5 = 2.5$	$(0, 2.5)$
1	$1 + 2.5 = 3.5$	$(1, 3.5)$
2	$2 + 2.5 = 4.5$	$(2, 4.5)$
3	$3 + 2.5 = 5.5$	$(3, 5.5)$

Guided Practice

1. $y = 3x$

Hours worked	Lawns mowed
0	0
1	3
2	6
3	9

2.

x	0	1	2	3
y	0	1.5	3	4.5

3.

Independent Practice

5.

Additional hours	0	5	10	15	20
Total hours	20	25	30	35	40

7. 20 hours; when 0 additional hours are worked, the total is 20 hours.

9.

11a.

Number of tickets, x	1	2	3	4	5
Total cost ($), y	9	18	27	36	45

b. Dependent: total cost; independent: number of tickets

UNIT 6 Selected Answers

MODULE 13

LESSON 13.1

Your Turn

2. 366 **3.** 210 **4.** 66.5 **5.** 90 **6.** 165

Guided Practice

1. 13; 9; 117 **2.** 14; 9; 15; 168
3. 18; 11; 99

Independent Practice

5. 84 cm² **7.** 936 in² **9.** 72 m²
11. 8.25 ft² **13.** 1,620 in² **15.** 57 ft²
17. 9 in. and 15 in.

LESSON 13.2

Your Turn

3. 59.5 in² **5.** 12 ft²

Guided Practice

1. 14; 8; 56 **2.** 12; 30; 80

Independent Practice

5. 240 ft² **7.** 288 ft² **9.** 71.5 in²
11. 20 ft² **13.** Monica forgot to
multiply by $\frac{1}{2}$. The area of the
fabric is 45 in². **17a.** 6 in. **b.** 1 in.
and 36 in., 2 in. and 18 in., 3 in. and
12 in., 4 in. and 9 in.

LESSON 13.3

Your Turn

1. 8 in. **3.** 4 ft **4.** 8 pallets

Guided Practice

1. $70 = \frac{1}{2}\left(8\frac{3}{4}\right) b$; 16 in. **2.** $791 = \frac{1}{2}h(26.5 + 30)$; 28 centimeters
3. area; $A = 42(28) = 1{,}176$ ft²;
number of gallons of paint;
$n = 1{,}176 \div 350 = 3.36$; 4

Independent Practice

5. $5\frac{1}{2}$ ft **7.** 1.2 cm **9.** 16 in. and
8 in. **11.** 128 patches **13a.** 702 ft²
b. 1,458 ft² **c.** 486 ft² **15a.** $3\frac{1}{2}$ yd
b. $10\frac{2}{3}$ yd²

LESSON 13.4

Your Turn

3. 44 square meters
4. 567 square inches
5. $3,348

Guided Practice

1. $\frac{1}{8}$ square unit **2.** 112 **3.** 196
4. 240 square feet; 3 cans of paint

Independent Practice

7a. about 60% **b.** $321.75
9a. 73.5 square inches
b. 21 inches by 21 inches
c. 8 banners; yes
11. 50 square inches

MODULE 14

LESSON 14.1

Your Turn

3. 9 units **4.** 5 units
5. 0.8 hours, or 48 minutes

Guided Practice

1. (5, 2) **2.** (6, 8) **3.** $|5| + |{-2}| = 5 + 2 = 7$ **4.** $|5| - |1| = 5 - 1 = 4$
5. 2 units **6.** 3 units

5–6.

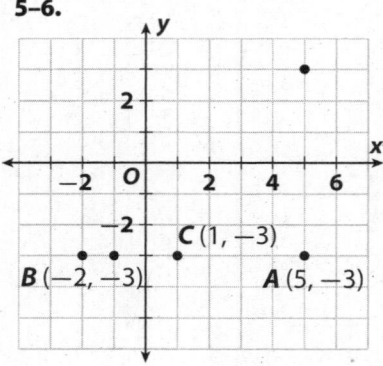

7. 5 blocks
8. 21 minutes; 4.5 minutes

Independent Practice

11. Place another point on the
other side of the y-axis the same
distance from the y-axis as point
A; (−1.5, −2.5); 3 units
13. (7, −3); 14 units **15.** (−2.4, −1);
4.8 units **17.** 3 hours

LESSON 14.2

Your Turn

2. 30 blocks **3.** 32 square units

Guided Practice

1. square

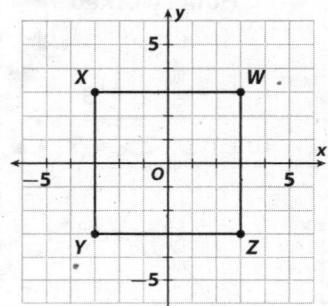

2. 6; 24 **3.** 36 square yards
4. L; 24 square inches

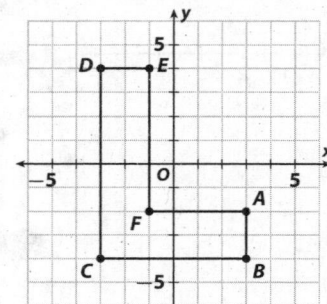

Independent Practice

7a. hexagon **b.** 18 units
c. trapezoid; 15 units
11. The octagon is a regular
octagon, so all the sides will have
the same length as the side whose
endpoints are given. Since that
side length $= |4| - |1| = 3$ units,
the perimeter of the octagon is
$8(3) = 24$ units.

MODULE

LESSON 15.1

Your Turn
4. 896 in² **6.** $7.92

Guided Practice
1. 1; 4 **2.** 36; 48; 84
3a. 248 square inches
b. 24,800 square inches **c.** 2 cans

Independent Practice
5. 272 in² **7.** 80 tiles
9. rectangular pyramid; triangular prism **11.** Sample answer: Decide whether the figure is a prism or a pyramid, and what the shapes of the bases and faces are. Make a net of the figure, and label the dimensions. Use appropriate area formulas to find the areas of the faces, and then find the sum of the areas.

LESSON 15.2

Your Turn
2. 75 cubic inches
3. $55\frac{1}{8}$ cubic inches
4. $393\frac{3}{4}$ cubic meters

Guided Practice
1. 2 **2.** 8
3. 10; 3.2; 5; 160 cubic meters
4. $7\frac{1}{4}$; 4; 29; 232 cubic meters
5. 277.5 cubic feet
6. $526\frac{1}{2}$ cubic inches
7. 357 cubic inches
9. 110.25 cubic inches
11. A: 120 in³; B: 960 in³; 8 times as great **13.** 58.5 cubic inches
15. $2\frac{47}{64}$ cubic feet
17. $\frac{1}{8}$ m; find a fraction that, when multiplied by itself 3 times, equals $\frac{1}{512}$ **19.** Both are correct.

LESSON 15.3

Your Turn
2. $\frac{5}{2}$ ft or $2\frac{1}{2}$ ft **3.** 1.5 feet

Guided Practice
1. $6{,}336 = 16(18)w$; $w = 22$ cm
2. $V = 72$ in³; 4 inches

Independent Practice
3. 12.4 inches
5. 6 centimeters
7. Volume: 2,000 mm³; weight: 1 ounce **9.** 1 inch; 25%
11. 42.9; 4.3; 30.0.

UNIT 7 Selected Answers

Selected Answers

MODULE 16

LESSON 16.1

Your Turn

3. median = 6.5 minutes

Guided Practice

1. 15; 5; 3; 3 **2a.** 42 **b.** No **3a.** mean: 8.5; median: 6 **b.** The median; sample answer: the median is closer to most of the data values than the mean is.

Independent Practice

5. Ten students were asked, because there are 10 data values in the list. **7.** 78.5; 80.5 **9.** Minutes and hours; convert all times to minutes. **11.** Median; it is closer to most of the data values; the data value for 1 hr (60 min) raises the mean. **13.** 95

LESSON 16.2

Your Turn

2. The MAD for Waiter A is 0.6 oz, and for Waiter B is 0.2 oz, so Barista B's smoothies showed less variability. **3.** A: MAD ≈ 0.0017; B: MAD ≈ 0.0063; A has less variability.

Guided Practice

1. did
a. 45.1 min
b. 0.4 min
2. 44.9; 0.733333; did not

Independent Practice

5. 1.6 people
7. The MAD at the beginning was about 3.7, and at the end it was about 2.1, so they made progress.
9. The mean for Austin is 31.855 in., and for San Antonio is 30.459 in.; Austin.
13a. mean = 1, MAD = 0; Because 1 is the only data value, it is the

mean of the data set and does not deviate from the mean.
b. mean = 1.5, MAD = 0.5; 1 + 2 = 3, and 3 ÷ 2 = 1.5. Also, both 1 and 2 are 0.5 away from 1.5.
c. Increase; the values are getting larger, so the mean increases, and they are getting more spread out, so the MAD increases.

LESSON 16.3

Your Turn

3. Group A IQR = $700. Group B IQR = $450. Group A's IQR is greater, so the salaries in the middle 50% for group A are more spread out than those for group B.
4. Miami = 15, Chicago = 53; Chicago

Guided Practice

1. 4; 10; 11; 13; 14; 15; 25; 29; 33; 33; 35; 43; 51; 58; 64 **2.** 29 **3.** 13 **4.** 43 **6.** 30 **7.** 60

Independent Practice

11. Sample answer: Students could have measured each others' heights. **13.** 0.3; 0.3 **15.** The IQRs are the same. The spreads of the middle 50% of the data values are the same for the two data sets. **17.** Yes

LESSON 16.4

Your Turn

4. 14 games; the value with the greatest frequency is 4; there were 4 games in which the team scored 4 runs. **5.** spread: 0 to 11.11 appears to be an outlier. The data has a cluster from 0 to 7 with one peak at 2. The distribution is not symmetric because the data is not clustered around the center of the distribution. **6.** Mean: about 3.3, median: 3.5, range: 5; sample

answer: between 3 and 4 runs. The mean and median are close in value, and there are no outliers.

Guided Practice

1. Variable data **3.** Mean: about 5.2; median = 5; range = 17.
4. spread: 0 to 17. 17 appears to be an outlier. The distribution is not symmetric.

Independent Practice

7. not statistical **9.** not statistical
11.

Days of Precipitation

15. The mean would change to about 9.3; the median would stay at 9.5; the range would change to 9 days. **19.** 5(2) + 6(2) + 7 + 8(3) + 9(2) + 10(5) + 11 + 12(3) + 13(2) + 15(2) + 22
21. Count the number of dots above a data value. **23.** 19; Each dot represents one game. **25.** Mean: about 3.9 runs; median: 4 runs; range: 11 runs **27a.** the units for the ages (years, months, weeks) **b.** No

LESSON 16.5

Your Turn

4.

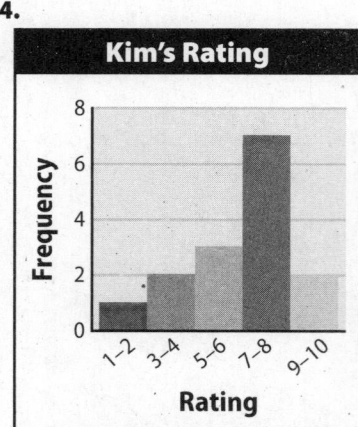

5. Sample answer: Kim gave ratings of 7 or 8 to 7 of 15 movies. She gave ratings of 9 or 10 to 2 of 15 movies.

Guided Practice

1.

Interval	Frequency
0–9	4
10–19	3
20–29	9
30–39	5

2. 1; 3; 4; 2

3. Sample answer: Only one cafe has less than 7 seats available. The bars increase in height until they

reach the interval for 15–21 seats, and then they decrease in height, showing that most cafes have 21 or fewer seats.

5.

Interval	Frequency
10–19	9
20–29	7
30–39	3
40–49	4
50–59	2

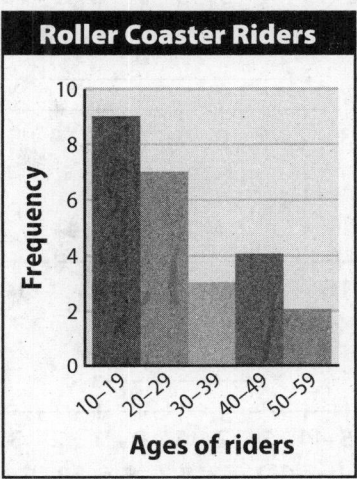

7a. 6 **b.** 3 bars; 9
c. box plot, dot plot

9. a.

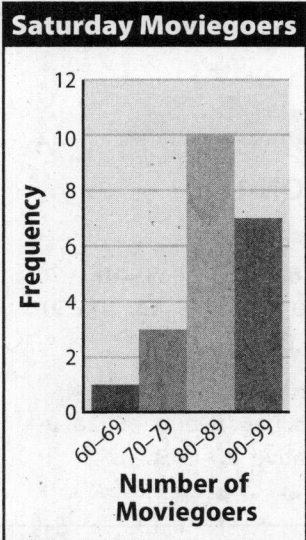

UNIT 8 Selected Answers

LESSON 17.1

Your Turn
7. −9 **8.** −10 **9.** −60 **10.** −70
11. 300 **12.** −145 **13.** −1,650
14. −1,000

Guided Practice
1a. 6 **b.** negative **c.** −6 **2a.** 9
b. negative **c.** −9 **3.** −7

4. −4

5. −10

6. −5

7. −4

8. −14

9. −9 **10.** −11 **11.** −10 **12.** −110
13. −100 **14.** 203 **15.** −15
16. −570

Independent Practice
19. −11 **21.** −54 **23.** −100 +
(−75) + (−85) = −260

LESSON 17.2

Your Turn
3. 4 **4.** −2 **5.** −6 **6.** −1 **7.** −28
8. −8 **9.** 0 **10.** −1

Guided Practice
1. 6

2. 5

3. −11

4. −3

5. 1 **6.** 0 **7.** −3 **8.** 4 **9.** 6 **10.** 2
11. −16 **12.** 0 **13.** −5 **14.** 24

Independent Practice
17. −8 **19.** 25 **21.** −95 **23.** −7
25. 100 **27.** −55 + 275 = 220. The
team's profit was $220.

LESSON 17.3

Your Turn
4. −9 **5.** 2 **6.** −2 **7.** −4

Guided Practice
1. −3 **2.** −2 **3.** (−5); −9 **4.** −4; −3
5. −3 **6.** 2 **7.** −6 **8.** −18 **9.** 5
10. 19 **11.** 14 **12.** 42 **13.** 38 **14.** 0

Independent Practice
17. −127 − (−225) = 98 feet
19. −150 points **21.** Diet Chow
25. −16, −21, −26

LESSON 17.4

Your Turn
1. −40 − 13 + 18; −35; 35 feet
below the cave entrance
3. −35 + (−45) + 180 = 100;
$100 increase **4.** Jim

Guided Practice
1. −15 + 9 − 12 = −18; 18 feet
below sea level **2.** −23 + 5 − 7 =
−25; −25 °F **3.** 50 − 40 + 87 −
30 = 67 **4.** 24 **5.** −12 **6.** 18 **7.** 21
8. 97 **9.** 27 **10.** (−12 + 6 − 4) <
(−34 − 3 + 39)
11. (21 − 3 + 8) > (−14 + 31 − 6)

Independent Practice
13a. 5 − 1 + 6 − 1 = 9 **b.** over par
c. yes **15.** The Commutative
Property does not apply to
subtraction. 3 − 6 + 5 = 2 and
3 − 5 + 6 = 4 **17a.** 3:00 to 4:00
b. 87 **19.** $24 **23.** The sum of the
absolute values of the other two
numbers must be greater than the
value of the first number.

MODULE 18

LESSON 18.1

Your Turn
4. −15 **5.** 20 **6.** −42 **7.** 0
8. 45 **9.** 32

Guided Practice
1. −9 **2.** −28 **3.** 54 **4.** −100
5. −60 **6.** 0 **7.** 49 **8.** −135
9. −96 **10.** 300 **11.** 0 **12.** −192
13. 7(−75) = −525; −$525
14. Start at zero and move 5 units
to the left 3 times. 3(−5) = −15;
−15 yards **15.** 6(−2) = −12;
−12 °F **16.** 4(−5) = −20; −$20
17. 5(−50) = −250; −250 feet

Independent Practice

19. No **21.** 5(−4) = −20; $20 decrease **23.** 7(−6) = −42; the cost of the jeans decreased by $42 over the 7 weeks. **25.** 7(−8) = −56; 7(−5) = −35; −56 + (−35) = −91. The savings decreased by $91. **27a.** −27 **b.** 27 **c.** −27 **d.** −81 **e.** 81 **f.** −81 **g.** negative; positive

LESSON 18.2

Your Turn

2. 0 **3.** −2 **4.** 13 **5.** Yolanda received the same number of penalties in each game; 5. −25 ÷ (−5) = 5 and −35 ÷ (−7) = 5.

Guided Practice

1. −7 **2.** −7 **3.** −2 **4.** 0 **5.** 9 **6.** −3 **7.** 11 **8.** 1 **9.** 0 **10.** 11 **11.** −12 **12.** −20 **13.** undefined **14.** 3 **15.** −40 ÷ (4) = −10; $10 **16.** −22 ÷ (11) = −2; 2 points **17.** −75 ÷ (−15) = 5; 5 targets **18.** −99 ÷ (−9) = 11; 11 times

Independent Practice

21. Elisa; Elisa made −140 ÷ (−20) = 7 withdrawals; Francis made −270 ÷ (−45) = 6 withdrawals, and 7 > 6. **23.** the first part **27.** False; division by 0 is undefined for any dividend. **29.** 12

LESSON 18.3

Your Turn

1. Reggie earned 110 points; 3(−30) + 200 = −90 + 200 = 110. **2.** −78 − 21 = −99 **4.** 0 **5.** 20 **6.** 22 **7.** −28 **8.** Will **9.** −7; −6; (−28) ÷ 4 + 1 **10.** −5; −6; 42 ÷ (−3) + 9

Guided Practice

1. 42 **2.** −21 **3.** −9 **4.** −32 **5.** −4 **6.** −1 **7.** 7(−5) + 20 = −15; 15 dollars less **8.** 7(−10) + (−100) = −170; 170 fewer points **9.** 6(−4) + 10 = −14; lost 14 points **10.** 4(−12) + 10 = −38;

$38 less **11.** > **12.** = **13.** > **14.** <

Independent Practice

17. 4 **19.** 0 **21.** 2 **23.** 5(−4) − 8 = −28 **25a.** 4(−35) − 9 = −149; $149 less **b.** Yes **29.** 80 inches

LESSON 19.1

Your Turn

4. 0.571428… **5.** 0.333… **6.** 0.45 **7.** 2.75; terminating decimal **8.** 7.333…; repeating decimal

Guided Practice

1. 0.6; terminating **2.** 0.89; terminating **3.** 0.333…; repeating **4.** 0.2525…; repeating **5.** 0.7777…; repeating **6.** 0.36; terminating **7.** 0.04; terminating **8.** 0.14204545…; repeating **9.** 0.012; terminating **10.** 11.166… **11.** 2.9 **12.** 8.23 **13.** 7.2 **14.** 54.2727… **15.** 3.0555… **16.** 3.666… **17.** 12.875

Independent Practice

19. $\frac{5}{11}$; 0.4545…; repeating **21.** $\frac{4}{11}$; 0.3636…; repeating **23.** $\frac{11}{11}$; 1; terminating **25a.** $\frac{39}{8}$ **b.** 4.875 **27.** Ben is taller because 5.3125 > 5.2916…. **29.** When the denominator is 3, 6, 7, or 9, the result will be a repeating decimal. **31.** No; although the digits follow a pattern, the same combination of digits do not repeat.

LESSON 19.2

Your Turn

2. $4\frac{1}{2}$

3. −7

---

6. −3

7. $-\frac{1}{4}$

8. 6

9. 0

10. 0

11. 4 **12.** −1 **13.** −1 **14.** 20

Guided Practice

1. −4.5

2. 5

3. $\frac{3}{4}$

4. −3

5. −2

6. 2.5

7. $0 **8.** $0 **9.** −4.5 **10.** 1 **11.** −2.2 **12.** 9 **13.** −12 **14.** $-\frac{1}{2}$ **15.** $-2\frac{1}{2}$ **16.** $-9\frac{1}{8}$

© Houghton Mifflin Harcourt Publishing Company

Selected Answers

Independent Practice

19. $12.75 **21.** $1\frac{1}{2}$ miles **23.** $30 + 15 + (-25) = 20$; the final score is 20 points **25.** June: $306.77, July: $301.50, Aug: $337.88 **27.** opposite or additive inverse

LESSON 19.3

Your Turn

1. -8.5

2.

2. $-\frac{1}{2}$

3. -7.75

4.

6. 1.75

7. $\frac{1}{4}$

Guided Practice

1. 13

2. -8

3. -11

4. -4

---

5. -36 **6.** -7.7 **7.** 1 **8.** 79
9. $2\frac{7}{9}$ **10.** $78\frac{1}{2}$ **11.** 1.5 meters
12. $17\frac{1}{2}$ yards loss **13.** 543 feet
14. took out $75.15

Independent Practice

17. $-25.65 - 16.5 + 12.45$; -29.7 ft; the diver is 29.7 ft below the surface. **19a.** $-$43.30
b. $-$68.30 **c.** $68.30
21. 65,233 ft; 96,000 ft; 96,000 ft (Mars); 30,767 ft
23a. $5 - 7.2 + 2.2$ **b.** He is exactly where he started because $5 - 7.2 + 2.2 = 0$.

LESSON 19.4

Your Turn

1. -7

2. 3.75

4. $-\frac{2}{7}$ **5.** $\frac{2}{5}$ **6.** $-\frac{1}{2}$

Guided Practice

1. $-3\frac{1}{3}$

2. $-\frac{3}{4}$

3. $1\frac{5}{7}$

4. 3

5. -12 **6.** -9 **7.** 6.8 **8.** 4.32
9. 6 **10.** -7.2 **11.** $\frac{1}{3}$; $\frac{1}{4}$ **12.** $\frac{12}{35}$; $-\frac{4}{5}$
13. $-\frac{5}{12}$ **14.** $\frac{2}{7}$ **15.** $4(-3.50) = -14$; $14 decrease

---

16. $18(-100) = -1,800$; $1,800 decrease

Independent Practice

21. The submarine would be 975 feet below sea level, or -975 feet. **25.** 13.5 points

LESSON 19.5

Your Turn

5. -0.7 **6.** $\frac{35}{48}$ **7.** -11

Guided Practice

1. -0.8 **2.** $-\frac{1}{7}$ **3.** -8 **4.** $-\frac{502}{3}$
5. -375 **6.** 7 **7.** $-\frac{4}{21}$ **8.** -400
9. -0.875 liter per day
10. $-45.75 \div 5 = -9.15$; $-$9.15 per day, on average **11.** -0.55 mile per minute

Independent Practice

13. -20 **15.** 20 **17.** -0.1
19. $\frac{5}{9}$ **21.** 4.5 **23.** $-1\frac{3}{4}$ yards
25a. $250 per day **b.** $1,050 per day **c.** $-$70 **31.** Yes, since an integer divided by an integer is a ratio of two integers and the denominator is not zero, the number is rational by definition.

LESSON 19.6

Your Turn

1. $5\frac{5}{8}$ min
2. 12 batches; $0.29 per batch
3. $1,070.72

Guided Practice

1. Step 1: $3\frac{1}{5}$ or 3.2 mi/h, 14.4 mi; Step 2: 14.4 mi, $3\frac{3}{5}$ or 3.6 mi/h, 4 h
2. Step 1: 25.68 in., -0.02375 in, -0.61 in.; Step 2: 25.68 in., 0.61 in., 25.07 in.

Independent Practice

5. $4\frac{1}{4}$ in. **7.** $29\frac{1}{8}$ yd
9. 5 more; $88\% = \frac{88}{100} = \frac{44}{50}$
11. Yes, because the product is negative and about half of 1.5.
13. Sample answer: Yes; $-0.7343 \approx -0.75$ **15.** Sample answer: (1) Convert the fraction to a decimal and find the sum of 27.6

and 15.9, then multiply the result by 0.37. (2) Convert the fraction, then use the Distributive Property. Multiply both 27.6 and 15.9 by 0.37, then add the products. The first method; there are fewer steps and so fewer chances to make errors.

LESSON 19.7

Your Turn
2. $10x - 4$ **3.** $-1.75x - 4.4$
5. $63k + 42m$ **6.** $0.6b - 3c$
7. $4e + 6f - 14g$ **9.** $2(x + 1)$
10. $3(x + 3)$ **11.** $5(x + 3)$
12. $4(x + 4)$

Guided Practice
1. Step 1: baseballs: $14 + 12n$, tennis balls: $23 + 16n$; Step 2: $14 + 12n + 23 + 16n$, $14 + 23 + 12n + 16n$, $37 + 28n$, $37 + 28n$ **2.** 289
3. $0.5(12m) - 0.5(22n)$, $6m - 11n$
4. $\frac{2}{3}(18x) + \frac{2}{3}(6z) = 12x + 4z$
5. $2(x + 6)$ **6.** $12(x + 2)$
7. $7(x + 5)$

Independent Practice
9. $15(100 + 5d) + 20(50 + 7d) = 2,500 + 215d$ **11.** 3 and $x + 2$; $3x + 6$ **13.** The area is the product of the length and width (6×9). It is also the sum of the areas of the rectangles separated by the

dashed line (6×5 and 6×4). So, $6(9) = 6(5) + 6(4)$.
15. $2x + 6$ **17.** $x^2 + 5x + 6$
19. (1) Think of 997 as $1,000 - 3$. So, $8 \times 997 = 8(1,000 - 3)$. By the Distributive Property, $8(1,000 - 3) = 8,000 - 24 = 7,976$. (2) Think of 997 as $900 + 90 + 7$. By the Distributive Property, $8(900 + 90 + 7) = 7,200 + 720 + 56 = 7,976$.

MODULE 20

LESSON 20.1

Your Turn

3. $\frac{1}{6} \div \frac{1}{4} = \frac{1}{6} \times \frac{4}{1} = \frac{4}{6} = \frac{2}{3}$; $\frac{2}{3}$ acre per hour **4.** 4 ounces **5.** the second tank

Guided Practice

2. $2\frac{4}{5}$ miles per hour **3.** $\frac{15}{16}$ page per minute **4.** $\frac{1}{2}$ foot per hour
5. $2\frac{1}{2}$ square feet per hour.
6. Brand A: 720 mg/pickle, Brand B: 650 mg/pickle; Brand B
7. Ingredient C: $\frac{3}{8}$ cup/serving, Ingredient D: $\frac{4}{9}$ cup/serving; Ingredient C

Independent Practice

9a. On Call: about $2.86 per hour; Talk Time: $2.50 per hour
b. Talk Time; their rate per hour is lower. **c.** Multiply 0.05 times 60 because there are 60 minutes in 1 hour. **d.** The unit rate is $3 per hour, so it is not a better deal. **11.** $\frac{5 \text{ songs}}{1 \text{ commercial}}$ **13.** Faster; he typed 50 words per minute in his first attempt and 60 words per minute in his second attempt.

LESSON 20.2

Your Turn

3. No; the rates are not equal because her speed changed.
4. Each rate is equal to $\frac{1 \text{ adult}}{12 \text{ students}}$. The relationship is proportional; $a = \frac{1}{12}s$.

Guided Practice

1. 45, $\frac{90}{2} = 45$; $\frac{135}{3} = 45$; $\frac{180}{4} = 45$; the relationship is proportional.
2. $k = 5$; $y = 5x$ **3.** $k = \frac{1}{4}$; $y = \frac{1}{4}x$

Independent Practice

5. $y = 18.50x$ **7.** Rent–All has the best deal because it has the lowest rate per day ($18.50).

9. The rates have the same unit rate, $6.25 per hour. **11.** x is the number of hours Steven babysits, and y is the amount he charges; the equation is $y = 6.25x$.
13. 150 feet per minute; 9,000 feet per hour **15.** Feet per minute

LESSON 20.3

Your Turn

1. No; A line drawn through the points does not go through the origin.

4a. The bicyclist rides 60 miles in 4 hours. **b.** 15 **c.** $y = 15x$

Guided Practice

1. 9; 195; 325; 650; proportional; pages is always 65 times the number of hours. **2.** 3; 8; 15; 37.50; proportional; earnings are always 7.5 times the number of hours. **3.** not proportional; the line will not pass through the origin. **4.** proportional; the line will pass through the origin.
5. $y = 3.5x$ **6.** $y = \frac{1}{4}x$

Independent Practice

9. Horse A takes about 4 minutes. Horse B takes about 2.5 minutes. **11.** Horse A: $y = 3$ miles; Horse B: $y = 4\frac{4}{5}$ miles
13. Yes; A graph of miles traveled compared to number of hours will form a line that passes through the origin.

15a.

b. Sample answer: (4, 20); 4 DVDs cost $20. **17.** Yes. The graph is a line that passes through the origin. **21.** If the values in the "Time" column are the same, each value in the "Distance" column for Car 4 will be twice the corresponding value for Car 2.

MODULE 21

LESSON 21.1

Your Turn

2. 23% **4.** 33% **5.** 37.5%
8. $548.90 **9.** $349.30

Guided Practice

1. 60% **2.** 50% **3.** 74% **4.** 11%
5. 8% **6.** 220% **7.** 78% **8.** 20%
9. 28% **10.** 50% **11.** 9% **12.** 67%
13. 100% **14.** 83% **15.** $9.90
16. 36 cookies **17.** 272 pages
18. 42 members **19.** $27,840
20. 1,863 songs **21.** 26 miles

Independent Practice

25a. Amount of change = 1; percent decrease = $\frac{1}{5}$ = 20%
27a. They have the same.
$100 + $10 = $110 and $100 + 10%($100) = $110. **b.** Sylvia has more. Leroi has $110 + $10 = $120, and Sylvia has $110 + 10%($110) = $121.

29. No. Only the first withdrawal is $10. Each withdrawal after that is less than $10 because it is 10% of the remaining balance. There will be money left after 10 withdrawals.

LESSON 21.2

Your Turn

2a. $1c + 0.1c$; $1.1c$ **b.** $30.80
3a. 200% **b.** $1c + 2c$; $3c$
5a.

0.24*b*   1*b*

1*b* − 0.24*b*

b. 0.76*b* **6a.** $1p - 0.05p$, $0.95p$
b. $14.25

Guided Practice

1a. 0.35*s* **b.** $1s + 0.35s$ or $1.35s$
c. $43.20 **d.** $11.20 **2.** $2.70;
$20.70 **3.** $9.45; $31.95 **4.** $25.31;
$59.06 **5.** $24.75; $99.74 **6.** $48.60;
$97.20 **7.** $231.25; $416.25 **8.** $35.10
9. $59.63 **10.** $13.43 **11.** $70.00

Independent Practice

13a. 0.46*b* **b.** $1b - 0.46b$ or $0.54b$
c. $15.66 **d.** $13.34 **17.** Either buy 3, get one free or $\frac{1}{4}$ off. Either case would result in a discount of 25%, which is better than 20%.
19. No; first change: 20.1% decrease; second change: 25.1% increase. The second percent change is greater.

LESSON 21.3

Your Turn

1. $1; $21 **3.** $80; $480 **4.** $34.13

Guided Practice

1. $1.50 **2.** $10.50 **3.** $0.40 **4.** $33
5. $0.80 **6.** $10 **7a.** $3.08 **b.** $47.07
8. $86.83 **9.** $700 **10.** $715 **11a.**
$18 **b.** $19.53 **12.** $37.86

Independent Practice

15. $82.58 **17.** $75.14 **19.** $1,076.25
21a. Multiply Sandra's height by 0.10 and add the product to 4 to get Pablo's height. Then multiply Pablo's height by 0.08 and add the product to Pablo's height to get Michaela's height. **b.** about 4 feet 9 inches **23a.** $101.49 **b.** $109.39 **c.** Digital camera; he can save $8. **d.** $109.61

Glossary/Glosario

A

ENGLISH	SPANISH	EXAMPLES
absolute value The distance of a number from zero on a number line; shown by | |.	**valor absoluto** Distancia a la que está un número de 0 en una recta numérica. El símbolo del valor absoluto es | |.	$\|-5\| = 5$
acute angle An angle that measures greater than 0° and less than 90°.	**ángulo agudo** Ángulo que mide más do 0° y menos de 90°.	
acute triangle A triangle with all angles measuring less than 90°.	**triángulo acutángulo** Triángulo en el que todos los ángulos miden menos de 90°.	
addend A number added to one or more other numbers to form a sum.	**sumando** Número que se suma a uno o más números para formar una suma.	In the expression $4 + 6 + 7$, the numbers 4, 6, and 7 are addends.
Addition Property of Opposites The property that states that the sum of a number and its opposite equals zero.	**Propiedad de la suma de los opuestos** Propiedad que establece que la suma de un número y su opuesto es cero.	$12 + (-12) = 0$
additive inverse The opposite of a number.	**inverso aditivo** El opuesto de un número.	-4 is the additive inverse of 4.
adjacent angles Angles in the same plane that have a common vertex and a common side.	**ángulos adyacentes** Ángulos en el mismo plano que comparten un vértice y un lado.	$\angle 1$ and $\angle 2$ are adjacent angles.
algebraic expression An expression that contains at least one variable.	**expresión algebraica** Expresión que contiene al menos una variable.	$x + 8$ $4(m - b)$
algebraic inequality An inequality that contains at least one variable.	**desigualdad algebraica** Desigualdad que contiene al menos una variable.	$x + 3 > 10$ $5a > b + 3$
alternate exterior angles For two lines intersected by a transversal, a pair of angles that lie on opposite sides of the transversal and outside the other two lines.	**ángulos alternos externos** Dadas dos rectas cortadas por una transversal, par de ángulos no adyacentes ubicados en los lados opuestos de la transversal y fuera de las otras dos rectas.	$\angle 4$ and $\angle 5$ are alternate exterior angles.

alternate interior angles For two lines intersected by a transversal, a pair of nonadjacent angles that lie on opposite sides of the transversal and between the other two lines.

ángulos alternos internos Dadas dos rectas cortadas por una transversal, par de ángulos no adyacentes ubicados en los lados opuestos de la transversal y entre las otras dos rectas.

$\angle 3$ and $\angle 6$ are alternate interior angles.

---

angle A figure formed by two rays with a common endpoint called the vertex.

ángulo Figura formada por dos rayos con un extremo común llamado vértice.

---

area The number of square units needed to cover a given surface.

área El número de unidades cuadradas que se necesitan para cubrir una superficie dada.

The area is 10 square units.

---

arithmetic sequence A sequence in which the terms change by the same amount each time.

sucesión aritmética Una sucesión en la que los términos cambian la misma cantidad cada vez.

The sequence 2, 5, 8, 11, 14 . . . is an arthmetic sequence.

Associative Property of Addition The property that states that for three or more numbers, their sum is always the same, regardless of their grouping.

Propiedad asociativa de la suma Propiedad que establece que agrupar tres o más números en cualquier orden siempre da como resultado la misma suma.

$2 + 3 + 8 = (2 + 3) + 8 = 2 + (3 + 8)$

Associative Property of Multiplication The property that states that for three or more numbers, their product is always the same, regardless of their grouping.

Propiedad asociativa de la multiplicación Propiedad que establece que agrupar tres o más números en cualquier orden siempre da como resultado el mismo producto.

$2 \cdot 3 \cdot 8 = (2 \cdot 3) \cdot 8 = 2 \cdot (3 \cdot 8)$

---

asymmetrical Not identical on either side of a central line; not symmetrical.

asimétrico Que no es idéntico a ambos lados de una línea central; no simétrico.

---

average The sum of the items in a set of data divided by the number of items in the set; also called *mean*.

promedio La suma de los elementos de un conjunto de datos dividida entre el número de elementos del conjunto. También se le llama *media*.

Data set: 4, 6, 7, 8, 10

Average: $\frac{4 + 6 + 7 + 8 + 10}{5} = \frac{35}{5} = 7$

---

axes The two perpendicular lines of a coordinate plane that intersect at the origin. singular: axis

ejes Las dos rectas numéricas perpendiculares del plano cartesiano que se intersecan en el origen.

Glossary/Glosario

Glossary/Glosario

bar graph A graph that uses vertical or horizontal bars to display data.

gráfica de barras Gráfica en la que se usan barras verticales u horizontales para presentar datos.

base (in numeration) When a number is raised to a power, the number that is used as a factor is the base.

base (en numeración) Cuando un número es elevado a una potencia, el número que se usa como factor es la base.

$3^5 = 3 \cdot 3 \cdot 3 \cdot 3 \cdot 3$; 3 is the base.

base (of a polygon or three-dimensional figure) A side of a polygon; a face of a three-dimensional figure by which the figure is measured or classified.

base (de un polígono o figura tridimensional) Lado de un polígono; la cara de una figura tridimensional, a partir de la cual se mide o se clasifica la figura.

 bases of a cylinder bases of a prism

 base of a cone base of a pyramid

bisect To divide into two congruent parts.

trazar una bisectriz Dividir en dos partes congruentes.

box plot A graph that shows how data are distributed by using the median, quartiles, least value, and greatest value; also called a box-and-whisker plot.

gráfica de caja Gráfica para demostrar la distribución de datos utilizando la mediana, los cuartiles y los valores menos y más grande; también llamado gráfica de mediana y rango.

break (graph) A zigzag on a horizontal or vertical scale of a graph that indicates that some of the numbers on the scale have been omitted.

discontinuidad (gráfica) Zig-zag en la escala horizontal o vertical de una gráfica que indica la omisión de algunos de los números de la escala.

capacity The amount a container can hold when filled.

capacidad Cantidad que cabe en un recipiente cuando se llena.

categorical data Data that consists of nonnumeric information.

datos categóricos Datos que constan de información no numérica.

Celsius A metric scale for measuring temperature in which 0°C is the freezing point of water and 100°C is the boiling point of water; also called *centigrade*.

Celsius Escala métrica para medir la temperatura, en la que 0° C es el punto de congelación del agua y 100° C es el punto de ebullición. También se llama *centígrado*.

center (of a circle) The point inside a circle that is the same distance from all the points on the circle.

centro (de un círculo) Punto interior de un círculo que se encuentra a la misma distancia de todos los puntos de la circunferencia.

center (of rotation) The point about which a figure is rotated.

centro (de una rotación) Punto alrededor del cual se hace girar una figura.

checking account An account at a financial institution that allows for withdrawals and deposits.

cuenta corriente Una cuenta en una institución financiera que permite para retiros y depósitos.

chord A line segment whose endpoints lie on a circle.

cuerda Segmento cuyos extremos se encuentran en un círculo.

circle The set of all points in a plane that are the same distance from a given point called the center.

círculo Conjunto de todos los puntos en un plano que se encuentran a la misma distancia de un punto dado llamado centro.

circle graph A graph that uses sections of a circle to compare parts to the whole and parts to other parts.

gráfica circular Gráfica que usa secciones de un círculo para comparar partes con el todo y con otras partes.

circumference The distance around a circle.

circunferencia Distancia alrededor de un círculo.

clockwise A circular movement in the direction shown.

en el sentido de las manecillas del reloj Movimiento circular en la dirección que se indica.

© Houghton Mifflin Harcourt Publishing Company

Glossary/Glosario

ENGLISH	SPANISH	EXAMPLES
clustering A method used to estimate a sum when all addends are close to the same value.	**agrupación** Método que se usa para estimar una suma cuando todos los sumandos se aproximan al mismo valor.	27, 29, 24, and 23 all cluster around 25.
coefficient The number that is multiplied by the variable in an algebraic expression.	**coeficiente** Número que se multiplica por la variable en una expresión algebraica.	5 is the coefficient in 5b.
combination An arrangement of items or events in which order does not matter.	**combinación** Agrupación de objetos o sucesos en la cual el orden no es importante.	For objects A, B, C, and D, there are 6 different combinations of 2 objects: AB, AC, AD, BC, BD, CD.
common denominator A denominator that is the same in two or more fractions.	**denominador común** Denominador que es común a dos o más fracciones.	The common denominator of $\frac{5}{8}$ and $\frac{2}{8}$ is 8.
common factor A number that is a factor of two or more numbers.	**factor común** Número que es factor de dos o más números.	8 is a common factor of 16 and 40.
common multiple A number that is a multiple of each of two or more numbers.	**múltiplo común** Un número que es múltiplo de dos o más números.	15 is a common multiple of 3 and 5.
Commutative Property of Addition The property that states that two or more numbers can be added in any order without changing the sum.	**Propiedad conmutativa de la suma** Propiedad que establece que sumar dos o más números en cualquier orden no altera la suma.	$8 + 20 = 20 + 8$
Commutative Property of Multiplication The property that states that two or more numbers can be multiplied in any order without changing the product.	**Propiedad conmutativa de la multiplicación** Propiedad que establece que multiplicar dos o más números en cualquier orden no altera el producto.	$6 \cdot 12 = 12 \cdot 6$
compatible numbers Numbers that are close to the given numbers that make estimation or mental calculation easier.	**números compatibles** Números que están cerca de los números dados y hacen más fácil la estimación o el cálculo mental.	To estimate $7{,}957 + 5{,}009$, use the compatible numbers 8,000 and 5,000: $8{,}000 + 5{,}000 = 13{,}000$.
compensation When a number in a problem is close to another number that is easier to calculate with, the easier number is used to find the answer. Then the answer is adjusted by adding to it or subtracting from it.	**compensación** Cuando un número de un problema está cerca de otro con el que es más fácil hacer cálculos, se usa el número más fácil para hallar la respuesta. Luego, se ajusta la respuesta sumando o restando.	
complement The set of all outcomes that are not the event.	**complemento** La serie de resultados que no están en el suceso.	When rolling a number cube, the complement of rolling a 3 is rolling a 1, 2, 4, 5, or 6.

Glossary/Glosario

complementary angles Two angles whose measures add to 90°.

ángulos complementarios Dos ángulos cuyas medidas suman 90°.

The complement of a 53° angle is a 37° angle.

---

complex fraction A fraction that contains one or more fractions in the numerator, the denominator, or both.

fracción compleja Fracción que contiene una o más fracciones en el numerador, en el denominador, o en ambos.

---

composite number A number greater than 1 that has more than two whole-number factors.

número compuesto Número mayor que 1 que tiene más de dos factores que son números cabales.

4, 6, 8, and 9 are composite numbers.

---

compound inequality A combination of more than one inequality.

desigualdad compuesta Combinación de dos o más desigualdades.

$-2 \leq x < 10$

---

cone A three-dimensional figure with one vertex and one circular base.

cono Figura tridimensional con un vértice y una base circular.

---

congruent Having the same size and shape.

congruentes Que tienen la misma forma y el mismo tamaño.

---

congruent angles Angles that have the same measure.

ángulos congruentes Ángulos que tienen la misma medida.

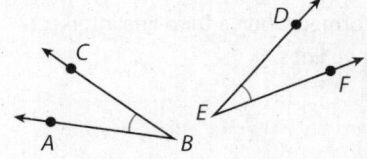

m ∠ABC = m ∠DEF

---

congruent figures Two figures whose corresponding sides and angles are congruent.

figuras congruentes Figuras que tienen el mismo tamaño y forma.

---

congruent line segments Two line segments that have the same length.

segmentos congruentes Dos segmentos que tienen la misma longitud.

---

conjecture A statement that is believed to be true.

conjetura Enunciado que se supone verdadero.

---

constant A value that does not change.

constante Valor que no cambia.

$3, 0, \pi$

ENGLISH	SPANISH	EXAMPLES
constant of proportionality A constant ratio of two variables related proportionally.	**constante de proporcionalidad** Razón constante de dos variables que están relacionadas en forma proporcional.	
coordinate grid A grid formed by the intersection of horizontal and vertical lines that is used to locate points.	**cuadrícula de coordenadas** **cuadrícula formada** por la intersección de líneas horizontales y líneas verticales que se usan por localizar puntos.	
coordinate plane A plane formed by the intersection of a horizontal number line called the *x*-axis and a vertical number line called the *y*-axis.	**plano cartesiano** Plano formado por la intersección de una recta numérica horizontal llamada eje *x* y otra vertical llamada eje *y*.	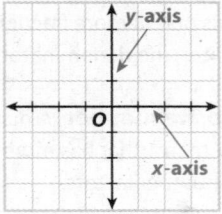
coordinates The numbers of an ordered pair that locate a point on a coordinate graph.	**coordenadas** Los números de un par ordenado que ubican un punto en una gráfica de coordenadas.	The coordinates of *B* are (−2, 3).
correspondence The relationship between two or more objects that are matched.	**correspondencia** La relación entre dos o más objetos que coinciden.	
corresponding angles (for lines) Angles in the same position formed when a third line intersects two lines.	**ángulos correspondientes (en líneas)** Ángulos en la misma posición formados cuando una tercera línea interseca dos líneas.	∠1 and ∠3 are corresponding angles.
corresponding angles (in polygons) Angles in the same relative position in polygons with an equal number of sides.	**ángulos correspondientes (en polígonos)** Ángulos que se ubican en la misma posición relativa en polígonos que tienen el mismo número de lados.	∠A and ∠D are corresponding angles.
corresponding sides Sides in the same relative position in polygons with an equal number of sides.	**lados correspondientes** Lados que se ubican en la misma posición relativa en polígonos que tienen el mismo número de lados.	$\overline{AB}$ and $\overline{DE}$ are corresponding sides.
counterclockwise A circular movement in the direction shown.	**en sentido contrario a las manecillas del reloj** Movimiento circular en la dirección que se indica.	

credit card A plastic card issued by a financial company allowing a customer to buy goods or services on credit.

tarjeta de crédito Tarjeta de pago plástica que un cliente puede utilizar para comprar bienes o servicios. El cliente puede pagar por las compras a plazos, pero pagará intereses en el saldo restante.

credit history Information about how a consumer has borrowed and repaid debt.

historia crediticia Información del buen manejo de dinero y pago de cuentas por parte de un cliente.

credit report A report containing detailed information on a person's credit history.

informe crediticio Informe que recopilan las agencias acerca de la historia crediticia de un cliente y que ayuda a los prestamistas a decidir si dan dinero a crédito a los clientes.

credit score A number based on information in a consumer's credit report that measures an individual's creditworthiness.

calificación crediticia Número basado en información de un informe crediticio de un cliente. Se usa para predecir la posibilidad de que una persona se retrase en hacer pagos o que no pague una deuda.

cross product The product of numbers on the diagonal when comparing two ratios.

producto cruzado El producto de los números multiplicados en diagonal cuando se comparan dos razones.

For the proportion $\frac{2}{3} = \frac{4}{6}$, the cross products are $2 \cdot 6 = 12$ and $3 \cdot 4 = 12$.

cube (geometric figure) A rectangular prism with six congruent square faces.

cubo (figura geométrica) Prisma rectangular con seis caras cuadradas congruentes.

cube (in numeration) A number raised to the third power.

cubo (en numeración) Número elevado a la tercera potencia.

$5^3 = 5 \cdot 5 \cdot 5 = 125$

cumulative frequency The frequency of all data values that are less than or equal to a given value.

frecuencia acumulativa Muestra el total acumulado de las frecuencias.

customary system The measurement system often used in the United States.

sistema usual de medidas El sistema de medidas que se usa comúnmente en Estados Unidos.

inches, feet, miles, ounces, pounds, tons, cups, quarts, gallons

cylinder A three-dimensional figure with two parallel, congruent circular bases connected by a curved lateral surface.

cilindro Figura tridimensional con dos bases circulares paralelas y congruentes, unidas por una superficie lateral curva.

debit card An electronic card issued by a financial institution that allows a customer to access their account to withdraw cash or pay for goods and services

tarjeta de débito Tarjeta de pago plástica que un cliente puede usar para pagar por bienes o servicios. El dinero se retira inmediatamente de la cuenta corriente o de ahorros del cliente.

degree The unit of measure for angles or temperature.

grado Unidad de medida para ángulos y temperaturas.

denominator The bottom number of a fraction that tells how many equal parts are in the whole.

denominador Número de abajo en una fracción que indica en cuántas partes iguales se divide el entero.

$\frac{3}{4}$ ← denominator

dependent events Events for which the outcome of one event affects the probability of the other.

sucesos dependientes Dos sucesos son dependientes si el resultado de uno afecta la probabilidad del otro.

A bag contains 3 red marbles and 2 blue marbles. Drawing a red marble and then drawing a blue marble without replacing the first marble is an example of dependent events.

dependent variable The output of a function; a variable whose value depends on the value of the input, or independent variable.

variable dependiente Salida de una función; variable cuyo valor depende del valor de la entrada, o variable independiente.

For $y = 2x + 1$, y is the dependent variable: input: x output: y.

diagonal A line segment that connects two nonadjacent vertices of a polygon.

diagonal Segmento de recta que une dos vértices no adyacentes de un polígono.

diameter A line segment that passes through the center of a circle and has endpoints on the circle, or the length of that segment.

diámetro Segmento de recta que pasa por el centro de un círculo y tiene sus extremos en la circunferencia, o bien la longitud de ese segmento.

difference The result when one number is subtracted from another.

diferencia El resultado de restar un número de otro.

dimension The length, width, or height of a figure.

dimensión Longitud, ancho o altura de una figura.

discount The amount by which the original price is reduced.

descuento Cantidad que se resta del precio original de un artículo.

Distributive Property The property that states if you multiply a sum by a number, you will get the same result if you multiply each addend by that number and then add the products.

Propiedad distributiva Propiedad que establece que, si multiplicas una suma por un número, obtendrás el mismo resultado que si multiplicas cada sumando por ese número y luego sumas los productos.

$5(20 + 1) = 5 \cdot 20 + 5 \cdot 1$

ENGLISH	SPANISH	EXAMPLES
dividend The number to be divided in a division problem.	**dividendo** Número que se divide en un problema de división.	In 8 ÷ 4 = 2, 8 is the dividend.
divisible Can be divided by a number without leaving a remainder.	**divisible** Que se puede dividir entre un número sin dejar residuo.	18 is divisible by 3.
divisor The number you are dividing by in a division problem.	**divisor** El número entre el que se divide en un problema de división.	In 8 ÷ 4 = 2, 4 is the divisor.
dot plot A visual display in which each piece of data is represented by a dot above a number line.	**diagrama de puntos** Despliegue visual en que cada dato se representa con un punto sobre una recta numérica.	
double-bar graph A bar graph that compares two related sets of data.	**gráfica de doble barra** Gráfica de barras que compara dos conjuntos de datos relacionados.	
double-line graph A graph that shows how two related sets of data change over time.	**gráfica de doble línea** Gráfica lineal que muestra cómo cambian con el tiempo dos conjuntos de datos relacionados.	

E

edge The line segment along which two faces of a polyhedron intersect.	**arista** Segmento de recta donde se intersecan dos caras de un poliedro.	Edge
elements The words, numbers, or objects in a set.	**elementos** Palabras, números u objetos que forman un conjunto.	Elements of A: 1, 2, 3, 4
empty set A set that has no elements.	**conjunto vacío** Un conjunto que no tiene elementos.	
endpoint A point at the end of a line segment or ray.	**extremo** Un punto ubicado al final de un segmento de recta o rayo.	
equally likely Outcomes that have the same probability.	**igualmente probables** Resultados que tienen la misma probabilidad de ocurrir.	When you toss a coin, the outcomes "heads" and "tails" are equally likely.

ENGLISH	SPANISH	EXAMPLES
equation A mathematical sentence that shows that two expressions are equivalent.	**ecuación** Enunciado matemático que indica que dos expresiones son equivalentes.	$x + 4 = 7$ $6 + 1 = 10 - 3$
equilateral triangle A triangle with three congruent sides.	**triángulo equilátero** Triángulo con tres lados congruentes.	
equivalent Having the same value.	**equivalentes** Que tienen el mismo valor.	
equivalent expression Equivalent expressions have the same value for all values of the variables.	**expresión equivalente** Las expresiones equivalentes tienen el mismo valor para todos los valores de las variables.	$4x + 5x$ and $9x$ are equivalent expressions.
equivalent fractions Fractions that name the same amount or part.	**fracciones equivalentes** Fracciones que representan la misma cantidad o parte.	$\frac{1}{2}$ and $\frac{2}{4}$ are equivalent fractions.
equivalent ratios Ratios that name the same comparison.	**razones equivalentes** Razones que representan la misma comparación.	$\frac{1}{2}$ and $\frac{2}{4}$ are equivalent ratios.
estimate (n) An answer that is close to the exact answer and is found by rounding or other methods.	**estimación** Una solución aproximada a la respuesta exacta que se halla mediante el redondeo u otros métodos.	
estimate (v) To find an answer close to the exact answer by rounding or other methods.	**estimar** Hallar una solución aproximada a la respuesta exacta mediante el redondeo u otros métodos.	
evaluate To find the value of a numerical or algebraic expression.	**evaluar** Hallar el valor de una expresión numérica o algebraica.	Evaluate $2x + 7$ for $x = 3$: $2x + 7$ $2(3) + 7$ $6 + 7$ 13
even number A whole number that is divisible by two.	**número par** Un número cabal que es divisible entre dos.	
event An outcome or set of outcomes of an experiment or situation.	**suceso** Un resultado o una serie de resultados de un experimento o una situación.	
expanded form A number written as the sum of the values of its digits.	**forma desarrollada** Número escrito como suma de los valores de sus dígitos.	236,536 written in expanded form is $200,000 + 30,000 + 6,000 + 500 + 30 + 6$.
experiment In probability, any activity based on chance.	**experimento** En probabilidad, cualquier actividad basada en la posibilidad.	Tossing a coin 10 times and noting the number of "heads"

Glossary/Glosario

experimental probability The ratio of the number of times an event occurs to the total number of trials, or times that the activity is performed.

probabilidad experimental Razón del número de veces que ocurre un suceso al número total de pruebas o al número de veces que se realiza el experimento.

Kendra attempted 27 free throws and made 16 of them. Her experimental probability of making a free throw is $\frac{\text{number made}}{\text{number attempted}} = \frac{16}{27} \approx 0.59$.

---

exponent The number that indicates how many times the base is used as a factor.

exponente Número que indica cuántas veces se usa la base como factor.

$2^3 = 2 \cdot 2 \cdot 2 = 8$; 3 is the exponent.

---

exponential form A number is in exponential form when it is written with a base and an exponent.

forma exponencial Cuando se escribe un número con una base y un exponente, está en forma exponencial.

4^2 is the exponential form for $4 \cdot 4$.

---

expression A mathematical phrase that contains operations, numbers, and/or variables.

expresión Enunciado matemático que contiene operaciones, números y/o variables.

$6x + 1$

face A flat surface of a polyhedron.

cara Lado plano de un poliedro.

Face

---

factor A number that is multiplied by another number to get a product.

factor Número que se multiplica por otro para hallar un producto.

7 is a factor of 21 since $7 \cdot 3 = 21$.

---

factor tree A diagram showing how a whole number breaks down into its prime factors.

árbol de factores Diagrama que muestra cómo se descompone un número cabal en sus factores primos.

```
    12
   /  \
  3 · 4
     / \
    2 · 2
```
$12 = 3 \cdot 2 \cdot 2$

Fahrenheit A temperature scale in which 32 °F is the freezing point of water and 212 °F is the boiling point of water.

Fahrenheit Escala de temperatura en la que 32 °F es el punto de congelación del agua y 212 °F es el punto de ebullición.

---

fair When all outcomes of an experiment are equally likely, the experiment is said to be fair.

justo Se dice de un experimento donde todos los resultados posibles son igualmente probables.

When tossing a fair coin, heads and tails are equally likely. Each has a probability of $\frac{1}{2}$.

---

formula A rule showing relationships among quantities.

fórmula Regla que muestra relaciones entre cantidades.

$A = \ell w$ is the formula for the area of a rectangle.

---

fraction A number in the form $\frac{a}{b}$ where $b \neq 0$.

fracción Número escrito en la forma $\frac{a}{b}$ donde $b \neq 0$.

---

frequency The number of times a data value occurs.

frecuencia Cantidad de veces que aparece el valor en un conjunto de datos.

In the data set 5, 6, 7, 8, 6, the data value 6 has a frequency of 2.

Glossary/Glosario

ENGLISH	SPANISH	EXAMPLES

frequency table A table that lists items together according to the number of times, or frequency, that the items occur.

tabla de frecuencia Una tabla en la que se organizan los datos de acuerdo con el número de veces que aparece cada valor (o la frecuencia).

Data set: 1, 1, 2, 2, 3, 4, 5, 5, 5, 6, 6
Frequency table:

Date	Frequency
1	2
2	2
3	1
4	1
5	3
6	2

---

front-end estimation An estimating technique in which the front digits of the addends are added.

estimación por partes Técnica en la que se suman sólo los números enteros de los sumandos y luego se ajusta la suma para tener una estimación mas exacta.

Estimate $25.05 + 14.671$ with the sum $25 + 14 = 39$. The actual value is 39 or greater.

---

function An input-output relationship that has exactly one output for each input.

función Relación de entrada-salida en la que a cada valor de entrada corresponde un valor de salida.

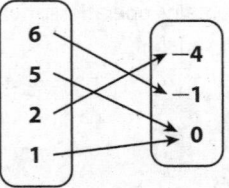

---

function table A table of ordered pairs that represent solutions of a function.

tabla de funciónes Tabla de pares ordenados que representan soluciones de una función.

x	3	4	5	6
y	7	9	11	13

G

grants Money awarded to students that does not need to be repaid.

beca Dinero que se otorga a estudiantes y el cual no se necesita devolver.

---

graph of an equation A graph of the set of ordered pairs that are solutions of the equation.

gráfica de una ecuación Gráfica del conjunto de pares ordenados que son soluciones de la ecuación.

---

greatest common factor (GCF) The largest common factor of two or more given numbers.

máximo común divisor (MCD) El mayor de los factores comunes compartidos por dos o más números dados.

The GCF of 27 and 45 is 9.

H

height In a triangle or quadrilateral, the perpendicular distance from the base to the opposite vertex or side. In a prism or cylinder, the perpendicular distance between the bases.

altura En un triángulo o cuadrilátero, la distancia perpendicular desde la base de la figura al vértice o lado opuesto. En un prisma o cilindro, la distancia perpendicular entre las bases.

ENGLISH	SPANISH	EXAMPLES

heptagon A seven-sided polygon.

heptágono Polígono de siete lados.

hexagon A six-sided polygon.

hexágono Polígono de seis lados.

histogram A bar graph that shows the frequency of data within equal intervals.

histograma Gráfica de barras que muestra la frecuencia de los datos en intervalos iguales.

Starting Salaries

Frequency: 40, 30, 20, 10, 0

Salary range (thousand $): 20–29, 30–39, 40–49, 50–59

hypotenuse In a right triangle, the side opposite the right angle.

hipotenusa En un triángulo rectángulo, el lado opuesto al ángulo recto.

Hypotenuse

I

Identity Property (for Addition) The property that states the sum of zero and any number is that number.

Propiedad de identidad (de la suma) Propiedad que establece que la suma de cero y cualquier número es ese número.

$7 + 0 = 7$
$-9 + 0 = -9$

Identity Property (for Multiplication) The property that states that the product of 1 and any number is that number.

Propiedad de identidad (de la multiplicación) Propiedad que establece que el producto de 1 y cualquier número es ese número.

$5 \times 1 = 5$
$-8 \times 1 = -8$

improper fraction A fraction in which the numerator is greater than or equal to the denominator.

fracción impropia Fracción cuyo numerador es mayor que o igual al denominador.

$\frac{5}{5}$

$\frac{7}{3}$

independent variable The input of a function; a variable whose value determines the value of the output, or dependent variable.

variable independiente Entrada de una función; variable cuyo valor determina el valor de la salida, o variable dependiente.

For $y = 2x + 1$, x is the dependent variable. Input: x output: y

indirect measurement The technique of using similar figures and proportions to find a measure.

medición indirecta La técnica de usar figuras semejantes y proporciones para hallar una medida.

inequality A mathematical sentence that shows the relationship between quantities that are not equal.

desigualdad Enunciado matemático que muestra una relación entre cantidades que no son iguales.

$5 < 8$
$5x + 2 \geq 12$

Glossary/Glosario

ENGLISH	SPANISH	EXAMPLES
input The value substituted into an expression or function.	**valor de entrada** Valor que se usa para sustituir una variable en una expresión o función.	For the rule $y = 6x$, the input 4 produces an output of 24.
integer A member of the set of whole numbers and their opposites.	**entero** Un miembro del conjunto de los números cabales y sus opuestos.	$\ldots -3, -2, -1, 0, 1, 2, 3, \ldots$
interest The amount of money charged for borrowing or using money, or the amount of money earned by saving money.	**interés** Cantidad de dinero que se cobra por el préstamo o uso del dinero, o la cantidad que se gana al ahorrar dinero.	
interquartile range (IQR) The difference of the third (upper) and first (lower) quartiles in a data set, representing the middle half of the data.	**rango intercuartil (RIC)** Diferencia entre el tercer cuartil (superior) y el primer cuartil (inferior) de un conjunto de datos, que representa la mitad central de los datos.	Lower half Upper half 18, (23), 28, 29, (36,) 42 First quartile Third quartile Interquartile range: $36 - 23 = 13$
intersecting lines Lines that cross at exactly one point.	**rectas secantes** Líneas que se cruzan en un solo punto.	m n
intersection (sets) The set of elements common to two or more sets.	**intersección (de conjuntos)** Conjunto de elementos comunes a dos o más conjuntos.	
interval The space between marked values on a number line or the scale of a graph.	**intervalo** El espacio entre los valores marcados en una recta numérica o en la escala de una gráfica.	
inverse operations Operations that undo each other: addition and subtraction, or multiplication and division.	**operaciones inversas** Operaciones que se cancelan mutuamente: suma y resta, o multiplicación y división.	
isosceles triangle A triangle with at least two congruent sides.	**triángulo isósceles** Triángulo que tiene al menos dos lados congruentes.	

L

lateral surface In a cylinder, the curved surface connecting the circular bases; in a cone, the curved surface that is not a base.	**superficie lateral** En un cilindro, superficie curva que une las bases circulares; en un cono, la superficie curva que no es la base.	Lateral surface
least common denominator (LCD) The least common multiple of two or more denominators.	**mínimo común denominador (m.c.d.)** El mínimo común múltiplo de dos o más denominadores.	The LCD of $\frac{3}{4}$ and $\frac{5}{6}$ is 12.

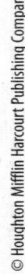

ENGLISH	SPANISH	EXAMPLES
least common multiple (LCM) The smallest number, other than zero, that is a multiple of two or more given numbers.	**mínimo común múltiplo (m.c.m.)** El menor de los múltiplos (distinto de cero) de dos o más números.	The LCM of 10 and 18 is 90.
like fractions Fractions that have the same denominator.	**fracciones semejantes** Fracciones que tienen el mismo denominador.	$\frac{5}{12}$ and $\frac{3}{12}$ are like fractions.
like terms Terms with the same variables raised to the same exponents.	**términos semejantes** Términos con las mismas variables elevadas a los mismos exponentes.	$3a^2b^2$ and $7a^2b^2$
line A straight path that has no thickness and extends forever.	**recta** Trayectoria recta que no tiene ningún grueso y que se extiende por siempre.	$\longleftrightarrow\ \ell$
line graph A graph that uses line segments to show how data changes.	**gráfica lineal** Gráfica que muestra cómo cambian los datos mediante segmentos de recta.	**Marlon's Video Game Scores**
line plot A number line with marks or dots that show frequency.	**diagrama de puntos** Recta numérica con marcas o puntos que indican la frecuencia.	X X / X X X / X X X X / 0 1 2 3 4 / **Number of Pets**
line of reflection A line that a figure is flipped across to create a mirror image of the original figure.	**línea de reflexión** Línea sobre la cual se invierte una figura para crear una imagen reflejada de la figura original.	**Line of reflection**
line of symmetry The imaginary "mirror" in line symmetry.	**eje de simetría** El espejo imaginario en la simetría axial.	
line segment A part of a line between two endpoints.	**segmento de recta** Parte de una línea con dos extremos.	A —— B
line symmetry A figure has line symmetry if one-half is a mirror image of the other half.	**simetría axial** Una figura tiene simetría axial si una de sus mitades es la imagen reflejada de la otra.	

Glossary/Glosario

ENGLISH	SPANISH	EXAMPLES
linear equation An equation whose solutions form a straight line on a coordinate plane.	**ecuación lineal** Ecuación en la que las soluciones forman una línea recta en un plano cartesiano.	$y = 2x + 1$

M

ENGLISH	SPANISH	EXAMPLES
mean The sum of the items in a set of data divided by the number of items in the set; also called *average*.	**media** La suma de todos los elementos de un conjunto de datos dividida entre el número de elementos del conjunto.	Data set: 4, 6, 7, 8, 10 Mean: $\frac{4+6+7+8+10}{5} = \frac{35}{5} = 7$
mean absolute deviation (MAD) The mean distance between each data value and the mean of the data set.	**desviación absoluta media (DAM)** Distancia media entre cada dato y la media del conjunto de datos.	
measure of center A measure used to describe the middle of a data set. Also called measure of central tendency.	**medida central** Medida que se usa para describir el centro de un conjunto de datos; la media, la mediana y la moda son medidas centrales. También se conocen como medidas de tendencia central.	
measure of spread A measure that describes how far apart the data are distributed.	**medida de dispersión** Medida que describe la separación en una distribución de datos.	
median The middle number or the mean (average) of the two middle numbers in an ordered set of data.	**mediana** El número intermedio o la media (el promedio) de los dos números intermedios en un conjunto ordenado de datos.	Data set: 4, 6, 7, 8, 10 Median: 7
metric system A decimal system of weights and measures that is used universally in science and commonly throughout the world.	**sistema métrico** Sistema decimal de pesos y medidas empleado universalmente en las ciencias y por lo general en todo el mundo.	centimeters, meters, kilometers, grams, kilograms, milliliters, liters
midpoint The point that divides a line segment into two congruent line segments.	**punto medio** El punto que divide un segmento de recta en dos segmentos de recta congruentes.	A B C B is the midpoint of $\overline{AC}$.
mixed number A number made up of a whole number that is not zero and a fraction.	**número mixto** Número compuesto por un número cabal distinto de cero y una fracción.	$5\frac{1}{8}$
mode The number or numbers that occur most frequently in a set of data; when all numbers occur with the same frequency, we say there is no mode.	**moda** Número o números más frecuentes en un conjunto de datos; si todos los números aparecen con la misma frecuencia, no hay moda.	Data set: 3, 5, 8, 8, 10 Mode: 8
multiple The product of a number and any nonzero whole number.	**múltiplo** El producto de un número y cualquier número cabal distinto de cero es un múltiplo de ese número.	

Glossary/Glosario

ENGLISH	SPANISH	EXAMPLES
Multiplication Property of Zero The property that states that the product of any number and 0 is 0.	**Propiedad de multiplicación del cero** Propiedad que establece que el producto de cualquier número y 0 es 0.	$6 \times 0 = 0$ $-5 \times 0 = 0$
multiplicative inverse One of two numbers whose product is 1.	**inverso multiplicativo** Uno de dos números cuyo producto es igual a 1.	The multiplicative inverse of $\frac{3}{4}$ is $\frac{4}{3}$.

negative number A number less than zero.	**número negativo** Número menor que cero.	-2 is a negative number.
net An arrangement of two-dimensional figures that can be folded to form a polyhedron.	**plantilla** Arreglo de figuras bidimensionales que se doblan para formar un poliedro.	
numerator The top number of a fraction that tells how many parts of a whole are being considered.	**numerador** El número de arriba de una fracción; indica cuántas partes de un entero se consideran.	$\frac{3}{4} \leftarrow$ numerator
numerical expression An expression that contains only numbers and operations.	**expresión numérica** Expresión que incluye sólo números y operaciones.	$(2 \cdot 3) + 1$

obtuse angle An angle whose measure is greater than 90° but less than 180°.	**ángulo obtuso** Ángulo que mide más de 90° y menos de 180°.	
obtuse triangle A triangle containing one obtuse angle.	**triángulo obtusángulo** Triángulo que tiene un ángulo obtuso.	
odd number A whole number that is not divisible by two.	**número impar** Un número cabal que no es divisible entre dos.	
opposites Two numbers that are an equal distance from zero on a number line; also called additive inverse.	**opuestos** Dos números que están a la misma distancia de cero en una recta numérica. También se llaman *inversos aditivos*.	5 and -5 are opposites.

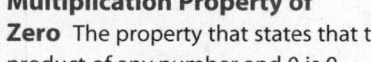

Glossary/Glosario

Glossary/Glosario

order of operations A rule for evaluating expressions: first perform the operations in parentheses, then compute powers and roots, then perform all multiplication and division from left to right, and then perform all addition and subtraction from left to right.

orden de las operaciones Regla para evaluar expresiones: primero se resuelven las operaciones entre paréntesis, luego se hallan las potencias y raíces, después todas las multiplicaciones y divisiones de izquierda a derecha y, por último, todas las sumas y restas de izquierda a derecha.

$3^2 - 12 \div 4$	Evaluate the power.
$9 - 12 \div 4$	Divide.
$9 - 3$	Subtract.
6	

ordered pair A pair of numbers that can be used to locate a point on a coordinate plane.

par ordenado Par de números que sirven para ubicar un punto en un plano cartesiano.

The coordinates of B are $(-2, 3)$.

origin The point where the *x*-axis and *y*-axis intersect on the coordinate plane; (0, 0).

origen Punto de intersección entre el eje *x* y el eje *y* en un plano cartesiano: (0, 0).

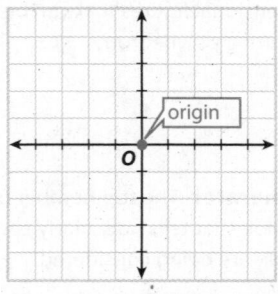

outcome A possible result of a probability experiment.

resultado Posible resultado de un experimento de probabilidad.

When rolling a number cube, the possible outcomes are 1, 2, 3, 4, 5, and 6.

outlier A value much greater or much less than the others in a data set.

valor atípico Un valor mucho mayor o menor que los demás valores de un conjunto de datos.

output The value that results from the substitution of a given input into an expression or function.

valor de salida Valor que resulta después de sustituir un valor de entrada determinado en una expresión o función.

For the rule $y = 6x$, the input 4 produces an output of 24.

overestimate An estimate that is greater than the exact answer.

estimación alta Estimación mayor que la respuesta exacta.

100 is an overestimate for the sum $23 + 24 + 21 + 22$.

P

parallel lines Lines in a plane that do not intersect.

rectas paralelas Líneas que se encuentran en el mismo plano pero que nunca se intersecan.

r
s

ENGLISH	SPANISH	EXAMPLES
parallelogram A quadrilateral with two pairs of parallel sides.	**paralelogramo** Cuadrilátero con dos pares de lados paralelos.	
pentagon A five-sided polygon.	**pentágono** Polígono de cinco lados.	
percent A ratio comparing a number to 100.	**porcentaje** Razón que compara un número con el número 100.	$45\% = \frac{45}{100}$
percent of decrease A percent change describing a decrease in a quantity.	**porcentaje de disminución** Porcentaje de cambio en que una cantidad disminuye.	An item that costs $8 is marked down to $6. The amount of the decrease is $2, and the percent of decrease is $\frac{2}{8} = 0.25 = 25\%$.
percent of increase A percent change describing an increase in a quantity.	**porcentaje de incremento** Porcentaje de cambio en que una cantidad aumenta.	The price of an item increases from $8 to $12. The amount of the increase is $4, and the percent of increase is $\frac{4}{8} = 0.5 = 50\%$.
perfect square A square of a whole number.	**cuadrado perfecto** El cuadrado de un número cabal.	$5^2 = 25$, so 25 is a perfect square.
perimeter The distance around a polygon.	**perímetro** Distancia alrededor de un polígono.	
permutation An arrangement of items or events in which order is important.	**permutación** Arreglo de objetos o sucesos en el que el orden es importante.	For objects *A*, *B*, and *C*, there are 6 different permutations: *ABC, ACB, BAC, BCA, CAB, CBA*.
perpendicular bisector A line that intersects a segment at its midpoint and is perpendicular to the segment.	**mediatriz** Línea que cruza un segmento en su punto medio y es perpendicular al segmento.	ℓ is the perpendicular bisector of $\overline{AB}$.
perpendicular lines Lines that intersect to form right angles.	**rectas perpendiculares** Líneas que al intersecarse forman ángulos rectos.	
pi (π) The ratio of the circumference of a circle to the length of its diameter; $\pi \approx 3.14$ or $\frac{22}{7}$.	**pi (π)** Razón de la circunferencia de un círculo a la longitud de su diámetro; $\pi < 3.14$ ó $\frac{22}{7}$	

© Houghton Mifflin Harcourt Publishing Company

Glossary/Glosario

ENGLISH	SPANISH	EXAMPLES
plane A flat surface that has no thickness and extends forever.	**plano** Superficie plana que no tiene ningún grueso y que se extiende por siempre.	plane *R* or plane *ABC*
point An exact location that has no size.	**punto** Ubicación exacta que no tiene ningún tamaño.	*P* • point *P*
polygon A closed plane figure formed by three or more line segments that intersect only at their endpoints.	**polígono** Figura plana cerrada, formada por tres o más segmentos de recta que se intersecan sólo en sus extremos.	
polyhedron A three-dimensional figure in which all the surfaces or faces are polygons.	**poliedro** Figura tridimensional cuyas superficies o caras tienen forma de polígonos.	
population The whole group being surveyed.	**población** El grupo completo que es objeto de estudio.	In a survey about eating habits of middle school students, the population is all middle school students.
positive number A number greater than zero.	**número positivo** Número mayor que cero.	2 is a positive number.
power A number produced by raising a base to an exponent.	**potencia** Número que resulta al elevar una base a un exponente.	$2^3 = 8$, so 2 to the 3rd power is 8.
prediction A guess about something that will happen in the future.	**predicción** Pronóstico sobre algo que puede ocurrir en el futuro.	
prime factorization A number written as the product of its prime factors.	**descomposición en factores primos** Un número escrito como el producto de sus factores primos.	$10 = 2 \cdot 5$ $24 = 2^3 \cdot 3$
prime number A whole number greater than 1 that has exactly two factors, itself and 1.	**número primo** Número cabal mayor que 1 que sólo es divisible entre 1 y él mismo.	5 is prime because its only factors are 5 and 1.
principal The initial amount of money borrowed or saved.	**capital** Cantidad inicial de dinero depositada o recibida en préstamo.	
prism A polyhedron that has two congruent, polygon-shaped bases and other faces that are all rectangles.	**prisma** Poliedro con dos bases congruentes con forma de polígono y caras con forma de rectángulos.	

Glossary/Glosario

probability A number from 0 to 1 (or 0% to 100%) that describes how likely an event is to occur.

probabilidad Un número entre 0 y 1 (ó 0% y 100%) que describe qué tan probable es un suceso.

A bag contains 3 red marbles and 4 blue marbles. The probability of randomly choosing a red marble is $\frac{3}{7}$.

---

product The result when two or more numbers are multiplied.

producto Resultado de multiplicar dos o más números.

The product of 4 and 8 is 32.

---

proper fraction A fraction in which the numerator is less than the denominator.

fracción propia Fracción en la que el numerador es menor que el denominador.

$\frac{3}{4}, \frac{1}{13}, \frac{7}{8}$

---

proportion An equation that states that two ratios are equivalent.

proporción Ecuación que establece que dos razones son equivalentes.

$\frac{2}{3} = \frac{4}{6}$

---

proportional relationship A relationship between two quantities in which the ratio of one quantity to the other quantity is constant.

relación proporcional Relación entre dos cantidades en que la razón de una cantidad a la otra es constante.

---

protractor A tool for measuring angles.

transportador Instrumento para medir ángulos.

---

pyramid A polyhedron with a polygon base and triangular sides that all meet at a common vertex.

pirámide Poliedro cuya base es un polígono; tiene caras triangulares que se juntan en un vértice común.

---

quadrant The x- and y-axes divide the coordinate plane into four regions. Each region is called a quadrant.

cuadrante El eje x y el eje y dividen el plano cartesiano en cuatro regiones. Cada región recibe el nombre de cuadrante.

---

quartile Three values, one of which is the median, that divide a data set into fourths.

cuartil Cada uno de tres valores, uno de los cuales es la mediana, que dividen en cuartos un conjunto de datos.

---

quotient The result when one number is divided by another.

cociente Resultado de dividir un número entre otro.

In $8 \div 4 = 2$, 2 is the quotient.

Glossary/Glosario

ENGLISH	SPANISH	EXAMPLES

radius A line segment with one endpoint at the center of a circle and the other endpoint on the circle, or the length of that segment.

radio Segmento de recta con un extremo en el centro de un círculo y el otro en la circunferencia, o bien la longitud de ese segmento.

---

range In statistics, the difference between the greatest and least values in a data set.

rango (en estadística) Diferencia entre los valores máximo y mínimo de un conjunto de datos.

---

rate A ratio that compares two quantities measured in different units.

tasa Una razón que compara dos cantidades medidas en diferentes unidades.

---

rate of change A ratio that compares the difference between two output values to the difference between the corresponding input values.

tasa de cambio Razón que compara la diferencia entre dos salidas con la diferencia entre dos entrados.

The cost of mailing a letter increased from 22 cents in 1985 to 25 cents in 1988. The rate of change was
$\frac{25 - 22}{1988 - 1985} = \frac{3}{3}$
= 1 cent per year.

---

rate of interest The percent charged or earned on an amount of money; see *simple interest*.

tasa de interés Porcentaje que se cobra por una cantidad de dinero prestada o que se gana por una cantidad de dinero ahorrada; ver *interés simple*.

---

ratio A comparison of two quantities by division.

razón Comparación de dos cantidades mediante una división.

12 to 25, 12:25, $\frac{12}{25}$

---

rational number A number that can be expressed as a ratio of two integers and can be written in the form $\frac{a}{b}$, where a and b are integers and $b \neq 0$.

número racional Número que se puede escribir como una razón de dos enteros y se puede expresar como $\frac{a}{b}$, donde a y b son números enteros y $b \neq 0$.

$3, 1.75, 0.\overline{3}, -\frac{2}{3}, 0$

---

ray A part of a line that starts at one endpoint and extends forever in one direction.

rayo Parte de una línea que comienza en un extremo y se extiende siempre en una dirección.

$\overset{\bullet}{\underset{D}{\longrightarrow}}$

---

reciprocal One of two numbers whose product is 1.

recíproco Uno de dos números cuyo producto es igual a 1.

The reciprocal of $\frac{2}{3}$ is $\frac{3}{2}$.

---

rectangle A parallelogram with four right angles.

rectángulo Paralelogramo con cuatro ángulos rectos.

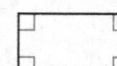

---

rectangular prism A polyhedron whose bases are rectangles and whose other faces are rectangles.

prisma rectangular Poliedro cuyas bases son rectángulos y cuyas caras tienen forma de rectángulos.

Glossary/Glosario

reflection A transformation of a figure that flips the figure across a line.

reflexión Transformación que ocurre cuando se invierte una figura sobre una línea.

regular polygon A polygon with congruent sides and angles.

polígono regular Polígono con lados y ángulos congruentes.

relative frequency The ratio of the number of times an event or data value occurs and the total number of events or data values.

frecuencia relativa La razón del número de veces que ocurre un evento o dato (frecuencia) al total del número de eventos o datos.

repeating decimal A decimal in which one or more digits repeat infinitely.

decimal periódico Decimal en el que uno o más dígitos se repiten infinitamente.

$0.75757575\ldots = 0.\overline{75}$

rhombus A parallelogram with all sides congruent.

rombo Paralelogramo en el que todos los lados son congruentes.

right angle An angle that measures 90°.

ángulo recto Ángulo que mide exactamente 90°.

right triangle A triangle containing a right angle.

triángulo rectángulo Triángulo que tiene un ángulo recto.

rotation A transformation in which a figure is turned around a point.

rotación Transformación que ocurre cuando una figura gira alrededor de un punto.

rotational symmetry A figure that can be rotated about a point by an angle less than 360° so that the image coincides with the preimage has rotational symmetry.

simetría de rotación Una figura que puede rotarse alrededor de un punto en un ángulo menor de 360° de forma tal que la imagen coincide con la imagen original que tenga simetría de rotación.

rounding Replacing a number with an estimate of that number to a given place value.

redondear Sustituir un número por una estimación de ese número hasta cierto valor posicional.

2,354 rounded to the nearest thousand is 2,000; 2,354 rounded to the nearest 100 is 2,400.

Glossary/Glosario

S

sales tax A percent of the cost of an item which is charged by governments to raise money.

impuesto sobre la venta Porcentaje del costo de un artículo que los gobiernos cobran para recaudar fondos.

---

sample A part of a group being surveyed.

muestra Parte de un grupo que es objeto de estudio.

In a survey about eating habits of middle school math students, a sample is a survey of 100 randomly chosen students.

---

sample space All possible outcomes of an experiment.

espacio muestral Conjunto de todos los resultados posibles de un experimento.

When rolling a number cube, the sample space is 1, 2, 3, 4, 5, 6.

---

scale The ratio between two sets of measurements.

escala La razón entre dos conjuntos de medidas.

1 cm: 5 mi

---

scale drawing A drawing that uses a scale to make an object proportionally smaller than or larger than the real object.

dibujo a escala Dibujo en el que se usa una escala para que un objeto se vea proporcionalmente mayor o menor que el objeto real al que representa.

A blueprint is an example of a scale drawing.

---

scale model A proportional model of a three-dimensional object.

modelo a escala Modelo proporcional de un objeto tridimensional.

---

scalene triangle A triangle with no congruent sides.

triángulo escaleno Triángulo que no tiene lados congruentes.

---

scholarship A monetary award to a student to support their education.

becas Dinero que se otorga a los estudiantes en base a logros.

---

scientific notation A method of writing very large or very small numbers by using powers of 10.

notación científica Método que se usa para escribir números muy grandes o muy pequeños mediante potencias de 10.

$12{,}560{,}000{,}000{,}000 = 1.256 \times 10^{13}$

---

segment A part of a line made of two endpoints and all points between them.

segmento Parte de una línea que consiste en dos extremos y todos los puntos entre éstos.

---

sequence An ordered list of numbers.

sucesión Lista ordenada de números.

2, 4, 6, 8, 10, . . .

---

set A group of items.

conjunto Un grupo de elementos.

ENGLISH	SPANISH	EXAMPLES

side A line bounding a geometric figure; one of the faces forming the outside of an object.

lado Línea que delimita las figuras geométricas; una de las caras que forman la parte exterior de un objeto.

significant figures The figures used to express the precision of a measurement.

dígitos significativos Dígitos usados para expresar la precisión de una medida.

similar Figures with the same shape but not necessarily the same size are similar.

semejantes Figuras que tienen la misma forma, pero no necesariamente el mismo tamaño.

simple event An event consisting of only one outcome.

suceso simple Suceso que tiene sólo un resultado.

In the experiment of rolling a number cube, the event consisting of the outcome 3 is a simple event.

simple interest A fixed percent of the principal. It is found using the formula $I = Prt$, where P represents the principal, r the rate of interest, and t the time.

interés simple Un porcentaje fijo del capital. Se calcula con la fórmula $I = Cit$, donde C representa el capital, i, la tasa de interés y t, el tiempo.

simplest form (of a fraction) A fraction is in simplest form when the numerator and denominator have no common factors other than 1.

mínima expresión (de una fracción) Una fracción está en su mínima expresión cuando el numerador y el denominador no tienen más factor común que 1.

Fraction: $\frac{8}{12}$
Simplest form: $\frac{2}{3}$

simplify To write a fraction or expression in simplest form.

simplificar Escribir una fracción o expresión numérica en su mínima expresión.

simulation A model of an experiment, often one that would be too difficult or too time-consuming to actually perform.

simulación Representación de un experimento, por lo regular de uno cuya realización sería demasiado difícil o llevaría mucho tiempo.

skew lines Lines that lie in different planes that are neither parallel nor intersecting.

líneas oblicuas Líneas que se encuentran en planos distintos, por eso no se intersecan ni son paralelas.

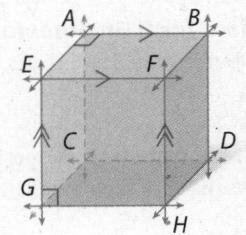

slope The constant rate of change of a line.

pendiente La tasa de cambio constante de una línea.

© Houghton Mifflin Harcourt Publishing Company

Glossary/Glosario

solid figure A three-dimensional figure.

cuerpo geométrico Figura tridimensional.

---

solution of an equation A value or values that make an equation true.

solución de una ecuación Valor o valores que hacen verdadera una ecuación.

Equation: $x + 2 = 6$
Solution: $x = 4$

---

solution of an inequality A value or values that make an inequality true.

solución de una desigualdad Valor o valores que hacen verdadera una desigualdad.

Inequality: $x + 3 \geq 10$
Solution set: $x \geq 7$

---

solution set The set of values that make a statement true.

conjunto solución Conjunto de valores que hacen verdadero un enunciado.

Inequality: $x + 3 \geq 5$
Solution set: $x \geq 2$

$-4\ -3\ -2\ -1\ \ 0\ \ 1\ \ 2\ \ 3\ \ 4\ \ 5\ \ 6$

---

solve To find an answer or a solution.

resolver Hallar una respuesta o solución.

---

square (geometry) A rectangle with four congruent sides.

cuadrado (en geometría) Rectángulo con cuatro lados congruentes.

---

square (numeration) A number raised to the second power.

cuadrado (en numeración) Número elevado a la segunda potencia.

In 5^2, the number 5 is squared.

---

square number A number that is the product of a whole number and itself.

cuadrado de un número El producto de un número cabal multiplicado por sí mismo.

25 is a square number since $5^2 = 25$.

---

square root A number that is multiplied by itself to form a product is called a square root of that product.

raíz cuadrada El número que se multiplica por sí mismo para formar un producto se denomina la raíz cuadrada de ese producto.

$16 = 4 \cdot 4$ and $16 = -4 \cdot -4$, so 4 and -4 are square roots of 16.

---

standard form (in numeration) A number written using digits.

forma estándar Una forma de escribir números por medio de dígitos.

Five thousand, two hundred ten in standard form is 5,210.

---

statistical question A question that has many different, or variable, answers.

pregunta estadística Pregunta con muchas respuestas o variables diferentes.

Glossary/Glosario

ENGLISH	SPANISH	EXAMPLES

straight angle An angle that measures 180°.

ángulo llano Ángulo que mide exactamente 180°.

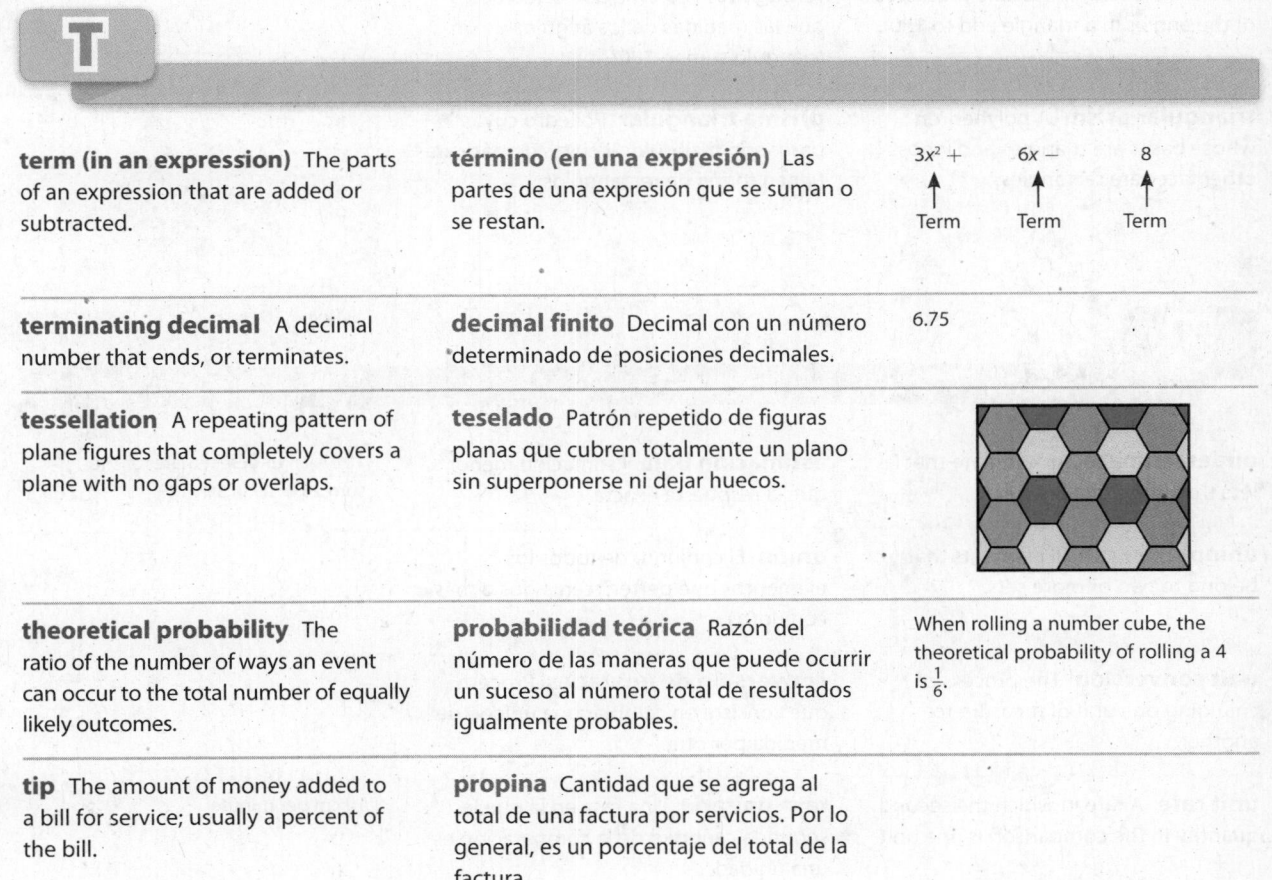

subset A set contained within another set.

subconjunto Conjunto que pertenece a otro conjunto.

substitute To replace a variable with a number or another expression in an algebraic expression.

sustituir Reemplazar una variable por un número u otra expresión en una expresión algebraica.

sum The result when two or more numbers are added.

suma Resultado de sumar dos o más números.

supplementary angles Two angles whose measures have a sum of 180°.

ángulos suplementarios Dos ángulos cuyas medidas suman 180°.

30° 150°

surface area The sum of the areas of the faces, or surfaces, of a three-dimensional figure.

área total Suma de las áreas de las caras, o superficies, de una figura tridimensional.

12 cm
6 cm
8 cm

Surface area = 2(8)(12) + 2(8)(6) + 2(12)(6) = 432cm²

T

term (in an expression) The parts of an expression that are added or subtracted.

término (en una expresión) Las partes de una expresión que se suman o se restan.

$3x^2 +$ $6x -$ 8
↑   ↑   ↑
Term   Term   Term

terminating decimal A decimal number that ends, or terminates.

decimal finito Decimal con un número determinado de posiciones decimales.

6.75

tessellation A repeating pattern of plane figures that completely covers a plane with no gaps or overlaps.

teselado Patrón repetido de figuras planas que cubren totalmente un plano sin superponerse ni dejar huecos.

theoretical probability The ratio of the number of ways an event can occur to the total number of equally likely outcomes.

probabilidad teórica Razón del número de las maneras que puede ocurrir un suceso al número total de resultados igualmente probables.

When rolling a number cube, the theoretical probability of rolling a 4 is $\frac{1}{6}$.

tip The amount of money added to a bill for service; usually a percent of the bill.

propina Cantidad que se agrega al total de una factura por servicios. Por lo general, es un porcentaje del total de la factura.

Glossary/Glosario

transformation A change in the size or position of a figure.

transformación Cambio en el tamaño o la posición de una figura.

---

translation A movement (slide) of a figure along a straight line.

traslación Desplazamiento de una figura a lo largo de una línea recta.

---

trapezoid A quadrilateral with exactly one pair of parallel sides.

trapecio Cuadrilátero con un par de lados paralelos.

---

tree diagram A branching diagram that shows all possible combinations or outcomes of an event.

diagrama de árbol Diagrama ramificado que muestra todas las posibles combinaciones o resultados de un suceso.

---

trial Each repetition or observation of an experiment.

prueba Cada repetición u observación de un experimento.

In the experiment of rolling a number cube, each roll is one trial.

---

triangle A three-sided polygon.

triángulo Polígono de tres lados.

Triangle Sum Theorem The theorem that states that the measures of the angles in a triangle add to 180°.

Teorema de la suma del triángulo Teorema que establece que las medidas de los ángulos de un triángulo suman 180°.

---

triangular prism A polyhedron whose bases are triangles and whose other faces are rectangles.

prisma triangular Poliedro cuyas bases son triángulos y cuyas demás caras tienen forma de rectángulos.

---

underestimate An estimate that is less than the exact answer.

estimación baja Estimación menor que la respuesta exacta.

100 is an underestimate for the sum 26 + 29 + 31 + 27.

---

union The set of all elements that belong to two or more sets.

unión El conjunto de todos los elementos que pertenecen a dos o más conjuntos.

---

unit conversion The process of changing one unit of measure to another.

conversión de unidades Proceso que consiste en cambiar una unidad de medida por otra.

---

unit rate A rate in which the second quantity in the comparison is one unit.

tasa unitaria Una tasa en la que la segunda cantidad de la comparación es una unidad.

10 cm per minute

Glossary/Glosario

ENGLISH	SPANISH	EXAMPLES

unlike fractions Fractions with different denominators.

fracciones distintas Fracciones con distinto denominador.

$\frac{3}{4}$ and $\frac{1}{2}$ are unlike fractions.

V

variable A symbol used to represent a quantity that can change.

variable Símbolo que representa una cantidad que puede cambiar.

In the expression $2x + 3$, x is the variable.

variation (variability) The spread of values in a set of data.

variación (variabilidad) Amplitud de los valores de un conjunto de datos.

The data set {1, 5, 7, 10, 25} has greater variation than the data set {8, 8, 9, 9, 9}.

Venn diagram A diagram that is used to show relationships between sets.

diagrama de Venn Diagrama que muestra las relaciones entre conjuntos.

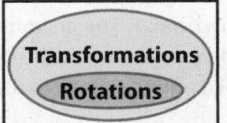

vertex (vertices) On an angle or polygon, the point where two sides intersect.

vértice (vértices) En un ángulo o polígono, el punto de intersección de dos lados.

A is the vertex of $\angle CAB$.

vertical angles A pair of opposite congruent angles formed by intersecting lines.

ángulos opuestos por el vértice Par de ángulos opuestos congruentes formados por líneas secantes.

$\angle 1$ and $\angle 3$ are vertical angles.
$\angle 2$ and $\angle 4$ are vertical angles.

volume The number of cubic units needed to fill a given space.

volumen Número de unidades cúbicas que se necesitan para llenar un espacio.

Volume $= 3 \cdot 4 \cdot 12 = 144 \text{ ft}^3$

W

work-study program A program in which students are able to work at jobs on campus to make money to pay their college tuition.

programas de trabajo y estudio Programas que permiten a los estudiantes universitarios trabajar a medio tiempo y así ganar dinero para las matrículas universitarias y los gastos.

ENGLISH	SPANISH	EXAMPLES

X

x-axis The horizontal axis on a coordinate plane.

eje x El eje horizontal del plano cartesiano.

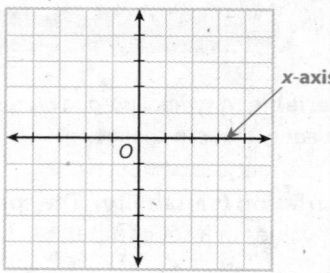

x-coordinate The first number in an ordered pair; it tells the distance to move right or left from the origin, (0, 0).

coordenada x El primer número en un par ordenado; indica la distancia que debes avanzar hacia la izquierda o hacia la derecha desde el origen, (0, 0).

Y

y-axis The vertical axis on a coordinate plane.

eje y El eje vertical del plano cartesiano.

y-coordinate The second number in an ordered pair; it tells the distance to move up or down from the origin, (0, 0).

coordenada y El segundo número en un par ordenado; indica la distancia que debes avanzar hacia arriba o hacia abajo desde el origen, (0, 0).

Z

zero pair A number and its opposite, which add to 0.

par nulo Un número y su opuesto, que sumados dan 0.

18 and −18

Glossary/Glosario

Index

A

absolute value, 2, 6, 46, 556, 566
  comparing, 21–22
  as distance from zero, 6
  in finding distance on coordinate plane, 402–404, 408
  instead of negative numbers, 20–21
  of rational numbers, 55

Active Reading, 5, 29, 45, 77, 105, 147, 171, 201, 235, 259, 295, 329, 369, 399, 417, 447, 493, 523, 547, 609, 633

addend, 555–558

addition
  additive inverse, 490, 558, 562
  algebraic expressions for, 261
  Associative Property of, 118, 277, 559, 589
  checking reasonableness of answers, 116
  Commutative Property of, 118, 277
  of decimals, 113–118
  of expressions, 589
  of fractions, using LCM in, 81–82
  Identity Property of, 277
  of integers
    application of properties to solve problems, 514
    with different signs, 501–504
    with same sign, 495–497
    solving multistep problems and, 513
  in order of operations, 249
  of rational numbers, 555–562
  repeated, multiplication as, 571
  solving equations containing, 305
  use Distributive Property to rewrite sums, 33

Addition Property of Equality, 305

additive inverse, 490, 494, 503, 558, 562

algebra
  The development of algebra skills and concepts is a central focus of this course and is found throughout the book.
  equations, 296, 297
    about area of shapes, 383–386, 390–394
    addition, solving by, 305
    algebraic, 296, 297–302
    checking solutions to, 299
    defined, 330
    division, solving by, 312
    with greatest common factor, 32–34, 36
    modeling, 303, 311
    multiplication, solving by, 313
    multistep, 573–575, 612–614, 619–620, 648, 649
    for proportional relationships, 619–620, 625, 626
    representing geometric concepts, 306
    for solving real-world problems, 314–315
    subtraction, solving by, 304
    with two variables, 345–348, 351–354
    for volume, 431–434
    writing from graphs, 351–354
    writing from tables, 345–348
    writing real-world problems for, 307
    writing to represent situations, 297–299
  expressions, 562, 568–570, 578, 589–594
    adding and subtracting, 589, 592
    for adding simple interest, 648
    algebraic, 261–268
    comparing using models, 263–264
    Distributive Property with, 589–592, 594
    equations and, 297
    equivalent, 260, 261, 263–264, 275–279
    evaluating, 269–271
    expanding, 590
    with exponents, 238, 240
    factoring, 591, 592
    generating equivalent, 275–279
    inequalities and, 321
    modeling equivalent, 261
    numerical, 250–253
    parts of, 279
    in problem solving, 97, 131
    rational number operations, 588
    removing parentheses from, 590
    representing word problems, 134
    simplifying, 249–253, 590, 592
    for total cost, 648
  inequalities, 296
    graphing solutions of, 320–321
    using to describe quantities, 319
    writing, 321–322
  multistep equations, 97–100, 573–575, 612–614, 619–620, 648, 649
  properties
    Addition Property of Equality, 305
    Associative, 118, 277, 559, 589
    Commutative, 118, 277, 278, 570, 589
    Distributive, 33, 277, 278, 589–592, 594
    Division Property of Equality, 312
    identifying equivalent expressions using, 278
    Identity, 277
    Inverse Property of Addition, 558, 562
    Multiplication Property of Equality, 313
    solving equations using, 304, 305, 312, 313
    Subtraction Property of Equality, 304
    writing equivalent expressions using, 277
    of zero as an exponent, 239
  proportions
    solving problems with, 179–184
    using to convert units, 186–187
  variables, 232, 261, 619
    independent and dependent in tables and, 337–341
    writing equations from tables and, 346–348

algebraic expressions, 232, 261–268
  for addition, 261
  bar models of, 262–265
  comparing using models, 263–264
  for division, 261
  equivalent, 263–264

algebra tiles, 276, 278, 281, 303, 311, 591, 593

algorithms, 106

Analyze Relationships, 8, 9, 11, 12, 13, 18, 19, 23, 48, 49, 52, 58, 64, 81, 92, 96, 118, 119, 130, 150, 154, 155, 162, 166, 177, 178, 184, 190, 196, 208, 217, 253, 338, 339, 343, 344, 351, 355, 382, 388, 456, 468, 496, 506, 512, 518, 530, 535, 554, 588, 615, 616, 621, 627, 646, 652

analyzing data, for proportional relationships, 625

angles, 306

Animated Math, 3, 27, 43, 75, 103, 145, 157, 199, 233, 257, 278, 293, 327, 367, 415, 420, 445, 491, 521, 545, 607, 624, 631

answers, assessing reasonableness of, 115, 116, 583–588

applications
  astronomy, 17, 568
  biology, 89
  chemistry, 11
  consumer math, 221
  earth science, 23, 111, 222
  financial literacy, 23, 24, 52, 57, 221, 561, 568, 575
  geography, 18, 561
  geometry, 254
  history, 433
  music, 83
  physical science, 433
  science, 11, 17, 18, 23, 89, 166, 222, 429, 568, 582
  sports, 517

approximation (≈), 191

area
  of parallelograms, 371, 389, 394, 409
  of polygons, 389–394, 409, 410
  of quadrilaterals, 371–374
  of rectangles, 409, 591, 593
  of a rhombus, 373–374
  solving equations for, 383–386
  solving problems involving, 93–96
  in square centimeters, 390
  in square feet, 193, 390, 391–392, 393, 612
  in square inches, 394
  in square meters, 193, 196, 391
  of squares, 410, 412
  of trapezoids, 372–373, 392, 394
  of triangles, 377–380, 389–392, 394, 412

area models, 119, 591
  for greatest common factor, 33
  grids as, 409

Are You Ready?, 4, 28, 44, 76, 104, 146, 170, 200, 234, 258, 294, 328, 368, 398, 416, 446, 492, 522, 546, 608, 632

assessment
  Are You Ready?, 4, 28, 44, 76, 104, 146, 170, 200, 234, 258, 294, 328, 368, 398, 416, 446, 492, 522, 546, 608, 632
  Assessment Readiness, 26, 42, 66, 71–72, 102, 136, 141–142, 168, 198, 224,

Index

229–230, 256, 284, 289–290, 326, 358, 363–364, 396, 414, 436, 441–442, 484, 487–488, 520, 544, 596, 603–604, 630, 654, 659–660

Mini-Tasks, 26, 42, 66, 72, 102, 136, 142, 168, 198, 224, 230, 256, 284, 290, 326, 358, 364, 396, 414, 436, 442, 484, 488, 520, 544, 596, 604, 630, 654, 660

Performance Tasks, 70, 140, 228, 288, 362, 440, 486, 601–602, 657–658

Ready to Go On?, 25, 41, 65, 101, 135, 167, 197, 223, 255, 283, 325, 357, 395, 413, 435, 483, 519, 543, 595, 629, 653

Study Guide Review, 67–69, 137–139, 225–228, 285–287, 359–362, 437–440, 485–486, 597–602, 655–658

Associative Property of Addition, 118, 277, 559, 589

Associative Property of Multiplication, 277

astronomy, 17, 568

Atlantic Basin, 639

axes, 292, 331, 340

B

bar diagrams, 156–159, 191, 611, 617
bar graphs, 639
bar models, 215, 220, 262–265, 641–643, 647
fraction bars, 85, 91
percent bars, 204
base, 232, 238, 241, 242
of prisms, 421, 426
of pyramids, 420
benchmark fractions, 80
benchmark percents, 205
biology, 89
booklets, 105, 295, 417, 493
box plots, 463–468

C

calculators, 585, 588
capacity, measurements of, 186
careers
bicycle tour operator, 605, 657
botanist, 291, 362
chef, 73, 140
climatologist, 1, 70
freelance computer programmer, 231, 288
geneticist, 443, 486
residential builder, 143, 228
theater set construction, 365, 440
urban planner, 489, 601
center, measures of, 449–452, 472
centimeters, 191, 194, 195, 424, 429, 432, 433
change
constant rates of, 617–622
percent, 637
markup and markdown, 641–646
percent increase and decrease, 635–640
Check for Reasonableness, 93, 112, 121, 124, 126, 219, 583–588, 616

chemistry, 11
clusters, 471
coefficients, 279
commission, 651
common factors, 31, 32, 34
on area models, 33
greatest. *See* greatest common factor (GCF)
common multiples, 38. *See also* least common multiple (LCM)
Communicate Mathematical Ideas, 12, 20, 24, 36, 40, 48, 53, 55, 59, 61, 64, 83, 86, 90, 91, 118, 120, 174, 178, 185, 192, 196, 214, 216, 217, 218, 237, 242, 245, 247, 248, 282, 302, 303, 304, 305, 318, 324, 332, 336, 350, 375, 377, 378, 382, 384, 406, 412, 424, 430, 431, 434, 452, 454, 482, 495, 496, 497, 500, 506, 508, 509, 514, 530, 536, 553, 554, 561, 562, 575, 594, 616, 622, 625, 628, 645
communicating math
arrange, 465
classify, 50, 52, 412
compare, 15, 16, 18, 25, 349, 350, 430, 464, 465, 467, 554
describe, 18, 24, 40, 49, 61, 101, 135, 174, 215, 242, 280, 324, 334, 335, 341, 342, 343, 350, 356, 424, 471, 473, 474, 475, 476, 504, 530, 561
draw, 281, 283, 308, 322, 352, 467
estimate, 121, 123, 126
evaluate, 275, 482, 516, 541
explain. *Explain appears in most lessons. See, for example,* 12, 13, 18, 19, 24, 36, 47, 52, 57, 65, 83, 86
give an example, 190, 319, 344, 510, 512, 518, 645
justify your answer, 355, 356, 382, 406, 473, 533, 535
list, 14, 16, 25, 51, 61, 243, 247
match, 275
Math Talk. *Math Talk appears in most lessons. See, for example,* 10, 14, 15, 20, 33, 48, 55, 61
order, 17, 18, 60, 61, 63, 64, 466
predict, 502
shade, 119, 125, 203, 206, 207, 210, 223
use an example, 118
Commutative Property, 118, 277, 278, 570, 589
comparisons, 15
with absolute values, 21–22
with equivalent ratios, 161–162, 164
of measures, 195
with mixed numbers, 613
with percent, 651
percent decrease, 636
percent increase, 635
with rates, 155
with rates of change, 618
with ratios, 149, 161–162, 164
values of expressions, 539
complementary angles, 306
complex fractions, 612, 613
constant of proportionality, 606, 610, 619–620
constant rates of change, 617–622
constants, 261, 610

Construct an Argument, 582
consumer math, 165, 221
conversion factors, 187–188, 192
conversions of units
using conversion factors, 187–188
using models, 185
using proportions and unit rates, 186–187
coordinate plane, 331
defined, 330
distance in, 401–406, 408
graphing on, 331–333
polygons in, 407–412
finding area, 409, 410
finding perimeter, 408
reflecting in, 401
coordinates, 292, 331
counters, 449, 495, 502, 526
Critical Thinking, 52, 57, 64, 107, 214, 242, 247, 302, 310, 318, 336, 350, 355, 356, 387, 412, 430, 454, 461, 476, 497, 506, 518, 582, 627, 640
Critique Reasoning, 12, 18, 24, 36, 52, 64, 112, 118, 129, 160, 184, 195, 204, 208, 248, 251, 268, 274, 309, 324, 376, 381, 424, 454, 468, 500, 529, 542, 575, 588, 621, 636, 646
cubes
as cubic units, 425
nets for, 419
surface area of, 423
volume of, 242, 425–426, 428
cubic centimeters, 429, 432
cubic feet, 428–430, 432, 433
cubic inches, 427–429, 432, 434
cubic meters, 426–428
cubic millimeters, 433
cubic units, 425
customary system of measurement, 185, 186

D

data
analyzing, 625
displayed in histograms, 480
grouping at intervals, 477–478
mean, absolute deviation of, 455–462
ordered pairs, 623, 624
decimal grids, 113–116, 119, 125
decimals, 549–552
adding, 113–118
aligning decimal points, 114
converting rational numbers to, 549–554
converting to solve problems, 132
dividing, 125–127
equivalent, 59, 132
fraction equivalents for, 549
modeling equivalencies with fractions and percents, 210
multiplying, 119–122
ordering, 59
repeating, 490, 550–554
subtracting, 115–118
terminating, 490, 550–554
writing fractions as, 132, 211–212
writing markdowns as, 645

© Houghton Mifflin Harcourt Publishing Company

writing markups as, 644
writing mixed numbers as, 551
writing percents as, 209
writing rational numbers as, 550–552
denominator, 74, 612
dependent variables, 337–338
depth, 585
difference, 564, 565, 569–570
direct variation. *See* proportional
relationships
discounts, 642
distance
in the coordinate plane, 401–406, 408
from Earth to Moon, 111
on a map, 181
on a number line, 566–567
and rate of change
constant rates, 617–618
unit rates, 611, 612, 614
distribution, histograms and, 479, 480
Distributive Property, 33, 277, 278,
589–592, 594
dividend, 74
division
algebraic expressions for, 261
converting mixed numbers to decimals, 551
converting rational numbers to decimals,
550, 552
of decimals, 125–127
of equations, 312
estimating quotients, 107, 110
to find equivalent ratios, 151
of fractions, 85–89
of integers, 47–48, 531–533
long, 108, 110
of mixed numbers, 91–93
of multi-digit whole numbers, 107–112
of numbers by factors, 243
in order of operations, 249
of rational numbers, 577–582
with remainders, 109
word problems with fractions and mixed
numbers, 97–100
Division Property of Equality, 312
divisor, 74
dot plots, 470–472, 477–478
double-door folds, 523
double number lines, 163, 205
Draw Conclusions, 40, 58, 63, 96, 160, 274,
388, 512, 518, 562, 594, 615, 622, 623,
627, 637
Driskill Mountain, Louisiana, 561

E

Earth, 568
earth science, 23, 111, 222
edge length, volume and, 425–426, 428
elevation, 7, 513, 531
equality
Addition Property of, 305
Division Property of, 312

Multiplication Property of, 313
Subtraction Property of, 304
equations, 296, 297
adding, 305
algebraic, 261–264
checking solutions to, 299
defined, 330
dividing, 312
with greatest common factor, 32–34, 36
modeling, 303, 311
multiplying, 313
multistep, 573–575, 612–614, 619–620,
648, 649
for proportional relationships, 619–620,
625, 626
representing geometric concepts, 306
subtracting, 304
using to find area of shapes, 383–386,
390–394
using to solve real-world problems, 314–315
for volume, 431–434
writing from graphs, 352
writing from tables, 345–350
writing real-world problems for, 307
writing to represent situations, 297–299
equilateral triangles, 379
equivalent decimals, 59, 132
equivalent expressions, 260, 261, 263–264
generating, 275–279
identifying, 275–276
modeling, 261, 276
using properties to identify, 278
using properties to write, 277
equivalent fractions, 59, 132, 180
equivalent rates, 157–158
and proportions, 179
to solve proportions, 180
equivalent ratios, 148, 151–152, 193
comparisons with, 161–162, 164
multiplicative relationship between, 152
solving proportions with, 179
solving real-world problems with, 162
equivalent values, reciprocals and, 87
Error Analysis, 84, 193, 276, 344, 356
Essential Question. *Essential Question appears
in every lesson. See, for example,* 7, 13, 19, 31,
47, 53, 59
estimation, 121, 123, 126
and actual averages, 108
in adding decimals, 114
in multiplying fractions and whole numbers, 80
of quotients, 107, 110
evaluating, 232
expanding expressions, 590
Explain the Error, 58, 96, 124, 134, 154, 214,
222, 248, 253, 254, 301, 335, 349, 406, 412,
476, 482, 512, 517, 562
Explore Activity, 7–8, 13, 19, 21–22, 31, 33, 37,
47–48, 53, 59, 85, 87, 91, 107, 113, 119, 125,
149, 155, 161–163, 173, 174, 185, 203, 204,
210, 215, 237, 244, 245, 249–250, 275–276,
303, 311, 337–339, 345, 352, 377–378, 389,
401, 407, 419–420, 425–426, 449–450,
451–452, 477–478, 617–618, 623

exponents, 232, 236–242
finding value of powers, 239, 240
with grouping symbols, 251
identifying repeated multiplication, 237
and order of operations, 249
simplifying expressions with, 249–251
using, 238, 240
expressions, 260, 562, 568–570, 578, 589–594
adding and subtracting, 589, 592
for adding simple interest, 648
algebraic, 261–268
comparing using models, 263–264
comparing values of, 515, 539
defined, 634
Distributive Property with, 589–592, 594
equations and, 297
equivalent, 260, 261, 263–264, 275–279
evaluating, 269–271
expanding, 590
with exponents, 238, 240
factoring, 591, 592
inequalities and, 321
numerical, 250–253
parts of, 279
in problem solving, 97, 131
rational number operations, 588
removing parentheses from, 590
representing price, 641–644
representing word problems, 134
simplifying, 249–253, 590, 592
for total cost, 648

F

faces
of cubes, 419
of prisms, 421, 423, 426
of pyramids, 420, 423
factor, 35, 243, 591
greatest common. *See* greatest common
factor (GCF)
multiplied by itself, 237
factoring, relationship of multiplying and, 592
factoring expressions, 591, 592
factorization, prime, 243–248
factor trees, 244
feet, 191, 193, 194, 196, 409, 411, 428–430,
432, 612
financial literacy, 23, 24, 52, 57, 221, 561,
568, 575
fluid ounces, 191
fractional edge lengths, finding volume with,
425–426
fraction bars, 85, 91
fractions, 78
adding, using LCM, 81–82
benchmark, 80
comparing, 554
complex, 612, 613
converting to solve problems, 132
decimal equivalents of, 549
dividing, 85–89
equivalent, 59, 132, 180

Index

improper, 551, 552
modeling equivalencies with decimals and
   percents, 210
multiplying, 79–82
   two fractions, 79–80
   using GCF in, 79–82
   whole numbers and fractions, 80–81
multistep problems, 97–100
ordering, 59
percents and, 204
reciprocals of, 86–88
representing division as, 47–48
subtracting, using LCM, 81–82
unit rates, 611–616
writing as decimals and percents, 211–212
writing decimals as, 132
writing percents as, 209
frequency, histograms and, 477–482

G

gallons, 191, 194–196, 432, 433, 434
GCF. *See* greatest common factor
geography, 18, 561
geometry, 254, 411
   *The development of geometry skills and concepts
   is a central focus of this course and is found
   throughout the book.*
   angles, 306
   area, 243, 246, 273
      of parallelograms, 371, 389, 394, 409
      of polygons, 389–394, 409, 410
      of quadrilaterals, 371–374
      of rectangles, 390–394, 409, 591, 593
      of a rhombus, 373–374
      solving equations for, 383–386
      solving problems involving, 93–96
      in square feet, 193, 390, 391–392, 393, 612
      in square inches, 394
      in square meters, 193, 196, 391
      of squares, 389, 390, 392, 393, 410, 412
      of trapezoids, 372–373, 394
      of triangles, 377–382, 389–392, 394, 412
   on coordinate plane, 407
   cubes
      as cubic units, 425
      nets for, 419
      surface area of, 423
      volume of, 242, 425–426, 428
   octagons, 412
   parallelograms, 371, 389, 394, 409
   pentagons, 412
   perimeter
      of hexagons, 411
      and length of side, 593
      of polygons in coordinate plane, 408
      of rectangles, 594
      of squares, 410
      of trapezoids, 411
   polygons
      area of, 389–394, 409, 410
      in the coordinate plane, 407–412
      perimeter of, 408

prisms
   nets for, 419
   surface area of, 421–424
   volume of, 425–434
pyramids, 201, 274
   defined, 420
   rectangular, 423
   square, 420, 422
   surface area of, 420
   triangular, 420
quadrilaterals, 371–374
rectangles, 243, 246, 371
   area of, 390–394, 409, 591, 593
   finding dimensions of, 254
   length of, 591
   perimeter of, 594
   width of, 591
rhombuses, 373–374
solving equations representing, 306
squares
   area of, 389, 390, 392, 393, 410, 412
   on coordinate plane, 407
   perimeter of, 410
surface area, 271
   of prisms, 421–424
   of pyramids, 420
trapezoids, 372–373, 384, 394, 411
triangles, 273, 377–380, 383
   area of, 389–392, 394, 412
volume, 274
   of cubes, 242, 425–426, 428
   of prisms, 425–430
   solving equations for, 431–434
grams, 191, 194, 195, 429
graphing
   on coordinate plane, 331–333. *See also*
      coordinate plane
   equations, 352–354
   histograms, 477–482
   independent and dependent variables and,
      338–341
   integers on number line, 9–10
   with ratios, 174
   representing algebraic relationships and,
      351–354
   representing rates and, 175
graph paper, 419
graphs
   analyzing proportional relationships, 625
   bar graphs, 639
   ordered pairs, 623, 624
   proportional relationships, 623–628
greater than, 15, 81, 319–322
greatest common factor (GCF), 2, 30–36, 78
   finding, 32
   in multiplying fractions
      fractions and whole numbers, 80–81
      two fractions, 79–80
   using Distributive Property, 33
grid paper, 33, 371, 377–378, 550
grids, 203
   as area models, 409
   decimal, 113, 116, 119, 125

ten-by-ten, 203, 210
   See also coordinate plane
grouping symbols, using exponents with, 251

H

height, volume and, 426–434
hexagons, 407, 411
histograms, 477–482
   analyzing, 479
   defined, 478
   grouping data, 477–478
history, 433
honey, 89
H.O.T. (Higher Order Thinking) problems.
   *H.O.T. problems are found in every lesson. See, for
   example,* 12, 18, 24, 52, 58, 64, 66, 84
Hot Tip, 229, 290, 363, 488, 604, 659, 660

I

Identify Patterns, 576
Identity Property, 277
improper fractions, 551, 552
inches, 191, 193–195, 410, 411, 422, 423,
   427–429, 432, 433
independent, 292
independent variables, 337–338
inequalities, 2, 15, 296
   graphing solutions of, 320–321
   using to describe quantities, 319
   writing, 321–322
integers, 2, 6, 8, 494, 524
   adding, 503
      with different signs, 501–504
      with same sign, 495–497
   application of properties to solve problems, 514
   comparing, 13
   comparing values of expressions, 515, 539
   defined, 490
   dividing, 531–533
   multiplying, 525–527
   negative, to represent quantities, 538–539
   on a number line, 9–10
   opposites, 8
   ordering, 14
   positive and negative numbers, 7–8, 13–15
   solving multistep problems, 513
   subtracting, 507–509
   using order of operations with, 537–538
   Venn diagram of, 49
   writing inequalities, 15
interest, simple, 606
Interpret the Answer, 37, 90, 109, 621
interquartile range (IQR), 464, 477
intervals
   grouping data at, 477–478
   histograms and, 478–482
IQR (interquartile range), 464, 477

Index

J

Justify Reasoning, 8, 19, 84, 90, 100, 208, 216, 242, 281, 530, 536, 594, 616

K

Kaktovik, Alaska, 570
key-term folds, 5, 259
kilograms, 191, 192, 194–196
kilometers, 191, 194–196

L

ladder diagrams, 245, 246
layered books, 77, 329, 447, 547
least common multiple (LCM), 30, 37–40, 78
  in adding and subtracting fractions, 81–82
  applying, 38
length
  of area model sides, 33
  in the coordinate plane, 408
  measurements of, 186
  and perimeter, 593
  of rectangles, 591
  and volume, 426–434
less than, 15, 81, 319–322
like terms, 232, 279
liters, 194, 195
long division, 108, 110
  converting mixed numbers to decimals, 551
  converting rational numbers to decimals, 550
Look for a Pattern, 18, 160, 173, 190, 208, 242, 248, 254, 273, 310, 311, 349, 406, 512, 553, 554, 570, 573, 640
lower quartile, 463

M

MAD (mean absolute deviation), 455–462
Make a Conjecture, 24, 58, 87, 174, 178, 190, 350, 401, 461, 462, 526, 530, 531, 549, 565, 570, 578, 617, 622, 628, 643
Make a Prediction, 90, 112, 149, 482, 502
manipulatives
  algebra tiles, 276, 278, 281, 303, 311, 591, 593
  area models, 119
  bar models, 215, 220, 262–265
  counters, 449, 495, 502, 526
  decimal grids, 113, 116, 119, 125
  double number lines, 163, 205
  fraction bars, 85, 91
  graph paper, 419
  grid paper, 33, 371, 377–378, 550
  ladder diagrams, 245, 246
  meter stick, 196
  nets, 419–424
  number lines. *See* number lines
  percent bars, 204
  rulers, 185, 194, 585
  square tiles, 241
  tangrams, 389
  ten-by-ten grids, 203, 210
  yard stick, 196, 588
maps
  coordinate planes as, 403–405
  proportional relationships to find distance on, 181
  scale of, 183
markdowns, 642–646
markups, 641–646
Mars, 568, 569
mathematical practices
  Mathematical practices are a central focus of this course and are found throughout the book.
  Analyze Relationships, 8, 9, 11, 12, 13, 18, 19, 23, 48, 49, 52, 58, 64, 81, 92, 96, 118, 119, 130, 150, 154, 155, 162, 166, 177, 178, 184, 190, 196, 208, 217, 253, 338, 339, 343, 344, 351, 355, 382, 388, 456, 468, 496, 506, 512, 518, 530, 535, 554, 588, 615, 616, 621, 627, 646, 652
  Check for Reasonableness, 93, 112, 121, 124, 126, 219, 583–588, 616
  Communicate Mathematical Ideas, 12, 20, 24, 36, 40, 48, 53, 55, 59, 61, 64, 83, 86, 90, 91, 118, 120, 174, 178, 185, 192, 196, 214, 216, 217, 218, 237, 242, 245, 247, 248, 282, 302, 303, 304, 305, 318, 324, 332, 336, 350, 375, 377, 378, 382, 384, 406, 412, 424, 430, 431, 434, 452, 454, 482, 495, 496, 497, 500, 506, 508, 509, 514, 530, 536, 553, 554, 561, 562, 575, 594, 616, 622, 625, 628, 645
  Construct an Argument, 582
  Consumer Math, 165
  Critical Thinking, 52, 57, 64, 107, 214, 242, 247, 302, 310, 318, 336, 350, 355, 356, 387, 412, 430, 454, 461, 476, 497, 506, 518, 582, 627, 640
  Critique Reasoning, 12, 18, 24, 36, 52, 64, 112, 118, 129, 160, 184, 195, 204, 208, 248, 251, 268, 274, 309, 324, 376, 381, 424, 454, 468, 500, 529, 542, 575, 588, 621, 636, 646
  Draw Conclusions, 40, 58, 63, 96, 160, 274, 388, 512, 518, 562, 594, 615, 622, 623, 627, 637
  Error Analysis, 84, 193, 276, 344, 356
  Explain the Error, 58, 96, 124, 134, 154, 214, 222, 248, 253, 254, 301, 335, 349, 406, 412, 476, 482, 512, 517, 562
  Identify Patterns, 576
  Interpret the Answer, 37, 90, 109, 621
  Justify Reasoning, 8, 19, 84, 90, 100, 208, 216, 242, 281, 530, 536, 594, 616
  Look for a Pattern, 18, 160, 173, 190, 208, 242, 248, 254, 273, 310, 311, 349, 406, 512, 553, 554, 570, 573, 640
  Make a Conjecture, 24, 58, 87, 174, 178, 190, 350, 401, 461, 462, 526, 530, 531, 549, 565, 570, 578, 617, 622, 628, 643
  Make a Prediction, 90, 112, 149, 482, 502
  Math Talk. *Math Talk appears in most lessons. See, for example,* 10, 14, 15, 20, 33, 48, 55, 61
  Multiple Representations, 8, 12, 17, 47, 58, 91, 100, 113, 117, 125, 134, 154, 156, 184, 207, 210, 214, 247, 282, 302, 356, 376, 434, 468, 481, 499, 530, 627, 628, 639
  Multistep, 51, 57, 83, 95, 123, 133, 153, 159, 165, 183, 189, 208, 222, 253, 267, 268, 310, 318, 343, 349, 356, 376, 381, 382, 387, 394, 434, 462, 476, 482, 499, 500, 505, 517, 535, 541, 575, 581, 615, 652
  Persevere in Problem Solving, 36, 160, 190, 254, 318, 356, 380, 388, 394, 412, 424, 430, 454, 536, 542, 569–570, 588, 594, 646
  Problem Solving, 18, 124, 130, 166, 268, 282, 302, 554, 561, 570, 646
  Reason Abstractly, 576
  Reflect. *Reflect appears in most lessons. See, for example,* 8, 9, 13, 19, 20, 22, 31, 32, 49, 53, 55, 61
  Represent Real-World Problems, 17, 20, 21, 84, 90, 100, 124, 130, 134, 166, 178, 214, 268, 309, 317, 318, 324, 336, 350, 434, 467, 499, 500, 506, 512, 518, 529, 536, 542, 554, 576, 582, 588, 615, 639, 646
  What If?, 12, 31, 63, 91, 92, 117, 118, 129, 134, 154, 159, 177, 195, 244, 268, 282, 299, 307, 345, 382, 451, 460, 462, 474, 476, 479, 496, 509, 511, 530, 538, 615, 625
Math On the Spot. *Math On the Spot is available online for every example.*
Math Talk. *Math Talk appears in most lessons. See, for example,* 10, 14, 15, 20, 33, 48, 55, 61
mean, 449, 451–452, 455–457, 477–478, 482
mean absolute deviation (MAD), 455–462
measurement
  capacity, 191
  customary, 191
  length, 191
  mass, 191
  mean absolute deviation, 455–462
  metric, 191
  weight, 191
measurement systems, 185, 186
  converting between, 191–196
    using conversion factors, 192
    using proportions, 193–194
  customary, 191
    comparing metric and, 195
    converting metric and, 191–196
  metric, 191
    comparing customary and, 195
    converting customary and, 191–196
measure of variability, 455–462
measures of center, 449–452, 472
measures of spread, 455, 464, 472
median, 450, 451–452, 477–478, 482
mental math, 594
meters, 191, 194–196, 426–428
metric system of measurement, 185, 186
miles, 191, 194–196
milliliters, 191
Mini-Tasks, 26, 42, 66, 72, 102, 136, 142, 168, 198, 224, 230, 256, 284, 290, 326, 358, 364, 396, 414, 436, 442, 484, 488, 520, 544, 596, 604, 630, 654, 660
mixed numbers, 74
  compare, 613
  dividing, 91–93

Index

multistep problems with fractions and, 97–100
as rational numbers, 550
writing as decimals, 551
writing as improper fractions, 552

Mixed Review, 71–72, 141–142, 229–230, 289–290, 363–364, 441–442, 487–488, 603–604, 659–660. *See also* assessment, Assessment Readiness

modeling
absolute value, 20
algebraic equations, 303, 311
algebraic expressions, comparing, 261, 264
algebra tiles, 275, 278, 281, 303, 311, 591, 593
area, 389, 409
bar models, 641–643, 647
to convert units, 185
decimal, fraction, and percent equivalencies, 210
decimal division, 125
decimal grids, 113–116, 119, 125
decimal multiplication, 119
equivalent fractions and decimals, 60
to find ratios, 152
fraction division, 85
greatest common factor, 33
grid paper, 33, 371, 377–378, 550
inequalities, 15
integer multiplication, 526
integer subtraction, 507–508
mixed number division, 91–92
order of operations, 249
percent problems, 215–216
of percents using grids, 203
of perimeter using grids, 408
positive and negative numbers, 9
rational numbers, 60
rational numbers and absolute values, 55
rational numbers and opposites, 54
relationships between rational numbers, integers, and whole numbers, 49, 50
to represent ratios, 149
sums of integers with different signs, 502–503
sums of integers with same sign, 495

models, strategic use of, 585

money. *See* Financial literacy

Moon, 103, 111

Multiple Representations, 8, 12, 17, 47, 58, 91, 100, 113, 117, 125, 134, 154, 156, 184, 207, 210, 214, 247, 282, 302, 356, 376, 434, 468, 481, 499, 530, 627, 628, 639

multiples, 37, 38
common, 38
least common, 37–40, 81–82

multiplication
algebraic expressions for, 261
Associative Property of, 277
Commutative Property of, 277
of decimals, 119–122
of equations, 313
of expressions, 590
to find equivalent ratios, 151
of fractions, 80–81
two fractions, 79–80

using GCF in, 79–82
whole numbers and fractions, 80–81
Identity Property of, 277
of integers, 525–527
in order of operations, 249
prime factorization and, 244
of rational numbers, 571–576
with different signs, 571
with the same sign, 572–573
three or more numbers, 573–574
using number lines, 571–572, 574
relationship of factoring and, 592
repeated, 237. *See also* exponents
as repeated addition, 571
rewriting division problems as, 577

Multiplication Property of Equality, 313

Multistep, 51, 57, 83, 95, 123, 133, 153, 159, 165, 183, 189, 208, 222, 253, 267, 268, 310, 318, 343, 349, 356, 376, 381, 382, 387, 394, 434, 462, 476, 482, 499, 500, 505, 517, 535, 541, 575, 581, 615, 652

multistep equations, 612–614, 619–620
for simple interest, 648
using multiple percents, 649

multistep problems, with fractions and mixed numbers, 97–100

music, 83

N

negative numbers, 2, 7, 13–15
absolute value instead of, 20–21
integers as quantities, 538–539
rational, 53
rational numbers, 549
adding, 555–562
dividing, 577–582
multiplying, 571–574
subtracting, 564, 568

nets, 419
and surface area, 419–424
of prisms, 421
of pyramids, 420
using, 419

New Orleans, Louisiana, 561

number lines
absolute value and, 19
distance on, 566–567
double, 163, 205
elevation and, 513, 531
equivalent fractions and decimals on, 59, 60, 132
inequalities and, 15, 319–321
integers on, 9–10
adding, 496, 501
multiplying, 525
subtracting, 508
opposites on, 9, 54
ordering integers on, 14
positive and negative numbers on, 7, 9, 13, 14
rational numbers on, 6, 54, 61
adding, 555–560
multiplying, 571–572, 574

subtracting, 563–567
representing rates on, 163
solving equations using, 305, 312, 313

numbers
additive inverse of, 558, 562
exponents representing, 237–242
finding distance between, 566
mixed, 74
dividing, 91–93
multistep problems with fractions and, 97–100
negative, 2, 7, 13–14, 20–21
positive, 7, 13–15
prime, 32
rational. *See* rational numbers
whole. *See* whole numbers

numerator, 612

numerical expressions
defined, 250
simplifying, 250–253

O

occupations. *See* careers

octagons, 407, 412

operations, 261
with fractions
GCF in multiplying fractions, 79–82
LCM in adding and subtracting fractions, 81–82
word problems with, 97–100
for multistep problems, 97
order of, 97, 98, 249–254
with rational numbers, 131–134, 583–588
converting fractions and decimals, 132
interpreting word problems, 131–132
See also individual operations

opposites, 6, 8, 277, 558, 575
addition of, 509
integers and, 537–538
on a number line, 9, 54
See also additive inverse

ordered pairs, 407, 623, 624

order of operations, 97, 98, 249–254
defined, 232, 236
exponents with grouping symbols, 251
in simplifying numerical expressions, 250–253
using, 249–250

origin, 292, 331, 623, 624

ounces, 191, 195

outliers, 471

P

parallelograms, 371, 389, 394, 409

parentheses, order of operations and, 97, 249, 251

patterns
in multiplying rational numbers, 573, 576
in ratios, 553
in repeated multiplication, 237

Index

© Houghton Mifflin Harcourt Publishing Company

in repeating decimals, 550, 554
in simplifying expressions, 570

peaks, 471

pentagons, 412

percent, 202, 203
applications of, 647–652
benchmarks and proportional reasoning and, 205
defined, 634
fractions and, 204
markup and markdown, 641–646
modeling equivalencies with decimals and fractions, 210
modeling with grids, 203
multiple percents, 649
percent decrease, 606, 636–640, 642–646
percent increase, 635, 637–640, 641–646
rewriting expressions of, 641–646
rounding, 638, 644
simple interest, 648
solving problems involving, 215–220
writing as decimals and fractions, 209
writing fractions as, 211–212

percent bars, 204

percent decrease, 606, 636–640
markdowns, 642–646

percent increase, 635, 637–640
markups, 641–646

Performance Tasks, 70, 140, 228, 288, 362, 440, 486, 601–602, 657–658

perimeter
of hexagons, 411
and length of side, 593
of polygons in coordinate plane, 408
of rectangles, 594
of squares, 410
of trapezoids, 411

Persevere in Problem Solving, 36, 160, 190, 254, 318, 356, 380, 388, 394, 412, 424, 430, 454, 536, 542, 569–570, 588, 594, 646

Personal Math Trainer. *Personal Math Trainer is available online for every lesson.*

physical science, 433

points (on coordinate plane), 331–333
finding distances between, 402–404
reflections of, 401, 402

polygons, 407
area of, 389–394, 409, 410
in the coordinate plane, 407–412
area of, 409, 410
perimeter of, 408
perimeter of, 408

positive numbers, 7, 13–15, 53
percent of change as, 637
rational
adding, 555–562
multiplying, 571–573, 575
subtracting, 563, 565–567

pounds, 191, 192, 195, 196

powers, 232, 238, 239
finding values of, 239, 240
reading, 238
See also exponents

precipitation records, 15

predictions
of quotients, 107
using rates to make, 163, 164
using ratios to make, 149

prices
comparing, 155
markup and markdown, 641–646
retail, 641
sale, 642–644
sales tax on, 647–650
total cost, 647–650
unit, 156–157

prime factorization, 243–248

prime numbers, 32

principal, 648

prisms
defined, 421
nets for, 419
rectangular
surface area of, 423, 424
volume of, 425–430
writing equations involving volume, 431–434
square, 421
surface area of, 421–424
triangular, 422–424
volume of, 425–430

Problem Solving, 18, 124, 130, 166, 268, 282, 302, 554, 561, 570, 646

problem solving
Problem solving is a central focus of this course and is found throughout the book.
assessing reasonableness of answers, 583–588
interpreting word problems, 131–132
rational numbers in any form, 585–586
use an equation, 190, 347, 385–386
use an expression, 97, 131, 515
use a property, 514, 515
use a ratio table, 166
use a relationship, 403
use logical reasoning, 584
use order of operations, 537–538
with proportions, 179–184
with unit rates, 157–158

problem solving plan
adding integers, 514
comparing values of expressions, 515
distance problems between points on a grid, 403
multiple percents, 649
order of operations, 97–98
solving equations using relationships in geometry, 385–386
using equations to solve problems, 314–315
using order of operations with integers and, 537–538
using rational numbers in any form, 584–585
using tables and equations to solve problems, 347

product, 571–574, 594
checking, 33
of fractions, 79–81

properties
Addition Property of Equality, 305
Associative, 118, 277, 559, 589
Commutative, 118, 277, 278, 570, 589
Distributive, 33, 277, 278, 589–592, 594
Division Property of Equality, 312
identifying equivalent expressions using, 278
Identity, 277
solving equations using, 304, 305, 312, 313
Subtraction Property of Equality, 304
writing equivalent expressions using, 277
of zero as an exponent, 239

proportionality
constant of, 610, 619–620
constant rates of change, 617–622
converting between measurement systems, 191–196
ratios, 617–622
unit rates, 611–616

proportional reasoning, 205, 216, 218–219

proportional relationships, 606, 618
constant of proportionality for, 619–620
constant rates of change, 617–622
discovering, 617–618
graphing, 623–628
identifying, 624
nonproportional relationships distinguished from, 624, 626
writing equations for, 619–620

proportions, 179, 618, 634
in converting measurements, 193–194
finding distance on a map with, 181
solving problems with, 179–184
using to convert units, 186–187

protractors, 585

pyramids, 201, 274, 369, 420
rectangular, 423
square, 420, 422
surface area of, 420
triangular, 420

quadrants, 292, 331

quadrilaterals, area of, 371–374

quantities
unit rates for, 156–158
using inequalities to describe, 319
using rates to compare, 149

quartiles, 463–464

quarts, 191, 195

quotients, 78, 106, 550, 577–582
estimating, 107, 110
and remainders, 109
using long division, 108, 110

range, 465–466, 477

rate of change
constant, 617–622
defined, 606, 618

rates, 148, 155–160, 172, 610
  comparing prices with, 155
  on double number lines, 163
  equivalent, 157–158, 180
  in forming proportions, 618
  to make predictions, 163, 164
  representing with graphs and tables, 175
  unit, 148, 156–158, 172, 180, 186–187, 610, 611–616

rational numbers, 2, 6, 46, 48, 490, 548, 549
  absolute values of, 55
  adding, 555–562
    additive inverse, 558, 562
    with different signs, 556–557
    with same sign, 555–556
    three or more numbers, 559
    using number lines, 555–560
  in any form, 584–585
  applying multiplication and division of, 131
  assessing reasonableness of answers, 583–588
  classifying, 49–50
  converting to decimals, 549–554
  dividing, 577–582
    negative signs in quotients, 578
    quotients of, 579–580
  mixed numbers, 550, 551
  multiplying, 571–576
    with different signs, 571
    with the same sign, 572–573
    three or more numbers, 573–574
  multistep problems with, 97–100
  negative, 549
  number lines and, 6
  operations with, 131–134
    converting fractions and decimals, 132
    interpreting word problems, 131–132
  positive and negative, 53
  representing division as a fraction, 47–48
  subtracting, 563–570
    by adding its opposite, 565
    negative numbers, 564, 568
    positive numbers, 563, 569
    using number lines, 563–567
  written as decimals, 550–552

ratios, 148–154, 172
  comparisons with, 161–162, 164
  constant rates of change, 617–622
  conversion factor, 192
  converting between measurement systems, 192–194
  defined, 634
  equivalent, 151–152, 161–162, 164, 179, 193
  finding from tables, 173
  in forming proportions, 618
  graphing with, 174
  patterns in, 553
  percents as, 203
  representing with models, 149
  writing, 150

Reading Start-Up, 5, 29, 45, 77, 105, 147, 171, 201, 235, 259, 295, 329, 369, 399, 417, 447, 493, 523, 547, 609, 633

Ready to Go On?, 25, 41, 65, 101, 135, 167, 197, 223, 255, 283, 325, 357, 395, 413, 435, 483, 519, 543, 595, 629, 653

Real World. *Real-world situations are a central focus of this course and are found throughout the book.*

Real-World Video, 3, 27, 43, 75, 103, 145, 169, 199, 233, 257, 293, 327, 367, 397, 415, 445, 491, 521, 545, 607, 631

reasonableness of answers, 115, 116, 583–588

Reason Abstractly, 576

reciprocals, 74, 86
  dividing fractions and, 86–88
  dividing mixed numbers and, 92–93
  equivalent values and, 87

rectangles, 243, 246, 371
  area of, 390–394, 409, 591, 593
  finding dimensions of, 254
  length of, 591
  perimeter of, 594
  width of, 591

rectangular prisms
  surface area of, 423, 424
  volume of, 425–430
  writing equations involving volume, 431–434

rectangular pyramids, 423

Reflect. *Reflect appears in most lessons. See, for example,* 8, 9, 13, 19, 20, 22, 31, 32, 49, 53, 55, 61

reflection
  in the coordinate plane, 401, 402
  finding distance with, 402–406

remainders, 74, 109

repeated addition, 571

repeated multiplication, 237.
  See also exponents

repeating decimals, 490, 550–554

Represent Real-World Problems, 17, 20, 21, 84, 90, 100, 124, 130, 134, 166, 178, 214, 268, 309, 317, 318, 324, 336, 350, 434, 467, 499, 500, 506, 512, 518, 529, 536, 542, 554, 576, 582, 588, 615, 639, 646

retail price, 641
  markups, 641–646
  tax on, 649

rhombuses, 373–374

right triangle, area of, 377

rounding
  in estimating quotients, 107, 110
  to nearest whole number, 455, 456
  percents, 638, 644
  in subtracting decimals, 115
  to two decimal places, 644

rulers, 185

S

sale price, 642–644
  markdowns, 642–646
  tax on, 649

sales tax, 647–650

sampling, 455–462

scale, 181, 183

scale drawing, 181

scales of axes, reading, 333

science, 11, 17, 18, 23, 89, 166, 222, 429, 568, 582

sides, perimeter and length of, 593

simple interest, 606

simplifying, 590, 592
  numerical expressions, 249–253
  product of two fractions, 79–82
  sums and differences, 81, 82

software, strategic use of, 585

solutions, 292, 297, 320, 353
  checking, 299
  of equations, 353
  of inequalities, 320
  reasonableness of, 115, 116, 583–588

sports, 517

spread, measures of, 464, 472

spreadsheets, mean absolute deviation on, 458–459

square centimeters, 390, 424

square feet, 193, 194, 390, 391–392, 393, 411, 612

square inches, 394, 410, 411, 422, 423

square meters, 193, 196, 391

square prisms, 421

square pyramids, 420, 422

squares
  area of, 389, 390, 392, 393, 410, 412
  on coordinate plane, 407
  perimeter of, 410

square tiles, 241

square units, 389, 392–394

square yards, 410

statistical questions, 469

Study Guide Review, 67–69, 137–139, 225–228, 285–287, 359–362, 437–440, 485–486, 597–600, 655–656

subtraction
  by adding the opposite, 565
  algebraic expressions for, 261
  checking reasonableness of answers, 115, 116
  of decimals, 115–118
  of expressions, 589
  of fractions, 81–82
  of integers, 507–509
  of negative numbers, 564, 568
  in order of operations, 249
  of positive numbers, 563, 569
  of rational numbers, 563–570
  solving equations containing, 304
  using number lines, 563–567

sum, 557, 559, 560, 565
  sign of, 555

Sunshine Skyway Bridge, 548

supplementary angles, 306

surface area, 271, 420
  and nets, 419–424
  of prisms, 421–424
  of pyramids, 420

symmetric distribution of data, 471

T

tables
- comparing prices with, 155
- comparing ratios with, 161–162, 164
- constant rate of change, 618, 619
- for equivalent ratios, 151, 154
- of exponential forms, 240
- finding ratios from, 173–174
- frequency, 477–482
- for greatest common factors, 31
- for identifying repeated multiplication, 237
- independent and dependent quantities on, 337–338, 340
- for interpreting word problems, 133, 134
- proportional relationships, 617, 623
- repeated multiplication and, 237
- representing algebraic relationships in, 351–354
- representing rates with, 158–160, 175
- writing equations from, 345–348

tangrams, 389

tape diagrams, 156–159, 191

tax, sales, 647–650

ten-by-ten grids, 203, 210

terminating decimals, 490, 550–554

terms, 150, 164, 279

test prep. *See* assessment, Assessment Readiness

test-taking tips. *See* Hot Tip

three-panel flip charts, 235, 609

time
- and rate of change
  - constant rates, 617–618, 620
  - unit rates, 611, 612, 614

tons, 433
- total cost
  - finding, 647–648
  - using multiple percents, 649

trapezoids, 372–373, 384
- area of, 394
- perimeter of, 411

triangles
- area of, 377–380, 383, 389–392, 394, 412
- problem solving using area of, 383

triangular prisms, 422–424

triangular pyramids, 420

tri-folds, 45, 171, 633

two-panel flip charts, 29, 147, 399

U

Understand Vocabulary, 29, 45, 77, 105, 147, 171, 201, 235, 259, 295, 329, 369, 399, 417, 447, 493, 523, 547, 609, 633

unit cost, 156

unit price, 156

unit rates, 148, 156, 172, 610, 611–616
- calculating, 156–157
- problem solving with, 157–158
- solving proportions with, 180
- using to convert units, 186–187

units
- converting using conversion factors, 187–188
- using models to convert, 185
- using proportions and unit rates to convert, 186–187

Unpacking the Standards, 6, 30, 46, 78, 106, 148, 172, 202, 236, 260, 296, 330, 370, 400, 418, 448, 494, 524, 548, 610, 634

upper quartile, 463

V

variability
- mean absolute deviation, 455–462
- measure of, 455

variable data, statistical questions and, 469

variables, 261
- defined, 232
- in equations with proportional relationships, 619
- independent and dependent, in tables and graphs, 337–344
- writing equations from tables and, 346–348

Venn diagrams, 2, 49

Venus, 568

vertices, 407
- of polygons, 407, 409, 410
- of triangles, 412

Video Tutor. *See* Math on the Spot

Visualize Vocabulary, 5, 29, 45, 77, 105, 147, 171, 201, 235, 259, 295, 329, 369, 399, 417, 447, 493, 523, 547, 609, 633

vocabulary, 22, 29, 36, 39, 45, 51, 56, 77, 105, 112, 171, 301, 329, 334, 349, 399, 411, 423, 474, 475, 554, 562
- Understand Vocabulary, 29, 45, 77, 105, 147, 171, 201, 235, 259, 295, 329, 369, 399, 417, 447, 493, 523, 547, 609, 633
- Visualize Vocabulary, 5, 29, 45, 77, 105, 147, 171, 201, 235, 259, 295, 329, 369, 399, 417, 447, 493, 523, 547, 609, 633
- Vocabulary Preview, 2, 74, 144, 232, 292, 366, 444, 490, 606

Vocabulary Preview, 2, 74, 144, 232, 292, 366, 444, 490, 606

volume
- of cubes, 425–426, 428
- of rectangular prisms, 425–434
- solving equations for, 431–434

W

weight, measurements of, 186

What If?, 12, 31, 63, 91, 92, 117, 118, 129, 134, 154, 159, 177, 195, 244, 268, 282, 299, 307, 345, 382, 451, 460, 462, 474, 476, 479, 496, 509, 511, 530, 538, 615, 625

whole numbers
- division
  - of decimals by whole numbers, 126
  - of multi-digit whole numbers, 107–112
- greatest common factor of, 31–36
- least common multiple, 37–40
- multiplying fractions and, 80–81
- Venn diagram of, 49

width
- of rectangles, 591
- volume and, 426–434

word problems
- expressions representing, 134
- with fractions and mixed numbers, 97–100
- interpreting, 131–134

X

x-axis, 331, 401, 404

x-coordinate, 331

Y

yards, 191, 194–196, 410

y-axis, 331, 401, 404

y-coordinate, 331

Yellowstone National Park, 637

Z

zero
- absolute value and, 6
- as additive inverse, 558
- as an exponent, 239
- division by, 532
- as placeholder, 114, 115
- points on axes and, 332
- properties of operations and, 277

zero pairs, 502

ASSESSMENT REFERENCE SHEET

TABLE OF MEASURES

Length

1 inch = 2.54 centimeters

1 meter ≈ 39.37 inches

1 mile = 5,280 feet

1 mile = 1,760 yards

1 mile ≈ 1.609 kilometers

1 kilometer ≈ 0.62 mile

Mass/Weight

1 pound = 16 ounces

1 pound ≈ 0.454 kilogram

1 kilogram ≈ 2.2 pounds

1 ton = 2,000 pounds

Capacity

1 cup = 8 fluid ounces

1 pint = 2 cups

1 quart = 2 pints

1 gallon = 4 quarts

1 gallon ≈ 3.785 liters

1 liter ≈ 0.264 gallon

1 liter = 1000 cubic centimeters

FORMULAS

Area

Parallelogram	$A = bh$
Circle	$A = \pi r^2$
Triangle	$A = \frac{1}{2} bh$

Volume

General prism	$V = Bh$

Circumference

Circle	$C = \pi d$ or $C = 2\pi r$

© Houghton Mifflin Harcourt Publishing Company